Rick Steves'

FLORENCE
& TUSCANY

Rick Steves & Gene Openshaw

2010

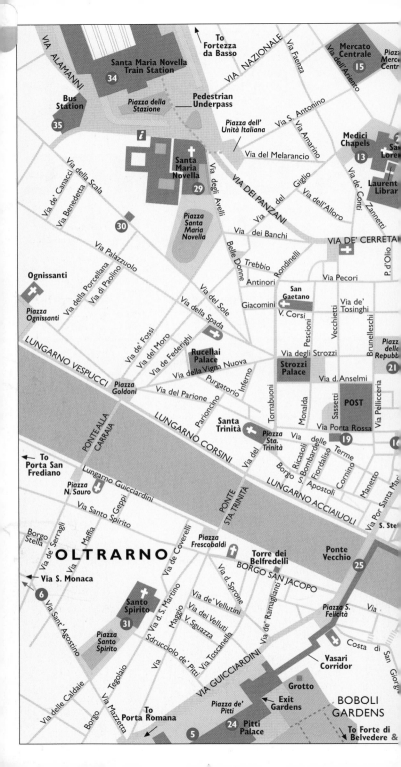

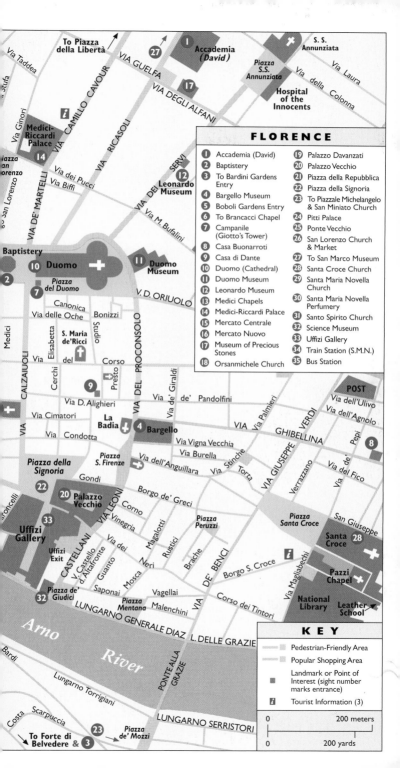

FLORENCE

1. Accademia (David)
2. Baptistery
3. To Bardini Gardens
4. Bargello Museum
5. Boboli Gardens Entry
6. To Brancacci Chapel
7. Campanile (Giotto's Tower)
8. Casa Buonarroti
9. Casa di Dante
10. Duomo (Cathedral)
11. Duomo Museum
12. Leonardo Museum
13. Medici Chapels
14. Medici-Riccardi Palace
15. Mercato Centrale
16. Mercato Nuovo
17. Museum of Precious Stones
18. Orsanmichele Church
19. Palazzo Davanzati
20. Palazzo Vecchio
21. Piazza della Repubblica
22. Piazza della Signoria
23. To Piazzale Michelangelo & San Miniato Church
24. Pitti Palace
25. Ponte Vecchio
26. San Lorenzo Church & Market
27. To San Marco Museum
28. Santa Croce Church
29. Santa Maria Novella Church
30. Santa Maria Novella Perfumery
31. Santo Spirito Church
32. Science Museum
33. Uffizi Gallery
34. Train Station (S.M.N.)
35. Bus Station

KEY

- Pedestrian-Friendly Area
- Popular Shopping Area
- Landmark or Point of Interest (sight number marks entrance)
- *i* Tourist Information (3)

| 0 | 200 meters |
| 0 | 200 yards |

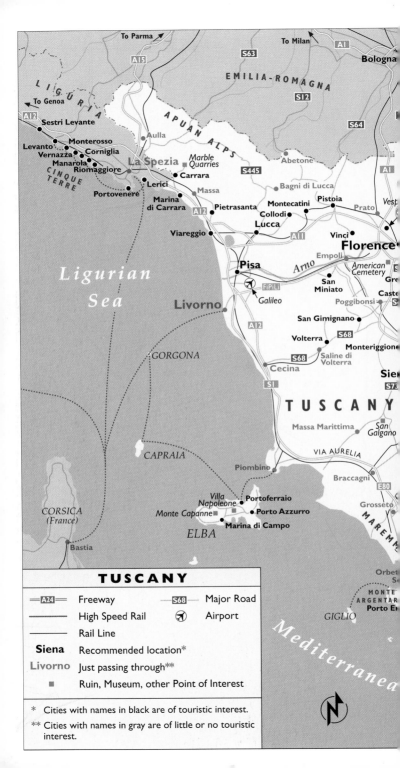

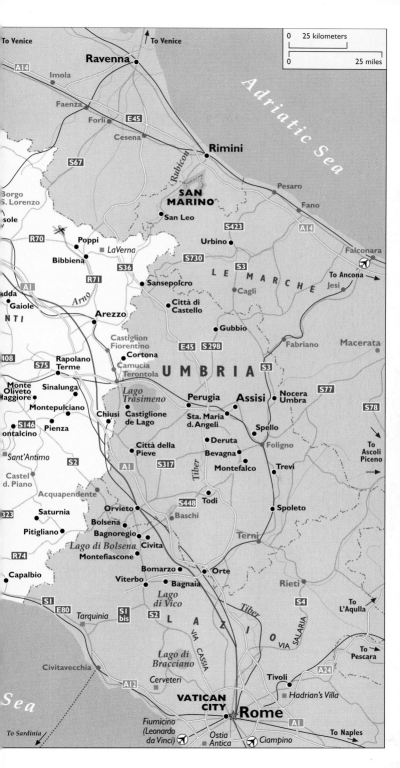

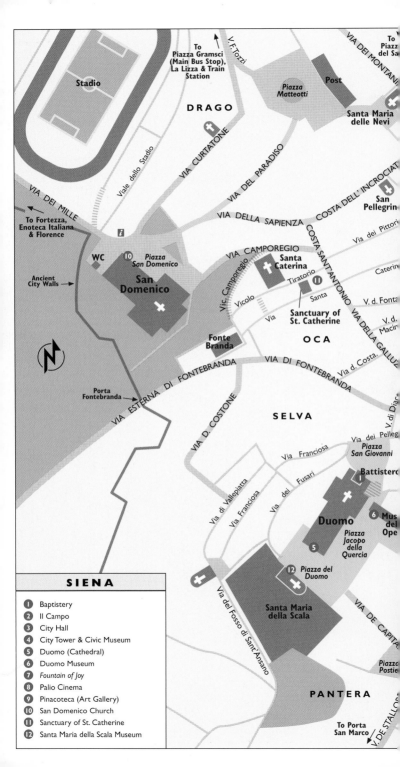

Stadio

DRAGO

To
Piazza Gramsci
(Main Bus Stop),
La Lizza & Train
Station

V. F. Tozzi

Piazza
Matteotti

Post

To
Piazza
del Sa...

VIA DEI MONTAN...

Santa Maria
delle Nevi

VIA CURTATONE

Viale dello Stadio

VIA DEL PARADISO

VIA DELL' INCROCIAT...

VIA DEI MILLE

To Fortezza,
Enoteca Italiana
& Florence

COSTA DELL'

San
Pellegrin...

VIA DELLA SAPIENZA

COSTA SANTANTONIO

Via dei Pittori

Ancient
City Walls

WC

10 Piazza
San Domenico

San
Domenico

VIA CAMPOREGIO

Santa
Caterina

Cateri...

Tiratorio 11

V. d. Fonta...

Vic. Camporegio

Vicolo

Santa

VIA DELLA GALLUZ...

Sanctuary of
St. Catherine

Via

V. d.
Macin...

OCA

Fonte
Branda

VIA ESTERNA DI FONTEBRANDA

VIA DI FONTEBRANDA

Via d. Costa...

Porta
Fontebranda

Via d. Diac...

VIA D. COSTONE

SELVA

Via dei Pelleg...

Via Franciosa

Piazza
San Giovanni

Battistero

Via di Vallepiatta

Via Franciosa

Via dei Fusari

1

Via del Fosso di Sant'Ansano

Duomo

6 Mus...
del
Ope...

Piazza
Jacopo
della
Quercia

5

12 Piazza del
Duomo

VIA DE CAPITA...

Santa Maria
della Scala

Piazza
Postie...

PANTERA

To Porta
San Marco

V. DE STALLO...

V. DE CAPITA...

SIENA

1 Baptistery
2 Il Campo
3 City Hall
4 City Tower & Civic Museum
5 Duomo (Cathedral)
6 Duomo Museum
7 *Fountain of Joy*
8 Palio Cinema
9 Pinacoteca (Art Gallery)
10 San Domenico Church
11 Sanctuary of St. Catherine
12 Santa Maria della Scala Museum

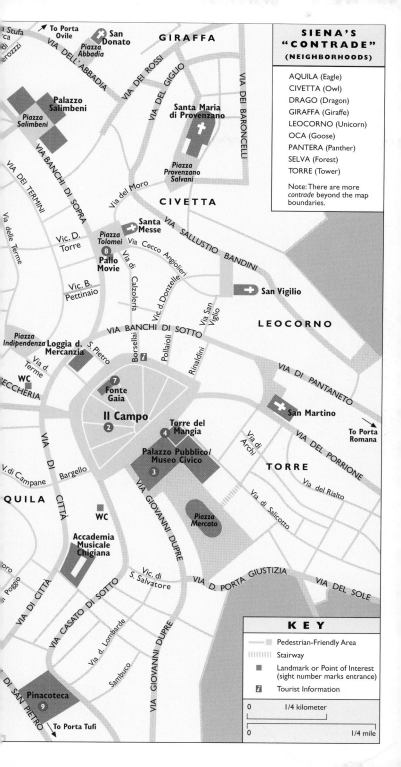

SIENA'S "CONTRADE"
(NEIGHBORHOODS)

AQUILA (Eagle)
CIVETTA (Owl)
DRAGO (Dragon)
GIRAFFA (Giraffe)
LEOCORNO (Unicorn)
OCA (Goose)
PANTERA (Panther)
SELVA (Forest)
TORRE (Tower)

Note: There are more *contrade* beyond the map boundaries.

GIRAFFA

To Porta Ovile
San Donato
Piazza Abbadia
VIA DELL'ABBADIA
VIA DEI ROSSI
VIA DEL GIGLIO
VIA DEI BARONCELLI
Palazzo Salimbeni
Piazza Salimbeni
Santa Maria di Provenzano
VIA BANCHI DI SOPRA
VIA DEI TERMINI
Via delle Terme
Via del Moro
Piazza Provenzano Salvani
CIVETTA
Vic. D. Torre
Piazza Tolomei
Santa Messe
Via Cecco Angolieri
VIA SALLUSTIO BANDINI
8 Palio Movie
Via di Calzoleria
Vic. B. Pettinaio
Vic. d. Donzelle
San Vigilio
Via San Vigilio
LEOCORNO
Piazza Indipendenza
Loggia d. Mercanzia
VIA BANCHI DI SOTTO
S. Pietro
Borsellai
Pollaioli
Rinaldini
Via d. Terme
ECCHERIA
WC
7 Fonte Gaia
VIA DI PANTANETO
San Martino
Il Campo **2**
Torre del Mangia **4**
Via di Archi
VIA DEL PORRIONE
To Porta Romana
V. di Campane
VIA DI CITTÀ
Bargello
Palazzo Pubblico/ Museo Civico **3**
TORRE
Via del Rialto
QUILA
WC
Accademia Musicale Chigiana
Piazza Mercato
Via di Salicotto
VIA GIOVANNI DUPRE
Vic. di S. Salvatore
VIA D. PORTA GIUSTIZIA
VIA DEL SOLE
VIA DI CITTÀ
VIA CASATO DI SOTTO
Via d. Lombarde
Sambuco
Pinacoteca **9**
DI SAN PIETRO
To Porta Tufi

KEY

Pedestrian-Friendly Area

Stairway

Landmark or Point of Interest (sight number marks entrance)

Tourist Information

0   1/4 kilometer

0   1/4 mile

Rick Steves'®

FLORENCE
& TUSCANY

2010

AVALON
TRAVEL

CONTENTS

INTRODUCTION

Florence is Europe's cultural capital. As the home of the Renaissance and the birthplace of the modern world, Florence practiced the art of civilized living back when the rest of Europe was rural and crude. Democracy, science, and literature, as well as painting, sculpture, and architecture, were all championed by the proud and energetic Florentines of the 1400s.

When the Florentine poet Dante first saw the teenaged Beatrice, her beauty so inspired him that he spent the rest of his life writing poems to her. In the same way, the Renaissance opened people's eyes to the physical beauty of the world around them, inspiring them to write, paint, sculpt, and build.

Today, Florence is geographically small but culturally rich, with more artistic masterpieces per square mile than anyplace else. In a single day, you could look Michelangelo's *David* in the eyes, fall under the seductive sway of Botticelli's *Birth of Venus*, and climb the modern world's first dome, which still dominates the skyline.

Of course, there's a reality here, too. As the historic center becomes increasingly filled with visitors, rents are rising and locals are fleeing to the suburbs, threatening to make Florence a kind of Renaissance theme park. Sure, Florence is touristy. But where else can you stroll the same pedestrian streets walked by Michelangelo, Leonardo, and Botticelli while savoring the world's best gelato?

To round out your visit, see Florence and then escape to the Tuscan countryside. With its manicured fields, rustic farms, and towns clinging to nearly every hill, Tuscany is our image of village Italy. Venture beyond the fringes of Florence and you'll find a series of sun- and wine-soaked villages, each with its own appeal. Stretching from the Umbrian border to the Ligurian Sea, the landscape changes from idyllic (Crete Senese) to mountainous (the Montagnola) to flat and brushed with sea breezes (Pisa).

During your visit, you'll discover that peaceful Tuscan villages and bustling Florence—with its rough-stone beauty, art-packed museums, children chasing pigeons, students riding Vespas, artisans sipping Chianti, and supermodels wearing Gucci fashions—offer many of the very things you came to Italy to see.

About This Book

Rick Steves' Florence & Tuscany 2010 is a personal tour guide in your pocket. Better yet, it's actually two tour guides in your pocket: The co-author of this book is Gene Openshaw. Since our first "Europe through the gutter" trip together as high school buddies in the 1970s, Gene and I have been exploring the wonders of the Old World. An inquisitive historian and lover of European culture, Gene wrote most of this book's self-guided museum tours and neighborhood walks. Together, Gene and I keep this book up-to-date and accurate (though for simplicity, from this point "we" will shed our respective egos and become "I").

This book is updated every year—but once you pin down Italy, it wiggles. For any updates that have occurred since our recent research, see www.ricksteves.com/update, and for a valuable list of reports and experiences—good and bad—from fellow travelers, check www.ricksteves.com/feedback.

The book is organized this way:

Orientation includes tips on public transportation, local tour options, helpful hints, and tourist information (note that tourist information is abbreviated **TI** in this book). The "Planning Your Time" section offers a suggested schedule for how to best use your limited time.

Sights provides a succinct overview of the most important sights, arranged by neighborhood, with ratings:

▲▲▲—Don't miss.
▲▲—Try hard to see.
▲—Worthwhile if you can make it.
No rating—Worth knowing about.

The self-guided **Renaissance Walk** takes you through the core of Renaissance Florence, starting with Michelangelo's *David* and cutting through the heart of the city to Ponte Vecchio on the Arno River. The **Oltrarno Walk** takes you into rustic, old Florence on the south side of the Arno, with river views, a peek at artisan workshops, and sights such as the Pitti Palace and Brancacci Chapel.

The **Self-Guided Tours** lead you through Tuscany's most important sights, with tours of Florence's Accademia (home to

Michelangelo's *David*), Uffizi Gallery, Bargello, Museum of San Marco, Duomo Museum, Medici Chapels, Medici-Riccardi Palace, Church of Santa Maria Novella, Santa Croce Church, Brancacci Chapel, Pitti Palace, and the Galileo Science Museum, as well as Siena's Duomo, Duomo Museum, and Civic Museum, and Pisa's Leaning Tower, Duomo, and Field of Miracles.

Sleeping is a guide to my favorite good-value hotels, conveniently located near the sights.

Eating serves up a range of options, from inexpensive eateries to splurges, with an emphasis on good value and quality.

Florence with Children includes my top recommendations for keeping your kids (and you) happy in Florence.

Shopping gives you tips for shopping painlessly and enjoyably, without letting it overwhelm your vacation or ruin your budget.

Nightlife is your guide to after-dark Florence, including concerts, theaters, pubs, and clubs.

Connections lays the groundwork for your smooth arrival and departure, covering transportation by train, bus, and plane.

Siena covers the highlights in this captivating Gothic city, from the stay-awhile central piazza to the 13th-century cathedral. **Pisa** takes you beyond the Leaning Tower. **Lucca** introduces you to the charms of this little-touristed, well-preserved city. And **Tuscan Hill Towns** brings you the best of village Italy, featuring San Gimignano, Volterra, Montalcino, Pienza, Montepulciano, and Cortona.

Florentine History takes you on a whirlwind tour through the ages, covering two millennia, from ancient Tuscany to the present.

The **appendix** is a traveler's tool kit, with telephone tips, useful phone numbers, recommended books and films, a festival list, climate chart, handy packing checklist, hotel reservation form, Italian survival phrases, and more.

Throughout this book, when you see a ✪ in a listing, it means that the sight is covered in much more detail in one of the tour chapters.

Browse through this book and choose your favorite sights. Then have a *buono* trip! Traveling like a temporary local, you'll get the absolute most out of every mile, minute, and euro. As you visit places I know and love, I'm happy you'll be meeting my favorite Florentines.

Planning

This section will help you get started on planning your trip—with advice on trip costs, when to go, and what you should know before you take off.

INTRODUCTION

Travel Smart

Many people travel through Italy and think it's a chaotic mess. They feel that any attempt at efficient travel is futile. This is dead wrong—and expensive. Italy, which seems as orderly as spilled spaghetti, actually functions well. Only those who understand this and travel smart can enjoy Italy on a budget.

This book can save you lots of time and money. But to have an "A" trip, you need to be an "A" student. Read it all before your trip, noting holidays, specifics on sights, and days when sights are closed. You can wait in line for two hours or more to get into the Uffizi—or you can book ahead, and walk right in. Saving Michelangelo's *David* for your trip finale is risky, and on Monday, impossible. (Florence's major sights, along with some minor ones, are closed on Mondays.) If you cut your Siena day trip short, you'll miss the city's medieval magic at twilight. A smart trip is a puzzle—a fun, doable, and worthwhile challenge.

Be sure to mix intense and relaxed periods in your itinerary. Every trip—and every traveler—needs slack time (picnics, laundry, people-watching, and so on). Pace yourself. Assume you will return.

As you travel, take advantage of the Internet and phones to make your trip run smoothly. By going online (at Internet cafés or your hotel) and using the phone (buy a phone card or carry a mobile phone), you can get tourist information, learn the latest on sights (special events, English tour schedule, etc.), book tickets and tours, make reservations, reconfirm hotels, research transportation connections, and keep in touch with your loved ones.

Connect with the culture. Set up your own quest for the best gelato, town square, *enoteca* (wine bar), or Renaissance painting or sculpture. Enjoy the friendliness of your Tuscan hosts. Slow down and be open to unexpected experiences. Ask questions—most locals are eager to point you in their idea of the right direction. Keep a notepad in your pocket for organizing your thoughts. Wear your money belt, and learn the local currency and how to estimate prices in dollars. Those who expect to travel smart, do.

Trip Costs

Six components make up your trip costs: airfare, surface transportation, room and board, sightseeing/entertainment, shopping/miscellany, and gelato.

Airfare: A basic, round-trip flight from the US to Florence should cost from $800 to $1,500, depending on where you fly from and when (flying into Milan or Rome is sometimes a little cheaper). If your trip covers a wide area, consider saving time and money in Europe by flying "open jaw" (into one city and out of another—e.g., into Rome and out of Milan).

Surface Transportation: Most of Florence's sights, clustered in the downtown core, are within easy walking distance of each other. If you'd rather use taxis than walk, allow $80–100 over the course of a one-week visit (taxis can be shared by up to four people). The cost of round-trip, second-class train transportation to the recommended nearby destinations is affordable (about $17 for a train ticket to Pisa or Siena, and less for a bus ticket to San Gimignano). For a one-way trip between Florence's airport and the city center, allow $7 by bus or $25 by taxi (can be shared). The other cities and villages covered in this book are made for walking.

Room and Board: You can easily manage in Tuscany in 2010 on $120 a day per person for room and board. This allows $15 for lunch, $30 for dinner, and $75 for lodging (based on two people splitting the cost of a $150 double room that includes breakfast). If you have more money, I've suggested great ways to spend it. Students and tightwads can enjoy Tuscany for as little as $60 a day ($30 for a bed, $30 for meals and snacks).

Sightseeing and Entertainment: Figure about $15–20 for major sights (Michelangelo's *David*, Uffizi Gallery), $5–10 for smaller ones (museums, climbing church towers), and $25–30 for splurge experiences (e.g., walking tours and concerts). An overall average of $35 a day works for most. Don't skimp here. After all, this category is the driving force behind your trip—you came to sightsee, enjoy, and experience Florence.

Shopping and Miscellany: Figure $3 per postcard, coffee, soft drink, or gelato. Shopping can vary in cost from nearly nothing to a small fortune. Good budget travelers find that this category has little to do with assembling a trip full of lifelong, wonderful memories.

When to Go

Tuscany's best travel months (also its busiest and most expensive) are May, June, September, and October.

The most grueling thing about travel in Tuscany is the summer heat in July and August, when temperatures hit the high 80s and 90s. Most mid-range hotels come with air-conditioning—a worthwhile splurge in the summer—but it's usually available only from June through September. By law, hotels cannot provide air-conditioning (or heating) outside of summer (or winter). In April and October, you'll generally need a sweater or light jacket in the evening, and in winter the temperatures can drop to the 40s or 50s (for more specifics, see the climate chart in the appendix).

Between November and April, you can usually expect pleasant weather and none of the sweat and stress of the tourist season. However, sights may have shorter hours, lunchtime breaks, and fewer activities. Confirm your sightseeing plans locally, especially when traveling off-season.

INTRODUCTION

Major Holidays and Weekends

Popular places are even busier on weekends...and inundated on three-day weekends. Holidays bring many businesses to a grinding halt. Plan ahead and reserve your accommodations and transportation well in advance.

Reserve ahead in Florence if you're traveling on major holidays—Easter and Easter Monday (April 4-5 in 2010), Liberation Day (April 25), Labor Day (May 1), Feast of the Ascension Day (May 13 in 2010), June 24 (Florence's patron saint day), All Saints' Day (November 1), Christmas (Dec 25-26), and on Fridays and Saturdays year-round. Siena's big event is the Palio, held every year on July 2 and August 16. Also check the list of festivals and holidays on page 473 of the appendix, but don't let it lull you into a false sense of security. Religious holidays can catch you by surprise anywhere in Italy.

Try to avoid Florence during the big events that bring enormous crowds. A huge fashion convention jam-packs the city twice a year (usually January and June). During Italy's Cultural Heritage Week (Settimana dei Beni Culturali), the museums are free, and the city is inundated with school groups (falls sometime in April 2010—confirm dates with TI).

Know Before You Go

Your trip is more likely to go smoothly if you plan ahead. Check this list of things to arrange while you're still at home.

You need a **passport**—but no visa or shots—to travel in Italy. You may be denied entry into certain European countries if your passport is due to expire within three to six months of your ticketed date of return. Get it renewed if you'll be cutting it close. It can take up to six weeks to get or renew a passport (for more on passports, see www.travel.state.gov). Pack a photocopy of your passport in your luggage in case the original is lost or stolen.

Check to see if you'll be visiting Tuscany during any **holidays or festivals** (such as during the Palio in Siena), when rooms can cost more and get booked up quickly. (See sidebar above.)

The popularity of Florence's top sights makes **reservations** for museums crucial: Book ahead for the Uffizi (Renaissance paintings) and Accademia (Michelangelo's *David*) to avoid standing in long lines and to guarantee that you'll get in. The Uffizi is often booked up a month or more in advance, while the Accademia is usually full at least a few days out. Make reservations for both as soon as you know when you'll be in town—your options are explained in detail on page 54. While reservations are mandatory for both the Brancacci Chapel and the Medici-Riccardi Palace, spots are generally available a day or two in advance.

Call your **debit and credit card companies** to let them know the countries you'll be visiting, so that they'll accept (and not deny) your international charges. Confirm the amount of your daily withdrawal limit, and consider asking to have it raised so you can take out more cash at each ATM stop. Ask about international transaction fees.

If you're interested in **travel insurance**, do your homework before you buy. Compare the cost of the insurance to the likelihood of your using it and your potential loss if something goes wrong. For details on the many kinds of travel insurance, see www .ricksteves.com/plan/tips/insurance.htm.

Try our **free Rick Steves audio tours** if you're bringing an iPod or other MP3 player. You can download free tours (verbal versions of several tours from this book) of Florence's major sights at www.ricksteves.com or from the iTunes Store; see page 469.

If you're planning on **renting a car** in Italy, technically you're required to have an International Driving Permit, available at your local AAA office for $15 plus the cost of two passport-type photos; see www.aaa.com. However, every time I've rented a car in Italy, I've traveled with just my US license without any problem.

If you're taking an **overnight train** and you need a couchette *(cuccetta)* or sleeper—and you must leave on a certain day—consider booking it in advance through a US agent (such as www .raileurope.com), even though it may cost more than buying it in Italy. Other Italian trains, like the high-speed ES trains, require a seat reservation, but for these it's usually possible to make arrangements in Italy just a few days ahead. (For more on train travel, see the Connections chapter and www.ricksteves.com/rail.)

Since **airline carry-on restrictions** are always changing, visit the Transportation Security Administration's website (www.tsa .gov/travelers) for an up-to-date list of what you can bring on the plane with you...and what you have to check.

Practicalities

Emergency Telephone Numbers: In Italy, dial 113 for English-speaking police help. To summon an ambulance, call 118. Or ask at your hotel for help. They'll know the nearest medical and emergency services.

Time: In Italy—and in this book—you'll use the 24-hour clock. It's the same through 12:00 noon, then keep going: 13:00,

Where Do I Find Information On...?

Credit Card Theft	See page 10.
Packing Light	See the packing list on page 479.
Phoning	See "How to Dial" on page 462.
Language	See page 481.
Making Hotel Reservations	See page 19.
Tipping	See page 11.
Tourist Information Offices	See page 461.
Updates to This Book	See www.ricksteves.com/update.

14:00, and so on. For anything past 12, subtract 12 and add p.m. (14:00 is 2:00 p.m.).

Italy, like most of continental Europe, is generally six/nine hours ahead of the East/West Coasts of the US. The exceptions are the beginning and end of Daylight Saving Time: Europe "springs forward" the last Sunday in March (two weeks after most of North America), and "falls back" the last Sunday in October (one week before North America). For a handy online converter, try www.timeanddate.com/worldclock.

Business Hours: Traditionally, Italy uses the siesta plan, though many businesses have adopted the government's recommended 8:00 to 14:00 workday. In tourist areas, shops are open longer. People usually work from about 9:00 to 13:00 and from 15:30 to 19:00. Stores are usually closed on Sunday, and often on Monday. Banking hours are generally Monday through Friday from 8:30 to 13:30 and 15:30 to 16:30, but they can vary wildly.

Saturdays are virtually weekdays, with earlier closing hours. Sundays have the same pros and cons as they do for travelers in the US: Sightseeing attractions are generally open, while shops and banks are closed. Rowdy evenings are rare on Sundays.

Watt's Up? Europe's electrical system is different from North America's in two ways: the shape of the plug (two round prongs) and the voltage of the current (220 volts, instead of 110 volts). For your North American plug to work in Europe, you'll need an adapter, sold inexpensively at travel stores in the US. As for the voltage, most newer electronics or travel appliances (such as hair dryers, laptops, and battery chargers) automatically convert the voltage—if you see a range of voltages printed on the item or its plug (such as "110–220"), it'll work in Europe. Otherwise, you can buy a converter separately in the US (about $20).

Discounts: Generally speaking, discounted admission fees are limited to European residents and countries that offer reciprocal deals (the US does not). However, museums in smaller towns are sometimes accommodating to non-European seniors, and it doesn't hurt to ask if you can get a reduced ticket *(biglietto ridotto)*.

News: Americans keep in touch via the *International Herald Tribune* (published almost daily throughout Europe and online at www.iht.com). Other newsy sites are http://news.bbc.co.uk and www.europeantimes.com. Every Tuesday, the European editions of *Time* and *Newsweek* hit the stands with articles of particular interest to European travelers. Sports addicts can get their daily fix online or from *USA Today*. Many hotels have CNN and BBC television channels.

Money

This section offers advice on getting cash, using credit and debit cards, dealing with lost or stolen cards, and tipping.

Cash from ATMs

Throughout Europe, cash machines (ATMs) are the standard way for travelers to get local currency. Traveler's checks are a waste of time in banks and a waste of money in fees.

Bring plastic—credit and/or debit cards—along with several hundred dollars as an emergency backup (in easy-to-exchange $20 bills). It's smart to bring two cards, in case one gets demagnetized or eaten by a temperamental machine. To use an ATM (known as a *bancomat*) to withdraw money from your account, you'll need a debit card (ideally with a Visa or MasterCard logo for maximum usability), plus a PIN code. Know your PIN code in numbers; there are only numbers—no letters—on European keypads.

Before you go, confirm with your bank that your card will work overseas, and alert them that you'll be making withdrawals in Europe. Otherwise, the bank may not approve transactions if it perceives unusual spending patterns. (Your credit-card company may do the same thing—let them know about your travel plans, too.) Also ask about international fees; see "Credit and Debit Cards" on the next page.

When using an ATM, try to take out large sums of money to reduce your per-transaction bank fees. If the machine refuses your request, try again and select a smaller amount (some cash machines limit the amount you can withdraw—don't take it personally). If that doesn't work, try a different machine. Also, be aware that some ATMs will tell you to take your cash within 30 seconds, and if you aren't fast enough, your cash may be sucked back into the machine...and you'll have a hassle trying to get it from the bank.

To keep your cash safe, use a money belt—a pouch with a strap that you buckle around your waist like a belt and wear under your clothes. Thieves target tourists. A money belt provides peace

Exchange Rate

1 euro (€) = about $1.40

To convert prices in euros to dollars, add about 40 percent: €20 = about $28; €50 = about $70. Just like the dollar, one euro is broken down into 100 cents. You'll find coins ranging from €0.01 to €2, and bills ranging from €5 to €500.

Look carefully at any €2 coin you get in change. Some unscrupulous merchants are giving out similar-looking, gold-rimmed old 500-*lire* coins (worth $0) instead of €2 coins (worth $2.80). You are now warned!

of mind, allowing you to carry lots of cash safely. Don't waste time every few days tracking down a cash machine—withdraw a week's worth of money, stuff it in your money belt, and travel!

Credit and Debit Cards

For purchases, Visa and MasterCard are more commonly accepted than American Express. Just like at home, credit or debit cards work easily at larger hotels and shops, but smaller businesses and many restaurants prefer—and sometimes require—payment in local currency (it's easier to pay with smaller bills; break large bills at a bank or larger store). If receipts show your credit-card number, don't toss these thoughtlessly.

Fees: Credit and debit cards—whether used for purchases or ATM withdrawals—often charge additional, tacked-on "international transaction" fees of up to 3 percent plus $5 per transaction. Note that if you use a credit card for ATM transactions, it's technically a "cash advance" rather than a "withdrawal"—and subject to an additional cash-advance fee.

To avoid unpleasant surprises, call your bank or credit-card company before your trip to ask about these fees. If the fees are too high, consider getting a card just for your trip: Capital One (www.capitalone.com) and most credit unions have low-to-no international transaction fees.

If merchants offer to convert your purchase price into dollars (called dynamic currency conversion, or DCC), refuse this "service." You'll pay even more in fees for the expensive convenience of seeing your charge in dollars.

Damage Control for Lost Cards

If you lose your credit, debit, or ATM card, you can stop people from using your card by reporting the loss immediately to the respective global customer-assistance centers. Call these 24-hour

US numbers collect: Visa (410/581-9994), MasterCard (636/722-7111), and American Express (623/492-8427).

At a minimum, you'll need to know the name of the financial institution that issued you the card, along with the type of card (classic, platinum, or whatever). Providing the following information will allow for a quicker cancellation of your missing card: full card number, whether you are the primary or secondary cardholder, the cardholder's name exactly as printed on the card, billing address, home phone number, circumstances of the loss or theft, and identification verification (your birth date, your mother's maiden name, or your Social Security number—memorize this, don't carry a copy). If you are the secondary cardholder, you'll also need to provide the primary cardholder's identification-verification details. You can generally receive a temporary card within two or three business days in Europe.

If you promptly report your card lost or stolen, you typically won't be responsible for any unauthorized transactions on your account, although many banks charge a liability fee of $50.

Tipping

Tipping in Italy isn't as automatic and generous as it is in the US, but for special service, tips are appreciated, if not expected. As in the US, the proper amount depends on your resources, tipping philosophy, and the circumstances, but some general guidelines apply.

Restaurants: Check the menu to see if the service is included (*servizio incluso*—generally 10–15 percent); if not, you could tip 5–10 percent for good service, though be advised that Italians rarely tip. For more specifics, see "Tipping in Restaurants" sidebar on page 22.

Taxis: To tip the cabbie, round up. For a typical ride, round up to the next euro on the fare (to pay a €4.50 fare, give €5). If the cabbie hauls your bags and zips you to the airport to help you catch your flight, you might want to toss in a little more. But if you feel like you're being driven in circles or otherwise ripped off, skip the tip.

Special Services: It's thoughtful to tip a couple of euros to someone who shows you a special sight and who is paid in no other way. Tour guides at sights sometimes hold out their hands for tips after they give their spiel; if I've already paid for the tour, I don't tip extra, though some tourists do give a euro or two, particularly for a job well done. At hotels, porters expect a euro for each bag they carry (another reason to pack light). Leaving the maid a euro per overnight at the end of your stay is a nice touch. In general, if someone in the service industry does a super job for you, a tip of a couple of euros is appropriate...but not required.

Cheap Tricks in Tuscany

Here are some ideas to help stretch your travel dollars.

Sightseeing

- Many of Florence's sights and activities are free. There is no charge for entry to the Duomo, Palazzo Davanzati, Orsanmichele Church, Santo Spirito Church, and San Miniato Church. It's free to visit the leather school at Santa Croce Church and the perfumery near the Church of Santa Maria Novella. The three markets (Centrale for produce, Nuovo and San Lorenzo for goods) are fun to browse through.

    Free public spaces include the Uffizi and Palazzo Vecchio courtyards; the art-filled loggia on Piazza della Signoria; and Piazzale Michelangelo, with glorious views over Florence. A walk across the picturesque Ponte Vecchio costs nothing at all—unless you suc-cumb to temptation at one of the many shops along the way. A stroll anywhere in Florence with a gelato in hand is an inexpensive treat. (This book contains information on all of these options.)
- If you're packing along an iPod or other MP3 player, you can

When in doubt, ask. If you're not sure whether (or how much) to tip for a service, ask your hotelier or the tourist information office; they'll fill you in on how it's done on their turf.

Getting a VAT Refund

Wrapped into the purchase price of your Italian souvenirs is a Value-Added Tax (VAT) of about 20 percent. If you purchase more than €155 (about $220) worth of goods at a store that participates in the VAT-refund scheme, you're entitled to get most of that tax back. Getting your refund is usually straightforward and, if you buy a substantial amount of souvenirs, well worth the hassle. If you're lucky, the merchant will subtract the tax when you make your purchase. (This is more likely to occur if the store ships the goods to your home.) Otherwise, you'll need to:

Get the paperwork. Have the merchant completely fill out the necessary refund document, called a "cheque." You'll have to present your passport.

Get your stamp at the border or airport. Process your cheque(s) at your last stop in the EU with the customs agent who download my free audio tours of the Renaissance Walk, Accademia, and Uffizi Gallery (see page 469). Audioguides at the museums cost about €5.50 apiece.

Hotels

- Choose hotels that offer a Rick Steves discount and/or offer to pay cash to get the lowest rate.
- Opt out of optional, overpriced hotel breakfasts, and grab a brioche and cappuccino with the locals at the corner bar instead.

Dining

- Don't order too much at restaurants. Servings are often big—and splittable. While restaurants frown on a couple splitting just one dish, if you and your travel partner order a few small dishes and enjoy them family-style, you can sample a few different things, save some euros, and still have room for gelato. Splitting a €6 pizza makes for a very cheap meal.
- Order take-out from delicatessens. Many shops have ready-to-eat entrées and side dishes, and will heat them up and send you on your way with plastic cutlery and napkins. Find a scenic picnic spot and enjoy your feast, having paid just a fraction of what you'd pay to eat in a restaurant.

deals with VAT refunds. It's best to keep your purchases in your carry-on for viewing, but if they're too large or dangerous (such as knives) to carry on, track down the proper customs agent to inspect them before you check your bag. You're not supposed to use your purchased goods before you leave. If you show up at customs wearing your new leather shoes, officials might look the other way—or deny you a refund.

Collect your refund. You'll need to return your stamped document to the retailer or its representative. Many merchants work with a service, such as Global Refund (www.globalrefund.com) or Premier Tax Free (www.premiertaxfree.com), which have offices at major airports, ports, and border crossings. These services, which extract a 4 percent fee, can refund your money immediately in your currency of choice or credit your card (within two billing cycles). If the retailer handles VAT refunds directly, it's up to you to contact the merchant for your refund. You can mail the documents from home, or, quicker, from your point of departure (using a stamped, addressed envelope you've prepared or one that's been provided by the merchant)—and then wait. It could take months.

Customs for American Shoppers

You are allowed to take home $800 worth of items per person duty-free, once every 30 days. The next $1,000 is taxed at a flat 3 percent. After that, you pay the individual item's duty rate. You can also bring in duty-free a liter of alcohol (slightly more than a standard-size bottle of wine, pack carefully in checked luggage; you must be at least 21), 200 cigarettes, and up to 100 non-Cuban cigars. You may take home vacuum-packed cheeses; dried herbs, spices, or mushrooms; and canned fruits or vegetables, including jams and vegetable spreads. Baked goods, candy, chocolate, oil, vinegar, mustard, and honey are OK. Fresh fruits or vegetables are not. Meats, even if canned, are generally not allowed. Note that you'll need to carefully pack any bottles of wine and other liquid-containing items in your checked luggage, due to limits on liquids in carry-ons. To check customs rules and duty rates, visit www.cbp.gov and click on "Travel," then "Know Before You Go."

Sightseeing

Sightseeing can be hard work. Use these tips to make your visits to Florence and Tuscany's finest sights meaningful, fun, efficient, and painless.

Plan Ahead

Set up an itinerary that allows you to fit in all your must-see sights. For a one-stop look at opening hours in Florence and Siena, see the "At a Glance" sidebars in their respective Orientation chapters. Most sights keep stable hours, but you can easily confirm the latest by checking with the local TI.

For Florence, make reservations for the Uffizi, Accademia *(David),* and Brancacci Chapel, plus the Medici-Riccardi Palace if you want to visit its Chapel of the Magi (see "Make Reservations to Avoid Lines" on page 54). Reserved entry times are available for other sights—including the Bargello, Medici Chapels, and Museum of San Marco—but are unnecessary.

If you'll be visiting during a holiday, find out if a particular sight will be open by phoning ahead or checking its website. And don't put off visiting a must-see sight—you never know when a place will close unexpectedly for a holiday, strike, or restoration.

When possible, visit the major sights in the morning (when your energy is best) and save other activities for the afternoon. Hit the highlights first, then go back to other things if you have the stamina and time.

Depending on the sight, there are ways to avoid crowds. This book offers tips on specific sights. Try visiting the sight very early, at lunch, or very late. Evening visits, when possible, are usually peaceful with fewer crowds.

Read ahead. To get the most out of the self-guided tours and sight descriptions in this book, read them before you visit.

At Sights

All sights have rules, and if you know about these in advance, they're no big deal. Some important sights use metal detectors or conduct bag searches that will slow your entry.

At churches—which generally offer interesting art (usually free) and a cool, welcome seat—a modest dress code is encouraged and often required (no shorts or bare shoulders). Coin boxes near a piece of art illuminate the art (and present a better photo opportunity). I pop in a coin whenever I can. It improves my experience, is a favor to other visitors trying to appreciate a great piece of art in the dark, and is a little contribution to that church and its work. Whenever possible, let there be light.

A few sights require you to check daypacks and coats. They'll be kept safely. If you have something you can't bear to part with, stash it in a pocket or purse. To avoid checking a small backpack, carry it under your arm like a purse as you enter. From a guard's point of view, a backpack is generally a problem while a purse is not.

Cameras are normally allowed, but not flashes or tripods (without special permission). Flashes damage oil paintings and distract others in the room. Even without a flash, a handheld camera will take a decent picture (or buy postcards or posters at the museum bookstore). If photos are allowed, video cameras are, too.

You'll likely have to pay cash for the admission fee; few sights take credit cards. Museums may have special exhibits in addition to their permanent collection. Some exhibits are included in the entry price, while others come at an extra cost (which you may have to pay even if you don't want to see the exhibit).

Many sights rent audioguides, which generally offer excellent recorded descriptions of the art (about $4–6). If you bring along your own pair of headphones and a Y-jack, you can sometimes share one audioguide with your travel partner and save. I have produced free audio tours of the major sights in this book (see page 469). Guided tours are most likely to be available during peak season (usually about €7 and widely ranging in quality).

Expect changes—artwork can be on tour, on loan, out sick, or shifted at the whim of the curator. To adapt, pick up any available free floor plans as you enter. Ask the museum staff if you can't find a particular painting. Say the title or artist's name, or point to the photograph in this book and ask, *"Dov'è?"* (doh-VEH, meaning "Where?").

It helps to know the terms. Art historians and Italians refer to the great Florentine centuries by dropping a thousand years. The Trecento (300s), Quattrocento (400s), and Cinquecento (500s) were the 1300s, 1400s, and 1500s. Also, in Italian museums, art is dated with *sec* for *secolo* (century, often indicated with Roman numerals), A.C. (for *Avanti Cristo,* or B.C.), and D.C. (for *Dopo Cristo,* or A.D.). O.K.?

Some important sights have an on-site café or cafeteria (usually a good place to rest and have a snack or light meal). The WCs are free and generally clean.

Many sights sell postcards and guidebooks that highlight their attractions. Before you leave, scan the postcards and thumb through the biggest guidebook (or skim its index) to be sure you haven't overlooked something that you'd like to see.

Most sights stop admitting people 30–60 minutes before closing time, and some rooms close early (generally about 45 minutes before the actual closing time). Guards usher people out, so don't save the best for last.

Every sight or museum offers more than what is covered in this book. Use the self-guided tours in this book as an introduction—not the final word.

Sleeping

For hassle-free efficiency, I favor hotels and restaurants that are handy to your sightseeing activities. Nearly all of my recommended accommodations are located in city or town centers, within minutes of the great sights. (To stay in the countryside, try *agriturismo* farmhouses; for more information on these rural B&Bs, see page 394.)

The hotel accommodations scene varies wildly with the season. Spring and fall are very tight and expensive, while mid-July through August is wide open and discounted. November through February is also generally empty. I've listed prices for peak season: April, May, June, September, and October.

With the economic downturn, no one really knows what prices the market will bear in the future, so many of the rates listed here are maximums. Many hotels may offer discounts. When emailing about their availablity, ask directly for their best deal—they want your business.

Prices at nearly any hotel can get soft if you do any of the following: Book direct, without using a pricey middleman like the TI or a Web booking service. If you pay cash, you'll get an additional 5–10 percent discount at most of these hotels—ask when you check in. Many of the listed hotels also offer my readers a "Rick Steves discount," but you must request it when you reserve;

it usually doesn't apply if you wait until check-out to bring it up. Other possibilities for price breaks: Stay at least three nights, and offer to skip breakfast for a better price. If you're on a budget, ask for a cheaper room or a discount. People traveling off-season can show up without reservations and find huge discounts.

In general, with good information and an email or phone call beforehand, you can find a stark, clean, and comfortable double with breakfast and a private bath for about €100 in Florence (less in smaller towns). You get elegance in peak season for €160. Some places listed are old and rickety, and I've described them as such. I like places that are clean, small, central, relatively quiet at night, traditional, inexpensive, and friendly—and not listed in other guidebooks. (In Florence and Tuscany, six out of eight means it's a keeper.)

Solo travelers find that the cost of a *camera singola* is often only 25 percent less than a *camera doppia*. Three or four people economize by sharing larger rooms. (If a Db is €110, a Qb would be about €150.) Most listed hotels have rooms for any size party from one to five people. If there's room for an extra cot, they'll cram it in for you (charging you around €25).

You'll save €30 if you request a room without a shower and just use the shower down the hall. Generally rooms with a bath or shower also have a toilet and a bidet (which Italians use for quick sponge baths). The cord that dangles over the tub or shower is not a clothesline. You pull it when you've fallen and can't get up.

Double beds are called *matrimoniale*, even though hotels aren't interested in your marital status. Twins are *due letti singoli*. Convents offer cheap accommodation but only *letti singoli*.

Because Europeans are generally careful with energy use, you'll find government-enforced limits on heating and air-conditioning. (There's a one-month period each spring and fall when neither is allowed.) Air-conditioning sometimes costs an extra per-day charge, is worth seeking out in summer (though it may be available only certain times of the day), and is rarely available from fall through spring.

Most hotel rooms with air-conditioners come with a control stick (like a TV remote) that generally has the same symbols and features: fan icon (click to toggle through wind power, from light to gale); louver icon (choose steady airflow or waves); snowflake and sunshine icons (cold air or heat, depending on season); clock ("O" setting: run x hours before turning off; "I" setting: wait x hours to start); and the temperature control (20–21 degrees Celsius is comfortable).

Fancier hotels usually come with air-conditioning (included in the price), a little safe, and a small stocked fridge called a *frigo bar* (FREE-goh bar; pay for what you use). Most hotel rooms have a TV and phone. Simpler places rarely have a phone.

Sleep Code

(€1 = about $1.40, country code: 39)
To help you easily sort through these listings, I've divided the rooms into three categories based on the price for a standard double room with bath during high season:

$$$ Higher Priced
$$ Moderately Priced
$ Lower Priced

To pack maximum information into a minimum of space, I use the following code to describe the recommended accommodations. Prices listed are per room, not per person. When a price range is given for a type of room (such as double rooms listing for €100–150), it means the price fluctuates with the season, size of room, or length of stay.

S = Single room (or price for one person in a double).
D = Double or Twin room. "Double beds" are often two twins sheeted together and are usually big enough for nonromantic couples.
T = Triple (generally a double bed with a single).
Q = Quad (usually two double beds).
b = Private bathroom with toilet and shower or tub.
s = Private shower or tub only (the toilet is down the hall).

According to this code, a couple staying at a "Db-€140" hotel would pay a total of €140 (about $195) for a double room with a private bathroom. Unless otherwise noted, breakfast is included, hotel staff speak basic English, and credit cards are accepted.

If I say "Internet access," there's a public terminal in the lobby for guests to use. If I say "Wi-Fi" or "cable Internet," you can generally access it in your room, but only if you have your own laptop.

When you check in, the receptionist will normally ask for your passport and keep it for a couple of hours. Hotels are legally required to register each guest with the local police. Relax. Americans are notorious for making this chore more difficult than it needs to be.

Assume that breakfast is included in the prices I've listed, unless otherwise noted. If breakfast is included but optional, you may want to skip it. While convenient, it's usually expensive—€8–10 for a simple continental buffet with ham, cheese, yogurt, and unlimited *caffè latte*. A picnic in your room followed by a coffee at the corner café can be lots cheaper.

Rooms are safe. Still, zip up camera bags and keep money out of sight. More pillows and blankets are usually in the closet or available on request. In Italy, towels and linen aren't always replaced every day. Hang your towel up to dry. Budget hotels often use "waffle," or very thin, tablecloth-type towels, which use less water and electricity to launder.

Your hotelier, a good source of advice, can direct you to the nearest launderette and Internet café.

To avoid the time-wasting line at the reception desk in the morning (or a last-minute dispute over the bill), settle your bill the evening before you leave.

Phoning

To call Italy from the US or Canada, dial 011-39 (the country code) and then the local number. If calling Italy from another European country, dial 00-39-local number. To call a Florence hotel from anywhere in Italy (including Florence), simply dial the 10-digit local number. Land lines start with 0; mobile lines start with 3. For more information on telephoning, see the appendix.

Making Reservations

Given the quality of the accommodations I've found for this book, I'd recommend that you reserve your rooms in advance, particularly if you'll be traveling during peak season. Book several weeks ahead, or as soon as you've pinned down your travel dates. Note that some national holidays jam things up and merit your making reservations far in advance (see "Major Holidays and Weekends," page 6). Just like at home, holidays that fall on a Monday, Thursday, or Friday can turn the weekend into a long holiday, so book the entire weekend well in advance.

Requesting a Reservation: To reserve, contact hotels directly by email, phone, or fax. Email is the clearest and most economical way to make a reservation. Or you can go straight to the hotel website; many have secure online reservation forms and can instantly inform you of availability and any special deals. But be sure you use the hotel's official site and not a booking agency's site—otherwise you may pay higher rates than you should. If you're phoning from the US, be mindful of time zones. Most hotels listed are accustomed to guests who speak only English.

The hotelier wants to know these key pieces of information (also included in the sample request form in the appendix):
- number and type of rooms
- number of nights
- date of arrival
- date of departure
- any special needs (e.g., bathroom in the room or down the hall, twin beds vs. double bed, air-conditioning, quiet, view, ground floor, etc.)

When you request a room, use the European style for writing dates: day/month/year. For example, for a two-night stay in July, I would request "1 double room for 2 nights, arrive 16/07/10, depart 18/07/10." (Consider carefully how long you'll stay; don't just assume you can extend your reservation for extra days after you arrive.)

If you don't get a reply to your email or fax, it usually means the hotel is already fully booked, but you can try sending the message again, or call to follow up. If they say they're booked up, mention that you're using this book.

Confirming a Reservation: If the hotel's response tells you its room availability and rates, it's not a confirmation. You must tell them that you want that room at the given rate. The hotelier will likely request your credit-card number for a one-night deposit to hold the room. While you can email your credit-card information (I do), it's safer to share that personal info via phone call, fax, two successive emails, or secure online reservation form (if the hotel has one on its website).

Canceling a Reservation: If you must cancel your reservation, it's courteous to do so with as much advance notice as possible—at least three days. Simply make a quick phone call or send an email. Family-run hotels lose money if they turn away customers while holding a room for someone who doesn't show up. Understandably, some hotels bill no-shows for one night.

Some hotels have strict cancellation policies: For example, you might lose a deposit if you cancel within two weeks of your reserved stay, or you might be billed for the entire visit if you leave early. Ask about cancellation policies before you book.

If canceling via email, request confirmation that your cancellation was received to avoid being accidentally billed.

Reconfirm Your Reservation: Always call to reconfirm your room reservation a few days in advance from the road. If you'll be arriving after 17:00, be sure to let your hotelier know. On the small chance that a hotel loses track of your reservation, bring along a hard copy of their emailed or faxed confirmation.

Reserving Rooms as You Travel: For more spontaneity, you can make reservations as you travel, calling hotels a few days to a week before your visit. If you prefer the flexibility of traveling without any reservations at all, you'll have greater success snaring rooms if you arrive at your destination early in the day. When you anticipate crowds (weekends are worst), call hotels at about 9:00 on the day you plan to arrive, when the hotel clerk knows who'll be checking out and just which rooms will be available; if you encounter a language barrier, ask the fluent receptionist at your current hotel to call for you. During less busy times, you'll find prices can be soft if you drop in and ask at the end of the day.

Eating

The Italians are masters of the art of fine living. That means eating...long and well. Lengthy, multicourse lunches and dinners and endless hours sitting in outdoor cafés are the norm. Americans eat on their way to an evening event and complain if the check is slow in coming. For Italians, the meal is an end in itself, and only rude waiters rush you. When you want the bill, mime-scribble on your raised palm or ask for it: *"Il conto?"*

Even those of us who liked dorm food will find that the local cafés, cuisine, and wines become a highlight of our Italian adventure. Trust me: This is sightseeing for your palate, and even if the rest of you is sleeping in cheap hotels, your taste buds will relish an occasional first-class splurge. You can eat well without going broke. But be careful: You're just as likely to blow a small fortune on a disappointing meal as you are to dine wonderfully for €25.

Restaurants

Good restaurants don't open for dinner before 19:00. Restaurants parked on famous squares generally serve bad food at high prices to tourists. Locals eat better at lower-rent locales. Family-run places operate without hired help and can offer cheaper meals. If the restaurants in Florence seem touristy at night there are likely two reasons: We tourists generally eat early and the locals fill the restaurants after 9:00, and a traffic law keeps locals with cars out of the city at night, causing most Florentines to opt for outlying restaurants that are Fiat-accessible.

The words *trattoria* and *osteria* (which historically meant a simple, local-style restaurant) can now mean that a place is just as elegant and pricey as a *ristorante*. While set-price meals can be cheap and easy, galloping gourmets order à la carte with the help of a menu translator. (The *Rick Steves' Italian Phrase Book & Dictionary* has a menu decoder with enough phrases for intermediate eaters.)

A full meal consists of an appetizer (antipasto, €3–6), a first course (*primo piatto*, pasta or soup, €5–12), and a second course (*secondo piatto*, expensive meat and fish dishes, €8–18). Vegetables *(contorni, verdure)* may come with the *secondo* or cost extra (€3–5) as a side dish.

The euros can add up in a hurry. Light and budget eaters get a *primo piatto* each and share an antipasto. Another good option is sharing an array of *antipasti*—either several specific dishes or a big plate of mixed delights assembled from a buffet. Italians admit that the *secondo* is the least interesting aspect of the local cuisine.

Restaurants normally pad the bill with a cover charge (*pane e coperto*—"bread and cover charge," about €2–3) and a service charge (*servizio*, 15 percent); these charges are listed on the menu.

Tipping in Restaurants

Tipping is an issue only at restaurants that have waiters and waitresses. If you order your food at a counter, don't tip. (Many Italians don't ever tip.)

In Italy, the service charge *(servizio)* is usually included and figured at 10 or 15 percent of your total bill. There's no need to tip beyond that. If service is included, the prices listed in the menu will either have this charge built in (the menu will say *servizio incluso)* or the service might show up as a separate line item at the end of your bill (in this case, the menu might say *servizio non incluso).* Check your bill. Fixed-price tourist deals *(menu turistico)* include service.

If service is not included, you could tip 5–10 percent by rounding up or leaving the change from your bill. Leave the tip on the table, or hand it to your server. It's best to tip in cash, even if you pay with your credit card; otherwise, the tip may never reach your server.

Wine Bars *(Enoteche)*

An *enoteca* is a popular, fast, and inexpensive option for lunch. Surrounded by the local office crowd, you can get a fancy salad, plate of meats and cheeses, and a glass of fine wine (see blackboards for the day's selection and price per glass—and go for the top end). A good *enoteca* aims to impress visitors with its wine, and will generally choose excellent-quality ingredients for the simple dishes it offers with the wine. Some of my favorite Italian eating experiences have been at *enoteche.*

Bars/Cafés

Italian "bars" are not taverns but cafés. These local hangouts serve coffee, mini-pizzas, sandwiches, and drinks from the cooler. Many dish up plates of fried cheese and vegetables from under the glass counter, ready to reheat. This budget choice is the Italian equivalent of English pub grub.

For quick meals, bars usually have trays of cheap, ready-made sandwiches *(panini or tramezzini)*—some kinds are delightful grilled. To save time for sightseeing and room for dinner, stop by a bar for a light lunch, such as a ham-and-cheese *panino* (called *toast;* have it grilled twice if you want it really hot). To get food "to go," say, *"Da portar via"* (for the road). All bars have a WC *(toilette, bagno)* in the back, and customers (and the discreet public) can use it.

Bars serve great drinks: hot, cold, sweet, or alcoholic. Chilled bottled water, still *(naturale)* or carbonated *(frizzante),* is sold cheap to go.

Eating with the Seasons

Italian cooks love to serve you fresh produce and seafood at its tastiest. If you must have porcini mushrooms outside of October and November, they'll be frozen. To get the freshest veggies at a fine restaurant, request *"Il piatto di verdure della stagione, per favore"* ("A plate of seasonal vegetables, please").

Here are a few examples of what's fresh when:

April–May:	Squid, green beans, asparagus, artichokes, and zucchini flowers
April, May, Sept, Oct:	Black truffles
May–June:	Asparagus, zucchini, cantaloupe, and strawberries
May–Aug:	Eggplant
Oct–Nov:	Mushrooms and white truffles
Fresh year-round:	Clams, meats, and cheese

Coffee: If you ask for *"un caffè,"* you'll get espresso. Cappuccino is served to locals before noon and to tourists any time of day. (To an Italian, cappuccino is a breakfast drink and a travesty after eating anything with tomatoes.) Italians like their coffee only warm—to get it hot, request *"molto caldo"* (very hot) or *"più caldo, per favore"* ("hotter, please"; pew KAHL-doh, pehr fah-VOH-ray).

Experiment with a few of the options:

- cappuccino: espresso with foamed milk on top
- *caffè latte:* tall glass with espresso and hot milk mixed (ordering just a "latte" gets you only milk)
- *caffè freddo:* iced sweet espresso
- cappuccino *freddo:* iced cappuccino
- *caffè hag:* instant decaf (any coffee drink is available decaffeinated; ask for it *decaffeinato:* day-kah-fay-een-AH-toh)
- *caffè macchiato:* with only a little milk
- *caffè americano:* espresso diluted with hot water
- *caffè corretto:* espresso with a shot of liqueur (normally grappa, amaro, or Sambuca)

Juice: *Spremuta* means freshly squeezed, as far as *succa* (fruit juice) is concerned. (Note: *Spumante* means champagne.)

Beer: Beer on tap is *alla spina.* Get it *piccola* (33 cl, 11 oz), *media* (50 cl, 17 oz), or *grande* (a liter).

Wine: To order a glass (*bicchiere;* bee-kee-AY-ray) of red *(rosso)* or white *(bianco)* wine, say, *"Un bicchiere di vino rosso/bianco."* *Corposo* means full-bodied. House wine *(vino della casa)* often comes in a quarter-liter carafe *(un quarto).*

Prices: You'll notice a two-tiered price system. Drinking a cup of coffee while standing at the bar is cheaper than drinking it at a table. If you're on a budget, don't sit without first checking out the financial consequences. Ask, "Same price if I sit or stand?" by saying, *"Costa uguale al tavolo o al banco?"* (KOH-stah oo-GWAH-lay ahl TAH-voh-loh oh ahl BAHN-koh?).

If the bar isn't busy, you'll often just order and then pay when you leave. Otherwise: 1) Decide what you want; 2) find out the price by checking the price list on the wall, the prices posted near the food, or by asking the barista; 3) pay the cashier; and 4) give the receipt to the barista (whose clean fingers handle no dirty euros) and tell him or her what you want.

Delis, Cafeterias, Pizza Shops, *Tavola Calda* ("Hot Table") Bars, and More

Tuscany offers many less-expensive alternatives to restaurants. Stop by a *rosticceria* for great cooked deli food, a self-service cafeteria (called "free flow" in Italian) for the basics without the add-ons, a *tavola calda* bar for an assortment of veggies, or a Pizza Rustica shop for stand-up or take-out pizza by the slice.

Pizza is cheap and everywhere. Key pizza vocabulary: *capricciosa* (generally ham, mushrooms, olives, and artichokes), *funghi* (mushrooms), *marinara* (tomato sauce, oregano, garlic, no cheese), *quattro formaggi* (four different cheeses), and *quattro stagioni* (different toppings on each of the four quarters, for those who can't choose just one menu item). If you ask for *peperoni* on your pizza, you'll get green or red peppers, not sausage. Kids like the bland *margherita* (cheese with tomato sauce) or *diavola* (the closest thing in Italy to American pepperoni). At Pizza Rustica take-out shops, slices are sold by weight (100 grams, or *un etto*, is a hot and cheap snack; 200 grams, or *due etti*, makes a light meal).

For a fast, economic, and healthy lunch, find a *tavola calda* bar with a buffet spread of meat and vegetables, and ask for a mixed plate of vegetables with a hunk of mozzarella *(piatto misto di verdure con mozzarella)*. Don't be limited by what's displayed. If you'd like a salad with a slice of cantaloupe and a hunk of cheese, they'll whip that up for you in a snap. Belly up to the bar and, with a pointing finger and key words from the chart in this chapter, you can get a fine plate of mixed vegetables. If something's a mystery, ask for *un assaggio* (oon ah-SAH-joh) to get a little taste.

Döner kebab places are popping up all over Florence (selling veal, chicken, or falafel and salad fixings wrapped in a tortilla)—understandably popular for a budget break from Italian food.

Ordering Food at *Tavola Caldas*

plate of mixed veggies	*piatto misto di verdure*	pee-AH-toh MEES-toh dee vehr-DOO-ray
"Heated, please."	*"Scaldare, per favore."*	skahl-DAH-ray, pehr fah-VOH-ray
"A taste, please."	*"Un assaggio, per favore."*	oon ah-SAH-joh, pehr fah-VOH-ray
artichoke	*carciofi*	kar-CHOH-fee
asparagus	*asparagi*	ah-SPAH-rah-jee
beans	*fagioli*	fah-JOH-lee
breadsticks	*grissini*	gree-SEE-nee
broccoli	*broccoli*	BROH-koh-lee
cantaloupe	*melone*	may-LOH-nay
carrots	*carote*	kah-ROT-ay
green beans	*fagiolini*	fah-joh-LEE-nee
ham	*prosciutto*	proh-SHOO-toh
mushrooms	*funghi*	FOONG-ghee
potatoes	*patate*	pah-TAH-tay
rice	*riso*	REE-zoh
spinach	*spinaci*	speen-AH-chee
tomatoes	*pomodori*	poh-moh-DOH-ree
zucchini	*zucchine*	zoo-KEE-nay

(Excerpted from *Rick Steves' Italian Phrase Book & Dictionary*)

Picnics

Throughout Tuscany, picnicking saves lots of euros and is a great way to sample local specialties. For a colorful experience, gather your ingredients in the morning at the local produce market (Florence's is Mercato Centrale, near the Church of San Lorenzo); you'll probably visit several market stalls to put together a complete meal. A local *alimentari* is your one-stop corner grocery store (most will slice and stuff your sandwich for you if you buy the ingredients there). The rare *supermercato* gives you more efficiency with less color for less cost.

Juice-lovers can get a liter of O.J. for the price of a Coke or coffee. Look for "100% *succo*" (juice) on the label. Hang onto the half-liter mineral-water bottles (sold everywhere for about €1). Buy juice in cheap liter boxes, drink some, and store the extra in your water bottle. (Like locals, I refill my water bottle with tap water—*acqua del rubinetto.*)

Picnics can be an adventure in high cuisine. Be daring. Try the fresh mozzarella, *presto* pesto, shriveled olives, and any UFOs the locals are excited about. Shopkeepers are happy to sell small quantities of produce. They seem to enjoy giving you a taste *(un assaggio)*. It is customary to let the merchant choose the produce for you. Say *"Per oggi"* (pehr OH-jee), or "For today," and he or she will grab you something ready to eat, weigh it, and make the sale. A typical picnic for two might be fresh rolls, 100 grams of cheese, 100 grams of meat *(un etto* = 100 grams = about a quarter pound), two tomatoes, three carrots, two apples, yogurt, and a liter box of juice. Total cost: about €10.

Florentine Cuisine

While many restaurants in Florence and Tuscany serve your basic Italian fare—pasta and pizza, veal cutlets, and mixed salad—there are a few local specialties you'll find without looking too hard. In general, Florentine cuisine is hearty, simple farmers' food: grilled meats, high-quality seasonal vegetables, fresh herbs, prized olive oil, and rustic bread. Tuscans are frugal, not wasting a single breadcrumb. They are also known as *mangiafagioli* (bean-eaters)—and upon sorting through the many beans on Florentine menus, you'll learn why. Florence is not a great pizza town.

Note that steak and seafood are often sold by weight (priced by the kilo—1,000 grams, or just more than 2 pounds; or by the *etto*—100 grams). Sometimes, especially for steak, restaurants require a minimum order of four or five etti. Beware, or be shell-shocked by €50 entrées. Make sure you're really clear on the price before ordering.

Here are some typical foods you'll encounter throughout Tuscany:

Appetizers *(Antipasti)*
Tuscan bread: Rustic-style breads (not baguettes) with a thick crust and chewy interior. It's a type of sourdough bread, unsalted and nearly flavorless, used almost like a utensil to sop up the heartier-flavored cuisine. Slathered with olive oil and salt, it is a popular afternoon snack. Locals describe the action of dipping their crust repeatedly into the treasured olive oil as "making the *scarpetta* (little shoe)."

Bruschetta: Toasted bread slices brushed with olive oil and rubbed with garlic, topped with chopped tomato, or a variety of spreads.

Crostini: Small toasted bread rounds topped with meat or vegetable pastes. *Alla Toscana* generally means with liver paste.

Lardo (pork lard) is also a favorite traditional spread.

Panzanella: A simple Tuscan salad, served only in the summer, that's made of chunks of day-old bread and chopped tomatoes, onion, and basil, tossed in a light vinaigrette.

Pecorino cheese: Fresh *(fresco)* or aged *(stagionato),* from ewe's milk.

Porcini mushrooms: Harvested in the fall and used in pasta and soups.

Finocchiona sbriciolona: A soft salami flavored with fennel seed.

First Course *(Primo Piatto)*

Ribollita: "Reboiled" soup traditionally made with leftovers, including white beans *(fagioli),* seasonal vegetables, and olive oil, with layers of day-old Tuscan bread slices.

Pappardelle sulla lepre: This broad noodle is served with a rich sauce made from wild hare.

Pici al ragù: A fat, spaghetti-like pasta served most often with a meat-tomato sauce.

Main Course *(Secondo Piatto)*

Bistecca alla fiorentina: A thick T-bone steak, grilled and lightly seasoned. (The best is from the white Chianina breed of cattle you'll see grazing throughout Tuscany.) This dish is often sold by weight (per *etto,* or 100 grams), not per portion; ask what the minimum amount costs.

Cinghiale: Wild boar, served grilled or in soups, stews, and pasta. It is also made into many varieties of sausage.

Arrosto misto: Mixed roast meats, or meats on a skewer *(spiedino).*

Various game birds: Squab, pheasant, and guinea hen.

Trippa alla fiorentina: Tripe (intestines) and vegetables sautéed in a tomato sauce, sometimes baked with parmesan cheese.

...alla fiorentina: Anything cooked "in the Florentine style." The phrase can mean almost anything, but often means it's cooked with vegetables, especially spinach.

Dessert *(Dolci)*

Panforte: Dense, dark, clove-and-cinnamon-spiced cake from Siena. *Panforte* makes a good, enduring gift.

Gelato: The Florentines claim they invented Italian-style ice cream. Many think they serve some of the world's best. Consider skipping dessert at the restaurant and stretching your legs before finding a good *gelateria.*

Cantucci and **Vin Santo:** Florentines love this simple way to end a meal, by dipping the crunchy almond biscotti in *vin santo* (literally "holy wine"), a sweet, golden dessert wine.

Wines (Vini)

For more on Tuscan wines, and how to decipher the labels, see page 394.

Brunello di Montalcino: One of Italy's greatest red wines, made from Sangiovese *grosso* grapes, comes from the slopes of Montalcino, south of Siena. This full-bodied wine is aged at least four years in wooden casks, resulting in a bold, smooth character. Called "the brunette," it's dark brownish-red and has a rich, robust, complex aroma that is suitable to pair with hearty, meaty food. Really savor this one; bottles typically start at €25.

Rosso di Montalcino: This lower-priced, younger version of Brunello—a.k.a. "baby Brunello"—is also made in Montalcino from Sangiovese grapes. It lacks Brunello's depth of flavor and complexity, but it's still a great wine at a bargain price, usually €8–15.

Chianti: This hearty red from the Chianti region (20 miles south of Florence), made mostly from the Sangiovese grape, is world-famous. "Chianti Classico," with a black rooster symbol on the bottle's neck, is usually the best. Cheap, €2 Chiantis are acidic, while better ones, starting at €8, can be flavorful, sometimes earthy or fruity.

Vino Nobile di Montepulciano: This high-quality, ruby red, dry wine—also made of Sangiovese grapes—goes well with meat dishes, especially chicken. Don't confuse this one with the inferior (but drinkable) Montepulciano wine available in most US grocery stores.

Super Tuscans: Ultra-expensive and rivaling the Brunello in taste, this newer breed of Italian wine is a creative mix of locally grown non-Italian grapes (usually from French grapes like Cabernet and Merlot), so the Italian regulating body does not rate them. Ask for help in choosing one of these at an *enoteca*. There are many choices, and at these prices, you don't want to be disappointed. Reliable brands are Sassicaia and Tignanello.

Vernaccia di San Gimignano: In Tuscany, this is the only choice for white-wine-lovers, but even finicky red wine fans will be able to down a glass of this medium-dry white, which pairs well with pasta and salad.

Transportation

The downtown core of Florence is walkable. For information on taking city buses and taxis, see "Getting Around Florence" in the Orientation to Florence chapter. If you have a car, park it. Drivers who don't follow the strict rules get fined (see page 286).

> ## How Was Your Trip?
>
> Were your travels fun, smooth, and meaningful? If you'd like to share your tips, concerns, and discoveries, please fill out the survey at www.ricksteves.com/feedback. I value your feedback. Thanks in advance—it helps a lot.

Getting around the Tuscan countryside is easiest by rental car and doable by bus and train; you'll find information in the Connections chapter on getting around Tuscany by car, bus, and train. Specifics on public transportation are also given per destination. If you need a travel agency in Florence, see page 40.

Traveling as a Temporary Local

We travel all the way to Italy to enjoy differences—to become temporary locals. You'll experience frustrations. Certain truths that we find "God-given" or "self-evident," such as cold beer, ice in drinks, bottomless cups of coffee, hot showers, and bigger being better, are suddenly not so true. One of the benefits of travel is the eye-opening realization that there are logical, civil, and even better alternatives. A willingness to go local ensures that you'll enjoy a full dose of Italian hospitality.

Americans are enjoying a surge in popularity in Europe these days. But if there is a negative aspect to Italians' image of Americans, it's that we are big, loud, aggressive, impolite, rich, and a bit naive. Think about the rationale behind "crazy" Italian decisions. For instance, many hoteliers turn off the heat in early April and can't turn on air-conditioning until June. The point is to conserve energy, and it's mandated by the Italian government. You could complain about being cold or hot...or bring a sweater in winter, and in summer, be prepared to sweat a little like everyone else.

Europeans place a high value on speaking quietly in nice restaurants and on trains. Listen while on the bus or in a restaurant—the place can be packed, but the decibel level is low. Try to adjust your volume accordingly to show respect for their culture.

While Italians, flabbergasted by our Yankee excesses, say in disbelief, *"Mi sono cadute le braccia!"* ("I throw my arms down!"), they nearly always afford us individual travelers all the warmth we deserve. Judging from all the happy feedback I receive from travelers who have used this book, it's safe to assume you'll enjoy a great, affordable vacation—with the finesse of an independent, experienced traveler.

Thanks, and *buon viaggio!*

Back Door Travel Philosophy
From Rick Steves' Europe Through the Back Door

Travel is intensified living—maximum thrills per minute and one of the last great sources of legal adventure. Travel is freedom. It's recess, and we need it.

Experiencing the real Europe requires catching it by surprise, going casual..."Through the Back Door."

Affording travel is a matter of priorities. (Make do with the old car.) You can eat and sleep—simply, safely, and enjoyably—anywhere in Europe for $120 a day plus transportation costs. In many ways, spending more money only builds a thicker wall between you and what you traveled so far to see. Europe is a cultural carnival, and time after time, you'll find that its best acts are free and the best seats are the cheap ones.

A tight budget forces you to travel close to the ground, meeting and communicating with the people. Never sacrifice sleep, nutrition, safety, or cleanliness to save money. Simply enjoy the local-style alternatives to expensive hotels and restaurants.

Connecting with people carbonates your experience. Extroverts have more fun. If your trip is low on magic moments, kick yourself and make things happen. If you don't enjoy a place, maybe you don't know enough about it. Seek the truth. Recognize tourist traps. Give a culture the benefit of your open mind. See things as different, but not better or worse. Any culture has plenty to share.

Of course, travel, like the world, is a series of hills and valleys. Be fanatically positive and militantly optimistic. If something's not to your liking, change your liking.

Travel can make you a happier American, as well as a citizen of the world. Our Earth is home to six and a half billion equally precious people. It's humbling to travel and find that other people don't have the "American Dream"—they have their own dreams. Europeans like us, but with all due respect, they wouldn't trade passports.

Thoughtful travel engages us with the world. In tough economic times, it reminds us what is truly important. By broadening perspectives, travel teaches new ways to measure quality of life.

Globetrotting destroys ethnocentricity, helping us understand and appreciate other cultures. Rather than fear the diversity on this planet, celebrate it. Among your most prized souvenirs will be the strands of different cultures you choose to knit into your own character. The world is a cultural yarn shop, and Back Door travelers are weaving the ultimate tapestry. Join in!

FLORENCE
Firenze

ORIENTATION

The best of Florence lies mostly on the north bank of the Arno River. The main historical sights cluster around the red-brick dome of the cathedral (Duomo). Everything is within a 20-minute walk of the train station, cathedral, or Ponte Vecchio (Old Bridge). The less impressive but more characteristic Oltrarno area (south bank) is just over the bridge. Though small, Florence is intense. Prepare for scorching summer heat, kamikaze motor scooters, slick pickpockets, few WCs, steep prices, and long lines.

Planning Your Time

Plan your sightseeing carefully: Opening hours can be erratic, and crowds can cause long lines. Before heading into Florence, carefully check all the opening and closing times of your must-see museums at the TI, by phone, or online. This is especially true if you'll be in town for only a day or two during the crowded summer months.

The Uffizi Gallery and Accademia (starring Michelangelo's *David*) nearly always have long ticket-buying lines, especially in peak season (April–Oct) and on holiday weekends. Crowds thin out weekdays in the off-season. Whatever time of year you visit, you can easily avoid the wait by making reservations (see page 54). Note that both of these major sights are closed on Monday.

The Museum of San Marco closes at 13:50 on weekdays and at 16:50 on weekends. Other museums close early only on certain days (e.g., the first Sunday of the month, second and fourth Monday, etc.). In general, Sundays and Mondays are bad, with many museums either closed or with shorter hours.

Set up a good itinerary in advance. Do my recommended Renaissance Walk in the morning or late afternoon to avoid heat and crowds. Stop often for gelato.

Florence Overview

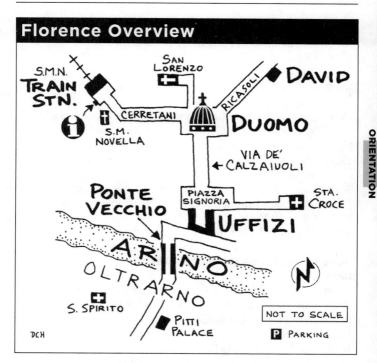

Florence in One Day

8:30   Accademia *(David)*—reserve in advance.

10:00 Renaissance Walk through town center, climb the Campanile.

12:00 Bargello (best statues), lunch afterward at Cantinetta dei Verrazzano (closed Sun) or in market neighborhood.

14:00 Shopping around San Lorenzo.

16:30 Uffizi Gallery (finest paintings)—reserve at least a month in advance (with your hotel's help, by phone, or online).

19:30 Dinner on or near Piazza della Signoria, or take the Oltrarno Walk (best local color) and have dinner across the river at 20:00.

Florence in Two Days

Day 1

8:30   Accademia (David)—reserve in advance.

10:00 Museum of San Marco (art by Fra Angelico).

12:00 Medici Chapels (Michelangelo, closes early in winter).

14:00 Lunch, market, wander, shop.

16:30 Baptistery (closes at 14:00 on Sun).

17:00 Climb the Campanile.

18:00 Renaissance Walk through heart of old town (Duomo interior closed in evening, but skippable).

20:00 Dinner near Piazza della Signoria.

Day 2

9:00 Bargello (great statues).

11:00 Duomo Museum (intriguing statues by Donatello and Michelangelo) or Galileo Science Museum.

13:00 Lunch, free to wander and shop.

15:00 Church of Santa Maria Novella (Masaccio painting) and old perfumery.

17:00 Uffizi Gallery (best paintings)—reserve at least a month in advance (through your hotel, by phone, or online).

19:00 Oltrarno Walk.

20:00 Dinner in Oltrarno.

Florence in Three (or More) Days

Day 1

8:30 Accademia (*David*)—reserve in advance.

10:00 Museum of San Marco (Fra Angelico).

12:00 Markets, shop, wander.

13:00 Lunch.

14:00 Medici Chapels (Michelangelo).

15:00 Church of Santa Maria Novella and old perfumery.

16:30 Baptistery (closes at 14:00 on Sun).

17:00 Climb the Campanile.

18:00 Renaissance Walk through heart of old town.

20:00 Dinner on or near Piazza della Signoria.

Day 2

9:00 Bargello (top statues).

11:00 Galileo Science Museum.

13:00 Lunch, free to wander and shop.

16:30　Uffizi Gallery (unforgettable paintings)—reserve at least a month in advance (through your hotel, by phone, or online).

19:00　Sunset at Piazzale Michelangelo (consider a dinner picnic).

Day 3

9:00　Duomo Museum.

11:00　Santa Croce Church (opens at 13:00 on Sun).

13:00　Lunch.

14:00　Pitti Palace, Boboli and Bardini Gardens.

18:00　Oltrarno Walk.

20:00　Dinner in Oltrarno.

Day 4

Side-trip to Siena (sights open daily; 1–2 hours away by bus), or consider an overnight stay to enjoy the town at twilight.

Day 5 (or More)

Visit your pick of Pisa, Lucca, and Tuscan hill towns.

Arrival in Florence

For a rundown on Florence's train station, the bus station (next to the train station), and nearby airports—as well as tips for arriving by car or cruise ship—see the Connections chapter.

Tourist Information

There are three TIs in Florence: across from the train station, near Santa Croce Church, and on Via Cavour.

The TI across the square from the train station is most crowded—expect long lines (Mon–Sat 8:30–19:00, Sun 8:30–14:00; with your back to tracks, exit the station—it's 100 yards away, across the square in wall near corner of church at Piazza Stazione 4; tel. 055-212-245, www.firenzeturismo.it). In the train station, avoid the Hotel Reservations "Tourist Information" window (marked *Informazioni Turistiche Alberghiere*) near the McDonald's; it's not a real TI but a hotel-reservation business instead.

The TI near Santa Croce Church is pleasant, helpful, and uncrowded (Mon–Sat 9:00–19:00, Sun 9:00–14:00, shorter hours off-season, Borgo Santa Croce 29 red, tel. 055-234-0444).

Another winner is the TI three blocks north of the Duomo (Mon–Sat 8:30–18:30, Sun 8:30–13:30, Via Cavour 1 red, tel. 055-290-832, international bookstore across street).

At any TI, pick up these handy resources:

• a free map (ask for the "APT" map, which has bus routes of interest to tourists on the back)

Daily Reminder

Sunday: The Duomo's dome, Galileo Science Museum, Museum of Precious Stones, and Mercato Centrale are closed. At the Church of Santa Maria Novella, the Museum and Cloisters are closed, but the church itself is open (13:00–17:00). These sights close early: Duomo Museum (at 13:40) and the Baptistery's interior (at 14:00). A few sights are open only in the afternoon: Duomo (13:30–16:45), Santa Croce Church (13:00–17:30), Church of San Lorenzo (13:30–17:00), Brancacci Chapel and Church of Santa Maria Novella (both 13:00–17:00), and Santo Spirito Church (16:00–17:30). The Museum of San Marco is closed on the first, third, and fifth Sundays of the month. Palazzo Davanzati and the Medici Chapels close on the second and fourth Sundays. Need a calendar? Look in the appendix.

It's not possible to reserve tickets by phone on Sunday for the major sights (Accademia and Uffizi Gallery) because the telephone-reservation office for both is closed; try other options instead (see page 54 for details).

Monday: The biggies are closed, including the Accademia (David) and the Uffizi Gallery, as well as the Orsanmichele Church, and the Pitti Palace's Palatine Gallery, Royal Apartments, and Modern Art Gallery.

The Museum of San Marco and the Bargello close on the second and fourth Mondays. At the Pitti Palace, the Argenti Museum and the Boboli and Bardini Gardens close on the first and last Mondays. Palazzo Davanzati is closed on the first, third, and fifth Mondays. The San Lorenzo Market is closed Monday in winter.

Target these sights on Mondays: Duomo and its dome, Duomo Museum, Campanile, Baptistery, Medici-Riccardi Palace, Brancacci Chapel, Mercato Nuovo, Mercato Centrale, Casa Buonarroti, Galileo Science Museum, Palazzo Vecchio, and churches (including Santa Croce and Santa Maria Novella). Or take a walking tour.

Tuesday: All sights are open, except Casa Buonarroti and the Brancacci Chapel. The Galileo Science Museum closes early (13:00).

- a current museum-hours listing (extremely important, since no guidebook—including this one—has ever been able to accurately predict the hours of Florence's sights for the coming year), and any information on entertainment, including the TI's monthly *Florence and Tuscany News* (good for events and entertainment listings); the free (and ad-driven) monthly *Florence Concierge Information* magazine (which lists museums, plus concerts, markets, sporting events, church services, shopping ideas, some bus and train connections, and an

Wednesday: All sights are open, except the Medici-Riccardi Palace and Santo Spirito Church.

Thursday: All sights are open. These sights close early: Duomo (15:30) and Palazzo Vecchio (14:00).

Friday: All sights are open except the Museum and Cloisters at the Church of Santa Maria Novella (church open 13:00–17:00).

Saturday: All sights are open, but the Science Museum closes at 13:00. The Duomo's dome closes at 17:40, and the Duomo closes early (15:30) on the first Saturday of the month.

Early-Closing Warning: Some of Florence's sights close surprisingly early every day (or most days). Palazzo Davanzati closes daily at 13:50, and the Museum of San Marco closes at 13:50 on weekdays (open later Sat and some Sun). The Museum of Precious Stones closes at 14:00 (Mon–Wed and Fri–Sat), as does the Mercato Centrale (open daily except Sun) and Casa Buonarroti (open daily except Tue).

State-run museums (including the Uffizi, Accademia, Bargello, Medici Chapels, Pitti Palace, and Museum of San Marco) have impromptu staff meetings (once a month or so) that temporarily close the sight and disrupt reservation schedules. If this happens during your visit to Florence, take a deep breath and be prepared to wait in line.

Late-Hours Relief: The Accademia, along with the Palatine Gallery in the Pitti Palace, is open until 18:50 daily except Monday.

Many sights are open until 19:00 on a particular day or more: Museum of Precious Stones (Thu), San Lorenzo Market (daily, but closed Mon in winter), Medici-Riccardi Palace (Thu–Tue), the Duomo's dome (Mon–Fri), Baptistery (Mon–Sat, except first Sat of month until 14:00), Mercato Nuovo (daily), Palazzo Vecchio (Fri–Wed), and San Miniato Church (daily but closes at 18:00 in winter).

These sights are open until 19:30: Campanile (daily), Duomo Museum (Mon–Sat), and the Boboli and Bardini Gardens at the Pitti Palace (daily, June–Aug only).

entire similar section on Siena); and *The Florentine* newspaper (published every other Thu in English, for expats and tourists, with great articles giving cultural insights; download latest issue at www.theflorentine.net). These English freebies are available at TIs and hotels all over town.

Helpful Hints

Theft Alert: Florence has particularly hardworking thief gangs who hang out where you do: near the train station, the station's underpass (especially where the tunnel surfaces), and major sights. American tourists—especially older ones—are considered easy targets. Some thieves even dress like tourists to fool you. Also be on guard at two squares frequented by drug pushers (Santa Maria Novella and Santo Spirito). Bus #7 (to Fiesole) is a favorite with tourists and, therefore, with thieves.

Medical Help: There's no shortage of English-speaking medical help in Florence. To reach a doctor who speaks English, call **Medical Service Firenze** at 055-475-411; the phone is answered 24/7. Rates are reasonable. For a doctor to come to your hotel within an hour of your call, you'd pay €100–200 (higher rates apply on Sun, holidays, or late visits). You pay only €50 if you go to the clinic when the doctor's in (Mon–Fri 11:00–12:00 & 17:00–18:00, Sat 11:00–12:00, closed Sun, no appointment necessary, Via L. Magnifico 59, near Piazza della Libertà). A second clinic is available at Via Porta Rossa 1 (Mon–Sat 13:00–16:00, closed Sun).

Dr. Stephen Kerr is an English doctor specializing in helping sick tourists. Near his clinic is a 24-hour pharmacy (clinic open for drop-ins Mon–Fri 15:00–17:00, other times by appointment, €60 per visit, Piazza Mercato Nuovo 1, between Piazza della Repubblica and Ponte Vecchio, tel. 055-288-055, mobile 335-836-1682, www.dr-kerr.com). The TI has a list of other English-speaking doctors.

There are 24-hour **pharmacies** at the train station and on Borgo San Lorenzo (near the Duomo).

Churches: Many churches now operate like museums, charging an admission fee to see their art treasures. Modest dress for men, women, and even children is required in some churches, and recommended for all of them—no bare shoulders, short shorts, or short skirts. Be respectful of worshippers and the paintings; don't use a flash. Churches usually close from 12:00 or 12:30 to 15:00 or 16:00.

Addresses: Street addresses list businesses in red and residences in black (color-coded on the actual street number and indicated by a letter following the number in printed addresses: "r" = red; no indication or "n" = black, for *nero*). *Pensioni* are usually black but can be either. The red and black numbers each appear in roughly consecutive order on streets but bear no apparent connection with each other. I'm lazy and don't concern myself with the distinction (if one number's wrong, I look for the other) and can easily find my way around.

Internet Access: In bustling, tourist-filled Florence, you'll see small Internet cafés on virtually every street (remember to bring your passport).

Internet Train is the dominant chain, with bright and cheery rooms, speedy computers, and long hours (€3.50/hr, reusable card good for any other Internet Train location, open daily roughly 9:00–20:00, www.internettrain.it). Find branches at the train station (downstairs), near Piazza della Repubblica (Via Porta Rossa 38 red), behind the Duomo (Via dell'Oriolo 40), on Piazza Santa Croce (Via de Benci 36 red), near David and recommended hotels (Via Guelfa 54 red), and near Ponte Vecchio (Borgo San Jacopo 30 red). Internet Train also offers Wi-Fi, phone cards, compact-disc burning, and other related services.

Bookstores: Local guidebooks (sold at kiosks) are cheap and give you a map and a decent commentary on the sights. For brand-name guidebooks in English, try **Feltrinelli International** (Mon–Sat 9:00–19:30, closed Sun, a few blocks north of the Duomo and across the street from TI and Medici-Riccardi Palace at Via Cavour 20 red, tel. 055-219-524); **Edison Bookstore** (also has CDs, plus novels on the Renaissance and much more on its four floors; Mon–Sat 9:00–24:00, Sun 10:00–24:00, facing Piazza della Repubblica, tel. 055-213-110); **Paperback Exchange** (cheaper, all books in English, bring in your used book for a discount on a new one, Mon–Fri 9:00–19:30, Sat 10:30–19:30, closed Sun, just south of the Duomo on Via delle Oche 4 red, tel. 055-293-460); or **BM Bookshop** (with perhaps the city's largest collection of English books and guidebooks—including mine; Mon–Sat 9:30–19:30, closed Sun, near Ponte alla Carraia at Borgognissanti 4 red, tel. 055-294-575).

Maps: While the city is awash in free tourist maps, which work fine for most visits, if you want to invest in a durable, detailed, and smartly designed map, consider Rough Guide's *Map of Florence & Siena* (€9).

Laundry: The **Wash & Dry Lavarapido** chain offers long hours and efficient, self-service launderettes at several locations (about €7 for wash and dry, daily 8:00–22:00, tel. 055-580-480). These are close to recommended hotels: Via dei Servi 105 red (and a rival launderette at Via Guelfa 55, off Via San Zanobi; both near David), Via del Sole 29 red and Via della Scala 52 red (between train station and river), Via Ghibellina 143 red (Palazzo Vecchio), Via Faenza 26 (near station), and Via dei Serragli 87 red (across the river in Oltrarno neighborhood).

Travel Agency: Get train tickets, reservations, and supplements at travel agencies rather than at the congested train station. The cost is often the same, though sometimes there's a minimal charge. Ask your hotel for the nearest travel agency.

Chill Out: Schedule several cool breaks into your sightseeing where you can sit, pause, and refresh yourself with a sandwich, gelato, or coffee.

Getting Around Florence

I organize my sightseeing geographically and do it all on foot.

I think of Florence as a Renaissance treadmill—it requires a lot of walking. Its buses don't really cover the old center well.

Of the many **bus** lines, I found these of most value for sightseeing: lines #7, #10, #31, and #32, which connect the train station, the Duomo, and Piazza San Marco. Bus #7 continues on to the Parterre parking lot at Piazza della Libertà and then on to Fiesole. Lines #12 and #13 go from the train station to Porta Romana, up to San Miniato Church and Piazzale Michelangelo, and on to Santa Croce.

Fun little *elettrico* **minibuses** wind through the tangled old center of town and up and down the river—just €1.20 gets you a 70-minute joyride. *Elettrico* A winds around the congested old center from the train station to Piazza Beccaria. *Elettrico* B goes up and down the Arno River from Ognissanti to Santa Croce Church. *Elettrico* D goes from the train station to Ponte Vecchio, cruising through Oltrarno, and finishing at Ponte San Niccolò. You'll likely be sitting with eccentric local seniors. The free TI map comes with a handy inset that shows all these bus routes.

Buy tickets in *tabacchi* (tobacco) shops, newsstands, or at the train station bus stop, as tickets bought on board are a little pricier (€2) and require exact change (€1.20/70 min, €4.50/4 tickets, €5/24 hrs, €12/3 days, validate in machine on the bus, route map available at TI, tel. 800-424-500). Follow general bus etiquette: Board at front or rear doors, exit out the center.

Hop-on, hop-off bus tours stop at the major sights (see "Hop-on, Hop-off Bus Tours," page 42).

The minimum cost for a **taxi** ride is €4, or €6 after 22:00 and on Sundays (rides in the center of town should be charged as tariff #1). A taxi ride from the train station to Ponte Vecchio costs about €9. Taxi fares and supplements (e.g., €2 extra if you call a cab rather than hail one) are clearly explained on signs in each taxi.

Tours in Florence

Tour companies big and small offer plenty of tours that go out to smaller towns in the Tuscan countryside (the most popular day trips: Siena, San Gimignano, Pisa, and into Chianti country for wine tasting). They also do city tours, but for most people, the city is really best on foot (and the book you're holding provides as much information as you'll get with a generic bus tour).

For extra insight with a personal touch, consider the tour companies and individual Florentine guides listed here. They are hardworking, creative, and offer a worthwhile array of organized sightseeing activities. Study their websites for details. If you're taking a city tour, remember that individuals save money with a scheduled public tour (such as those offered daily by Walking Tours of Florence, see below). If you're traveling as a family or small group, however, you're likely to save money by booking a private guide (since rates are based on roughly €55/hour for any size of group).

Walking Tours of Florence—This company offers a variety of tours (up to 12/day year-round) featuring downtown Florence, museum highlights, and Tuscany day trips. Their guides are native English-speakers. The three-hour "Original Florence" walk hits the main sights but gets offbeat to weave a picture of Florentine life in medieval and Renaissance times. Tours go rain or shine with as few as four participants (€25, daily at 9:15). They also offer tours of the Uffizi (€39, includes admission, 2 hours), Accademia (called "Original *David*" tour, €35, includes admission, 1 hour), and "Original Florence in One Day" (€94, includes admission to Uffizi and Accademia, 6 hours). Their "Florence Orientation" talk starts in their office and is followed by a wine-tasting in an atmospheric bar (€10, daily at 17:00). Reservations are necessary for all tours. For schedule details, pick up their extensive brochure in your hotel lobby or their office (Mon–Sat 8:00–18:00, Sun 8:30–13:30 but off-season closed Sun and for lunch, near Piazza della Repubblica at Via dei Sassetti 1, second floor, above Odeon Cinema, tel. 055-264-5033 during day or mobile 329-613-2730 18:00–20:00, www.italy.artviva.com, staff@artviva.com).

Florentia—Top-notch, private walking tours—geared for thoughtful, well-heeled travelers with longer-than-average attention spans—are led by local scholars. The tours range from introductory city walks and museum visits to in-depth thematic walks, such as the Golden Age of Florence, the Medici Dynasty, and side-trips into Tuscany (tours-€250/half-day, reserve in advance, tel. 338-890-8625, www.florentia.org, info@florentia.org).

Context Florence—This group of graduate students and professors lead "walking seminars" as scholarly as Florentia's (above). Their tours include a three-hour Michelangelo seminar—an in-depth study of the artist's work and influence (€85.50/person, includes Accademia admission), a two-hour evening orientation stroll (€35/person), and a fascinating three-hour fresco workshop (€75/person, you take home a fresco you make yourself). See their website for other innovative offerings: Medici walk, lecture series, food walks, kids' tours, and programs in Venice, Rome, Naples, London, and Paris (tel. 06-482-0911, US tel. 888-467-1986, www.contexttravel.com, info@contexttravel.com).

Local Guides—Good guides include **Paola Barubiani** and her art historian partners at Walks Inside Florence (€60/hr for up to 4 people, €55/person for semi-private 3-hour tour, €180/group of 2–6 people for private 3-hour tour, family tours, mobile 335-526-6496, www.walksinsideflorence.it, barubiani.paola@walksinsideflorence .it). **Alessandra Marchetti**, a Florentine who has lived in the US, gives private walking tours of Florence and driving tours of Tuscany (€60–75/hr, mobile 347-386-9839, aleoberm@tin.it). **Antonia Lanza d'Ajeta**, a native of England who has lived most of her life in Florence, has a knack for sharing her adopted home-town with a passion for art and culture (€50/hr, tel. 055-247-8002, mobile 347-549-1085, antonialanzadajeta@alice.it).

Paola Migliorini and her partners at Tuscany Tours offer museum tours, city walking tours, private cooking classes, and Tuscan excursions by van (you can tailor tours as you like). Go any-where in the center of Florence by van and enjoy the city nearly sweat-free (€55/hr, €65/hr in an 8-seat van, tel. 055-472-448, mobile 347-657-2611, www.florencetour.com, info@florencetour.com).

Hop-on, Hop-off Bus Tours—Around town, you'll see big double-decker sightseeing buses double-parking near major sights. Tourists on the top deck can listen to brief recorded descriptions of the sights, snap photos, and enjoy an effortless drive-by look at the major landmarks. Tickets cost €20 (good for 24 hours, first bus at 9:30, last bus at 18:00, pay as you board, tickets include two bus lines—Blue is one hour with a trip up to Piazzale Michelangelo, Green is 2 hours with a side-trip to Fiesole, www.firenze.city -sightseeing.it). As the name implies, you can hop off when you want and catch the next bus (usually every 30 min, depending on the season). Hop-on stops include the train station, Duomo, and Pitti Palace. As most sights are buried in the old center where big buses can't go, Florence doesn't really lend itself to this kind of tour bus. Look at the route map before committing.

SIGHTS IN FLORENCE

In this chapter, Florence's most important museums have the shortest listings and are marked with a ✪. These sights are covered in much more detail in one of the self-guided tours included in this book.

The Renaissance Walk chapter connects a number of Florence's major sights, from Michelangelo's *David* (also covered by a separate tour in this book) to Ponte Vecchio over the Arno River. To avoid lines, you should book ahead to visit the Accademia and Uffizi Gallery (see page 54 for details).

Check opening hours carefully and plan your time well. Many museums have somewhat erratic hours (e.g., closed the first Sun of the month), and others require a reservation (Brancacci Chapel and the Medici-Riccardi Palace's Chapel of the Magi). Also, Florence—more than most cities—has a tendency to change its opening hours from season to season, so it's always wise to get the most up-to-date info possible at the TI, by phone, or online (www.firenzeturismo.it).

Price Hike Alert: Some of Florence's museums have found a clever way to squeeze more money out of visitors. They host a special exhibit (which no tourist really cares to pay for) and require that you pay for this extra ticket along with the permanent collection. This means already steep admission fees jump by about €3. A prime example: The Uffizi Gallery is technically only €6.50. But for most of the year, temporary exhibits raise the price to a mandatory €10. Expect this practice at the Bargello, Pitti Palace, Medici Chapels, and others...and consider yourself lucky if you happen to visit when it's the normal price. If you make a reservation at a major museum, you'll also pay a €4 booking fee, but it can be worth the money for the peace of mind of an assured entry time.

Florence

SIGHTS IN FLORENCE

North of the Duomo (Cathedral)

▲▲▲**Accademia (Galleria dell'Accademia)**—This museum houses Michelangelo's *David,* the consummate Renaissance statue of the buff, biblical shepherd boy ready to take on the giant. Nearby are some of the master's other works, including his powerful (unfinished) *Prisoners, St. Matthew,* and a *Pietà* (possibly by one of his disciples). Florentine Michelangelo Buonarroti, who would work tirelessly through the night, believed that the sculptor was a tool of God, responsible only for chipping away at the

stone until the intended sculpture emerged. Beyond the magic marble are some mildly interesting pre-Renaissance and Renaissance paintings, including a couple of lighter-than-air Botticellis, the plaster model of Giambologna's *Rape of the Sabines,* and a musical instrument collection with an early piano.

Cost, Hours, Location: €6.50, plus €4 fee for recommended reservation (see page 88 for details), Tue–Sun 8:15–18:50, last entry 30 min before closing, closed Mon (Via Ricasoli 60, tel. 055-238-8609 or 055-294-883, www.polomuseale.firenze.it).

SIGHTS IN FLORENCE

✪ See the Accademia Tour chapter.

Nearby: Piazza S.S. Annunziata, behind the Accademia, displays lovely Renaissance harmony. Facing the square are two fine buildings: the 15th-century Santissima Annunziata church (worth a peek) and Filippo Brunelleschi's Hospital of the Innocents (Spedale degli Innocenti, not worth going inside), with terra-cotta medallions by Luca della Robbia. Built in the 1420s, the hospital is considered the first Renaissance building. I love sleeping on this square (at Hotel Loggiato dei Serviti, listed in the Sleeping in Florence chapter) and picnicking here during the day (with the riff-raff, who remind me of the persistent gap—today as in Medici times—

between those who appreciate fine art and those just looking for some cheap wine).

▲▲Museum of San Marco (Museo di San Marco)—Located one block north of the Accademia, this 15th-century monastery houses the greatest collection anywhere of frescoes and paintings by the early Renaissance master Fra Angelico. The ground floor features

the monk's paintings, along with some works by Fra Bartolomeo. Upstairs are 43 cells decorated by Fra Angelico and his assistants. While the monk/painter was trained in the medieval religious style, he also learned and adopted Renaissance techniques and sensibilities, producing works that blended Christian symbols and Renaissance

Florence at a Glance

▲▲▲**Accademia** Michelangelo's *David* and powerful (unfinished) *Prisoners*. Reserve ahead. **Hours:** Tue–Sun 8:15–18:50, closed Mon. See page 44.

▲▲▲**Uffizi Gallery** Greatest collection of Italian paintings anywhere. Reserve at least one month in advance. **Hours:** Tue–Sun 8:15–18:50, closed Mon. See page 58.

▲▲▲**Duomo Museum** Underrated cathedral museum with sculptures. **Hours:** Mon–Sat 9:00–19:30, Sun 9:00–13:40. See page 50.

▲▲▲**Bargello** Underappreciated sculpture museum (Michelangelo, Donatello, Medici treasures). **Hours:** Tue–Sun April–Oct 8:15–17:00, Nov–March 8:15–13:50; also open first, third, and fifth Mon of each month—until 17:00 April–Oct or 13:50 Nov–March. See page 53.

▲▲**Museum of San Marco** Best collection anywhere of artwork by the early Renaissance master Fra Angelico. **Hours:** Tue–Fri 8:15–13:50, Sat 8:15–16:50; also open 8:15–16:50 on second and fourth Sun and 8:15–13:50 on first, third, and fifth Mon of each month. See page 45.

▲▲**Medici Chapels** Tombs of Florence's great ruling family, designed and carved by Michelangelo. **Hours:** Tue–Sat April–Oct 8:15–16:50, Nov–March 8:15–13:50; also open first, third, and fifth Sun and second and fourth Mon of each month. See page 49.

▲▲**Duomo (Santa Maria del Fiore)** Gothic cathedral with colorful facade and the first dome built since ancient Roman times. **Hours:** Mon–Wed and Fri 10:00–17:00, Thu 10:00–15:30, Sat 10:00–16:45 except first Sat of month 10:00–15:30, Sun 13:30–16:45. See page 50.

▲▲**Galileo Science Museum** Fascinating old clocks, telescopes, maps, and Galileo's finger. **Hours:** Mon and Wed–Fri 9:30–17:00, Tue and Sat 9:30–13:00, closed Sun. See page 61.

▲▲**Santa Croce Church** Fourteenth-century church with precious art, tombs of famous Florentines, and Brunelleschi's Pazzi Chapel. **Hours:** Mon–Sat 9:30–17:30, Sun 13:00–17:30. See page 62.

▲▲**Church of Santa Maria Novella** Thirteenth-century Dominican church with Masaccio's famous 3-D painting. **Hours:** Mon–Thu and Sat 9:00–17:00, Fri and Sun 13:00–17:00. See page 63.

▲▲**Pitti Palace** Several museums in lavish palace plus sprawling Boboli and Bardini Gardens. **Hours:** Palatine Gallery, Royal Apartments, and Modern Art Gallery: Tue–Sun 8:15–18:50, closed Mon; Argenti Museum, Costume Gallery, Porcelain Museum, and Boboli and Bardini Gardens: Daily 8:15–18:30, until 19:30 June–Aug, closed first and last Mon of the month, shorter hours in winter. See page 64.

▲▲**Brancacci Chapel** Works of Masaccio, early Renaissance master who reinvented perspective. **Hours:** Mon and Wed–Sat 10:00–17:00, Sun 13:00–17:00, closed Tue. Reservations required. See page 64.

▲▲**San Miniato Church** Sumptuous Renaissance chapel and sacristy showing scenes of St. Benedict. **Hours:** Daily April–Oct 8:00–19:00, Nov–March 8:00–13:00 & 14:30–18:00. See page 66.

▲**Medici-Riccardi Palace** Lorenzo the Magnificent's home, with fine art, frescoed ceilings, and a lovely Chapel of the Magi. **Hours:** Thu–Tue 9:00–19:00, closed Wed. See page 50.

▲**Climbing the Duomo's Dome** Grand view into the cathedral, close-up of dome architecture, and, after 463 steps, a glorious Florence vista. **Hours:** Mon–Fri 8:30–19:00, Sat 8:30–17:40, closed Sun. Long and slow lines, go early, no reservations accepted. See page 52.

▲**Campanile** Views similar to Duomo's, 50 fewer steps, and fewer lines. **Hours:** Daily 8:30–19:30. See page 52.

▲**Baptistery** Bronze doors fit to be the gates of paradise. **Hours:** Doors always viewable; interior open Mon–Sat 12:15–19:00 except first Sat of month 8:30–14:00, Sun 8:30–14:00. See page 52.

▲**Palazzo Vecchio** Fortified palace, once the home of the Medici family, wallpapered with history and Renaissance themes. **Hours:** Fri–Wed 9:00–19:00, Thu 9:00–14:00. See page 59.

▲**Ponte Vecchio** Famous bridge lined with gold and silver shops. **Hours:** Bridge always open (shops closed at night). See page 61.

▲**Casa Buonarroti** Early, lesser-known works by Michelangelo. Hours: Wed–Mon 9:30–14:00, closed Tue. See page 62.

▲**Piazzale Michelangelo** Hilltop square with stunning view of Duomo and Florence. **Hours:** Always open. See page 66.

SIGHTS IN FLORENCE

realism. Don't miss the cell of Savonarola, the charismatic monk who rode in from the Christian right, threw out the Medicis, turned Florence into a theocracy, sponsored "bonfires of the vanities" (burning books, paintings, and so on), and was finally burned himself when Florence decided to change channels (€4, Tue–Fri 8:15–13:50, Sat 8:15–16:50; also open 8:15–16:50 on second and fourth Sun and 8:15–13:50 on first, third, and fifth Mon of each month; last entry 30 min before closing, reservations possible but unnecessary, on Piazza San Marco, tel. 055-238-8608, www.polomuseale.firenze.it).

○ See the Museum of San Marco Tour chapter.

Museum of Precious Stones (Museo dell'Opificio delle Pietre Dure)

—This unusual gem of a museum features room after room of exquisite mosaics of inlaid marble and stones. Upstairs, you'll see remnants of the Medici workshop from 1588, including 500 different precious stones and the tools used to cut and inlay them. The helpful loaner booklet available next to the ticket window describes it all in English (€4, Mon–Wed and Fri–Sat 8:15–14:00, Thu 8:15–19:00, closed Sun, around corner from Accademia at Via degli Alfani 78, tel. 055-26-511).

Church of San Lorenzo

—This red-brick dome—which looks like the Duomo's little sister—is the Medici church and the burial place of the family's founder, Giovanni di Bicci de' Medici (1360–1429). The facade is big, ugly, and unfinished, because Pope Leo X (also a Medici) pulled the plug on the project due to dwindling funds—after Michelangelo had labored on it for four years (1516–1520). Inside, though, is the spirit of Florence in the 1420s, with gray-and-white columns and arches in perfect Renaissance symmetry and simplicity. The Brunelleschi-designed church is lit by an even, diffused light. The Medici coat of arms (with the round pills of these "medics") decorates the ceiling, and everywhere are images of St. Lawrence, the Medici patron saint who was martyred on a grill.

Highlights of the church include two finely sculpted Donatello pulpits (in the nave). In the Martelli Chapel (left wall of the left transept), Filippo Lippi's *Annunciation* features a smiling angel greeting Mary in a sharply 3-D courtyard. Light shines through the vase in the foreground, like the Holy Spirit entering Mary's womb. The Old Sacristy (far left corner), designed by Brunelleschi, was the burial chapel for the Medicis. Bronze doors by Donatello flank the sacristy's small altar. Overhead, the dome above the altar shows the exact arrangement of the heavens on July 4, 1442, leaving scholars to hypothesize about why that particular date was used. Back in the nave, the round inlaid marble in the floor before the main altar marks where Cosimo the Elder—Lorenzo the Magnificent's grandfather—is buried (€3.50; March–Nov Mon–Sat 10:00–17:00, Sun 13:30–17:00; closed Dec–Feb, free information brochure).

Outside the church, along the left side, is a cloister with peek-a-boo Duomo views and two sights: The San Lorenzo Museum (of fancy reliquaries) is included in your church admission, but is hardly worth the walk, except to see Donatello's grave. Next door is the Laurentian Library (*Biblioteca Laurenziana,* not included in church entry), starring Michelangelo's impressive staircase entrance. The library is worthwhile if it's open (€3, only opens during special exhibits, generally 9:30–13:00).

Around the back end of the church is the entrance to the Medici Chapels (see below) and the New Sacristy, designed by Michelangelo for a later generation of dead Medicis.

▲▲Medici Chapels (Cappelle Medicee)—The burial site of the ruling Medici family in the Church of San Lorenzo includes the dusky Crypt; the big, domed Chapel of Princes; and the magnificent, all-Michelangelo New Sacristy, featuring the master's architecture, tombs, and statues. The Medicis made their money in textiles and banking and patronized a dream team of Renaissance artists that put Florence on the cultural map. Michelangelo, who spent his teen years living with the Medicis, was commissioned for the family's final tribute (€4 but usually about €6 with mandatory special exhibits; Tue–Sat April–Oct 8:15–16:50, Nov–March 8:15–13:50; also open first, third, and fifth Sun and second and fourth Mon of each month; last entry 30 min before closing, confirm latest hours at TI or chapel, tel. 055-294-883 or 055-238-8602, www.polomuseale.firenze.it). Don't make a pricey (and unnecessary) reservation to visit this sight.

○ See the Medici Chapels Tour chapter.

▲San Lorenzo Market—Florence's vast open-air market sprawls around the Church of San Lorenzo. Most of the leather stalls are run by Iranians selling South American leather that was tailored in Italy. Prices are soft (daily 9:00–19:00, closed Mon in winter, between the Duomo and train station).

▲Mercato Centrale (Central Market)—Florence's giant iron-and-glass-covered central market, a wonderland of picturesque produce, is fun to explore. While the nearby San Lorenzo Market—with its garment stalls in the streets—feels

like a step up from a haphazard flea market, the Mercato Centrale retains a Florentine elegance. Wander around. You'll see parts of the cow you'd never dream of eating (no, that's not a turkey neck), enjoy generous free samples, watch pasta making, and have your pick of plenty of fun eateries sloshing out cheap and tasty pasta to locals (Mon–Sat 7:00–14:00, closed Sun). For eating ideas in and around the market, see the Eating in Florence chapter.

▲Medici-Riccardi Palace (Palazzo Medici-Riccardi)— Lorenzo the Magnificent's home is worth a look for its art. The tiny Chapel of the Magi contains colorful Renaissance gems like the *Procession of the Magi* frescoes by Benozzo Gozzoli. The former library has a Baroque ceiling fresco by Luca Giordano, a prolific artist from Naples known as "Fast Luke" *(Luca fa presto)* for his ambidextrous painting abilities. While the Medicis originally occupied this 1444 house, in the 1700s it became home to the Riccardi family, who added the Baroque flourishes. As only eight people are allowed into the Chapel of the Magi every seven minutes, it's smart to call for a reservation if you want to avoid a wait (€5, €7 with mandatory special exhibits; Thu–Tue 9:00–19:00, last entry 30 min before closing, closed Wed; kitty-corner from Church of San Lorenzo, one long block north of Duomo, ticket entrance is north of the main gated entrance, Via Cavour 3, tel. 055-276-0340).

○ See the Medici-Riccardi Palace Tour chapter.

Leonardo Museum—This small, entrepreneurial venture is fun for anyone who wants to crank the shaft and spin the ball bear-

ings of Leonardo's genius inventions. While there are no actual historic artifacts, it shows about 30 of Leonardo's inventions and experiments made into models. You'll see a full-size armored tank, walk into a chamber of mirrors, operate a rotat-ing crane, and watch experiments in flying. Each is described in English. What makes this exhibit special is that you're encouraged to touch and play with the models—it's great for kids (€6, daily 10:00–19:00, Via dei Servi 66 red, tel. 055-282-966).

Duomo and Nearby

▲▲Duomo (Santa Maria del Fiore)— Florence's Gothic cathedral has the third-longest nave in Christendom. The church's noisy neo-Gothic facade from the 1870s is covered with pink, green, and white Tuscan marble. Since nearly all of its great art is stored in the Duomo Museum (behind the church), the best thing about the interior is the shade.

Heart of Florence

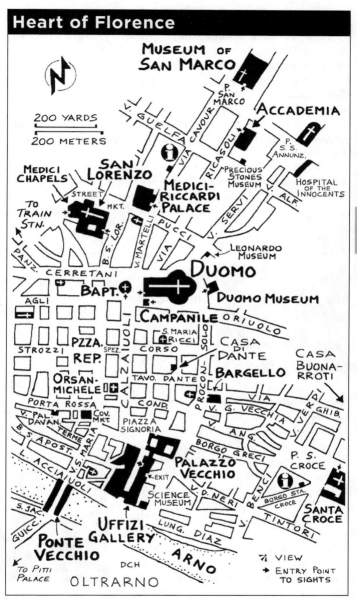

The inside of the dome is decorated by one of the largest paintings of the Renaissance, a huge *Last Judgment* by Giorgio Vasari and Federico Zuccari. Note: The massive crowds that overwhelm the entrance in the morning clear out by late afternoon (free, Mon–Wed and Fri 10:00–17:00, Thu 10:00–15:30, Sat 10:00–16:45 except first Sat of month 10:00–15:30, Sun 13:30–16:45, modest dress code enforced, tel. 055-230-2885).

The cathedral's claim to artistic fame is Brunelleschi's magnificent dome—the first Renaissance dome and the model for domes to follow.

✪ See page 74 of the Renaissance Walk chapter.

▲**Climbing the Duomo's Dome**—For a grand view into the cathedral from the base of the dome, a peek at some of the tools used in the dome's construction, a

chance to see Brunelleschi's "dome-within-a-dome" construction, a glorious Florence view from the top, and the equivalent of 463 plunges on a StairMaster, climb the dome. To avoid the long, dreadfully slow-moving line, arrive by 8:30 or drop by very late (€8, Mon–Fri 8:30–19:00, Sat 8:30–17:40, last entry 40 min before closing, closed Sun, enter from outside church on north side, tel. 055-230-2885).

✪ See page 76 of the Renaissance Walk chapter.

▲**Campanile (Giotto's Tower)**—The 270-foot bell tower has 50 fewer steps than the Duomo's dome (but that's still 414 steps—no elevator); offers a faster, less-crowded climb; and has a view of the Duomo to boot, but the cage-like top makes taking good photographs difficult (€6, daily 8:30–19:30, last entry 40 min before closing).

✪ See page 76 of the Renaissance Walk chapter.

▲**Baptistery**—Michelangelo said its bronze doors were fit to be the gates of paradise. Check out the gleaming copies of Lorenzo Ghiberti's bronze doors facing the Duomo. Making a breakthrough in perspective, Ghiberti used mathematical laws to create the illusion of receding distance on a basically flat surface.

The doors on the north side of the building were designed by Ghiberti when he was young; he'd won the honor and opportunity by beating Brunelleschi in a competition (the rivals' original entries are in the Bargello).

Inside, sit and savor the medieval mosaic ceiling, where it's always Judgment Day and Jesus is giving the ultimate thumbs-up and thumbs-down (€4, interior open Mon–Sat 12:15–19:00 except first Sat of month 8:30–14:00, Sun 8:30–14:00, last entry 30 min before closing; bronze doors are on the outside, so always "open"; original panels are in the Duomo Museum).

○ See page 127 of the Bargello Tour chapter and page 150 of the Duomo Museum Tour chapter.

▲▲▲**Duomo Museum (Museo dell'Opera del Duomo)**—The underrated cathedral museum, behind the church (at Via del Proconsolo 9), is great if you like sculpture. On the ground floor, look for a late Michelangelo *Pietà*, the eight restored panels of Ghiberti's north doors for the Baptistery, and statues from the original Baptistery facade. Upstairs, you'll find Brunelleschi's models for his dome, as well as Donatello's anorexic *Mary Magdalene* and playful choir loft. The museum features most of Ghiberti's original "Gates of Paradise" panels; the panels on the Baptistery's doors today

are copies (€6, Mon–Sat 9:00–19:30, Sun 9:00–13:40, last entry 40 min before closing, one of the few museums in Florence open on Mon, Via del Proconsolo 9, tel. 055-230-2885 or 055-264-7287).

○ See the Duomo Museum Tour chapter.

Between the Duomo and Piazza della Signoria

▲▲▲**Bargello (Museo Nazionale)**—This underappreciated sculpture museum is in a former police station-turned-prison that looks like a mini–Palazzo Vecchio. It has Donatello's painfully beautiful *David* (the very influential first male nude to be sculpted in a thousand years), works by Michelangelo, and rooms of Medici treasures

explained only in Italian (politely suggest to the staff that English descriptions would be wonderful). Moody Donatello, who embraced realism with his lifelike statues, set the personal and artistic style for many Renaissance artists to follow. The best works are in the ground-floor room at the foot of the outdoor staircase

Make Reservations to Avoid Lines

Florence has a reservation system for its state-run sights, which include the Accademia, Uffizi Gallery, Bargello, Medici Chapels, and Pitti Palace. I highly recommend getting reservations for the Accademia (Michelangelo's *David*) and the Uffizi (Renaissance paintings), but not the others. While you can generally get an entry time for the Accademia within a few days, the Uffizi can be booked more than a month in advance. Your best strategy is to get reservations for both as soon as you know when you'll be in town.

If you're in Florence off-season (Oct–March), you can probably get into the Uffizi or Accademia without a reservation in the late afternoon (after 16:00). At worst, you can make a reservation for later that day or the next day. But why hassle with it when making a reservation in advance is so easy? After learning how simple this is and seeing hundreds of bored, sweaty tourists waiting in lines without the reservation, it's hard not to be amazed at their cluelessness.

There are several ways to make a reservation: Have your hotelier arrange it, call the reservation number directly, book online, use an online booking service, take a tour, or go in person in advance to one of the museums or the Orsanmichele Church ticket window. Here are details on the options:

• When you make your hotel reservation, ask if they can book your museum reservations for you (some hoteliers will do this for free; others charge a €3–5 fee).

• Reserve by phone before you leave the States (from the US, dial 011-39-055-294-883, or within Italy call 055-294-883; €4/ ticket reservation fee; booking office open Mon–Fri 8:30–18:30, Sat 8:30–12:30, closed Sun). The reservation line is often busy, and even if you get through, you may be disconnected while on hold. Try again. When you do get through, an English-speaking operator walks you through the process, and a few minutes later you say *grazie,* with an appointment and a six-digit confirmation number. Bring the confirmation(s) with you and pay cash at the

and in the room directly above (€4, but mandatory special exhibitions often increase the price to €7; Tue–Sun April–Oct 8:15–17:00, Nov–March 8:15–13:50; also open first, third, and fifth Mon of each month—until 17:00 April–Oct or until 13:50 Nov–March; last entry 30 min before closing, reservations possible but unnecessary, Via del Proconsolo 4, info tel. 055-282-902, reservation tel. 055-238-8606, www.polomuseale.firenze.it).

○ See the Bargello Tour chapter.

sight(s). The advantage to phoning versus booking online is that you pay nothing upfront when you phone.

• You can book your museum visit online with a credit card by using the official website for Florence museums: www .b-ticket.com/b-ticket/Uffizi (€4/ticket reservation fee). To use the site, start by choosing a museum from the list. A color-coded calendar shows how many tickets are available for any given date and time slot. Select the month, date, time, and number of tickets that you want. To purchase, you'll need to create a log-in ID (when it asks for your country of residence, pick *"Stati Uniti"*— Italian for the US). If the site reverts to Italian, note that *"Invio"* means "send" (and *"Annulia Operazione"* means "cancel"). Some readers have reported difficulty with this site, such as not being able to book a time before noon, or not receiving the vouchers they've paid for. If you don't receive your voucher, report it to the email address given on the site (if it's working).

As an alternative to the official website, you could try a third-party booking agency such as Weekend a Firenze (www .weekendafirenze.com; €5/person booking fee).

• Take a tour that includes your museum admission. Walking Tours of Florence offers tours of the Uffizi (€39/person, 2 hours), Accademia (€35/person, 1 hour), and both museums (€94/person, 6 hours; see listing on page 41, or visit www.italy.artviva .com).

• If you arrive in Florence without a reservation, you can try to make one by phone, by asking your hotelier for help, by going directly to the Uffizi ticket office, or using the booking window at Orsanmichele Church (daily 10:00–17:00; see location on map on page 80).

Reservations are mandatory (and free) for the Brancacci Chapel (you must reserve in advance, even off-season) and the Medici-Riccardi Palace (where you can often just show up and still get in). You can make reservations for these two sights either online (www.b-ticket.com/b-ticket/Uffizi) or by phone (phone numbers are included in the sight listings in this chapter). Spots are generally available a day or two in advance.

Ticket phone numbers are often busy; be persistent. The best time to call is around 14:00–15:00 or just before closing.

Casa di Dante (Dante's House)—Dante Alighieri (1265–1321), the poet who gave us *The Divine Comedy*, is the Shakespeare of Italy, the father of the modern Italian language, and the face on the country's €2 coin. However, most Americans know little of him, and this museum is not the ideal place to start. Even though it has English information, this small museum (in a building near where he likely lived) assumes visitors have prior knowledge of Dante. Exhibits are as much about medieval

Florence as they are about the man. Still, Dante lovers can trace his interesting life and works through pictures, models, and artifacts, and novices can learn a little about Dante and the city he lived in.

Cost, Hours, Location: €4, summer daily 10:00–18:00; winter Tue–Sun 10:00–17:00, closed Mon; last entry 30 min before closing, near the Bargello at Via Santa Margherita 1, tel. 055-219-416.

➲ **Self-Guided Tour:** Begin on the **first floor.** In the first room, you'll see a sketch of Florence's Baptistery. Born in 1265, Dante was baptized there, and later trained as a doctor (glass case of herbs).

In the two rooms to the left, a model of Dante's Florence shows it as a walled city of many towers, housing feuding clans. Dante's life changed dramatically when he set eyes on Beatrice (look for her starry-sky picture), and fell in love with her. They ended up marrying other people, but Beatrice remained Dante's muse, inspiring him to write lofty poetry. Dante entered civic life, serving as the ambassador to Pope Boniface VIII (photo of the statue in Duomo Museum, see page 147). He served in Florence's army (toy soldiers in glass case) at the decisive Battle of Campaldino, which established the city's dominance.

Exhibits on the **second floor** explain the confusing politics that divided Florence between the victorious Black Guelphs and the defeated Whites, which included Dante. Politically incorrect Dante was exiled (see the *Book of the Nail—"Libro del Chiodo"*—that condemns him), and he would never again return to his beloved Florence. Look for the painting of him in red, forlorn, with his distinctive ear-flap cap, hooked nose, and jutting chin.

Dante roamed Italy and was received by nobles (see paintings in the next room). He worked on his magnum opus, *The Divine Comedy,* before he died and was buried in Ravenna in 1321 (see photos of the tomb and of his memorial in Florence's Santa Croce Church—see page 185).

Dante's most enduring legacy is the poem *The Divine Comedy.* The entire poem is displayed on the **top floor** wall alongside pictures of Dante's cosmos: Hell (a spiral-shaped hole through the earth), Purgatory (a spiral-shaped mountain), and Paradise (the concentric orbits of satellites that surround earth). Copies of paintings by famous artists and a video of scenes from *The Divine Comedy* demonstrate just how much Dante inspired the imagination of later artists. Some call him the father of the Renaissance.

▲**Orsanmichele Church**—In the ninth century, this loggia (covered courtyard) was a market used for selling grain (stored upstairs). Later, it was enclosed to make a church.

Outside are dynamic, statue-filled niches, some with accompanying symbols from the guilds that sponsored the art. Donatello's *St. Mark* and *St. George* (on the northeast and northwest corners) step out boldly in the new Renaissance style.

The interior has a glorious Gothic tabernacle (1359) housing the painted wooden panel that depicts *Madonna delle Grazie* (1346). The iron bars spanning the vaults were the Italian Gothic answer to the French Gothic external buttresses. Look for the rectangular holes in the piers—these were once wheat chutes that connected to the upper floors (church is free, Tue–Sun 10:00–17:00, closed Mon, niche sculptures always viewable from the outside). You can give the *Madonna della Grazie* a special thanks if you're in town when an evening concert is held inside the Orsanmichele (tickets sold on day of concert from door facing Via de' Calzaiuoli; also sells Uffizi and Accademia tickets, ticket window open daily 10:00–17:00).

✪ See page 80 of the Renaissance Walk chapter.

The museum upstairs, currently closed, holds many of the church's precious originals. Someday, tourists might be able to enjoy the fine statues by Ghiberti, Donatello, and company.

A block away, you'll find the...

▲**Mercato Nuovo (a.k.a. the Straw Market)**—This market loggia is how Orsanmichele looked before it became a church. Originally a silk and straw market, Mercato Nuovo still functions as a rustic yet touristy market (at the intersection of Via Calimala and Via Porta Rossa). Prices are soft, but the San Lorenzo Market (listed above) is much better for haggling. Notice the circled X in the center, marking the spot where people hit after being hoisted up to the top and dropped as punishment for bankruptcy. You'll also find *Porcellino* (a statue of a wild boar nicknamed "little pig"), which people rub and give coins to in order to ensure their return to Florence. This new copy, while only a few years old, already has a polished snout. At the back corner, a wagon sells tripe (cow innards) sandwiches—a local favorite (daily 9:30–19:00).

▲**Piazza della Repubblica and Nearby**—This large square sits on the site of Florence's original Roman Forum. The lone column—nicknamed "the belly button of Florence"—once marked the intersection of the two main Roman roads. All that survives of Roman Florence is its grid street plan and this column. Look at any map of Florence today (there's one by the benches—where the old boys hang out to talk sports and politics), and you'll see the ghost

of Rome in its streets: a grid-plan city center surrounded by what was the Roman wall. Roman Florence was a garrison town, a rectangular fort with this square marking the intersection of the two main roads (Via Corso and Via Roma).

Today's piazza, framed by a triumphal arch, is a nationalistic statement celebrating the unification of Italy. Florence, the capital of the country (1865–1870) until Rome was "liberated" (from the Vatican), lacked a square worthy of this grand new country. So the neighborhood here—once the Jewish quarter—was razed to open up an imposing, modern forum surrounded by stately circa-1890 buildings.

Between here and the river, you'll find characteristic parts of the medieval city that give a sense of what this neighborhood felt like before it was bulldozed. Back in the Middle Ages, writers described Florence as so densely built up that when it rained, pedestrians didn't get wet. Torches were used to light the lanes in midday. The city was prickly with noble families' towers (like San Gimignano) and had *Romeo and Juliet*–type family feuds. But with the rise of city power (c. 1300), no noble family was allowed to have an architectural ego trip taller than the City Hall, and nearly all other towers were taken down.

Venerable cafés and stores line the square. The La Rinascente department store, facing Piazza della Repubblica, is one of the city's mainstays (WC on fourth floor, continue up the stairs from there to the bar with a view terrace).

▲**Palazzo Davanzati**—This five-story, late-medieval tower house offers a rare look at a noble dwelling built in the 14th century. It may

become a museum of medieval Florence someday, but currently only the ground and first floors are open to visitors. Like other buildings of the age, the exterior is festooned with 14th-century horse-tethering rings made out of iron, torch holders, and poles upon which to hang laundry and fly flags. Inside, though the furnishings are pretty sparse, you'll see richly painted walls, a long chute that functioned as a well, plenty of fireplaces, a lace display, and even a modern toilet (free; Tue–Sat 8:15–13:50; also open second and fourth Mon and first, third, and fifth Sun; Via Porta Rossa 13, tel. 055-238-8610).

On and near Piazza della Signoria

▲▲▲**Uffizi Gallery**—This greatest collection of Italian paintings anywhere features works by Giotto, Leonardo, Raphael, Caravaggio, Rubens, Titian, and Michelangelo, and a roomful of Botticellis, including his *Birth of Venus*. Start with Giotto's early stabs at Renaissance-style realism, then move on through the 3-D experimentation of the early 1400s to the real thing rendered by the likes of Botticelli and Leonardo. Finish off with the High Renaissance—Michelangelo, Rubens, and Titian. Because only 600 visitors are allowed inside the building at any one time, there's generally a very long wait. The good news: no Louvre-style mob scenes. The museum is nowhere near as big as it is great. Few tourists spend more than two hours inside. The paintings are displayed on one comfortable, U-shaped floor in chronological order from the 13th through 17th centuries. The left wing, starring the Florentine Middle Ages to the Renaissance, is the best. The connecting corridor contains sculpture, and the right wing focuses on the High Renaissance and Baroque.

Cost, Hours, Reservations: €6.50 but mandatory special exhibits generally bump the price to €10, extra €4 for recommended reservation, cash required to pick up reserved tickets, Tue–Sun 8:15–18:50, last entry 30 min before closing, closed Mon, tel. 055-238-8651, www.polomuseale.firenze.it. After entering, take the elevator or climb four long flights of stairs. To avoid the long ticket lines, get reservations at least a month ahead in high season. For details on making reservations, check the sidebar on page 54.

○ See the Uffizi Gallery Tour chapter.

In the Uffizi's Courtyard: Enjoy the courtyard (free), full of artists and souvenir stalls. (Swing by after dinner when it's completely empty.) The surrounding statues honor earthshaking Florentines: artists (Michelangelo), philosophers (Niccolò Machiavelli), scientists (Galileo), writers (Dante), explorers (Amerigo Vespucci), and the great patron of so much Renaissance thinking, Lorenzo "the Magnificent" de' Medici.

○ See page 86 of the Renaissance Walk chapter.

▲**Palazzo Vecchio**—With its distinctive castle turret, this fortified palace—the Town Hall, officially called the Palazzo della

Signoria—is a Florentine landmark. But if you're visiting only one palace interior in town, the Pitti Palace is better. The Palazzo Vecchio interior is best for fans of coffered and gilded ceilings, of Florentine history, or of the artist Giorgio Vasari, who wallpapered the place with mediocre magnificence.

Highlights include the 13,000-square-foot Grand Hall (Sala Grande), lined with huge Vasari paintings of Florence at war. The central ceiling painting shows Cosimo I de' Medici, the patron who financed Vasari's work. (A controversy is brewing over whether to try to remove some of Vasari's work along the entrance wall to reveal what may be Leonardo da Vinci's famous *Battle of Anghiari*.)

In the hall stands Michelangelo's statue of *Victory* (*La Vittoria,* 1533–1534), showing a young man triumphing over an older man. This was the prototype of the many spiral-shaped statues by other artists that also line the Grand Hall.

Go upstairs from the Grand Hall and circle through a dozen richly decorated rooms to the Room of the Lilies (Sala dei Gigli), with Duomo views and Donatello's bronze statue of *Judith and Holofernes.* The statue was commissioned by the Medicis, who saw themselves as the noble Judith slaying their (drunken, sleepy) enemies. When the Medicis were driven out, the Florentines took it from the Medici-Riccardi Palace and placed it at the Palazzo Vecchio doorway (where the fake *David* stands) as a symbol of their triumph over the corrupt family. A decade later, it was replaced by Michelangelo's *David* as the symbol of Florence victorious.

The adjoining Chancery Room (Cancelleria) was once Machiavelli's office. In the nearby Map Chamber (Sala delle Carte Geografiche), Texans and Southern Californians can find their hometowns on maps (far right corner, upper level) that chart the known world in the 16th century.

Cost, Hours, Location: €6, €8 combo-ticket with Brancacci Chapel, Fri–Wed 9:00–19:00, Thu 9:00–14:00, ticket office closes one hour earlier (Piazza della Signoria, tel. 055-276-8224). The Palazzo Vecchio offers many kids' activities (call or ask at the reception by the ticket office). Skip the €4.10 audioguide (ID required) unless you want to know the fine details of Florentine political leaders. But do take advantage of the nifty computer screens scattered throughout the museum, with mini-documentaries on the transporting of *David* to Piazza della Signoria and the sculptural highlights within the *palazzo.* Free tours in English are offered daily, but the schedule varies and you must reserve (call to arrange).

There are two entrances: the crowded one next to the fake *David* and a less-crowded one around the left side of the building. Both have metal-detector checkpoints that can create long lines. Entry to the ground floor **courtyard** is free, so even if you don't go upstairs to the museum, you can step inside and feel the essence of the Medicis. Until 1873, Michelangelo's *David* stood at the entrance, where the copy is today.

✪ See page 84 of the Renaissance Walk chapter.

▲▲Galileo Science Museum (Museo Galilei e Istituto di Storia della Scienza)—This recently renovated museum should be completely open by spring of 2010. When we think of the Florentine Renaissance, we think of visual arts: painting, mosaics, architecture, and sculpture. But when the visual arts declined in the 1600s (abused and co-opted by political powers), music and science flourished in Florence. The first opera was written here. And Florence hosted many scientific breakthroughs, as you'll see in this fascinating collection of Renaissance and later clocks, telescopes, maps, and ingenious gadgets. Trace the technical innovations as modern science emerges from 1000 to 1900. One of the most talked-about bottles in Florence is the one here that contains Galileo's finger. Exhibits include various tools for gauging the world, from a compass and thermometer to Galileo's telescopes. Other displays delve into clocks, pumps, medicine, and chemistry. Loaner English guide booklets are available. It's friendly, comfortably cool, never crowded, and just a block east of the Uffizi on the Arno River (€4, rising to €6–8 after reopening; Mon and Wed–Fri 9:30–17:00, Tue and Sat 9:30–13:00, closed Sun; Piazza dei Giudici 1, tel. 055-265-311, www.imss.fi.it).

○ See the Galileo Science Museum Tour chapter.

▲Ponte Vecchio—Florence's most famous bridge is lined with shops that have traditionally sold gold and silver. A statue of Benvenuto Cellini, the master goldsmith of the Renaissance, stands in the center, ignored by the flood of tacky tourism.

○ See page 87 of the Renaissance Walk chapter.

Notice the "prince's passageway" above the bridge, called the **Vasari Corridor.** In less-secure times, the city leaders had a fortified passageway connecting the Palazzo Vecchio and Uffizi with the mighty Pitti Palace, to which they could flee in times of attack. This passageway is technically open to the public, but a visit is almost impossible to arrange, and if you do manage it, it's usually a disappointment (open sporadically, check at the Uffizi to see if it's open or try a private tour company such as Weekend a Firenze—see www.weekendafirenze.com).

▲▲**Santa Croce Church**—This 14th-century Franciscan church, decorated with centuries of precious art, holds the tombs of great

Florentines. The loud 19th-century Victorian Gothic facade faces a huge square ringed with tempting shops and littered with tired tourists. Escape into the church and admire its sheer height and spaciousness. Your ticket also includes the Pazzi Chapel and a small museum (€5, Mon–Sat 9:30–17:30, Sun 13:00–17:30, last entry 30 min before closing, audioguide-€4, modest dress code is enforced, tel. 055-246-6105). The leather school is free and sells tickets to the church. If the church has a long line, come here (daily 9:30–18:00, has own entry behind church plus an entry within the church, www.leatherschool.com).

○ See the Santa Croce Tour chapter.

▲ **Casa Buonarroti (Michelangelo's House)**—Fans enjoy a house standing on property once owned by Michelangelo. The house was built after Michelangelo's death by the artist's grand-nephew, who turned it into a little museum honoring his famous relative. You'll see some of Michelangelo's early, less-than-monumental statues and a few sketches. Be warned: Michelangelo's descendants attributed everything they could to their famous relative, but very little here (beyond two marble relief panels and a couple of sketches) is actually by Michelangelo (€6.50, Wed–Mon 9:30–14:00, closed Tue, English descriptions, Via Ghibellina 70, tel. 055-241-752).

○ **Self-Guided Tour:** Climb the stairs to the first-floor landing, where you come face-to-face with portraits (by his contemporaries) of 60-year-old Michelangelo, the Buonarroti family walking sticks, and some leather shoes thought to be Michelangelo's.

The room to the left of the landing displays two relief panels, Michelangelo's earliest known sculptures. Teenage Michelangelo carved every inch of the *Battle of the Centaurs* (1490–1492). This squirming tangle of battling nudes shows Michelangelo's fascination with anatomy. He kept this in his personal collection all his life. *The Madonna of the Stairs* (c. 1490) is as contemplative as the *Centaurs* is dramatic. Throughout his long career, bipolar Michelangelo veered between these two styles—moving or still, emotional or thoughtful, pagan or Christian.

In an adjoining room is the big wooden model of a project Michelangelo took on but never completed: the facade of the Church of San Lorenzo (which remains bare brick to this day). The

reclining river god was a model for one of the statues in the Medici Chapels.

The small room adjoining the landing is for the museum's vast collection of Michelangelo's sketches. Unfortunately, only a handful of works are displayed at a time. Vasari claimed that Michelangelo wanted to burn his preliminary sketches, lest anyone think him less than perfect.

The room to the right of the landing displays small clay and wax models—some by Michelangelo, some by pupils—that the artist used to sketch out ideas for his statues.

And finally, true Michelangelomaniacs can complete their visit by exiting outside to gaze at Via Ghibellina 67 (next door to a *farmacia*). This humble doorway, lined with gray-green stone, was once the entrance to Michelangelo's actual residence, circa 1520.

Near the Train Station

▲▲**Church of Santa Maria Novella**—This 13th-century Dominican church is rich in art. Along with crucifixes by Giotto and Brunelleschi, there's every textbook's example of the early Renaissance mastery of perspective: *The Holy Trinity* by Masaccio. The exquisite chapels trace art in Florence from medieval times to early Baroque. The outside of the church features a dash of Romanesque (horizontal stripes), Gothic (pointed arches), Renaissance (geometric shapes), and Baroque (scrolls). Step in and look down the 330-foot nave for a 14th-century optical illusion (€2.50, Mon–Thu and Sat 9:00–17:00, Fri and Sun 13:00–17:00, last entry 30 min before closing).

◆ See the Santa Maria Novella Tour chapter.

Nearby: A palatial **perfumery** (Farmacia di Santa Maria Novella) is a block from Piazza Santa Maria Novella, 100 yards down Via della Scala at #16 (free but shopping encouraged, inconsistent hours but likely daily 10:30–19:30, located on map on page 44, tel. 055-216-276). Thick with the lingering aroma of centuries of spritzes, it started as the herb garden of the Santa Maria Novella monks. Well-known even today for its top-quality products, it is extremely Florentine. Pick up the history sheet at the desk, and wander deep into the shop. From the back room, you can peek at one of Santa Maria Novella's cloisters with its dreamy frescoes and imagine a time before Vespas and tourists.

You can get a closer look inside the **Museum and Cloisters,** adjacent to the church, but they're definitely lesser sights (€2.70, entry to the left of the church's facade; Mon–Thu and Sat 9:00–17:00, closed Fri and Sun).

South of the Arno River

▲▲**Pitti Palace**—The imposing Pitti Palace, several blocks southwest of Ponte Vecchio, has several separate museums and two gardens. The main reason to visit is to see the Palatine Gallery, but if you want to see all of the Pitti Palace, you'll need to buy two different combo-tickets. Ticket #1 includes the Palatine Gallery, Royal Apartments, and Modern Art Gallery (€8.50 but often €12 with mandatory special exhibits, Tue–Sun 8:15–18:50, closed Mon,

tel. 055-238-8614, www.polomuseale.firenze.it). Ticket #2 covers the Boboli and Bardini Gardens, Argenti Museum (the Duke's treasures), Costume Gallery, and Porcelain Museum (€6, more with special exhibits, daily 8:15–18:30, until 19:30 June–Aug, gardens close as early as 16:30 in winter, last entry 30–60 min before closing, closed first and last Mon of the month, same phone and website as above). If there's a long line, bypass it by buying a reservation for immediate entry at the ticket window (€3 reservation fee).

○ See the Pitti Palace Tour chapter.

▲▲**Brancacci Chapel**—For the best look at Masaccio's works (he's the early Renaissance master who reinvented perspective),

see his restored frescoes here. Instead of medieval religious symbols, Masaccio's paintings feature simple, strong human figures with facial expressions that reflect their emotions. The accompanying works of Masolino and Filippino Lippi provide illuminating contrasts (€4, free reservations required— it's very easy...just call, €8 combo-ticket with Palazzo Vecchio, both tickets include worthwhile 40-min film in English—reserve film when you book entry, limit of 30 visitors every 15 minutes, Mon and Wed–Sat 10:00–17:00, Sun 13:00–17:00, closed Tue, ticket office closes at 16:30; cross Ponte Vecchio and turn right

Oltrarno, South of the Arno River

on Borgo San Jacopo, walk 10 min, then turn left into Piazza del Carmine; tel. 055-276-8224 or 055-276-8558).

○ See the Brancacci Chapel Tour chapter.

The neighborhoods around the church are considered the last surviving bits of old Florence.

Santo Spirito Church—This church has a classic Brunelleschi interior and a painted, carved wooden crucifix attributed to 17-year-

old Michelangelo. The sculptor donated this early work to the monastery in appreciation for allowing him to dissect and learn about bodies. The Michelangelo *Crocifisso* is displayed in the sacristy, through a door midway down the left side of the nave (if it's closed, ask someone to let you in). Copies of Michelangelo's *Pietà* and *Risen Christ* flank the nave. Beer-drinking, guitar-playing rowdies decorate the church steps (free, Mon–Tue and Thu–Sat 9:30–12:30 & 16:00–17:30, Sun 16:00–17:30 only, closed Wed, Piazza Santo Spirito, tel. 055-211-716).

▲**Piazzale Michelangelo**—Overlooking the city from across the river (look for the huge statue of *David*), this square is worth the 30-minute hike, drive (free parking), or bus ride (either #12 or #13 from the train station—takes a long time) for the view of Florence and the stunning dome of the Duomo (see photo on page 74). It makes sense to take a taxi or ride the bus up, and then enjoy the easy

downhill walk back into town. An inviting café with great views is just below the overlook. The best photos are taken from the street immediately below the overlook (go around to the right and down a few steps). Off the west side of the piazza is a somewhat hidden terrace, an excellent place to retreat from the mobs. After dark, the square is packed with local school kids licking ice cream and each other. About 200 yards beyond all the tour groups and teenagers is the stark, beautiful, crowd-free, Romanesque San Miniato Church (next listing).

The hike down is quick and enjoyable. Take the steps between the two bars on the San Miniato Church side of the parking lot (via San Salvatore al Monte), and in a couple minutes you walk through the old wall (Porta San Miniato) and emerge in the delightful little Oltrarno neighborhood of San Niccolò.

▲▲**San Miniato Church**—According to legend, the martyred St. Minias—this church's namesake—was beheaded on the banks

of the Arno in A.D. 250. He picked up his head and walked here (this was before the #12 bus), where he died and was buried in what became the first Christian cemetery in Florence. In the 11th century, this church was built to house Minias' remains. Imagine this fine church all alone—without out any nearby buildings or fancy stairs—a peaceful refuge where white-robed Benedictine monks could pray and work (their motto: *ora et labora*).

Cost, Hours, Location: Free, daily April–Oct 8:00–19:00, Nov–March 8:00–13:00 & 14:30–18:00, Gregorian chants April–Sept daily at the 17:30 Mass—17:00 in winter, 200 yards above Piazzale Michelangelo, bus #12 or #13 from train station, tel. 055-234-2731.

○ Self-Guided Tour: For a thousand years, San Miniato Church—still part of a functioning monastery—has blessed the city that lies at the foot of its hill. Carved into the marble of its threshold is the Genesis verse *"Haec est Porta Coeli"* ("This is the Gate of Heaven").

Facade: The church's green-and-white marble facade (12th century) is classic Florentine Romanesque, one of the oldest in town. The perfect symmetry is a reminder of the perfection of God. The central mosaic shows Christ flanked by Mary and St. Minias. Minias, who was King of Armenia before his conversion, offers his secular crown to the heavenly king. The eagle on top, with bags of wool in his talons, reminds all who approach the church who paid for it—the wool guild.

Nave: Stepping inside, you enter the closest thing to a holy space that medieval Florentines could create. The "carpet of marble" dates from 1207. The wood ceiling is painted as it was originally. The glittering 13th-century golden mosaic that dominates the nave repeats the scene on the church's facade: St. Minias offering his paltry secular crown to the king in heaven.

The Renaissance tabernacle front and center was built by the Medicis. It's a résumé of early Renaissance humanism, with experiments in 3-D paintings (including St. Minias, in red) and a plush canopy of glazed terra-cotta panels by Luca della Robbia.

On the left side of the nave is an exquisite chapel dedicated to Cardinal Jacopo of Portugal. When 26-year-old Jacopo died in Florence (1459), his wealthy family mourned him by adding a chapel to the church (by cutting a hole in the church wall) and hiring the best artists of the day to decorate it. The family could enter their private chapel, take a seat on the throne (on the left), and meditate on the tomb of Jacopo (on the right).

Crypt: The church is designed like a split-level rambler, with staircases on either side of the altar, leading upstairs and down. Downstairs in the crypt, an alabaster window helps create a quiet and mysterious atmosphere. The forest of columns and capitals are all recycled...each from ancient Rome and each different. The floor is paved with the tombstones of long-forgotten big shots. Look through the window in the marble altar to see St. Minias' name, carved on the box that holds his mortal remains.

Upstairs to the Sacristy: At the staircase to the right of the main altar, notice the sinopia on the wall. A sinopia is a pattern that guides the fresco artist, and that allows the patron to have a peek at what the artist intends to create before it's set in hard plaster. There's a sinopia behind every surviving fresco in Florence.

Step upstairs. Before entering the sacristy, peek through the window into the cloister of the Benedictines who live and work here. Then enter the sacristy, which is beautifully frescoed with scenes from the life of St. Benedict (circa 1350, by a follower of Giotto). Drop a euro into the box to light the room for five minutes. The elegantly bearded patron saint of Europe was the founder of the vast network of monasteries that gave the Continent some cohesiveness in the cultural darkness that followed the collapse of Rome. Benedict is shown as an active force for good, with his arm always outstretched: busy blessing, being kissed, preaching, helping, chasing the devil, bringing a man (crushed by a fallen tower) back to life, reaching out even on his death bed. Notice Benedict on the ramp, scooting up to heaven to be welcomed by an angel. And, overseeing everything, in the starry skies of the ceiling, are the four evangelists—each with his book, pen, and symbolic sidekicks.

Outside the Church: Before leaving, stroll through the cemetery behind the church to marvel at the showy crypts and headstones of Florentine hotshots from the last two centuries. And savor the views of Florence.

Near Florence: Fiesole

Perched on a hill overlooking the Arno valley, Fiesole gives weary travelers a break in the action and—during the heat of summer— a breezy location from which to admire the city below. It's a small town with a main square, a few restaurants and shops, a few minor sights, and a great view. The ancient Etruscans knew a good spot when they saw one, and chose to settle here, establishing Fiesole about 400 years before the Romans founded

Florence. Wealthy Renaissance families in pre-air-conditioning days also chose Fiesole (fee-AY-zoh-lay) as a preferred vacation spot, building villas in the surrounding hillsides. Later, 19th-century Romantics spent part of the Grand Tour admiring the vistas, much like the hordes of tourists do today. Most come here for the view—the actual sights pale in comparison to those in Florence. Shutterbugs visit in the morning for the best light.

Getting to Fiesole: From the Florence train station, Duomo, or Piazza San Marco, take bus #7—enjoying a peek at gardens, vineyards, orchards, and villas—to the last stop, Piazza Mino (4/ hr, fewer after 20:00, 30 min, €1.20; departs Florence from the line of buses, just out of the east exit of train station and also from south side of Piazza San Marco; wear your money belt—thieves frequent this bus). Taxis from Florence cost about €20 (ride to highest point you want to visit—La Reggia Ristorante for view terrace or Church of San Francesco—then explore downhill).

Tourist Information: The TI is immediately to the right of the Roman Archaeological Park (listed below), at Via Portigiani 3 (daily 9:30–18:30, tel. 055-598-720).

Market Day: A modest selection of food and household items fills Piazza Garibaldi on Saturdays (8:00–13:00).

Sights in Fiesole

Fiesole's main sights are either free or covered under one €7 combo-ticket, available at the Roman Theater (described below).

▲▲**Terrace with a View**—Catch the sunset (and your breath) from the view terrace just below La Reggia Ristorante. It's a steep seven-minute hike from the Fiesole bus stop: Face the bell tower and take Via San Francesco, on the left. (For similar views and a peek at residential Fiesole, climb up the opposite side of the square, along the road hugging the ridgeline.)

Church of San Francesco—For even more hill-climbing, continue up from the view terrace to this charming little church. The small scale and several colorful altar paintings make this church more enjoyable than Fiesole's Duomo (free, Mon–Sat 8:00–12:00 & 15:00–19:00, Sun 7:00–11:00 & 15:00–19:00, Via San Francesco 13).

Ethnographic Missionary Museum—This eclectic little collection, hidden beneath the church of San Francesco, includes an Egyptian mummy, ancient coins, Chinese Buddhas, and the *in situ* ruins of a third-century Etruscan wall (donation suggested, Tue–Sat 10:30–12:00 & 15:00–19:00, Sun open 15:00–19:00 only, closed Mon, unmarked door inside church leads to cloisters and museum).

Duomo—While this church has a drab, 19th-century exterior, the interior is worth a look, if only for the blue-and-white glazed Giovanni della Robbia statue of St. Romulus over the entry door (free, daily 8:00–12:00 & 15:00–18:00, across Piazza Mino from the bus stop).

Roman Theater and Archaeological Park—Occasionally used today for plays, this well-preserved theater held up to 2,000 people. The site's other ruins are, well, ruined, and lacking in explanation. But the valley view and peaceful setting are lovely (€10 combo-ticket also covers Civic and Bandini museums, Wed–Mon 10:00–18:00, closed Tue; from the bus stop cross Piazza Mino, heading toward the back of the Duomo). Warning: They have a greedy habit of forcing visitors to pay more for special exhibits (often totaling around €13)—more than this sight is worth.

Civic Museum—Located within the Archaeological Park, the museum imparts insight into Fiesole's Etruscan and Roman roots with well-displayed artifacts and with a few English description sheets in the corners (covered by €10 combo-ticket, Wed–Mon 10:00–18:00, closed Tue).

Bandini Museum—This petite museum displays the wooden panels of lesser-known Gothic and Renaissance painters as well as the glazed terra-cotta figures of Andrea della Robbia (covered by €10 combo-ticket, Wed–Mon 10:00–18:00, closed Tue, behind Duomo at Via Dupre 1).

Sleeping in Fiesole

(€1 = about $1.40, country code: 39)

$$ Villa le Scalette has six clean, tidy rooms a short distance from the bus stop on Piazza Mino (Db-€100, family deals, air-con, Via Cannelle 1, tel. 055-597-8484, fax 055-597-9970, www.villascalette .it, info@villascalette.it). From the square, take Via Portigiani to Via Cannelle, a stepped alleyway. The hotel is at #1.

$ Hotel Villa Bonelli in Fiesole has three stars, 20 dim, outdated rooms, an abandoned ambience, and a good price (Sb-€70, Db-€90, Tb-€100, air-con, free Wi-Fi, 250 yards from bus stop up Via Gramsci, go right on Via Poeti to #1, tel. 055-59-513, fax 055-598-942, www.hotelvillabonelli.com, info@hotelvilla bonelli.com).

Eating in Fiesole

These two restaurants are on Piazza Mino, where the bus from Florence stops.

Ristorante Perseus, a local favorite, serves authentic Tuscan dishes at a fair price in a rambling interior. They also have seating at a few sidewalk tables or on a shady garden terrace in fair weather (daily 12:30–14:30 & 19:30–23:00, tel. 055-59-143).

Ristorante Aurora is an upscale alternative with a view terrace overlooking the city of Florence (daily 12:00–14:30 & 19:00–22:30, tel. 055-59-363).

Picnics: Fiesole is made-to-order for a scenic and breezy picnic. Grab a pastry at Fiesole's best *pasticceria,* **Alcedo** (head up the main drag from the bus stop to Via Gramsci 27). Round out your goodies at the **Co-op** supermarket on Via Gramsci before walking up to the panoramic terrace. Or, for more convenience and less view, picnic at the shaded park on the way to the view terrace (walk up Via San Francesco about halfway to the terrace, and climb the stairs to the right).

RENAISSANCE WALK

*From the Duomo
to the Arno River*

After centuries of labor, Florence gave birth to the Renaissance. We'll start with the soaring church dome that stands as the proud symbol of the Renaissance spirit. Next door, you'll find the Baptistery doors that opened the Renaissance. Finally, we'll reach Florence's political center, dotted with monuments of that proud time. Great and rich as this city is, it's easily covered on foot. This walk through the top sights is less than a mile long, running from the Duomo to the Arno River.

Orientation

Duomo (Cathedral): Free, Mon–Wed and Fri 10:00–17:00, Thu 10:00–15:30, Sat 10:00–16:45 except first Sat of the month 10:00–15:30, Sun 13:30–16:45. A modest dress code is enforced. Tel. 055-230-2885, www.duomofirenze.it.

    Mass in English is held in the cathedral on Sat at 17:00 (except the first Sat, when it's in a side chapel that you enter from south side, near the tower).

Climbing the Dome: €8, Mon–Fri 8:30–19:00, Sat 8:30–17:40, last entry 40 min before closing, closed Sun. Enter from outside the church on the north side. To avoid a long wait in line, arrive by 8:30 or drop by very late. You might prefer to climb the adjacent Campanile instead.

Campanile (Giotto's Tower): €6, daily 8:30–19:30, last entry 40 min before closing.

Baptistery: €4, interior open Mon–Sat 12:15–19:00 except first Sat of month 8:30–14:00, Sun 8:30–14:00, last entry 30 min before closing. The famous bronze doors are on the outside so they're always "open" (viewable) and free. The original panels are in the Duomo Museum.

Medici-Riccardi Palace: €5, €7 with mandatory special exhibits; Thu–Tue 9:00–19:00, last entry 30 min before closing, closed Wed, Via Cavour 3. Reservations are recommended for the palace's Chapel of the Magi (call ahead, tel. 055-276-0340).

Orsanmichele Church: Free, Tue–Sun 10:00–17:00, closed Mon. Niche sculptures are always viewable from the outside. The church hosts evening concerts; tickets are sold on the day of the concert from the door facing Via de' Calzaiuoli.

Information and Services: The nearest TI is on Via Cavour, two blocks north of the Duomo (ask for updates of museum hours). WCs are in cafés along the walk.

Audio Tour: If you're packing along an iPod or other MP3 player, you can download a free audio tour to accompany this walk at www.ricksteves.com (see page 469).

Length of This Tour: Allow two hours.

Photography: In churches and other sights along this walk, photos without a flash are generally OK.

Cuisine Art: You'll find plenty of cafés, self-service cafeterias, bars, and gelato shops along the route. Many good eateries along this walk are described in the Eating chapter (including Self-Service Ristorante Leonardo near the Duomo, and the famous L'Antico Trippaio tripe-selling sandwich cart a block east of Orsanmichele). For an inexpensive drink a half-block north of the Duomo, sneak up to the quiet upstairs café at the Libreria Martelli bookstore (26 Via de' Martelli).

Starring: Brunelleschi's dome, Ghiberti's doors, the Medicis' palaces, and the city of Florence—old and new.

The Tour Begins

Overview

The Duomo, the cathedral with the distinctive red dome, is the center of Florence and the orientation point for this walk. If you ever get lost, home's the dome. We'll start here, see several sights in the area, and then stroll down the city's pedestrian-only main street to the Palazzo Vecchio and the Arno River. Consider prefacing this walk with a visit to the ultimate Renaissance man: Michelangelo's *David*.

(❖ See the Accademia Tour chapter.)

The Florentine Renaissance (1400–1550)

In the 13th and 14th centuries, Florence was a powerful center of banking, trading, and textile manufacturing. The resulting wealth fertilized the cultural soil. Then came the Black Death in 1348.

Renaissance Walk

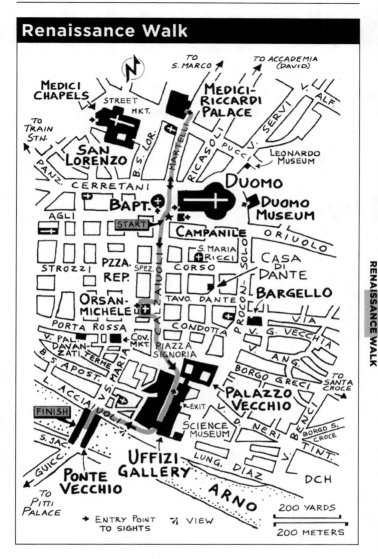

Nearly half of the population died, but the infrastructure remained strong, and the city rebuilt better than ever. Led by Florence's chief family, the art-crazy Medicis, and with the naturally aggressive and creative spirit of the Florentines, it's no wonder that the long-awaited Renaissance finally took root here.

The Renaissance—the "rebirth" of Greek and Roman culture that swept across Europe—started around 1400 and lasted about 150 years. In politics, the Renaissance meant democracy; in science, a renewed interest in exploring nature. The general mood was optimistic and "humanistic," with a confidence in the power of the individual.

In medieval times, poverty and ignorance had made life "nasty, brutish, and short" (for lack of a better cliché). The church was the people's opiate, and their lives were only a preparation for a happier time in heaven after leaving this miserable vale of tears.

Medieval art was the church's servant. The noblest art form was architecture—churches themselves—and other arts were considered most worthwhile if they embellished the house of God. Painting and sculpture were narrative and symbolic, designed to tell Bible stories to the devout and illiterate masses.

As prosperity rose in Florence, so did people's confidence in life and themselves. Middle-class craftsmen, merchants, and bankers felt they could control their own destinies, rather than be at the whim of nature. They found much in common with the ancient Greeks and Romans, who valued logic and reason above superstition and blind faith.

Renaissance art was a return to the realism and balance of Greek and Roman sculpture and architecture. Domes and round arches replaced Gothic spires and pointed arches. In painting and sculpture, Renaissance artists strove for realism. Merging art and science, they used mathematics, the laws of perspective, and direct observation of nature to paint the world on a flat surface.

This was not an anti-Christian movement, though it was a logical and scientific age. Artists saw themselves as an extension of God's creative powers. At times, the church even supported the Renaissance and commissioned many of its greatest works— Raphael frescoed Plato and Aristotle on the walls of the Vatican. But for the first time in Europe since Roman times, we also find rich laymen who wanted art simply for art's sake.

After 1,000 years of waiting, the smoldering fires of Europe's classical heritage burst into flame in Florence.

• *The dome of the Duomo is best viewed just to the right of the facade on the corner of the pedestrian-only street.*

The Duomo—Florence's Cathedral

The dome of Florence's cathedral—visible from all over the city— inspired Florentines to do great things. The big but unremarkable church itself (called the Duomo) is Gothic, built in the Middle Ages by architects who left it unfinished.

Think of the confidence of the age: The Duomo was built with a big hole in its roof awaiting

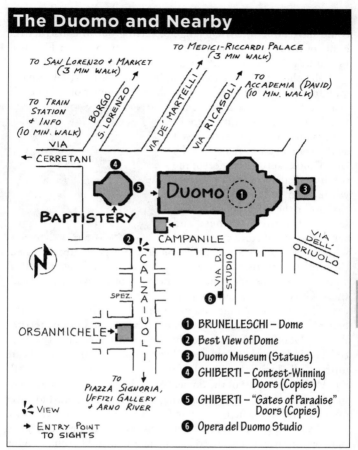

The Duomo and Nearby

TO MEDICI-RICCARDI PALACE (3 MIN. WALK)

TO SAN LORENZO + MARKET (3 MIN. WALK)

TO TRAIN STATION + INFO (10 MIN. WALK)

TO ACCADEMIA (DAVID) (10 MIN. WALK)

BORGO S. LORENZO

VIA DE' MARTELLI

VIA RICASOLI

VIA CERRETANI

BAPTISTERY

DUOMO

CAMPANILE

VIA DELL' ORIUOLO

CALZAIUOLI

SPEZ.

VIA D. STUDIO

ORSANMICHELE

TO PIAZZA SIGNORIA, UFFIZI GALLERY + ARNO RIVER

VIEW

ENTRY POINT TO SIGHTS

❶ BRUNELLESCHI – Dome
❷ Best View of Dome
❸ Duomo Museum (Statues)
❹ GHIBERTI – Contest-Winning Doors (Copies)
❺ GHIBERTI – "Gates of Paradise" Doors (Copies)
❻ Opera del Duomo Studio

RENAISSANCE WALK

a dome. This was before the technology to span it with a dome was available. *No problema.* They knew that someone soon could handle the challenge. In the 1400s, the architect Filippo Brunelleschi was called on to finish the job. Brunelleschi capped the church Roman-style—with a tall, self-supporting dome as grand as the ancient Pantheon's, which he had studied.

He used a dome within a dome. First, he built the grand white skeletal ribs, which you can see, then filled them in with interlocking bricks in a herringbone pattern. The dome grew upward like an igloo, supporting itself as it proceeded from the base. When they reached the top, Brunelleschi arched the ribs in and fixed them in place with the lantern. His dome, built in only 14 years, was the largest since Rome's Pantheon.

Brunelleschi's dome was the wonder of the age, the model for many domes to follow, from St. Peter's to the US Capitol. People gave it the ultimate compliment, saying, "Not even the ancients could have done it." Michelangelo, setting out to construct the dome of St. Peter's, drew inspiration from the dome of Florence. He said, "I'll make its sister...bigger, but not more beautiful."

The church's facade looks old, but is actually Neo-Gothic—only from 1870. The facade was rushed to completion (about 600 years after the building began) to celebrate Italian unity, here in the city that for a few years served as the young country's capital. Its "retro" look captures the feel of the original medieval facade—green, white, and pink marble sheets that cover the brick construction; Gothic (pointed) arches; and three horizontal stories decorated

with mosaics and statues. Still, the facade is generally ridiculed. (While one of this book's authors thinks it's the most beautiful church facade this side of heaven, the other one naively agrees with those who call it "the cathedral in pajamas.")

The interior is a bit disappointing, as it still feels bare after being cleaned out during the Neoclassical age and by the terrible flood of 1966 (free, but not worth a long wait; remember the dress code: no bare shoulders or knees). Inside, the structural elements are unabashedly highlighted by the gray stone and cream-colored filling. Walk to the base of the dome. Notice how the crossing expands to include half the transepts, making the hole they needed to cover even larger. The dome is decorated with Giorgio Vasari's vast *Last Judgment* from the late 1570s. From their graves, the dead rise into a multilevel heaven to be judged by a radiant Christ. Descend into the crypt (staircase in nave) to see the floor of the previous church and the tomb of Brunelleschi (€3, but it's free to peek at the tomb from the bookshop down the stairs). To climb the dome (€8), enter from outside the church on the north side.

Campanile (Giotto's Tower)

The bell tower (to the right of the facade) offers an easier, less crowded, and faster climb than the Duomo's dome, though the unobstructed views from the Duomo are better. Giotto, like any good Renaissance genius, wore several artistic hats. Considered the father of modern painting, he designed this 270-foot-tall bell tower for the Duomo two centuries before the age of Michelangelo. In his day, Giotto was called the ugliest man to ever walk the streets of Florence, but he designed for the city what many in our day call the most beautiful bell tower in all of Europe.

The bell tower served as a sculpture gallery for Renaissance artists—notice Donatello's four prophets on the side that faces out (west). These are copies, but the originals are at the wonderful Duomo Museum, just behind the church. (❂ See the Duomo Museum Tour chapter.) In the museum, you'll also get a close-up look at Brunelleschi's wooden model of his dome, Ghiberti's doors (described next), and a late *Pietà* by Michelangelo. A couple of blocks away, at the Opera del Duomo Studio, workers sculpt and restore statues for the cathedral (Via dello Studio 23a—see location on map; you can peek through the doorway).

• *The Baptistery is the small octagonal building in front of the church.*

Baptistery and Ghiberti's Bronze Doors

Florence's Baptistery is dear to the soul of the city. In medieval and Renaissance times, the locals—eager to link themselves to the classical past—believed (wrongly) that this was a Roman building. It is, however, Florence's oldest building (11th century). Most festivals and parades either started or ended here. Go inside (for a modest €4 fee) for a fine example of pre-Renaissance mosaic art (1200s–1300s) in the Byzantine style. Workers from St. Mark's in Venice came here to make the remarkable ceiling mosaics (of Venetian glass) in the late 1200s.

The Last Judgment on the ceiling gives us a glimpse of the medieval worldview. Life was a preparation for the afterlife, when

you would be judged and saved or damned, with no in-between. Christ, peaceful and reassuring, would bless you with heaven (on his right hand, thumbs up) or send you to hell (below Christ's ultimate thumbs down) to be tortured by demons and gnashed between the teeth of monsters.

This hellish scene looks like something right out of the *Inferno* by Dante...who was dipped into the baptismal waters right here.

The Baptistery's bronze doors bring us out of the Middle Ages and into the Renaissance. Some say the Renaissance began precisely in the year 1401, when Florence staged a competition to find the best artist to create the Baptistery's north doors (on the right side as you face the Baptistery with the Duomo at your back). Florence had strong civic spirit, with different guilds (powerful business associations) and merchant groups embellishing their city with great art. All the greats entered the contest, but 25-year-old Lorenzo Ghiberti won easily, beating out heavyweights such as Brunelleschi (who,

Ghiberti's Bronze Doors

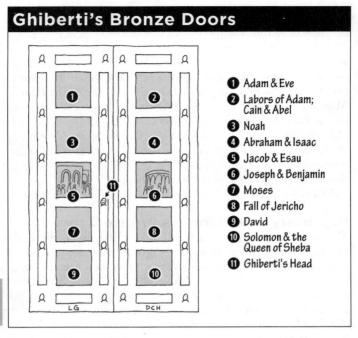

1. Adam & Eve
2. Labors of Adam; Cain & Abel
3. Noah
4. Abraham & Isaac
5. Jacob & Esau
6. Joseph & Benjamin
7. Moses
8. Fall of Jericho
9. David
10. Solomon & the Queen of Sheba
11. Ghiberti's Head

having lost the Baptistery gig, was free to go to Rome, study the Pantheon, and later design the Duomo's dome). The original entries of Brunelleschi and Ghiberti are in the Bargello, where you can judge them for yourself.

Later, in 1425, Ghiberti was given another commission, for the east doors (facing the church). This time there was literally no contest. The bronze panels of these doors (the ones with the crowd of tourists looking on) added a whole new dimension to art—depth. Michelangelo said these doors were fit to be the gates of paradise. (These panels are copies; the originals are in the nearby Duomo Museum. For more detailed descriptions of the panels, see page 150 of the Duomo Museum Tour chapter.) Here we see how the Renaissance was a merging of art and science. Realism was in, and Renaissance artists used math, illusion, and dissection to get it.

In the "Jacob and Esau" panel (just above eye level on the left), receding arches, floor tiles, and banisters create a background for a realistic scene. The figures in the foreground stand and move like real people, telling the Bible story with human

details. Amazingly, this spacious, 3-D scene is made from bronze only a few inches deep.

Ghiberti spent 27 years (1425–1452) working on these panels. That's him in the center of the door frame, atop the second row of panels—the head on the left with the shiny, male-pattern baldness.

• *Before we head south to the river, detour a block north up Via de' Martelli (which becomes Via Cavour). At the intersection with Via dei Pucci is the imposing Medici-Riccardi Palace.*

Medici-Riccardi Palace

Renaissance Florence was ruled by the rich banking family, the Medicis, who lived here. Studying this grand Florentine palace, you'll notice fortified lower walls and elegance limited to the fancy upper stories. The Medici family may have been the local Rockefellers but, having self-made wealth rather than actual noble blood, they were always a bit defensive. The Greek motifs along the eaves highlight the palace's Renaissance roots. Back then, rather than having parking spots, grand buildings came with iron rings to which you'd tether your horse.

You can step into the doorway at Via Cavour 1 and view the courtyard through an iron gate (though the entrance is farther up the street). If you pay admission, you get access to a quintessential Florentine palazzo with a courtyard and a couple of impressive rooms, most notably the sumptuous little Chapel of the Magi (reservations required). ❂ See the Medici-Riccardi Palace Tour chapter.

• *Though we won't visit them on this walk, one block west of here are the Church of San Lorenzo (page 48), San Lorenzo street market (page 49), and Medici Chapels (❂ Medici Chapels Tour chapter). For now, return to the Duomo and continue south, entering the pedestrian-only street that runs from here toward the Arno River.*

Via de' Calzaiuoli

The pedestrian-only Via de' Calzaiuoli (kahlts-ay-WOH-lee) is lined with high-fashion shops, as Florence is a trend-setting city in trend-setting Italy. This street has always been the main axis of Florence, and it was part of the ancient Roman grid plan that became Florence. In medieval times, this street connected the religious center

(sidebar) RENAISSANCE WALK

(where we are now) with the political center (where we're heading), a five-minute walk away. In the 20th century, this historic core was a noisy snarl of car traffic. However, traffic jams have been replaced by potted plants, and now this is a pleasant place to stroll, people-watch, window-shop, lick the drips on your gelato cone, and wonder why American cities can't become more pedestrian-friendly.

And speaking of gelato...**Grom,** which keeps its *gelati* in covered metal bins, the old-fashioned way, is just a half-block detour away (daily 10:30–24:00, take your first left, to Via delle Oche 24a; see the Eating in Florence chapter). Or you could drop by any of the several nearby gelato shops. *Perché no?* (Why not?)

Continue down Via de' Calzaiuoli. Two blocks down from the Baptistery, look right on Via degli Speziali to see a triumphal arch that marks Piazza della Repubblica. The arch celebrates the unification of Italy in 1870 and stands as a reminder that, in ancient Roman times, this piazza was the city center.

• *A block farther, at the intersection with Via Orsanmichele, is the...*

Orsanmichele Church— Florence's Medieval Roots

The Orsanmichele Church provides an interesting look at Florentine values. It's a combo church/granary. Originally, this was an open loggia (covered porch) with a huge grain warehouse upstairs. The arches of the loggia were artfully filled in (14th century), and the building gained a new purpose—as a church. This was prime real estate on what had become the main drag between the church and palace.

The niches in the walls stood empty for decades while they waited for sponsors to fill them with statues. That job fell to the rising middle class of merchants and their guilds.

Florence in 1400 was a republic, a government working for the interests not of a king, but of these guilds (much as modern America caters to corporate interests). Over time, various guilds commissioned statues as PR gestures, hiring the finest artists of the generation. As a result, the statues that ring the church (generally copies of originals stored safely in nearby museums) function as a textbook of the evolution of Florentine art.

Orsanmichele Exterior

In earlier Gothic times, statues were set deep into church niches, simply embellishing the house of God. Here at the Orsanmichele Church, we see statues—as restless as man on the verge of the Renaissance—stepping out from the protection of the Church.

• *Circle the church exterior counterclockwise, enjoying the statues.*

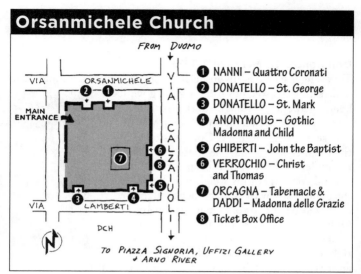

Orsanmichele Church

FROM DUOMO

VIA ORSANMICHELE

MAIN ENTRANCE

VIA LAMBERTI

VIA CALZAIUOLI

DCH

N

TO PIAZZA SIGNORIA, UFFIZI GALLERY & ARNO RIVER

① NANNI – Quattro Coronati
② DONATELLO – St. George
③ DONATELLO – St. Mark
④ ANONYMOUS – Gothic Madonna and Child
⑤ GHIBERTI – John the Baptist
⑥ VERROCHIO – Christ and Thomas
⑦ ORCAGNA – Tabernacle & DADDI – Madonna delle Grazie
⑧ Ticket Box Office

Nanni di Banco's *Quattro Coronati* (c. 1400)

These four early Christians were sculptors martyred by the Roman emperor Diocletian because they refused to sculpt pagan gods. They seem to be contemplating the consequences of the fatal decision they're about to make. Beneath some of the niches, you'll find the symbol of the guilds that paid for the art. Art historians differ here. Some think the work was commissioned by the carpenters' and masons' guild. Others contend it was by the guys who did discount circumcisions.

Donatello's *St. George* (c. 1417)

George is alert, perched on the edge of his niche, scanning the horizon for dragons, and announcing the new age with its new outlook. His knitted brow shows there's a drama unfolding. Sure, he's anxious, but he's also self-assured. Comparing this Renaissance-style *St. George* to *Quattro Coronati,* you can psychoanalyze the heady changes underway. This is humanism.

This *St. George* is a bronze copy of the marble original (located in the Bargello, and described in the Bargello Tour chapter).

• *Continue around the corner of the church, bypassing the entrance for now.*

Donatello's *St. Mark* (1411–1413)

The evangelist cradles his gospel in his strong, veined hand and gazes out, resting his weight on the right leg while bending the left. Though subtle, St. Mark's *contrapposto* pose (weight on one foot) was the first seen since antiquity. Commissioned by the linen-sellers' guild, the statue has elaborately detailed robes that drape around the natural contours of his weighty body. When the guild first saw the statue, they thought the oversized head and torso made it top-heavy. Only after it was lifted into its raised niche did Donatello's cleverly designed proportions look right—and the guild accepted it. Eighty years after young Donatello carved this statue, a teenage Michelangelo Buonarroti stood here and marveled.

Gothic *Madonna and Child* (1399)

This poor copy (made by an anonymous artist) of the oldest statue decorating the Orsanmichele Church shows the serene but unrealistic style that Renaissance artists were so ready to improve. The inscription says that in 1493, a Jew who desecrated this statue was tortured and killed.

Ghiberti's *John the Baptist* (c. 1415)

This statue of the patron saint of Florence is considered the first freestanding bronze since antiquity. It was also the largest bronze cast of its day, a triumph of technology that made Florentines proud of their know-how.

• *On the way to the next statue, you'll pass the ticket box office (where you can make reservations for the Uffizi if you haven't already).*

Verrochio's *Christ and Thomas* (1476–1483)

Doubting Thomas just has to touch Jesus' side wound. With one foot in the heavenly niche and one in our real world...Thomas is one of us. Sculpted a full generation after Donatello, this artwork has more motion, more emotion, and a full sense of the bodies under the heavy robes.

• *Now, noticing how big the church is compared to anything else around, circle back and enter the...*

Orsanmichele Interior

Here's a chance to step into Florence, circa 1350. The church has a double nave because it was adapted from a granary. Look for the pillars (on the left) with rectangular holes in them about three feet off the ground. These were once used as chutes for delivering grain from the storage rooms upstairs. Look up to see the rings hanging from the ceiling, which were likely used to make pulleys for lifting grain, and the iron bars spanning the vaults for support.

The fine **tabernacle** is by Andrea Orcagna. Notice how it was designed exactly for this space: Like the biggest Christmas tree possible, it's capped by an angel whose head touches the ceiling. Take in the Gothic tabernacle's medieval elegance. What it lacks in depth and realism it makes up for in color, with an intricate assemblage of marble, glass, gold, and expensive lapis lazuli. Florence had just survived the terrible bubonic plague of 1348, which killed half the population. The elaborate tabernacle was built to display Bernardo Daddi's *Madonna delle Grazie,* which received plague survivors' grateful prayers. While it's great to see art in museums, it's even better to enjoy it in its original setting—or "in situ"—where the artist intended it. When you view similar altarpieces out of context in the Uffizi, think back on the candlelit medieval atmosphere that surrounds this altarpiece. Consider returning for one of the church's evening concerts.

• *Florence's best collection of sculpture, the Bargello (◎ see the Bargello Tour chapter), is a few blocks east, down Via dei Tavolini. But let's continue down the mall 50 more yards, to the huge and historic square.*

Palazzo Vecchio—Florence's Political Center

The main civic center of Florence is dominated by the Palazzo Vecchio, the Uffizi Gallery, and the marble greatness of old Florence littering the cobbles. This square still vibrates with the echoes of Florence's past—executions, riots, and great celebrations. There's even Roman history: Look for the chart showing the ancient city (on a waist-high, freestanding display to your right as you enter the square). Today, it's a tourist's world with pigeons, postcards, horse buggies, and tired hubbies. And, if it would make your tired spouse happy, stop in at the ritzy **Rivoire** café to enjoy its fine  desserts, pudding-thick hot chocolate, and the best view seats in town (expensive, closed Sun).

Before you towers the Palazzo Vecchio, the Medicis' palatial City Hall—a fortress designed to contain riches and survive the

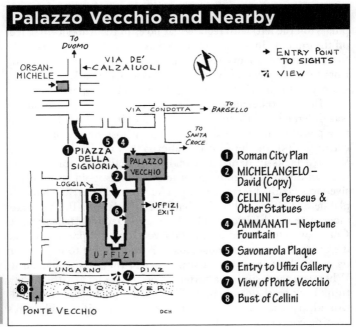

Palazzo Vecchio and Nearby

→ ENTRY POINT TO SIGHTS
↗ VIEW

TO DUOMO
ORSAN-MICHELE
VIA DE' CALZAIUOLI
VIA CONDOTTA → TO BARGELLO
TO SANTA CROCE
PIAZZA DELLA SIGNORIA
PALAZZO VECCHIO
LOGGIA
UFFIZI EXIT
UFFIZI
LUNGARNO   DIAZ
ARNO RIVER
PONTE VECCHIO
DCH

1. Roman City Plan
2. MICHELANGELO – David (Copy)
3. CELLINI – Perseus & Other Statues
4. AMMANATI – Neptune Fountain
5. Savonarola Plaque
6. Entry to Uffizi Gallery
7. View of Ponte Vecchio
8. Bust of Cellini

many riots that went with local politics. The windows are just beyond the reach of angry stones, the tower was a handy look-out post, and justice was doled out sternly on this square. Until 1873, Michelangelo's *David* stood where the replica stands today. The original *David,* damaged in a 1527 riot (when a bench thrown out of a palace window knocked its left arm off), was moved indoors for its own protection.

While the palace interior is not worth touring on a short visit, be sure to step past the replica *David* through the front door into the Palazzo Vecchio's courtyard (free). This palace was Florence's civic center. You're surrounded by art for art's sake—a statue frivolously marking the courtyard's center, and ornate walls and columns. Such luxury was a big change 500 years ago. The squiggly wall painting is called *grotteschi,* inspired by the art that decorated the walls of ancient Roman villas being excavated at the time (c. 1500, named for "grotto" because the ancient villas were actually well below 15th-century Roman street level).

• *Back outside, check out the statue-filled Loggia.*

The Loggia, once a forum for public debate, was perfect for a city that prided itself on its democratic traditions. But later, when the Medicis figured that good art was more desirable than free speech, it was turned into an outdoor sculpture gallery. Notice the squirming Florentine themes—conquest, dominance, rapes, and severed heads. The statues lining the back are Roman originals brought back to Florence by a Medici when he moved home after living in Rome. Two statues in the front deserve a closer look.

The Rape of the Sabines, with its pulse-quickening rhythm of muscles, is from the restless Mannerist period following the stately and confident Renaissance (c. 1560). The sculptor, Giambologna, proved his mastery of the medium by sculpting three entangled bodies from one piece of marble. The composition is best viewed from below and in front.

The relief panel below shows a wider view of the terrible scene. Note what looks like an IV tube on the arm of the horrified husband. It's an electrified wire that effectively keeps the pigeons away.

Benvenuto Cellini's *Perseus,* the Loggia's most noteworthy piece, shows the Greek hero who decapitated the snake-headed Medusa. They say Medusa was so ugly she turned humans who looked at her to stone—though one of this book's authors thinks she's kinda cute.

• *Cross the square to the big fountain of Neptune by Bartolomeo Ammanati that Florentines (including Michelangelo) consider a huge waste of marble—though one of this book's authors...*

The guy on the horse, to the left, is Cosimo I, one of the post-Renaissance Medici. Find the round bronze plaque on the ground 10 steps in front of the fountain.

Savonarola

The Medici family was briefly thrown from power by an austere monk named Savonarola, who made Florence a constitutional republic. He organized huge rallies lit by roaring bonfires here on the square where he preached. While children sang hymns, the devout brought their rich "vanities" (such as paintings, musical instruments, and playing cards) and threw them into the flames.

But not everyone wanted a return to the medieval past. Encouraged by the pope, the Florentines fought back and arrested Savonarola. For two days, they tortured him, trying unsuccessfully to persuade him to see their side of things. Finally, on the very spot where Savonarola's followers had built bonfires of vanities, the monk was burned. The bronze plaque, engraved in Italian *("Qui dove...")*, reads, "Here, Girolamo Savonarola and his Dominican brothers were hanged and burned" in the year "MCCCCXCVIII" (1498). For help in deciphering Roman numerals, see page 475 in the appendix.

• *Stay cool, we have 200 yards to go. Follow the gaze of the fake* David *into the courtyard of the two-tone horseshoe-shaped building...*

Uffizi Courtyard— The Renaissance Hall of Fame

RENAISSANCE WALK

The top floor of this building, known as the *uffizi* ("offices") during Medici days, is filled with the greatest collection of Florentine painting anywhere. It's one of Europe's top four or five art galleries (**○** see the Uffizi Gallery Tour chapter).

The Uffizi courtyard, filled with merchants and hustling young artists, is watched over by 19th-century statues of the great figures of the Renaissance. Tourists zero in on the visual accomplishments of the era—not realizing that it was many-faceted. Let's pay tribute to the nonvisual Renaissance as well, as we wander through Florence's Hall of Fame.

• *Stroll down the left side of the courtyard from the Palazzo Vecchio to the river, noticing...*

1. **Lorenzo the Magnificent**—whose statue is tucked under the arcade, by an Uffizi doorway—was a great art patron and cunning power broker. Excelling in everything except modesty, he set the tone for the Renaissance.

2. **Giotto,** an architect (he holds the plan to the city's great bell tower—named for him), was the first great modern painter.

3. **Donatello,** the sculptor who served as a role model for Michelangelo, holds a hammer and chisel.

4. **Alberti** wrote a famous book, *On Painting*, which taught early Renaissance artists the mathematics of perspective.

5. **Leonardo da Vinci** was a scientist, sculptor, musician, engineer...and not a bad painter either.

6. **Michelangelo** ponders the universe and/or stifles a belch.

7. **Dante,** with the laurel-leaf crown and lyre of a poet, says,

"I am the father of the Italian language." He was the first Italian to write a popular work *(The Divine Comedy)* in non-Latin, using the Florentine dialect, which soon became "Italian" throughout the country.

8. The poet **Petrarch** wears laurel leaves from Greece, a robe from Rome, and a belt from Wal-Mart.

9. **Boccaccio** wrote *The Decameron,* stories told to pass the time during the 1348 Black Death.

10. The devious-looking **Machiavelli** is hatching a plot—his book *The Prince* taught that the end justifies the means, paving the way for the slick-and-cunning "Machiavellian" politics of today.

11. **Vespucci** (in the corner) was an explorer who gave his first name, Amerigo, to a fledgling New World.

12. **Galileo** (in the other corner) holds the humble telescope he used to spot the moons of Jupiter.

• *Pause at the Arno River, overlooking Ponte Vecchio.*

RENAISSANCE WALK

Ponte Vecchio

Before you is Ponte Vecchio (Old Bridge). A bridge has spanned this narrowest part of the Arno since Roman times. While Rome

"fell," Florence really didn't, remaining a bustling trade center along the river. To get into the exclusive little park below (on the north bank), you'll need to join the Florence rowing club.

• *Finish your walk by hiking to the center of the bridge.*

A fine bust of the great gold-smith, Cellini, graces the central point of the bridge. This statue is a reminder that, in the 1500s, the Medicis booted out the bridge's butchers and tanners and installed the gold- and silversmiths who still tempt visitors to this day. This is a very romantic spot late at night (when lovers gather, and a top-notch street musician performs).

Look up to notice the Medicis' protected and elevated passageway that led from the Palazzo Vecchio through the Uffizi, across Ponte Vecchio, and up to the immense Pitti Palace, four blocks beyond the bridge. During World War II, the local German commander was instructed to blow the bridge up. But even some Nazis appreciated history—he blew up the buildings at either end, leaving the bridge impassable but intact. *Grazie.*

ACCADEMIA TOUR: MICHELANGELO'S *DAVID*

Galleria dell'Accademia

One of Europe's great thrills is actually seeing Michelangelo's *David* in the flesh. Seventeen feet high, gleaming white, and exalted by a halo-like dome over his head, *David* rarely disappoints, even for those with high expectations. And the Accademia doesn't stop there. With a handful of other Michelangelo statues and a few other interesting sights, it makes for an uplifting visit that isn't overwhelming. *David* is a must-see on any visit to Florence, so plan for it (and consider reserving an entry time—see page 54 for info).

Orientation

Cost: €6.50 (plus €4 fee for recommended reservation).

Hours: Tue–Sun 8:15–18:50, last entry 30 min before closing, closed Mon.

Reservations: It's smart and easy to reserve ahead. Your hotelier may be able to make the reservation for you (request this service when you book your room). As an alternative, book the tickets yourself by phone by calling 011-39-055-294-883 from the US, or online at www.b-ticket.com/b-ticket/Uffizi (both charge a €4/ticket reservation fee). For details on all of your reservation options, see page 54. During the off-season (Oct–March) on weekdays after 16:00, you can often get in with no reservation and no lines.

When to Go: The museum is most crowded on Sun, Tue, and right when it opens.

Getting There: It's at Via Ricasoli 60, a 15-minute walk from the train station or a 10-minute walk northeast of the Duomo. Taxis are reasonable.

Information: Tel. 055-238-8609 or 055-294-883, www.polomuseale.firenze.it.

Audioguides: The museum rents a €5.50 audioguide (€8/2 people). If you're packing an iPod or other MP3 player, you can also download a free audio tour of the Accademia at www.rick steves.com.

Length of This Tour: While *David* and the *Prisoners* can be seen in 30 minutes, allow an hour if you wish to linger and explore other parts of the museum.

Services: WCs are downstairs. You'll find a small shop in the museum plus several shops outside where you can purchase postcards, books, and posters.

Cuisine Art: Gran Caffè San Marco, around the corner on Piazza San Marco, is a great place for a coffee and *dolce* (but not ideal for a meal). Gelateria Carabè, popular for its sumptuous *granita* (Italian ice) is nearby; from the Accademia, it's a block toward the Duomo, at Via Ricasoli 60 red. Also see "Budget Lunches near the Accademia and Museum of San Marco" (in the Eating chapter).

Photography: No photos or videos are allowed.

Starring: Michelangelo's *David* and *Prisoners*.

The Tour Begins

• *From the entrance lobby, show your ticket, turn left, and look right down the long hall with* David *at the far end, under a halo-like dome. Yes, you're really here. With* David *presiding at the "altar," the* Prisoners *lining the "nave," and hordes of "pilgrims" crowding in to look, you've arrived at Florence's "cathedral of humanism."*

    Start with the ultimate...

ACCADEMIA

David (1501–1504)

When you look into the eyes of Michelangelo's *David*, you're looking into the eyes of Renaissance man. This 17-foot-tall sym-

bol of divine victory over evil represents a new century and a whole new Renaissance outlook. This is the age of Columbus and classicism, Galileo and Gutenberg, Luther and Leonardo—of Florence and the Renaissance.

    In 1501, Michelangelo Buonarroti, a 26-year-old Florentine, was commissioned to carve a large-scale work for the Duomo. He was given a block of marble that other sculptors had rejected as too tall, shallow, and flawed to be of any value. But Michelangelo picked up his hammer and chisel, knocked a knot off what became *David*'s heart, and started to work.

    The figure comes from a Bible story. The Israelites, God's chosen people, are surrounded by

ACCADEMIA

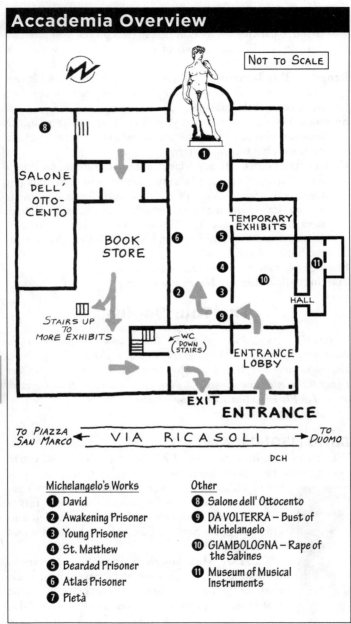

Accademia Overview

NOT TO SCALE

SALONE DELL' OTTOCENTO

BOOK STORE

TEMPORARY EXHIBITS

STAIRS UP TO MORE EXHIBITS

WC (DOWN STAIRS)

HALL

ENTRANCE LOBBY

EXIT

ENTRANCE

TO PIAZZA SAN MARCO ← VIA RICASOLI → TO DUOMO

DCH

Michelangelo's Works
1 David
2 Awakening Prisoner
3 Young Prisoner
4 St. Matthew
5 Bearded Prisoner
6 Atlas Prisoner
7 Pietà

Other
8 Salone dell' Ottocento
9 DA VOLTERRA – Bust of Michelangelo
10 GIAMBOLOGNA – Rape of the Sabines
11 Museum of Musical Instruments

barbarian warriors led by a brutish giant named Goliath. The giant challenges the Israelites to send out someone to fight him. Everyone is afraid except for one young shepherd boy—David. Armed only with a sling, which he's thrown over his shoulder, David gathers five smooth stones from the stream and faces Goliath.

The statue captures David as he's sizing up his enemy. He stands relaxed but alert, leaning on one leg in a classical pose known as *contrapposto*. In his powerful right hand, he fondles the handle of the sling, ready to fling a stone at the giant. His gaze is steady—searching with intense concentration, but also with extreme confidence. Michelangelo has caught the precise moment when David is saying to himself, "I can take this guy."

Note that while the label on *David* indicates that he's already slain the giant, the current director of the Accademia believes, as I do, that Michelangelo has portrayed David facing the giant. Unlike most depictions of David after the kill, this sculpture does not show the giant's severed head. There's also a question of exactly how David's sling would work. Is he holding the stone in his right or left hand? Does the right hand hold the sling's pouch or the retention handle of a sling? Scholars debate Sling Theory endlessly.

David is a symbol of Renaissance optimism. He's no brute. He's a civilized, thinking individual who can grapple with and overcome problems. He needs no armor, only his God-given body and wits. Look at his right hand, with the raised veins and strong, relaxed fingers—many complained that it was too big and overdeveloped. But this is the hand of a man with the strength of God. No mere boy could slay the giant. But David, powered by God, could...and did.

Originally, the statue was commissioned to stand along the southern roofline of the Duomo. But during the three years it

took to sculpt, they decided instead to place it guarding the entrance of the Town Hall, or Palazzo Vecchio. (If the relationship between *David*'s head and body seems a bit out of proportion, it's because Michelangelo designed it to be seen "correctly" from far below the rooftop of the church.)

The colossus was placed standing up in a cart and dragged across rollers from Michelangelo's workshop (behind the Duomo) to the Palazzo Vecchio, where the statue replaced a work by Donatello. There *David* stood—naked and outdoors—for 350 years. In the right light, you can see signs of weathering on his shoulders. Also, note the crack in *David*'s left arm where it was broken off

ACCADEMIA

David, David, David, and *David*

Several Italian masters produced iconic sculptures of David—all of them different. Compare and contrast the artists' styles. How many ways can you slay a giant?

Donatello's *David* (1430, Bargello, Florence)

Donatello's *David* is young and graceful, casually gloating over the head of Goliath, almost Gothic in its elegance and smooth lines. While he has a similar weight-on-one-leg *(contrapposto)* stance as Michelangelo's later version, Donatello's *David*

seems feminine rather than masculine. (For further description, see the Bargello Tour chapter.)

Andrea del Verrocchio's *David* (c. 1470, Bargello, Florence)

Wearing a military skirt and armed with a small sword, Verrocchio's *David* is just a boy. The statue is only four feet tall—light years from Michelangelo's monumental version. (For more, see the Bargello Tour chapter.)

Michelangelo's *David* (1501–1504, Accademia, Florence)

Michelangelo's *David* is pure Renaissance: massive, heroic in size, and superhuman in strength and power. The tensed right

during a 1527 riot near the Palazzo Vecchio. In 1873, to conserve the masterpiece, the statue was finally replaced with a copy and moved here (see photo on the previous page). The real *David* now stands under a wonderful Renaissance-style dome designed just for him.

Renaissance Florentines could identify with *David.* Like him, they considered themselves God-blessed underdogs fighting their city-state rivals. In a deeper sense, they were civilized Renaissance people slaying the ugly giant of medieval superstition, pessimism, and oppression.

• *Hang around a while. Eavesdrop on tour guides. The Plexiglas shields at the base of the statue went up after an attack by a frustrated artist, who smashed the statue's feet in 1991.*

Lining the hall leading up to David *are other statues by Michelangelo—his* Prisoners, St. Matthew, *and* Pietà. *Start with the* Awakening Prisoner, *the statue at the far end of the nave (farthest from* David*). He's on your left as you face* David.

hand, which grips a stone in readiness to hurl at Goliath, is more powerful than any human hand. It's symbolic of divine strength. A model of perfection, Michelangelo's _David_ is far larger and grander than we mere mortals. We know he'll win. Renaissance man has arrived.

Gian Lorenzo Bernini's _David_ (1623, Borghese Museum, Rome)

Flash forward more than a century. In this self-portrait, 25-year-old Bernini is ready to take on the world, slay the pretty-boy _David_s of the Renaissance, and invent Baroque. Unlike Michelangelo's rational, cool, restrained _David,_ Bernini's is a doer: passionate, engaged, dramatic. While Renaissance _David_ is simple and unadorned—carrying only a sling— Baroque Dave is "cluttered" with a braided sling, a hairy pouch, flowing cloth, and discarded armor. Bernini's _David,_ with his tousled hair and set mouth, is one of us; the contest is less certain than with the other three _David_s.

To sum up: Donatello's _David_ represents the first inkling of the Renaissance; Verrocchio's is early Renaissance in miniature; Michelangelo's is textbook Renaissance; and Bernini's is the epitome of Baroque.

ACCADEMIA

The _Prisoners (Prigioni,_ c. 1516–1534)

These unfinished figures seem to be fighting to free themselves from the stone. Michelangelo believed the sculptor was a tool of God, not creating but simply revealing the powerful and beautiful figures that God put in the marble. Michelangelo's job was

to chip away the excess, to reveal. He needed to be in tune with God's will, and whenever the spirit came upon him, Michelangelo worked in a frenzy, often for days on end without sleep.

The _Prisoners_ give us a glimpse of this fitful process, showing the restless energy of someone possessed, struggling against the rock that binds him. Michelangelo himself fought to create the image he saw in his mind's eye. You can still see the grooves from the chisel, and you can picture Michelangelo hacking away in a cloud of dust. Unlike most sculptors, who built a model

More Michelangelo

If you're a fan of Earth's greatest sculptor, you won't leave Florence until there's a check next to each of these:

- **Bargello:** Several Michelangelo sculptures, including the *Bacchus* (pictured here; see the Bargello Tour chapter).
- **Duomo Museum:** Another moving *pietà* (see the Duomo Museum Tour chapter).
- **Medici Chapels:** The *Night* and *Day* statues, plus others done for the Medici tomb, located at the Church of San Lorenzo (see the Medici Chapels Tour chapter).
- **Laurentian Library:** Michelangelo designed the entrance staircase, located at the Church of San Lorenzo.
- **Palazzo Vecchio:** His *Victory* statue (see page 60).
- **Uffizi:** A rare Michelangelo painting (see the Uffizi Gallery Tour chapter).
- **Casa Buonarroti:** Built on property Michelangelo once owned, at Via Ghibellina 70, containing some early works (see page 62).
- **Santa Croce Church:** Michelangelo's tomb (see page 188).
- **Santo Spirito Church:** Wooden crucifix thought to be by him.

ACCADEMIA

and then marked up their block of marble to know where to chip, Michelangelo always worked freehand, starting from the front and working back. These figures emerge from the stone (as his colleague Vasari put it) "as though surfacing from a pool of water."

The so-called *Awakening Prisoner* (the names are given by scholars, not Michelangelo) seems to be stretching after a long nap, still tangled in the "bedsheets" of uncarved rock. He's more block than statue.

On the right, the *Young Prisoner* is more finished. He buries his face in his forearm, while his other arm is chained behind him.

The *Prisoners* were designed for the never-completed tomb of Pope Julius II (who also commissioned the Sistine Chapel ceiling). Michelangelo may have abandoned them simply because the project itself petered out, but he may have deliberately left them unfinished. Having satisfied himself that he'd accomplished what he set out to do, and seeing no point in polishing them into their shiny, finished state, he went on to a new project.

Walking up the nave toward *David*, you'll pass by Michelangelo's **St. Matthew** (1503). Though not one of the *Prisoners* series, he is also unfinished, perfectly illustrating Vasari's "surfac-ing" description.

The next statue, the ***Bearded Prisoner,*** is the most finished of the four, with all four limbs, a bushy face, and even a hint of daylight between his arm and body.

Across the nave on the left, the ***Atlas Prisoner*** carries the unfinished marble on his stooped shoulders, his head still encased in the block.

As you study the *Prisoners,* notice Michelangelo's love and understanding of the human body. His greatest days were spent sketching the muscular, tanned, and sweating bodies of the workers in the Carrara marble quarries. The prisoners' heads and faces are the least-developed part—they "speak" with their poses. Comparing the restless, claustrophobic *Prisoners* with the serene and confident *David* gives an idea of the sheer emotional range in Michelangelo's work.

Pietà

In the unfinished *Pietà* (the threesome closest to *David*), the figures struggle to hold up the sagging body of Christ. Michelangelo (or, more likely, one of his followers) emphasizes the heaviness of Jesus' dead body, driving home the point that this divine being suffered a very human death. Christ's massive arm is almost the size of his bent and bro-ken legs. By stretching his body—if he stood up, he'd be more than seven feet tall—the weight is exaggerated.
• *After getting your fill of Michelangelo, consider taking a spin around...*

ACCADEMIA

The Rest of the Accademia

Michelangelo's statues are far and away the highlight here, but the rest of this small museum—housed in a former convent/hospice—has a few bonuses. Browse the pleasant-but-underwhelming col-lection of **paintings.**

At the end of the hall to the left of *David* is the **Salone dell' Ottocento,** a long room crammed with plaster statues and busts that were the Academy art students' "final exams." An art school has been attached to the museum for centuries, and you may see the next Michelangelo wandering the streets nearby.

At the end of the nave (farthest from *David*) is a bronze **bust** of a craggy, wrinkled Michelangelo, age 89, by Daniele da Volterra. (Da Volterra, one of Michelangelo's colleagues and friends, is best known as the one who painted loincloths on the private parts of Michelangelo's nudes in the Sistine Chapel.) As a teenager, Michelangelo got his nose broken in a fight with a rival artist. Though Michelangelo went on to create great beauty, he was never classically handsome.

In the room near the museum entrance is Giambologna's **Rape of the Sabines** (1582). This full-size plaster model guided the artist's assistants in completing the marble version in the Loggia (next to the Palazzo Vecchio, described on page 84). A Roman warrior tramples a fighter from the Sabine tribe and carries off the man's wife. Husband and wife exchange one final, anguished glance. Circle the statue and watch it spiral around its axis. Giambologna was clearly influenced (as a plaque with photo points out) by Michelangelo's groundbreaking *Victory* in the Palazzo Vecchio (1533–1534, described on page 60). Michelangelo's statue of a man triumphing over a fallen enemy introduced both the theme and the spiral-shaped pose that many artists imitated.

The **Museum of Musical Instruments** (in two rooms down a short hallway) displays late-Renaissance cellos, dulcimers, violins, and harpsichords. Between 1400 and 1700, Florence was one of Europe's most sophisticated cities, and the Medici rulers were trendsetters. Musicians like Scarlatti and Handel flocked to the court of Prince Ferdinando (1663–1713). As you enter, look for the two paintings of the prince (he's second from the right in both paintings, with the yellow bowtie) hanging out with his musician friends. The gay prince played a mean harpsichord, and he helped pioneer new variations. In the adjoining room, you'll see several experimental keyboards, including some by Florence's keyboard pioneer, Bartolomeo Cristofori. The tall piano on display is considered by some to be the world's first upright piano.

• *The tour is finished. From here, it's a 10-minute walk to the Duomo.*

UFFIZI GALLERY TOUR

Galleria degli Uffizi

In the Renaissance, Florentine artists rediscovered the beauty of the natural world. Medieval art had been symbolic, telling Bible stories. Realism didn't matter. But Renaissance people saw the beauty of God in nature and the human body. They used math and science to capture the natural world on canvas as realistically as possible.

The Uffizi Gallery (oo-FEED-zee) has the greatest overall collection anywhere of Italian painting. We'll trace the rise of realism and savor the optimistic spirit that marked the Renaissance.

> *My eyes love things that are fair,*
> *and my soul for salvation cries.*
> *But neither will to Heaven rise*
> *unless the sight of Beauty lifts them there.*
> — Michelangelo Buonarroti, sculptor, painter, poet

Orientation

Cost: €6.50, but mandatory special exhibitions generally bump the price to €10; plus there's a €4 fee for optional but highly recommended reservations. If you've reserved tickets, you'll need to bring cash to pick them up.

Hours: Tue–Sun 8:15–18:50, last entry 30 min before closing, closed Mon.

Reservations: It's smart to book ahead. There are infamously long lines to get in. During summer and on weekends, the Uffizi can be booked up several months in advance, and you'll generally find lines until late afternoon even on winter weekdays. The busiest days are Tue, Sat, and Sun. Avoid the three-hour peak-season wait by reserving ahead.

There are several ways to make reservations: through your hotel, by calling the museum, or by booking online. For details on these options, see the "Making Reservations" sidebar on page 54.

If you arrive in Florence without a reservation for the Uffizi, try booking directly at the Uffizi's ticket office for later that day or the next day (enter the left side of door #2—labeled *Unreserved Ticket Entrance*, pay cash for a ticket up front, same hours as museum). There's also a booking office outside the Orsanmichele Church (€4 reservation fee, open daily 10:00–17:00, along Via Calzaiuoli, the main pedestrian street). Sometimes, by the end of the day (an hour before closing), there are no lines and you can just walk right in.

Getting In: After you have your reservation (or voucher), go to the Uffizi 10 minutes before your appointed time. You'll notice that there are several entrances. Walk briskly across the courtyard from the 200-yard-long ticket-buying line—pondering the IQ of this gang—to the reserved-ticket pickup desk at door #3 (labeled *Picking Up Service*, see map on facing page). Give your reservation number or voucher, pay in cash (if you didn't already pay when you made the reservation), and get your ticket. Then take it back across the courtyard again to door #1 (labeled *Reservation Entrance*), close to the Palazzo Vecchio. There are two lines: one for groups and one for individuals. Show your ticket and walk in.

Getting There: It's on the Arno River between the Palazzo Vecchio and Ponte Vecchio, a 15-minute walk from the train station.

Ongoing Renovation: The Uffizi is undergoing a massive, years-long renovation to create new exhibition space and new entrances. The construction and reshuffling may affect your visit in 2010.

Information: There's no English (or Italian) information in the museum's rooms. You can buy cheap Uffizi guidebooks from street vendors. Tel. 055-238-8651, www.polomuseale.firenze.it.

Audioguide Tours: The museum rents an audioguide (€5.50, €8/2 people, 1.5 hours, must leave ID). If you're traveling with an iPod or other MP3 player, you can download my free audio tour of the Uffizi at www.ricksteves.com.

Length of This Tour: Allow two hours.

Cloakroom: You'll find the baggage check at the start of this tour, far from the finish. No bottled liquids are allowed inside the museum.

Uffizi Gallery Overview

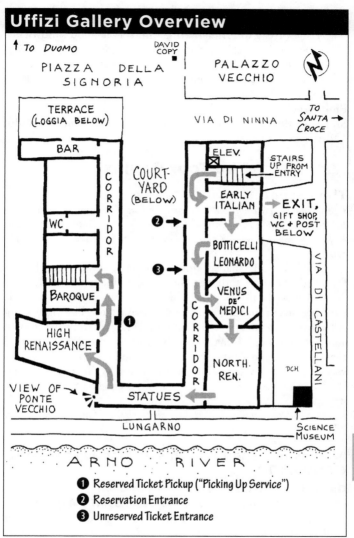

To Duomo

PIAZZA DELLA SIGNORIA

DAVID COPY

PALAZZO VECCHIO

TERRACE (LOGGIA BELOW)

VIA DI NINNA

TO SANTA CROCE

BAR

CORRIDOR

COURT-YARD (BELOW)

ELEV.

STAIRS UP FROM ENTRY

EARLY ITALIAN

EXIT, GIFT SHOP, WC & POST BELOW

WC

❷

BOTTICELLI LEONARDO

❸

BAROQUE

VENUS DE' MEDICI

CORRIDOR

HIGH RENAISSANCE

❶

NORTH. REN.

DCH

VIA DI CASTELLANI

VIEW OF PONTE VECCHIO

STATUES

LUNGARNO

SCIENCE MUSEUM

ARNO RIVER

❶ Reserved Ticket Pickup ("Picking Up Service")
❷ Reservation Entrance
❸ Unreserved Ticket Entrance

UFFIZI GALLERY

Services: The Uffizi has a post office and gift shop (at exit on ground floor, has public entrance and WC). The two, often-crowded WCs within the collection are located at the end of this self-guided tour on the way to the exit.

Cuisine Art: The simple café at the end of the gallery has reasonably priced salads, desserts, and fruit cups (for eating indoors), and a pricier outdoor terrace with a Duomo/Palazzo Vecchio view. A €5 cappuccino here is one of Europe's great treats.

A block away, a quiet wine-and-olive-oil shop called 'Ino Bottega di Alimentari e Vini serves good sandwiches (Tue–Sat 11:00–20:00, Sun 12:00–17:00, closed Mon; walking from the Uffizi along the Arno to Ponte Vecchio, take the first right to Via dei Georgofili 3 red). See page 258 for details on this and other nearby restaurants.

Photography: No photos allowed.

Starring: Botticelli, Venus, Raphael, Giotto, Titian, Leonardo, and Michelangelo.

The Tour Begins

The Ascent

• *Buy your ticket, then walk up the four long flights of the monumental staircase to the top floor (or take the elevator). Your brain should be fully aerated from the hike up. Past the ticket-taker, look out the window.*

The Uffizi is U-shaped, running around the courtyard. Except for a little Baroque spillover, the entire collection is on this one floor, displayed chronologically. This left wing contains Florentine paintings from medieval to Renaissance times. The right wing (which you can see across the courtyard) has art from the Roman and Venetian High Renaissance, works from the Baroque period that followed, and a café terrace facing the Duomo. A short hallway with sculpture connects the two wings. We'll concentrate on the Uffizi's forte, the Florentine section, then get a taste of the art it inspired.

• *Down the hall, enter the first door on the left and face Giotto's giant Madonna and Child.*

Medieval—When Art Was as Flat as the World (1200–1400)

Giotto (c. 1266–1337)—*Madonna and Child*
(Madonna in trono col Bambino Gesù, Santi e Angeli)

Mary and baby Jesus sit on a throne in a golden never-never land symbolizing heaven. It's as if medieval Christians couldn't imagine holy people inhabiting our dreary material world. It took Renaissance painters to bring Mary down to Earth and give her human realism. For the Florentines, "realism" meant "three-dimensional." In this room, pre-Renaissance paintings show the slow process of learning to paint a 3-D world on a 2-D surface.

Before concentrating on the Giotto, look at some others in the room. The **crucifixion** (on your right as you face the Giotto) was medieval 3-D—paint a crude two-dimensional work...then physically tilt the head forward. Nice try.

The three similar-looking Madonna-and-Bambinos in this room—all painted within a few decades of each other in about the year 1300—show baby steps in the march to realism. **Duccio**'s piece (on the left as you face Giotto) is the most medieval and two-dimensional. There's no background. The angels are just stacked one on top of the other, floating in the golden atmosphere. Mary's throne is crudely drawn—the left side is at a three-quarters angle while the right is practically straight on. Mary herself is a wispy cardboard-cutout figure seemingly floating just above the throne.

On the opposite wall, the work of **Cimabue**—mixing the iconic Byzantine style with budding Italian realism—is an improvement. The large throne creates an illusion of depth. Mary's foot actually sticks out over the lip of the throne. Still, the angels are stacked totem-pole-style, serving as heavenly bookends.

Giotto (JOT-oh) employs realism to make his theological points. He creates a space and fills it. Like a set designer, he builds a three-dimensional "stage"—the canopied throne—then peoples it with real beings. The throne has angels in front, prophets behind, and a canopy over the top, clearly defining its three dimensions. The steps up to the throne lead from our space to Mary's, making the scene an extension of our world. But the real triumph here is Mary herself—big and monumental, like a Roman statue. Beneath her robe, she has a real live body, with knees and breasts that stick out at us. This three-dimensionality was revolutionary in its day, a taste of the Renaissance a century before it began.

Giotto was one of the first "famous" artists. In the Middle Ages, artists were mostly unglamorous craftsmen, like carpenters or cable-TV repairmen. They cranked out generic art and could have signed their work with a bar code. But Giotto was recognized as a genius, a unique individual. He died in a plague that devastated Florence. If there had been no plague, would the Renaissance have started 100 years earlier?

• *Enter Room 3, to the left of Giotto.*

Medieval Art

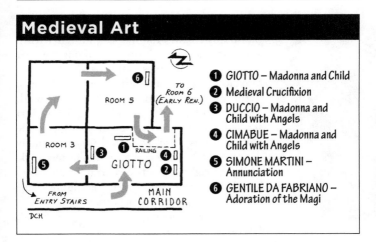

ROOM 5

TO
ROOM 6
(EARLY REN.)

ROOM 3

RAILING

GIOTTO

MAIN
CORRIDOR

FROM
ENTRY STAIRS

DCH

❶ GIOTTO – Madonna and Child
❷ Medieval Crucifixion
❸ DUCCIO – Madonna and Child with Angels
❹ CIMABUE – Madonna and Child with Angels
❺ SIMONE MARTINI – Annunciation
❻ GENTILE DA FABRIANO – Adoration of the Magi

Simone Martini (c. 1285–1344)—Annunciation
(Annunciazione con i Santi Ansano e Massima)

Simone Martini boils things down to the basic figures needed to get the message across: (1) The angel appears to sternly tell (2) Mary

that she'll be the mother of Jesus. In the center is (3) a vase of lilies, a symbol of purity. Above is (4) the Holy Spirit as a dove about to descend on her. If the symbols aren't enough to get the message across, Simone Martini has spelled it right out for us in Latin: *"Ave Gratia Plena..."* or, "Hail, favored one, the Lord is with you." Mary doesn't exactly look pleased as punch.

This is not a three-dimensional work. The point was not to re-create reality but to teach religion, especially to the illiterate masses. This isn't a beautiful Mary or even a real Mary. She's a generic woman without distinctive features. We know she's pure—not from her face, but only because of the halo and symbolic flowers. Before the Renaissance, artists didn't care about the beauty of individual people.

Simone Martini's *Annunciation* has medieval features you'll see in many of the paintings in the next few rooms: (1) religious subject, (2) gold background, (3) two-dimensionality, and (4) meticulous detail.

• Pass through Room 4, full of golden altarpieces, stopping at the far end of Room 5.

UFFIZI GALLERY

Gentile da Fabriano (c. 1370–1427)—
Adoration of the Magi (Adorazione dei Magi)

Look at the incredible detail of the Three Kings' costumes, the fine horses, and the cow in the cave. The canvas is filled from top to bot-

tom with realistic details—but it's far from realistic. While the Magi worship Jesus in the foreground, their return trip home dangles over their heads in the "background."

This is a textbook example of the International Gothic style popular with Europe's aristocrats in the early 1400s:

well-dressed, elegant people in a colorful, design-oriented setting. The religious subject is just an excuse to paint secular luxuries such as jewelry and clothes made of silk brocade. And the scene's background and foreground are compressed together to create an overall design that's pleasing to the eye.

Such exquisite detail work raises the question: Was Renaissance three-dimensionality truly an improvement over Gothic, or simply a different style?

• *Exit to your right and hang a U-turn left into Room 7.*

Early Renaissance (mid-1400s)
Paolo Uccello (1397–1475)—*The Battle of San Romano*
(La Battaglia di San Romano)

In the 1400s, painters worked out the problems of painting realisti-cally, using mathematics to create the illusion of three-dimension-ality. This colorful battle scene, which may be out for restoration in 2010, is not so much a piece of art as an exercise in perspective. Paolo Uccello (oo-CHEL-loh) has challenged himself with every possible problem.

The broken lances at left set up a 3-D "grid" in which to place this crowded scene. The fallen horses and soldiers are experiments in "foreshortening"—shortening the things that are farther away from us (which appear smaller) to create the illusion of distance.

Some of the figures are definitely A-plus mate-rial, like the fallen gray horse in the center and the white horse at the far right walking away. But some are more like B-minus work—the kicking red horse's legs

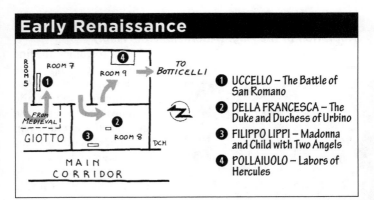

Early Renaissance

- **1** UCCELLO – The Battle of San Romano
- **2** DELLA FRANCESCA – The Duke and Duchess of Urbino
- **3** FILIPPO LIPPI – Madonna and Child with Two Angels
- **4** POLLAIUOLO – Labors of Hercules

look like ham hocks at this angle, and the fallen soldier at far right would be only child-size if he stood up.

And then there's the D-minus "Are you on drugs?" work. The converging hedges in the background create a nice illusion of a distant hillside maybe 250 feet away. So what are those soldiers the size of the foreground figures doing there? And jumping the hedge, is that rabbit 40 feet tall?

Paolo Uccello almost literally went crazy trying to master the three dimensions (thank God he was born before Einstein discovered one more). Uccello got so wrapped up in it he kind of lost... perspective.

• *Enter Room 8. In the center of the room stands a double portrait.*

Piero della Francesca (c. 1412–1492)— *The Duke and Duchess of Urbino (Ritratti dei Duchi di Urbino)*

In medieval times, only saints and angels were worthy of being painted. In the humanistic Renaissance, however, even non-religious folk like this husband and wife had their features preserved for posterity. Renaissance artists discovered the beauty in ordinary people and painted them, literally, warts and all.

Fra Filippo Lippi (1406–1469)—*Madonna and Child with Two Angels (Madonna col Bambino e Due Angeli)*

Compare this Mary with the generic female in Simone Martini's *Annunciation*. We don't need the wispy halo over her head to tell us she's holy—she radiates sweetness and light from her divine face. Heavenly beauty is expressed by a physically beautiful woman.

Fra (Brother) Lippi, an orphan raised as a monk, lived a less-than-monkish life. He lived with a nun who bore him two children. He spent his entire life searching for the perfect Virgin.

UFFIZI GALLERY

Through his studio passed Florence's prettiest girls, many of whom decorate the walls here in this room.

Lippi painted idealized beauty, but his models were real flesh-and-blood human beings. You could look through all the thousands of paintings from the Middle Ages and not find anything so human as the mischievous face of one of Lippi's little angel boys.

• *Enter Room 9, with two small works by Pollaiuolo in the glass case between the windows.*

Antonio Pollaiuolo (c. 1431–1498)—*Labors of Hercules (Fatiche di Ercole)*

Hercules gets a workout in these two small panels showing the

human form at odd angles. The poses are the wildest imaginable, to show how each muscle twists and tightens. While Uccello worked on perspective, Pollaiuolo studied anatomy. In medieval times, dissection of corpses was a sin and a crime (the two were the same then). Dissecting was a desecration of the human body, the temple of God. But Pollaiuolo was willing to sell his soul to the

devil for artistic knowledge. He dissected.

There's something funny about this room that I can't put my finger on...I've got it—no Madonnas. Not one. (No, that's not a Madonna; she's a Virtue.)

We've seen how Early Renaissance artists worked to conquer reality. Now let's see the fruits of their work, the flowering of Florence's Renaissance.

• *Enter the large Botticelli room and take a seat.*

Florence—The Renaissance Blossoms (1450–1500)

Florence in 1450 was in a Firenz-y of activity. There was a can-do spirit of optimism in the air, led by prosperous merchants and bankers and a strong middle class. The government was reasonably democratic, and Florentines saw themselves as citizens of a strong republic—like ancient Rome. Their civic pride showed in the public monuments and artworks they built. Man was leaving the protection of the church to stand on his own two feet.

Lorenzo de' Medici, head of the powerful Medici family, epitomized this new humanistic spirit. Strong, decisive, handsome, poetic, athletic, sensitive, charismatic, intelligent, brave, clean, and reverent, Lorenzo was a true Renaissance man, deserving of the nickname he went by—the Magnificent. He gathered Florence's best and brightest around him for evening wine and discussions of great ideas. One of this circle was the painter Botticelli (bot-i-CHEL-ee).

Sandro Botticelli (1445–1510)—*Allegory of Spring (Allegoria della Primavera)*

It's springtime in a citrus grove. The winds of spring blow in (Mr. Blue, at right), causing the woman on the right to sprout flowers from her lips as she morphs into Flora, or Spring—who walks by, spreading flowers from her dress. At the left are Mercury and the Three Graces, dancing a delicate maypole dance. The Graces may be symbolic of the three forms of love—love of beauty, love of people, and sexual love, suggested by the raised intertwined fingers. (They forgot love of peanut butter on toast.) In the center stands Venus, the Greek goddess of love. Above her flies a blindfolded Cupid, happily shooting his arrows of love without worrying whom they'll hit.

Here is the Renaissance in its first bloom, its "springtime" of innocence. Madonna is out, Venus is in. Adam and Eve hiding their nakedness are out, glorious flesh is in. This is a return to the pre-Christian pagan world of classical Greece, where things of the

UFFIZI GALLERY

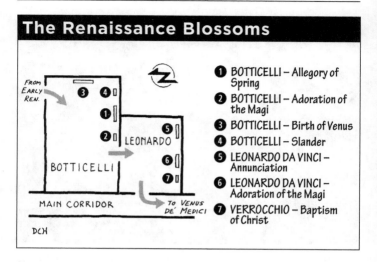

The Renaissance Blossoms

FROM
EARLY
REN.

BOTTICELLI

MAIN CORRIDOR

TO VENUS
DE' MEDICI

LEONARDO

DCH

❶ BOTTICELLI – Allegory of Spring

❷ BOTTICELLI – Adoration of the Magi

❸ BOTTICELLI – Birth of Venus

❹ BOTTICELLI – Slander

❺ LEONARDO DA VINCI – Annunciation

❻ LEONARDO DA VINCI – Adoration of the Magi

❼ VERROCCHIO – Baptism of Christ

flesh are not sinful. But this is certainly no orgy—just fresh-faced innocence and playfulness.

Botticelli emphasizes pristine beauty over gritty realism. The lines of the bodies, especially of the Graces in their see-through nighties, have pleasing, S-like curves. The faces are idealized but have real human features. There's a look of thoughtfulness and even melancholy in the faces—as though everyone knows that the innocence of spring will not last forever.

· *Look at the next painting to the right.*

Botticelli—*Adoration of the Magi (Adorazione dei Magi)*

Here's the rat pack of confident young Florentines who reveled in the optimistic pagan spirit—even in a religious scene. Botticelli included himself among the adorers, looking vain in the yellow robe at far right. Lorenzo's the Magnificent-looking guy at the far left.

UFFIZI GALLERY

Botticelli—*Birth of Venus (Nascita di Venere)*

According to myth, Venus was born from the foam of a wave. Still only half awake, this fragile, newborn beauty floats ashore on a clam shell, blown by the winds, where her maid waits to dress her. The pose is the same S-curve of classical statues (as we'll soon see). Botticelli's pastel colors make the world itself seem fresh and newly born.

This is the purest expression of Renaissance beauty. Venus' naked body is not sensual, but innocent. Botticelli thought that physical beauty was a way of appreciating God. Remember Michelangelo's poem: Souls will never ascend to heaven "...until the sight of Beauty lifts them there."

Botticelli finds God in the details—Venus' windblown hair, the translucent skin, the maid's braided hair, the slight ripple of the wind god's abs, and the flowers tumbling in the slowest of slow motions, suspended like musical notes, caught at the peak of their brief life.

Mr. and Mrs. Wind intertwine—notice her hands clasped around his body. Their hair, wings, and robes mingle like the wind. But what happened to those splayed toes?

• *"Venus on the Half-Shell" (as many tourists call this) is one of the masterpieces of Western art. Take some time with it. Then find the small canvas on the wall to the right, near the* Allegory of Spring.

Botticelli—*Slander (La Calunnia)*

The spring of Florence's Renaissance had to end. Lorenzo died young. The economy faltered. Into town rode the monk Savonarola, preaching medieval hellfire and damnation for those who embraced the "pagan" Renaissance spirit. "Down, down with all gold and decoration," he roared. "Down where the body is food for the worms." He presided over huge bonfires, where the people threw in

their fine clothes, jewelry, pagan books...and paintings.

Slander spells the end of the Florentine Renaissance. The setting is classic Brunelleschian architecture, but look at what's taking place beneath those stately arches. These aren't proud Renaissance men and women but a ragtag, medieval-looking bunch, a Court of Thieves in an abandoned hall of justice. The accusations fly, and everyone is condemned. The naked man pleads for mercy, but the hooded black figure, a symbol of his execution, turns away. The figure of Truth (naked Truth)—straight out of *The Birth of Venus*—looks up to heaven as if to ask, "What has happened to us?" The classical statues in their niches look on in disbelief.

Botticelli listened to Savonarola. He burned some of his own paintings and changed his tune. The last works of his life were darker, more somber, and pessimistic about humanity.

The German poet Heinrich Heine said, "When they start by burning books, they'll end by burning people." After four short years of power, Savonarola was burned on his own bonfire in Piazza della Signoria, but by then the city was in shambles. The first flowering of the Renaissance was over.

• *Enter the next room.*

Leonardo da Vinci (1452–1519)—*Annunciation*

A scientist, architect, engineer, musician, and painter, Leonardo was a true Renaissance man. He worked at his own pace rather

than to please an employer, so he often left works unfinished. The two paintings in this room aren't his best, but even a lesser Leonardo is enough to put a museum on the map, and they're definitely worth a look.

Gabriel has walked up to Mary, and now kneels on one knee like an ambassador, saluting her. See how relaxed his other hand is, draped over his knee. Mary, who's been reading, looks up with a gesture of surprise and curiosity.

Leonardo constructs a beautifully landscaped "stage" and puts his characters in it. Look at the bricks on the right wall. If you extended lines from them, the lines would all converge at the center of the painting, the distant blue mountain. Same with the edge of the sarcophagus and the railing. Subconsciously, this subtle touch creates a feeling of balance, order, and spaciousness.

Think back to Simone Martini's *Annunciation* to realize how much more natural, relaxed, and realistic Leonardo's version is. He's taken a miraculous event—an angel appearing out of the blue—and presented it in a very human way.

UFFIZI GALLERY

Leonardo da Vinci—*Adoration of the Magi*

Leonardo's human insight is even more apparent here, in this unfinished work. The poor kings are amazed at the Christ child—

even afraid of him. They scurry around like chimps around a fire. This work is as agitated as the *Annunciation* is calm, giving us an idea of Leonardo's range. Leonardo was pioneering a new era of painting, showing not just the outer features but the inner personality.

The next painting to the right, *Baptism of Christ,* is by Andrea del Verrocchio, Leonardo's teacher. Leonardo painted the angel on the far left when he was only 14 years old. Legend has it that when Verrocchio saw that some kid had painted an angel better than he ever would...he hung up his brush for good.

Florence saw the first blossoming of the Renaissance. But when the cultural climate turned chilly, artists flew south to warmer climes. The Renaissance shifted to Rome.

• *Exit into the main hallway. Breathe. Sit. Admire the ceiling. Look out the window. See you in five.*

Back already? Now continue down the hallway and turn left into the octagonal Venus de' Medici *room (they allow only 25 people in at a time). If you skip this because there's a line, you'll also be missing the next five rooms, which include works by Cranach, Dürer, Memling, Holbein, Giorgione, and others.*

Classical Sculpture

If the Renaissance was the foundation of the modern world, the foundation of the Renaissance was classical sculpture. Sculptors, painters, and poets alike turned for inspiration to these ancient Greek and Roman works as the epitome of balance, 3-D perspective, human anatomy, and beauty.

Venus de' Medici, or Medici Venus (*Venere de' Medici,* Ancient Greece)

Is this pose familiar? Botticelli's *Birth of Venus* has the same position of the arms, the same S-curved body, and the same lifting of the right leg. A copy of this statue stood in Lorenzo the Magnificent's garden, where Botticelli used to hang out. This one is a Roman copy of the lost original by the great Greek sculptor Praxiteles. The *Venus de' Medici* is a balanced, harmonious, serene statue from Greece's "Golden Age," when balance was admired in every aspect of life.

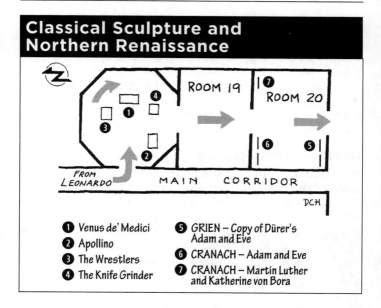

Classical Sculpture and Northern Renaissance

ROOM 19
ROOM 20

FROM LEONARDO   MAIN   CORRIDOR

DCH

1 Venus de' Medici
2 Apollino
3 The Wrestlers
4 The Knife Grinder
5 GRIEN – Copy of Dürer's Adam and Eve
6 CRANACH – Adam and Eve
7 CRANACH – Martin Luther and Katherine von Bora

Perhaps more than any other work of art, this statue has been the epitome of both ideal beauty and sexuality. In the 18th and 19th centuries, sex was "dirty," so the sex drive of cultured aristocrats was channeled into a love of pure beauty. Wealthy sons and daughters of Europe's aristocrats made the pilgrimage to the Uffizi to complete their classical education...where they swooned in ecstasy before the cold beauty of this goddess of love.

Louis XIV had a bronze copy made. Napoleon stole her away to Paris for himself. And in Philadelphia in the 1800s, a copy had to be kept under lock and key to prevent the innocent from catching the Venere-al disease. At first, it may be difficult for us to appreciate such passionate love of art, but if any generation knows the power of sex to sell something—be it art or underarm deodorant—it's ours.

The Other Statues

Venus de' Medici's male counterpart is on the right, facing Venus. *Apollino* (a.k.a. "Venus with a Penis") is also by the master of smooth, cool lines: Praxiteles.

The other works are later Greek (Hellenistic), when quiet balance was replaced by violent motion and emotion. *The Wrestlers*, to the left of Venus, is a study in anatomy and twisted limbs—like Pollaiuolo's paintings a thousand years later.

The drama of *The Knife Grinder* to the right of Venus stems from the off-stage action—he's sharpening the knife to flay a man alive.

This fine room was a showroom, or a "cabinet of wonders," back when this building still functioned as the Medici offices. Filled with family portraits, it's a holistic statement that symbolically links the Medici family with the four basic elements: air (weathervane in the lantern), water (inlaid mother of pearl in the dome), fire (red wall), and earth (inlaid stone floor).

• *When you reach the baby with the bird, exit the octagonal room and pass through Room 19 into Room 20.*

Northern Renaissance

Hans Baldung Grien (c. 1484-1545)— Copy of Dürer's *Adam and Eve*

The warm spirit of the Renaissance blew north into Germany. Albrecht Dürer (1471–1528), the famous German painter and

engraver, traveled to Venice, where he fell in love with all things Italian. Returning home, he painted the First Couple in the Italian style—full-bodied, muscular (check out Adam's abs and Eve's knees), "carved" with strong shading, fresh-faced, and innocent in their earthly Paradise.

This copy of Dürer's original (now in the Prado) by Hans Baldung Grien was a training exercise. Like many of Europe's artists—including Michelangelo and Raphael—Baldung Grien learned technique by studying Dürer's meticulous engravings, spread by the newly invented printing press.

Lucas Cranach (1472-1553)— *Adam and Eve*

Eve sashays forward, with heavy-lidded eyes, to offer the forbidden fruit. Adam stretches to display himself and his foliage to Eve. The two panels are linked by smoldering eye contact, as Man and Woman awaken to their own nakedness. The Garden of Eden is about to be rocked by new ideas that are both liberating and troubling.

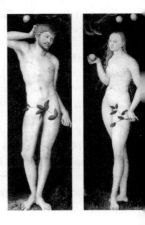

Though the German Lucas Cranach occasionally dabbled in the "Italian style," he chose to portray his Adam and Eve in

UFFIZI GALLERY

the now-retro look of International Gothic.

They are slimmer than Dürer's, as well as smoother, more S-shaped, elegant, graceful, shapely, and erotic, with the dainty pinkies of the refined aristocrats signing Cranach's paycheck.

Though life-size, Adam and Eve are not lifelike, not monumental, not full-bodied or muscular, and are not placed in a real-world landscape with distant perspectives. Even so, Cranach was very much a man of the Renaissance, a friend of Martin Luther, and a champion of humanism.

• *Find a small, two-panel portrait featuring Martin Luther with his wife (or possibly a panel featuring Luther's colleague, Melanchthon; the museum rotates these two).*

Cranach—*Martin Luther*

Martin Luther—German monk, fiery orator, and religious whistle-blower—sparked a century of European wars by speaking out against the Catholic Church.

Luther (1483–1546) lived a turbulent life. In early adulthood, the newly ordained priest suffered a severe personal crisis of faith, before finally emerging "born again." In 1517, he openly protested against Church corruption and was excommunicated. Defying both the pope and the emperor, he lived on the run as an outlaw, watching as his ideas sparked peasant riots. He still found time to translate the New Testament from Latin to modern German, write hymns such as "A Mighty Fortress," and spar with the humanist Erasmus and fellow-Reformer Zwingli.

Now 46 years old, Martin Luther is easing out of the fast lane. Recently married to an ex-nun, he has traded his monk's habit for street clothes, bought a house, had several kids...and has clearly been enjoying his wife's home cooking and home-brewed beer.

Cranach—*Katherine von Bora* (Luther's wife)

When "Katie" decided to leave her convent, the famous Martin Luther agreed to help find her a husband. She rejected his nominees, saying she'd marry no one...except Luther himself. In 1525, the 42-year-old ex-priest married the 26-year-old ex-nun "to please my father and annoy the pope." Martin turned his checkbook over to "my lord Katie," who also ran the family farm, raised their six children and 11 adopted orphans, and hosted Martin's circle of friends (including Cranach) at loud, chatty dinner parties.

• *Pass through the next couple of rooms, exiting to a great view of the Arno and Ponte Vecchio. Stroll through the hall with sculpture.*

The Sculpture Hall

A hundred years ago, no one even looked at Botticelli—they came to the Uffizi to see the sculpture collection. And today, these 2,000-year-old Roman copies of 2,500-year-old Greek originals are hardly noticed...but they should be. The purple statue in the center of the hall—headless and limbless—is a female wolf (or "Lupa"), the animal that raised Rome's legendary founders and became the city's symbol. Look up as you go. Along the ceiling are portraits of leading citizens, as well as an ornate patterned ceiling decor in the "grotesque" style inspired by frescoes discovered in Nero's Golden House (in Rome). The entire Greek and Roman pantheon were present here—a design meant to humble visiting dignitaries and diplomats.

• *Grab a seat at one of the benches scattered throughout the hall for a...*

View of the Arno

Enjoy Florence's best view of the Arno and Ponte Vecchio. You can also see the red-tiled roof of the Vasari Corridor, the "secret" passage connecting the Palazzo Vecchio, Uffizi, Ponte Vecchio, and Pitti Palace on the other side of the river—a half-mile in all. This was a private walkway, wallpapered in great art, for the Medici family's commute from home to work.

As you appreciate the view (best at sunset), remember that it's this sort of pleasure that Renaissance painters wanted you to get from their paintings. For them, a canvas was a window you looked through to see the wide world. Their paintings re-create natural perspective: Distant objects (such as bridges) are dimmer and higher up the "canvas," while closer objects are clearer and lower.

We're headed down the home stretch now. If your little U-feetsies are killing you, and it feels like torture, remind yourself that it's a pleasant torture and smile...like the statue next to you.

• *In the far hallway, turn left into the first room (#25) and grab a blast of cold from the air-conditioning vent on the floor to the left.*

High Renaissance

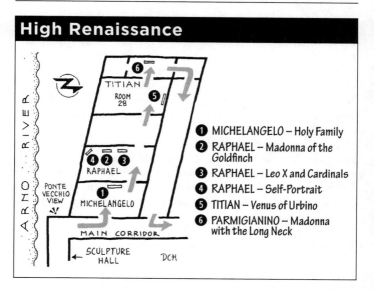

TITIAN

ROOM 28

PONTE VECCHIO VIEW

RAPHAEL

MICHELANGELO

MAIN CORRIDOR

SCULPTURE HALL

ARNO RIVER

DCH

1 MICHELANGELO – Holy Family

2 RAPHAEL – Madonna of the Goldfinch

3 RAPHAEL – Leo X and Cardinals

4 RAPHAEL – Self-Portrait

5 TITIAN – Venus of Urbino

6 PARMIGIANINO – Madonna with the Long Neck

High Renaissance (1500–1550)—Michelangelo, Raphael, Titian

Michelangelo Buonarroti (1475–1564)—*Holy Family (Sacra Famiglia)*

This is the only completed easel painting by the greatest sculptor in history. Florentine painters were sculptors with brushes. This shows it. Instead of a painting, it's more like three clusters of statues with some clothes painted on.

The main subject is the holy family—Mary, Joseph, and baby Jesus—and in the background are two groups of nudes looking like classical statues. The background represents the old pagan world, while Jesus in the foreground is the new age of Christianity. The figure of young John the Baptist at right is the link between the two.

This is a "peasant" Mary, with a plain face and sunburned arms. Michelangelo shows her from a very unflattering angle—we're looking up her nostrils. But Michelangelo himself was an ugly man, and he was among the first artists to recognize the beauty in everyday people.

Michelangelo was a Florentine—in fact, he was like an adopted son of the Medicis, who recognized his talent—but much of his greatest work was done in Rome as part of the Pope's face-lift of the city. We can see here some of the techniques he used on the Sistine Chapel ceiling that revolutionized painting—monumental figures; dramatic angles (looking up Mary's nose); accentuated, rippling muscles; and bright, clashing colors (all the more apparent since both this work and the Sistine Chapel ceiling have recently been cleaned). These elements added a dramatic tension that was lacking in the graceful work of Leonardo and Botticelli.

Michelangelo painted this for Angelo Doni for 70 ducats. (Michelangelo designed, but didn't carve, the elaborate frame.) When the painting was delivered, Doni tried to talk Michelangelo down to 40. Proud Michelangelo took the painting away and would not sell it until the man finally agreed to pay double...140 ducats.

• *Enter Room 26 and welcome back Raphael's* Madonna of the Goldfinch *after a laborious 10-year restoration.*

Raphael (Raffaello Sanzio, 1483–1520)— *Madonna of the Goldfinch (La Madonna del Cardellino)*

Raphael (roff-eye-ELL) brings Mary and Bambino down from heaven and into the real world of trees, water, and sky. He gives baby Jesus (right) and John the Baptist a realistic, human playfulness. It's a tender scene painted with warm colors and a hazy background that matches the golden skin of the children.

Raphael perfected his craft in Florence, following the graceful style of Leonardo. In typical Leonardo fashion, this group of Mary, John the Baptist, and Jesus is arranged in the shape of a pyramid, with Mary's head at the peak.

The two halves of the painting balance perfectly. Draw a line down the middle, through Mary's nose and down through her knee. John the Baptist on the left is balanced by Jesus on the right. Even the trees in the background balance each other, left and right. These things aren't immediately noticeable, but they help create the subconscious feelings of balance and order that reinforce the atmosphere of maternal security in this domestic scene—pure Renaissance.

Raphael—*Leo X and Cardinals (Ritratta di Papa Leone X con i Cardinali)*

Raphael was called to Rome at the same time as Michelangelo, working next door while Michelangelo painted the Sistine

UFFIZI GALLERY

Six Degrees of Leo X

This sophisticated, luxury-loving pope was at the center of an international, Renaissance world that spread across Europe. He crossed paths with many of the Renaissance men of his generation. Based on the theory that any two people are linked by only "six degrees of separation," let's link Leo X with the actor Kevin Bacon:

- Leo X's father was Lorenzo the Magnificent, patron of Botticelli and Leonardo.
- When Leo X was age 13, his family took in 13-year-old Michelangelo.
- Michelangelo inspired Raphael, who was later hired by Leo X.
- Raphael exchanged masterpieces with fellow genius Albrecht Dürer, who was personally converted by Martin Luther (who was friends with Lucas Cranach), who was excommunicated by…Leo X.
- Leo X was portrayed in the movie *The Agony and the Ecstasy,* which starred Charlton Heston, who was in *Planet of the Apes* with Burgess Meredith, who was in *Rocky* with Sylvester Stallone, who was in *Cop Land* with Robert De Niro, who was in *Sleepers* with…Kevin Bacon.

Chapel ceiling. Raphael peeked in from time to time, learning from Michelangelo's monumental, dramatic figures, and his later work is grittier and more realistic than the idealized, graceful, and "Leonardoesque" Madonna.

Pope Leo X is big, like a Michelangelo statue. And Raphael captures some of the seamier side of Vatican life in the cardinals' eyes—shrewd, suspicious, and somewhat cynical. With Raphael, the photographic realism pursued by painters since Giotto was finally achieved.

The Florentine Renaissance ended in 1520 with the death of Raphael. Raphael (see his **self-portrait** to the left of the Madonna) is considered both the culmination and conclusion of the Renaissance. The realism, balance, and humanism we associate with the Renaissance are all found in Raphael's work. He combined the grace of Leonardo with the power of Michelangelo. With his death, the Renaissance shifted again—to Venice.

• *Pass through the next room and enter Room 28.*

Titian (Tiziano Vecellio, c. 1490–1576)—*Venus of Urbino* (*La Venere di Urbino*)

Compare this *Venus* with Botticelli's newly hatched *Venus,* and you get a good idea of the difference between the Florentine and Venetian Renaissance.

Botticelli's was pure, innocent, and otherworldly. Titian's should have a staple in her belly button. This isn't a Venus, it's a centerfold—with no purpose but to please the eye and other organs. While Botticelli's allegorical Venus is a message, this is a massage. The bed is used.

Titian and his fellow Venetians took the pagan spirit pioneered in Florence and carried it to its logical hedonistic conclusion. Using bright, rich colors, they captured the luxurious life of happy-go-lucky Venice.

While Raphael's *Madonna of the Goldfinch* was balanced with a figure on the left and one on the right, Titian balances his painting in a different way—with color. The canvas is split down the middle by the curtain. The left half is dark, the right half warmer. The two halves are connected by a diagonal slash of luminous gold—the nude woman. The girl in the background is trying to find her some clothes.

By the way, visitors from centuries past also panted in front of this Venus. The poet Byron called it "*the* Venus." With her sensual skin, hey-sailor look, and suggestively placed hand, she must have left them blithering idiots.

• Find the n-n-n-next painting...in Room 29.

Parmigianino (1503–1540)—*Madonna with the Long Neck* (*Madonna della Collo Lungo*)

Raphael, Michelangelo, Leonardo, and Titian mastered reality. They could place any scene onto a canvas with photographic accuracy. How could future artists top that?

Mannerists such as Parmigianino tried, by going beyond realism, exaggerating it for effect. Using brighter colors and twisting poses (two techniques explored by Michelangelo), they created scenes more elegant and more exciting than real life.

By stretching the neck of his Madonna, Parmigianino (like the cheese) gives her an unnatural, swanlike beauty. She has the same pose and position of hands as Botticelli's *Venus* and the *Venus de' Medici*. Her body forms an arcing S-curve—down her neck as far as her elbow, then back the other way along Jesus' body to her knee, then down to her foot. The baby Jesus seems to be blissfully gliding down this slippery slide of sheer beauty.

In the Uffizi, we've seen many images of female beauty: from ancient goddesses to medieval Madonnas to wicked Eves, from Botticelli's pristine nymphs to Michelangelo's peasant Mary, from Raphael's Madonna-and-baby to Titian's babe. Their physical beauty expresses different aspects of the human spirit.

• *Pass through several rooms, returning to the main hallway.*

The Rest of the Uffizi

As art moved into the Baroque period, artists took Renaissance realism and exaggerated it still more—more beauty, more emotion, more drama. There's lots of great stuff in the following rooms, and I'd especially recommend Room 42 (The Sky Is Falling), Rooms 43 and 44 (Rembrandt self-portraits), and the shocking ultra-realism of Caravaggio's *Bacchus* and *Abraham Sacrificing Isaac* (downstairs on the way out). If there are newly restored paintings, the Uffizi shows them off in Room 38 (near the exit stairs) with an English description of the work done. WCs are downstairs, as you head for the exit. (If the first one is too crowded, there's another farther along.)

• *But first, head to the end of the hallway for a true aesthetic experience.*

The Little Cappuccin Monk (Cappuccino)

This drinkable art form, born in Italy, is now enjoyed all over the world. It's called "The Little Cappuccin Monk" because the coffee's frothy light- and dark-brown foam looks like the two-toned cowls of the Cappuccin order. Sip it on the terrace in the shadow of the towering Palazzo Vecchio, and be glad we live in an age where you don't need to be a Medici to enjoy all this fine art. *Salute.*

BARGELLO TOUR

The Renaissance began with sculpture. The great Florentine painters were "sculptors with brushes." You can see the birth of this revolution of 3-D in the Bargello (bar-JEL-oh), which boasts the best collection of Florentine sculpture. It's a small, uncrowded museum and a pleasant break from the intensity of the rest of Florence.

Orientation

Cost: €4 (but mandatory special exhibitions often raise the price to €7).

Hours: Tue–Sun April–Oct 8:15–17:00, Nov–March 8:15–13:50; also open first, third, and fifth Mon of each month—until 17:00 April–Oct or 13:50 Nov–March; last entry 30 min before closing).

Getting There: It's located at Via del Proconsolo 4, a three-minute walk northeast of the Uffizi. Facing the Palazzo Vecchio, go behind the Palazzo and turn left. Look for a rustic brick building with a spire that looks like a baby Palazzo Vecchio. If lost ask, *"Dov'è Bargello?"* (doh-VEH bar-JEL-oh).

Information: Tel. 055-282-902, www.polomuseale.firenze.it. You can reserve an entrance time (tel. 055-238-8606), but it's unnecessary.

Security: You must pass through a metal detector to enter. No liquids are allowed in the museum.

Length of This Tour: Allow one hour.

Cuisine Art: Inexpensive bars and cafés await in the surrounding streets. See recommended eateries on pages 256–257.

Photography: Permitted only in the courtyard.

Starring: Michelangelo, Donatello, Brunelleschi, Ghiberti, and four different *David*s.

The Tour Begins

Sculpture in Florence

• *Buy your ticket and take a seat in the courtyard.*

The Bargello, built in 1255, was an early Florence police station *(bargello)* and later served as a prison. The heavy fortifications

tell us that politics in medieval Florence had its occupational hazards.

The Bargello, a three-story rectangular building, surrounds this cool and peaceful courtyard. The best statues are found in two rooms—one on the ground floor at the foot of the outdoor staircase, and another one flight up,

directly above. We'll proceed from Michelangelo to Donatello to Verrocchio.

But first, meander around this courtyard and get a feel for sculpture in general and the medium of stone in particular. Sculpture is a much more robust art form than painting. Think of just the engineering problems of the sculpting process: quarrying and cutting the stone, transporting the block to the artist's studio, all the hours of chiseling away chips, then the painstaking process of sanding the final product by hand. A sculptor must be strong enough to gouge into the stone, but delicate enough to groove out the smallest details. Think of Michelangelo's approach to sculpting: He wasn't creating a figure—he was liberating it from the rock that surrounded it.

If the Renaissance is humanism, then sculpture is the perfect medium in which to express it. It shows the human form, standing alone, independent of church, state, or society, ready to create itself.

Finally, a viewing note. Every sculpture has an invisible "frame" around it—the stone block it was cut from. Visualizing this frame helps you find the center of the composition.

• *Begin here on the ground floor, in the room at the foot of the courtyard's grand staircase.*

Michelangelo—*Bacchus* (*Baccho,* c. 1497)

Bacchus, the god of wine and revelry, raises another cup to his lips, while his little companion goes straight for the grapes.

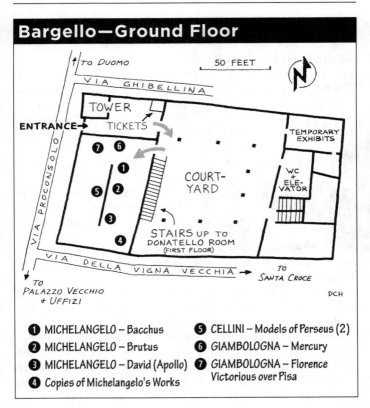

Bargello—Ground Floor

TO DUOMO

50 FEET

N

VIA GHIBELLINA

TOWER

ENTRANCE→   TICKETS

TEMPORARY EXHIBITS

VIA PROCONSOLO

❼ ❻

❶

COURT-YARD

WC & ELE-VATOR

❺ ❷

❸

❹

STAIRS UP TO DONATELLO ROOM (FIRST FLOOR)

VIA DELLA VIGNA VECCHIA →

TO SANTA CROCE

↓
TO PALAZZO VECCHIO & UFFIZI

DCH

❶ MICHELANGELO – Bacchus
❷ MICHELANGELO – Brutus
❸ MICHELANGELO – David (Apollo)
❹ Copies of Michelangelo's Works

❺ CELLINI – Models of Perseus (2)
❻ GIAMBOLOGNA – Mercury
❼ GIAMBOLOGNA – Florence Victorious over Pisa

Maybe Michelangelo had a sense of humor after all. Mentally compare this tipsy Greek god of wine with his sturdy, sober *David,* begun a few years later. Raucous *Bacchus* isn't nearly so muscular, so monumental...or so sure on his feet. Hope he's not driving. The pose, the smooth muscles, the beer belly, and swaying hips look more like Donatello's boyish *David.*

This was Michelangelo's first major commission. He often vacillated between showing man as strong and noble, or as weak and perverse. This isn't the nobility of the classical world, but the decadent side of orgies and indulgence.

• *Just to the left, you'll find...*

Michelangelo—*Brutus* (*Bruto,* 1540)

Another example of the influence of Donatello is this so-ugly-he's-beautiful bust by Michelangelo. His rough intensity gives him the look of a man who has succeeded against all odds, a dignity and

heroic quality that would be missing if he were too pretty.

The subject is Brutus, the Roman who, for the love of liberty, murdered his friend and dictator, Julius Caesar *("Et tu...?")*. Michelangelo could understand this man's dilemma. He himself was torn between his love of the democratic tradition of Florence and loyalty to his friends the Medicis, who had become dictators.

So he gives us two sides of a political assassin. The right profile (the front view) is heroic. But the hidden side, with the drooping mouth and squinting eye, makes him more cunning, sneering, and ominous.

Michelangelo—*David* (also known as *Apollo*, 1530–1532)

This restless, twisting man is either David or Apollo. (Is he reaching for a sling or a quiver?) This is the first of several *David*s in the Bargello. This demure statue (left unfinished) is light years away from Michelangelo's famous *David* in the Accademia, which is so much larger than life in every way.

In the glass cases in the corner are small-scale copies of some of Michelangelo's most famous works. Nearby, there's a bust of Michelangelo by his fellow sculptor Daniele da Volterra, capturing Michelangelo's broken nose and brooding nature.

• *Doubling back toward the entrance, you'll find...*

Cellini—*Models of Perseus (Perseo)*

The life-size statue of Perseus slaying Medusa, located in the open-air loggia next to the Palazzo Vecchio, is cast bronze. Benvenuto Cellini started with these smaller models (one in wax, one in bronze) to get the difficult process down. When it came time to cast the full-size work, everything was going fine...until he realized he didn't have enough metal! He ran around the studio, gathering up pewterware and throwing it in, narrowly avoiding a mess-terpiece.

Giambologna—*Mercury*

Catch this statue while you can—he's got flowers waiting to be delivered. Despite all the bustle and motion, *Mercury* has a solid

Renaissance core: the line of balance that runs straight up the center, from toes to hip to fingertip. He's caught in mid-stride. His top half leans forward, counterbalanced by his right leg in back, while the center of gravity rests firmly at the hipbone. Down at the toes, notice the cupid practicing up for the circus.

Giambologna—*Florence Victorious over Pisa (Firenze Trionfa su Pisa)*

This sculpture shows the fierce Florentine chauvinism that was born in an era when Italy's cities struggled for economic and political dominance...and Florence won.

• *To see the roots of Florence's Renaissance, climb the courtyard staircase to the next floor up and turn right into the large Donatello room. Pause at Donatello's painted bust of* Niccolò da Uzzano.

Donatello—*Niccolò da Uzzano* (c. 1420)

Not an emperor, not a king, not a pope, saint, or prince, this is one of Florence's leading businessmen in a toga, portrayed in the style of an ancient Roman bust. In the 1400s, when Florence was inventing the Renaissance that all Europe would soon follow, there was an optimistic spirit of democracy that gloried in everyday people. With wrinkles, a quizzical look, and bags under the eyes, Donatello has portrayed this man literally wart (left cheek) and all.

• *To the left stands a life-size white marble statue.*

Donatello—An early *David* (marble, 1408)

This is young Donatello's first take on the popular subject of *David* slaying Goliath. His dainty pose makes him a little unsteady on his feet. He's dressed like a medieval knight (fully clothed but showing some leg through the slit skirt). The generic face and blank, vacant eyes give him the look not of a real man but of an anonymous decoration on a church facade. At age 22, Donatello still had one foot in the old Gothic style. To tell the story of David, Donatello plants a huge rock right in the middle of Goliath's forehead.

• *At the far end of the room,* St. George *stands in a niche in the wall.*

BARGELLO

Bargello—Donatello Room

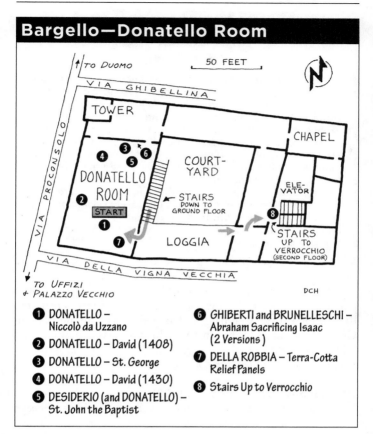

TO DUOMO

50 FEET

VIA GHIBELLINA

TOWER

VIA PROCONSOLO

CHAPEL

DONATELLO ROOM

COURT-YARD

START

STAIRS DOWN TO GROUND FLOOR

ELE-VATOR

LOGGIA

STAIRS UP TO VERROCCHIO (SECOND FLOOR)

VIA DELLA VIGNA VECCHIA

TO UFFIZI & PALAZZO VECCHIO

DCH

❶ DONATELLO – Niccolò da Uzzano

❷ DONATELLO – David (1408)

❸ DONATELLO – St. George

❹ DONATELLO – David (1430)

❺ DESIDERIO (and DONATELLO) – St. John the Baptist

❻ GHIBERTI and BRUNELLESCHI – Abraham Sacrificing Isaac (2 Versions)

❼ DELLA ROBBIA – Terra-Cotta Relief Panels

❽ Stairs Up to Verrocchio

Donatello—*St. George* (*S. Giorgio*, 1416)

The proud warrior has both feet planted firmly on the ground and stands on the edge of his niche looking out alertly. He tenses his powerful right hand as he prepares to attack. George, the Christian slayer of dragons, was just the sort of righteous warrior proud Renaissance Florentines could rally around in their struggles with nearby cities. Nearly a century later, Michelangelo's *David* replaced *George* as the unofficial symbol of Florence, but *David* was clearly inspired by *George*'s relaxed intensity and determination. (This is the original marble statue. A bronze version stands in its original niche at Orsanmichele Church—see page 81.)

Donatello
(1386–1466)

Donatello was the first great Renaissance genius, a model for Michelangelo and others. He mastered realism, creating the first truly lifelike statues of people since ancient times. Donatello's work is highly personal. Unlike the ancient Greeks—but like the ancient Romans—he often sculpted real people, not idealized versions of pretty gods and goddesses. Some of these people are downright ugly. In the true spirit of Renaissance humanism, Donatello appreciated the beauty of flesh-and-blood human beings.

Donatello's personality was also a model for later artists. He was moody and irascible, purposely setting himself apart from others in order to concentrate on his sculpting. He developed the role of the "mad genius" that Michelangelo would later perfect.

The relief panel below shows George doing what he's been pondering. To his right, the sketchy arches and trees create the illusion of a distant landscape. Donatello, who apprenticed in Ghiberti's studio, is credited with teaching his master how to create 3-D illusions like this.

• *On the floor to your left, you'll find...*

Donatello—*David* (bronze, c. 1430)

He's naked. Donatello, who never married, sees David as a teenage boy wearing only a helmet, boots, and sword. The smooth-skinned

warrior sways gracefully, poking his sword playfully at the severed head of the giant Goliath. His *contrapposto* stance is similar to Michelangelo's *David*, resting his weight on one leg in the classical style, but it gives him a feminine rather than masculine look. Gazing into his coy eyes and at his bulging belly is a very different experience from confronting Michelangelo's older and sturdier Renaissance Man.

This *David* paved the way for Michelangelo's. Europe hadn't seen a free-standing male nude like this in a thousand years. In the Middle Ages, the human body was considered a dirty thing, a symbol of man's weakness, something to be covered up in shame. The church prohibited exhibitions of nudity like this one, and certainly would never decorate a church with it. But in the Renaissance, a new class of rich and powerful merchants appeared who bought art for personal enjoyment. Reading Plato's *Symposium*, they saw the ideal of Beauty in the form of a young man. This particular statue stood in the Medicis' palace (today's Medici-Riccardi Palace)...where Michelangelo, practically an adopted son, grew up admiring it.

As we see the different *David*s in the Bargello, compare and contrast the artists' styles.
• St. John the Baptist, *begun by Donatello and finished by his student, is to the right of the boyish, naked* David.

Desiderio da Settignano (and Donatello)—*St. John the Baptist (San Giovannino)*

John the Baptist was the wild-eyed, wildcat prophet who lived in the desert preaching, living on bugs 'n' honey, and baptizing Saviors of the world. Donatello, the mad prophet of the coming Renaissance, might have identified with this original eccentric.
• *On the wall next to* George, *you'll find some bronze relief panels. Don't look at the labels just yet.*

Ghiberti and Brunelleschi— Baptistery Door Competition Entries (two different relief panels, titled *Sacrificio di Isacco,* 1401)

Some would say these two panels are the first works of the Renaissance. These two versions of *Abraham Sacrificing Isaac* were finalists in a contest held in 1401 to decide who would do the bronze doors of the Baptistery. The contest sparked citywide excitement, which evolved into the Renaissance spirit. Lorenzo Ghiberti won, and later did the doors known as the Gates of Paradise. Filippo Brunelleschi lost—fortunately for us—freeing him to design the Duomo's dome.

Both artists catch the crucial moment when Abraham, obeying God's orders, prepares to slaughter and burn his only son as a sacrifice. At the last moment—after Abraham passed this test of faith—an angel of God appears to stop the bloodshed.

Let's look at the composition of the two panels: One is integrated and cohesive, while the other is a balanced knickknack shelf of segments. Human drama: One has bodies and faces that speak. The boy's body is a fine classical nude in itself, so real and vulnerable. Abraham's face is intense and ready to follow God's will. Perspective: An angel zooms in from out of nowhere to save the boy in the nick of time.

Is one panel clearly better than the other? You be the judge. Pictured below are the two finalists for the Baptistery door competition—Ghiberti's and Brunelleschi's. Which do you like best?

Ghiberti's, on the left, won.

It was obviously a tough call, but Ghiberti's was chosen, perhaps because his goldsmith training made him better suited for the technical end.

• *Along the walls back near the entrance, you'll find several colorful terra-cotta reliefs.*

Luca della Robbia—Terra-Cotta Relief Panels

Mary and baby Jesus with accompanying angels look their most serene in these panels by the master of painted, glazed porcelain. Polished blue, white, green, and yellow, they have a gentle and feminine look that softens the rough masculine stone of this room. Luca was just one of a family of della Robbias who pioneered art in terra-cotta.

• *Exit the Donatello room through the same door you entered. Cross to the rooms on the other side of the courtyard. Take your first left, then immediately turn right and climb the carpeted stairs to the second floor. At the top of the stairs, turn left, then left again. Verrocchio's David stands in the middle of the room.*

Andrea del Verrocchio—*David* (c. 1470)

Verrocchio (1435–1488) is best known as the teacher of Leonardo da Vinci, but he was also the premier sculptor of the generation between Donatello and Michelangelo. Now's a good time to compare the four different *Davids* that we've seen. Verrocchio's saucy, impertinent *David* has more attitude than Donatello's generic warrior, and is younger and more masculine than Donatello's girlish, gloating *David*. He's more vigorous than Michelangelo's unfinished *David/Apollo* but he's a far cry from Michelangelo's monumental version. This one is definitely the shepherd "boy" described in the Bible. He leans on one leg, not with a firm, commanding stance but a nimble one (especially noticeable from behind). Compare the smug smile of the victor with Goliath's "Oh, have I got a headache" expression.

• *Go back through the doorway you entered earlier, and head straight to a room of glass cases filled with small statues. In the center of the room you'll find...*

Antonio Pollaiuolo—*Hercules and Antaeus* (*Ercole e Anteo,* 1498)

Antaeus was invincible as long as he was in contact with the Earth, his mother. So Hercules just picked him up like a Renaissance World Wrestling champ and crushed him to death.

More than any early artist from this period, Antonio Pollaiuolo studied the human body in motion. These figures are not dignified Renaissance Men. Yet, in this tangled pose of flailing arms and legs, there still is a Renaissance sense of balance—all the motion spins around the center of gravity where their bodies grind together.

• *In glass cases to either side are small-scale, alternate versions of works by Giambologna, including his* Mercury.

The Rest of the Bargello

Browse around the two upper floors, filled with objects that provide a look at life in Renaissance Florence. On the top floor, you'll likely find armor, medallions, and terra-cotta Mary-with-baby-and-angel panels by other members of the della Robbia clan. On the first floor are ivories, jewelry, and Renaissance dinnerware.

From swords to statues, from *Brutus* to Brunelleschi, from *David* to *David* to *David* to *David*—the Bargello's collection of civilized artifacts makes it clear why Florence dominated the Italian Renaissance.

MUSEUM OF SAN MARCO TOUR

Museo di San Marco

Two of Florence's brightest lights lived in the San Marco Monastery, a reminder that the Renaissance was not just a secular phenomenon. At the Museum of San Marco, you'll find these two different expressions of 15th-century Christianity—Fra Angelico's radiant paintings, fusing medieval faith with Renaissance realism, and Savonarola's moral reforms, fusing medieval faith with modern politics.

Orientation

Cost: €4.

Hours: Tue–Fri 8:15–13:50, Sat 8:15–16:50; also open 8:15–16:50 on second and fourth Sun and 8:15–13:50 on first, third, and fifth Mon of each month; last entry 30 min before closing.

Getting There: It's on Piazza San Marco, around the corner from the Accademia, and several long blocks northeast of the Duomo (head up Via Ricasoli or Via Cavour).

Information: Tel. 055-238-8608, www.polomuseale.firenze.it. Consider picking up the compact, worthwhile, official guide (€10) at the bookstore. You can reserve an entrance time, but it's unnecessary.

Baggage Check: None is available, and large bags are not allowed in the museum.

Length of This Tour: Allow one hour.

Cuisine Art: See "Budget Lunches near the Accademia and Museum of San Marco" in the Eating in Florence chapter.

Photography: Not allowed.

Starring: Fra Angelico's paintings and Savonarola's living quarters.

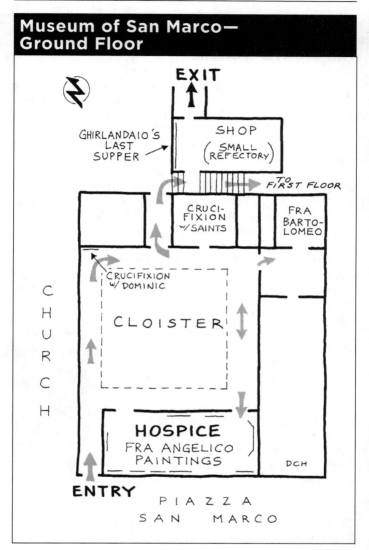

Museum of San Marco— Ground Floor

EXIT

GHIRLANDAIO'S
LAST
SUPPER

SHOP
(SMALL
REFECTORY)

TO
FIRST FLOOR

CRUCI-
FIXION
w/ SAINTS

FRA
BARTO-
LOMEO

CRUCIFIXION
w/ DOMINIC

C
H
U
R
C
H

CLOISTER

HOSPICE
FRA ANGELICO
PAINTINGS

DCH

ENTRY

PIAZZA
SAN MARCO

The Tour Begins

Overview

The ground floor features the world's best collection of Fra Angelico paintings. The upstairs contains the monks' cells (living quarters), decorated by Fra Angelico, and the cell of the most famous resident, Savonarola.

• *Buy your ticket and enter the courtyard/cloister.*

Ground Floor

The Courtyard/Cloister

Stepping into the cloister, you can feel the spirituality of this place, a respite from the hubbub of modern Florence. You'll see Renaissance arches frame Gothic cross-vaulting—an apt introduction to a monastery built during an optimistic time, when Renaissance humanism dovetailed with medieval spirituality.

In 1439, Cosimo de' Medici (Lorenzo the Magnificent's grandpa) hired the architect Michelozzo to build the monastery, and invited Fra Angelico's Dominican community to move here from Fiesole. Fra Angelico turned down an offer to be archbishop of Florence, instead becoming prior (head monk). He quickly began decorating the monastery walls with frescoes.

• *On the wall at the end of the first corridor is...*

Fra Angelico—*Crucifixion with St. Dominic*

The fresco by Fra Angelico (in the corner of the cloister, straight ahead from the entrance) shows Dominic, the founder of the order, hugging the bloody cross like a groupie adoring a rock star. Monks who lived here—including Fra Angelico, Savonarola, and Fra Bartolomeo—renounced money, sex, ego, and pop music to follow a simple, regimented life, meditating on Christ's ultimate sacrifice.

Fra Angelico considered painting to be a form of prayer. He worked to bridge the gap between the infinite (Christ) and the finite (a mortal's ability to relate to God) by injecting an ethereal atmosphere into his frescoes.

• *Now enter the Hospice (Ospizio).*

The Hospice (Ospizio), with Paintings by Fra Angelico (Beato Angelico)

Fra Angelico (c. 1400–1455)—equal parts monk and painter—fused early-Renaissance technique with medieval spirituality. His works can be admired for their beauty or contemplated as spiritual visions. Browse the room, and you'll find serene-faced Marys, Christs, and saints wearing gold halos (often painted on altarpieces), bright primary colors (red-blue-yellow/gold), evenly lit scenes, and meticulous detail—all creating a mystical world of their own, glowing from within like stained-glass windows.

• *Start with the large altarpiece—showing the* Deposition—*at the end of the room.*

Fra Angelico—*Deposition of Christ from the Cross (Pala di Santa Trinità)*

Christ's body is lowered from the cross, mourned by haloed women (on the left) and contemporary Florentines (right). There's a clearly

defined foreground (the kneeling, curly-headed man and the woman with her back to us), background (the distant city and hills), and middle distance (the trees).

Though trained in medieval religious painting, Fra Angelico never closed his eyes to the innovations of the budding Renaissance, using both styles all his life. There are Gothic elements, such as the altarpiece frame, inherited from his former teacher (who painted the pinnacles on top). The holy wear halos, and the stretched-out "body of Christ" is symbolically "displayed" like the communion bread.

But it's truly a Renaissance work. The man in green, lowering Christ, bends forward at a strongly foreshortened (difficult to draw) angle. Christ's toes, kissed by Mary Magdalene, cross the triptych wall, ignoring the frame's traditional three-arch divisions. Fra Angelico was boldly "coloring outside the lines" to create a single, realistic scene.

And the holy scene has been removed from its golden heaven and placed in the first great Renaissance landscape—on a lawn, among flowers, trees, cloud masses, real people, and the hillsides of Fiesole overlooking Florence. Fra Angelico, the ascetic monk, refused to renounce one pleasure—his joy in the natural beauty of God's creation.

• *Moving counterclockwise around the room, you'll find the following works (among others).*

Fra Angelico—*Triptych of St. Peter the Martyr (Trittico di San Pietro Martire)*

In this early, more "medieval" work, Fra Angelico sets (big)

Mary and Child in a gold background flanked by (small) saints standing obediently in their niches. Having recently joined the Dominican community in Fiesole, young Brother Giovanni (as he was known in his lifetime) is now dressed like these famous Dominicans—white robe, blue cape, and tonsured haircut.

Peter the Martyr (next to Mary, with bloody head) exemplified the unbending Dominican spirit. Attacked by heretics (see the scene above Peter), he was hacked in the head with a dagger but died still preaching, writing with his own blood: *"Credo in Deum"* ("I believe in God").

• *Continuing counterclockwise...*

Fra Angelico—Two Panels: *Wedding and Funeral of the Virgin (Sposalizio e Funerali della Vergine)*

Fra Angelico's teenage training was as a miniaturist, so even these small predella panels (part of a larger altarpiece) are surprisingly

realistic—the folds in the clothes, the gold-brocade hemlines, and the precisely outlined people, as though etched in glass. Notice the Renaissance perspective tricks he was exploring, setting the wedding in front of receding buildings and the funeral among candles that get shorter at the back of the scene.

Fra Angelico—*Last Judgment (Giudizio Universale)*

Despite the Renaissance, Florence in the 1420s was still a city in the

Christian universe described by Dante. Hell (to the right) is a hierarchical barbecue where sinners are burned, boiled, and tortured by a minotaur-like Satan, who rules the bottom of the pit. The blessed in heaven (left) play ring-around-the-rosy with angels. In the center,

a row of open tombs creates a 3-D highway to hell, stretching ominously to that final Judgment Day.

Fra Angelico (and assistants)—*Thirty-Five Scenes Painted on Doors of a Silverware Storeroom (Panelli dell'Armadio degli Argenti)*

The first nine scenes in this life of Christ are by Fra Angelico himself (the rest by assistants). Like storyboards for a movie, these natural, realistic, and straightforward panels "show" through action, they don't just "tell" through symbols. (The Latin inscription beneath each panel is redundant.) The miraculous is presented as an everyday occurrence.

MUSEUM OF SAN MARCO

1. The Wheel of Ezekiel (OK, that's medieval symbolism) prophesies Christ's coming.
2. In the Annunciation, the angel gestures to tell Mary that she'll give birth.
3. Newborn Jesus glows, amazing his parents, while timid shepherds sneak a peek.
4. Precocious Jesus splays himself and says, "Cut me."
5. One of the Magi kneels to kiss the babe's foot.
6. In the temple, the tiny baby is dwarfed by elongated priests and columns.
7. Mary and the baby ride, while Joseph carries the luggage.

8. Meanwhile, babies are slaughtered in a jumble of gore, dramatic poses, and agonized faces.
9. The commotion contrasts with the serenity of child Jesus in the temple.

This work by 50-year-old Fra Angelico—master of many styles, famous in Italy, recently returned from a gig in the Vatican—has the fresh, simple, spontaneous storytelling of a children's book.

Fra Angelico—*Lamentation (Compianto sul Cristo Morto)*

This painting of the executed Christ being mourned silently by loved ones was the last thing many condemned prisoners saw during

their final hours. It once hung in a church where the soon-to-be executed were incarcerated.

The melancholy mood is understated, suggested by a series of horizontal layers—Christ's body, the line of mourners, the city walls, landscape horizon, layered clouds, and the crossbar. It's as though Christ is being welcomed into peaceful rest, a comforting message from Fra Angelico to the condemned.

"Fra Angelico" (Angelic Brother) is a nickname that describes his reputation for sweetness, humility, and compassion. It's said he couldn't paint a crucifixion without crying. In 1984, he was beatified by Pope John Paul II and made patron of artists.

• *At the far end of the room hangs the...*

Fra Angelico—*Altarpiece of the Linen-Drapers (Tabernacolo dei Linaioli)*

This work may be out for restoration when you visit, but if it's here, check out its impressive size and marble frame (by Ghiberti), which attest to Fra Angelico's worldly success and collaboration with the Renaissance greats. The monumental Mary and Child, as well as the saints on the doors, are gold-backed and elegant, to please conservative patrons. In the three predella panels below, Fra Angelico gets to display his Renaissance chops, showing

haloed saints mingling with well-dressed Florentines amid local cityscapes and landscapes. (Find Ghiberti in the left panel, kneeling, in blue.)

• *On the long wall are three similar-looking altarpieces. Move left to right, watching the...*

Evolution of the *Sacra Conversazione*

Fra Angelico (largely) invented what became a common Renaissance theme: Mary and Child surrounded by saints "conversing" informally about holy matters. Four examples in this room show how Fra Angelico, exploring Renaissance techniques, developed the idea over his lifetime.

Fra Angelico—*Annalena Altarpiece (Pala d'Annalena)*

In the *Annalena Altarpiece*—considered Florence's first true *sacra conversazione*—the saints flank Mary in a neat line, backed by medieval gold in the form of a curtain. Everyone's either facing out or in profile—not the natural poses of a true crowd. There's little eye contact, and certainly no "conversation."

Mary and Jesus direct our eye to Mary's brooch, the first in a series of circles radiating out from the center: brooch, halo, canopy arch, circle of saints. Set in a square frame, this painting has the circle-in-a-square composition that marks many *sacra conversazione*s.

Fra Angelico—*San Marco Altarpiece (Pala di San Marco)*

Cosimo de' Medici commissioned this painting as the center-piece of the new church (next door). For the dedication Mass, Fra Angelico theatrically "opens the curtain," revealing a stage set with a distant backdrop of trees, kneeling saints in the foreground, and a crowd gathered around Mary and Child at center stage on a raised, canopied throne. The carpet makes a chessboard-like pattern to establish 3-D perspective. The altarpiece was like a window onto a marvelous world where holies mill about on Earth as naturally as mortals.

To show just how far we've come from Gothic, Fra Angelico gives us a painting-in-a-painting—a crude, gold-backed crucifixion.

Fra Angelico—*Bosco ai Frati Altarpiece (Pala di Bosco ai Frati)*

This altarpiece is Fra Angelico's last great work, and he uses every stylistic arrow in his quiver: detailed friezes of the miniaturist; medieval halos and gold backdrop; monumental, naturally posed figures in the style of Masaccio (especially St. Francis, on the left, with his relaxed *contrapposto*); 3-D perspective established by the floor tiles; and Renaissance love of natural beauty (the trees and sky).

Fra Angelico's bright colors are eye-catching. The gold backdrop sets off the red-pink handmaidens, which set off Jesus' pale skin. The deep blue of Mary's dress, frosted with a precious gold hem, turns out at her feet to show a swath of the green inner lining, suggesting the 3-D body within.

Despite Renaissance realism, Fra Angelico creates a world of his own—perfectly lit, with no moody shadows, dirt, frayed clothing, or imperfection. The faces are certainly realistic, but they express no human emotion. These mortals, through sacrifice and meditation, have risen above the petty passions celebrated by humanist painters, to achieve a serenity that lights them from within.

• *Exit the Hospice back into the courtyard, and enter the next set of rooms (marked* Lavabo e Refettorio*). The small room on the left has paintings and fresco fragments by...*

Fra Bartolomeo

Fra Bartolomeo (1473–1517) lived and worked in this monastery a generation after the "Angelic" brother. ***Ecce Homo*** shows the kind of Christ that young, idealistic Dominican monks (like Fra Bartolomeo) adored in their meditations—curly-haired, creamy-faced, dreamy-eyed, bearing the torments of the secular world with humble serenity.

Fra Bartolomeo—*St. Dominic* *(San Domenico)*

St. Dominic holds a finger to his lips— "Shh! We have strict rules in my order." Dominic (c. 1170–1221), a friend of St. Francis of Assisi, formed his rules after seeing the austere *perfetti* (perfect ones) of the heretical Cathar sect of southern France. He figured they could only be converted by someone just as extreme, following Christ's simple, possession-free lifestyle. Nearing 50, Dominic made a 3,400-mile preaching tour—on foot, carrying his luggage—from Rome to Spain to Paris and back. Dominic is often portrayed with the star of revelation over his head.

Fra Bartolomeo—*St. Thomas Aquinas* *(San Tommaso d'Aquino)*

St. Thomas Aquinas (c. 1225–1274, wearing a hood)—the intellectual giant of the U. of Paris—used logic and Aristotelian models to defend and explain Christianity (building the hierarchical belief system known as Scholasticism). He's often shown with a heavy build and the sun of knowledge burning in his chest.

Fra Bartolomeo—*Portrait of Savonarola* *(Ritratto di Fra Girolamo Savonarola)*

This is the famous portrait—in profile, hooded, with big nose and

clear eyes, gazing intently into the darkness—of the man reviled as the evil opponent of Renaissance goodness. Would it surprise you to learn that it was Savonarola who inspired Fra Bartolomeo's art? Bartolomeo was so moved by Savonarola's sermons that he burned his early nude paintings (and back issues of *Penthouse*), became a monk, gave up painting for a few years...then resurfaced to paint the simple, sweet frescoes we see here.

MUSEUM OF SAN MARCO

• *Leaving the world of Fra Bartolomeo, return to the courtyard and continue to the next room (Capitolo), which contains the large wall fresco...*

Fra Angelico—*Crucifixion with Saints (Crocifissione dell'Angelico)*

This crucifixion, against a bleak background, is one of more than 20 versions of Christ's torture/execution in the monastery. It was

in this room that naughty monks were examined and judged.

Among the group of hermits, martyrs, and religious extremists who surround the cross, locate Dominic (kneeling at the foot of the cross, in Dominican white robe, blue cape, and tonsured hair, with star on head), Peter the Martyr (kneeling in right corner, with bloody head), and Thomas Aquinas (standing behind Peter, with jowls and sun on chest).

The bell in the room is the original church bell, the one that rang a warning to Savonarola the night he was arrested. (The mob was so enraged that they exiled the bell for 10 years.)

• *Return to the courtyard and head upstairs to the first floor, where you'll come face-to-face with Fra Angelico's Annunciation.*

First Floor

Fra Angelico—*The Annunciation*

Sway back and forth and watch the angel's wings sparkle (from glitter mixed into the fresco) as he delivers "the good news" to the very humble and accepting Virgin. Mary is under an arcade that's remarkably similar to the one in the monastery courtyard. Fra Angelico literally brings this scene home to the monks.

Paintings such as this one made Fra Angelico so famous that the pope called on him to paint the Vatican. Yet this work, like the other frescoes here, was meant only for the private eyes of humble monks. Monks gathered near *The Annunciation* for common prayers, contemplating Christ's life from beginning *(Annunciation)* to end *(Crucifixion with St. Dominic,* over your shoulder). The caption reads: Remember to say your Hail Marys.

The Monastery's Living Quarters

This floor is lined with the cells (bedrooms) of those who lived in the monastery: monks (in the corridor to your left), novice monks (farther down), and lay people and support staff (to your right). We'll see Savonarola's quarters in the far corner. Each room was frescoed by Fra Angelico or his assistants.

After a long day of prayer, meditation, reading, frugal meals, chopping wood, hauling water, translating Greek, attending Mass, and more prayer, a monk retired to one of these small,

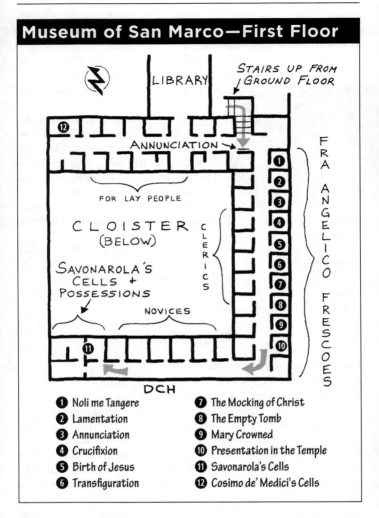

Museum of San Marco—First Floor

STAIRS UP FROM GROUND FLOOR

LIBRARY

ANNUNCIATION

FOR LAY PEOPLE

CLOISTER (BELOW)

SAVONAROLA'S CELLS + POSSESSIONS

CLERICS

NOVICES

DCH

FRA ANGELICO FRESCOES

❶ Noli me Tangere
❷ Lamentation
❸ Annunciation
❹ Crucifixion
❺ Birth of Jesus
❻ Transfiguration
❼ The Mocking of Christ
❽ The Empty Tomb
❾ Mary Crowned
❿ Presentation in the Temple
⓫ Savonarola's Cells
⓬ Cosimo de' Medici's Cells

bare, lamp-lit rooms. His "late-night TV" was programmed by the prior—Fra Angelico—in the form of a fresco to meditate on before sleep. In monastic life, everything is a form of prayer. Pondering these scenes, monks learned the various aspects of worship: humility, adoration, flagellation, reflection, and so on.

• *From* The Annunciation, *take a few steps to the left, and look down the (east) corridor lined with monks' cells to find...*

Fra Angelico's Frescoes

All in all, 43 cells were decorated in the early 1440s by Fra Angelico and his assistants. Many feature a crucifix and St. Dominic, but each shows Dominic in a different physical posture (kneeling, head bowed, head raised, hands folded), which the monks copied in order to attain a more spiritual state. Some of Fra Angelico's best work is found in the 10 cells along the left-hand side.

Cell ❶—*Noli me Tangere:* In the first of 10 rooms on the left-hand side of the corridor, the resurrected Jesus, appearing as a hoe-carrying gardener, says, "Don't touch me" and gingerly sidesteps Mary Magdalene's grasp. The flowers and trees represent the blossoming of new life, and they're about the last we'll see. Most scenes have stark, bare backgrounds, to concentrate the monk's focus on just the essential subject.

Cell ❷—*Lamentation:* Christ and mourners are a reverse image of the *Lamentation* downstairs. Christ levitates, not really supported by the ladies' laps. The colors are muted grays, browns, and pinks. Dominic (star on head) stands contemplating, just as the monk should do, by mentally transporting himself to the scene.

Cell ❸—*Annunciation:* The painting's arches echo the room's real arch. (And they, in turn, harmoniously "frame" the "arch" of Mary and the angel bending toward each other to talk.) Peter the Martyr (bloody head) looks on.

You can't call these cells a wrap until you've found at least six crosses, three Dominics, three Peters, and a Thomas Aquinas. Ready...go.

Cell ❹—*Crucifixion:* That's one. And another Dominic.

Cell ❺—*Birth of Jesus:* And there's your second Peter.

Cell ❻—*Transfiguration:* Forsaking Renaissance realism, Fra Angelico emphasizes the miraculous. In an aura of blinding light, Christ spreads his arms cross-like, dazzling the three witnesses at the bottom of the "mountain." He's joined by disembodied heads of prophets, all spinning in a circle echoed by the room's arch. These rooms, which housed senior monks, have some of the most complex and intellectually demanding symbolism.

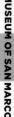

MUSEUM OF SAN MARCO

Cell ❼—*The Mocking of Christ:* From Renaissance realism to Dalí surrealism. Dominic, while reading the Passion, conjures an image of Christ—the true king, on a throne with a globe and scepter—now blindfolded, spit upon, slapped, and clubbed by...a painting of medieval symbols of torment. This must have been a puzzling riddle from the Master to a fellow monk.

Cell ❽—*The Empty Tomb:* The worried women are reassured by an angel that "he is risen." Jesus, far away in the clouds, seems annoyed that they didn't listen to him.

Cell ❾—*Mary Crowned:* ...triumphantly in heaven, while Dominic, Peter, Aquinas, Francis, and others prepare to celebrate with high-fives.

Cell ❿—*Presentation in the Temple:* Baby Jesus is swaddled like a mummy. And there's your final Peter.

• *Continue around the bend—Savonarola's three rooms are at the far end of the corridor. Stop at the last room on the right.*

Girolamo Savonarola (1452–1498)—His Rooms and Possessions *(Celle del Savonarola)*

⓫—Savonarola's Cells

You'll find a number of Savonarola's possessions scattered about this cluster of rooms, his living quarters. Browse around while reading about his life.

Last Room in the Corridor

The room displays Savonarola's **blue cloak** and personal **crucifix**. Home-schooled by his Scholastic grandfather, the 22-year-old's life was changed when he heard a sermon on repentance. He traded his scholar's robes for the blue cloak of a simple Dominican monk. He quickly became known for his asceticism, devotion, and knowledge of the Bible.

• *Now enter the Celle del Savonarola.*

First Room of Savonarola's Living Quarters

The **portrait bust** shows the hooded monk, whose personal charisma and prophetic fervor led him from humble scholar to celebrity preacher to prior of San Marco to leader of Florence to controversial martyr. The **relief** under the portrait bust shows Savonarola at his greatest moment. He stands before the Florence city council and pledges allegiance to Florence's constitution, assuming control of the city after the exile of the Medici (1494).

Reviled as a fanatical, regressive tyrant and praised as a saint, reformer, and champion of democracy, Savonarola was a complex man in turbulent times.

Various **paintings** depict Savonarola in action, including one by Federico Andreotti, which shows the powerful monk reproaching two troublemakers in his study.

• *The next room is...*

Savonarola's Study (Studiolo)

Seated at this **desk,** in his ecclesiastical folding **chair** (La sedia del Savonarola), Savonarola scoured his **Bible** for clues to solve Florence's civic strife.

In 1482 at age 30, the monk had come to San Marco as a lecturer. He was bright, humble...and boring. Then, after experiencing divine revelations, he spiced his sermons with prophecies of future events...which started coming true. His sermons on Ezekiel, Amos, Exodus, and the Apocalypse predicted doom for the Medici family. He made brazen references to the pope's embezzling and stable of mistresses, and preached hope for a glorious future after city and church were cleansed.

Packed houses heard him rail against the "prostitute church... the monster of abomination." Witnesses wrote that "the church echoed with weeping and wailing," and afterward "everyone wandered the city streets dazed and speechless." From this humble desk, he corresponded with the worldly pope, the humanist Pico della Mirandola, and fans, such as Lorenzo the Magnificent, who begrudgingly admired his courage.

Lorenzo died, the bankrupt Medicis were exiled, and Florence was invaded by France...as Savonarola had prophesied. In the power vacuum, the masses saw Savonarola as a moderate voice who championed a return to Florence's traditional constitution. He was made head of a Christian commonwealth.

Room with Savonarola's Possessions (Le Reliquie di Savonarola)

Savonarola's personal moral authority was unquestioned, as his simple **wool clothes** and **rosary** attest.

At first, his rule was just. He cut taxes, reduced street crime, shifted power from rich Medicis to citizens, and even boldly proposed banning Vespas from tourist zones.

However, Savonarola had an uncompromising and fanatical side, as his **hair-shirt girdle** attests. His government passed strict morality laws against swearing, blasphemy, gambling, and ostentatious clothes, which were enforced by gangs of thuggish teenagers. At the height of the Christian Republic, during Lent of 1497, followers built a huge "bonfire of vanities" on Piazza della

MUSEUM OF SAN MARCO

Signoria, where they burned wigs, carnival masks, dice, playing cards, musical instruments, and discredited books and paintings.

In 1498, several forces undermined Savonarola's Republic: scheming Medicis, crop failure, rival cities, a pissed-off pope threatening excommunication for Savonarola and political isolation for Florence, and a public tiring of puritanism. Gangs of opponents (called Arrabbiati, "Rabid Dogs") battled Savonarola's supporters (the "Weepers"). Meanwhile, Savonarola was slowly easing out of public life, refusing to embroil the church in a lengthy trial, retiring to his routine of study, prayer, and personal austerity.

During Lent, a Franciscan monk challenged a Dominican to a public ordeal by fire to prove Savonarola right or wrong. (The righteous one supposedly would survive.) The Franciscan chickened out, but a bloodthirsty mob—with the blessing of city leaders and the pope—marched on San Marco to arrest Savonarola. Arrabbiati fought monks with clubs (imagine it in the **courtyard** out the window), while the church bells clanged and the monks shouted, *"Salvum fac populum tuum, Domine!"* ("Save thy people, Lord!"). The Arrabbiati stormed up the stairs to this floor, and Savonarola was handed over to the authorities. He was taken to the Palazzo Vecchio, tortured, tried, and sentenced.

On May 23, 1498 (see the **painting** *Supplizio del Savonarola in Piazza della Signoria*), before a huge crowd in the square in front of the Palazzo Vecchio (where today there's a memorial plaque embedded in the pavement in front of the Neptune fountain), Savonarola was publicly defrocked, then publicly forgiven by a papal emissary. Then he was hanged—not American execution-style, where the neck snaps, but slowly strangled, dangling from a rope, while teenage boys hooted and threw rocks.

The crowd looked upon the lifeless body of this man who had once captivated their minds, as they lit a pyre under the scaffold—see the **stick** *(palo)* from the fire. The flames rose up, engulfing the body, when suddenly...his arm shot upward!—like a final blessing or curse—and the terrified crowd stampeded, killing several. His ashes were thrown in the Arno.

The Rest of the Museum

The corridor near Fra Angelico's *Annunciation* has the Library (also designed by Michelozzo), which contains music and other manuscripts. In a cell across the hall is Fra Angelico's *Kiss of Judas* fresco—a theme that proved prophetic, since it was outside that cell that Savonarola was arrested. At the end of the corridor (right side) are ❷ the cells where Cosimo de' Medici—the founder of the Medici ruling dynasty and builder of this monastery—often retired for spiritual renewal. Inside, the painting of the Magi includes a kneeling Magus kissing the baby's little holy toes—a portrait of Cosimo.

• *To exit, return to the stairway and descend. Take a right at the bottom into a bookshop decorated with a fine Ghirlandaio* Last Supper *fresco (are you as tired as John is?), then through corridors filled with a hodgepodge of architectural fragments and on to the exit. On the street, turn right, then right again, and you'll see the Duomo.*

DUOMO MUSEUM TOUR

Museo dell'Opera del Duomo

Brunelleschi's dome, Ghiberti's bronze doors, and Donatello's statues—these creations define the 1400s (the Quattrocento) in Florence, when the city blossomed and classical arts were reborn. All are featured at the Duomo Museum, plus a Michelangelo *Pietà* intended as his sculptural epitaph. While copies now decorate the exteriors of the Duomo (cathedral), Baptistery, and Campanile (bell tower, called Giotto's Tower), the original sculptured master-pieces of the complex are now restored and displayed safely indoors, filling the Duomo Museum. This recently refurbished museum is a delight, though it's overlooked by most visitors to Florence. There's never a line.

Orientation

Cost: €6.

Hours: Mon–Sat 9:00–19:30, Sun 9:00–13:40, last entry 40 min before closing. Note that this is one of the few museums in Florence open on Monday.

Getting There: The museum is across the street from the Duomo on the east side, at Via del Proconsolo 9.

Information: The audioguide costs €4. Tel. 055-230-2885 or 055-264-7287.

Length of This Tour: Allow 90 minutes.

Photography: Allowed, but no flash around paintings.

Starring: Brunelleschi, Ghiberti, Donatello, and Michelangelo.

The Tour Begins

Ghiberti's doors are on the ground floor, while Donatello's statues are on the first floor. The *Pietà* is on a landing halfway between floors.

Ground Floor

The Medieval Cathedral
• *Browse the first few small rooms.*
Roman sarcophagi, Etruscan fragments, a chronological chart, and broken **Baptistery statues** attest to the 2,000-year history of Florence's Duomo, Baptistery, and Campanile. The Baptistery

was likely built on the site of a pagan Roman temple. It was flanked by a humble church that, by the 1200s, was not big enough to contain the exuberant spirit of a city growing rich from the wool trade and banking. In 1296, the cornerstone was laid for a huge church—today's Duomo—intended to be the biggest in Christendom.
• *The first large room (with a pope sitting at one end) is lined with statues from the original facade. On the long wall you'll find...*

Madonna with the Glass Eyes
(Madonna in Trono col Bambino)
This room displays the statues that sat in niches on the original facade (1296–1587), designed by the church's architect, Arnolfo di Cambio. The church was dedicated to Mary—starry-eyed over

the birth of baby Jesus. She sits, crowned like a chess-set queen, above the main door, framed with a dazzling mosaic halo. She's accompanied (to our right) by St. Zenobius, Florence's first bishop during Roman times, whose raised hand consecrates the formerly pagan ground as Christian.

Large, Seated Statue of Pope Boniface VIII
Despised by Dante for his meddling in politics, this pope paid 3,000 florins to get his image in a box seat on the facade. His XL

shirt size made him look correct when viewed from below. Though the statue is stylized, Arnolfo di Cambio realistically shows the pope's custom-made, extra-tall hat and bony face. (Most of the room's statues are straight-backed to hang on the facade.)

• *On the long wall opposite the Madonna, find...*

Donatello—*St. John the Evangelist (San Giovanni Evangelista)*

A hundred years later, di Cambio's medieval facade became a showcase for Renaissance sculptors.

John sits gazing at a distant horizon, his tall head rising high above his massive body. This visionary foresees a new age...and the

coming Renaissance. The right hand is massive—as relaxed as though it were dangling over the back of a chair, but full of powerful tension. Like the mighty right hand of Michelangelo's *David,* and the beard of Michelangelo's *Moses,* this work is a hundred years ahead of its time.

At 22 years old, Donatello (c. 1386–1466) sculpted this just before becoming a celebrity for his inspiring statue of *St. George* (original in the Bargello, copy on the exterior of the Orsanmichele Church). Donatello, like most early Renaissance artists, was a blue-collar worker, raised as a workshop apprentice among knuckle-dragging musclemen. He proudly combined physical skill with technical know-how to create beauty (Art + Science = Renaissance Beauty). His statues are thinkers with big hands who can put theory into practice.

• *To the right of the Madonna, in an adjoining room, find a...*

Scale Model (1:20) of the Duomo's Original Facade (by Franco Gizdulich)

In Renaissance times, this is what the Duomo would have looked like. The glassy-eyed Madonna was over the main doorway, Pope Boniface was to the left, high up, and Donatello's St. John was to the left, farther down. You can see that only the bottom third was ever completed

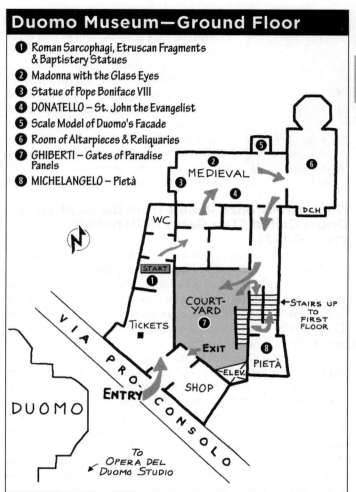

Duomo Museum—Ground Floor

1 Roman Sarcophagi, Etruscan Fragments & Baptistery Statues
2 Madonna with the Glass Eyes
3 Statue of Pope Boniface VIII
4 DONATELLO – St. John the Evangelist
5 Scale Model of Duomo's Facade
6 Room of Altarpieces & Reliquaries
7 GHIBERTI – Gates of Paradise Panels
8 MICHELANGELO – Pietà

with marble facing—the upper part was bare brick. Had Arnolfo's design been completed, the three-story facade would have looked much like today's colorful, Neo-Gothic version, with pointed arches and white, pink, and green marble, studded with statues and gleaming with gold mosaics. In 1587, the still-incomplete facade was torn down.

• *Up a few steps at the end of the long statue room is a...*

Room of Altarpieces and Reliquaries

These medieval altarpieces, which once adorned chapels and altars inside the Duomo, show saints and angels suspended in a gold never-never land. In the adjoining room, the ornate reliquaries

hold bones and objects of the saints (Peter's chains, Jerome's jawbone, and so on), many bought from a single, slick 14th-century con artist preying on medieval superstition.

In the 1400s, tastes changed, and these symbols of crude medievalism were purged from the Duomo and stacked in storage. Soon artists replaced the golden heavenly scenes with flesh-and-blood humans who inhabited the physical world of rocks, trees, and sky...the Renaissance.

• *In the ground-floor courtyard, you'll find...*

Ghiberti—Bronze Panels from the Baptistery Doors Called "The Gates of Paradise" (1425–1452)

The Renaissance began in 1401 with a citywide competition to build new doors for the Baptistery. Lorenzo Ghiberti (c. 1378–1455) won the job and built the doors (now on the Baptistery's north side), which everyone loved. He then was hired to make another set of doors—these panels—for the main entrance facing the Duomo. These "Gates of Paradise" revolutionized the way Renaissance people saw the world around them.

These are the original panels, which were removed from the Baptistery for preservation. (Copies now adorn the Baptistery itself—see the graphic on page 78 for the original layout.) Of the 10 panels from "The Gates of Paradise," the museum generally displays a half-dozen or so, while others are being cleaned. Restoration is difficult, because the corrosive oxides gather inside, between the bronze panel and gilding. (Even these cleaned panels are pitted and blotched.) The panels are under glass to protect against natural light, and gassed with nitrogen to protect them against oxygen and humidity.

• *Some of the panels that may be on display are...*

Joseph and Benjamin (Storie di Giuseppe e Beniamino)

With just the depth of a thumbnail, Ghiberti creates a temple in the round inhabited by workers. This round temple wowed Florence. Armed with the rules of perspective, Ghiberti rendered reality with a mathematical precision we don't normally impose on what we see, when our eyes and minds settle for ballpark estimates about relative size and distance.

For Florentines, suddenly the world acquired a whole new dimension—depth.

Adam and Eve
(La Creazione e Storie di Adamo ed Eva)

Ghiberti tells several stories in one panel—a common medieval technique—using different thickness in the relief. In the sketchy background (very low relief), God in a bubble conducts the Creation. In the center (a little thicker), Eve springs from Adam's side. Finally, in the lower left (in high relief), an elegantly robed God pulls Adam, as naked as the day he was born, from the mud.

Ghiberti welcomed the innovations of other artists. See the angel flying through an arch (right side). This arch is in very low relief but still looks fully 3-D because it's rendered sideways, using painters'-perspective tricks—a relief technique Ghiberti learned from one of his employees, the young Donatello.

Jacob and Esau (Storie di Giacobbe ed Esau)

The "background" arches and the space they create are as interesting as the scenes themselves. At the center is the "vanishing point" on the distant horizon, where all the arches and floor tiles converge. This calm center gives us an eye-level reference point for

all the figures. Those closest to us are big, clearly defined, and at the bottom of the panel. Distant figures are smaller, fuzzier, and higher up.

Ghiberti has placed us about 20 feet away from the scene, part of this casual crowd of holy people—some with their backs to us—milling around an arcade.

Labors of Adam, and Cain and Abel (Il lavoro dei progenitori e Storie di Caino e Abele)

On one mountain, we see Cain and Abel offering a sacrifice at the top, Adam waving at the bottom, and the first murder in between. In early panels such as this one (pictured at top of next page), Ghiberti used only a sketchy landscape as a backdrop for human activities.

Ghiberti, the illegitimate son of a goldsmith, labored all his working life (more than 50 years) on the two Baptistery doors.

These were major manufacturing jobs, employing a large workshop of artists and artisans for each stage of the process: making the door frames that hold the panels, designing and making models of the panels (forming them in wax in order to cast them in bronze), gilding the panels (by bathing them in powdered gold dissolved in mercury, then heating until the gold and bronze blended), polishing the panels, mounting them, installing the doors...and signing paychecks for everyone along the way. Ghiberti was as much businessman as artist.

Solomon and the Queen of Sheba

The receding arches stretch into infinity, giving the airy feeling that we could see forever. All of the arches and steps converge at the center of the panel, where the two monarchs meet, uniting their respective peoples. Ghiberti's subject was likely influenced by the warm ecumenical breeze blowing through Florence in 1439, as religious leaders convened here in an attempt to reunite the eastern (Constantinople) and western (Rome) realms of Christendom.

If the Renaissance began in 1401 with Ghiberti's doors, it ended in 1555 with Michelangelo's *Pietà*.

• In the courtyard are two staircases almost side by side. Ascend the old (not new) staircase to the first landing.

Michelangelo—*Pietà* (1547–1555)

Aging Michelangelo (1475–1564) was designing his own tomb, with this as the centerpiece. He was depressed by old age, the recent death of his soul mate, and the grim reality that by sculpting this statue he was writing his own obituary. It was done without a commission. As Michelangelo envisioned this for his own tomb, it's fair to consider it an introspective and very personal work.

Three mourners tend the broken body of the crucified Christ. We see Mary, his mother (the shadowy figure on our right); Mary Magdalene (on the left, polished up by a pupil); and Nicodemus, the converted Pharisee, whose face is clearly that of Michelangelo himself. The polished body of Christ stands out from the unfinished background. Michelangelo (as Nicodemus), who spent a lifetime bringing statues to life by "freeing" them

from the stone, looks down at what could be his final creation, the once-perfect body of Renaissance man that is now twisted, disfigured, and dead.

Seen face-on, the four figures form a powerful geometric shape of a circle inside a triangle, split down the middle by Christ's massive (but very dead) arm. Seen from the right side, they seem to interact with each other, their sketchy faces changing emotions from grief to melancholy to peaceful acceptance.

Fifty years earlier, a confident Michelangelo had worked here on these very premises, skillfully carving *David* from an imperfect block. But he hated this marble for the *Pietà;* it was hard and grainy and gave off sparks when hit wrong. (The chisel grooves in the base remind us of the sheer physical effort of a senior citizen sculpting.) Worst of all, his housekeeper kept bugging him with the same question that Pope Julius II used to ask about the Sistine Chapel—"When will you finish?" Pushed to the edge, Michelangelo grabbed a hammer and attacked the flawed marble statue, hacking away and breaking off limbs, then turned to the servant and said, "There! It's finished!" (An assistant later repaired some of the damage, but cracks are still visible in Christ's left arm and only leg.)

• *Continue upstairs to the first floor, entering a large room lined with statues and two balconies. Donatello's four prophets are at the far end.*

First Floor

Room of the Cantorie *(Le Cantorie)*— Donatello's Prophets

The room displays the original 16 statues (by several sculptors) that ring the bell tower's third story (where copies stand today). Donatello did five of them, plus some others in collaboration.

Donatello ("Little Donato") invented the Renaissance style that Michelangelo would later perfect—powerful statues that are ultra-realistic, even ugly, sculpted in an "unfinished" style by an artist known for experimentation and his prickly, brooding personality. Both men were famous but lived like peasants, married only to their work.

Donatello—*Habakkuk (Abacuc)*

Donatello's signature piece shows us the wiry man beneath the heavy mantle of a prophet. His rumpled cloak falls down the front, dividing the body lengthwise. From the deep furrows emerges a bare arm with well-defined tendons and that powerful right hand.

His long, muscled neck leads to a bald, pumpkin-like head (the Italians call the statue *Lo Zuccone*).

The ugly face, with several days' growth of beard, crossed eyes, and tongue-tied mouth, looks crazed. This is no confident Charlton Heston prophet, but a man who's spent too much time alone, fasting in the wilderness, searching for his calling, and who now returns to babble his vision on a street corner.

Donatello, the eccentric prophet of a new style, identified with this statue, talking to it, swearing at it, yelling at it: "Speak!"

• *Nearby, look for...*

Donatello—*Jeremiah (Geremia)*

(Note: Jeremiah may be under restoration during your visit.) Watching Jerusalem burn in the distance, the ignored prophet reflects on why the Israelites wouldn't listen to his warning. He

purses his lips bitterly, and his downturned mouth is accentuated by his plunging neck muscle and sagging shoulders. The folds in the clothes are very deep, evoking the anger, sorrow, and disgust that Jeremiah feels but cannot share, as it is too late.

Movement, realism, and human drama were Donatello's great contributions to sculpture.

• *The two balconies in Room 12 are two* cantorie—*Donatello's on the right (from the entrance), Luca della Robbia's on the left. Della Robbia's is a reconstruction from casts, with the original 10 panels below.*

Luca della Robbia—*Cantoria* (1431–1438)

After almost 150 years of construction, the cathedral was nearly

done, and they began preparing the interior for the celebration. Brunelleschi hired a little-known sculptor, 30-year-old Luca della Robbia, to make this choir box—a balcony for singers next to the organ in the cathedral—and it summed up the exuberance of the Quattrocento. The panels are a celebration of music, song, and dance performed by toddlers, children, and teenagers.

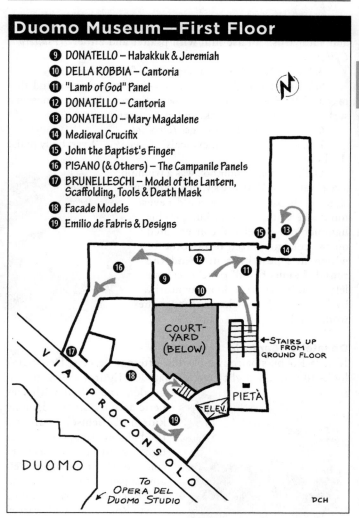

Duomo Museum—First Floor

⑨ DONATELLO – Habakkuk & Jeremiah
⑩ DELLA ROBBIA – Cantoria
⑪ "Lamb of God" Panel
⑫ DONATELLO – Cantoria
⑬ DONATELLO – Mary Magdalene
⑭ Medieval Crucifix
⑮ John the Baptist's Finger
⑯ PISANO (& Others) – The Campanile Panels
⑰ BRUNELLESCHI – Model of the Lantern, Scaffolding, Tools & Death Mask
⑱ Facade Models
⑲ Emilio de Fabris & Designs

COURT-YARD (BELOW)

←STAIRS UP FROM GROUND FLOOR

PIETÀ

ELEV.

VIA PROCONSOLO

DUOMO

To OPERA DEL DUOMO STUDIO

DCH

The *cantoria* brings Psalm 150 to life like an MTV video. Latin speakers can read the text, while the rest can follow along with the pictures. Start in the upper left (or view the panel copies, at eye level):

"*Laudate D.N.M.*" reads the banner along the top—"Praise the Lord." "Praise him in his holy place, in the firmament *(Firmamento)* for his mighty deeds *(Virtu)* and greatness *(Magnitudinus)*." Then come the panels:

1. (Upper-left panel): Children laugh and dance to the sound of trumpets, as the text reads, "Praise him with the sound of trumpets" *(sono Tubae)*.

2. and **3.** Babysitters put down infants and pick up guitars and autoharps: "Praise him with psalter and zither" (*Psaltero et Cythera*).

4. "... Praise him with tambourines..." *(Timpano)*.

5. "...and dancing" *(Choro)*. Seven kids dance ring-around-the-rosy as della Robbia sculpts a scene in the round on an almost-flat surface, showing front, back, and in-between poses.

6. "...with pipes and strings" *(Organo)*.

7. "...and with jubilant cymbals" *(Cimbales)*. "Everybody praise the Lord!"

Della Robbia's choir box was a triumph, a celebration of Florence's youthful boom time. Perhaps sensing he could never top it, the young sculptor hung up his hammer and chisel and concentrated on the colorful glazed terra-cotta for which he's best known. (Find the **round "Lamb of God" panel** over your left shoulder, above a doorway nearby, by Luca's nephew, who took over the workshop.)

Donatello—*Cantoria*

If della Robbia's balcony looks like afternoon recess, Donatello's looks like an all-night rave. Donatello's figures are sketchier,

murky, and filled with frenetic activity, as the dancing kids hurl themselves around the balcony. Imagine candles lighting this as they seem to come to life. If the dance feels almost pagan, there's a reason.

Recently returned from a trip to Rome, Donatello carved in the style of classical friezes of dancing *putti* (chubby, playful toddlers). This choir box stood in a dark area of the Duomo, so Donatello chose colorful mosaics and marbles to catch the eye, while purposely leaving the dancers unfinished and shadowy, tangled figures flitting inside the columns. In the dim light, worshippers swore they saw them move.

• *Enter an adjoining room to see bishops' robes, a half-ton silver altarpiece, and...*

Donatello—*Mary Magdalene (Maddalena)*

Carved out of white poplar, originally painted with realistic colors (like the **medieval crucifix** displayed nearby), this statue is less

a Renaissance work of beauty than a medieval object of intense devotion.

Mary Magdalene—the prostitute rescued from the streets by Jesus—folds her hands in humble prayer. Her once-beautiful face and body have been scarred by the fires of her own remorse, fasting, and repentance. The matted hair sticks to her face; veins and tendons line the anorexic arms and neck. The rippling hair suggests emotional turmoil within. But from her hollow, tired eyes, a new beauty shines, an enlightened soul that doesn't rely on the external beauty of human flesh.

The man who helped re-birth the classical style now shocked Florence by turning his back on it. Picking up a knife, he experimented in the difficult medium of wood carving, where subtlety can get lost when the wood splits off in larger-than-wanted slivers.

Sixty-five-year-old Donatello had just returned to Florence, after years away. His city had changed. Friends were dying (Brunelleschi died before they could reconcile after a bitter fight), favorite pubs were overrun with frat boys, and Florence was gaga over Greek gods in pretty, gleaming marble. Donatello fell into a five-year funk, completing only two statues, including this one.

• *In the display case to the left of* Mary, *you'll find...*

John the Baptist's Finger in a Reliquary (Artista fiorentino: Reliquario Del Dito Indice di S. Giovanni Battista)

The severed index finger of the beheaded prophet is the most revered relic of all the holy body parts in this museum.

• *Pass back through the large room of the* cantorie *and into the next room. Work clockwise from the entrance.*

Andrea Pisano (and others)—The Campanile Panels (c. 1334–1359)

These 28 hexagonal and 28 diamond-shaped, blue-glazed panels decorated Giotto's Tower, seven per side (where copies stand today). The original design scheme was perhaps Giotto's, but most were executed by his successor, Andrea Pisano, and assistants.

The panels celebrate technology, showing workers, inventors, and thinkers. Allegorically, they depict humanity's long march to "civilization"—a

Pop. 100,000...but still a small town

At the dawn of the Renaissance, Florence was bursting with creative geniuses, all of whom knew each other and worked together. For example, when Ghiberti won the bronze-door competition, Brunelleschi lost and took teenage Donatello with him to Rome. Donatello returned to join Ghiberti's workshop. Ghiberti helped Brunelleschi with dome plans. Brunelleschi, Donatello, and Luca della Robbia collaborated on the Pazzi Chapel. And so on, and so on.

blend of art and science, brain and brawn. But realistically, they're snapshots of that industrious generation that helped Florence bounce back ferociously from the Black Death of 1348.

The lower, **hexagonal panels** (reading clockwise from the entrance) show God starting the chain of creation by inventing (1) man and (2) woman, then (3) Adam and Eve continuing the work, (4) Jabal learning to domesticate sheep, (5) Jubal blowing a horn, inventing music...

• *Continuing along the next wall...*

(6) Tubalcain the blacksmith and (7) Noah inventing wine and Miller Time. (8) An astronomer sights along a quadrant to chart the heavens and the (round, tilted-on-axis, pre-Columbian) earth, (9) a master builder supervises his little apprentices building a brick wall, (10) a doctor holds a flask of urine to the light for analysis, and so on.

• *On the fourth wall, check out...*

(20) The invention of sculpture, as a man chisels a figure to life.

The upper **diamond-shaped panels,** of marble on blue majolica (tin-glazed pottery tinged blue with copper sulfate), add religion (sacraments and virtues) to the civilization equation.

• *Enter the next, narrow room to find tools, scaffolding, and, at the end of the corridor, a wooden model of the cathedral dome's lantern.*

Brunelleschi's Dome—Model of the Lantern (Cupola di S. Maria del Fiore)

Look at this model of the dome's top portion (or look out the window at the real thing). Brunelleschi's dome put mathematics in stone, a feat of engineering that was functional and beautiful. It rises 330 feet from the ground, with eight white, pointed-arch ribs, filled in with red brick and capped with a "lantern" to hold it all in place.

In designing the dome, Brunelleschi faced a number of challenges: The dome had to cover a gaping 140-foot hole in the roof of the church (a drag on rainy Sundays), a hole too wide to be spanned by the wooden scaffolding traditionally used to support a dome while it was being built. (An earlier architect suggested supporting the dome with a great mound of dirt inside the church...filled with coins, so peasants would later cart it away for free.) In addition,

the eight-sided "drum" that the dome was to rest on was too weak to support a heavy dome, and there were no side buildings on the church on which to attach Gothic-style buttresses.

The solution was a dome within a dome, leaving a hollow space between to make it lighter. And the dome had to be self-supporting, both while being built and when finished, so as not to require buttresses.

Brunelleschi used wooden models such as these to demonstrate his ideas to skeptical approval committees.

• *In the display cases are scaffolding and tools.*

Scaffolding

Although no scaffolding supported the dome itself, the stone masons needed exterior scaffolding to stand on as they worked. Support timbers were stuck into postholes in the drum (some are visible on the church today).

The dome rose in rings. First, they'd stack a few blocks of white marble to create part of the ribs, then connect the ribs with horizontal crosspieces, then fill in the space with red brick in a herringbone pattern. When the ring was complete and self-supporting, they'd move the scaffolding up and do another section.

Tools

The dome weighs 80 million pounds—as much as the entire population of Florence—so Brunelleschi had to design special tools and machines to lift and work all that stone. (The lantern alone—which caps the dome—is a marble building nearly as tall as the Baptistery.) You'll see sun-dried bricks, brick molds, rope, a tool belt, compasses, stone pincers, and various pulleys for lifting. Brunelleschi also designed a machine (not on display) where horses turned a shaft that reeled in rope, lifting heavy loads.

The dome was completed in 16 short years, capping 150 years of construction on the church. Brunelleschi enjoyed the dedication ceremonies, but he died before the lantern was completed. His legacy is a dome that stands as a proud symbol of man's ingenuity, proving that art and science can unite to make beauty.

• *Next to the lantern model, find...*

Brunelleschi's Death Mask *(Anonimo: Maschera Funebre)*

Filippo Brunelleschi (1377–1446) was uniquely qualified to create the dome. Trained in sculpture, he gave it up in disgust after losing the Baptistery-door gig. In Rome, he visualized placing the Pantheon on top of Florence's Duomo, and dissected the Pantheon's mathematics and engineering.

Back home, he astounded Florence with a super-realistic painting of the Baptistery, as seen from the Duomo's front steps. Florentines lined up to see the painting (now lost) displayed side by side with the real thing, marveling at the 3-D realism. (Brunelleschi's mathematics of linear perspective were later expanded and popularized by Alberti.)

In 1420 Brunelleschi was declared *capomaestro* of the dome project. He was a jack-of-all-trades and now master of all as well, overseeing every aspect of the dome, the lantern, and the machinery to build them. Despite all of his planning, it's clear from documentary evidence that he was making it up as he went along, exuding confidence to workers and city officials while privately improvising.

• *The models you'll find two rooms farther along represent the...*

Facade from the 16th to the 19th Centuries

The church wasn't done. In 1587, the medieval facade by di Cambio was considered hopelessly outdated and was torn down like so much old linoleum. But work on a replacement never got off the ground, and the front of the church sat bare for nearly 300 years while they debated proposal after proposal (like the models in this room) by many famous architects. Most versions champion the Renaissance style to match Brunelleschi's dome, rather than Gothic to fit the church.

• *Two rooms later, we reach the conclusion to the Duomo's long history.*

The 19th-Century Facade

Finally, in the 1800s, as Italy was unifying and filled with a can-do spirit, there was a push to finish the facade. **Emilio de Fabris (portrait)** won a competition, and began to build a neo-Gothic facade that echoed the original work of di Cambio. The new-old facade was dedicated in 1887. Notice that even de Fabris changed designs as he went—the spikes along the roofline in some of the designs are not there today.

Critics may charge that de Fabris' facade is too retro, but it was the style of the church beloved by Ghiberti, Donatello,

Brunelleschi, and the industrious citizens of Florence's Quattro-cento, who saw it as Florence's finest art gallery.

The Opera del Duomo Today

If you climb the stairs to the sparse third-floor landing, you might see lab-coated workers busy in the restoration studio. They belong to the Opera del Duomo, the organization that does the continual work required to keep the cathedral's art in good repair (*opera* is Italian for "work"). For another behind-the-scenes peek, make one more stop after leaving the Duomo Museum: Head to the left

around the back of the Duomo to find Via dello Studio (near the south transept), then walk a block toward the river to #23a (see map on page 75). You can look through the open doorway of the Opera del Duomo art studio and see workers sculpting new statues, restoring old ones, or making exact copies. They're

carrying on an artistic tradition that dates back to the days of Brunelleschi. The "opera" continues.

MEDICI CHAPELS TOUR

Cappelle Medicee

The Medici (MED-ee-chee) Chapels contain tombs of Florence's great ruling family, from Lorenzo the Magnificent to those less so. The highlight is a chapel designed by Michelangelo at the height of his creative powers. This is Renaissance man's greatest "installation," a room completely under one artist's control, featuring innovative architecture, tombs, and sculpture. His statues tell of a middle-aged man's brooding meditation on mortality, the fall of the Medici Golden Age, and the relentless passage of time—from *Dawn* to *Day* to *Dusk* to *Night*.

Orientation

Cost: €4, but mandatory special exhibits usually raise the price to about €6.

Dress Code: No tank tops, short shorts, or short skirts.

Hours: Tue–Sat April–Oct 8:15–16:50, Nov–March 8:15–13:50; also open first, third, and fifth Sun and second and fourth Mon of each month—until 16:50 April–Oct or 13:50 Nov–March; last entry 30 min before closing. Confirm the latest opening hours from the TI or by calling the chapel.

Getting There: It's in the Church of San Lorenzo—the one with the smaller dome on Florence's skyline (5-min walk northwest of Duomo). The bustling outdoor market almost obscures the chapel entrance at the back (west end) of the church. See page 48 for more about the Church of San Lorenzo and page 49 for the open-air market.

Information: The audioguide costs €5.50 (€8/2 people). Tel. 055-294-883 or 055-238-8602, www.polomuseale.firenze.it.

Length of This Tour: Allow one hour.

Photography: Prohibited.
Starring: Michelangelo's statues *Day, Night, Dawn,* and *Dusk.*

The Tour Begins

Overview

The Medici Chapels consist of three burial places: the unimpressive Crypt; the large and gaudy Chapel of Princes; and—the highlight—Michelangelo's New Sacristy, a room completely designed by him, with architecture, tombs, and statues to honor four Medicis.

• *Enter the Chapel and buy tickets. Immediately after you show your ticket, you're in...*

The Crypt

This gloomy, low-ceilinged room with gravestones underfoot reminds us that these "chapels" are really tombs. You'll see a few Lorenzos buried in this room (after all, "Laurentius," or Lawrence, was the family's patron saint)...but none that is "Magnificent" (he's later). The collection of ornate silver and gold reliquaries is appropriately macabre and worth a quick look.

• *Head upstairs via the staircase on the right into the large, domed, multicolored...*

Chapel of Princes
(La Cappella dei Principi, 1602–1743)

The impressive **dome** overhead (seen from outside, it's the big, red-brick "mini-Duomo") tops an octagonal room that echoes the

Baptistery and Duomo drum. It's lined with six tombs of Medici rulers and is decorated everywhere with the **Medici coat of arms**—a shield with six balls representing the pills of doctors *(medici),* their original occupation. Along with many different-colored marbles, geologists will recognize jasper, porphyry, quartz, alabaster, coral, mother-of-pearl, and lapis lazuli.

Sixteen shields ring the room at eye level, each representing one of the Tuscan cities ("Civitas") ruled by Florence's dukes. Find Florence, with its fleur-de-lis ("Florentiae"), and Pisa ("Pisarum"), both just left of the altar.

The bronze **statues** honor two of the "later" Medicis, the cultured but oppressive dukes who ruled Florence after the city's glorious Renaissance. Ferdinando I (ruled 1587–1609), in ermine cape and jewels, started the work on this Chapel of Princes and tore down the Duomo's medieval facade. His son, Cosimo II (ruled

MEDICI CHAPELS

1609–1621, to the right), appointed Galileo "first professor" of science at Pisa U., inspiring him to label the moons of Jupiter "the Medici Stars."

The **altar** was finished in 1939 for a visit from Hitler and Mussolini. The altar itself is the only Christian symbolism in this spacious but stifling temple to power, wealth, and mediocre Medicis.

(*Psst.* There's a room of relics behind the altar. It also displays the pastoral staff of Pope Leo X, who was Lorenzo the Magnificent's son and Michelangelo's classmate.)

• *Continue down the hall, passing statues of Roman armor with worms sprouting out, to Michelangelo's New Sacristy.*

New Sacristy (Sacrestia Nuova)—Michelangelo

The entire room—architecture, tombs, and statues—was designed by Michelangelo over a 14-year period (1520–1534) to house the bodies of four of the Medici family. Michelangelo, who spent his teen years in the Medici household and personally knew three of the four family members buried here, was emotionally attached to the project. This is the work of a middle-aged man (age 45–59) reflecting on his contemporaries dying around him, and on his own mortality.

• *There are tombs decorated with statues against three of the walls, and an altar on the fourth. Start with the tomb on the left wall (as you enter and face the altar).*

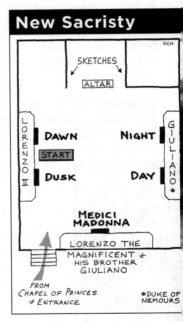

Tomb of Lorenzo II, Duke of Urbino

Lorenzo II—the grandson of Lorenzo the Magnificent—is shown as a Roman general, seated, arm resting on a Medici-bank money box, and bowing his head in contemplation. He had been the model for Machiavelli's *The Prince*, and when he died at 27 (of tuberculosis and syphilis) without a male heir, the line of great princes stretching back to Cosimo the Elder died with him.

His sarcophagus, with a curved, scrolled lid, bears the reclining statues that Michelangelo named *Dusk* and *Dawn*.

Dusk (the man), worn out after a long day, slumps his chin on his chest and reflects on the day's events. **Dawn** (the woman) stirs restlessly after a long night, with an anguished face, as though waking from a bad dream. *Dusk* and *Dawn*, with their counterparts *Day* and *Night* (opposite wall), represented to Michelangelo the swift passage of time, which kills everyone and causes our glorious deeds on earth to quickly fade.

During the years he worked here, Michelangelo suffered the deaths of his father, his favorite brother, and his unofficial step-brother, Pope Leo X Medici. In addition, plagues in 1522 and 1527 killed thousands in Florence. In 1527, his adoptive city of Rome was looted by mercenaries. Michelangelo's letters reveal that, upon turning 50, he was feeling old, tired ("If I work one day, I need four to recuperate"), and depressed (he called it *mio pazzo*, "my madness"), facing the sad fact that the masterpiece of his youth—the grand tomb of Pope Julius II—was never going to be completed.

Overachievers in severe midlife crises may wish to avoid the Medici Chapels.

• *On the opposite wall is the...*

Tomb of Giuliano, Duke of Nemours

Overshadowed by his famous father (Lorenzo the Magnificent) and big brother (Pope Leo X), **Giuliano** led a wine-women-and-song life, dying young without a male heir. His statue as a Roman general, with scepter, powerful Moses-esque pose, and alert, intelligent face, looks in the direction of the Madonna statue, as though asking forgiveness for a wasted life. The likeness is not at all accurate.

Michelangelo said, "In a thousand years, no one will know how they looked."

Giuliano's "active" pose complements the "contemplative" one of Lorenzo, showing the two elements (thought + action) that Plato and Michelangelo believed made up the soul of man.

Night (the woman) does a crossover sit-up in her sleep, toning the fleshy abs that look marvelously supple and waxlike, not like hard stone. She's highly polished, shimmering, and finished with minute details. Michelangelo's females—musclemen with coconut-shell breasts—are generally more complete and (some think) less interesting than his men.

Michelangelo was homosexual. While his private sex life (or lack thereof) remains a mystery, his public expressions of affection were clearly weighted toward men. Some say he was less interested in female bodies and felt he could easily sum them up in a statue.

Day (the man) works out a crick in his back, each limb twisting a different direction, turning away from us. He looks over his shoulder with an expression (suspicious? angry? arrogant?) forever veiled behind chisel marks suggestive of Impressionist brush strokes. In fact, none of the four reclining statues' faces expresses a clear emotion, as all are turned inward, letting body language speak.

If, as some say, Michelangelo purposely left these statues "unfinished" while liberating them from their stone prison, it certainly adds mystery and a contrast in color and texture. *Night*'s moonlit clarity and *Day*'s rough-hewn grogginess may also reflect Michelangelo's own work schedule—a notorious day-sleeper and guilt-ridden layabout ("Dear to me is sleep") who, when inspired (as a friend wrote), "works much, eats little, and sleeps less."

Among *Night*'s symbols (the crescent moon on her forehead, owl under knee, and poppies underfoot) is a grotesque **mask** with, perhaps, a self-portrait. Michelangelo, a serious poet (so much so that he almost considered sculpting his "day job"), has *Night* say in one of his poems: "As long as shame and sorrow exist / I'd rather not see or hear / So speak softly and let me sleep."

Day, Night, Dawn, and *Dusk*—brought to life in this room where Michelangelo had his workshop, and where they've been ever since—meditate eternally on Death, squirming restlessly, unable to come to terms with it.

• *On the entrance wall is the...*

Tomb of Lorenzo the Magnificent and his Brother Giuliano

As the tomb was never completed, all that really marks where The Magnificent One's body lies is a marble slab, now topped with a statue of the Madonna flanked by saints. Perhaps Michelangelo was working up to the grand finale to honor the man who not only was the greatest Medici, but who also plucked a poor 13-year-old Michelangelo from an obscure apprenticeship to dine at the Medici table with cardinals and kings.

Lorenzo's beloved younger brother, Giuliano, died in 1478 in a "hit" by a rival family, stabbed to death before the altar of the Duomo during Easter Mass. (Lorenzo, wounded, drew his sword and backpedaled to safety. Enraged supporters grabbed the assassins—including two priests planted there by the pope—and literally tore them apart.)

The **Medici Madonna,** unlike many Michelangelo women, is thin, vertical, and elegant, her sad face veiled under chisel marks.

She tolerates the squirming, two-year-old Jesus, who still seems to want to breast-feed, aware of the hard life her son has ahead of him. Mary's right foot is still buried in stone, so this unfinished statue was certainly meant to be worked on more. The saints **Cosmas** and **Damian** were done by assistants.

The Unfinished Project

The Chapel project (1520–1534) was plagued by delays: design changes, late shipments of Carrara marble, the death of patrons, Michelangelo's other obligations (including the Laurentian Library next door), his own depression, and...revolution.

In 1527, Florence rose up against the Medici pope and declared itself an independent republic. Michelangelo, torn between his love of Florence and loyalty to the Medicis of his youth, walked a fine line. He continued to work for the pope while simultaneously designing fortified city walls to defend Florence from the pope's troops. In 1530, the besieged city fell, republicans were rounded up and executed, and Michelangelo went into hiding (perhaps in the chapel basement, down the steps to the left of the altar). Fortunately, his status both as artist and staunch Florentine spared him from reprisals.

In 1534, a new pope enticed Michelangelo to come back to Rome with a challenging new project: painting the *Last Judgment* over the altar in the Sistine Chapel. Michelangelo left, never to return to the Medici Chapels. Assistants gathered up statues and fragments from the chapel floor (and the Madonna from Michelangelo's house) and did their best to assemble the pieces according to Michelangelo's designs.

• *The apse is the area behind the altar. This has the best view of the chapel as a whole.*

The Medicis in a Minute and a Half

The Medici family—part *Sopranos,* part Kennedys, part John-D-and-Catherine-T art patrons—dominated Florentine politics for 300 years (c. 1434–1737). Originally a hardworking, middle-class family in the cloth, silk, and banking businesses, they used their wealth, blue-collar popularity, and philanthropy to rise into Europe's nobility, producing popes and queens.

1400s: The Princes

Lorenzo the Magnificent (ruled 1469–1492), Cosimo the Elder's grandson, epitomized the Medici ruling style: publicly praising Florence's constitution while privately holding the purse strings. A true Renaissance Man, Lorenzo's personal charisma, public festivals, and support of da Vinci, Botticelli, and teenage Michelangelo made Florence Europe's most enlightened city.

1494–1532: Exile in Rome

After Lorenzo's early death, the family was exiled by the Florentines. The Medicis became victims of bank failure, Savonarola's reforms, and the Florentine tradition of democracy. They built a power base in Rome under Lorenzo's son (Pope Leo X, who made forays into Florence) and nephew (Pope Clement VII, who finally invaded Florence and crushed the republic).

1537–1737: The Grand Duchy—Mediocre Medicis

Backed by Europe's popes and kings, the "later" Medicis—descendants of Cosimo the Elder's brother—ruled Florence and Tuscany as just another duchy. Politically repressive but generous patrons of the arts and sciences (the Uffizi, Pitti Palace, Cellini, Galileo), they married into Europe's royal families (Catherine and Marie de' Medici were queens of France) while Florence declined as a political and economic power.

Sketches on the Walls of the Apse

Michelangelo's many design changes and improvisational style come to life in these (dimly lit and hard to see behind Plexiglas) black chalk and charcoal doodles, presumably by Michelangelo and assistants.

• *Starting on the left wall and working clockwise at about eye level...*

Look at all the marks: hash marks counting off days worked,

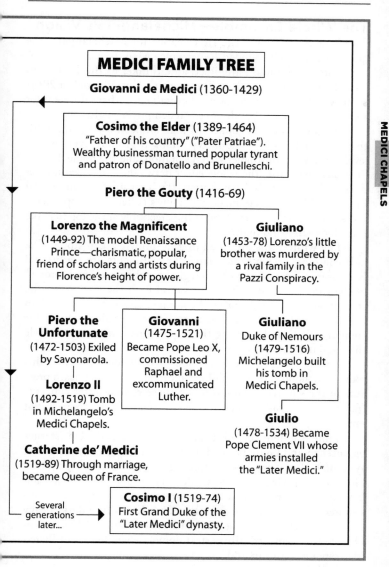

MEDICI FAMILY TREE

Giovanni de Medici (1360-1429)

Cosimo the Elder (1389-1464)
"Father of his country" ("Pater Patriae").
Wealthy businessman turned popular tyrant
and patron of Donatello and Brunelleschi.

Piero the Gouty (1416-69)

Lorenzo the Magnificent
(1449-92) The model Renaissance
Prince—charismatic, popular,
friend of scholars and artists during
Florence's height of power.

Giuliano
(1453-78) Lorenzo's little
brother was murdered by
a rival family in the
Pazzi Conspiracy.

Piero the Unfortunate
(1472-1503) Exiled
by Savonarola.

Lorenzo II
(1492-1519) Tomb
in Michelangelo's
Medici Chapels.

Giovanni
(1475-1521)
Became Pope Leo X,
commissioned
Raphael and
excommunicated
Luther.

Giuliano
Duke of Nemours
(1479-1516)
Michelangelo built
his tomb in
Medici Chapels.

Giulio
(1478-1534) Became
Pope Clement VII whose
armies installed
the "Later Medici."

Catherine de' Medici
(1519-89) Through marriage,
became Queen of France.

Several
generations
later...

Cosimo I (1519-74)
First Grand Duke of the
"Later Medici" dynasty.

a window frame for the Laurentian Library, scribbles, a face, an arch, a bearded face, and (on the right wall) a horse, a nude figure crouching under an arch, a twisting female nude with her dog, and a tiny, wacky, cartoon Roman soldier with shield and spurs. You really do get a sense of Michelangelo and staff working, sweating, arguing, and just goofing off as the hammers pound and dust flies.

The Whole Ensemble—Michelangelo's Vision

The New Sacristy was the first chance for Michelangelo, the quintessential well-rounded Renaissance Man, to use his arsenal of talents—as sculptor, architect, and Thinker of Big Ideas—on a single, multimedia project. The resulting "installation" (a 20th-century term) produces a powerful overall effect that's different for everyone—"somber," "meditative," "redemptive," "ugly."

The room is a cube topped with a Pantheon-style dome, with three distinct stories—the heavy tombs at ground level, upper-level windows with simpler wall decoration, and the dome, better-lit and simpler still. The whole effect draws the eye upward, from dark and "busy" to light and airy. (It's intensified by an optical illusion—Michelangelo made the dome's coffers, the upper windows, and round lunettes all taper imperceptibly at the top to make them look taller and higher.)

The white walls are lined in gray-brown-green stone. The half columns, arches, and triangular pediments are traditional Renaissance forms, but with no regard for the traditional "orders" of the time (matching the right capital with the right base, the correct width-to-height ratio of columns, upper story taller than lower, etc.). Michelangelo had Baroque-en the rules, baffling his contemporaries and pointing the way to a new, more ornate style that used old forms as mere decoration.

Finally, Michelangelo, a serious neo-Platonist, wanted this room to symbolize the big philosophical questions that death presents to the survivors. Summing up these capital-letter concepts (far, far more crudely than was ever intended), the room might say:

Time (the four reclining statues) kills Mortal Men (statues of Lorenzo and Giuliano) and mocks their Glory (Roman power symbols). But if we Focus (Lorenzo and Giuliano's gaze) on God's Grace (Madonna and Child), our Souls (both Active and Contemplative parts) can be Resurrected (the Chapel was consecrated to this) and rise from this drab Earth (the dark, heavy ground floor) up into the Light (the windows and lantern) of Heaven (the geometrically perfect dome), where God and Plato's Ideas are forever Immortal.

And that, folks, is a Mouthful.

MEDICI-RICCARDI PALACE TOUR

Palazzo Medici-Riccardi

Cosimo (the Elder) de' Medici, the founder of the ruling family dynasty, lived here with his upwardly mobile clan, including Lorenzo the Magnificent. Besides the immediate family, the palace also hosted many famous Florentines: teenage Michelangelo, who lived almost as an adopted son; Leonardo da Vinci, who played lute for Medici parties; and Botticelli, who studied the classical sculpture that dotted the gardens. The historical ambience is captured in a few well-preserved rooms and in a 15th-century fresco that brings the colorful Medici world to life.

Orientation

Cost: €5; €7 with mandatory special exhibits.

Hours: Thu–Tue 9:00–19:00, last entry 30 minutes before closing, closed Wed. Only eight people are allowed into the lavish Chapel of the Magi every seven minutes; to avoid a wait to see the chapel, call a day in advance to make a reservation (tel. 055-276-0340). Weekdays off-season (Nov–March) and late in the day, you may be able to just walk right in or reserve a time when you buy your ticket, and sightsee the rest of the palace while you wait your turn for the chapel.

Getting There: It's one block north of the Duomo at Via Cavour 3. Note that the ticket entrance is a bit north of what appears to be the main entrance (which is often gated shut).

Information: The €1 brochure in the bookshop is worth considering.

Length of This Tour: Allow an hour.

Photography: Not allowed in the Chapel of the Magi (Cappella di Gozzoli), but photos without flash allowed elsewhere.

MEDICI-RICCARDI PALACE

Starring: Cosimo de' Medici and Lorenzo the Magnificent as depicted in Gozzoli's colorful Magi frescoes.

The Tour Begins

Exterior

Cosimo de' Medici hired the architect Michelozzo to build the palace (1444), whose three-story facade set the tone throughout Florence—rough stones at bottom, rising to smooth and elegant on top. Two generations later, Michelangelo added the distinctive "kneeling windows" (with scrolls), an innovation that cropped up on palaces the world over. In the 1700s, the palace was extended northward (keeping the same style) by the next owners, the Riccardi family.

• *Buy your ticket, pass through one small courtyard, and continue into the...*

Courtyard

As with many Italian homes, the courtyard served as an open-air

meeting point and "living room" for the extended family. The statue of Orpheus (who calmed wild animals with his harp) reminded visitors that the Medici family calmed wild Florence with smart and soothing politics. Find the family shield above the arches, with the six pills of these doctors *(medici)* turned cloth merchants turned international bankers. The Riccardi family later gilded this Renaissance lily with Baroque decor and adorned this courtyard with their collection of classical sculpture.

Garden

Pop into the fragrant garden with its greenhouse for lemon trees. This tiny oasis is a mere fraction of the once-spacious gardens that stretched for a city block to the north. In the past, the grounds were studded with many more fountains and statues, including the *Venus de' Medici* (Uffizi). Donatello's *David* (Bargello) likely stood in the courtyard. Teenage

Michelangelo studied sculpture and liberal arts in the family school located in the gardens.

• *Enter the room to Orpheus' left.*

Lorenzo's Workshop/"Virtual Visit"

This room was once Lorenzo the Magnificent's public office. It now houses a multimedia "Star Wars meets art history" setup that allows you to see close-ups of Gozzoli's Magi frescoes. Stand on the lighted square and point at marked areas of the large video screen. It zooms in, and a narrator explains the selected detail. A smaller plasma screen takes you through what Lorenzo's workshop would have been like in 1492.

• *Check out any temporary exhibits (in the room to Orpheus' right), then head upstairs. From the courtyard, one stairway leads to the Chapel of the Magi (signed as* Benozzo Gozzoli*). The other stairway, just off the courtyard, goes to the Luca Giordano–decorated library. Both are on the first floor.*

Chapel of the Magi (Cappella di Gozzoli)

This sumptuous little room was the nuclear family's private chapel, where they could kneel at the altar and pray to a *Madonna and Child* by Fra Filippo Lippi (where a copy stands now). At the time, it was rare and highly prestigious for a family to have a private chapel (this is one of only three in Florence). But Cosimo was the pope's banker—he even bankrolled one of the Crusades. He could afford it.

The three walls around the altar display *The Journey of the Magi,* or three kings—one king per wall—by Benozzo Gozzoli (1459). Each wall has a dominant color of white, green, or red: the Medici family colors.

On the biggest wall, a curly-haired young king, dressed in white and riding a white horse, leads a parade of men through a rocky landscape. (Some scholars have suggested that the young Magus may be Lorenzo the Magnificent, but others dismiss the idea. Lorenzo is pictured elsewhere—see below.) The scene takes you not to Bethlehem, but to 15th-century Medici-populated Tuscany. Riding behind the king are Cosimo (in red hat, riding modest brown donkey) and his son Piero (red hat, gray-white horse), who succeeded Cosimo as ruler of Florence. In the line of red-hatted young men behind them, find Piero's 10-year-old son and future ruler—Lorenzo the Magnificent (sixth in from the left, in red cap, with scoop nose, brown bowl-cut hair, and intense gaze). Little Lorenzo grew up looking at these beautiful frescoes that celebrate the natural world. One day, he would commission his own great art.

Above Lorenzo (and slightly to the right) is Gozzoli himself. The sour-faced man in the cap above Gozzoli is Pope Pius II, often called "the first humanist" (see "Piccolomini Library" on page 315). Lost? Ask the attendant (with the red-tipped pointer) where they are: *"Dov'è* (doh-VEH) *Benozzo Gozzoli? Dov'è Cosimo? Dov'è Lorenzo?"*

The next wall (working clockwise) sets the king and his entourage in a green, spacious, and obviously Tuscan landscape. The men wear colorful clothes that set trends throughout Europe. Every year on Epiphany (January 6), the Medici men would actually dress up like this and parade through the streets to celebrate the holiday of the three kings.

On the last wall, notice that the white-bearded king on his white donkey (far left) got cut off when the room was later remodeled. But the fresco was preserved—find the horse's ass on the other side of the doorway.

Gozzoli's crystal-clear, shadowless scenes reflect the style of his teacher, Fra Angelico. The portraits are realistic, showing the leading characters of 1459 Florence.

The room itself functioned both as a chapel and as the place where Cosimo received VIPs. By portraying his own family in this religious setting, Cosimo made a classy display of cool power and sophistication. When learned rival powers came here, they thought, "Damn, these Medicis are good."

• *Exit the Gozzoli room into several...*

Palatial Rooms with Temporary Exhibitions

Though the displays change often, the rooms themselves give a small sense of the former luxury of the palace—suggested now by a few chandeliers and furnishings. Today, the palace is a functioning county government building. As you wander around, notice the bureaucrats at work. Occasionally, the provincial council meeting room is open for viewing.

• *Eventually you'll reach a room displaying a painting.*

Fra Filippo Lippi—*Madonna and Child*

Lippi's cheek-to-cheek *Madonna and Child* demonstrates Lippi's specialty—humanizing the son of God and the Virgin. Baby Jesus' transparent shirt, Mary's transparent scarf, and their transparent halos make this late Lippi work especially ethereal. Mary's eyes are sad, while Jesus stares into his spiritual future. She gives him a tender hug before he's off on his mission.

• *Nearby is the entrance to the...*

Luca Giordano Room

This Baroque, Versailles-like former reception hall was added by the Riccardi family. The ceiling (*The Apotheosis of the Medici Family*, frescoed in 1685 by the Naples artist Luca Giordano) features Medici big shots (with starbursts over their heads) frolicking with Greek gods. Walk slowly toward the center of the room and watch as the Medici appear to rise

up into heaven to be crowned by Zeus. Ringing the base of the ceiling are various Greek myths—find Poseidon with his trident (to the left) and Hades carrying off Persephone (to the right). The blue-robed woman over the entrance is Florence—mother of the Renaissance—immersed in the nobility of the classical world.

Your tour is done. Now head back out onto the streets, where the noble city retains its Renaissance heritage while immersed in the reality of today's world.

SANTA MARIA NOVELLA TOUR

The Church of Santa Maria Novella, chock-full of groundbreaking paintings and statues, is a reminder that the Renaissance was not simply a secular phenomenon. Many wealthy families paid for chapels inside the church that today are appreciated for their fine art.

Masaccio's fresco *The Trinity* (1427), the first painting of modern times to portray three-dimensional space, blew a "hole in the wall" of this church. From then on, a painting wasn't just a decorated panel, but a window into the spacious 3-D world of light and color. With Masaccio's *Trinity* as the centerpiece, the church traces Florentine art from the medieval to the Quattrocento (1400s) to the onset of Baroque.

Orientation

Cost: €2.50.

Hours: Mon–Thu and Sat 9:00–17:00, Fri and Sun 13:00–17:00, last entry 30 min before closing.

Dress Code: No bare shoulders or short skirts or short shorts for adults. Your clothing must cover your knees. Free poncho-like coverings are available.

Getting There: It's on Piazza Santa Maria Novella, a block south of the train station.

Nearby: Ardent art lovers can seek out the adjacent **Museum and Cloisters** (€2.70, entry to the left of the church's facade; Mon–Thu and Sat 9:00–17:00, closed Fri and Sun). You'll see a Daddi polyptych, some Uccello frescoes, and the Chapel of the Spaniards, notable for Bonaiuto's fresco *Allegory of the Dominican Order*.

Santa Maria Novella

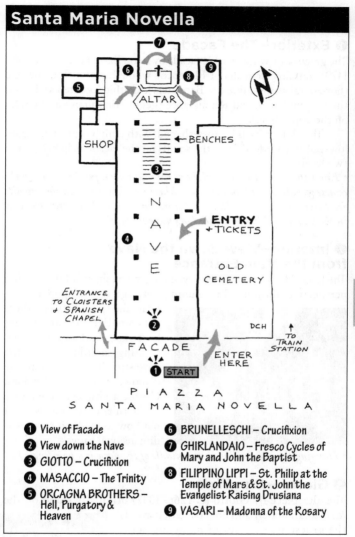

ALTAR

SHOP

← BENCHES

ENTRY + TICKETS

NAVE

OLD CEMETERY

ENTRANCE TO CLOISTERS & SPANISH CHAPEL

DCH

TO TRAIN STATION

FACADE

ENTER HERE

START

PIAZZA SANTA MARIA NOVELLA

- ❶ View of Facade
- ❷ View down the Nave
- ❸ GIOTTO – Crucifixion
- ❹ MASACCIO – The Trinity
- ❺ ORCAGNA BROTHERS – Hell, Purgatory & Heaven
- ❻ BRUNELLESCHI – Crucifixion
- ❼ GHIRLANDAIO – Fresco Cycles of Mary and John the Baptist
- ❽ FILIPPINO LIPPI – St. Philip at the Temple of Mars & St. John the Evangelist Raising Drusiana
- ❾ VASARI – Madonna of the Rosary

SANTA MARIA NOVELLA

A block away from Piazza Santa Maria Novella is a fancy **perfumery**—a store that feels like a small museum—that's free and fun to visit (Mon–Sat 9:30–19:30, Sun 10:30–18:30, Via della Scala 16, tel. 055-216-276); see page 63 for details.

Length of This Tour: Allow one hour.

Photography: Prohibited.

Starring: The early Renaissance—Masaccio, Giotto, Brunelleschi, and Ghirlandaio.

The Tour Begins

❶ Exterior—The Facade

The green-and-white marble facade by Leon Battista Alberti (1456–1470) contains elements of Florence's whole history: Romanesque (horizontal stripes, like the Baptistery), Gothic (pointed arches on the bottom level), and Renaissance (geometric squares and circles on the upper level).

The church itself is cross-shaped, with a high central nave and low-ceilinged side aisles—the scrolls on the facade help bridge the two levels.

• *Enter the courtyard to the right of the main door, passing through the cemetery, where you'll pay to enter. Masaccio's* Trinity *is on the opposite wall from the entrance. But we'll start our tour at the central doorway in the facade, looking down the long nave to the altar.*

❷ Interior—View down the Nave from the Main Entrance

The long, 330-foot nave looks even longer, thanks to a 14th-century perspective illusion. The columns converge as you approach the

altar, the space between them gets smaller, the arches get lower, and the floor gets higher, creating the illusion that the nave stretches farther into the distance than it actually does. Gothic architects were aware of the rules of perspective, just not how to render it on a two-dimensional canvas.

• *Hanging from the ceiling in the middle of the nave is a painting by...*

❸ Giotto—*Crucifixion*

The altarpiece by Giotto (c. 1266–1337) originally stood on the main altar. Stately and understated, it avoids the gruesome excesses of many medieval crucifixes. The tragic tilt of Christ's head, the parted lips, and the stretched rib cage tell more about human suffering than the excessive spurting of blood.

On either side of the crossbar, Mary and John sit in a golden iconic heaven, but they are fully human, turned at a three-quarter angle, with knowing, sympathetic expressions. Giotto, the proto-Renaissance experimenter in perspective, creates the illusion that Christ's hands are actually turned out, palms down, not hammered flat against the cross.

• *Masaccio's* Trinity *is on the left wall, about midway along the nave (opposite the entrance). For the best perspective, stand about 20 feet from it, then take four steps to your left, standing on the shield with a crown. Masaccio positioned it to be seen by the faithful as they dipped fingers into a (missing) font and crossed themselves—"Father, Son, and Holy Ghost."*

❹ Masaccio—*The Trinity* (1425–1427)

In his short but influential five-year career, Masaccio (1401–1428) was the first painter since ancient times to portray Man in Nature—real humans with real emotions, in a spacious three-dimensional world. (Unfortunately for tourists, he did the best 3-D space here, and the best humans in the Brancacci Chapel across the river.)

With simple pinks and blues (now faded), Masaccio creates the illusion that we're looking into a raised, cube-shaped chapel (about nine feet tall) topped with an arched ceiling and framed at the entrance with classical columns. Inside the chapel, God the Father stands on an altar, holding up the cross of Christ. (Where's the dove of the Holy Spirit? Why is God's "white collar" crooked?) John looks up at Christ while Mary looks down at us. Two donors (husband and wife, most likely) kneel on the front step outside the chapel, their cloaks spilling out of the niche. Below this fake chapel sits a fake tomb with the skeleton of Adam; compare it with the real tomb and niche to the right.

The checkerboard-coffered ceiling creates a 3-D tunnel effect, with rows of panels that appear to converge at the back, the panels getting smaller, lower, and closer together. Earlier painters had played with tricks like this, but Masaccio went further. He gave such thought to the proper perspective that we, as viewers, know right where we stand in relation to this virtual chapel.

He knew that, in real life, the rows of coffers would, if extended, stretch to the distant horizon. Lay a mental ruler along them, and you'll find the "vanishing point"—where all the lines intersect—all the way down below the foot of the cross. Masaccio places us there, looking "up" into the chapel.

Having fixed where the distant horizon is and where the viewer is, Masaccio draws a checkerboard grid in between, then places the figures on it (actually underneath it) like chess pieces.

What's truly amazing is that young Masaccio seemed to grasp this stuff intuitively—a "natural," eyeballing it and sketching freehand what later artists would have to work out with a pencil and paper.

What Masaccio learned intuitively, Brunelleschi analyzed mathematically, and Alberti (who did the facade) codified in his famous 1435 treatise, *On Painting*. Soon, artists everywhere were drawing Alberti checkerboards on the ground, creating spacious, perfectly lit, 3-D scenes filled with chess-piece humans.

• *The Orcagna Chapel is at the far end of the left transept. As you approach, view the chapel from a distance. This is the illusion that Masaccio tried to create—of a raised chapel set in a wall with people inside—using only paint on a flat surface. Climb the steps to see...*

❺ Orcagna Brothers— Frescoes of the Last Judgment: *Hell, Purgatory,* and *Heaven* (*Inferno, Purgatorio,* and *Paradiso,* 1340–1357)

In 1347–1348, Florence was hit with the terrible Black Death (bubonic plague) that killed half the population. Here, in the Orcagna Chapel, the fading frescoes from that grim time show hundreds of figures, and not a single smile.

It's the Day of Judgment (center wall), and God (above the stained-glass window) spreads his hands to divide the good and evil. God has selected Dante as the interior decorator for heaven and hell. (Find Dante all in white, with his ear-flap cap, among the crowd to the left of the window, about a third of the way up.) Notice that God is bigger than the angels, who dwarf the hallowed saints, who are bigger than ordinary souls such as Dante, mirroring the feudal hierarchy of king, nobles, knights, and serfs.

In *Heaven* (left wall), Hotel Paradiso is *completo*, stacked with gold-haloed saints. *Hell* (faded right wall) is a series of layers, the descending rings of Dante's Inferno. A river of fire runs through it, dividing *Purgatory* (above) and *Hell* (below). At the bottom of the pit, where dogs and winged demons run wild, naked souls in caves beg for mercy and get none.

• *In a chapel to the left of the church's main altar, you'll find...*

❻ Filippo Brunelleschi—*Crucifixion*

Filippo Brunelleschi (1377–1446)—architect, painter, sculptor— used his skills as an analyst of nature to carve (in wood) a perfectly

realistic *Crucifixion*, neither prettified nor with the grotesque exaggeration of medieval religious objects. His Christ is buck naked, not particularly muscular or handsome, with bulging veins, armpit hair, tensed leg muscles, and bent feet. The tilt of Christ's head frees a tendril of hair that directs our eye down to the wound and the dripping blood, dropping straight from his side to his thigh to his calf—a strong vertical line that sets off the curve of Christ's body. Brunelleschi carved this to outdo his friend Donatello's crucifix in Santa Croce. Donatello's is an agonized peasant; Brunelleschi's a dignified noble.

• *In the choir area behind the main altar are Ghirlandaio's 21 frescoes, stacked seven to a wall. We'll concentrate on just the six panels on the bottom.*

❼ Domenico Ghirlandaio—Fresco Cycles of Mary and John the Baptist (1485–1490)

At the peak of Florence's power, wealth, and confidence, Domenico Ghirlandaio (1449–1494) painted portraits of his fellow Florentines in their Sunday best, inhabiting video-game landscapes of mixed classical and contemporary buildings, rubbing shoulders with saints and angels. The religious subjects get lost in the colorful scenes of everyday life—perhaps a metaphor for how Renaissance humanism was marginalizing religion.

• *Start with the left wall and work clockwise along the bottom. The first scene shows the...*

Expulsion of Joachim from the Temple

Proud, young Florentine men (the group at left) seem oblivious to bearded, robed saints rushing from the arcade. There's Ghirlandaio himself (in the group on the right) looking out at

us, with one hand proudly on his hip and the other gesturing, "I did this." The scene is perfectly lit, almost shadow-free, allowing us to look deep into the receding arches.

• *The next scene, on the right, is the...*

SANTA MARIA NOVELLA

Birth of the Virgin

Five beautiful young women, led by the pregnant daughter of
Ghirlandaio's patron, parade up to newborn
Mary. The pregnant girl's brocade dress is
a microcosm of the room's decorations.
Dancing babies in the room's classical frieze
celebrate Mary's birth, obviously echoing
Donatello's beloved *cantoria* in Florence's
Duomo Museum.

True, Ghirlandaio's works are "busy"—
each scene crammed with portraits, designs,
fantasy architecture, and great costumes—
but if you mentally frame off small sections,
you discover a collection of mini-master-
pieces.

• *On the lowest part of the center wall, flanking the stained-glass window, are two matching panels.*

Giovanni Tornabuoni Kneeling and
Francesca Tornabuoni (his wife) Kneeling

Giovanni Tornabuoni, who paid for these frescoes, was a successful
executive in the Medici Company (and Lorenzo the Magnificent's
uncle). However, by the time these frescoes were being finished,
the Medici bank was slipping seriously into the red, and soon the
family had to flee Florence, creditors on their heels.

• *On the right wall...*

Mary Meets Elizabeth

In a spacious, airy landscape (with the pointed steeple of Santa
Maria Novella in the distance), Mary and Elizabeth embrace,

uniting their respective
entourages. The parade
of ladies in contemporary
dress echoes the one on
the opposite wall. This
panel celebrates youth,
beauty, the city, trees,
rocks, and life.

A generation after
Brunelleschi and Alberti, all artists—including the near-genius
Ghirlandaio—had mastered perspective tricks. Here, Alberti's
famed checkerboard is laid on its side, making a sharply receding
wall to create the illusion of great distance.

Ghirlandaio employed many assistants in his productive workshop: "Johnson, you do the ladies' dresses. Anderson, you're great
at birds and trees. And Michelangelo...you do young men's butts."

The three small figures leaning over the wall (above Mary and Elizabeth) were likely done by 13-year-old Michelangelo, an apprentice here before being "discovered" by Lorenzo the Magnificent. Relaxed and natural, they cast real shadows, as true to life as anyone in Ghirlandaio's perfect-posture, face-the-camera world.

Ghirlandaio was reportedly jealous (and talented Michelangelo contemptuous), but, before they parted ways, Michelangelo learned how to lay fresco from the man who did it as well as anyone in Florence.

• *On the far right, find the...*

Appearance of an Angel to Zechariah

In a crowded temple, old Zechariah is going about his business, when an angel strolls up. "Uh, excuse me..." The event is supposedly miraculous, but there's nothing supernatural about this scene: no clouds of fire or rays of light. The crowd doesn't even notice the angel. Ghirlandaio presents the holy in a completely secular way.

• *In the chapel to the right of the altar, Filippino Lippi did the frescoes on the left and right walls. Look first at the right wall, lower level (there's a decent view from the altar steps)...*

❽ Filippino Lippi

St. Philip at the Temple of Mars

In an elaborate shrine, a statue of the angry god Mars waves his broken lance menacingly. The Christian Philip points back up and

says, "I'm not afraid of him—that's a false god." To prove it, he opens a hole in the base of the altar, letting out a little dragon, who promptly farts (believe it when you see it), causing the pagan king's son to swoon and die. The overcome spectators clutch their foreheads and noses.

If Ghirlandaio was "busy," Lippi is downright hyperactive, filling every square inch with something frilly—rumpled hair, folds in clothes, dramatic gestures, twisting friezes, windblown flags, and gassy dragons.

• *On the left wall, lower level, is...*

St. John the Evangelist Raising Drusiana from the Dead

The miracle takes place in a spacious 3-D architectural setting, but Lippi has all his actors in a chorus line across the front of the stage. Filippino Lippi (1457–1504, the son of the more famous Fra Filippo Lippi) was apprenticed to Botticelli and exaggerated his bright colors, shadowless lighting, and elegant curves.

The sober, dignified realism of Florence's Quattrocento was ending. Michelangelo would extend it, building on Masaccio's spacious, solemn, dimly lit scenes. But Lippi championed a style (later called Mannerism, leading to Baroque) that loved color, dramatic excitement, and the exotic.

• *In the next chapel to the right of the altar, on the central wall, find...*

❾ Giorgio Vasari—*Madonna of the Rosary*

The picture-plane is saturated with images from top to bottom. Saints and angels twist and squirm around Mary (the red patch in the center), but their body language is gibberish, just an excuse for Vasari to exhibit his technique.

Giorgio Vasari (1511–1574), best known as the writer of *The*

Lives of the Artists, was a prolific artist himself. As a Mannerist, he copied the "manner" of, say, a twisting Michelangelo statue, but violated the sober spirit, multiplying by 100 and cramming the canvas. I've tried to defend Vasari from the art critics who unanimously call his art superficial and garish...but doggone it, they're right.

With Vasari, who immortalized the Florentine Renaissance with his writing, the Renaissance ended.

SANTA CROCE TOUR

Chiesa di Santa Croce

Santa Croce, one of Florence's biggest and oldest churches, gives us a glimpse into the medieval roots of the Renaissance. The centerpiece of a monastery for Franciscans, the church was built by Arnolfo di Cambio, who also designed the Duomo, and frescoed by Giotto, the proto-Renaissance pioneer.

In the cloisters is a small chapel that some consider the finest example of early-Renaissance architecture. The church was host to many famous Florentines, including Michelangelo and Galileo, who are both buried here. Today, the church complex houses a leather school, a display on the disastrous 1966 flood, and a museum housed in the monks' former dining hall.

Orientation

Cost: €5, includes the church, Pazzi Chapel, and museum. The leather school is always free.

Hours: Church—Mon–Sat 9:30–17:30, Sun 13:00–17:30 (last entry 30 min before closing); leather school—daily 9:30–18:00.

Dress Code: A modest dress code (no short shorts or bare shoulders) is enforced.

Getting There: It's a 10-minute walk east of the Palazzo Vecchio along the street called Borgo de' Greci.

Crowd Control: A limited number of people are allowed to enter at one time, sometimes resulting in waits of up to 40 minutes in summer. Go early or late in the day, or use the...

    Back Door Entrance: The leather school, tucked in the back of the church, is never crowded, and also sells entrance tickets to the church (which don't seem to count toward the church's admission limit). To find the school, walk west along the left side of the church, and enter the doorway at Via San Giuseppe 5 red.

Follow *Scuola del Cuoio* signs through the small garden to the low-key entrance of the school. Once inside, pass through the workshops and displays to the room with the cash register, and tell the cashier you want a church ticket. From there, enter the church's bookstore, and find your way to the nave to start this tour (see my Santa Croce map—when you enter from the leather school, you'll be at #12).

Information: The audioguide is €4. Tel. 055-246-6105. The leather school has its own website (www.leatherschool.com).

Cuisine Art: Recommended eateries are nearby (see "Dining near Santa Croce Church" in the Eating chapter.

Starring: Tombs of Michelangelo and Galileo, Giotto's frescoes, Francis' robe, and Brunelleschi's Pazzi Chapel.

The Tour Begins

• *Begin on the square in front of the church.*

Piazza Santa Croce

Santa Croce Church was built from 1294 to 1442. Architect Arnolfo di Cambio's design was so impressive, the city also hired him to do the Duomo and the Palazzo Vecchio.

The church's colorful marble facade, left unfinished for centuries, was finally added in the 1850s. A statue of the medieval poet Dante adorns the church steps.

The church presides over a vast square ringed with a few old palazzos, notably the late-Renaissance building at the far end. Piazza Santa Croce has always been one of Florence's gathering spots, for Carnival, May Day, and community events. If you're here in the third week of June, the square is covered with dirt and surrounded by bleachers for the annual soccer/rugby match, which since 1530 has pitted neighborhood against neighborhood.

If you were here on November 4, 1966, you would have found the square covered with 15 feet of water. The Arno flooded that day, submerging the church steps and rising halfway up the central doorway. (More on the flood later.)

• *Buy your ticket and enter. Start at the far end of the nave (farthest from the altar). Face the altar and gaze down the long nave.*

The Nave

The effect is one of great spaciousness. The nave is 375 feet long, lined with columns that are tall, slender, and spaced far apart, supporting wide, airy arches. As in most Gothic

Santa Croce

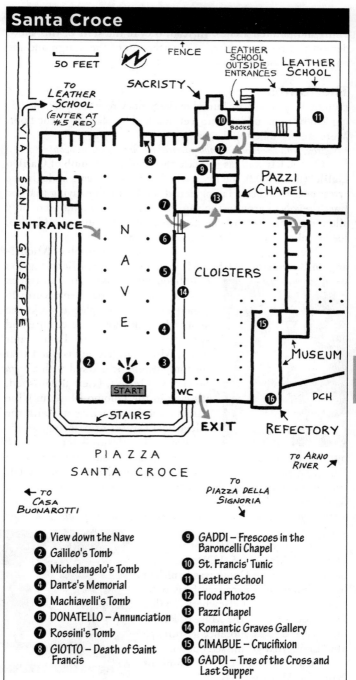

50 FEET

FENCE

LEATHER SCHOOL OUTSIDE ENTRANCES

LEATHER SCHOOL

SACRISTY

TO LEATHER SCHOOL (ENTER AT #5 RED)

VIA SAN GIUSEPPE

ENTRANCE

NAVE

BOOKS

PAZZI CHAPEL

CLOISTERS

MUSEUM

START

WC

STAIRS

EXIT

REFECTORY

DCH

SANTA CROCE

PIAZZA SANTA CROCE

← TO CASA BUONAROTTI

TO PIAZZA DELLA SIGNORIA

TO ARNO RIVER ↗

1. View down the Nave
2. Galileo's Tomb
3. Michelangelo's Tomb
4. Dante's Memorial
5. Machiavelli's Tomb
6. DONATELLO – Annunciation
7. Rossini's Tomb
8. GIOTTO – Death of Saint Francis
9. GADDI – Frescoes in the Baroncelli Chapel
10. St. Francis' Tunic
11. Leather School
12. Flood Photos
13. Pazzi Chapel
14. Romantic Graves Gallery
15. CIMABUE – Crucifixion
16. GADDI – Tree of the Cross and Last Supper

churches, there's no attempt to hide the structural skeleton of columns and pointed arches. Instead, they're the stars of this show, demonstrating the mathematic perfection of the design and the builders' technical prowess.

The Tombs

Hundreds of people are buried in the Santa Croce complex, including 276 of them under your feet, marked by plaques in the floor. More famous folk line the walls.

• *Nearby, find the tombs of two particularly well-known people.*

On the left wall (as you face the altar) is the **tomb of Galileo Galilei** (1564–1642), the Pisan who lived his last years under house arrest near Florence. Having defied the Church by saying that the Earth revolved around the sun, his heretical remains were only allowed in the church long after his death. (For more on Galileo, see his relics in the Galileo Science Museum.)

Directly opposite (on the right wall) is the **tomb of Michelangelo Buonarroti** (1475–1564). Santa Croce was Michelangelo's

childhood church, as he grew up a block west of here at Via dei Bentaccordi 15 (where nothing but a plaque marks the spot). He took Florentine culture and spread it across Europe. In his later years, Michelangelo envisioned that his tomb would be marked with a *pietà* he carved himself. (Left unfinished, it's now in the Duomo Museum.) The garish tomb he actually got—with the allegorical figures of painting, architecture, and sculpture—was designed by Michelangelo's great admirer, the artist/biographer Giorgio Vasari. Vasari also did the series of paintings that line the left side of the nave, using the twisting poses and bulky muscles that Michelangelo pioneered.

• *Stroll up the nave, finding more tombs and monuments along the right wall.*

At the memorial to the poet **Dante Alighieri** (1265–1321), there's no body inside, since Dante was banished by his hometown because of his politics and was buried elsewhere. Exiled Dante looks weary, the Muse of Poetry mourns, and Lady Florence gestures to say, "Look what we missed out on."

Two tombs ahead, the **tomb of Niccolò Machiavelli** (1469–1527)

features Lady Justice presenting a medallion with his portrait on it. Machiavelli, a champion of democratic Florence, opposed the Medicis as tyrants. When they returned to power, he was arrested and tortured. He retired to his farm to write *The Prince*, a how-to manual on hardball politics.

Next, Donatello's carved gray-and-gold **relief** (1430–1435) depicting the Annunciation shows a kneeling angel gently breaking the news to an astonished Mary. Notable for its then-unprecedented realism, the wispy Mary (on the right) is considered one of the artistic breakthroughs that marked the beginning of the long-overdue Renaissance.

Two tombs up is **Gioacchino Rossini** (1792–1868), the Italian composer of many operas and the *William Tell Overture* (a.k.a. the *Lone Ranger* theme). Rossini died in Paris, but his body was later moved here, to his homeland, during a wave of Italian nationalism in the late 19th century.

• *Head for the main altar. In the first chapel to the right of the altar are the...*

Giotto Frescoes in the Bardi Chapel (c. 1325)

The left wall has the famous *Death of Saint Francis*. With simple but eloquent gestures, Francis' brothers bid him a sad farewell.

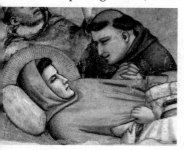

One folds his hands and stares longingly at Francis' serene face. Another bends to kiss Francis' hand, while others raise their arms in grief. It's one of the first expressions of human emotion in modern painting. It's also one of the first to create a real three-dimensional grouping of figures. Giotto places three kneeling men (with their backs to us) in the foreground, some others stand behind Francis, and the rest are turned to profile.

Giotto and his army of assistants were hired to plaster much of the church in colorful frescoes. But over the years, most were chiseled off, replaced by more modern works (like Vasari's). This chapel was only whitewashed over, and the groundbreaking frescoes were rediscovered in the 19th century.

• *Facing the altar, turn right, and head into the right (south) transept. At the far end, enter the chapel decorated with colorful frescoes.*

Gaddi Frescoes in the Baroncelli Chapel (c. 1328–1338)

After assisting Giotto in the Bardi Chapel, Taddeo Gaddi (1300–1366)—Giotto's beloved godson—was charged with painting this chapel. His lively frescoes cover both the wall to the left (as you enter), and the wall straight ahead (with stained-glass windows by Gaddi and an altar by Giotto).

Start with the wall to the left. The story of Mary, the mother of Jesus, unfolds from top to bottom, left to right. At the very top

(under the pointed arch), is a temple scene. Mary's future dad, Joachim (with a beard and a halo), is turned away from the temple because he's childless. Ashamed, he retreats to the wilderness (right side), where an angel promises him a daughter. Overjoyed, Joachim rushes to his wife, Anna, and they embrace (next level down, left panel). Anna soon gives birth to baby Mary (badly damaged panel, right side). Still a child, Mary climbs the steps of the temple (bottom level, left panel; most of her body is missing from peeling plaster) to the chief priest (cone-shaped hat), who would raise her. When it comes time for Mary to marry, the priest assembles all the eligible bachelors (bottom-right panel). Joseph's staff sprouts leaves and a dove (center of scene, to left of priest), signaling that he is chosen. In the foreground, a sore loser bends over and breaks his own staff.

Mary's life continues on the altar/stained-glass wall. At the top left, an angel swoops down to tell Mary that she'll give birth to Jesus. Perhaps Gaddi's most impressive scene is just below: A sleeping shepherd is awakened by an angel announcing that Christ is born. Gaddi, an early pioneer in lighting effects, placed these windows where the natural light coming through would mix with the supernatural light from the radiant angel. (It's said that Gaddi studied solar eclipses to the point of near-blindness.) Finally, Mary's story comes to its culmination (right of window): She gives birth in a stable to the Son of God.

• *Exit out the right transept and turn left at the first door, entering the sacristy.*

St. Francis' Tunic

In a glass case along the wall, find a bit of **St. Francis' tunic** (*Parte della Tonaca,* scrunched up in a small gold frame). Francis (c. 1182–1226), a monk from nearby Assisi, caused a stir by challenging the decadence of Church government and society in

Floods in Florence

Summer visitors to Florence gaze at the lazy green creek called the Arno River and have a tough time imagining it being a destructive giant. But rare, powerful flooding is a part of life in Florence. The Arno River washed away Ponte Vecchio in 1177 and 1333. And on November 4, 1966, a huge rain turned the Arno into a wall of water, inundating the city with mud stacked as high as 20 feet. Nearly 14,000 families were left homeless, and a huge amount of art was destroyed or damaged.

Almost as impressive as the flood was the huge outpouring of support, as the art-loving world came to the city's rescue. While money poured in from far and wide, volunteers, nicknamed "mud angels," mopped things up. After the flood, scientists made great gains in restoration techniques as they cleaned and repaired masterpieces from medieval and Renaissance times. Cimabue's *Crucifixion*, now displayed in Santa Croce's Refectory, is a prime example.

Today, you'll see plaques around town showing the high-water marks (about six feet high at the Duomo). Now that a dam has tamed the Arno, kayakers glide peacefully on the river, sightseers enjoy the great art with no thought of a flood, and locals...still get nervous after every heavy rain.

general. Adopting the poor, wandering lifestyle of Jesus Christ, he preached a message of non-materialism and love. His charismatic presence and stirring sermons attracted many followers, including the monks who founded Santa Croce. Francis' humanistic outlook and appreciation for the beauty of nature helped sow the seeds that would bloom into the Florentine Renaissance. Also displayed is a Papal Bull *(Regula Ordinis)*, which finally legitimized the once-controversial Franciscan movement.

• *The sacristy leads into the bookstore, which leads to the...*

Leather School *(Scuola del Cuoio)*

After World War II, the Franciscan monks created a "Boys Town" here to give war orphans a trade: making leather products. It was the first shop of what is now a popular leather district. The Gori family of merchants helped found the school and still runs it today. Wander through the former dorms for monks, watch the leather-working in action, and browse the finished products—for sale, of course. They also sell church admission tickets.

• *Backtrack through the bookstore, which spills out into a hallway that features a display on...*

Flood Photos

Located close to the Arno, Santa Croce was especially hard-hit by the devastating flood of November 1966. Water spilled into the church complex (including the museum/refectory we'll see later), carrying off furnishings and artwork, and leaving several feet of mud in its wake. Cimabue's famous *Crucifixion* was badly damaged, but survived (you'll see it in the refectory—described below).

• *Return to the nave and exit between the Rossini and Machiavelli tombs into the cloister (open-air courtyard). Descend the stairs and turn left into the...*

Pazzi Chapel

Begun in 1430 by Brunelleschi, this small chapel captures the Renaissance in miniature. As with his Duomo dome, Brunelleschi was inspired by Rome's ancient Pantheon. The circle-in-square design reflects the ancient Romans' (and Renaissance Florentines') belief in the unity and harmony of perfect shapes. Notice how the color scheme of white plaster and gray sandstone accentuates the architectural lines, so that only a little decoration is needed. The creamy colors help diffuse the light from the dome's windows, making the chapel evenly lit and meditative. The four medallions showing

the evangelists (at the base of the dome) may be by Donatello; the medallions of apostles (on the walls) are by Luca della Robbia. While originally used as a monk's assembly room (chapter house), this later became the Pazzi family's private chapel. Imagine how modern this chapel must have seemed after Brunelleschi capped it with a dome.

• *Exiting into the courtyard, notice the long building on the right that houses the Romantic Graves Gallery (19th-century headstones), which is also included in your church admission. On the left is the entrance to the...*

Museum *(Museo)* and Refectory

Stroll through several rooms of paintings, statues, medieval altarpieces, and frescoes, until you come out into the large room that was originally the monks' refectory, or dining hall.

Cimabue's *Crucifixion* (1423) was heavily damaged in the 1966 flood, and most of Christ's face and body were washed away.

Rescued and restored (as best they could), it became a symbol of the flood's destruction and the international community's efforts to rebuild the historic city.

The refectory's entire far wall is frescoed with the impressive, 1,300-square-foot *Tree of the Cross and Last Supper*, by Taddeo Gaddi. A crucifix sprouts branches blossoming with medieval symbolism, which dining monks ate up. Francis kneels at the base of the cross and makes sympathetic eye contact with Jesus. In one of the scenes that flank the cross (upper left), Francis has a vision in which he receives the stigmata—the same wounds in his hands, feet, and side that Christ suffered when he was crucified. Beneath the Tree of the Cross is the Last Supper, a scene that gave the monastery's residents the illusion that they were eating in the symbolic company of Jesus and the apostles.

OLTRARNO WALK

From Ponte Vecchio to Porta San Frediano

Staying in the tourist zone leaves you with an incomplete impression of Florence. Most of its people live and work outside of the touristy center. The best place to get a sense of rustic, old Florence is in the Oltrarno neighborhood, south of the Arno River. While the essence of the Oltrarno is best enjoyed by simply wandering, this walk gives you a structure in which to cover its highlights. We'll start at Ponte Vecchio, walk to the Pitti Palace, explore some colorful (and slightly seedy) back streets, and end at the medieval wall. This walk is a helpful way to link the Pitti Palace, Santo Spirito Church, and Brancacci Chapel.

Orientation

Pitti Palace: Palatine Gallery, Royal Apartments, and Modern Art Gallery: €8.50, but often €12 with mandatory special exhibits; Tue–Sun 8:15–18:50, closed Mon. Argenti Museum, Costume Gallery, Porcelain Museum, and Boboli and Bardini Gardens: €6, more with special exhibits; daily 8:15–18:30, until 19:30 June–Aug, closed first and last Mon of the month. Tel. 055-238-8614, www.polomuseale.firenze.it.

Santo Spirito Church: Free, Mon–Tue and Thu–Sat 9:30–12:30 & 16:00–17:30, Sun 16:00–17:30 only, closed Wed, tel. 055-211-716.

Brancacci Chapel: €4, Mon and Wed–Sat 10:00–17:00, Sun 13:00–17:00, closed Tue, free reservations required and easy by phone, tel. 055-276-8224 or 055-276-8558.

Getting There: Start at Ponte Vecchio, which crosses the Arno River (a 10-minute walk south of the Duomo).

Length of This Tour: Allow two hours.

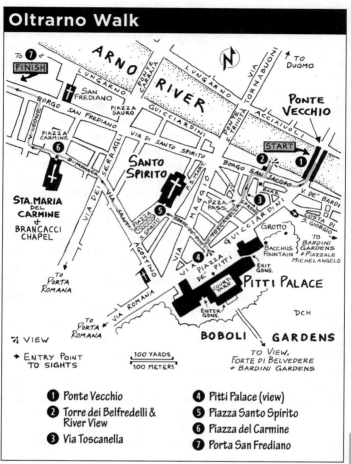

Oltrarno Walk

🥾 VIEW

→ ENTRY POINT
   TO SIGHTS

100 YARDS
100 METERS

❶ Ponte Vecchio

❷ Torre dei Belfredelli &
   River View

❸ Via Toscanella

❹ Pitti Palace (view)

❺ Piazza Santo Spirito

❻ Piazza del Carmine

❼ Porta San Frediano

Cuisine Art: You'll pass a number of recommended eateries, all described in "Dining in the Oltrarno" in the Eating in Florence chapter.

Starring: Views of the Arno, Florence's medieval past, present-day artisans at work, and few tourists.

The Tour Begins

What you'll see on this walk varies with the time of day. In the morning, shops and artisans dominate the scene. In the evening, cafés, restaurants, and strolling people—both locals and tourists—leave the strongest impression.

• *Start in the middle of Ponte Vecchio.*

Ponte Vecchio

The Arno River separates the city center from the Oltrarno—the neighborhood on the "other" (oltre) side of the river. The two sides have historically been connected by this oldest bridge—Ponte Vecchio—lined with its characteristic shops.

Florence was born on the north bank (founded by the Romans in the first century B.C.) and, ever since, the Oltrarno has been its poorer, working-class cousin. As the Oltrarno grew in medieval times, the wooden walls were replaced by stone, and two more bridges were added, connecting it with the city center. Looking upstream (east), you'll see the lone crenellated tower that marks the wall that once defined the medieval city. By Michelangelo's day, the Oltrarno had grown enough that this bridge was about midtown.

Look above to see the Vasari Corridor, the personal passage-way the Medici family built to give them a private commute from the Uffizi (center of city government) to the Pitti Palace, their palatial home (which we'll see a bit later). The corridor, built in five months in 1565, drilled straight through people's homes. The only detour is just to the right—notice how it curves around the tower at the end of the bridge. The family who lived there must have had clout. With Medici princes prancing back and forth in their corridor, the smell of the traditional shops had to go. That's when Ponte Vecchio's original merchants—butchers and fish mongers—were replaced by today's gold- and silversmiths.

Ponte Vecchio has seen a lot of turmoil. The plaque above the crowds on the uphill side honors Gerhard Wolf, a Nazi ambassador. In August 1944, as Hitler's occupying troops fled the city, they were ordered to destroy all of Florence's bridges to cover their retreat. Ponte Santa Trinità was demolished (rebuilt in 1958), and Ponte Vecchio was next in line. But thankfully, Wolf understood the bridge's historic value, and instead blew up buildings at each end of the bridge to render it impassable. Even more violent was the flood of 1966, which inundated the city, destroying still more bridges and sending entire trees like spears through buildings on Ponte Vecchio.

• *Cross the bridge, turn right on Borgo San Jacopo, and walk past ugly buildings from the 1950s and older structures that still bear the scars of WWII-era bombs. Stop at the tower on the first corner on the left.*

Torre dei Belfredelli and River View

The tower of the Belfredelli family is typical of countless towers that created Florence's 12th-century skyline. Across the street is the tower of the Barbadori family, another noble family. Just as the Montagues and Capulets feuded in nearby Verona, neighbors here also needed to fortify their mansions. Notice the high-water mark from the 1966 flood.

Step out to Hotel Lungarno's little riverside viewpoint for a good look at Ponte Vecchio. Envision a city turned inward, facing its main commercial artery, the river. Barges of goods from Pisa moored here through the ages (loaded with cargo, including marble for artists such as Michelangelo). Today's strict building codes leave the view essentially the same as you see in engravings from 1700.

• *Continue down Borgo San Jacopo to where the street narrows. In the 1950s, the former pedestrian promenade was widened to accommodate modern traffic. At the first corner (Via Toscanella), look above the street to find a little statue of a woman holding her nose—a garbage can used to be left there. Turn left on Via Toscanella and follow the lane away from the river, deeper into the Oltrarno.*

Via Toscanella

Now you'll find yourself on a quiet and characteristic lane typical of the Oltrarno. A high stone wall hides a private garden (common in this city). The street is named for the family of Paolo Toscanelli (1397–1482), the scientist who used Brunelleschi's dome as a giant sundial and convinced Columbus to reach the East by sailing west.

You'll pass many artisan shops on this street and neighboring streets. Their doors are open to welcome browsers. Be comfortable stepping in and enjoying the proud work of the artisan. It's polite to say *"Buon giorno"* and *"Ciao."* "Can I take a look?" is *"Posso guardare?"* (POH-soh gwahr-DAH-ray). Long a working-class neighborhood, the Oltrarno is where artisans still ply the traditional trades of their forebears. You'll find handmade furniture, jewelry, leather items, shoes, pottery, and picture frames in a centuries-old style. Craftsmen still bind books and make marbled paper. Antique pieces are refurbished by people who've become curators of the dying techniques of gilding, engraving, etching, enameling, mosaics, and repoussé metal work.

For a taste of the clothing styles of today's locals, look up and see the laundry. The classic little Café of the Artisans is a reminder of the earthy pride of this rustic district.

The little square ahead, formally Canto ai Quattro Pagoni, is nicknamed Piazza della Passera (a rude reference to its vaginal shape). The recommended Trattoria 4 Leoni dominates the square.

• *Continue to the end of Via Toscanella. Detour left to see the huge palace.*

Pitti Palace

The massive palace, with its rusticated stonework so pleasing to noble egos, sits conveniently in front of the quarry from where all that stone was cut. This behemoth shows the Renaissance esthetics of symmetry and mathematical order on a giant scale. In the 15th century, the Oltrarno became a fashionable spot for Florentine nobles to build palaces. Originally built for the Pitti family (15th century), the palace was later bought and enlarged by the Medici (16th century). In the 1860s, when Florence briefly ruled Italy as the interim capital, the palace was the "White House" for the ruling Savoy family. While stark on the outside, it was  much warmer on the inside and hides the lush Boboli Garden. It's been a museum since the early 1900s (see the ✪ Pitti Palace Tour chapter).

• *With your back to the Pitti Palace, head west down the street called Sdrucciolo de Pitti (enjoy wrapping your tongue around the word with its "sdr"), passing the Pitti Vintage clothes shop. You'll come to a big church facing a square.*

Piazza Santo Spirito

Piazza Santo Spirito, with its bald-faced church, is the community center, hosting a colorful produce market in the morning. Hat-

makers have long sold their wares in and around the square. Santo Spirito Church is worth a visit (see page 65) for its Brunelleschi-designed interior and crucifix by Michelangelo. As a teenager, Michelangelo was allowed to dissect bodies from the adjacent monastic mortuary in order to learn the secrets of anatomy—something he considered key to portraying bodies accurately. As thanks, he made the crucifix.

The church's blank facade prompted the neighborhood to have a contest to design a fun finish: The nearby Ricchi Caffè displays the hundred or so entries on its walls. Choose your favorite while enjoying an ice cream or drink. While the square is pleasant in the mornings, later in the day addicts and winos move in. Steer clear of any seedy characters camping out near the fountain.

OLTRARNO WALK

• *From the end of the square (opposite the church), turn right on Via Sant'Agostino. Stroll westward for 5 or 10 minutes, enjoying more people-watching and small antique and fashion shops, until you reach a big square.*

Piazza del Carmine

Piazza del Carmine (the ugliest square in Florence) hosts the Church of Santa Maria del Carmine, with its famous Brancacci Chapel and Masaccio frescoes—some of the most exquisite art in Florence (see the ✪ Brancacci Chapel Tour chapter). Just a few years ago, most of Europe's main squares were parking lots just like this. Now this square is an exception.

It's clear that the Oltrarno has some rough edges. It's an area in transition. Demographically, the Oltrano is an interesting melting pot of traditional craftspeople, immigrants, retired people, and yuppies.

• *Continue straight across the square one block to Via del Leone. (Note: Elettrico minibus D goes from Piazza del Carmine to the train station, and the recommended Ristorante Enoteca la Barrique is to the left on Via del Leone.) Turn right on Via del Leone, then left on the big, noisy, and frightening Borgo San Frediano.*

The pedestrian-unfriendly Borgo San Frediano leads to the town gate, in the distance, where this walk ends. Stay on the narrow sidewalks. If a pedestrian strays into the road and is hit, as far as local insurance is concerned...she's jaywalking and it's her fault. Also remember that motorbike thieves love to swipe purses that dangle on the roadside.

Porta San Frediano

As you walk along Borgo San Frediano, look for little architectural details. Tiny shrines protect the corners of many blocks. Once upon a time, the iron spikes on the walls impaled huge candles, which provided a little light. Electricity changed all that. And today most wires are under the streets.

Borgo San Frediano is lined with apartment buildings punctuated by the occasional palazzo. The skyline and architecture are typical of the 13th to 16th centuries. Huge palazzi (recognized by their immense doors, lush courtyards, and grand stonework) were for big-shot merchants. Some have small wooden service doors disguised to look like stones. While originally for one family, these buildings are now subdivided, as evidenced by the banks of doorbells at the door. At #127, pop in to the classic butcher shop.

Porta San Frediano (c. 1333) is one of the gates in Florence's medieval wall, which stretches impressively from here to the river. This gate straddled the road to Pisa. In medieval times, a three-quarter-mile-wide strip outside the wall was cleared to deny attackers any cover. The tower was originally twice as high, built when gravity ruled warfare. During the Renaissance, when gunpowder became the weapon of choice, the tower—now just an easy target—was lopped. Florence's symbol, the lily (fleur-de-lis), decorates the top of the tower. The 40-foot doors weigh 16 tons each, and are studded with fat iron nails to withstand battering rams. Take a close look at the hardware. Touch it. Clang a ring.

• *This tour is over. The colorful Trattoria Sabatino is just outside the wall, and you passed several recommended eateries along the way. Ciao.*

BRANCACCI CHAPEL TOUR

Cappella Brancacci

In the Brancacci (bran-KAH-chee) Chapel, Masaccio created a world in paint that looked like the world we inhabit. For the first time in a thousand years, Man and Nature were frozen for inspection. Masaccio's painting techniques were copied by many Renaissance artists, and his people—sturdy, intelligent, and dignified, with an expression of understated astonishment—helped shape Renaissance men and women's own self-images.

Orientation

Cost: €4, or €8 combo-ticket with Palazzo Vecchio.

Dress Code: Shorts and bare shoulders are OK in the chapel, but modest dress is requested when visiting the rest of the church.

Reservations: Call the chapel for free, mandatory reservations, often available for the same day. But for weekends and peak months (April–June), reserve at least one day ahead (tel. 055-276-8224 or 055-276-8558, English spoken, line is frequently busy, but keep trying—it's best to call around 14:00–15:00 Italian time). When you call to reserve, you can also book a time to see the film (see "Film," next page). Reservation times for the chapel begin every 15 minutes, with a maximum of 30 visitors per time slot. You have 15 minutes in the chapel itself.

Hours: Mon and Wed–Sat 10:00–17:00, Sun 13:00–17:00, closed Tue, ticket office closes at 16:30. The chapel is accessible only through the paid entrance to the right of the church.

Getting There: The Brancacci Chapel is in the Church of Santa Maria del Carmine, on Piazza del Carmine, in the Oltrarno neighborhood south of the Arno River. It's about a 20-minute walk or short taxi ride (about €11) from downtown Florence.

From Ponte Vecchio cross to the Oltrarno side, turn right on Borgo San Jacopo, walk 10 minutes, then turn left at Piazza del Carmine.

Film: Your ticket includes a 40-minute film in English on the church, the frescoes, and Renaissance Florence (reserve a viewing time when you book your entry). The film starts promptly at the top of the hour. Computer animation brings the paintings to life—making them appear to move and giving them 3-D depth—while narration describes the events depicted in the panels. Yes, it's a long time commitment, and the film takes liberties with the art. But it's visually interesting and your best way to see the frescoes close up. The film works great either before or after you visit the frescoes.

Length of This Tour: Allow 30 minutes (plus 40 minutes if you see the film).

Photography: Allowed without a flash.

Starring: Masaccio, Masolino, and Filippino Lippi.

The Tour Begins

Overview

The chapel has frescoes that tell the story of Peter—half are by Masaccio and half by either Masolino or Filippino Lippi (the son of Filippo Lippi). Although Masaccio is the star, the panels by his colleagues are interesting and provide a good contrast in styles. Masaccio's works are sprinkled among the others, mostly on the left and center walls.

The panels are displayed roughly in the order they were painted, from upper left to lower right—the upper six by Masaccio and Masolino (1424–1425), the lower ones by Masaccio (1426–1427) and Filippino Lippi (1481–1485).

• *Start with the left wall, the small panel in the upper left.*

Masaccio—*Adam and Eve Banished from Eden*

Renaissance man and woman—as nude as they can be—turn their backs on the skinny, unrealistic, medieval Gate of Paradise and take their first step as mortal humans in the real world. For the first time in a thousand years of painting, these figures cast a realistic shadow, seemingly lit by the same light we are—the natural light through the Brancacci Chapel's window.

Eve wails from deep within. (The first time I saw her, I thought

Brancacci Chapel

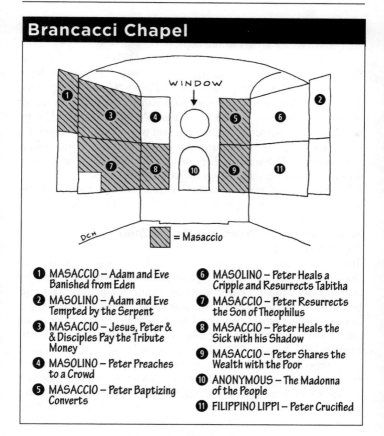

WINDOW

DCM ▨ = Masaccio

❶ MASACCIO – Adam and Eve Banished from Eden

❷ MASOLINO – Adam and Eve Tempted by the Serpent

❸ MASACCIO – Jesus, Peter & & Disciples Pay the Tribute Money

❹ MASOLINO – Peter Preaches to a Crowd

❺ MASACCIO – Peter Baptizing Converts

❻ MASOLINO – Peter Heals a Cripple and Resurrects Tabitha

❼ MASACCIO – Peter Resurrects the Son of Theophilus

❽ MASACCIO – Peter Heals the Sick with his Shadow

❾ MASACCIO – Peter Shares the Wealth with the Poor

❿ ANONYMOUS – The Madonna of the People

⓫ FILIPPINO LIPPI – Peter Crucified

Eve's gaping mouth was way over the top, until I saw the very same expression on someone dealing with a brother's death.) Adam buries his face in shame. These simple human gestures speak louder than the religious symbols of medieval art.

• *Compare Masaccio's* Adam and Eve *with the one on the opposite wall, by his colleague Masolino.*

Masolino—*Adam and Eve Tempted by the Serpent*

Masolino's elegant, innocent First Couple float in an ethereal Garden of Eden with no clear foreground or background (Eve hugs a tree or she'd float away). Their bodies are lit evenly by a pristine, all-encompassing, morning-in-springtime light

that casts no shadows. Satan and Eve share the same face—a motif later Renaissance artists would copy.

In 1424, Masolino da Panicale (1383–1435) was hired by the Brancacci family to decorate this chapel with the story of Peter (beginning with the Original Sin that Peter's "Good News" saves man from). Masolino, a 40-year-old contractor with too many other commitments, invited 23-year-old Masaccio (1401–1428) to help him. The two set up scaffolding and worked side by side—the older, workmanlike master and the young, intuitive genius—in a harmonious collaboration. They just divvied up the panels, never (or rarely) working together on the same scene.

• *Return to the left wall, upper level. From here, we'll work clockwise around the chapel. After* Adam and Eve, *the second panel is...*

Masaccio—*Jesus, Peter, and the Disciples Pay the Tribute Money*

The tax collector (in red miniskirt, with his back to us) tells Jesus that he must pay a temple tax. Jesus gestures to say, "OK, but the money's over there." Peter, his right-hand man (gray hair and beard, brown robe), says, "Yeah, over there." Peter goes over there to the lake (left side of panel), takes off his robe, stoops down at an odd angle, and miraculously pulls a coin from the mouth of a fish. He puts his robe back on (right side of panel) and pays the man.

Some consider this the first modern painting, placing real humans in a real setting, seen from a single viewpoint—ours. Earlier painters had done far more detailed landscapes than Masaccio's sketchy mountains, lake, trees, clouds, and buildings, but they never fixed where the viewer was in relation to these things.

Masaccio tells us exactly where we stand—near the crowd, farther from the trees, with the sun to our right casting late-afternoon shadows. We're no longer detached spectators, but an extension of the scene. Masaccio lets us stand in the presence of the human Jesus. While a good attempt at three-dimensionality, Masaccio's work is far from perfect. Later artists would perfect mathematically what Masaccio eyeballed intuitively.

The disciples all have strong, broad-shouldered bodies, but each face is unique. Blond, curly-haired, clean-shaven John is as handsome as the head on a Roman coin (Masaccio had just returned from Rome). Thomas (far right, with a five-o'clock shadow) is intense. Their different reactions—with faces half in shadow, half in light—tell us that they're divided over paying the tax.

Masaccio's people have one thing in common—a faraway look in the eye, as though hit with a spiritual two-by-four. They're deep in thought, reflective, and awestruck, aware they've just experienced something miraculous. But they're also dazzled, glazed over, and a bit disoriented, like tourists at the Brancacci Chapel.

• *Continuing clockwise, we move to the next panel, on the center wall.*

Masolino—*Peter Preaches to a Crowd*

Masolino and Masaccio were different in so many ways, but they were both fans of Giotto (c. 1266–1337), who told stories with simple gestures and minimal acting, adding the human drama by

showing the reaction of bystanders. Here, the miraculous power of the sermon is not evident in Peter (who just raises his hand) but in the faces of the crowd. The lady in the front row is riveted, while others close their eyes to meditate. The big nun (far right) is skeptical, but wants to hear more. The tonsured monk's mouth slips open in awe, while the gentleman to the left finds it interesting enough to come a little closer.

Masolino never mastered 3-D space like Masaccio. Peter's extreme profile is a cardboard cutout, his left leg stands too high to plant him realistically on flat ground, the people in the back have their gazes fixed somewhere above Peter, and the "Masacciesque" mountains in the background remain just that, background.

• *Continuing clockwise to the other side of the window, come to…*

Masaccio—*Peter Baptizing Converts*

A muscular man kneels in the stream to join the cult of Jesus. On

the bank (far right), another young man waits his turn, shivering in his jockstrap. Among the crowd, a just-baptized man wrestles with his robe, while the man in blue, his hair still dripping, buttons up.

The body language is eloquent: The strongman's humility, the shivering youth's uncertainty, and the bowed heads of the just-baptized communicate their reflection on the life-altering choice they've just made.

Masaccio builds these bodies with patches of color (an especially effective technique in fresco, where colors can bleed together). He knew that a kneeling man's body, when lit from the left (the direction of the chapel window), would look like a patchwork of bright hills (his pecs) and dark crevasses (his sternum). He assembles the pieces into a sculptural, 3-D figure, "modeled" by light and shade.

Again, Masaccio was the first artist to paint real humans—with 3-D bodies and individual faces, reflecting inner emotions—in a real-world setting.

• *Continue clockwise to the right wall.*

Masolino—*Peter Heals a Cripple* (left side) and *Resurrects Tabitha* (right side)

Masolino takes a crack at the 3-D style of his young partner, setting two separate stories in a single Florentine square, defined by an arcade on the left and a porch on the right. Crude elements of the future Renaissance style abound: The receding buildings establish the viewer's point of reference; the rocks scattered through the square define 3-D space; there are secular details in the background (mother and child, laundry on a balcony, a monkey on a ledge); and the cripple (left) is shown at an odd angle (foreshortening). Masaccio may have helped on this panel.

But the stars of the work are the two sharply dressed gentlemen strolling across the square, who help to divide (and unite) the two stories of Peter. The patterned coat is a textbook example of the International Gothic style that was the rage in Florence—elegant, refined, graceful, with curvy lines creating a complex, pleasing pattern. The man walking is at a three-quarters angle, but Masolino shows the coat from the front to catch the full display. The picture is evenly lit, with only a hint of shadow, accentuating the colorful clothes and cheerful atmosphere.

In mid-project (1426), Masolino took another job in Hungary, leaving Masaccio to finish the lower half of the chapel. Masolino never again explored the Renaissance style, building a successful career with the eternal springtime of International Gothic.

• *Move to the lower level. Start on the left wall with the second panel and work clockwise.*

Masaccio—*Peter Resurrects the Son of Theophilus*

Peter (in that same brown robe...like Masaccio, who was careless about his appearance) raises the boy from the world of bones, winning his freedom from stern Theophilus (seated in a niche to the left).

The courtyard setting is fully 3-D, Masaccio having recently learned a bit of perspective mathematics from his (older) friends

Brunelleschi and Donatello. At the far right of the painting are three of the Quattrocento (1400s) giants who invented painting perspective (from right to left): Brunelleschi, who broke down reality mathematically; Alberti, who popularized the math with his book, *On Painting;* and Masaccio himself (looking out at us), who opened everyone's eyes to the psychologically powerful possibilities.

Little is known of Masaccio's short life. "Masaccio" is a nickname (often translated as "Lumbering Antonio") describing his

personality—stumbling through life with careless abandon, not worrying about money, clothes, or fame...a lovable doofus.

Next to Masaccio's self-portrait is a painting within a painting of Peter on a throne. On a flat surface with a blank background, Masaccio has created a hovering hologram, a human more 3-D than even a statue made in medieval times.

"Wow," said Brother Philip, a 20-year-old Carmelite monk stationed here when Masaccio painted this. Fra Filippo ("Brother Philip") Lippi was inspired by these frescoes and went on to become a famous painter himself. At age 50, while painting in a convent, he fell in love with a young nun, and they eloped. Nine months later, "Little Philip" was born, and he too grew to be a famous painter—Filippino Lippi, who in 1481 was chosen to complete the Brancacci Chapel.

Filippino Lippi painted substantial portions of this fresco, including the group in the far left (five heads but only eight legs).
• *Moving clockwise to the center wall, find...*

Masaccio—*Peter Heals the Sick with his Shadow*
Peter is a powerful Donatello statue come to life, walking toward us along a Florentine street. Next to him, in the red cap, is bearded Donatello, Masaccio's friend and mentor.

Masaccio inspired more than painters. He gave ordinary people a new self-image of what it is to be human. Masaccio's people are individuals, not generic Greek gods, not always pretty (like the old bald guy) but still robust and handsome in their own way. They exude a seriousness that makes them very adult. Compare these street people with Masolino's two well-dressed dandies, and you see the difference between Florence's working-class, urban, "democratic" spirit (Guelphs) and the courtly grace of Europe's landed gentry (Ghibellines).

• *The next panel, on the other side of the altar, is...*

Masaccio—*Peter Shares the Wealth with the Poor*

Early Christians practiced a form of communal sharing. The wealthy Ananias lies about his contribution, and he drops dead

at Peter's feet. Peter takes the missing share and gives it to a poor lady who can't even afford baby pants. The shy baby, the grateful woman, and the admiring man on crutches show Masaccio's blue-collar sympathies.

The scene reflects an actual event in Florence—a tax-reform measure to make things equal for everyone. Florentines were championing a new form of government where, if we all contribute our fair share through taxes, we don't need kings and nobles.

• *The altar under the window holds a painting that is not by Masaccio, Masolino, or Lippi.*

Anonymous (possibly Coppo di Marcovaldo)— *The Madonna of the People*

This medieval altarpiece replaces the now-destroyed fresco by Masaccio that was the centerpiece of the whole design—Peter's crucifixion.

With several panels still unfinished, Masaccio traveled to Rome to meet up with Masolino. Masaccio died there (possibly poisoned) in 1428, at age 27. After his death, the political and artistic climate changed, the chapel was left unfinished (the lower right wall), and some of his frescoes were scraped off whole (his *Crucifixion of Peter*) or in part (in *Peter Resurrects the Son of Theophilus,* several exiled Brancaccis were erased from history, later to be replaced).

Finally, in 1481, new funding arrived and Filippino Lippi, the son of the monk-turned-painter, was hired to complete the blank panels and retouch some destroyed frescoes.

• *The right wall, lower section, contains two panels by Filippino Lippi. The first and biggest is...*

Filippino Lippi—*Peter Crucified*

Lippi completes the story of Peter with his upside-down cruci-fixion. Lippi tried to match the solemn style of Masaccio, but the compositions are busier, and his figures are less statuesque, and more colorful and detailed. Still, compared with Lippi's other, more hyperactive works found elsewhere, he's reined himself in admirably to honor the great pioneer.

In fact, while Masaccio's perspective tech-niques were enormously influential, learned by every Tuscan artist, his sober style was not terribly popular. Another strain of Tuscan painting diverged from Masaccio. From Fra Filippo Lippi to Botticelli, Ghir-landaio, and Filippino Lippi, artists mixed in the bright colors, line patterns, and even lighting of International Gothic. But Masaccio's legacy remained strong, emerg-ing in the grave, statuesque, harsh-shadow creations of two Florentine giants—Leon-ardo da Vinci and Michelangelo.

PITTI PALACE TOUR

Palazzo Pitti, Galleria Palatina

The Pitti Palace offers many reasons for a visit: the palace itself, with its imposing exterior and lavish interior; the second-best collection of paintings in town; the statue-dotted Boboli Gardens; and a host of secondary museums. However, seeing it all is impossible, and choosing where to spend your time can be confusing. I recommend sticking to the Palatine Gallery, which has the painting collection, plus the sumptuous rooms of the Royal Apartments. The paintings pick up where the Uffizi leaves off, at the High Renaissance. Lovers of Raphael's Madonnas and Titian's portraits will find some of the world's best at the Pitti Palace.

Orientation

Cost: Ticket #1 (the tour described in this chapter) costs €8.50, but mandatory special exhibitions often raise the price to €12. This ticket covers the recommended Palatine Gallery, Royal Apartments, and Modern Art Gallery.

Ticket #2 is €6, but can cost more with mandatory special exhibitions. This ticket covers the Boboli and Bardini Gardens, Argenti Museum (the Duke's treasures), Costume Gallery, and Porcelain Museum. To see everything, you have to buy both tickets. And if you want to see only one sight, you still need to buy one of the combo-tickets (individual tickets aren't sold for specific sights).

Hours: Palatine Gallery, Royal Apartments, and Modern Art Gallery Tue–Sun 8:15–18:50, closed Mon; Argenti Museum, Boboli and Bardini Gardens, Costume Gallery, and Porcelain Museum daily 8:15–18:30, until 19:30 June–Aug, gardens close as early as 16:30 in winter, last entry 30–60 min before closing, closed first and last Mon of the month.

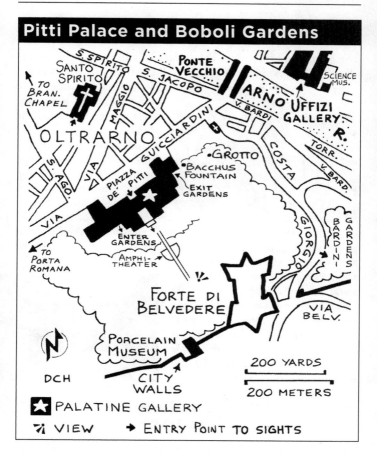

Pitti Palace and Boboli Gardens

Reservations: Not necessary. If there's a long line, bypass it by making a reservation at the ticket window (€3 reservation fee) for immediate entry.

Getting There: The Pitti Palace is located several blocks southwest of Ponte Vecchio, in the Oltrarno neighborhood.

Information: Tel. 055-238-8614, www.polomuseale.firenze.it. Each room has some descriptions in English, though the paintings themselves have limited English labels.

Length of This Tour: Allow one hour for the Palatine Gallery and Royal Apartments.

Cuisine Art: Across the plaza is a cozy wine-by-the-glass bar, Pitti Gola e Cantina, that also serves a few €10 antipasti plates and salads (Piazza Pitti 16, tel. 055-212-704).

Photography: No photos in the Palatine Gallery.

Starring: Raphael, Titian, and the most ornate palace you can tour in Florence.

The Tour Begins

The plain and brutal Pitti Palace facade is like other hide-your-wealth palace exteriors in Florence. The Pitti family (rivals of the

Medici) began building it in 1458 but ran out of money. It sat unfinished until the Medicis bought it, expanded it, and moved in during the mid-1500s, choosing to keep the name. It's an imposing facade—more than two football fields long, made of heavy blocks of unpolished stone, and set on a hill. For nearly two centuries (1549–1737), this palace was arguably Europe's cultural center, setting trends in the arts, sciences, and social mores.

• *Enter the palace (passing through the metal detector) into the courtyard. The Palatine Gallery entrance is to your right, the Boboli Gardens entrance is straight ahead, and the Argenti Museum is to the left. Climb the stairs to the Palatine Gallery (Galleria Palatina), housed in the Royal Apartments.*

Palatine Gallery and Royal Apartments

The collection is all on one floor. To see the highlights, walk straight down the spine through a dozen or so rooms. (Avoid the rooms that branch off to the side.) At the far end, make a U-turn left and double back. After the Galleria Palatina, the route flows naturally into the even-more-lavish rooms of the Royal Apartments.

You'll walk through one palatial room after another, with frescoed ceilings that celebrate the Medici family and give the room its name (the Venus Room, Apollo Room, and so on). The walls sag with floor-to-ceiling paintings in gilded frames, stacked three and four high, different artists and time periods all jumbled together. It's difficult to pick out the masterpieces from the minor pieces, so focus on my recommended highlights first, then let yourself browse.

• *Enter Room 1 of the Palatine Gallery. (If there's a temporary exhibit, your visit may begin in the large white ballroom, which then leads into Room 1.)*

Pitti Palace—Palatine Gallery

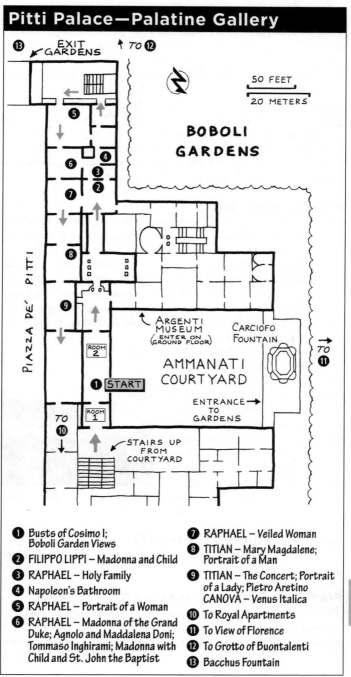

1 Busts of Cosimo I; Boboli Garden Views

2 FILIPPO LIPPI – Madonna and Child

3 RAPHAEL – Holy Family

4 Napoleon's Bathroom

5 RAPHAEL – Portrait of a Woman

6 RAPHAEL – Madonna of the Grand Duke; Agnolo and Maddalena Doni; Tommaso Inghirami; Madonna with Child and St. John the Baptist

7 RAPHAEL – Veiled Woman

8 TITIAN – Mary Magdalene; Portrait of a Man

9 TITIAN – The Concert; Portrait of a Lady; Pietro Aretino CANOVA – Venus Italica

10 To Royal Apartments

11 To View of Florence

12 To Grotto of Buontalenti

13 Bacchus Fountain

Rooms 1 and 2
Two Bronze Busts of Cosimo I

Thank Cosimo I Medici (1519–1574, with beard and crown) for this palace. Cosimo I (not to be confused with Cosimo the Elder, the 15th-century founder of the Medici clan) was the first Grand Duke and the man who revived the Medici family's dominance a generation after the death of Lorenzo the Magnificent. Cosimo's wife, Eleanor, bought the palace from the Pittis and convinced Cosimo and their 11 children to move there from their home in the Palazzo Vecchio. They used their wealth to expand the Pitti, building the gardens and amassing the rich painting collection. This would be the Medici family home for the next 200 years.

Boboli Garden Views

Dotted with statues and fountains, the gardens seem to stretch forever. The courtyard below (by Ammanati) is surrounded by the palace on three sides; the fourth side opens up theatrically onto the gardens, which rise in terraces up the hillside. Cosimo and his descendants could look out their windows at eye level onto the garden's amphitheater, ringed with seats around an obelisk that once stood in the Temple of Ramses II in Egypt. At this amphitheater the Medici enjoyed plays and spectacles, including perhaps the first opera, *Euridice* (1600).

From the amphitheater, the central axis of the Boboli Gardens stairsteps up to the top of the hill (where there are great views of Florence and beyond). The gardens' expansive sightlines, sculpted foliage, geometric patterns, Greek statues, and bubbling fountains would serve as the model a century later for the gardens at Versailles.

• *Continue straight ahead through a handful of rooms until you reach #17, a room virtually wallpapered with paintings.*

Sala di Prometeo (Room 17)

Inside this room, look for the fireplace topped with a round-framed painting.

Fra Filippo Lippi—*Madonna and Child* (c. 1452)

This pure, radiant Virgin cradles a playful Jesus eating a pomegranate. Lippi's work combines medieval piety with new Renaissance techniques. It may be Florence's first *tondo* (circular artwork), an innovative format that soon became a Renaissance staple. Seed-eating Jesus adds a human touch, but the pomegranate was also a medieval symbol for new life and the Resurrection. In medieval style, the background relates episodes from different places and times, including Mary's birth to Anne (in bed, at left) and the meeting of Mary's parents (distant background, right). But these stories are set in rooms that are textbook Renaissance 3-D, with floor tiles and ceiling coffers that create the illusion of depth. The ladies bringing gifts to celebrate Mary's birth add another element of everyday Renaissance realism.

Compare Lippi's Madonna with two by Lippi's star pupil, **Botticelli** (one on the left wall, one on the right, both hung high). Botticelli borrowed much from Lippi, including the same facial features, pale skin, precise lines, and everyday details.

• *The next room (on the other side of the fireplace) is the...*

Sala di Ulisse (Room 22)

This was the Grand Duke's bedroom. One of Cosimo's favorite paintings hangs above the fireplace.

Raphael (Raffaello Sanzio)—*Holy Family (Sacra Famiglia,* a.k.a. *Madonna dell'Impannata,* 1512–1514)

This work introduces us to the range of this great artist. There's the creamy, rosy beauty of the Virgin alongside the gritty wrinkles

of St. Anne/Elizabeth. At first glance, it seems like a stately scene, until you notice that Jesus is getting tickled. Everyone is in motion— gazes pointed in all different directions—but they're also posed in a harmonious pyramid with Jesus' crotch at the center. Little John the Baptist

sticks a foot in our face and points to Jesus as The One. Also typical of the always-busy Raphael: The work was probably completed by some of his 50-plus assistants.

• *The next small room you pass by is known as...*

Raphael
(1483–1520)

Raffaello Sanzio (like most Renaissance greats, known by a single name—Raphael) is considered the culmination of the High Renaissance. (Note that the museum uses his Italian name Raffaello, or Raffaello Sanzio.) He combined symmetry, grace, beauty, and emotion. With his debonair personality and lavish lifestyle, Raphael also epitomized the worldly spirit of the Renaissance.

Born in the sophisticated city of Urbino, the son of the court painter, he was raised among the dukes and duchesses who taught the rest of Europe the fine art of living. He spent his early twenties in Florence, soaking up the style of Leonardo da Vinci's graceful Madonnas. By 1508 he was in Rome, learning from the larger-than-life scale and dramatic motion of Michelangelo's Sistine ceiling.

Raphael lived a charmed life. Handsome and sophisticated, he quickly became a celebrity in the Medici family's high-living circle of bankers, princes, and popes. He painted masterpieces by day and partied by night. Both in his life and art, he exuded what his contemporaries called *sprezzatura*—an effortless, unpretentious elegance. In a different decade, he might have been thrown out of the Church as a great sinner, but his love affairs and devil-may-care personality were perfectly in keeping with the optimism of the times.

Raphael employed a wide range of styles and techniques, but there are some recurring elements. His paintings are bathed in an even light, with few shadows. His brushwork is smooth and

Napoleon's Bathroom (Sala da Bagno)

The white-marble luxury and sarcophagus-shaped bathtub were intended for the great French conqueror, Napoleon Bonaparte, when he ruled Florence (1799–1814). Napoleon installed his little sister Elisa as Grand Duchess, and she spent her years here redecorating the palace awaiting her brother's return. But Napoleon was not destined to meet this water loo. After he was toppled from power, the palace returned to its previous owners.

Over the centuries, the palace hosted several rulers: 200 years of Medicis (c. 1549–1737); 100 years of Austrians (the Habsburg-Lorraines, 1737–1860); a decade of Napoleon (1799–1814); and 60 years under the Savoy, Italy's first royal family (1860–1919), who made the Pitti their "White House" when Florence was briefly the capital of modern Italy.

• Pass through the final rooms and exit out the far end into the stairwell. Ahhh. Admire the views of the Duomo, Palazzo Vecchio, and green hills of Fiesole in the distance. The Medici could commute from here to blended, and colors are restrained. Works from the Florence years (1504–1508) show Leonardo's influence: Mona Lisa poses, *sfumato* brushwork (vague outlines), and lots of sweet Madonnas and Holy Families in a pyramid format. On the other hand, Raphael's portraits are never saccharin. The poses are natural, and individual quirks are never glossed over. He captures the personality without a hint of caricature.

In his later years, Raphael experimented with more complex compositions and stronger emotions. In group scenes, Raphael wants you to follow his subjects' gazes as they exchange glances or look off in different directions. This adds a sense of motion and psychological tension to otherwise well-balanced scenes. Raphael's compositions always have a strong geometric template. Figures are arranged into a pyramid or a circle. Human bodies are composed of oval faces, cylindrical arms, and arched shoulders. Subconsciously, this creates the feeling that God's created world is geometrically perfect. But Raphael always lets a bit of messy reality spill over the lines so his scenes don't appear static. His work comes across as simple and unforced... *sprezzatura*.

When Raphael died in 1520, he was one of Europe's most celebrated painters (along with Michelangelo and Titian). His style went out of fashion with the twisted forms of Mannerism and over-the-top drama of Baroque. The 1700s saw a revival, and today's museums are stuffed with sappy Madonnas by Raphael's many imitators. It's easy to dismiss his work and lump him in with his wannabes. Don't. This is the real deal.

---

downtown Florence by way of a private, covered passageway (Vasari Corridor) that goes from the Pitti Palace and across Ponte Vecchio to Palazzo Vecchio. If you look down into the Boboli Gardens, you can see the melted-frosting entrance to the Buontalenti Grotto.

Double back through the second half of the collection. The first room you enter is the...

Sala d'Iliade (Room 27)

This is the first of several former state rooms, used for grand public receptions. For centuries, Europe's nobles, ladies, and statesmen passed through these rooms as they visited the Medicis. They wrote home with wonder about the ceiling frescoes and masterpiece-covered walls. The ceiling frescoes depict the Greek gods cavorting with Medici princes, developing the idea of rule by divine right—themes that decades later would influence the decoration of Versailles. Turn your attention to the painting by the entrance door.

Raphael—*Portrait of a Woman*
(*Ritratto di Donna*, a.k.a. *La Gravida*, 1505–1506)

This rather plain-looking woman has one hand on her stomach and a serious expression on her face. She's pregnant. Though she

is no Madonna, and her eyes don't sparkle, the woman has presence. Raphael's sober realism cuts through the saccharin excesses of the surrounding paintings.

As one of Raphael's earliest portraits, from his time in Florence, it shows the influence of Leonardo da Vinci. Like Mona Lisa, she's a human pyramid turned at a three-quarters angle, supporting her arm on an armrest that's almost at the level of the frame itself. It's as if she's sitting near the edge of an open window, looking out at us.

• *Enter the next room.*

Sala di Saturno (Room 28)

This room boasts the second-biggest Raphael collection in the world—the Vatican beats it by one. A half-dozen Raphael paintings ring the room at eye level, ranging from dreamy soft-focus Madonnas to down-to-earth, five-o'clock-shadow portraits.

Raphael—*Madonna of the Grand Duke*
(*Madonna del Granduca*, 1505)

Raphael presents Mary in an unusually simple pose—standing, cradling baby Jesus under his bum. With no background, the

whole focus is on Mother, lost in thought, and Child, looking right at us. Mary's dreamy face and Jesus' golden body seem to emerge from the shadows. Try as you might, you can't quite discern the outlines of the figures, as they blend seamlessly into the dark background (Leonardo's *sfumato* technique).

The apparently simple pose is actually a skillful, geometric composition. Mary's head and flowing mantle form a triangle. The triangle's base is, first, the neckline of her dress, then her belt, then the horizontal line formed by her arm and Jesus' thighs. The geometric symmetry is livened by an off-kilter touch of reality: Mary's head tilts ever-so-slightly to the side.

This Madonna radiates tenderness and holiness, the divine embodied in human form. The iconic face, the pale colors, the simple pose, the geometric perfection—all are classic Raphael.

Raphael—*Portrait of Tommaso Inghirami* (c. 1510)

Wearing his bright red Cardinal's suit, Tommaso was the friend and librarian of the Medici pope, Leo X. Raphael captures him during an unposed moment, as he pauses to think while writing. Without glossing over anything, Raphael shows us the man just as he was, complete with cleft chin, jowls, lazy eye, and all.

Raphael—Two Companion Portraits (Ritratto) of Agnolo and Maddalena Doni (c. 1505–1506)

These portraits are as crystal clear as the *Madonna del Granduca* is hazy. They're a straightforward look at an upwardly mobile Florentine couple. He was a successful businessman in the textile trade (who commissioned Michelangelo's *Holy Family* in the Uffizi), and she was the daughter of one of the city's richest families. Raphael places them right at the edge of the picture plane, showing off his fine clothes and her jewelry.

Raphael—*Madonna with Child and St. John the Baptist* (*Madonna dell' Seggiola*, c. 1514–1516)

This colorful, round-framed painting (also known as the Madonna of the Chair) is one of Raphael's best-known and most-copied works. Mary hugs baby Jesus, squeezing him along with little John the Baptist. This Mary is no distant Madonna; she wears a peasant's scarf and a colorful dress and looks directly out at us with a cheerful half-smile. The composition plays on the theme of circles and spheres. The whole canvas is patterned after round sculpture-relief tondi. Mary's halo is a circle, her scarf forms a half-circle, and her face is an oval. Mother and child fit together like interlocking half-circles. As in a cameo, the figures seem to bulge out from the surface, suggesting roundness. Bathed in a golden glow, Mary enfolds her child into the safe circle of motherly love.

• *Head into the next room.*

Sala di Giove (Room 29)

Here in the throne room, the Grand Duke once saw visitors beneath a ceiling fresco showing Jupiter receiving legendary guests.

Raphael—*Veiled Woman* (*La Velata*, 1514–1515)

The dark-haired beauty's dark eyes stare intently at the viewer. The elaborate folds of her shiny silk dress contrast with her creamy complexion. It's a study in varying shades of white and brown, bathed in a diffuse golden glow. A geometric perfection underlies this woman's soft, flesh-and-blood beauty: her ovoid face, almond eyes, arch-shaped eyebrows, and circular necklace are all framed by a triangular veil. She is the very picture of perfection...except for that single wisp of loose hair that gives her the added charm of human imperfection.

Who is she? She may be the same woman Raphael depicted topless for a painting in Rome and as a Virgin (in Dresden). The biographer Vasari claims (and scholars debate) that La Velata is Raphael's beloved girlfriend Margherita Luti, known to history as La Fornarina, or the baker's daughter. Raphael became so obsessed with her that he had to have her near him to work. Vasari says that Raphael's sudden and premature death at age 37 came after a night of wild sex with her. Whoever La Velata is, she's one of the beauties of Western art.

• *Pass through the Sala di Marte (which may be closed for restoration in 2010) and into the Sala di Apollo. Two paintings by Titian (or Tiziano Vecellio) flank the entrance door.*

Sala di Apollo (Room 31)
Titian—*Mary Magdalene* (*La Maddalena*, c. 1530–1535)

According to medieval lore (but not the Bible), Mary Magdalene was a prostitute who repented when she heard the message of

Jesus. Titian captures her right on the cusp between whore and saint. She's naked, though covered by her hair, which she pulls around her like a cloak as she gazes heavenward, lips parted. Her hair is a rainbow of red, gold, and brown, and her ample flesh radiates gold. The rippling locks (echoed by gathering clouds in the background) suggest the inner turmoil and spiritual awakening of this passionate soul.

Among the upper classes in

Renaissance times, Mary Magdalene was a symbol of how sensual enjoyment (food, money, sex) could be a way of celebrating God's creation. The way this Mary Magdalene places her hand to her breast and gathers her hair around her is also the classic "Venus Pudica" pose of many ancient Greek statues. It's simultaneously a gesture of modesty and a way of drawing attention to her voluptuous nudity.

Titian—*Portrait of a Man* (*Ritratto Virile*, c. 1545)

This unknown subject has so mesmerized viewers that his portrait has become known by various monikers, including *The Young Englishman, The Gray-Eyed Nobleman*, and *Doctor McDreamy's Evil Twin*. The man is dressed in dark clothes and set against a dim background, so we only really see his face and hands, set off by a ruffled collar and sleeves. He nonchalantly places his hand on his hip while holding a glove, and stares out. The man is unforgettable, with a larger-than-life torso and those piercing blue-gray eyes that gaze right at us with extreme intensity. Scholars have speculated that the man could be a well-known lawyer... eternally cross-examining the museum-goers.

• *In the next room you'll find several more Titians.*

Sala di Venere (Room 32)
Titian—*The Concert* (*Concerto*, 1510–1512)

An organ-playing man leans back toward his fellow musician (a monk), who's put down his cello to tap him on the shoulder. A young dandy in fancy clothes and a feathered cap looks on. The meaning of the work is a puzzle, perhaps intentionally so. Titian may have collaborated on this early painting with his colleague Giorgione, who specialized in enigmatic works used by cultured hosts as conversation starters.

Maybe it's just a slice-of-life snapshot of Venetian musicians briefly united in their common task. Or maybe it's a philosophical metaphor, in which a middle-aged man, blithely engaged in the gay music of his youth, is interrupted by a glimpse at his future— the bass notes and receding hairline of old age.

Titian—*Portrait of a Lady*
(*Ritratto di Donna*, a.k.a. *La Bella*, c. 1536)

Titian presents a beautiful *(bella)* woman in a beautiful dress to create a beautiful ensemble of colors: the aqua-and-brown dress,

the gold necklace, pearl earrings, creamy complexion, auburn hair, and dark jewel-like eyes. She embodies the sensual, sophisticated, high-society world that Titian ran around in. The woman is likely Titian's *Venus of Urbino* standing up with her clothes on (see page 118). Scholars speculate on who she really was; perhaps she's Eleonora the Duchess of Urbino, or the mistress of the previous Duke, or maybe she's just a paid model that Titian found to be...beautiful.

Titian—*Portrait of Pietro Aretino* (c. 1545)

The most notorious and outrageous figure in Renaissance high society was the writer Pietro Aretino (1492–1556). In 1527, he fled Rome, having scandalized the city with a col-lection of erotic/pornographic sonnets known as the *Sixteen Ways* (or sex positions). He took refuge in luxury-loving Venice, where he befriended Titian, a fellow connoisseur of eroticism and the arts. Titian and Aretino were both commoners, but they moved eas-ily in court circles: Titian the diplomat and Aretino the fiery satirist who tweaked the noses of arrogant princes. (In fact, Aretino was part of the Rat Pack of rowdy Medicis that included the father of Cosimo I.)

This portrait captures the self-confidence that allowed Aretino to stand up to royalty. Titian portrays him with the bearded face of an ancient satyr (a lecherous, untamed creature in Greek mythology). His torso is huge, like a smoldering volcano of irreverence that could erupt at any moment. Rather than the seamless brushstrokes and elaborate detail of Titian's earlier works, the figure of Aretino is composed of many rough strokes of gold and brown paint. Around age 60, Titian radically altered his style, adopting this "unfinished" look that the Impressionists would elaborate on centuries later. Aretino joked when he saw the portrait: "It breathes and moves as I do in the flesh. But perhaps [Titian] would have spent more time on my fine clothes—the robe, the silk, the gold chain—if I'd paid him more." Aretino gave the portrait to Cosimo as a gift.

Canova—*Venus Italica (Venere,* 1810)

In the middle of the Sala di Venere stands Antonio Canova's *Venus Italica.* This pure white marble statue of Venus looks like the *Venus*

Titian
(c. 1490–1576)

Titian the Venetian (the museum uses his Italian name Tiziano or Tiziano Vecellio) captures the lusty spirit of his hometown. Titian was one of the most prolific painters ever, cranking out a painting a month for almost 80 years. He excelled in every subject: portraits of kings, racy nudes for bedrooms, creamy-faced Madonnas for churches, and pagan scenes from Greek mythology. He was cultured and witty, a fine musician and businessman—an all-around Renaissance kind of guy. Titian was famous and adored by high society, including Cosimo I and other Medicis.

Titian's style changed over his long career. In his youth, he painted alongside Giorgione, even working on the same canvases (scholars still debate who did what). When he reached middle age, he found his voice: bright colors (particularly the famed "Titian red"), large-scale canvases, exuberant motion, and complex compositions, rebelling against the strict symmetry of early Renaissance. In his sixties, his technique became more impressionistic. He applied the paint in rough, thick brushstrokes, even using his fingers. In these late works, his figures don't pop from the background; instead they blend in, creating a moody atmosphere.

Throughout his life, his bread and butter were portraits of Europe's movers and shakers—kings, popes, countesses, mistresses, artists, and thinkers. Without ever making his sitters more handsome or heroic than they were, he captured both their outer likeness and their inner essence. Their clothes and accessories tell us about their social circle, so collectively, his portraits are a chronicle of the Renaissance in all its sensual glory.

de' Medici with a sheet (see page 110). Like the Medici Venus, she's nude, modestly crossing her hands in front of her (the "Venus Pudica" pose), while turning her head to the side. But Canova's Venus clutches a garment, which only highlights her naked vulnerability.

In 1796, a young French general named Napoleon Bonaparte toured the Uffizi and fell in love with the *Venus de' Medici*. A few years later, when he conquered Italy, he carried Venus off with him to Paris. To replace it, the great Venetian sculptor Canova was asked to make a copy. He refused to make an exact replica, but he agreed to do his own interpretation, combining motifs from many ancient Venuses of the Pudica (modest) and Callipigia (ample derriere) style. Canova's *Venus Italica* stood in the Uffizi until Napoleon was conquered and *Venus de' Medici* returned.

• *From here, the rooms of the Palatine Gallery lead into the...*

Royal Apartments

These 14 rooms (of which only a few are open at any one time) are where the Pitti's rulers lived in the 18th and 19th centuries. By then, power had shifted from Italy to France, which is why these rooms mimic the Versailles style. You'll see velvety wallpaper, heavy curtains, white-and-gold stucco ceilings, chandeliers, and Louis XIV–style chairs, beds, clocks, and candelabras. Each room features a different color and time period. Here, you get a real feel for the splendor of the dukes' world.

The Rest of the Pitti Palace

If you've got the energy, it'd be a Pitti to miss the palace's other offerings.

Ticket #2 costs €6, but can increase with mandatory special exhibitions. This ticket covers the Boboli and Bardini Gardens, Argenti Museum (the Duke's treasures), Costume Gallery, and Porcelain Museum.

Other Palatine Gallery Works

Art lovers can hunt down Titian's *Portrait of Filippo II of Spain* and *Portrait of Ippolito de' Medici;* Giorgione's *Three Ages of Man;* Caravaggio's *Sleeping Cupid;* and many more.

Modern Art Gallery

On the second floor, this gallery features Romantic, Neoclassical, and Impressionist works by 19th- and 20th-century Tuscan painters.

Argenti Museum (Museo degli Argenti)

This Medici treasure chest (on the ground and mezzanine floors) holds items such as jeweled crucifixes, exotic porcelain, and gilded ostrich eggs, made to entertain fans of the applied arts.

Boboli and Bardini Gardens

Two adjoining gardens are located behind the palace. Enter the Boboli Gardens from the Pitti Palace courtyard. The less-visited Bardini Gardens are behind the Boboli, rising in terraces toward Piazzale Michelangelo. Both gardens are similar, providing a pleasant and shady refuge from the city heat, with statues, fountains, and scenic vistas down tree-lined avenues.

In the Boboli Gardens, the sightseeing highlights include a panoramic view of Florence (straight up the hill from the palace) and the Porcelain Museum (just beyond the hillcrest). The Grotto of Buontalenti, located to the left/ north of the palace, is an artificial cave crusted with fake stalactites and copies of Michelangelo's *Prisoners,* which once stood here (and are now in the Accademia). And just to the left of the palace is the much-photographed Bacchus Fountain (Fontana di Bacco, 1560), starring Cosimo's fat dwarf jester straddling a turtle—a fitting metaphor for this heavyweight palace.

GALILEO SCIENCE MUSEUM TOUR

*Museo Galilei e Istituto
di Storia della Scienza*

Enough art, already! Forget the Madonnas and Venuses for a while to ponder weird contraptions from the birth of modern science. The same spirit of discovery that fueled the artistic Renaissance helped free the sciences from medieval mumbo jumbo. This museum offers a historical overview of technical innovations from roughly A.D. 1000 to 1900, featuring early telescopes, clocks, experiments, and Galileo's finger in a jar.

English majors will enjoy expanding their knowledge. Art lovers can admire the sheer beauty of functional devices. Engineers will be in hog heaven among endless arrays of gadgets. Everyone will be fully amused by my feeble attempts to explain technical concepts.

Note: The Galileo Science Museum is set to reopen in spring of 2010 after an extensive renovation. Though the collection remains the same, the new layout will be different, so this chapter does not provide a room-by-room tour. It does, however, give a good overview of the collection itself. Read the chapter ahead of time, then visit and be amazed by what you see.

Orientation

Cost: €4, rising to €6-8 after reopening.

Hours: Mon and Wed–Fri 9:30–17:00, Tue and Sat 9:30–13:00, closed Sun.

Getting There: The museum is located one block east of the Uffizi on the north bank of the Arno River at Piazza dei Giudici 1.

Information: Tel. 055-265-311, www.imss.fi.it. Check the website for updates on the re-opening, hours, and cost.

Photography: Prohibited.

Starring: Galileo's telescopes, experiment models, and finger.

Overview

Since the collection's layout for 2010 is unpredictable due to renovation, take advantage of the helpful English-speaking docents. They're available to answer questions about how these scientific gadgets work and may be able to demonstrate one or two as well. In fact, the staff is happy that you're there to see this museum, and not just lost on your way to the nearby Uffizi.

The following information is presented not as a tour of the museum displays, but as helpful background material.

Mathematical Instruments— Quadrants, Globes, Astrolabes

Many of the museum's objects measured the world around us—the height of distant mountains, the length of a man's arm, the movement of the stars across the sky. In fact, one of the bold first steps in science was to observe nature and measure it. What scientists found is that nature—seemingly ever-changing and chaotic— actually behaves in an orderly way, following rather simple mathematical formulas.

In medieval times, traders needed navigational devices to help them find their way at sea. They mapped the constellations as a starting point. Next they had to figure out where they stood in relation to those stars.

Quadrants

A *quad*-rant is one-*fourth* of a 360-degree circle, or 90 degrees. You'd grab this wedge-shaped object by its curved edge, point it away from you, and sight along the top edge toward, say, a distant tower or star. Then you'd read the scale etched along the curved edge to find how many degrees above the horizon the object was.

A quadrant *(quadrante)* measured the triangle formed by you, the horizon, and a distant object. Once you knew at least three of the triangle's six variables (three angles and three sides), you

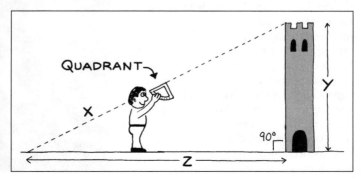

could calculate the others. (That's trigonometry.)

Armed with this knowledge, you could use the quadrant to measure all kinds of things. On land, you could calculate how high or how far away a building was. At sea, you could figure your position relative to the sun and stars.

Arab Astrolabes

Astrolabes—invented by the ancient Greeks and pioneered by medieval Arab sailors—combined a quadrant with a map of the sky (a star chart), allowing you to calculate your position against the stars without doing all of the math. You'd hang the metal disk from your thumb and sight along the central crossbeam, locate a star, then read its altitude above the horizon on the measuring scale etched around the rim.

Next, you'd enter this information by turning a little handle on the astrolabe's face. This set the wheels-within-wheels into motion,

and the constellations would spin across a backdrop of coordinates. You'd keep turning until the astrolabe mirrored the current heavens. With your known coordinates dialed in, the astrolabe calculated the unknowns, and you could read out your position along the rim.

Knowing the position of the stars and sun also revealed the current time of day, which was especially useful for Arab traders (i.e., Muslims) in their daily prayers.

Galileo

Galileo Galilei (1564–1642) is known as the father of modern science. His discoveries pioneered many scientific fields, and he was among the first to blend mathematics with hands-on observation of nature to find practical applications. Raised in Pisa, he achieved fame teaching at the University of Padua before working for the Grand Duke of Florence. The museum displays several of his possessions (lens, two telescopes, compass, and thermometer), models illustrating his early experiments, and his finger, preserved in a jar.

Galileo's Finger

Galileo is, perhaps, best known as a martyr for science. He popularized the belief (conceived by the Polish astronomer Nicolaus Copernicus in the early 1500s) that the Earth orbits around the sun. At the time, the Catholic Church (and most of Europe) preached an Earth-centered universe. At the age of 70, Galileo was hauled before the Inquisition in Rome and forced to kneel and publicly proclaim that the Earth did not move around the sun. As he walked away, legend has it, he whispered to his followers, "But it does move!"

His students preserved this finger bone *(Dito Medio della Mano Destra di Galileo)*, displayed on an alabaster pedestal, as a kind of sacred relic in this shrine to science. Galileo's beliefs eventually triumphed over the Inquisition, and, appropriately, we have his right middle finger raised upward for all those blind to science.

Galileo's Telescope Lens

Galileo was the first earthling to see the moons of Jupiter. With a homemade telescope (see next page), he looked through this lens *(Lente obiettiva di Galileo,* displayed in an ivory frame) and saw three moons lined up next to Jupiter (the lens wasn't cracked then). This discovery also irked the Church, which insisted that all heavenly bodies orbited the Earth. You could see Jupiter's moons with your own eyes if you simply looked through the telescope, but few church scholars bothered to do so, content to believe what they'd read in ancient books.

Pendulum Clock Model

It's said that during a church service in Pisa, Galileo looked up to see the cathedral's chandelier swaying slowly back and forth, like a pendulum. He noticed that a wide-but-fast arc took the same amount of time as a narrow-but-slow arc. "Hmmm. Maybe that regular pendulum motion could be used to time things..."

Thermometer / Thermoscope

Galileo also invented the thermometer *(termoscopio*—similar to this 19th-century replica), though his glass tube filled with air would later be replaced by thermometers of mercury.

Inclined Plane

Legend has it that Galileo dropped cannonballs from the Leaning Tower of Pisa to see whether heavier objects fall faster than lighter ones, as the ancient philosopher Aristotle (and most people) believed. In fact, Galileo probably did not drop objects from the Leaning Tower, but likely rolled them down a wooden ramp like this reconstructed one. If a docent is nearby, ask for a demonstration.

Rolling balls of different weights down the ramp, he timed them as they rang the bells posted along the way. (The bells are spaced increasingly farther apart, but a ball—accelerating as it drops—will ring them at regular intervals.) What Galileo found is that—if you discount air resistance—all objects fall at the same rate, regardless of their weight. (It's the air resistance, not the weight, that makes a feather fall more slowly than a cannonball.)

He also found that falling objects accelerate at a regular rate (9.8 meters per second faster every second), summed up in a mathematical formula (distance is proportional to the time squared).

Model of Water-Lifting Device

The horses in this toy-like device *(Macchina da Alzare Acqua)* walk in a circle, rocking the two cross-bars back and forth. The cross-bars alternately lift and lower buckets in wells, allowing the two horses to draw water from four wells. Galileo was among the first research scientists to suggest practical applications of his principles.

Galileo's Telescopes

Galileo built these telescopes, based on reports he'd read from Holland. He was the first person to seriously study the heavens with telescopes. Though these only magnified the image about 30 times ("30 power," which is less than today's binoculars), he saw Jupiter's four largest moons, Saturn's rings, the craters of the moon (which he named "seas"), and blemishes (sunspots) on the supposedly perfect sun.

A telescope is essentially an empty tube with a lens at the far end to gather light and another lens at the near end to magnify the image. The farther apart the lenses, the greater the magnification, prompting telescopes to get bigger and bigger. The longest ever built was 160 feet, but the slightest movement jiggled the image.

Galileo used a "refracting telescope," made with lenses that bend (refract) light. Later on, scientists started using "reflecting telescopes," which were often thick-barreled, with the eyepiece sticking out the side. These telescopes use mirrors (not lenses) to bounce light rays back and forth through several lenses, thereby increasing magnification without the long tubes and distortion of refractors.

Mapping the World: Maps and Armillary Spheres

Thanks to Columbus' voyages, the Europeans' world suddenly got bigger and rounder. Increasingly, maps started to portray the

spherical world on a flat surface. (In some early maps, south is up.)

An armillary sphere was a model of the universe as conceived by ancient Greeks and medieval Europeans. You'd turn a crank and watch the stars and planets orbit around the Earth in the center. This Earth-centered view of the universe—which matches

our common-sense observations of the night sky—was codified by Ptolemy, a Greek-speaking Egyptian of the second century A.D.

Ptolemy (silent P) summed up Aristotle's knowledge of the heavens and worked out the mathematics explaining its movements. His math was complex, especially when trying to explain the planets, which occasionally lag behind the stars in their paths across the night sky. (We now know it's because fast-orbiting Earth passes the outer planets in their longer, more time-consuming orbits around the sun.)

Ptolemy's system dominated Europe for 1,500 years. It worked most of the time and fit well with medieval Christianity's human-centered theology. But, finally, Nicolaus Copernicus (and Galileo) made the mental leap to a sun-centered system. This simplified the math, explained the movement of planets, and—most importantly—changed earthlings' conception of themselves forever.

Microscopes

The inner world was expanding, too. One day, a Dutchman picked something from his teeth, looked at it under his crude microscope, and discovered a mini-universe, crawling with thousands of "very

little animalcules, very prettily a-moving" (i.e., bacteria and protozoa). Antonie van Leeuwenhoek (1632–1723) popularized the microscope, finding that fleas have fleas, semen contains sperm, and one-celled creatures are our fellow animals.

Microscopes can be either simple *(semplice)* or compound *(composto)*. A simple one is just a single convex lens—what we'd call a magnifying glass. A compound contains two (or more) lenses in a tube, working like a telescope: one lens magnifies the object, and the eyepiece lens magnifies the magnified image. Van Leeuwenhoek opted for a simple microscope (not in this museum), since early compound ones often blurred and colored objects around the edges. His glass-bead-size lens could make a flea look 275 times bigger.

Thermometers and Barometers

Even nature's most changeable force—the weather—was analyzed by human reason.

You'll likely see many interesting thermometers *(termometri)*—spiral ones, tall ones, and skinny ones on distinctive bases. All operate on the basic principle that heat expands things. So, liquid in a closed glass tube will expand and climb upward as the temperature rises.

Galileo's early thermometer held air, and was not hermetically sealed, so it was too easily affected by changing air pressure. So scientists experimented with various liquids in a vacuum tube—first water, then alcohol. Finally, Gabriel Fahrenheit (1686–1736) tried mercury, the densest liquid, which expands evenly. He set his scale to the freezing point of a water/salt/ice mixture (zero degrees) and his own body temperature (96 degrees). With these parameters, water froze at 32 degrees and boiled at 212 degrees. Anders Celsius (1701–1744) used water as the standard, and called the freezing point 0 and the boiling point 100.

To make a barometer, take a long, skinny glass tube (like the ones in the wood frames), fill it with liquid mercury, then turn it upside-down and put the open end into a bowlful of more mercury. The column of mercury does not drain out, because the air in the room "pushes back," pressing down on the surface of the mercury in the bowl.

Changing air pressure signals a shift in the weather. Hot air expands, pressing down harder on the mercury's surface, thereby causing the mercury column to rise above 30 inches; this indicates the "pushing away" of clouds and points to good, dry weather. Low pressure lets the mercury drop, warning of rain. If

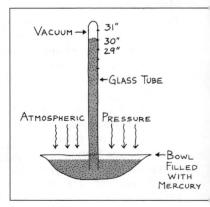

you have a barometer at home, it probably has a round dial with a needle (or a digital readout), but it operates on a similar principle.

Clocks

In an ever-changing universe, what is constant enough to measure the passage of time? The sun and stars passing over every 24 hours work for calendar time, but not for hours, minutes, or seconds. Since the time of the Greeks, man used sundials, or the steady flow of water or sand through an opening, but these were only approximate.

By the 1600s, with overseas trade booming, there was a crying need for an accurate and durable clock to help in navigation. Sighting by the stars told you your latitude but was less certain on whether you were near Florence, Italy (latitude 44), or Portland, Maine (also latitude 44). You needed a way to time Earth's 24-hour rotation, to know exactly where you were on that daily journey—i.e., your longitude. Reward money was offered for a good clock that could be taken to sea, and science sprang into action.

The large planetary clock displayed at the museum (a replica of a 1510 original) is essentially a crude grandfather clock. It's powered by suspended weights that slowly "fall," producing enough energy to turn a series of cogwheels that methodically move the clock hands around the dial. The whole thing is regulated by a horizontal ring (at the top) rocking back and forth, once a second. This model demonstrates three essential components of clocks:

1. Power (falling weights).
2. An "escapement" (the cogs that transform the "falling" power into turning power).
3. A regulator (swinging pendulum or rocking ring) that keeps the gears turning evenly.

Unfortunately, a "grandfather" clock powered by dangling weights wasn't going to work on a rocking ship. Later clocks were powered by a metal spring that slowly uncoiled (also used in most watches). The power was regulated by a pendulum—Galileo's contribution. Unfortunately, a rocking pendulum on a rocking ship wasn't going to work either.

The longitude problem was finally solved—and a £20,000 prize won—by John Harrison of England (1693–1776), who developed the "chronometer" (not in this museum), a spring-driven clock in a suspension device to keep it horizontal. It was accurate within three seconds a day, far better than any clock displayed here.

During the so-called Age of Reason (1600s) and Age of Enlightenment (1700s), the clock was the perfect metaphor for the orderly workings of God's well-crafted universe. So, wondered the philosopher/scientists, would the universe eventually wind down like an old clock? In fact, in every energy exchange (as stated in the second law of thermodynamics), a certain amount of energy is transformed into nonrecyclable heat, meaning a perpetual motion machine is impossible. This principle of entropy (the trend toward dissipation of energy) has led philosophers to ponder the eventual cold, lifeless fate of the universe itself.

Electricity
(or, more precisely, Electromagnetism)

Lightning, magnets, and static cling mystified humans for millennia. Little did they know that these quite different phenomena are all generated by the same invisible force—electromagnetism.

In the 1700s, scientists began to study, harness, and play with electricity. As a popular party amusement, they devised big

static-electricity-generating machines. You turned a crank to spin a glass disk, which rubbed against silk cloth and generated static electricity. The electricity could then be stored in a glass Leyden jar (a jar coated with metal and filled with water). A metal rod sticking out of the top of the jar gave off a small charge when touched, enough to create a spark, shock a party guest, or tenderize a turkey (as Ben Franklin attempted one Thanksgiving). But such static generators could never produce enough electricity for practical use.

Alessandro Volta (1745–1827) built the first battery in Europe. (Although the museum does not have one of Volta's batteries, it does have similar devices.) A battery generates electricity from a chemical reaction. Volta (and others) stacked metal disks of zinc and copper between disks of cardboard soaked with salt water. The zinc slowly dissolves, releasing electrons into the liquid.

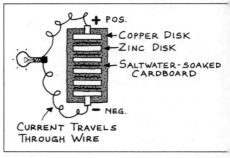

Hook a wire to each end of the battery, and the current flows. When the zinc is gone, your battery is dead.

England's Michael Faraday (c. 1831) created the first true electric motor, which could generate electricity by moving a magnet through a coil of copper wire. This invention soon led to the production of electricity on a large scale.

The Archimedes Screw Models (Modelo di Vite d'Archimede)

Back in third-century B.C. Greece, Archimedes—the man who gave us the phrase "Eureka!" ("I've found it!")—invented a way to pump water that's still occasionally used today. It's a screw in a cylinder. Simply turn the handle and the screw spins, channeling the water up in a spiral path. Dutch windmills powered big Archimedes screws to push water over dikes, reclaiming land from the sea.

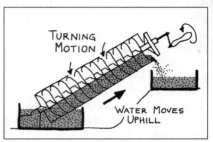

TURNING MOTION

WATER MOVES UPHILL

Models for Demonstrating Newton's Mechanics

Isaac Newton (1642–1727) explained all of the universe's motion ("mechanics")—from spinning planets to rolling rocks—in a few simple mathematical formulas.

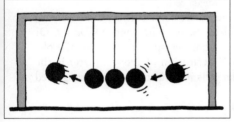

The museum's collision balls (the big wooden frame with hanging balls), a popular desktop toy in the 1970s, demonstrate Newton's three famous laws.

1. **Inertia:** The balls just sit there unless something moves them, and once they're set in motion, they'll keep moving the same way until something stops them.
2. **Force = Mass × Acceleration:** The harder you strike the balls, the more they accelerate (change speeds). Strike with two balls to pack twice the punch.
3. **For every action, there's an equal and opposite reaction:** When one ball swings in and strikes the rest, the ball at the other end swings out, then returns and strikes back.

Medicine

Back when the same guy who cut your hair removed your appendix, surgery was crude. In the 1700s, there were no anesthetics beyond a bottle of wine, nor was there any knowledge of antiseptics. The best they could do was resort to the healing powers of herbs and plants. Consider what was thought to be therapeutic in the 1700s:

cocaine *(Coca Boliviana)*, anise, poisonous plants *(Belladonna)*, tea *(The)*, and ipecac *(Ipecacuana)*.

Chemistry

Antoine Lavoisier (1743–1794) was the Galileo of chemistry, introducing sound methodology and transforming the mumbo jumbo of medieval alchemy into hard science. He created the precursor to our modern periodic table of the elements, and used the standardized terminology of suffixes that describe the different forms a single element can take (sulfur, sulf-ide, sulf-ate, sulf-uric, etc.).

Weights and Measures

Much of the purpose of science is to use constants to measure an ever-changing universe. For centuries, one of these constants was the meter-long metal rod, established in 1790 as the fundamental unit by which all distances are measured.

The rod is exactly one meter. Or 39.37 inches. Or 1/1,000th of the distance from the Galileo Science Museum to *David*. Or 1/10,000,000th of the distance from the equator to the North Pole. Or, according to the updated definition of 1960, a meter is the length of 1,650,763.73 wavelengths in a vacuum of the orange-red radiation of krypton 86.

Ain't science wonderful?

SLEEPING IN FLORENCE

I like hotels that are handy to the great sights. Nearly all of my recommended accommodations are located in the center of Florence.

For an overview of pricing, getting deals, making reservations, seasonal differences (peak season versus off-season), and much more, see page 16 of the Introduction.

Florence is notorious for its mosquitoes. If your hotel lacks air-conditioning, request a fan and don't open your windows, especially at night. Many hotels furnish a small plug-in bulb *(zanzariere)*—usually set in the ashtray—that helps keep the blood-suckers at bay. If not, you can purchase one cheaply at any pharmacy *(farmacia)*.

If you arrive on an overnight train, your room may not be ready. Drop your bag at the hotel and dive right into Florence.

Museum-goers take note: When you book your room, ask if your hotelier will book entry times for you to visit the popular Uffizi Gallery and the Accademia (Michelangelo's *David*). This service is fast, easy, and offered free or for a small fee by most hotels—the only requirement is advance notice. Ask them to make appointments for you any time the day after your arrival for the Uffizi and the Accademia. If your hotel does charge a fee, you'll usually save several euros per reservation by booking it yourself, but it may not be worth the hassle. For details, see page 16.

Between the Station and Duomo

$$ Hotel Accademia, which comes with marble stairs, parquet floors, and attractive public areas, has 21 pleasant rooms and a floor plan that defies logic (Db-€150, Tb-€180, 5 percent cash discount with this book, air-con, Wi-Fi, Via Faenza 7, tel. 055-293-451, fax 055-219-771, www.hotelaccademiafirenze.com, info@hotel accademiafirenze.com, Tea, Francesca, and Paolo).

$$ Residenza dei Pucci rents 12 tastefully decorated rooms—in soothing earth tones—with aristocratic furniture spread over three floors (Sb-€135, Db-€150, Tb-€170, Qb-€238, 10 percent discount with cash and this book, air-con, reception open 9:00–20:00—let them know if you'll arrive late, Via dei Pucci 9, tel. 055-281-886, fax 055-264-314, www.residenzadeipucci.com, residenzadeipucci@residenzadeipucci.com, Mirella).

$$ Hotel Centrale, with 20 spacious rooms, is indeed central (Db-€150, Tb-€182, 5 percent discount with this book, ask for Rick Steves rate when you reserve, air-con, elevator, Internet access, Via dei Conti 3, tel. 055-215-761, fax 055-215-216, www.hotelcentrale firenze.it, info@hotelcentralefirenze.it, Margherita and Roberto).

$$ Hotel Duomo, big and venerable, rents 24 rooms four floors up. The Duomo looms like a monster outside the hotel's windows. The rooms, while pretty forgettable, are comfortable enough and the location can't be beat (Db-€100–150, 10 percent cash discount with this book, Internet access, Piazza del Duomo 1, tel. 055-219-922, www.hotelduomofirenze.it, info@hotelduomo firenze.it, Alberto).

$ Katti House and the nearby **Soggiorno Annamaria** are run by house-proud mama-and-daughter team Maria and Katti, who keep their 15 rooms spotless, inviting, and well-maintained. While both offer equal comfort, Soggiorno Annamaria has a more historic setting, with frescoed ceilings, unique tiles, timbered beams, and quieter rooms (Db-€70–100, ask for Rick Steves cash-discount rate when you reserve, air-con, Internet access and Wi-Fi, Via Faenza 21, tel. & fax 055-213-410, www.kattihouse.com, info @kattihouse.com).

Near the Mercato Centrale

After dark, this neighborhood can feel a little sketchy, but I've never heard of anyone running into harm here. It's a short walk from the train station and an easy stroll to all the sightseeing action. Plenty of good budget restaurants and markets are nearby.

$$ Galileo Hotel, a classy business hotel of 31 rooms, is run with familial warmth (Db-€130, Tb-€150, ask for 10 percent Rick Steves discount when you book direct, quadruple-pane windows effectively shut out street noise, Wi-Fi, Via Nazionale 22a, tel. 055-496-645, fax 055-496-447, www.galileohotel.it, info@galileo hotel.it, Rhuna).

$ Hotel Il Bargellino, run by Bostonian Carmel and her Italian husband Pino, is a bit farther out and consequently feels like it's in a residential neighborhood. They rent 10 summery rooms decorated with funky antique furniture and Pino's modern paintings. Guests enjoy relaxing with Carmel on her big, breezy, momentum-slowing terrace. To avoid street noise, ask for a quiet

---

Sleep Code

(€1 = about $1.40, country code: 39)
To help you easily sort through these listings, I've divided the rooms into three categories based on the price for a standard double room with bath during high season:

$$$ Higher Priced—Most rooms €165 or more.
 $$ Moderately Priced—Most rooms between €100–165.
  $ Lower Priced—Most rooms €100 or less.

You can assume a hotel takes credit cards unless you see "cash only" in the listing. Unless otherwise noted, hotel staff speak basic English and breakfast is included.

---

room (S-€45, D-€75, Db-€85, extra bed-€25, air-con-€10, no breakfast, north of the train station at Via Guelfa 87, tel. & fax 055-238-2658, www.ilbargellino.com, carmel@ilbargellino.com).

$ Hotel Enza rents 19 relaxing rooms (Sb-€55, Db-€80, prices promised through 2010 with this book and cash, extra bed-€20, optional breakfast by request only-€5, air-con, Internet access and Wi-Fi, Via San Zanobi 45 black, tel. 055-490-990, fax 055-473-672, www.hotelenza.it, info@hotelenza.it, Katia).

$ Casa Rabatti is the ultimate if you always wanted to have a Florentine mama. Its four simple, clean rooms are run with warmth by Marcella, who speaks minimal English. Seeing 17 years of my family Christmas cards on their walls, I'm reminded of how long she has been keeping budget travelers happy (D-€50, Db-€60, €25 extra per bed in shared quad or quint, prices good with this book, cash only but secure reservation with credit card, no breakfast, fans available, 5 blocks from station at Via San Zanobi 48 black, tel. 055-212-393, casarabatti@inwind.it).

If Marcella's booked, she'll put you up in her daughter's place nearby, at Via Nazionale 20 (five big, airy, family-friendly rooms; €25/person, fans, no breakfast, closer to the station). While daughter Patrizia works, her mom runs the B&Bs. Getting bumped to Patrizia's gives you slightly more comfort and slightly less personality...certainly not a net negative.

$ Soggiorno Magliani is central and humble, with six no-frills rooms (sharing two baths) that feel and smell like a great-grandmother's home. It's run by the friendly duo Vincenza and her English-speaking daughter, Cristina, and the price is right (S-€39, D-€49, T-€65, cash only but secure reservation with credit card, no breakfast, near Via Guelfa at Via Santa Reparata 1, tel. 055-287-378, hotel-magliani@libero.it).

Florence Hotels

TO 29 & PIAZZA D. LIBERTÀ

TO FORTEZZA DI BASSO

S.M.N. TRAIN STATION

P. ADUA

BUS STN.

S. MARIA NOVELLA

MERCATO CENTRALE

MEDICI CHAPELS

SAN LORENZO

STREET MKT.

MEDICI-RICCARDI PALACE

DUOMO

CERRETANI

BAPT.

CAMPANILE

PZZA. REP.

ORSAN-MICH.

CORSO

CASA DI DANTE

DANTE

PIAZZA SIGNORIA

S. TRINITA

P. GOLD.

VIGNA NUOVA

A R N O

PONTE VECCHIO

OLTRARNO

UFFIZI GALLERY

SCIENCE MUSEUM

PALAZZO VECCHIO

TO PITTI PALACE

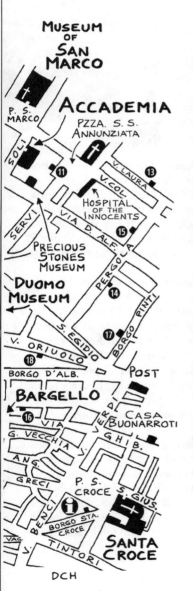

1 Hotel Accademia
2 Residenza dei Pucci
3 Hotel Centrale
4 Hotel Duomo
5 Katti House & Soggiorno Annamaria
6 Galileo Hotel
7 Hotel Il Bargellino
8 Hotel Enza
9 Casa Rabatti
10 Soggiorno Magliani
11 Hotel Loggiato dei Serviti
12 Palazzo Niccolini al Duomo
13 Hotel Morandi alla Crocetta
14 Panella's Residence
15 Residenza il Villino
16 B&B Il Bargello
17 Hotel Cardinal of Florence & Oblate Sisters of the Assumption
18 Hotel Dalí
19 Hotel Pendini
20 B&B Dei Mori
21 Hotel Axial & Hotel Maxim
22 Soggiorno Battistero
23 Albergo Firenze
24 Hotel Torre Guelfa & Hotel Alessandra
25 In Piazza della Signoria B&B
26 Hotel Davanzati
27 Bellevue House
28 Hotel Sole
29 To Villa Camerata & Hostel 7 Santi

200 YARDS

200 METERS

Elegant Splurges East of the Duomo

$$$ Hotel Loggiato dei Serviti, at the most prestigious address in Florence on the most Renaissance square in town, gives you Old World romance with hair dryers.

Stone stairways lead you under open-beam ceilings through this 16th-century monastery's monumental public rooms—it's so artful, you'll be snapping photos everywhere. The 33 cells—with air-conditioning, TVs, mini-bars, and telephones—would be unrecognizable to their original inhabitants. The hotel staff is both professional and warm (Sb-€120, Db-€160–180, superior Db-€205, family suites from €263, ask for their Rick Steves rate when you book, elevator, Piazza S.S. Annunziata 3, tel. 055-289-592, fax 055-289-595, www .loggiatodeiservitihotel.it, info@loggiatodeiservitihotel.it, Fabio, Chiara, and Simonetta). When full, they rent five spacious and sophisticated rooms in a 17th-century annex a block away. While it lacks the monastic mystique, the annex rooms are bigger, gorgeous, and cost the same.

$$$ Palazzo Niccolini al Duomo, one of five elite Historic Residence Hotels in Florence, is run by Sra. Niccolini da Camugliano. The lounge is palatial, and the 10 rooms are big and splendid, with original 16th-century frescoes. If you have the money and want a Florentine palace to call home, this is a very good bet, located just one block from the Duomo (Db-€220 and up, fancier and pricier suites, ask for 10 percent Rick Steves discount when you book, check online to choose a room and consider last-minute deals, Via dei Servi 2, tel. 055-282-412, fax 055-290-979, www.niccolinidomepalace.com, info@niccolini domepalace.com).

$$ Hotel Morandi alla Crocetta, a former convent, envelops you in a 16th-century cocoon. Located on a quiet street with 12 rooms, period furnishings, parquet floors, and wood-beamed ceilings, it takes you back a few centuries (Sb-€100, Db-€160, breakfast not worth €12, air-con, a block off Piazza S.S. Annunziata at Via Laura 50, tel. 055-234-4747, fax 055-248-0954, www .hotelmorandi.it, welcome@hotelmorandi.it, well run by Maurizio, Rolando, and Frank).

Other Hotels East of the Duomo

$$ Panella's Residence, once a convent and today part of owner Graziella's extensive home, is a classy B&B, with six chic and romantic rooms, antique furnishings, and historic architectural touches (Db-€140 with cash, discounts for 3 or more nights, air-con, Via della Pergola 42, tel. 055-234-7202, fax 055-247-9669, www.panellaresidence.com, panella_residence@yahoo.it).

$$ Residenza il Villino, popular and friendly, aspires to offer a Florentine home. It has 10 rooms and a picturesque, peaceful little courtyard (small Db-€110, Db-€130, Qb/family suite-€170, 5 percent discount with cash and this book, air-con, Internet access and Wi-Fi, just north of Via degli Alfani at Via della Pergola 53, tel. 055-200-1116, fax 055-200-1101, www.ilvillino.it, info @ilvillino.it, Sergio, Elisabetta, and son Lorenzo).

$ B&B Il Bargello is a home away from home, run by friendly and helpful Canadian expat Gabriella. Hike up three long flights to reach Gabriella's six smart, relaxing rooms. She offers a cozy communal living room, kitchen access, book exchange, Internet access and Wi-Fi, and an inviting rooftop terrace with close-up views of Florence's towers (Db-€100, ask for the Rick Steves rate when you book direct and pay cash, air-con, 20 yards off Via Proconsolo at Via de' Pandolfini 33 black, tel. 055-215-330, mobile 339-175-3110, www .firenze-bedandbreakfast.it, info@firenze-bedandbreakfast.it).

$ Hotel Cardinal of Florence is a third-floor walk-up with 17 new, tidy, and sun-splashed rooms overlooking either a silent courtyard (many with views of Brunelleschi's dome) or quiet street. Relax and enjoy Florence's rooftops from the sun terrace (Sb-€60, Db-€95, these prices for Rick Steves readers, additional €5 cash discount, €15/day limited parking—request when you reserve, Borgo Pinti 5, tel. 055-234-0780, fax 055-234-3389, www.hotel cardinalofflorence.com, info@hotelcardinalofflorence.com).

$ Hotel Dalí has 10 decent, basic rooms with new baths in a nice location for a great price. Samanta and Marco run this guesthouse with a charming passion; they offer no Wi-Fi "because it burns your brains" (S-€40, D-€65, Db-€80, extra bed-€25, no breakfast, fans but no air-con, request quiet room when you book, free parking, 2 blocks behind the Duomo at Via dell'Oriuolo 17, tel. & fax 055-234-0706, hoteldali@tin.it).

$ Oblate Sisters of the Assumption run an institutional 30-room hotel in a Renaissance building with a dreamy garden, great public spaces, appropriately simple rooms, and a quiet, prayerful ambience (S-€40, Db-€80, Tb-€120, Qb-€160, cash only, single beds only, optional breakfast-€5, air-con, elevator, €10/ day limited parking—request when you book, Borgo Pinti 15, tel. 055-248-0582, fax 055-234-6291, sroblateborgopinti@virgilio.it, sisters are likely to speak French but not English, Sister Theresa is very helpful).

Near Piazza della Repubblica

These are the most central of my accommodations recommendations (and therefore a little overpriced). While worth the extra cost for many, given Florence's walkable core nearly every hotel can be considered central.

$$ Hotel Pendini, with three tarnished stars, fills the top floor of a grand building constructed to celebrate Italian unification in the late 19th century. It overlooks Piazza della Repubblica, and as you walk into the lobby, you feel as if you are walking back in time. Its 50 rooms are well-worn and pretty stodgy but memorable—and a good value (Db-€120, Internet access and Wi-Fi, Via Strozzi 2, tel. 055-211-170, www.florenceitaly.net, pendini @florenceitaly.net).

$$ B&B Dei Mori, a peaceful haven, has five newly remodeled rooms ideally located on a quiet pedestrian street near the Casa di Dante. Accommodating hostess Suzanne offers lots of tips on dining and sightseeing in Florence (D-€100, Db-€120, air-con extra, 10 percent discount for my readers—ask when you book, reception open 8:00–19:00, Via Dante Alighieri 12, tel. 055-211-438, www.deimori.com, deimori@bnb.it).

$$ Hotel Axial (run by the same folks who own Hotel Maxim, below) offers 15 soundproofed, tidy, and plain rooms on Florence's main pedestrian drag (Sb-€89–109, Db-€139, 5 percent discount if you book on their website, another 5 percent off for cash, check for website promotions, air-con, elevator, Wi-Fi, Via de' Calzaiuoli 11, tel. 055-218-984, fax 055-211-733, www.hotel axial.it, info@hotelaxial.it).

$$ Hotel Maxim, right on Via de' Calzaiuoli, is a big and institutional-feeling place warmly run by a family team: father Paolo, son Nicola, and daughter Chiara. Its halls are narrow, but the 26 basic rooms are comfortable and well-maintained (Sb-€75, Db-€110, Tb-€138, Qb-€155, 10 percent discount with cash and this book, air-con, elevator, Internet access and Wi-Fi, Via de' Calzaiuoli 11, tel. 055-217-474, fax 055-283-729, www.hotelmaxim firenze.it, reservation@hotelmaximfirenze.it).

$$ Soggiorno Battistero rents seven simple, airy rooms, most with great views, literally overlooking the Baptistery and the Duomo square. Choose a view or a quieter room in the back when you book by email. It's a pristine, fresh, and minimalist little place run by Italian Luca and his American wife Kelly, who makes the hotel particularly welcoming (Sb-€78, Db-€103, Tb-€140, Qb-€150, prices good with this book, 5 percent cash discount, breakfast served in room, air-con, Wi-Fi, Piazza San Giovanni 1, third floor—no elevator, tel. 055-295-143, fax 055-268-189, www .soggiornobattistero.it, info@soggiornobattistero.it).

$ Albergo Firenze, a big, efficient place, offers 58 basic rooms in a central locale two blocks behind the Duomo. It's institutional and often busy with big groups (Sb-€84, Db-€114, Tb-€147 but these are wishful-thinking prices—ask for a discount, air-con, elevator, noisy, at Piazza Donati 4 across from Via del Corso 8, tel. 055-214-203, fax 055-212-370, www.albergofirenze.org, info @albergofirenze.org).

Near Piazza della Signoria and Ponte Vecchio

$$$ **Hotel Torre Guelfa** is topped by a fun medieval tower with a panoramic rooftop terrace and a huge living room. Its 24 pricey rooms vary wildly in size. Room 15, with a private terrace (€245), is worth reserving several months in advance (standard Db-€170–190, Db junior suite-€235, family deals, 5 percent discount with cash, air-con, elevator, a couple blocks northwest of Ponte Vecchio, Borgo S.S. Apostoli 8, tel. 055-239-6338, fax 055-239-8577, www.hoteltorreguelfa.com, info@hoteltorreguelfa.com, Sabina, Giancarlo, and Sandro).

$$$ **In Piazza della Signoria B&B,** overlooking Piazza della Signoria, is peaceful, refined, and homey at the same time. Fit for a honeymoon, the 10 rooms come with all the special touches and little extras you'd expect in a top-end American B&B—such as being served fresh-squeezed orange juice for breakfast (viewless Db-€220, view Db-€250, Tb-€280, ask for 10 percent discount when you book direct with this book, family apartments, lavish bathrooms, air-con, tiny elevator, Internet access and Wi-Fi, Via dei Magazzini 2, tel. 055-239-9546, mobile 348-321-0565, fax 055-267-6616, www.inpiazzadellasignoria.com, info@inpiazzadella signoria.com, Sonia and Alessandro).

$$$ **Hotel Davanzati,** bright and shiny with artistic touches, has 19 cheerful rooms with all the comforts. The place is a family affair, thoughtfully run by friendly Tommaso and father Fabrizio, who offer drinks and snacks each evening at their candlelit happy hour (Sb-€122, Db-€189, Tb-€259, these rates good with this book though prices soft off-season, 10 percent cash discount; PlayStation 2, DVD player, and laptop with free Wi-Fi in every room; air-con, Via Porta Rossa 5, tel. 055-286-666, fax 055-265-8252, www.hotel davanzati.it, info@hoteldavanzati.it).

$$ **Hotel Alessandra** is 16th-century, tranquil, and sprawling, with 27 big, tasteful rooms (S-€67, Sb-€110, D-€110, Db-€150, Tb-€195, Qb-€215, 5 percent cash discount, air-con, Borgo S.S. Apostoli 17, tel. 055-283-438, fax 055-210-619, www.hotelalessandra .com, info@hotelalessandra.com, Anna and son Andrea).

Near the Train Station

As with any big Italian city, the area around the train station is a magnet for hardworking pickpockets on the alert for lost, vulnerable tourists with bulging money belts hanging out of their khakis.

$ **Bellevue House** is a third-floor (no elevator) oasis of tranquility, with six spacious rooms flanking a long, mellow-yellow lobby. It's a peaceful time warp thoughtfully run by Rosanna and Antonio di Grazia (Db–€70–90, family deals, 5 percent cash discount, optional €3 breakfast in street-level bar, Via della Scala 21, tel. 055-260-8932, mobile 333-612-5973, fax 055-265-5315, www .bellevuehouse.it, info@bellevuehouse.it).

$ Hotel Sole is a basic place with eight clean, functional rooms (Sb–€50, Db–€80, Tb–€110, no breakfast, air-con, elevator, a block toward river from Piazza Santa Maria Novella at Via del Sole 8, tel. & fax 055-239-6094, htlsole@tiscali.it).

Oltrarno, South of the River

Across the river in the Oltrarno area, between the Pitti Palace and Ponte Vecchio, you'll still find small, traditional crafts shops, neighborly piazzas, and family eateries. The following places are an easy walk from Ponte Vecchio. Only the first one is a real hotel—the rest are a ragtag gang of budget alternatives.

$$$ Hotel Silla, a classic three-star hotel with 35 cheery, spacious, pastel, and modern rooms, faces the river and overlooks a park opposite the Santa Croce Church (Db–€180, Tb–€220, ask for Rick Steves rate when you book, air-con, elevator, Wi-Fi, Via dei Renai 5, tel. 055-234-2888, fax 055-234-1437, www.hotelsilla.it, hotelsilla@hotelsilla.it, Laura, Chiara, Massimo, and Stefano).

$ Istituto Gould is a Protestant Church–run place with 40 clean and spartan rooms with twin beds and modern facilities (Sb–€44, Db–€56–66, Tb–€75, Qb–€92, breakfast extra, quieter rooms in back, no air-con but rooms have fans, Via dei Serragli 49, tel. 055-212-576, fax 055-280-274, www.istitutogould.it, foresteria firenze@diaconiavaldese.org). You must arrive when the office is open (Mon–Fri 8:45–13:00 & 15:00–19:30, Sat 9:00–13:30 & 14:30–18:00, no check-in Sun or holidays).

$ Soggiorno Alessandra has five bright, comfy, and smallish rooms. Because of its double-paned windows, you'll hardly notice the traffic noise (D–€58–73, Db–€78, Tb–€98, Qb–€128, 5 percent discount with 2-night stay, air-con–€8, just past the Carraia Bridge at Via Borgo San Frediano 6, tel. 055-290-424, fax 055-218-464, www.soggiornoalessandra.it, info@soggiornoalessandra .it, Alessandra).

$ Casa Santo Nome di Gesù is a grand, 29-room convent whose sisters—Franciscan Missionaries of Mary—are thankful to rent rooms to tourists. Staying in this 15th-century palace, you'll be immersed in the tranquil atmosphere created by a huge, peaceful garden, generous and prayerful public spaces, and smiling nuns (D–€70, Db–€85, elevator, no air-con but rooms have fans, twin beds only, memorable convent-like breakfast room, strict 23:29 curfew, Piazza del Carmine 21, tel. 055-213-856, fax 055-281-835, www.fmmfirenze.it, info@fmmfirenze.it).

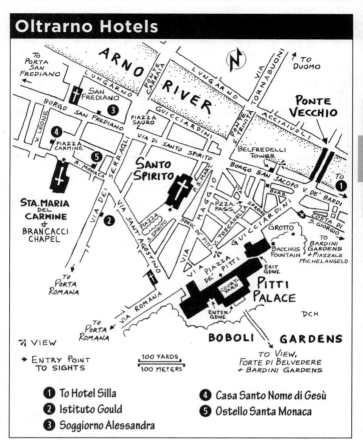

Oltrarno Hotels

1 To Hotel Silla
2 Istituto Gould
3 Soggiorno Alessandra
4 Casa Santo Nome di Gesù
5 Ostello Santa Monaca

Hostels

$ Ostello Santa Monaca, a well-run hostel a long block south of the Brancacci Chapel in the Oltrarno area, attracts a young backpacking crowd (€17–20/bed with sheets, 4- to 20-bed dorms, 10:00–14:00 lock-out, 2:00 curfew, free Internet access, self-serve laundry, Via Santa Monaca 6, tel. 055-268-338, fax 055-280-185, www.ostello.it, info@ostello.it).

$ Villa Camerata, classy for an IYHF hostel, is in a pretty villa three miles northeast of the train station, on the outskirts of Florence (€20/bed with breakfast, 4- to 8-bed rooms, must have hostel membership card or pay additional €3/night, self-serve laundry; take bus #17 from the train station, Duomo, or Piazza San Marco to Salviatino stop; Via Righi 2, tel. 055-601-451, fax 055-610-300, www.hihostels.com, firenze@ostellionline.org).

$ Hostel 7 Santi calls itself a "travelers' haven." It fills a former convent, but you'll feel like you're in an old school. Still, it offers some of the best cheap beds in town; is friendly to older travelers; and comes with the services you'd expect in a big, modern hostel, including free Wi-Fi and a self-serve laundry. It's in a more residential neighborhood near the Campo di Marte stadium, about a 10-minute bus ride from the center (260 beds in 60 rooms, mostly 4- or 6-bed dorms with a floor of doubles and triples, €16/dorm bed, Sb-€30, Ds-€45, Db-€50; includes breakfast, sheets, and towels; no curfew; from the station, Duomo, or Piazza San Marco, take bus #10 or #17 direction: Campo di Marte to bus stop Sette Santi; Viale dei Mille 11, tel. 055-504-8452, www.7santi.com, info@7santi.com).

EATING IN FLORENCE

Florence is a Tuscan tour for your taste buds, but be warned: My readers fill many of the mom-and-pop eateries listed here. But even when packed with travelers, these personality-driven places are a fine value and offer high quality. If you want to steer away from my readers, grab another spot. If it's in the center, it'll probably have less value and just as many tourists. To really escape from the crowds, you need to get away from the town center...though I'd rather stick around. You may have the best luck finding a local ambience at lunch, since that's when many restaurants in the center cater to office workers. For dinner, the locals flee, and those same places fill with tourists. If you're on a budget and are planning to visit any small Tuscan towns, your splurge dollars will go further than in expensive Florence. For an overview of restaurants, other eateries, tips on tipping, and Florentine cuisine, see page 21.

To save money and time for sights, keep lunches fast and simple, eating in one of the countless pizzerias and self-service cafeterias (or picnicking your way though the Mercato Centrale). For dessert, it's gelato (see end of this chapter).

North of the River

Restaurants near Piazza Santa Maria Novella and the Train Station

Trattoria al Trebbio serves traditional food with simple Florentine elegance in its candlelit interior. Tables spill out onto a romantic little square—an oasis of Roman Trastevere-like charm (€8 pastas, €13 *secondi,* daily 12:00–15:00 & 19:15–23:00, reserve for outdoor seating, half a block off of Piazza Santa Maria Novella at Via delle Belle Donne 47, tel. 055-287-089, Antonio).

Trattoria "da Giorgio" is a family-style diner serving up piping-hot, delicious home cooking to happy locals and tourists

EATING IN FLORENCE

Florence Restaurants

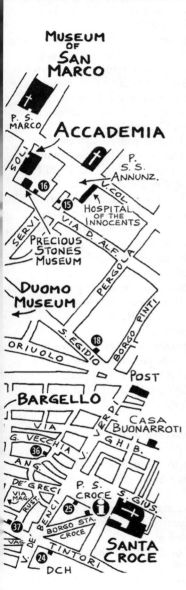

1. Trattoria al Trebbio
2. Trattoria "da Giorgio"
3. Osteria Belle Donne
4. Trattoria Marione
5. Trattoria Sostanza-Troia
6. Trattoria 13 Gobbi
7. Trattoria Zà-Zà & Trattoria Mario's
8. Trattoria la Burrasca
9. Osteria la Congrega
10. Osteria Vineria i'Brincello
11. Trattoria Nerone Pizzeria
12. Il Pirata
13. Mercato Centrale & Nerbone in the Market
14. Casa del Vino
15. Pasticceria Robiglio
16. La Mescita Fiaschetteria
17. Self-Service Rist. Leonardo
18. The Oil Shoppe
19. Rivoire Café
20. Frescobaldi Ristorante & Wine Bar
21. Ristorante Paoli & Cantinetta dei Verrazzano
22. Trattoria Nella
23. Trattoria Icche C'è C'è
24. Ristorante del Fagioli
25. Boccadama Enoteca Ristorante
26. Trattoria Anita
27. Osteria Vini e Vecchi Sapori
28. I Fratellini
29. L'Antico Trippaio
30. 'Ino Bottega di Alimentari e Vini
31. Gelateria Grom
32. Gelateria Carrozze
33. Gelateria Carabè
34. Festival del Gelato
35. Perchè No! Gelateria
36. Vivoli's Gelateria
37. Gelateria de' Neri
38. Il Centro Supermarcati

EATING IN FLORENCE

alike. Their three-course, fixed-price meal is a great value for €12, including water and a drink. Choose from among the daily specials or the regular menu (Mon–Sat 12:00–14:30 & 18:00–22:00, closed Sun, Via Palazzuolo 100 red, tel. 055-284-302).

Osteria Belle Donne makes you feel like you're eating dinner in a crowded terrarium piled high with decorative knickknacks. Old-fashioned Tuscan food is served on tight tables, with a few tables spilling onto a tiny deck outside. They take no reservations and tend to steamroll tourists; arrive early or wait (€10 pastas, €12 *secondi*, daily 12:00–15:00 & 19:00–23:00, Via delle Belle Donne 16 red, tel. 055-238-2609, run by sprightly Giacinto).

Trattoria Marione serves sincerely home-cooked-style meals to a mixed group of tourists and locals in a happy, crowded, food-loving, and steamy ambience (€8 pastas, €10 *secondi*, daily 12:00–15:00 & 19:00–22:30, Via della Spada 27 red, tel. 055-214-756, Fabio).

Trattoria Sostanza-Troia, characteristic and well-established, is famous for its beef. Hearty steaks and pastas are splittable. Whirling ceiling fans and walls strewn with old photos evoke earlier times, while the artichoke pies remind locals of grandma's cooking. Crowded, shared tables with paper tablecloths give this place a bistro feel. They offer two dinner seatings, at 19:30 and 21:00, which require reservations (dinners for about €30 plus wine, cash only, lunch Mon–Sat 12:30–14:00, closed Sun, closed Sat in off-season, Via del Porcellana 25 red, tel. 055-212-691).

Trattoria 13 Gobbi ("13 Hunchbacks") is a trendy favorite, glowing with candles around a tiny garden. Romantic in front and kid-friendly in back, it serves beautifully presented, Tuscan food on big, fancy plates to a mostly tourist crowd (€8.50 pastas, €15 *secondi*, Tue–Sun 12:00–15:00 & 19:30–23:00, closed Mon, Via del Porcellana 9 red, tel. 055-284-015, Enrico).

Restaurants near Mercato Centrale and San Lorenzo Market

The following market neighborhood eateries are distinct but within a hundred yards of each other. Scout around and choose your favorite.

Trattoria Zà-Zà is a fun, characteristic, high-energy place facing the Mercato Centrale. It's a family-friendly festival of standard Tuscan dishes such as *ribollita* and *bistecca alla fiorentina*, plus a variety of big, splittable salads. Locals lament the invasion of tourists, but everyone's happy, and the food is still great. Arrive early or make a reservation, especially for the wonderful outdoor piazza seating. Understand your itemized bill (as they are reportedly arithmetic-challenged), and don't mistake their outside seating with the neighboring restaurant (daily 11:30–23:00, Piazza del Mercato Centrale 26 red, tel. 055-215-411).

Döner Kebab—Cheap, Fast, and Not a Hint of Pasta

Because of the influx of Middle Eastern immigrants into Italy, "ethnic cuisine" has become more prevalent in recent years. Today, shops selling döner kebab (roasted meat wrapped in thin bread) are sprouting up everywhere.

Döner kebab shops offer cheap, filling, healthy alternatives to your average slice of pizza or ham-and-cheese panino. The kebab itself consists of chicken or veal and turkey, which has been cut into thick slabs, piled high onto a skewer, and slow-roasted on a vertical spit. Once it's cooked, the rich, savory meat is sliced ultra-thin with a razor and stuffed into your choice of pita bread (panino) or a wrap *(piadina)*, along with tomatoes, onions, lettuce, tangy yogurt sauce, and (optional) hot chili sauce.

A vegetarian alternative is falafel (a fried garbanzo-bean patty) served with the same works. Both cost about €3–4, and shops are generally open from 11:00 in the morning until midnight.

Trattoria la Burrasca is Flintstone-chic. Friendly duo Elio and Simone offer a limited menu with daily specials of rib-stickin' Tuscan home cooking. It's small—10 tables—and often filled with my readers. If Archie Bunker were Italian, he'd eat at this *trattoria* for special nights out (€7 pastas, €10 *secondi*, Tue–Sun 12:00–15:30 & 19:00–23:00, closed Mon, Via Panicale 6, north corner of Mercato Centrale, tel. 055-215-827).

Osteria la Congrega brags that it's "a Tuscan wine bar designed to help you lose track of time." In a fresh, imaginative, two-level setting, chef/owner Mahyar takes pride in his fun, easy menu, which features modern Tuscan cuisine, top-notch meat, and seasonal produce. He offers quality vegetarian dishes, creative salads, and an inexpensive but excellent house wine. With just 10 tables, reservations are required for dinner (€8 pastas, €12 nightly specials, daily 12:00–15:00 & 19:00–23:00, closed Sun in winter, a block from Mercato Centrale, Via Panicale 43 red, tel. 055-264-5027). Mahyar offers fine wines by the glass (see list on blackboard) and occasional live jazz. Between meals, he teaches cooking classes here (www.osterialacongrega.it).

Osteria Vineria i'Brincello—a bright, happy, no-frills diner with lots of spirit and friendly service—is great for a simple lunch. Notice the list of Tuscan daily specials on the blackboard hanging from the ceiling (€7 pastas, daily 12:00–15:00 & 18:30–23:00, corner of Via Nazionale and Via Chiara at Via Nazionale 110 red, tel. 055-282-645, Freddie cooks while Claudia and Max serve).

Trattoria Nerone Pizzeria serves up cheap, hearty Tuscan dishes and decent pizzas. The lively, flamboyantly outfitted space (once the garden courtyard of a convent) feels like a good but kitschy American Italian chain restaurant (€7 pizzas, €7 pastas, €10 *secondi,* daily 12:00–15:00 & 18:30–23:00, just north of Via Nazionale at Via Faenza 95 red, tel. 055-291-217, Tulio).

Il Pirata, a deli and rotisserie, puts out a €6 all-you-can-eat buffet each evening (18:00–22:00). They offer budget travelers an array of homemade Italian dishes and roasted meats for take-out or to dine-in at their counter. Pick up a plastic plate, fill it, get it microwaved if you like, grab a stool, and chow down (closed Sun, 2 blocks from the Accademia at Via de' Ginori 56 red, tel. 055-218-625). You don't want to linger here...but you'll fill your stomach.

Lunching Cheap and Simple in or near the Mercato Centrale and San Lorenzo Market

Mercato Centrale (Central Market) is great for an ad-lib lunch. It offers colorful piles of picnic produce, people-watching, and rustic sandwiches (Mon–Sat 7:00–14:00, closed Sun, a block north of San Lorenzo street market). Meat, fish, and cheese are sold on the ground level, with fruit and veggies mostly upstairs. The thriving ground-level eateries within the market (such as Nerbone, described next) serve some of the cheapest hot meals in town. The fancy deli, Perini, is famous for its quality products and generous free samples. Buy a picnic of fresh mozzarella cheese, olives, fruit, and crunchy bread to munch on the steps of the nearby Church of San Lorenzo, overlooking the bustling street market.

Nerbone in the Market is a venerable café and the best place for a sit-down meal within Mercato Centrale. Join the shoppers and workers who crowd up to the bar to grab their €5 plates—tripe is very big here—and then find an informal table to eat at nearby. Of the several cheap market diners, this feels the most authentic (lunch only, cash only, inside Mercato Centrale on the side closest to the Church of San Lorenzo, tel. 055-219-949).

Trattoria Mario's, around the corner from Trattoria Zà-Zà (above), has been serving hearty lunches to market-goers since 1953 (Fabio and Romeo are the latest generation). Their simple formula: bustling service, old-fashioned good value, a lunch-only fixed-price meal, and shared tables. It's *cucina casalinga*—home cooking *con brio.* This place is extremely popular, and their best dishes often sell out first, so go early. If there's a line, put your name on the list (€5 pastas, €8 *secondi,* cash only, Mon–Sat 12:00–15:30, closed Sun, no reservations, Via Rosina 2, tel. 055-218-550).

Casa del Vino, Florence's oldest operating wine shop, offers glasses of wine from among 25 open bottles. Owner Gianni, whose family has owned the Casa for 70 years, is a class act

(Mon–Fri 9:30–16:30, closed Sat–Sun, hidden behind stalls of the San Lorenzo Market at Via dell'Ariento 16 red). Gianni's *carta dei panini* lists many delightful €3.50 sandwiches, and the opened bottles behind the counter are marked with prices for wine by the glass. During busy times, it's a mob scene. You'll eat standing outside, with local workers on a quick lunch break.

Budget Lunches near the Accademia and Museum of San Marco

Pasticceria Robiglio, a smart little café, opens up its stately dining area and sets out a few tables on the sidewalk for lunch on workdays. They have a small menu of daily pasta and *secondi* specials, and seem determined to do things like they did in the elegant, pre-tourism days (generous €8 plates, a great €7.50 *niçoise*-like "fantasy salad," pretty pastries, good wines by the glass, smiling service, daily 12:00–15:00, longer hours as a café, a block toward the Duomo off Piazza S.S. Annunziata at Via dei Servi 112 red, tel. 055-212-784). Before you leave, be tempted by their pastries—famous among Florentines.

La Mescita Fiaschetteria is a characteristic hole-in-the-wall just around the corner from *David*—but a world away from all the tourism. It's where locals and students enjoy daily pasta specials and hearty sandwiches with good €1 house wine. You can trust Mirco; just point to what looks good (such as their €4 pasta plate) and eat lunch quickly, well, and inexpensively. The place can either be mobbed by local students or in a peaceful time warp, depending upon when you stop by (Mon–Sat 12:00–16:00, closed Sun, Via degli Alfani 70 red, mobile 347-795-1604).

Picnic on the Ultimate Renaissance Square: A handy supermarket across from the Accademia *(David)* happily makes sandwiches to your specs (Il Centro Supermarcati, Mon–Sat 8:00–20:00, Sun 10:00–19:00, Via Ricasoli 109). Choose your fresh bread and tasty meat and cheese (assembled and sold by the weight); embellish with some veggies, milk, yogurt, or juice; and hike around the block to Piazza S.S. Annunziata, the first Renaissance square in Florence. There's a fountain for washing fruit on the square. Grab a stony seat anywhere you like, and savor one of my favorite cheap Florence eating experiences. (Or, drop by either of the two places listed above for a sandwich and juice to go.)

Eating Fast and Cheap near the Duomo

Self-Service Ristorante Leonardo is inexpensive, air-conditioned, quick, and handy. Eating here, you'll get the sense that they're passionate about the quality of their food. It's just a block from the Duomo, southwest of the Baptistery (tasty €4 pastas, €5 main courses, Sun–Fri 11:45–14:45 & 18:45–21:45, closed Sat, upstairs at

Via Pecori 11, tel. 055-284-446). Luciano (like Pavarotti) runs the place with enthusiasm, and puts out free pitchers of tap water.

The Oil Shoppe cobbles together huge gourmet hot and cold sub sandwiches *all'Italiana* from creative ingredients, or build your own salad and pair it with a homemade soup of the day for a fast, cheap, and hearty lunch. Eat at the skinny counter or take your food to go (Mon–Fri 11:00–20:00, Sun 12:00–18:00, closed Sat, 2 long blocks east of the Duomo at Via S. Egidio 22 red, tel. 055-200-1092, cheery Alberto runs the show).

Dining near the Palazzo Vecchio

Piazza della Signoria, the scenic square facing the Palazzo Vecchio, is ringed by beautifully situated yet touristy eateries serving overpriced, bad-value, and probably microwaved food. If you're determined to eat on the square, have pizza at Ristorante il Cavallino or bar food from the Irish pub next door. The Piazza della Signoria's saving grace is **Rivoire** café, famous for its fancy desserts and thick hot chocolate. While obscenely expensive, it has the best view tables on the square (Mon–Sat 7:40–24:00, closed Sun, tel. 055-214-412).

Frescobaldi Ristorante and Wine Bar, the showcase of Italy's aristocratic wine family, is a good choice for a formal dinner in Florence. Candlelight reflects on glasses, and high-vaulted ceilings complement the sophisticated dishes and fine wines. They offer the same menu in three different dining areas: cozy interior, woody wine bar, and breezy terrace. If coming for dinner, dress up, make a reservation, and hit an ATM (€12 appetizers and pastas, €20 *secondi*, lunch salads, Mon–Sat 12:00–14:30 & 19:00–23:00, closed Sun and Aug; air-con, half a block north of the Palazzo Vecchio at Via dei Magazzini 2–4 red, tel. 055-284-724). Don't let them railroad you into ordering things you don't want.

Ristorante Paoli dishes up wonderful local cuisine to loads of cheerful eaters being served by jolly little old men under a richly frescoed Gothic vault. Because of its fame and central location, it's filled mostly with tourists, but for a sophisticated, traditional Tuscan splurge meal, this is a fine choice. Salads are dramatically cut and mixed from a trolley right at your table. The walls are sweaty with memories that go back to 1824, and the service is flamboyant and fun-loving (but don't get taken—confirm prices). Woodrow Wilson slurped spaghetti here—his bust looks down on you as you eat (€11 pastas, €15 *secondi*, €25 tourist fixed-price meal, Wed–Mon 12:00–15:00 & 19:00–22:30, closed Tue, reserve for dinner, between Piazza della Signoria and the Duomo at Via dei Tavolini 12 red, tel. 055-216-215).

Trattoria Nella serves good, typical Tuscan cuisine at affordable prices. Twin brothers Federico and Lorenzo carry on their father Sergio's tradition of keeping their clientele well-fed and happy. Their ravioli with walnuts is a hit with regulars (daily specials, €9 pastas, €14 *secondi*, Mon–Sat 12:00–15:00 & 19:00–22:00, closed Sun, reserve for dinner, 3 blocks northwest of Ponte Vecchio, Via delle Terme 19 red, tel. 055-218-925).

Dining near Santa Croce Church

Trattoria Icche C'è C'è (EE-kay chay chay; dialect for "whatever there is, there is") is a small, family-style restaurant where fun-loving Gino and his wife Mara serve quality, local food, including a €13 three-course, fixed-price meal (€6 pastas, €10 *secondi*, Tue–Sun 12:30–14:30 & 19:30–22:30, closed Mon and two weeks in Aug, midway between Bargello and river at Via Magalotti 11 red, tel. 055-216-589).

Ristorante del Fagioli is an enthusiastically run eatery where you feel the heritage. The dad, Gigi, commands the kitchen while sons Antonio and Simone keep the throngs of loyal locals returning. The cuisine: home-style bread soups, hearty steaks, and Florentine classics (€9 pastas, €9 *secondi*, closed Sat–Sun, reserve for dinner, cash only, between Santa Croce Church and the Alle Grazie bridge at Corso dei Tintori 47, tel. 055-244-285). Don't worry—while *fagioli* means "beans," that's the family name, not the extent of the menu.

Boccadama Enoteca Ristorante is a stylish, shabby-chic wine bistro serving creative Tuscan fare based on seasonal produce. Eat in the intimate candlelit dining room or at a few tables lining tranquil Piazza Santa Croce. Reservations are smart (€9 *primi*, €14 *secondi*, daily 11:00–15:00 & 19:00–22:30, on south side of Piazza Santa Croce at 25–26 red, tel. 055-243-640).

Trattoria Anita, midway between the Uffizi and Santa Croce, offers a good lunch special: three hearty Tuscan courses—antipasto, pasta, and *secondi*—for €9 (Mon–Sat 12:00–14:30, closed Sun, on the corner of Via Vinegia and Via del Parlagio at #2 red, tel. 055-218-698).

Eating Cheap and Simple near the Palazzo Vecchio and Uffizi Gallery

Cantinetta dei Verrazzano, a long-established bakery/café/wine bar, serves delightful sandwich plates in an old-time setting. Their *specialità Verrazzano* is a fine plate of four little crostini (like mini-bruschetta) proudly featuring different breads, cheeses, and meats from the Chianti region (€7.50). The *tagliere di focacce* (confirm the €6.50-per-person price), a sampler plate of mini-focaccia sandwiches, is also fun. Add a glass of Chianti to either of these dishes to make a fine, light meal. Office workers pop in for a quick lunch, and it's traditional to share tables (Mon–Sat 8:00–21:00, closed Sun, just off Via de' Calzaiuoli on a side street across from Orsanmichele Church at Via dei Tavolini 18, tel. 055-268-590). They also have benches and tiny tables for eating at "take out" prices. Simply step to the back and point to the hot *focacce* sandwich (€3) you'd like, order a drink at the bar, and take away your food or sit with locals and watch the action while you munch.

Osteria Vini e Vecchi Sapori, half a block north of the Palazzo Vecchio, is a colorful 16-seat hole-in-the-wall serving Tuscan food, including plates of mixed crostini (€1 each—step right up and choose at the bar) and €10 daily specials. Be sure to try their raspberry *(lampone)* tiramisu. In the evening, it becomes a little restaurant with a fun, accessible menu of delicious €8 pastas and *secondi* (Tue–Sat 12:30–15:00 & 19:30–22:00, Sun 12:30–15:00, closed Mon, reserve for dinner; facing the bronze equestrian statue in Piazza della Signoria, go behind its tail into the corner and to your left; Via dei Magazzini 3 red, tel. 055-293-045, run by Mario while wife Rosanna cooks and son Thomas serves).

I Fratellini is an informal little eatery where the "little brothers" have served peasants 29 different kinds of sandwiches and cheap glasses of Chianti wine (see list on wall) since 1875. Join the local crowd to order, then sit on a nearby curb or windowsill to munch, placing your glass on the wall rack before you leave (€4 for sandwich and wine, Mon–Sat 9:00–20:00 or until the bread runs out, closed Sun, 20 yards in front of Orsanmichele Church on Via dei Cimatori, tel. 055-239-6096). Be adventurous with the menu (easy-order by number). Consider *finocchiona* (the special local salami), *lardo di Colonnata* (lard aged in Carrara marble), and *cinghiale piccante* (spicy wild boar) sandwiches. Order the most expensive wine they're selling by the glass (Brunello for €4; bottles are labeled).

L'Antico Trippaio, an antique tripe stand, is a fixture in the town center (on Via Dante Alighieri, mobile 339-742-5692). Cheap and authentic as can be, this is where locals come daily for €3.50 sandwiches (panino) featuring specialties like *trippa alla fiorentina* (tripe), *lampredotto* (cow's stomach), and a list of more appetizing sandwiches. Roberto offers a free plastic glass of his Chianti with each sandwich for travelers with this book. The best people-watching place to munch your sandwich is three blocks away, on Piazza della Signoria.

'Ino Bottega di Alimentari e Vini is a mod little shop filled with gifty edibles. Serena and Alessandro serve sandwiches and wine—you'll get your €5–7 sandwich on a napkin with an included glass of their wine of the day as you perch on a tiny stool. They can also make a fine *piatto misto* of cheeses and meats; just say how much you'd like to spend (Tue–Sat 11:00–20:00, Sun 12:00–17:00, closed Mon, immediately behind Uffizi Gallery on Ponte Vecchio side, Via dei Georgofili 3 red, tel. 055-219-208).

Oltrarno, South of the River
Dining with a Ponte Vecchio View

Golden View Open Bar is a lively, trendy bistro, good for a romantic meal or just a salad, pizza, or pasta with fine wine and a fine view of Ponte Vecchio and the Arno River. Reservations for window tables are essential (reasonable prices, €10 pizzas and big salads, daily 11:30–24:00, impressive wine bar, 50 yards upstream from Ponte Vecchio at Via dei Bardi 58, tel. 055-214-502, run by Francesco, Antonio, Marco, and Tomaso). They have four seating areas (with the same menu and prices) for whatever mood you're in: a riverside pizza place, a classier restaurant, jazzy lounge, and a wine bar (serving a buffet of appetizers free with your drink 19:00–22:00). Mixing their fine wine, river views, and live jazz makes for a wonderful evening (jazz nightly at 21:00 except Tue and Thu off-season).

Dining in the Heart of the Oltrarno

Of the many good and colorful restaurants in Oltrarno, these are my favorites. You can survey most of these while following the route in the Oltrarno Walk chapter before making a choice. Reservations are smart in the evening.

Ristorante Enoteca la Barrique, with eight tables, offers a delightful, quiet, intimate break from traditional Italian cuisine. The Japanese chef fuses Tuscan and Asian with a fun, inviting menu. The list is short as everything is fresh and seasonal. While the candlelit interior is calm and sweet, the garden out back is a welcome option on a hot summer night (€10 homemade pastas, €14 *secondi*, €2 cover, closed Mon, two blocks beyond Piazza del Carmine at Via del Leone 40, tel. 055-224-192, Allessandro). If la Barrique doesn't work for you, **Ristorante Pandemonio,** a block farther down the street, is also good (closed Sun, Via del Leone 50, tel. 055-224-002).

Trattoria 4 Leoni creates the quintessential Oltrarno dinner scene. The food is Tuscan with an innovative twist and an appreciation for vegetables. You'll enjoy the fun energy and characteristic seating, both inside and on the colorful square, Canto ai Quattro Pagoni (informally known as Piazza della Passera). While the wines by the glass are pricey, the house wine is very good (€10 pastas, €15 *secondi*, nightly from 19:00; from Ponte Vecchio walk four blocks up Via de' Guicciardini, turn right on Via dello Sprone, then slightly left to Via de' Vellutini 1; tel. 055-218-562).

Olio & Convivium Gastronomia started as an elegant deli whose refined oil-tasting room morphed into a romantic, aristocratic restaurant. Their three intimate rooms are surrounded by fine *prosciutti*, cheeses, and wine shelves. It's an intimidating place and a little pretentious, but one that foodies will appreciate for its quiet atmosphere. Use it for a special evening. Their list of €13–20

EATING IN FLORENCE

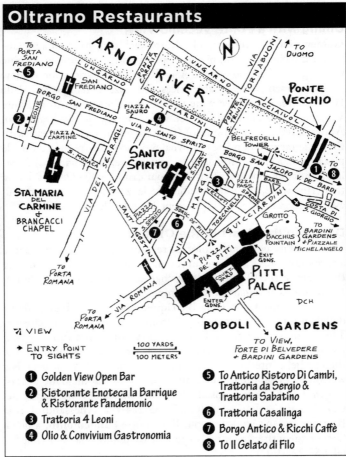

Oltrarno Restaurants

Legend:

1. Golden View Open Bar
2. Ristorante Enoteca la Barrique & Ristorante Pandemonio
3. Trattoria 4 Leoni
4. Olio & Convivium Gastronomia
5. To Antico Ristoro Di Cambi, Trattoria da Sergio & Trattoria Sabatino
6. Trattoria Casalinga
7. Borgo Antico & Ricchi Caffè
8. To Il Gelato di Filo

gastronomia plates offers an array of taste treats and fine wines by the glass (€14 pastas, €18 *secondi*, stylish €18 lunches, €3 cover, Tue–Sat 12:00–14:30 & 19:00–22:30, Mon lunch only, closed Sun, strong air-con, Via di Santo Spirito 4, tel. 055-265-8198).

Antico Ristoro Di Cambi is a meat-lover's dream—thick with Tuscan traditions, rustic touches, and T-bone steaks. The bustling scene has a memorable, beer-hall energy. As you walk in, you'll pass a glass case filled with red chunks of Chianina beef. These cost €40 each, and can be split by two or even more—a good chance to enjoy the famous *bistecca alla fiorentina*. You can enjoy the convivial woody interior, or sit outside on a square (€8 pastas, €12 *secondi*, closed Sun, reserve on weekends and to sit outside, Via Sant'Onofrio 1 red, one block south of Ponte Amerigo Vespucci, tel. 055-217-134, run by Stefano and Fabio, the Cambi cousins).

Trattoria da Sergio, a tiny eatery about a block before Porta San Frediano, has charm and a strong local following—reservations are a must. The food is on the gourmet side of home-cooking—mama's favorites with a modern twist—and therefore a bit more expensive (€10 pastas, €15 *secondi*, Mon–Sat 19:30–23:00, closed Sun, Borgo San Frediano 145 red, tel. 055-223-449, Sergio and Marco).

Eating Cheaply in the Oltrarno

Trattoria Sabatino, farthest away and least touristy of my Oltrarno listings, is a spacious, brightly lit mess hall—disturbingly cheap—with family character and a simple menu. It's a super place to watch locals munch. You'll find it just outside the Porta San Frediano, one of Florence's medieval gates, a 15-minute walk from Ponte Vecchio (€4 pastas, €5 *secondi*, Mon–Fri 12:00–15:00 & 19:00–22:00, closed Sat–Sun, Via Pisana 2 red, tel. 055-225-955, little English spoken). Let eating here be your reward after following the stroll in my Oltrarno Walk chapter.

Trattoria Casalinga, an inexpensive standby, comes with aproned women bustling around the kitchen. Locals and tourists alike pack the place and leave full and happy, with euros to spare for gelato (€6 pastas, €7 *secondi,* Mon–Sat 12:00–14:30 & 19:00–21:30, after 20:00 reserve or wait, closed Sun and Aug, just off Piazza Santo Spirito, near the church at Via de' Michelozzi 9 red, tel. 055-218-624).

Borgo Antico is the hit of Piazza Santo Spirito, with enticing pizzas, big deluxe plates of pasta, a delightful setting, and a trendy and boisterous young local crowd (€9 pizza and pasta, €16 *secondi*, daily 12:00–24:00, best to reserve for a seat on the square, Piazza Santo Spirito 6 red, tel. 055-210-437).

Ricchi Caffè, next to Borgo Antico, has fine gelato, homemade desserts, shaded outdoor tables, and pasta dishes at lunch (Mon–Sat 7:00–24:00, closed Sun, tel. 055-215-864). After noting the plain facade of the Brunelleschi church facing the square, step inside the café and pick your favorite picture of the many ways it might be finished.

Gelato

Gelato is an edible art form. Italy's best ice cream is in Florence—one souvenir that can't break and won't clutter your luggage. But beware of scams at touristy joints on busy streets that turn a simple request for a cone into a €10 "tourist special" rip-off.

A key to gelato appreciation is sampling liberally and choosing flavors that go well together. Ask, as the locals do, for *"Un assaggio, per favore?"* (A taste, please?; oon ah-SAH-joh pehr fah-VOH-ray) and *"Che si sposano bene?"* (What marries well?; kay see spoh-ZAH-noh BEN-ay).

Artiginale, nostra produzione, and *produzione propia* mean gelato is made on the premises, and gelato displayed in covered metal tins (rather than white plastic) is more likely to be homemade. Gelato aficionados avoid colors that don't appear in nature—for fewer chemicals and real flavor, go for mellow hues (bright colors attract children). These places are open daily for long hours.

Near the Duomo: The new favorite in town, **Grom** uses organic ingredients and seasonal fresh fruit. Their traditional approach and quality gives locals déjà vu, reminding them of the good old days and the ice cream of their childhood. Mario, who really cares, sees "gelato as cuisine," and adjusts the menu monthly to fit what's in season (daily 10:30–24:00, Via delle Oche 24a). Their licorice is worth a sample.

Near Ponte Vecchio: **Gelateria Carrozze** is a longtime local favorite (daily 11:00–20:00, until 1:00 in the morning in summer, on riverfront 30 yards from Ponte Vecchio toward the Uffizi at Piazza del Pesce 3).

Near the Accademia: A Sicilian choice on a tourist thoroughfare, **Gelateria Carabè** is particularly famous for its luscious *granite*—Italian ices made with fresh fruit. Antonio, whose family has made ice cream the Sicilian way for more than 100 years, can tell you why that's important (daily 11:00–20:00; from the Accademia, it's a block toward the Duomo at Via Ricasoli 60 red).

Near Orsanmichele Church: For gelato served in a brash, neon environment, it's **Festival del Gelato** or **Perchè No!**, located just off the busy main pedestrian drag (Via de' Calzaiuoli). They serve a stunning array of brightly colored, kid-pleasing flavors (Festival del Gelato is at Via del Corso 75; Perchè No! is at Via dei Tavolini 19).

Near the Church of Santa Croce: The venerable favorite, **Vivoli's** still serves great gelato—but it's more expensive and stingy in its servings (closed Mon, Aug, and Jan; opposite the Church of Santa Croce, go down Via Torta a block and turn right on Via Stinche). Before ordering, try a free sample of their rice flavor—*riso*. Locals flock to **Gelateria de' Neri** (Via de' Neri 26 red), also owned by Vivoli's.

Across the River: If you want an excuse to check out the little village-like neighborhood across the river from Santa Croce, enjoy a gelato at the tiny **Il Gelato di Filo** (named for Filippo and Lorenzo) at Via San Miniato 5 red, a few steps toward the river from Porta San Miniato. Gelato chef Edmir is proud of his fruity sorbet as well.

FLORENCE WITH CHILDREN

Florence with kids: not ideal. But it's certainly good for them! Here are a few thoughts on family fun in the art capital of Europe.

- Book ahead to avoid lines whenever possible, especially at the Uffizi and *David* (see page 89 for more info). Long museum lines add insult to injury for the preteen dragged into another old building filled with more old paintings.
- Avoid the midday heat by planning on a cool break such as an air-conditioned, kid-friendly place for lunch.
- Public WCs are hard to find: Try museums, bars, gelato shops, and fast-food restaurants.
- The smart tour guide/parent incorporates the child's interests into each day's plans. When a child is unhappy, no one has fun.
- Guidebooks can make history more accessible for kids. Try *Florence: A Young Traveller's Guide* (ages 6–9) or *Florence: Just Add Water* (excellent for travelers aged 10 to adult); both are easy to find in Florence. (See bookstores listed under "Helpful Hints" in the Orientation chapter.) The spiral-bound *Kids Go Europe: Treasure Hunt Florence*, available in the US, encourages youngsters to journal and sketch.
- Context Florence offers a children's tour program run by scholarly guides who make the city's great art and culture accessible to kids (contact info on page 41).
- Kids love computers. Buy a big fat Internet Train card and give your kids some surfing time to break up the sightseeing (see "Helpful Hints" in the Orientation chapter).
- Riding the little *elettrico* minibuses around the old town and up and down the river could be entertaining to some children. Propose the challenge of covering as many routes on the A, B, and D lines as you can in 70 minutes—the amount of time a ticket is valid.

- If you're taking the train to another city, ask for the family discount ("Offerta Familia") when buying tickets at a counter. Or, at a ticket machine, click "Yes" to the "Do you want ticket issue?" cue, then click "Familia." With the discount, families of three to five people with at least one kid (age 12 or under) get 50 percent off the kids' tickets, and 20 percent off the adults'. The deal doesn't apply to all trains at all times, but it's worth checking out.

Sights and Activities

After touring a bunch of hands-off museums, squirming kids will enjoy the hands-on activities at the **Leonardo Museum,** where all that human energy can be used to power modern recreations of da Vinci's machines (see page 50).

Climbing the dome of the cathedral is almost like climbing an urban mountain—you'll spiral up in a strange dome-within-a-dome space, see some musty old tools used in the construction, get a bird's-eye peek into the nave from way up, and then pop out to see the best city view in town. Arrive by 8:30 to beat the crowds; otherwise it may not be worth the long, slow-moving line (closed Sun; see page 52).

Every kid will want to see Michelangelo's *David* (closed Mon; see the ✪ Accademia Tour chapter). But the most interesting collection of statues—with many bizarre poses—is in the **Bargello** (see the ✪ Bargello Tour chapter).

The **Children's Museum** (Museo dei Ragazzi), in the Palazzo Vecchio, offers activities (for ages 4 to teens) on a reservation-only basis. The kids can take a guided English tour with a historically costumed character, or make their own fresco on a souvenir tile (€6 plus €2/activity, family rates, no reservation fee, call to reserve, daily 9:00–19:00 except Thu 9:00–14:00, tel. 055-276-8325).

The **Galileo Science Museum** has Galileo's finger on display, plus cool old telescopes and early chemical and science lab stuff. Be warned that some parents find the museum's displays on childbirth inappropriate for children (closed Sun; see the Galileo Science Museum Tour chapter).

The **Museum of Precious Stones** displays 500 different semi-precious stones and then demonstrates the fascinating techniques of inlay and mosaic work (closed Sun, around corner from *David*; see page 48).

The **Uffizi courtyard** is ringed by statues of all the famous Florentines (Amerigo Vespucci, Machiavelli, Leonardo, and so on)—great for putting a face on a sweep through history (see page 86 of the Renaissance Walk chapter).

Florence's various **open-air markets** are fun for kids (see Shopping chapter). Remember to haggle.

The **Boboli Gardens** (and adjacent Bardini Gardens) are landscaped wonderlands. While designed to give adults a break from the city, they are kid-friendly compared to streets and museums (closed first and last Mon of the month; see the ✪ Pitti Palace Tour chapter). To get to Florence's sprawling public park, **Parco delle Cascine,** head west of the old center along the north side of the river (10-min walk, lots of grass, playground, swimming pool open June–Sept).

The peaceful and breezy **Piazza d'Azeglio** park—complete with playground—can be a welcome refuge from touring madness (daily dawn to dusk, 15-min walk east from Duomo or take bus #12 or #13 from train station or from Via Cavour bus stop just north of Duomo).

Older kids may enjoy hiking up to **Piazzale Michelangelo** for the view, or taking a **bike tour** through the countryside. Florence by Bike rents two-wheelers of all sizes and city bikes

with rear child seats (€3/ hr, €8/5 hours, includes bike lock and helmet, daily 9:00–19:30, Via San Zanobi 120 red, tel. 055-488-992, www.florence bybike.it); another bike-rental place is 50 yards in front of the train station. While it's possible to bike through Florence, it's far from safe.

For kids running on their gelato buzz well into the evening hours, the vibrant **Piazza della Repubblica** has a sparkling carousel and lively street musicians.

Of all the side trips, a jaunt to see the Leaning Tower in **Pisa** is probably the most interesting for kids (see page 351; note that kids under 8 aren't allowed to climb the tower).

Eating

Eat dinner early (at about 19:00), and you'll miss the romantic crowd. (Restaurants are less kid-friendly after 21:00.) Skip the famous places. Look instead for self-serve cafeterias, bars (children are welcome), or fast-food restaurants where kids can move around without bothering others. Picnic lunches and dinners work well. For ready-made picnics, drop by a *rosticceria* (deli) or a Pizza Rustica shop (cheap take-out pizza; *diavola* is the closest thing on the menu to kid-friendly pepperoni).

For fast and kid-approved meals in the old center, there are plenty of hamburger and pizza joints. For a good cafeteria, try Self-Service Ristorante Leonardo (a block from the Duomo; see listing in the Eating in Florence chapter). *Gelaterie* such as Festival del Gelato (Via del Corso 75 red) and Perchè No! (Via dei Tavolini 19 red) are brash and neon, providing some of the best high-calorie memories in town.

SHOPPING IN FLORENCE

Florence is a great shopping town—known for its sense of style since the Medici days. Many people spend entire days shopping. Stores are generally open 9:00–13:00 and 15:30–19:30, usually closed on Sunday, often closed on Monday, and sometimes closed for a couple of weeks around August 15. Many stores have promotional stalls in the market squares.

For shopping ideas, ads, and a list of markets, see *The Florentine* newspaper or *Florence Concierge Information* magazine (free from TI and many hotels). For a list of bookstores, see "Helpful Hints" in the Orientation chapter. For information on VAT refunds and customs regulations, see page 12.

Markets

Busy street scenes and markets abound. Prices are soft in the markets—go ahead and bargain. Perhaps the biggest market is the one

that fills the streets around the Church of San Lorenzo (see page 49), with countless stalls selling lower-end leather, clothing, T-shirts, handbags, and souvenirs (daily 9:00–19:00, closed Mon in winter, between the Duomo and train station). Beware of fake "genuine" leather and "Venetian" glass. The neighboring Mercato Centrale (Central Market) is a giant covered food market (see "Edible Goodies," later in this chapter).

Other popular shopping centers are the Santa Croce area (known for leather; check out the leather school, which is actually inside the Santa Croce Church—enter to the right of the altar or use the outside entrance); Ponte Vecchio (traditional spot for gold and silver); and the old, covered Mercato Nuovo (three blocks north of Ponte Vecchio, described on page 57).

For antiques, artisan shops, and fashionable clothing boutiques, wander the city's "Left Bank," the Oltrarno (south side of river—see the Oltrarno Walk chapter).

A **flea market** litters Piazza dei Ciompi with antiques and odds and ends daily, but is only really big on the last Sunday of each month (9:00–20:00, near Piazza Santa Croce).

Boutiques and High Fashion

The entire area between the river and the cathedral is busy with inviting boutiques that show off ritzy Italian fashions. The street Via de' Tornabuoni is best for boutique browsing.

The main **Ferragamo** store fills a classy 800-year-old building with a fine selection of shoes and boots (daily 10:00–19:30, Via de' Tornabuoni 2). They have an interesting, four-room shoe museum (€5, Wed–Mon 10:00–18:00, closed Tue, near the Santa Trinità bridge at Piazza Santa Trinità 5, tel. 055-336-0846). For more boutiques, meander the streets Via della Vigna Nuova (runs west from Via de' Tornabuoni), Via del Parione, and Via Strozzi (runs east from Via de' Tornabuoni to Piazza della Repubblica).

Department Stores

Typical chain department stores are **Coin,** the local equivalent of Macy's (Mon–Sat 10:00–20:00, Sun 10:30–20:00, on Via de' Calzaiuoli, near Orsanmichele Church); the similar, upscale **La Rinascente** (Mon–Sat 9:00–21:00, Sun 10:00–20:00, on Piazza della Repubblica); and **Oviesse,** the local JCPenney, a discount clothing chain (Mon–Sat 9:00–19:30, Sun 10:00–19:30, near train station at intersection of Via Panzani and Via del Giglio).

Souvenir Ideas

Shoppers in Florence can easily buy art reproductions (posters, calendars, books, prints, and so on—a breeze to find in and near the Uffizi and Accademia museums). With its tradition as a literary center, Florence offers traditional marbled stationery and leather-bound journals (try the Il Papiro chain stores), plus reproductions of old documents, maps, and manuscripts. Find silk ties, scarves, and Tuscan ceramics at the San Lorenzo street market, where haggling is expected. Goofy knickknacks featuring Renaissance

masterpieces are fun gifts: Botticelli mouse pads, Raphael lipstick-holders, and plaster *David*s. For soaps, skin creams, herbal remedies, and perfumes, sniff out the antique and palatial perfumery, **Farmacia di Santa Maria Novella** (Via della Scala 16, see page 63).

Edible Goodies

The **Mercato Centrale** is a prime spot for stocking up on culinary souvenirs (Mon–Sat 7:00–14:00, closed Sun, a block north of the Church of San Lorenzo). Classic purchases include olives, Parmigiano-Reggiano cheese, unusually shaped and colored pasta, and jars of pestos and sauces (such as pesto *genovese* or *tartufo*—truffle).

Upstairs, where produce and bulk products are sold, the price of the dried porcini mushrooms is less than a quarter of what you'll find at the airport Duty Free. While many bring home a special bottle of Chianti Classico or Brunello di Montalcino, I take home only the names of my favorite wines—and buy them later at my local wine shop (rather than flying with hard-to-pack bottles).

NIGHTLIFE IN FLORENCE

With so many American and international college students in town, Florence by night can have a frat-party atmosphere. For me, nighttime is for eating a late meal, catching a concert, attending a lecture, strolling through the old-town pedestrian zone and piazzas, or hitting one of the many pubs.

The latest on nightlife and concerts is listed in several publications available free at the TI (such as the bi-weekly *The Florentine*) or for a small price at newsstands (consider the monthly *Firenze Spettacolo,* which has an English section). The TI prints a daily listing of musical events. Also check www.firenzeturismo.it.

Strolling

The historic center has a good floodlit ambience ideal for strolling. The entire pedestrian zone along Via de' Calzaiuoli, between the Uffizi and the Duomo, is lively with people. Piazza della Repubblica, lined with venerable 19th-century cafés, offers good people-watching. In the evening, it's a hub of activity with opera singers, violinists, harpists, bizarre street performers, and a cover band that plays cheesy tunes for the seating area of one of the piazza's bars. Ponte Vecchio is a popular place to enjoy river views (and kiss). Some squares feel creepy after dark. Use good judgment. I'd skip the seedy area north of the Mercato Centrale.

Piazzale Michelangelo, perched on a hilltop across the river (bus #12 or #13 from the train station), is awesome for sunset-watching; it's packed with local Romeos and Juliets on weekend evenings. The

nearby San Miniato Church is quieter and comes with the same commanding view. If you're going after dark, it's more efficient to zip up there by taxi (rather than take a 60-min round-trip hike). While side-tripping out to **Fiesole** for the sunset is popular (described at the end of the Sights in Florence chapter), I'd stick with Piazzale Michelangelo.

Live Music

Frequent **live concerts** enhance Florence's beautiful setting. In the summertime, piazzas host a wide range of performers, including pop bands on temporary stages. The lovely sounds of classical music fill churches year-round for special performances.

Orsanmichele Church regularly holds concerts under its Gothic arches. Tickets are sold on the day of the concert from the door facing Via de' Calzaiuoli.

Santa Maria de' Ricci Church, a delightful and intimate Baroque space, hosts a variety of hour-long concerts practically every night, usually at 21:15 (€11 tickets generally available at the door, some concerts are free, between Duomo and Palazzo Vecchio on Via del Corso, tel. 055-215-044).

Orchestra della Toscana presents classical concerts from November to May in the Teatro Verdi (box office open Mon–Fri 10:00–13:00 & 15:00–18:00, closed Sat–Sun, near Bargello at Via Ghibellina 99 red, tel. 055-212-320, www.orchestradellatoscana.it).

The **Golden View Open Bar** complements its Arno River views with live jazz (nightly at 21:00, no jazz off-season Tue and Thu; near Ponte Vecchio—see listing in Eating in Florence chapter).

The **Box Office** sells tickets for rock concerts and theater productions in Italian (Mon–Sat 10:00–20:00, closed Sun, on road that runs along west side of train station, Via Alamanni 39, tel. 055-210-804).

Ponte Vecchio hosts a fine street musician late each evening in summer. He plugs in his amp, while young locals get comfortable on the curb. There's generally a street concert nightly in the **Uffizi courtyard.**

Wine Bars

A wine bar *(enoteca)* is fun for sampling local wines and enjoying regional munchies, especially pre-dinnertime. Throughout the old town, *enoteche* serve fine Italian wines by the glass with memorable atmosphere.

Le Volpi e l'Uva, specializing only in small wine producers, has a cozy interior and romantic seating on a quiet little piazza. They have 40 open bottles to choose from and a short menu of appropriate dishes. For maximum tasting, they are happy to arrange a set of half-glasses and make a little plate of mixed meats and cheese (Mon–Sat 11:00–21:00, closed Sun, 65 yards south of Ponte Vecchio—walk through Piazza Santa Felicità to Piazza dei Rossi 1, tel. 055-239-8132, run by wine experts Riccardo, Ciro, and Emilio).

Movies

Find first-run films in their original languages—including English—on Monday, Tuesday, and Thursday at Odeon Cinema, a half-block west of Piazza della Repubblica (Via Sassetti 1, tel. 055-214-068, www.cinehall.it; for schedule of original-language films, choose *"Programmazione,"* then look under *"Odeon Original Sound"*).

Late-Night Local Scenes

American university students in Florence seem to do more drinking than studying during their semesters abroad. Apparently it's tough for young people not to overreact when suddenly they're in a land that doesn't make them wait until they are 21 to legally drink.

Piazza Santa Croce: This square becomes a hangout at night, often with concerts in front of the church. The neighboring Via de' Benci is busy with night spots. **Moyo**—a slick, goldenly lit lounge—is a chandeliers-and-thongs kind of place, perfect for a high school prom. They offer a happy-hour buffet at 19:00 (Sun–Thu 8:00–24:00, Fri–Sat 8:00–2:00 in the morning, just off Piazza Santa Croce at Via de' Benci 23 red, tel. 055-247-738).

Piazza Demidoff: To rub elbows with the locals, head across the river toward tiny Piazza Demidoff (cross the bridge east of Ponte Vecchio and turn left). These two places have outdoor seating, chichi interiors, and Florentines flaunting their latest shoe purchases: **Negroni** (Mon–Fri 8:30–2:00 in the morning, Sat–Sun 19:00–2:00, Via dei Renai 17 red, tel. 055-243-647) and **Zoe** (Tue–Sat 8:00–2:00, Sun 18:00–2:00, closed Mon, Via dei Renai 13 red, tel. 055-243-111).

Piazza Santo Spirito: While this square—long known for its riff-raff and druggies—retains an edge, it's becoming a more mainstream place to enjoy the evening. It's lined with lively bars and restaurants. Hobos and drunks just BYOB and camp for the evening around the delightful little fountain at the center of the square. **Pop Café** serves a free vegetarian buffet with drinks from 20:00 to 22:00. It feels trendy, but is plastic-plate simple, with local students getting comfortable on the curbs and cobbles (Piazza Santo Spirito 18, tel. 055-213-852).

CONNECTIONS

Florence is Tuscany's transportation hub, with fine train, bus, or plane connections to virtually anywhere in Italy. The city has several train stations, a bus station (next to the main train station), and an airport (plus Pisa's airport nearby).

Trains

Main Station

Florence's main station is Santa Maria Novella (*Firenze S.M.N.* on schedules and signs). Built in Mussolini's "Rationalism" style back between the wars, in some ways the station seems to have changed little—notice the 1930s-era lettering and architecture.

Florence also has two suburban train stations: Firenze Rifredi and Firenze Campo di Marte. Note that some trains don't stop at the main station—before boarding, confirm that you're heading for S.M.N. or you may overshoot the city. (If this happens, don't panic; the other stations are a short taxi ride from the center.)

Minimize time in the main station—doing business here is generally intense, crowded, and overpriced. It's also rife with pickpockets. The banks of user-friendly automated ticket machines are handy. They take euros and credit cards, display schedules, issue tickets, and even make reservations for railpass-holders. Still, it can be quicker to get tickets and train info from travel agencies in town. Ask about discounts for families (see page 264), students, and seniors. For more on your ticket-buying options, see "Tickets," later in this chapter.

With your back to the tracks, look left to see a 24-hour pharmacy (*Farmacia*, near McDonald's), the fake "Tourist Information" office (funded by hotels), city buses, bus ticket booth, the taxi stand (fast-moving line, except on holidays), and the entrance to the

Italy's Public Transportation

CONNECTIONS

NOT TO SCALE

— RAIL   ⊥ PRIVATE RAIL   •••• SHIP   --- BUS

⊞ AIRPORT (NOT ALL SHOWN)

Train Costs in Italy

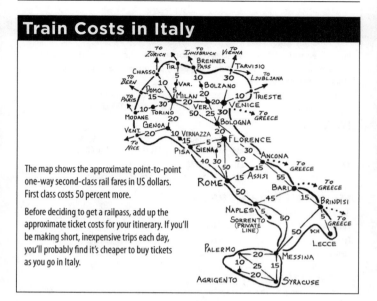

The map shows the approximate point-to-point one-way second-class rail fares in US dollars. First class costs 50 percent more.

Before deciding to get a railpass, add up the approximate ticket costs for your itinerary. If you'll be making short, inexpensive trips each day, you'll probably find it's cheaper to buy tickets as you go in Italy.

Galleria S.M. Novella underground mall/passage that leads from the station under the square to the Church of Santa Maria Novella. (Note: Pickpockets—often dressed as tourists—frequent this tunnel, especially the surface point near the church.) Baggage check is near track 16 (€4/5 hours, then €0.60/hr for 6–12 hours and €0.20/hr for 13-plus, daily 6:00–23:50, passport required, maximum 40 pounds, no explosives—sorry).

Getting to the TI: With your back to the tracks, exit the train station to the left (going straight out the station leads you to an uninviting wasteland of construction). The real TI is across the square by the stone church, 100 yards in front of the station (see page 35). Pick up picnic supplies at the Conad supermarket, located along the west side of the station on Via Luigi Alamanni (Mon–Sat 8:00–20:00, closed Sun). Most recommended hotels are within a 10- or 15-minute walk from the station. The Duomo, though not visible from here, is located to the left (east) down busy Via dei Panzani, a 10-minute walk away.

Railpasses

Most people traveling within Italy find that the Italy Pass for Italian State Railways saves neither time nor hassle. Use the price map above to add up your ticket costs. Although the pass covers the full cost of getting you from A to B on many trains in Italy, it doesn't cover the cost of seat reservations or overnight berths. Reservations are optional for many trains, but are required for the fastest trains between major Italian cities (see "Types of Trains,"

Railpasses

Prices listed are for 2009 and are subject to change. For the latest prices, details, and train schedules (and easy online ordering), see my comprehensive *Guide to Eurail Passes* at www.ricksteves.com/rail.

"Saver" prices are per person for two or more people traveling together. "Youth" means under age 26. The fare for children 4–11 is half the adult individual fare or Saver fare. Kids under age 4 travel free.

ITALY PASS

	Individual 1st Class	Individual 2nd Class	Saver 1st Class	Saver 2nd Class	Youth 2nd Class
3 days in 2 months	$259	$221	$211	$179	$171
Extra rail days (max 7)	$33-33	$25-28	$23-27	$19-22	$20-22

ITALY RAIL & DRIVE PASS

Any 3 rail days and 2 car days in 2 months.

Car Category	1st Class	2nd Class	Extra Car Day
Economy	$343	293	$70
Compact	361	310	88
Intermediate	387	336	114
Extra rail days (max 7)	35	26	

Prices are per person, two traveling together. Solo travelers pay about 20 percent more. To order a Rail & Drive pass, call your travel agent or Rail Europe at 800-438-7245. *This pass is not sold by Europe Through the Back Door.*

FRANCE–ITALY PASS

	Individual 1st Class	Individual 2nd Class	Saver 1st Class	Saver 2nd Class	Youth 2nd Class
4 days in 2 months	$372	$325	$325	$287	$246
Extra rail days (max 6)	43	37	37	32	29

Be aware of your route. Many daytime connections from Paris to Italy pass through Switzerland (an additional $60 2nd class or $90 1st class if not covered by your pass). Routes via Nice, Torino, or Modane will bypass Switzerland. Direct Paris–Italy day or night trains are covered by the pass, regardless of their route.

GREECE–ITALY PASS

	Individual 1st Class	Individual 2nd Class	Saver 1st Class	Saver 2nd Class	Youth 2nd Class
4 days in 2 months	$362	$289	$307	$246	$236
Extra rail days (max 6)	36	30	32	25	23

Covers deck passage on overnight Superfast Ferries between Patras, Greece and Bari or Ancona, Italy (starts use of one travel day). Or 30-50% discount on Hellenic Mediterranean Line ferry with basic cabin Patras-Corfu-Brindisi (does not use a travel day). Does not cover travel to or on Greek islands, except a 30% discount on Blue Star Ferries.

SELECTPASS

This pass covers travel in three adjacent countries. Please visit **www.ricksteves.com/rail** for four- and five-country options.

	Individual 1st Class	Saver 1st Class	Youth 2nd Class
5 days in 2 months	$461	$392	$300
6 days in 2 months	509	481	334
8 days in 2 months	604	561	392
10 days in 2 months	700	638	453

below). While the pass does save you from having to buy each train ticket as you go, if you'll be taking a few fast trains, you'll still have to spend time in line—essentially eliminating the point of buying this pass.

For travel exclusively in Italy, a 21-country **Eurail Global Pass** is a bad value. If you're branching out beyond Italy, the **Eurail Selectpass** allows you to tailor a pass to your trip, provided you're traveling in three, four, or five adjacent countries directly connected by rail or ferry. For instance, with a three-country pass allowing 10 days of train travel within a two-month period ($700 for a single adult in 2009), you could choose France–Italy–Greece or Germany–Austria–Italy. A **France and Italy Pass** combines just those two countries and covers night trains to and from Paris via Switzerland (but if your route crosses Switzerland by day, you'll pay extra—so the Selectpass is a better choice if you want to see the Alps). Before you buy a Selectpass or France and Italy Pass, think carefully how many travel days you'll really need. Use the pass only for travel days that involve long hauls or several trips. Pay out of pocket for tickets on days you're taking only short, cheap rides.

For a summary of railpass deals and the latest prices, check my Guide to Eurail Passes at www.ricksteves.com/rail. If you decide to get a railpass, this guide will help you know you're getting the right one for your trip.

Types of Trains

You'll encounter several types of trains in Italy: pokey, milk-run trains *(regionali)*, slow IR *(interregionali)* and *diretto* trains, the medium *espresso*, the fast IC *(Intercity)*, and the space-age ES *(Eurostar Italia)*. All of these trains are fully covered by a railpass (except the ES and a few IC, EC, and international trains—which require railpass-holders to purchase a €15–20 seat reservation). For point-to-point tickets, you'll pay more the faster you go, but even the fastest trains are still affordable (for example, a second-class ticket on a Florence–Venice express train costs about €34; first class costs about €51).

Tickets

Avoid big-city train station ticket lines whenever possible by using automated ticket machines (in train stations) or going to local travel agencies. You'll be able to easily purchase tickets, make seat reservations, and even book a *cuccetta* (koo-CHEHT-tah; overnight berth).

Automated ticket machines are user-friendly and found in all but the tiniest stations in Italy. You can pay by cash (they give change) or by debit or credit card. Select English, then wade through a menu of destinations. If you don't see the city you're

CONNECTIONS

Anatomy of an Italian Train Ticket

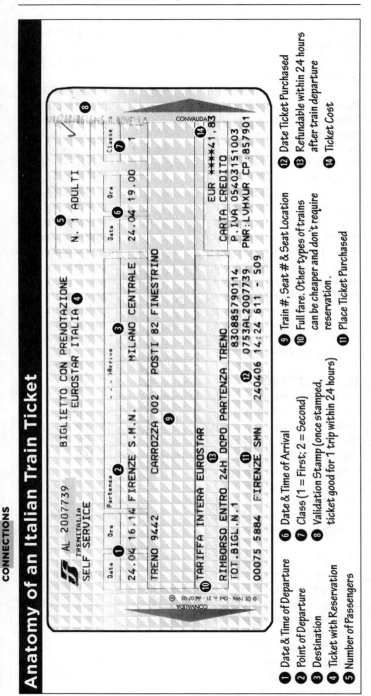

1 Date & Time of Departure
2 Point of Departure
3 Destination
4 Ticket with Reservation
5 Number of Passengers
6 Date & Time of Arrival
7 Class (1 = First; 2 = Second)
8 Validation Stamp (once stamped, ticket good for 1 trip within 24 hours)
9 Train #, Seat # & Seat Location
10 Full fare. Other types of trains can be cheaper and don't require reservation.
11 Place Ticket Purchased
12 Date Ticket Purchased
13 Refundable within 24 hours after train departure
14 Ticket Cost

traveling to, keep keying in the spelling until it's listed. You can choose from first- and second-class seats, request tickets for more than one traveler, and (on the high-speed Eurostar trains) choose an aisle or window seat. When the machine prompts you—"Fidelity Card?"—choose no. Americans will need to select full-price tickets, since we're not eligible for any EU or resident discounts. You can even validate your ticket in the same machine if you're boarding your train right away.

At **local travel agencies,** whether in the station or around town, you'll pay either the same or a little bit more (about €3) than at the train station ticket window, and encounter shorter lines and less of a language barrier.

You can try to buy tickets **online** through www.trenitalia.it if you're Web-savvy, patient, prepared (you have only a 15-minute window of time to place your order), and certain of your needs (don't expect to make changes to your ticket afterward). You usually won't save money booking online, but you'll be able to nail your major trips down well in advance and have e-tickets that won't require validation at the station. The website only accepts American credit cards that have "Verified by Visa" or "Mastercard SecureCode" features. Credit-card approval is often a problem, and the site's rules and features are subject to constant change—causing many readers throw their hands up in defeat.

First-class tickets cost 50 percent more than **second-class.** While second-class cars go as fast as their first-class neighbors, Italy is one country where I would consider the splurge of first class. The easiest way to "upgrade" a second-class ticket once on board a crowded train is to nurse a drink in the snack car.

Before boarding the train, you must **validate** (stamp) your train documents in the yellow box near the platform. This includes whatever you need to take a particular trip, which can be as simple as a single ticket, but can also involve a supplement, seat reservation, or *cuccetta* reservation on an overnight train. If you forget to stamp your ticket, go right away to the train conductor—before he comes to you—or you'll pay a fine. Note that you don't need to stamp a railpass or e-ticket.

Reservations

Trains can fill up, even in first class. If you're on a tight schedule, you'll want to reserve a few days ahead for fast trains (€4 for most trains, or €15–20 for railpass-holders on the Eurostar Italia). Purchasing required seat reservations onboard a train comes with a nasty penalty. Buying them at the station can be a time-waster unless you use the automatic ticket machines.

If you don't have a reservation, and if your train originates at your departure point (e.g., you're catching the Florence–Rome train in Florence), arriving at least 15 minutes before the departure time will help you snare a seat.

Some major stations have train composition posters on the platforms showing where first- and second-class cars are located when the trains arrive (letters on the poster are supposed to correspond to letters posted over the platform—but they don't always). Since most trains now allow you to make reservations up to the time of departure, conductors are no longer marking reserved seats with a card—instead, they simply post a list of the reservable and non-reservable seat rows (sometimes in English) in each train car's vestibule. This means that if you board a crowded train and get one of the last seats, you may be ousted when the reservation holder comes along.

Baggage Storage, Theft Concerns, and Strikes

Many stations have *deposito bagagli* where you can safely leave your bag for €8 per 12-hour period (payable when you pick up the bag, double-check closing hours). Due to security concerns, no Italian stations have lockers.

Italian trains are famous for their thieves. Never leave a bag unattended. I've noticed that police now ride the trains, and things seem more controlled. Still, for an overnight trip, I'd feel safe only in a *cuccetta* (a bunk in a special sleeping car with an attendant who keeps track of who comes and goes while you sleep—approximately €20 in a six-bed compartment, €25 in a less-cramped four-bed compartment).

Strikes, which are common, generally last a day. Train employees will simply explain, "*Sciopero*" (strike). But in actuality, sporadic trains, following no particular schedule, lumber down the tracks during most strikes. When a strike is pending, travel agencies (and Web-savvy hoteliers) can check the Web for you to see when the strike goes into effect and which trains will continue to run. If I need to get somewhere and know a strike is imminent, I leave early (heading off the strike, which often begins at 9:00), or I just go to the station with extra patience in tow and hop on anything rolling in the direction I want to go.

Schedules

At the train station, the easiest way to check schedules is at a handy automated ticket machine. Enter the desired date, time, and destination to view all your options. The machines take euros or credit cards (clearly marked), issue tickets, and make reservations for railpass-holders. Printed schedules are also posted at the station (departure posters are always yellow).

Deciphering Italian Train Schedules

At the station, look for the big yellow posters labeled *Partenze*—Departures (ignore the white posters, which show arrivals).

Schedules are listed chronologically, hour by hour, showing the trains leaving the station throughout the day. Each schedule has columns:

- The first column (Ora) lists the time of departure.
- The next column (Treno) shows the type of train.
- The third column (Classi Servizi) lists the services available (first- and second-class cars, dining car, cuccetta berths, etc.) and, more importantly, whether you need reservations (usually denoted by an R in a box). Note that all Eurostar (ES) trains, many InterCity (IC) and EuroCity (EC) trains, and most international trains require reservations.
- The next column lists the destination of the train (Principali Fermate Destinazioni), often showing intermediate stops, followed by the final destination, with arrival times listed throughout in parentheses. Note that your final destination may be listed in fine print as an intermediate destination. If you're going from Florence to Cortona, scan the schedule and you'll notice that many trains that terminate in Rome stop in Cortona en route (and fast trains stop in Terontola, near Cortona). Travelers who read the fine print end up with a far greater choice of trains.
- The next column (Servizi Diretti e Annotazioni) has pertinent notes about the train, such as "also stops in..." (ferma anche a...), "doesn't stop in..." (non ferma a...), "stops in every station" (ferma in tutte le stazioni), "delayed..." (ritardo...), and so on.
- The last column lists the track (Binario) the train departs from. Confirm the binario with an additional source: a ticket seller, the electronic board that lists immediate departures, TV monitors on the platform, or the railway officials who are usually standing by the train unless you really need them.

For any odd symbols on the poster, look at the key at the end. Some of the phrasing can be deciphered easily, such as *servizio periodico* (periodic service—doesn't always run). For the trickier ones, ask a local or railway official, try your *Rick Steves* phrasebook, or simply take a different train.

You can also check schedules—for trains anywhere in Italy, not just from the station you're currently in—at the handy ticket machines. Enter the date and time of your departure (to or from any Italian station), and you can view all your options.

Newsstands sell up-to-date regional and all-Italy time-tables (€5, ask for the *orario ferroviaro*). On the Web, check http ://bahn.hafas.de/bin/query.exe/en (Germany's excellent all-Europe schedule website) or www.trenitalia.it/en/index.html. There is also a single all-Italy telephone number for train information (24 hours daily, tel. 892-021, Italian only, consider having your hotelier call for you).

From Florence by Train to: Pisa (2–3/hr, 1.25 hrs, €6), **Lucca** (2/hr, 1.5 hrs, €5), **Siena** (direct trains hourly, 1.5 hrs, €6; bus is better because Siena's train station is far from the center), **Livorno**—port of call for many cruise ships (hourly, 1.5 hrs), **La Spezia** (for the Cinque Terre, 5/day direct, 2.5 hrs, nearly hourly with change in Pisa), **Milan** (hourly, 2 hrs), **Venice** (nearly hourly, 3–3.5 hrs), **Assisi** (8/day direct, 2–3 hrs), **Orvieto** (hourly, 2 hrs, some with change in Campo di Marte or Rifredi station), **Rome** (at least hourly, 2 hrs, many stop at Orvieto en route, most connections require seat reservations), **Naples** (hourly, 3.5–5 hrs, some change in Rome), **Brindisi** (3/day, 9 hrs with change in Bologna or Rome), **Frankfurt** (9/day, 12 hrs, 1–3 changes), **Paris** (7/day, 12–15 hrs, 1–2 changes, important to reserve overnight train ahead), **Vienna** (1 direct overnight train, or 9/day with 1–3 changes, 10–16 hrs).

Buses

The SITA bus station (100 yards west of the Florence train station on Via Santa Caterina da Siena) is traveler-friendly—a big, old-school lot with numbered stalls and all the services you'd expect. Schedules for regional trips are posted everywhere, and TV monitors show imminent departures. Bus service drops dramatically on Sunday.

By Bus to: San Gimignano (hourly, 1.25 hrs, change in Poggibonsi, €6), **Siena** (2/hr, 1.25-hr *corse rapide* buses are faster than the train, avoid the 2-hr *diretta* scenic-but-slow buses, €7), **Volterra** (4/day, 2/day Sun, 2 hrs, change in Colle Val d'Elsa, €7.50), and the **airport** (2/hr, 20 min, €4.50). Buy tickets in the station if possible, as you'll pay 30 percent more if you buy tickets on the bus (except for the airport bus). Bus info: tel. 800-373-760 (Mon–Fri 8:30–18:30, Sat 8:30–12:30, closed Sun); some schedules are listed in the *Florence Concierge Information* magazine.

Taxis

For small groups with more money than time, zipping to nearby towns by taxi can be a good value (e.g., €120 from your Florence hotel to your Siena hotel).

Flights

Florence's Amerigo Vespucci Airport is several miles northwest of Florence (open 5:10–24:00, no overnighting allowed, TI, cash machines, car-rental agencies, airport info tel. 055-306-1630, flight info tel. 055-306-1700—domestic only, www.aeroporto .firenze.it). Shuttle buses (far right of airport as you exit arrivals hall) connect the airport with Florence's SITA bus station, 100 yards west of the train station on Via Santa Caterina da Siena (2/hr, 30 min, daily 5:30–23:30, €4.50). Allow about €20 and 30 minutes for a taxi.

Pisa's Galileo Galilei Airport handles more and more international and domestic flights (TI open daily 11:00–23:00, cash machine, car-rental agencies, baggage storage from 8:00–20:00 only, €7/bag; self-service cafeteria, general info tel. 050-502-518, flight info tel. 050-849-300, www.pisa-airport.com).

You can connect to Florence easily by train (2/hr, 90 min, €5.50, most transfer at Pisa Centrale) or by Terravision bus (about hourly, 1.25 hours, €10 one-way, ticket kiosk is at the right end of the arrivals hall as you're facing the exits, catch bus outside and to the far right of the bus parking lot). To get to Pisa, you can take bus LAM Rossa (4–6/hr, after 20:00 3/hr, 15 min; depart from in front of the arrivals hall); a train (depart from the far left of the arrivals hall as you face the exits); or a taxi (€10–12).

Cheap Flights: If Florence is just one stop on a longer European trip, you might want to look into flying one of the affordable intra-European airlines. While trains are still the best way to connect places that are close together, a flight can save both time and money on long journeys. When comparing a flight versus a train trip, consider the time it takes to get to the airport and how early you'll need to arrive to check in before the flight. Most flights make sense only as an alternate to a train ride five or more hours in length.

One of the best places to look to compare inexpensive flights is www.skyscanner.net. Other comparison search engines include www.mobissimo.com and www.wegolo.com. Budget airlines out of Florence include Belle Air (www.belleair.it), Flybaboo (www .flybaboo.com), and Cimber Sterling (www.cimber.dk).

Even more cheapo airlines fly into Pisa, including well-known carriers easyJet and Ryanair (see www.pisa-airport.com for full list) and the Italian-based discount airline Air One (www.flyairone.it).

Remember that Florence is well-connected by train to plenty of airports—giving you more options—including Parma, Perugia, Bologna, and Rimini (which all have budget flights available). Rome, Milan, and Venice are only a two-hour train ride away.

Be aware of the potential drawbacks of flying on the cheap: nonrefundable and nonchangeable tickets, rigid baggage restrictions (and fees if you have more than what's officially allowed), use of airports far outside town, tight schedules that can mean more delays, little in the way of customer assistance if problems arise, and, of course, no frills. To avoid unpleasant surprises, read the small print—especially baggage policies—before you book.

Cruising

If you're coming to Florence by cruise ship, you'll get off the boat in the coastal town of **Livorno,** Florence's official port and cruise ship dock, located about 60 miles west of the city.

A branch TI may be open at the port in summer (tel. 0586-895-320). The main TI is located in the town center on Piazza Municipio (daily 9:00–17:00, tel. 0586-204-611, www.costa deglietruschi.it). Livorno and Florence are most easily connected by train (hourly, 1.5 hours, some change in Pisa, Lucca connection possible). Most cruise ships offer a shuttle to the train station. You can also take a taxi between the port and station for about €10–20, depending on where your ship is docked.

Driving

To Drive or Not to Drive?

The answer is a resounding yes if you want to get off the beaten path, free yourself from bus and train schedules, and stop on a whim for that perfect photo of undulating, cypress-lined hills. But don't rent a car if you find driving stressful or if your destinations are easily accessible by public transportation. If your itinerary includes only Lucca, Florence, and Siena, a rental car would be an unnecessary cost and hassle. However, if you want to stay in an out-of-the-way *agriturismo* and focus on isolated hill towns and Etruscan tombs, having your own wheels will save you time and headaches. For information on driving in the Tuscan countryside, see page 392.

Renting a Car

To drive in Italy, you need only your US driver's license. Although an International Driving Permit is technically required, I've never gotten or needed one ($15 plus the cost of two passport photos at local AAA office; www.aaa.com). To rent a car in Italy, you must be at least 18 years old and have held your license for one year. Drivers under the age of 25 may incur a young-driver surcharge, and some rental companies do not rent to anyone 75 and over. Seatbelts are mandatory. Roads and parking spaces are narrow in

Driving in Tuscany

To Cinque Terre (La Spezia)

To Milan

To Venice

EMILIA-ROMAGNA

50m•1h
50m•1h
50m•1h

50m•1h Lucca

190m•3.5h
160m•3.5h

20m .5h

70m•1.25h Florence

Pisa

70m•1.5h

40m•.75h

45m•1h

55m•1.5h

60m•1.25h San Gimignano

45m•2h (via S-222)

75m•1.5h

20m•.5h

30m•.75h

Volterra

Cortona 40m 1h

45m•1h

Siena

50m•1h

To Assisi

30m•.75h

40m•1h

20m•.75h

30m•1h

35m•1h

10m .25h Montepulciano

San Galgano Monastery

55m•1.5h

15m•.5h Pienza

15m•.5h Chiusi

Montalcino

UMBRIA

210m•4h

60m•1.5h

105m•2h Orvieto

m = miles
h = hours
Note: Your times may vary based on traffic, construction, and road conditions.

TUSCANY

75m•1.5h

To Rome

LAZIO

To Rome

Tuscany, so you'll do yourself a favor by renting the smallest car that meets your needs.

Car Insurance Options

Accidents can happen anywhere, but when you're on vacation, the last thing you need is stress over car insurance. Limit your financial risk by choosing one of these two options: buy Collision Damage Waiver (CDW) coverage from the car-rental company, or get coverage through your credit card (free, but more complicated).

While each rental company has its own variation, the basic **CDW** costs $15–25 a day (figure roughly 25 percent extra) and reduces your liability, but does not eliminate it. When you pick up the car, you'll be offered the chance to "buy down" the basic deductible to zero (for an additional $10–30/day; sometimes called "super CDW").

If you opt for **credit-card coverage,** there's a catch. You'll technically have to decline all coverage offered by the car-rental company, which means they can place a hold on your card

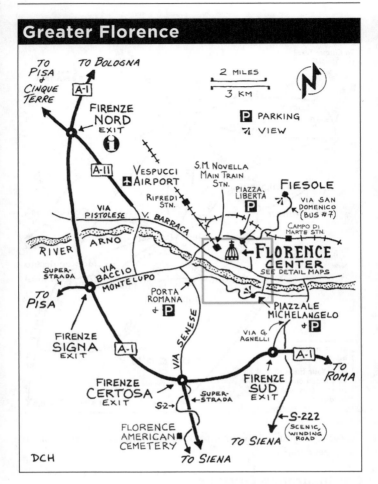

Greater Florence

(which can be up to the full value of the car). In case of damage, it can be time-consuming to resolve the charges with your credit-card company. Before you decide on this option, quiz your credit-card company about how it works.

Note that **theft insurance** (separate from CDW insurance) is mandatory in Italy. The insurance usually costs about $15–20 a day, payable when you pick up the car.

For more fine print about car-rental insurance, see www.rick steves.com/cdw.

Driving and Parking in Florence

After driving around and trying to park in Florence, you'll understand why Leonardo never invented the car. Cars flatten the charm of the city.

The autostrada has several exits for Florence. Get off at the Nord, Sud, or Certosa exits and follow signs toward—but not into—the Centro.

Don't even attempt driving into the city center. Florence has a traffic-reduction system that's complicated and confusing even to locals. Every car passing into the *Zona Traffico Limitato (ZTL)* is photographed; those that haven't jumped through bureaucratic hoops to get a permit are fined in the mail about €100 per infraction; if you get lost and cross the line several times...you get several fines. The no-go zone (defined basically by the old medieval wall,

now a boulevard circling the historic center of town—watch for *Zona Traffico Limitato* signs) is roughly the area between the river, main train station, Piazza della Libertà, Piazza Donatello, and Piazza Beccaria.

Fortunately, the city center is ringed with big, efficient parking lots (signposted with the standard big *P*), each with taxi and bus service into the center. I just head for "Parcheggio Parterre," just beyond Piazza della Libertà (€1.50/hr, €18/day, €65/week, open 24 hours daily, tel. 055-500-1994, 600 spots, automated, pay with cash or credit card, never fills up completely). From the freeway, follow the signs to *Centro*, then *Stadio*, then *P*; at the elevator exit, you'll see a taxi stand and the bus stop for the #7, which heads to Piazza San Marco, the Duomo, and the train station.

You can park for free along any suburban curb near a bus stop that feels safe, and take the bus into the city center from there. Check for signs that indicate parking restrictions—for example, a circle with a slash through it and "*dispari giovedi, 0,00–06,00*" means don't park on Thursdays between midnight and six in the morning. Signs showing a street cleaner and a day of the week indicate which day the

street is cleaned; there's a €100 tow-fee incentive to learn the days of the week in Italian.

Free parking is easy up at Piazzale Michelangelo (see page 66), but don't park where the buses drop people off; park on the side of the piazza farthest from the view. To get from Piazzale Michelangelo to the center of town, take bus #12 or #13 (see "Getting Around Florence," page 40).

If you're picking up a rental car upon departure, don't struggle with driving into the center. Taxi with your luggage to the car-rental office, and head out from there.

TUSCANY
Toscana

Tuscany

EMILIA-ROMAGNA

TO BOLOGNA

TO RAVENNA

LIG.
LA SPEZIA
APUAN ALPS
CARRARA
CINQUE TERRE
PISTOIA
LUCCA
VESPUCCI
FIESOLE
FLORENCE
VIAREGGIO
VINCI
ARNO
TO URBINO
LE MARCHE
PISA
ARNO
GALILEO EMPOLI
U.S. CEM.
POGG.
CHIANTI
SAN-SEPOLCRO
AREZZO
Livorno
SAN GIMIGNANO
S-222
CAST.
UMBRIA
VOLTERRA
S-68
SIENA
CORTONA
LISCIANO
MONTE-RIGGIONE
ANCAIANO
S-326
ASSISI
SAN GALGANO
S-438
S-2
ASCIANO
TER.
LAKE TRAS.
MONTALCINO
S-146
PIENZA
MONTE-PULCIANO
SANT'ANTIMO
CHIUSI
ORVIETO
PIOMBINO
VIA CASSIA
TODI
PORTO-FERRAIO
GROSSETO
BAG.
ELBA
MAREMMA
MEDITERRANEAN SEA
MONTE ARGENTARIO
LAKE BOLSENA
LAZIO
TO ROME

AUTOSTRADA
OTHER ROADS
RAIL
BORDER OF PROVINCE
AIRPORTS

30 MILES
50 KM
DCH

SIENA

Siena was medieval Florence's archrival. And while Florence ultimately won the battle for political and economic superiority, Siena still competes for the tourists. Sure, Florence has the heavyweight sights. But Siena seems to be every Italy connoisseur's favorite pet town. In my office, whenever Siena is mentioned, someone moans, "Siena? I looove Siena!"

Once upon a time (about 1260–1348), Siena was a major banking and trade center, and a military power in a class with Florence, Venice, and Genoa. With a population of 60,000, it was even bigger than Paris. Situated on the north–south road to Rome (the Via Francigena), Siena traded with all of Europe. Then, in 1348, the Black Death (bubonic plague) that swept through Europe hit Siena and cut the population by more than a third. Siena never recovered. In the 1550s, Florence, with the help of Philip II's Spanish army, conquered the flailing city-state, forever rendering Siena a non-threatening backwater. Siena's loss became our sightseeing gain, as its political and economic irrelevance pickled the city in a purely medieval brine. Today, Siena's population is still 60,000, compared with Florence's 420,000.

Siena's thriving historic center, with red-brick lanes cascading every which way, offers Italy's best medieval city experience. Most people do Siena, just 35 miles south of Florence, as a day trip, but it's best experienced at twilight. While Florence has the blockbuster museums, Siena has an easy-to-enjoy soul: Courtyards sport flower-decked wells, alleys dead-end at rooftop views, and the sky is a rich blue dome.

For those who dream of a Fiat-free Italy, pedestrians rule in the old center of Siena. Sit at a café on the main square. Wander narrow streets lined with colorful flags and iron rings to tether horses. Take time to savor the first European city to eliminate

...mobile traffic from its main square (1966) and then, just to be ...ly, wonder what would happen if they did it in your hometown.

Planning Your Time

On a quick trip, consider spending two nights in Siena (or three nights with a whole-day side trip into Florence). Whatever you do, enjoy a sleepy medieval evening in Siena. The next morning, you can see the city's major sights in half a day.

Orientation to Siena

Siena lounges atop a hill, stretching its three legs out from Il Campo. This main square, the historic meeting point of Siena's neighborhoods, is pedestrian-only. And most of those pedestrians are students from the local university.

Just about everything mentioned in this chapter is within a 15-minute walk of the square. Navigate by three major landmarks (Il Campo, Duomo, and Church of San Domenico), following the excellent system of street-corner signs. The typical visitor sticks to the Il Campo–San Domenico axis. Make a point to stray from the current of this main artery.

Siena itself is one big sight. Its individual sights come in two little clusters: the square (Civic Museum and City Tower) and the cathedral (Baptistery and Duomo Museum with its surprise viewpoint). Check these sights off, and then you're free to wander.

Tourist Information

The TI on Il Campo can be an exasperating place, but you can pick up some good handouts and buy a €0.50 map (daily 9:00–19:00, on Il Campo at #56, tel. 0577-280-551, www.terresiena.it, incoming @terresiena.it). The helpful booklet *Terre di Siena* lists current hours and prices for sights in Siena and outlying towns. The TI organizes walking tours of the old town and of San Gimignano (€20, daily April–Sept).

There's also a little TI, which is primarily for hotel promotion, across the street from the Church of San Domenico, and a TI at the train station (daily 9:30–13:30, tel. 0577-270-600).

Arrival in Siena

By Train: The small train station, located on the edge of town, has a bar, a TI, a bus office (daily 6:15–20:15), and a newsstand (which

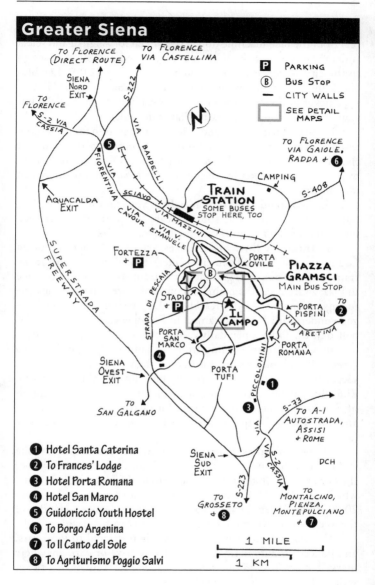

Greater Siena

P PARKING
B BUS STOP
— CITY WALLS
☐ SEE DETAIL MAPS

TO FLORENCE (DIRECT ROUTE)
TO FLORENCE VIA CASTELLINA
SIENA NORD EXIT
TO FLORENCE
S-2 VIA CASSIA
S-222
VIA BANDELLI
AQUACALDA EXIT
VIA FIORENTINA
VIA SCIAVO
SUPERSTRADA FREEWAY
VIA CAVOUR EMANUELE
VIA V. MAZZINI

TRAIN STATION SOME BUSES STOP HERE, TOO
CAMPING
S-408
TO FLORENCE VIA GAIOLE, RADDA & ❻

FORTEZZA ♦ **P**
B
STADIO ♦ **P**
★ **IL CAMPO**
STRADA DI PESCAIA
PORTA OVILE
PIAZZA GRAMSCI MAIN BUS STOP
PORTA PISPINI
VIA ARETINA
TO ❷
PORTA ROMANA
PORTA SAN MARCO
❹
PORTA TUFI
VIA PICCOLOMINI
❶
❸
SIENA OVEST EXIT
TO SAN GALGANO
SIENA SUD EXIT
S-223
S-73 TO A-1 AUTOSTRADA, ASSISI & ROME
VIA S-2 CASSIA
DCH
TO GROSSETO ♦ ❽
TO MONTALCINO, PIENZA, MONTEPULCIANO ♦ ❼

❶ Hotel Santa Caterina
❷ To Frances' Lodge
❸ Hotel Porta Romana
❹ Hotel San Marco
❺ Guidoriccio Youth Hostel
❻ To Borgo Argenina
❼ To Il Canto del Sole
❽ To Agriturismo Poggio Salvi

1 MILE
1 KM

sells bus tickets), but no baggage check or lockers (check bags at Piazza Gramsci, see "By Intercity Bus" on next page). A new shopping mall is right in front of the station.

To get from the station to the city center by **city bus,** exit the station, go left 15 yards, and head across the road to the shopping mall, a brick-and-glass building labeled *Galleria Porta Siena*. Enter the right-hand glass door and use the elevator to go down one floor.

If you didn't buy bus tickets in the train station, you can get tickets (€1) from the blue machine (touch the screen for English and select "urban" for type of ticket). Most orange or red-and-silver buses go to the city center (6/hr, fewer on Sun and after 22:00). Double-check the destination with the driver by asking *"Centro?"* Punch your ticket in the machine onboard to validate it. Ride to the last stop, Piazza Gramsci (or nearby Piazza del Sale).

If you're leaving Siena and you need to get to the train station, catch a city bus from Piazza Gramsci. Confirm with the driver that the bus is going to the *stazione* (stat-zee-OH-nay); remember to purchase your ticket in advance from a *tabacchi* shop and punch it on board.

The **taxi stand** is to your far right as you exit the train station, but the city is chronically short on cabs, so getting one here can take forever (about €9 to Il Campo, taxi tel. 0577-49-222).

By Intercity Bus: Some buses arrive in Siena at Piazza Gramsci (a few blocks from city center), though most arrive at the train station. Some will go first to the train station, then continue to Piazza Gramsci. The main bus companies are Sena and the confusingly named Tra-In (TRAH-in). Day-trippers can store baggage underneath Piazza Gramsci in Sottopassaggio la Lizza (€3/half-day, €5.50/day, open daily 7:00–19:00, no overnight storage).

By Car: Drivers coming from the autostrada take the *Siena Ovest* exit and follow signs for *Centro*, then *Stadio* (stadium). The soccer-ball signs take you to the stadium lot (Parcheggio Stadio, €1.60/hr, pay when you leave) near the huge, bare-brick Church of San Domenico. The Fortezza lot nearby charges the same amount. The Il Campo parking lot has a special rate of €25/day (ask at your hotel).

On parking spots, blue stripes mean "pay and display"; white stripes mean free parking. You can park for free in the lot west of the Fortezza; in white-striped spots behind the Hotel Villa Liberty, which is behind the Fortezza; and overnight in most city lots from 20:00–8:00. Watch for signs showing a street cleaner and a day of the week—that's when the street is closed to cars for cleaning.

Driving within Siena's city center is restricted to local cars, and policed by automatic cameras. If you drive or park anywhere marked *Zona Traffico Limitato (ZTL)*, you'll likely have a ticket waiting for you in the mail back home.

Technically, hotel customers are allowed to drop off bags at their hotel before finding a place to park overnight, but getting permission to do so isn't worth the trouble.

Helpful Hints

Combo-Tickets: A deranged person cobbled together a pile of illogically paired combo-tickets to give some travelers a small savings.

SIENA

Nothing covers everything, and you'll save money only if you visit every sight listed in this chapter. The meager savings are just not worth the brainpower it takes to figure out the system. The only worthwhile combo-ticket is "My Name is Duccio" (DOO-choh), which covers the Duomo, Duomo Museum, and Baptistery (buy at museum to skip line at Duomo).

Wednesday Morning Market: The weekly market (clothes, knick-knacks, and food) sprawls between the Fortezza and Piazza Gramsci along Viale Cesare Maccari and the adjacent Viale XXV Aprile.

Internet Access: In this university town, there are lots of places to get plugged in. **Internet Train,** near Il Campo at Via di Città 121, is part of a chain; buying a card here gives you access all over Italy (Mon–Sat 10:00–20:00, Sun 14:00–19:00, tel. 0577-226-366). **Cheap Phone Center** is hidden in a small shopping mall at Via Angiolieri Cecco 16 (€2/hr to use their terminals, €1/hr to access Wi-Fi with your laptop, Mon–Sat 10:00–22:00, Sun 11:00–23:00; coming from Il Campo, go uphill past recommended Albergo Tre Donzelle, turn left, and look for *Buffet Restaurant* sign on your left.

Post Office: It's on Piazza Matteotti (Mon–Fri 8:15–19:00, Sat 8:15–13:30, closed Sun).

Books: Libreria Senese sells books (including my guidebooks), newspapers, and magazines in English, with an emphasis on Italian-related topics (daily 9:00–20:00, Via di Città 62, tel. 0577-280-353). The **Feltrinelli** bookstore also sells books and magazines in English (Mon–Sat 9:00–19:30, closed Sun, Banchi di Sopra 52, tel. 0577-44009).

Laundry: Two modern, self-service launderettes are **Express Wash** (near Logge del Papa at Via di Pantaneto 38) and **Onda Blu** (50 yards from Il Campo at Via del Casato di Sotto 17). Both are open daily 8:00–22:00 with last loads at 21:00.

Travel Agency: Palio Viaggi, on Piazza Gramsci, sells train and plane tickets but no bus tickets (Mon–Fri 9:00–13:00 & 15:00–19:00, Sat 9:00–13:00, closed Sun, opposite the columns of NH Excelsior Hotel at La Lizza 12, tel. 0577-280-828, info@palioviaggi.it).

Local Guides: Roberto Bechi, a hardworking Sienese guide, specializes in off-the-beaten-path tours of the surrounding countryside by minibus (up to eight passengers, convenient pick up at hotel). Married to an American (Patti) and having run restaurants in Siena and the US, Roberto communicates well with Americans. His passions are Sienese culture, Tuscan history, and local cuisine. It's ideal to book well in advance, but you might be able to schedule a tour if you call the day before (seven different tours: full-day tours are €90/person with discounts

Siena at a Glance

▲▲▲Il Campo Best square in Italy. **Hours:** Always open. See page 297.

▲▲▲Duomo Art-packed cathedral with mosaic floors and statues by Michelangelo and Bernini. **Hours:** March–Sept Mon–Sat 10:30–17:30, June until 20:00, Sun 13:30–17:30; Oct–Feb Mon–Sat 10:30–18:00, Sun 13:30–17:30. See page 302.

▲▲Duomo Museum Displays cathedral art (including Duccio's *Maestà*) and offers sweeping Tuscan view. **Hours:** Daily March–Sept 9:30–20:00, Oct–Feb 10:00–17:00. See page 309.

▲Civic Museum City museum in City Hall with Sienese frescoes of Good and Bad Government. **Hours:** Daily March–Oct 10:00–19:00, Nov–Feb 10:00–17:15. May be open later in summer. See page 300.

▲City Tower 330-foot tower climb. **Hours:** Daily March–Oct 10:00–19:00, Nov–Feb 10:00–16:00. See page 300.

▲Pinacoteca Fine Sienese paintings. **Hours:** Sun–Mon 9:00–13:00, Tue–Sat 10:00–18:00. See page 301.

▲Baptistery Cave-like building has baptismal font decorated by Ghiberti and Donatello. **Hours:** Daily March–Sept 9:30–19:00, Oct–Feb 9:30–19:00. See page 303.

▲Santa Maria della Scala Museum with vibrant ceiling and wall frescoes depicting day-to-day life in a medieval hospital, much of the original *Fountain of Joy,* and an Etruscan artifact exhibit. **Hours:** Daily 10:30–18:30. See page 304.

Church of San Domenico Huge brick church with St. Catherine's head and thumb. **Hours:** Daily March–Oct 7:00–18:30, Nov–Feb 9:00–18:00. See page 307.

Sanctuary of St. Catherine Home of St. Catherine. **Hours:** Daily 9:30–18:00. See page 307.

once the van fills up, off-season 4-hour tours are €60/person, entry fees are extra; assistant Anna can schedule city tours as well as other guides if Roberto is booked; tel. 0577-321-004, Anna's mobile 320-147-6590, Roberto's mobile 328-425-5648, www.toursbyroberto.com, info@toursbyroberto.com).

Federica Olla is a smart young guide with a knack for creative teaching (€55/hr, mobile 338-133-9525, info @ollaeventi.com).

Esperienze Culturali runs half-day bus tours from Siena into Chianti country—including winery visits and tastings, and the Tuscan countryside (€36, 10 percent discount with this book, Mon-Sat 14:00–19:00, four different 5-hour tours, live guides, leave from Piazza Gramsci, office at Via Il Casato di Sotto 12, tel. 0577-46-091, www.enocuriosi.com, escult @gmail.it).

High Adventure: Siena Ballooning provides hot-air balloon flights over the countryside for adventurous travelers and includes a Tuscan breakfast and a Prosecco toast (€220/ person, 3–4 hour excursion with 1-hour flight, mobile 338-896-4607, www.sienaballooning.com, info@sienaballooning .com, Jennie).

Sights in Siena

▲▲▲Il Campo: Siena's Main Square

Il Campo is the heart—geographically and metaphorically—of Siena. The square fans out from the City Hall (Palazzo Pubblico)

to create an amphitheater, where the citizens are the stars.

Originally, this area was just a field *(campo)* located outside the former city walls. You can still see some of the old tuff-stone blocks incorporated into today's red-brick Caffè Fonte Gaia (along the right side of the square as you face City Hall).

As the city expanded, Il Campo eventually became the historic junction of Siena's various competing districts, or *contrade,* and the old marketplace. The brick surface is divided into nine sections, representing the council of nine merchants and city bigwigs who ruled medieval Siena. The square and its buildings are the color of the soil upon which they stand... a color known to artists and Crayola-users as "Burnt Sienna."

The City Hall and its 330-foot tower dominate the square. In medieval Siena, this secular building was the center of the city, and the whole focus of Il Campo still flows down to it.

The City Hall features the various symbols of the city. The sun on the facade remembers St. Bernardino of Siena. Born on the day that St. Catherine of Siena died, he grew up here and went on to travel throughout Italy, giving spirited and humorous sermons that preached peace between warring political factions. His sermons often ended with reconciling parties exchanging a *bacio di pace* (kiss of peace). In Siena he would stand in front of the Palazzo and preach to crowds

discreetly segregated by gender with a curtain down the middle. Bernardino personally designed the sun logo to attract crowds, and later he became the patron saint of advertising (and of Siena).

To either side of the sun logo, she-wolf gargoyles lean out and snarl, "Don't mess with Siena, Mister Pope!" This Ghibelline city prided itself on its political independence from the papacy; it embraced as a city symbol the pagan she-wolf who suckled Romulus and Remus (Remus' son was Siena's legendary founder). The black-and-white shields over the windows are another city symbol. Near ground level, the metal rings are for tying your horse, while the fixtures above held flags.

The City Hall's 330-foot-tall **City Tower** (Torre del Mangia), Italy's tallest secular tower, was named after a hedonistic watchman who consumed his earnings like a glutton consumes food—his chewed-up statue is in the courtyard, to the left as you enter. (See tower admission details later in this chapter.)

The chapel located at the base of the tower was built in 1348 as thanks to God for ending the Black Death (after it killed more than a third of the population). It should also be used to thank God that the tower—just plunked onto the building with no extra foundation—still stands. These days, the chapel is used solely to bless the Palio contestants, and the tower's bell only rings for the race.

The *Fountain of Joy (Fonte Gaia)* by Jacopo della Quercia marks the square's high point. Find the snake-handler woman, the two naked guys about to be tossed in, and the pigeons politely waiting their turn to tightrope gingerly down slippery spouts to slurp a drink from wolves' snouts. The relief panel on the left (as you face

Siena

1. Sottopassaggio la Lizza (Underground Bus Depot, Bag Storage & Bus Tickets)
2. Palio al Cinema
3. Esperienze Culturali Tours
4. Palio Viaggi Travel Agency
5. Libreria Senese Bookstore
6. Feltrinelli Bookstore

the fountain) shows God creating Adam by helping him to his feet. It's said that this reclining Adam influenced Michelangelo when he painted his Sistine Chapel ceiling. This fountain is a copy—you can see most of the original fountain in an interesting exhibit at Siena's Santa Maria della Scala, described later in this chapter.

To say that Siena and Florence have always been competitive is an understatement. In medieval times, a statue of Venus stood on Il Campo. After the plague hit Siena, the monks blamed the pagan statue. The people cut it to pieces and buried it along the walls of Florence.

Picture Il Campo during the famous Palio horse races (every year on July 2 and Aug 16). Ten snorting horses and their nervous riders (selected from 17 *contrade*, or neighborhoods) line up near the Antica Siena shop (right side of square) to await the starting signal. Then they race like crazy three times around the perimeter (the gray pavement), which is covered with dirt. Mattresses pad the sharpest turns. Spectators wav-

ing the banners of their neighborhoods cram (for free) into the center of the square or, if they have the money, watch from temporary bleachers or the balconies above. Every possible vantage point and perch is packed with people straining to see the action. The winner crosses the line, and 1/17th of Siena goes berserk for the next 365 days. For more on the Palio, see the sidebar on page 304.

▲**Civic Museum *(Museo Civico)*—**At the base of the tower is Siena's City Hall, the spot where secular government got its start in early Renaissance Europe. There you'll find city government still at work, along with a sampling of local art, including Siena's first fresco (with a groundbreaking down-to-earth depiction of the Madonna). Stroll through the dramatic halls for more frescoes and portraits extolling Siena's greats, saints, and the city-as-utopia (€7.50, €12 combo-ticket includes City Tower, €11 combo-ticket includes Santa Maria della Scala, daily March–Oct 10:00–19:00—may be open later in summer, Nov–Feb 10:00–17:15, last entry 45 min before closing, tel. 0577-292-615).

🔾 See the Civic Museum Tour chapter.

▲**City Tower *(Torre del Mangia)*—**Siena gathers around its City Hall more than its church. Medieval Siena was a proud republic, and this tall tower is the exclamation point of its "declaration of independence." Its 300 steps get pretty skinny at the top, but the reward is one of Italy's best views (€7, €12 combo-ticket includes Civic Museum, daily March–Oct 10:00–19:00, Nov–Feb 10:00–16:00, last entry 45 min before closing, closed in rain, limited to 30 tourists at a time so be prepared for long lines—avoid midday crowds, often sold out, free and mandatory bag check).

Near Il Campo

Via Banchi di Sopra and Via Banchi di Sotto—These main drags in town are named "upper row of banks" and "lower row of banks." They were once lined with market tables *(banchi)*, and rents were paid to the city for a table's position along the street. If the owner of a *banco* neglected to pay the rent for his space, thugs came along and literally broke *(rotto)* his table. It is from this practice—*banco rotto,* or broken table—that we get the English word "bankrupt."

In medieval times, these two streets were part of the Via Francigena, the main thoroughfare between Rome, London, and Santiago de Compostela in Spain. The medieval Sienese traded wool with passing travelers, requiring money-changers, which led to banks. As Siena was a secular town, local Christians were allowed to loan money and be bankers. Today, strollers out each evening for their *passeggiata* fill Via Banchi di Sopra.

▲Pinacoteca—If you're into medieval art, you'll likely find this quiet, uncrowded, colorful museum delightful. The museum walks you through Siena's art chronologically, from the 12th through the 16th century, when a revolution in realism was percolating in Tuscany.

Cost, Hours, Location: €4, Sun–Mon 9:00–13:00, Tue–Sat 10:00–18:00, last entry 30 min before closing, free and mandatory bag check, tel. 0577-281-161 or 0577-286-143. To reach the museum from Il Campo, walk out Via di Città and go left on Via San Pietro.

Here are a few highlights from this large collection:

Room 1 (ascend two floors and go up a little landing to your right) features the art world pre-Duccio. (Duccio created the *Maestà* in the Duomo Museum, the Duomo's big stained-glass window, and a fresco in the Civic Museum.) Altarpieces emphasize the heavenly and otherworldly, rather than the human realism that Duccio helped to pioneer.

Rooms 2–4 contain a number of works by Duccio (and assistants), whose groundbreaking innovations are subtle to the layman's eyes: less gold-leaf background, fewer gold creases in robes, transparent garments, inlaid-marble thrones, and a more human Mary and Jesus.

In **Room 5** are works by Duccio's assistant, Simone Martini, including his *St. Augustine of Siena*. The saint's life is set in pretty realistic Sienese streets, buildings, and landscapes. The saint occasionally pops out at the oddest (difficult to draw) angles to save the day. (Simone Martini also did the *Maestà* and Guidoriccio frescoes in the Civic Museum.)

Room 7 includes religious works by the Lorenzetti brothers, best known for the secular masterpiece, *Effects of Good and Bad Government*, in the Civic Museum. The rest of the rooms on this floor are a menagerie of gold-backed saints and Madonnas.

In **Room 12** are two famous small wooden panels by Sienese painter Ambrogio Lorenzetti: *La Città sul Mare (City by the Sea)* and *Castello in Riva al Lago (Castle on the Lakeshore)*. These works feature the strange, medieval Cubism seen in his contemporary Simone Martini's *Guidoriccio da Fogliano* (in the Civic Museum). Notice the weird, melancholy light that captures the sense of the Dark Ages. These images are replicated on postcards found throughout the city.

Descend one floor down to **Room 20,** and suddenly the gold is gone—Madonna is set on earth. See works by the painter/biographer Giorgio Vasari **(Room 22),** a stunning view out the window **(Room 26),** and several colorful rooms **(Rooms 27–30)** dedicated to Domenico Beccafumi (1486–1551). Beccafumi designed many of the Duomo's inlaid pavement panels (including *Slaughter of the Innocents*), and his original cartoons are displayed in **Room 30.** With strong bodies, twisting poses, and dramatic gestures, Beccafumi's works epitomize the Mannerist style.

Room 31 has "Il Sodoma's" sympathetic *Christ on the Column,* and the long **Room 32** displays large-scale works by Il Sodoma, Beccafumi, and others. And finally, Bernardino Mei **(Room 33)** gives a Sienese take on the wrinkled saints and dark shadows of Caravaggio.

Siena's Cathedral Area

▲▲▲**Duomo**—This 13th-century Gothic cathedral, with its six-story striped bell tower—Siena's ultimate tribute to the Virgin Mary—is heaped with statues, plastered with frescoes, and paved with art. Soak up the richly ornamented facade before venturing inside, where 1,000 years of popes keep watch from on high. The interior is a Renaissance riot

of striped columns, intricate marble inlays, Michelangelo statues, and Bernini sculptures. The Piccolomini Library features a series of 15th-century frescoes chronicling the adventures of Siena's philanderer-turned-pope, Aeneas Piccolomini.

Cost, Hours, Information: €3 includes cathedral and Piccolomini Library, €10 "My Name is Duccio" combo-ticket includes the Duomo Museum (sold 100 yards away at the museum, allows you to skip cathedral line) and Baptistery. There's a €4 audioguide for the church and the library; a €6 combo-audioguide also covers the Duomo Museum (ID required for deposit). The Duomo and library are both open March–Sept Mon–Sat 10:30–17:30—in June until 20:00, Sun 13:30–17:30; Oct–Feb Mon–Sat 10:30–18:00, Sun 13:30–17:30; last entry 30 min before closing. Modest dress is required to enter, but paper ponchos are provided if needed.

○ See the Siena Duomo Tour chapter.

▲▲**Duomo Museum (*Museo dell'Opera e Panorama*)**—On the Il Campo side of the church (look for the yellow signs), Siena's most enjoyable museum was built to house the cathedral's art. Upstairs is Duccio's *Maestà* (*Enthroned Virgin*, 1311), one of the great pieces of medieval art. The flip side of the *Maestà* (displayed on the opposite wall) has 26 panels—the medieval equivalent of pages—showing scenes from the Passion of Christ.

Climb onto the Panorama dal Facciatone. From the first landing, take the skinnier second spiral for Siena's surprise view (€10 "My Name is Duccio" combo-ticket includes the Duomo and Baptistery; €3 worthwhile 40-min audioguide; €6 combo-audioguide also includes Duomo—rentable only at the Duomo, ID required for deposit; daily March–Sept 9:30–20:00, Oct–Feb 10:00–17:00, tel. 0577-283-048, www.operaduomo.siena.it, operaduomo@operaduomo.siena.it).

○ See the Siena Duomo Museum Tour chapter.

▲**Baptistery**—Siena is so hilly that there wasn't enough flat ground on which to build a big church. What to do? Build a big church anyway and prop up the overhanging edge with the Baptistery. This dark and quietly tucked-away cave of art is worth a look for its cool tranquility bronze panels and angels by Ghiberti, Donatello, and others that adorn the pedestal of the baptismal font (€3, €10 "My Name is Duccio" combo-ticket includes Duomo and Duomo Museum, daily March–Sept 9:30–19:00, Oct–Feb 9:30–19:00).

The nearby cathedral "crypt" is important archaeologically—several frescoed rooms have been discovered here within the last 10 years. It may be of little interest to the average tourist, but fresco fans will enjoy it (included with €10 "My Name is Duccio" combo-ticket, otherwise €6).

Siena's Palio

In the Palio, the feisty spirit of Siena's 17 *contrade* (neighborhoods) lives on. Each *contrada* has a parish church, well, or fountain, and sometimes even a historical museum. Each is represented by a mascot (porcupine, unicorn, wolf, etc.) and unique colors worn proudly by residents.

Contrada pride is evident year-round in Siena's parades and colorful banners, lamps, and wall plaques. (If you hear the thunder of distant drumming, run to it for some medieval action, often featuring flag-throwers.) You are welcome to participate in these lively neighborhood festivals. Buy a scarf in *contrada* colors, grab a glass of Chianti, munch on some *panforte,* and join in the merriment.

Contrada passion is most visible twice a year—on July 2 and August 16—when the city erupts during its world-famous horse race, the Palio di Siena. Ten of the 17 neigh-borhoods compete (chosen by rotation and lot), hurling themselves with medieval abandon into several days of trial races and traditional revelry. Jockeys—usually from out of town—are considered hired guns...paid mercenaries. Bets are placed on which *contrada* will win...and lose. Despite the shady behind-the-scenes dealing, on the big day the horses are taken into their *contrada*'s church to be blessed. ("Go and return victorious," says the priest.) It's considered a sign of luck if a horse leaves droppings in the church.

On the evening of the race, Il Campo is stuffed to the brim with locals and tourists. Dirt is brought in and packed down to create the track's surface, while mattresses pad the walls of surrounding buildings. The most treacherous spots are the sharp

▲**Santa Maria della Scala**—This museum (opposite the Duomo entrance) was used as a hospital until the 1980s. Its labyrinthine 12th-century cellars—carved out of volcanic tuff and finished with brick—go down several floors, and during medieval times were used to store supplies for the hospital upstairs. Today, the hospital and its cellars are filled with museum exhibits, including these main attractions: the fancily frescoed Pellegrinaio Hall (ground floor), most of the original *Fountain of Joy*, St. Catherine's Oratory chapel (first basement), and the Etruscan collection in the Archaeological Museum (second basement).

Cost and Hours: €6, €11 combo-ticket includes Civic Museum, daily 10:30–18:30, last entry 30 min before closing, tel.

corners, where many a rider bites the dust. One lap around the course is about a third of a mile (350 meters); three laps make a full circuit. In this literally no-holds-barred race—which lasts just over a minute—a horse can win even without its rider (jockeys perch precariously without saddles on the sweaty horses' backs, and often fall off).

The winning neighborhood is the scene of grand celebrations afterward. Winners receive a *palio* (banner), typically painted by a local artist and always featuring the Virgin Mary. But the true prize is proving that your *contrada* is *numero uno,* and mocking your losing rival.

All over town, sketches and posters depict the Palio. This is not some folkloristic event. It's a real medieval moment. If you're packed onto the square with 60,000 people, all hungry for victory, you won't see much, but you'll feel it. Bleacher and balcony seats are expensive, but it's free to join the masses in the square. Be sure to go with an empty bladder as there are no WCs, and be prepared to surrender any sense of personal space.

While the actual Palio packs the city, you could side-trip in from Florence to see the horse-race trials—called *prove*—on any of the three days before the main event (usually at 9:00 and about 19:30, free seats in bleachers). For more information, visit www.ilpalio.org.

▲**Palio al Cinema**—This 20-minute film, *Siena, the Palio, and Its History,* helps re-create the craziness, but it may close in 2010. If it's still showing, see it at the air-conditioned Cinema Moderno in Piazza Tolomei, two blocks from Il Campo (€5.25, ask for Rick Steves discount with this book—€4.25/person or €8/two people, €10 for DVD, film shows June–Aug Mon–Sat, closed Sun; usually 9 English showings a day—generally hourly at half past the hour, schedule may change, call or drop by to confirm—times posted on door; tel. 0577-289-201 or mobile 349-896-7494).

0577-224-811. The church just inside the door to your left is free (English description inside church entrance on left).

Pellegrinaio Hall: Sumptuously frescoed, this hall shows medieval Siena's innovative health care and social welfare system in action (c. 1442, wonderfully described in English). Starting in the 11th century, the hospital nursed the sick and cared for abandoned children, as is vividly portrayed in these frescoes. The good works paid off, as bequests and donations poured in, creating the wealth that's evident throughout this building.

Fountain of Joy **Exhibit:** Downstairs you'll find an engaging exhibit on Jacopo della Quercia's early 15th-century *Fountain of Joy (Fonte Gaia)*—and the disassembled pieces of the original fountain

St. Catherine of Siena
(1347–1380)

The youngest of 25 children born to a Sienese cloth dyer, Catherine began experiencing heavenly visions as a child. At 16 she became a Dominican nun, locking herself away for three

years in a room in her family's house. She lived the life of an ascetic, which culminated in a vision wherein she married Christ. Catherine emerged from solitude to join her Dominican sisters, sharing her experiences, caring for the sick, and gathering both disciples and enemies. At age 23, she lapsed into a spiritual coma, waking with the heavenly command to spread her message to the world. She wrote essays and letters to kings, dukes, bishops, and popes, imploring them to find peace for a war-ravaged Italy. While visiting Pisa during Lent of 1375, she had a vision in which she received the stigmata, the wounds of Christ.

Still in her twenties, Catherine was invited to Avignon, France, where the pope had taken up residence. With her charm, sincerity, and reputation for holiness, she helped convince Pope Gregory XI to return the papacy to the city of Rome. Catherine also went to Rome, where she died young. She was canonized in the next generation (by a Sienese pope), and her relics were distributed to churches around Italy.

itself. In the 19th century, after serious deterioration, the ornate fountain was dismantled and plaster casts were made. (From these casts, they formed the replica that graces Il Campo today.) Here you'll see the eroded original panels paired with their restored casts, along with the original statues that once stood on the edges of the fountain.

On the same floor, pop into **St. Catherine's Oratory,** the small chapel where she prayed and received visions. A holy nail thought to be from Jesus' cross is on the altar.

Archaeological Museum: Descend into the cavernous second basement under groin vaults to be alone with piles of ancient Etruscan stuff excavated from tombs dating centuries before Christ (displayed in a labyrinthine exhibit). Remember, the Etruscans dominated this part of Italy before the Roman Empire swept through—some historians think even Rome originated as an Etruscan town.

Siena's San Domenico Area

Church of San Domenico—This huge brick church is worth a quick look. The spacious, plain interior (except for the colorful flags of the city's 17 *contrade,* or neighborhoods) fits the austere philosophy of the Dominicans and invites meditation on the thoughts and deeds of St. Catherine. Walk up the steps in the rear to see paintings from the life of St. Catherine, patron saint of Siena. Halfway up the church on the right, find a metal bust of St. Catherine, a small case housing her thumb

(sometimes loaned out to other churches), and a reliquary on the lowest shelf containing the chain she used to scourge herself. In the chapel (15 feet to the left) surrounded with candles, you'll see Catherine's actual head atop the altar (free, daily March–Oct 7:00–18:30, Nov–Feb 9:00–18:00, tel. 0577-280-893, WC for €0.50 at far end of parking lot to the right when facing church entrance).

Sanctuary of St. Catherine—Step into Catherine's cool and peaceful home. Siena remembers its favorite hometown gal, a simple, unschooled, but mystically devout soul who, in the mid-1300s, helped convince the pope to return from France to Rome. This schism split the Continent in the 14th century, but because of her intervention, Catherine is honored today as Europe's patron saint. Pilgrims have visited her home since 1464, and architects and artists have greatly embellished what was probably once a humble home (her family worked as wool-dyers). Enter through the courtyard, and walk down the stairs at the far end. The church on your right contains the wooden crucifix upon which Catherine was meditating when she received the stigmata. The chapel on your left was originally the kitchen. Go down the stairs to the left of the kitchen to reach the saint's room. Catherine's bare cell is behind wrought-iron doors. Much of the art throughout the sanctuary depicts scenes from her life (free, daily 9:30–18:00, a few downhill blocks toward the center from San Domenico—follow signs to *Santuario di Santa Caterina*—at Costa di Sant'Antonio 6).

Shopping and Nightlife in Siena

Shopping

The main drag, Via Banchi di Sopra, is a cancan of fancy shops. The big local department store is **Upim** (Mon–Sat 8:30–20:00, Sun 10:00–20:00, Piazza Matteotti).

For easy-to-pack souvenirs, get some of the large, colorful scarves/flags that depict the symbols of Siena's 17 different neighborhoods (such as the wolf, the turtle, and the snail). Pick up a few extra to decorate your home (€7 each for large size, sold at souvenir stands).

Local Sweets: All over town, **Prodotti Tipici** shops sell Sienese specialties. Siena's claim to caloric fame is its *panforte,* a rich, chewy concoction of nuts, honey, and candied fruits that impresses even fruitcake-haters. There are a few varieties. *Margherita,* dusted in powdered sugar, is more fruity while *panpepato* has a spicy, peppery crust. Locals prefer a chewy, white macaroon-and-almond cookie called *ricciarelli.*

Nightlife

Join the evening *passeggiata* (peak strolling time is 19:00) along Via Banchi di Sopra with gelato in hand.

The **Enoteca Italiana** is a good wine bar in a cellar in the Fortezza. To get there, enter the Fortezza via the bridge, cross the running track, and—after passing a tree—go left down a ramp (sample glasses in three different price ranges: €3, €4, and €6.50; Mon–Sat 12:00–24:00, closed Sun; bottles available from all over Italy, snacks served when the bar's pricey restaurant is between mealtimes; outside terrace, tel. 0577-228-832).

SIENA DUOMO TOUR

The Duomo sits atop Siena's highest point, with one of the most extravagant facades in all of Europe. And this ornate but surprisingly secular shrine to the Virgin Mary is stacked with colorful art inside and out, from the inlaid-marble floors to the stained-glass windows. Along with sculptures by Bernini and Michelangelo, the church features the Piccolomini Library, where a series of captivating frescoes by the Umbrian painter Pinturicchio tells the story of Aeneas Piccolomini, Siena's consummate Renaissance man, who became Pope Pius II.

Orientation

Cost: €3, €10 "My Name is Duccio" combo-ticket includes Duomo Museum and Baptistery (purchase it at Duomo Museum to skip the line at the Duomo and walk directly in—use the group lane on the left).

Dress Code: Modest dress is required, but paper ponchos are provided if needed.

Hours: March–Sept Mon–Sat 10:30–17:30—in June until 20:00, Sun 13:30–17:30; Oct–Feb Mon–Sat 10:30–18:00, Sun 13:30–17:30; last entry 30 min before closing.

Getting There: Just look up and head for the green-and-white-striped tower.

Information: The €4 audioguide covers the church and library (€6/2 people), or rent the €6 combo-audioguide, which includes the Duomo Museum (€8/2 people, ID required for deposit). Inside the Duomo there are €1 video terminals that give a history of the cathedral floor.

Photography: No flash permitted.

Length of This Tour: Allow one hour.

The Tour Begins

Exterior

Grab a spot on a stone bench opposite the entry to take in this architectural festival of green, white, pink, and gold. Like a medieval altarpiece, the facade is divided into sections, each frame filled with patriarchs and prophets, studded with roaring gargoyles, and topped with prickly pinnacles.

The current structure dates back to 1215, with the major decoration done during Siena's heyday from 1250–1350. The lower story, by Giovanni Pisano (who worked from 1284–1297), features remnants of the fading Romanesque style (round arches over the doors) topped with the pointed arches of the new Gothic style seeping in from France. The upper half, in full-blown Gothic, was designed and built a century later.

The six-story bell tower (c. 1315) looks even taller, thanks to an optical illusion: The white marble stripes get narrower toward the top, making the upper part seem farther away.

On columns flanking the entrance are statues of the Roman she-wolf suckling Romulus and Remus, the mythical founders of Rome. Legend has it that Remus' son Senio ("Siena") rode north on a black horse to found the city of Siena. Step inside. (With a maximum capacity of 700 visitors, you may have to wait—the current number is indicated on a computer screen at the turnstile.)

Interior—Nave

The heads of 172 popes—who reigned from Peter to the 12th century—peer down from above, looking over the fine inlaid art on the floor. With a forest of striped columns, a coffered dome, a large stained-glass window at the far end (it's a copy—the original is viewable up close in the nearby Duomo Museum), and an art gallery's worth of early Renaissance art, this is one busy interior. If you look closely at the popes, you'll see the same four faces repeated over and over.

For almost two centuries (1373–1547), 40 artists paved the marble floor with scenes from the Old Testament, allegories, and intricate patterns. The earliest designs are simple black-and-white with engraved details, but the later ones use inlay technique with many colored marbles. The series starts near the entrance with historical allegories; the larger, more elaborate scenes surrounding the altar are mostly stories from the Old Testament. Many of the floor panels are roped off to prevent further wear and tear.

• On the floor, find the second pavement panel from the entrance.

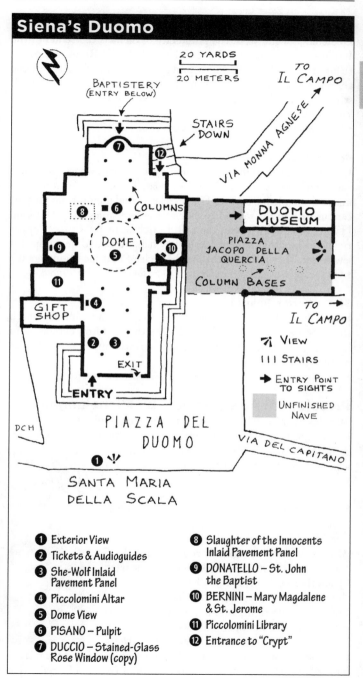

Siena's Duomo

SIENA DUOMO

20 YARDS
20 METERS

TO IL CAMPO

BAPTISTERY (ENTRY BELOW)

STAIRS DOWN

VIA MONNA AGNESE

7

12

8 **6** COLUMNS

DUOMO MUSEUM

PIAZZA JACOPO DELLA QUERCIA

9 DOME **5** **10**

COLUMN BASES

11

TO → IL CAMPO

GIFT SHOP **4**

2 **3**

EXIT

ENTRY

7· VIEW
||| STAIRS
→ ENTRY POINT TO SIGHTS
    UNFINISHED NAVE

DCH

PIAZZA DEL DUOMO

VIA DEL CAPITANO

1 ↯

SANTA MARIA DELLA SCALA

1 Exterior View
2 Tickets & Audioguides
3 She-Wolf Inlaid Pavement Panel
4 Piccolomini Altar
5 Dome View
6 PISANO – Pulpit
7 DUCCIO – Stained-Glass Rose Window (copy)

8 Slaughter of the Innocents Inlaid Pavement Panel
9 DONATELLO – St. John the Baptist
10 BERNINI – Mary Magdalene & St. Jerome
11 Piccolomini Library
12 Entrance to "Crypt"

She-Wolf Inlaid Pavement Panel

Depicted as a she-wolf, the proud city of Siena is the center of the Italian universe, orbited by such lesser lights as Roma, Florentia (Florence), and Pisa. This is pretty pagan stuff for such prime church real estate. Five yards to the left and right are panels with still more pre-Christian imagery—the ancient Greek prophetesses known as the sibyls.

• *The fourth pavement panel from the entrance is the...*

Fortune Panel

Lady Luck (lower right) parachutes down to earth, where she teeters back and forth on a ball and a tipsy boat. The lesson? Fortune is an unstable foundation for life. Truth-seekers wind their way up the precarious path to the top, where Socrates accompanies Lady Wisdom. Having attained wisdom, the world's richest man ("Crates," upper right) realizes that money doesn't buy happiness, and he dumps his jewels out. They fall to earth, and the cycle of Fortune begins again.

• *On the right wall hangs a dim painting (fourth from entrance).*

St. Catherine Painting

Siena's homegrown saint (see page 306) had a vision in which she mystically married Christ. Here's the wedding ceremony in heaven. Jesus places the ring on Catherine's finger as her future mother-in-law, Mary, looks on.

• *On the opposite wall is a marble altarpiece decorated with statues.*

Piccolomini Altar—in Part by Michelangelo

The Piccolomini Altar was designed for the tomb of the Sienese-born Pope Pius III. It was commissioned when he was the cardinal of Siena, but because he later became a pope (see the fresco of his coronation with Pius wearing the golden robe—above and to the right of the Michelangelo statue), he was buried in the Vatican and this fancy tomb was never used. It's most interesting for its statues—one by Michelangelo, three by his students. Michelangelo was originally contracted to do 15 statues, but the marble blocks had been started by another sculptor, and his heart was never in the project. He personally finished only one—St. Paul (lower right, who is clearly more interesting than the bland, bored popes above him).

Paul has the look of Michelangelo's *Moses,* the broken-nosed self-portrait of the sculptor himself, and the relaxed hand of his *David.* It was the chance to sculpt *David* in Florence that convinced Michelangelo to abandon the Siena project.

Dome

Grab a seat under the dome. It sits on a 12-sided base, but its "coffered" ceiling is actually a painted illusion.

Get oriented to the array of sights by thinking of the church floor as a big 12-hour clock. You're the middle, and the altar is high noon: You'll find the *Slaughter of the Innocents* roped off on the floor at 10:00, Pisano's pulpit between two pillars at 11:00, a copy of Duccio's round stained-glass window at high noon, Bernini's chapel at 3:00, the Piccolomini Altar with the Michelangelo statue (next to doorway leading to a shop, snacks, and WC) at 7:00, the Piccolomini Library at 8:00, and a Donatello statue at 9:00.

Attached to columns (at 7:00 and 5:00) are two 65-foot wooden poles—dear to any Sienese heart. These were the **flagpoles** bearing the Florentine flag, captured during the pivotal Battle of Montaperti (1260, fought near Siena), when 20,000 Sienese squared off against 35,000 soldiers from their archrival Florence. The two armies battled back and forth all day, until one of the Florentine soldiers—actually, a Sienese spy under cover—attacked the Florentine standard-bearer from behind. Florence's flag fell to the ground, the army lost its bearings and confidence, and Siena seized the moment to counterattack and win. It was the city's finest hour, ushering in its 80-year Golden Age.

The church was intended to be much larger. Look into the right transept and mentally blow a hole in the wall. You'd be looking down the nave of the massive extension of the church—that is, if the original grandiose plan had been completed (see "Siena's Big Plans and Slow Fade" sidebar on the next page).

Pisano's Pulpit

The octagonal Carrara marble pulpit (1268) rests on the backs of lions, symbols of Christianity triumphant. Like the lions, the Church eats its catch (devouring paganism) and nurses its cubs.

The seven relief panels tell the life of Christ in rich detail. (Buy light from the coin-op machine.) The pulpit is the work of Nicola Pisano (c. 1220–1284), the "Giotto of sculpture," whose revival of classical forms (columns, sarcophagus-like relief panels) signaled the coming Renaissance. His son Giovanni (c. 1250–1314) carved many of the panels, mixing his dad's classicism and realism with the decorative detail and curvy lines of French Gothic—a style that would influence Donatello and the other Florentines.

Siena's Big Plans and Slow Fade

After rival republic Florence began its grand cathedral (1296), proud Siena planned to build one even bigger, the biggest church in all Christendom. Construction began in the 1330s on an extension off the right side of the existing Duomo (today's cathedral would have been used as a transept). The vision was grand, but it underestimated the complexity of constructing such a building without enough land for it to sit upon. That, coupled with the devastating effects of a plague, killed the city's ability and will to finish the project. Many Sienese saw the plague as a sign from God, punishing them for their pride. They canceled their plans and humbly faded into the background of Tuscan history.

The Crucifixion panel (facing the nave under the eagle) is proto-Renaissance. Christ's anatomy is realistic. Mary (bottom left) swoons into the arms of the other women, a very human outburst of emotion. And a Roman soldier (to the right, by Giovanni) turns to look back with an easy motion that breaks the stiff, frontal Gothic mold.

If you plan to visit Pisa, you'll see two similar Pisano pulpits there. (See pages 357 and 364 for more on the Pisanos and their pulpits.)

Duccio's Stained-Glass Rose Window

This is a copy of the original window, which was moved to the Duomo Museum a couple of years ago. The famous rose window was created in 1288 and dedicated to the Virgin Mary (read the complete description in the next chapter).

Slaughter of the Innocents Inlaid Pavement Panel

Herod (left), sitting enthroned amid Renaissance arches, orders the massacre of all babies to prevent the coming of the promised Messiah. It's a chaotic scene of angry soldiers, grieving mothers, and dead babies, reminding locals that a republic ruled by a tyrant will experience misery.

The work was designed by the Sienese Matteo di Giovanni (late 1400s) and inlaid with a colorful array of marble, including yellow marble, a Sienese specialty quarried nearby.

• Step into the chapel to the right of the library to see...

Donatello's *St. John the Baptist*

The rugged saint in his famous rags stands in a chapel to the right of the library. Donatello, the aging Florentine sculptor, whose style was now considered passé in Florence, came here to build bronze doors for the church (similar to Ghiberti's in Florence). He didn't complete the door project, but he did finish this bronze statue (1457).

• *Cross beneath the dome to find the...*

Bernini Chapel

To understand why Bernini is considered the greatest Baroque sculptor, step into his sumptuous chapel. This last work in the cathedral (1659) is enough to make even a Lutheran light a candle. Move up to the altar and look back at the two Bernini statues: Mary Magdalene in a state of spiritual ecstasy, and St. Jerome playing the crucifix like a violinist lost in beautiful music.

The chapel is classic Baroque, combining colored marble, statues, stained glass, a dome, and golden angels holding an oil painting, creating a multimedia extravaganza that offers a glimpse of heaven.

Over the altar is the *Madonna del Voto,* a Madonna and Child painted by Duccio and adorned with a real crown of gold and jewels. In typical medieval fashion, the scene is set in the golden light of heaven. Mary has the almond eyes, long fingers, and golden folds in her robe that are found in orthodox icons of the time. Still, this Mary tilts her head and looks out sympathetically, ready to listen to the prayers of the faithful. This is the Mary to whom the Palio is dedicated, dear to the hearts of the Sienese.

• *The faithful's prayers to Mary are accompanied by offerings, found outside the chapel, hanging on the wall to the left as you exit.*

Offerings to the *Madonna del Voto*

For untold generations, the Sienese have prayed to the *Madonna del Voto* for her help. In thanks, they give offerings, many of which hang now on the church wall. They express their thanks with silver hearts and medallions, helmets from non-fatal motorbike accidents, and neighborhood scarves from winners of the Palio. Want to leave an offering yourself? Light a candle for a €0.50 donation.

• *Cross back to the other side of the church to find the...*

Piccolomini Library

While the facade of the Piccolomini Library may be hidden behind scaffolding in 2010, the interior is open—and it's what's inside that matters. If there are crowds, spend your waiting time by reading ahead. Brilliantly frescoed, the library captures the exuberant, optimistic spirit of the 1400s, when humanism and the Renaissance were born. The never-restored frescoes look nearly as vivid now as the day they were finished 550 years ago. (With the bright window light, candles were not necessary in this room—and didn't sully the art with soot.) The painter Pinturicchio (c. 1454–1513) was hired to celebrate the life of one of Siena's hometown boys—a man many call "the first humanist," Aeneas Piccolomini (1405–1464), who became Pope Pius II. Each of the 10 scenes is framed with an arch, as if Pinturicchio were opening a window onto the spacious 3-D world we inhabit. The line of viewers moves counterclockwise; start at the window, letting your eyes follow the frescoes clockwise to trace the following progression:

1. Leaving for Basel: Twenty-seven-year-old Aeneas, riding a white horse and decked out in an  outrageous hat, pauses to take one last look back as he leaves Siena to charge off on the first of many adventures in his sometimes sunny, sometimes stormy life. Born poor but noble, he got all A's in his classics classes in Siena. Now, having soaked up all the secular knowledge available, he leaves home to crash a church council in Switzerland, where he would take sides against the pope.

2. Meeting James II of Scotland: Aeneas (with long brown hair) charmed King James and the well-dressed, educated, worldly crowd of Europe's courts. Among his many travels, he visited London (writing home about Westminster Abbey and St. Paul's), barely survived a storm at sea, negotiated peace between England and France, and fathered (at least) two illegitimate children.

3. Crowned Poet by Frederick III: Next we find Aeneas in Vienna, working as secretary to the German king. Aeneas kneels to ceremonially receive the laurel crown of a poet. Aeneas wrote love poetry, bawdy stories, and a play, and is best known for his candid autobiography. Everyone was talking about Aeneas—a writer, speaker, diplomat, and lover of the arts and pretty women, who was the very essence of the *uomo universale,* or Renaissance Man.

4. Submitting to Pope Eugene IV: At age 40, after a serious illness, Aeneas changes his life. He journeys to Rome and kisses the pope's foot, apologizing for his heretical opposition. He repents for his wild youth and becomes a priest. (In his autobiography, he says it was time to change anyway, as women no longer aroused him...and he no longer attracted them.)

5. Introducing Frederick III and Eleanora: Quickly named Bishop of Siena, Aeneas (in white pointed bishop's hat) makes his hometown a romantic getaway for his friend Frederick and his fiancée. Notice the Duomo's bell tower in the distance and the city walls (upper left). Aeneas always seemed to be present at Europe's most important political, religious, and social events.

6. Made Cardinal: Kneeling before the pope, with shaved head and praying hands, Aeneas receives the flat red hat of a cardinal. In many of these panels, the artist Pinturicchio uses all the latest 3-D effects—floor tiles and carpets, distant landscapes, receding lines—to suck you into the scene. He tears down palace walls and lets us peek inside into the day's centers of power.

7. Made Pope: In 1458, at age 53, Aeneas is elected to be Pope Pius II. Carried in triumph, he blesses the crowd. One of his first acts as pope is to declare as heresy the anti-pope doctrines he championed in his youth. (Pius II fans can visit his birthplace in Pienza, described in the Tuscan Hill Towns chapter.)

8. Proclaims a Crusade: He calls on all of Europe to liberate the Christian city Constantinople, which had recently fallen in 1453 to the Ottoman Turks. Europe is reluctant to follow his call, but Aeneas pushes the measure through.

9. Canonizes St. Catherine: From his papal throne, Aeneas looks down on the mortal remains of Catherine (clutching her symbol, the lily) and proclaims his fellow Sienese a saint. The well-dressed candle-holders in the foreground pose proudly.

10. Arrival in Ancona: Old and sick, the pope has to be carried everywhere on a litter because of rheumatic feet. He travels to Ancona, ready to board a ship to go fight the Turks. But only a handful of Venetian galleys arrive at the appointed time, the crusade peters out, and Aeneas, disheartened, dies. He wrote: "I do not deny my past. I have been a great wanderer, wandering away from the right path. But at least I know it, and hope the knowledge has not come too late."

The library also contains intricately decorated, illuminated music scores, and a statue (a Roman copy of a Greek original) of the Three Graces.

• *Exit the Duomo and make a U-turn to the left, walking alongside the church to Piazza Jacopo della Quercia.*

The Unfinished Church

The nave of the Duomo was supposed to be where the piazza is today. Worshippers would have entered the church from the far end of the piazza through the unfinished wall. (Look way up at the highest part of the wall. That's the viewpoint accessible from inside the Duomo Museum.) Some of the nave's green-and-white-striped columns were built, and are now filled in with a brick wall. Round white stones in the pavement mark where a row of pillars would have been. Look through the unfinished entrance facade, note blue sky where the stained-glass windows would have been, and ponder the struggles, triumphs, and failures of the human spirit.

SIENA DUOMO MUSEUM TOUR

Museo dell'Opera e Panorama

Siena's most enjoyable museum was built to house the cathedral's art. Stand eye-to-eye with the saints and angels who once languished unknown in the church's upper reaches (where copies are found today). The museum's centerpiece—an altarpiece by Duccio—once stood in the center of the church. And the museum's high point is one of the loftiest in town, offering expansive views of the church and the city.

Orientation

Cost: €6, €10 "My Name is Duccio" combo-ticket includes the Duomo (buy it at the museum to skip the ticket-buying line at the Duomo) and the Baptistery.

Hours: Daily March–Sept 9:30–20:00, Oct–Feb 10:00–17:00.

Getting There: It's next to the Duomo, in the skeleton of the unfinished part of the church on the Il Campo side; look for the yellow signs.

Information: There's a good 40-minute audioguide for €3. A €6 combo-audioguide available only at the Duomo includes the museum, the Duomo, and its library (€8/2 people, ID required for deposit). Tel. 0577-283-048, www.operaduomo.siena.it.

Length of This Tour: Allow one hour.

Starring: Duccio, the Virgin Mary, and the Tuscan view.

The Tour Begins

Ground Floor

The ground floor houses the church's original statues, mainly from the facade and exterior. After descending a few steps, turn your back on the hall of statues and wrought-iron gate.

• *You're now face-to-face with...*

Donatello's *Madonna and Child*

In this round, carved relief, a slender and tender Mary gazes down at her chubby-cheeked baby. The thick folds of her headdress stream down around her smooth face. Her sad eyes say that she knows the eventual fate of her son. Donatello creates the illusion of Mary's three-dimensional "lap" using only a few inches of depth cut into the creamy-rose stone.

• *On the opposite side of the room is...*

Duccio's Stained-Glass Rose Window

Until a couple of years ago, this original window was located above and behind the Duomo's altar. Now the church has a copy, and art lovers can enjoy a close-up look at this masterpiece. The rose window—20 feet across, made in 1288—is dedicated (like the church and the city itself) to the Virgin Mary. In the window's bottom panel, Mary (in blue) lies stretched across a red coffin while a crowd of mourners looks on. Miraculously, Mary was spared the pain of death (the Assumption, central panel), and winged angels carry her up in a holy bubble to heaven (top panel), where Christ sets her on a throne beside him and crowns her.

The work was designed by Siena's most famous artist, Duccio di Buoninsegna (c. 1225–1319). Duccio combined elements from rigid Byzantine icons (Mary's almond-shaped bubble, or *mandorla*, and the full-frontal saints that flank her) with a budding sense of 3-D realism (the throne turned at a three-quarter angle to simulate depth, with angels behind). Also notice how the angels in the central panel spread their wings out beyond the border of the window frame.

The Sienese army defeated Florence in the bloody battle of Montaperti, thanks, many believed, to the divine intervention of the Virgin. For the next 80 years of prosperity, Sienese artists cranked out countless Madonnas as a way of saying *grazie*. Bear in mind that the Duomo's main altar was originally dominated by Duccio's *Maestà*, a huge golden altarpiece of the Virgin in Majesty (which you'll see upstairs) that was bathed in the golden-blue light from this window.

• *Lining this main room are...*

Giovanni Pisano's Statues

Pisano spent a decade (c. 1285–1296) carving and orchestrating the decoration of the cathedral—saints, prophets, sibyls, animals, and the original she-wolf with Romulus and Remus. These life-size, robed saints stand in a relaxed *contrapposto*, with open mouths and expressive gestures. Their heads jut out—Pisano's way of making them more visible from below. Some turn and seem to converse with their neighbors, especially evident with Moses *(Mose)* and the sister who raised him like a mother, Miriam *(Maria di Mose,* on the left side of the room). The copies of these two stand on the right side of the church, where they appear to interact.

Down a few steps in Rooms 11 and 12 are the two lions that once looked down from the church's main entrance, and Pisano's 12 apostles who originally lined the nave. (See old photos on the wall.) Tastes changed over the centuries, and the apostles were later moved up to the roof, where they eroded. Pisano's relaxed realism and expressive gestures were a major influence on later Florentine sculptors such as Donatello.

• *Retrace your steps and go upstairs. To the left awaits a private audience with Duccio's Madonna.*

Duccio di Buoninsegna—Altarpiece Panels (*Maestà* and 26 Passion panels, 1311)

The panels in this room were once part of the Duomo's main altar-piece. Grab a seat and study one of the great pieces of medieval art. Although the former altarpiece was disassembled (and the frame was lost), most of the pieces are displayed here, with the front side (*Maestà*, with Mary and saints, pronounced my-STAH) at one end of the room, and the back side (Passion panels) at the other.

Imagine these separate panels pieced together, set into their original gold, prickly, 15-by-15-foot wood frame and placed on the main altar in the Duomo. For two centuries it gave the congregation something to look at while the priests turned their backs at Communion time. The Christ child stared back.

Maestà (**Enthroned Virgin**): At the center of the front side sit the Virgin and Child, surrounded by angels and saints. Mary's a melancholy queen on an inlaid-marble throne. Young angels lean their elbows on the back of the throne and sigh. We see the throne head-on, unnaturally splayed open (a Byzantine style popular at the time in Siena). Mary is massive, twice the size of the saints around her, and she clearly stands out from the golden background. Unlike traditional full-frontal Byzantine icons, she turns slightly sideways to touch her baby, who does not bless us.

The city of Siena is dedicated to this Lady, who backed the Sienese against Florence in the bloody battle of Montaperti in 1260. Here, she's triumphant, visited by Siena's four patron saints (kneeling in front), John the Baptist and other saints (the first choir row), more angels in a row (soprano section), and, chiming in from up in the balcony, James the Great and the 12 apostles.

The painting was revolutionary for the time in its sheer size and opulence, and in Duccio's budding realism that broke standard conventions. Duccio (c. 1225–1319), at the height of his powers, used every innovative arrow in his quiver. He replaced the standard gold-leaf background (symbolizing heaven) with a gold, intricately patterned curtain draped over the throne. Mary's blue robe opens to reveal her body, and the curve of her knee suggests real anatomy beneath the robe. Baby Jesus wears a delicately transparent garment. Their faces are modeled with light—a patchwork of bright flesh and shadowy valleys, as if lit from the left (a technique he likely learned from his contemporary Giotto during a visit to Florence).

Along the base of Mary's throne is an inscription (*"Mater sancta dei..."* or "Holy Mother of God...") asking Mary to bring peace to Siena *(Senis)* and long life to Duccio *(Ducio)*—quite a tribute in a time when painters were usually treated as anonymous craftsmen.

• *Look on the opposite wall to find...*

Scenes from the Passion of Christ: The flip side of the altarpiece featured 26 smaller panels—the medieval equivalent of pages—showing colorful scenes from the Passion of Christ.

The panels showcase the budding Tuscan style—realism and storytelling. It doesn't take a Bible scholar to "read" these panels, left to right. Christ on a donkey (lower left) makes his triumphal entry into the city gate of Jerusalem (or is it Siena?). Next, he washes his disciples' feet in a realistic, three-dimensional room. But Duccio hasn't fully mastered perspective—in the Last Supper, we see Christ eye-to-eye, but view the table from above. Christ is arrested in Gethsemane, and so on, until the climactic Crucifixion. The Crucifixion is given the standard gold background, but the cross is set on a terraced hillside, amid the crowd. Jesus' followers express human emotion rarely seen in earlier art.

The Passion panels' crowd scenes aren't arranged in neat choir rows, but in more natural-looking groups. Duccio sets figures in motion, with individual faces expressing sorrow, anger, and agitation. Duccio's human realism would be taken to the next level by his Florentine counterpart Giotto, often called the first proto-Renaissance painter.

Duccio and assistants (possibly including Simone Martini) spent three years on this massive altarpiece. It was a triumph, and at its dedication the satisfied Sienese marched it around the Campo and into the church in a public procession.

But by 1506, at the height of the Renaissance, Duccio's medieval altarpiece looked musty and old-fashioned, and was moved to a side altar. In 1771 it was disassembled and stored in the church offices (today's Duomo Museum). Today, scholars debate how to reassemble it accurately, and hail it as a quantum leap in the evolution of art.

Room 9, to the left and behind the *Maestà*, contains wooden models of the Duomo's inlaid-marble floor and close-ups of the individual panels for easier inspection.

• *Return to the stairs and continue up. Take a right at the first landing. At the landing just before the top floor, turn right and walk past the rooms, going through the small doorway to the stairwell. Climb down the steps and then up about 60 claustrophobic spiral stairs to the first viewpoint. You can continue up another similar spiral staircase to reach the very top.*

Panorama del Facciatone

Standing on the wall from this high point in the city, you're rewarded with a stunning view of Siena...and an interesting perspective.

Look toward the Duomo and remember this: To outdo Florence, Siena had planned to enlarge this cathedral by turning it into a transept and constructing an enormous nave (see sidebar on page 314). You're standing on top of what would have been the new entrance facade (see map on page 311). The white stones in the pavement mark where columns would have stood. Had the church been completed, you'd be looking straight down the nave toward the altar.

CIVIC MUSEUM TOUR

Museo Civico

The City Hall (Palazzo Pubblico), at the base of the City Tower, stands as a symbol of a republic independent from the pope and the Holy Roman Emperor, and of the rising secular society that appeared first in Tuscany before spreading throughout Europe in the Renaissance. Still the seat of city government, the City Hall also has a fine and manageable museum that displays a good sample of Sienese art. Stroll through this civic center and let its fine day-in-the-life frescoes take you back to a time when this proud town understandably considered itself the vanguard of Western civilization.

Orientation

Cost: €7.50, €12 combo-ticket includes City Tower, €11 combo-ticket includes Santa Maria della Scala but not City Tower.

Hours: Daily March–Oct 10:00–19:00 (may be open later in summer), Nov–Feb 10:00–17:15, last entry 45 min before closing.

Getting There: As the focus of the main square, it's hard to miss.

Photography: Not allowed.

Length of This Tour: Allow one hour.

The Tour Begins

• *Climb two flights of stairs (elevator on request—ask at ticket desk), pass through the gift shop, and enter the...*

Hall of Italian Unification (Sala del Risorgimento)

This hall has dramatic scenes of the 19th-century unification of Italy (surrounded by statues that don't seem to care). See Victor

CIVIC MUSEUM

Siena's Civic Museum

PIAZZA DEL MERCATO

SALA DELLA PACE

GIFT SHOP

VIA SALICOTTO

COURT-YARD

SALA DEL MAPPAMONDO

CHAPEL

START

SALA DEL RISORG.

SALA DI BALIA

WC

VIA GIOVANNI DUPRÈ

TORRE DEL MANGIA (TOWER)

PIAZZA DEL CAMPO

DCH

20 YARDS

20 METERS

❶ Victor Emmanuel II at Battle of San Martino

❷ Victor Emmanuel II Receives Politicians

❸ Chapel

❹ MARTINI – Maestà

❺ MARTINI – Guidoriccio da Fogliano

❻ DUCCIO – The Surrender of the Castle of Giuncarico

❼ St. Catherine & St. Bernardino Frescoes

❽ LORENZETTI – Good Government

❾ LORENZETTI – Bad Government

Emmanuel II (left wall as you enter, with beard and pointy moustache), king of a small northern Italian province, on horseback at the Battle of San Martino (1859) while leading a united Italian nation against its Austrian oppressors. Beneath that, you'll see the coat he's wearing in the painting. Next (clockwise above the windows), the king's red-shirted troops cheer as he shakes hands with the dashing general Giuseppe Garibaldi. Victorious, the king receives politicians (next painting), who bow and present the election results that made Italy united and democratic, with Victor Emmanuel II as a symbolic head. When he died in 1878 (see his funeral procession passing through Rome's Pantheon portico filled with real portraits on the far wall), Italy was well on the way to modern nationhood.

• *Pass through the hallway to the left, and walk through the Sala di Balia (may be under partial restoration). In the next room, turn left to find the chapel where the city's governors and bureaucrats prayed. Continue into the large...*

Sala del Mappamondo

This room, where the Grand Council met, pumped up governors and citizens alike with its images of military victories and the blessings of Mary. On opposite ends of the room, you'll find two large frescoes by Siena's great Simone Martini (c. 1280–1344). His *Maestà* (*Enthroned Virgin*, 1315) was the secular counterpart to Duccio's *Maestà* in the Duomo (now in the Duomo Museum). Mary sits on a throne under a red silk canopy, a model to Siena's city council of what a just ruler should be. Siena's black-and-white coat of arms is woven into both the canopy and the picture frame. Mary is surrounded by saints and angels, clearly echoing the *Maestà* of Simone's teacher, Duccio.

But this is a groundbreaking work. It's Siena's first fresco showing a Madonna not in a faraway, gold-leaf heaven, but under the blue sky of the real world that we inhabit. The canopy creates a 3-D stage, with saints in front of, behind, and underneath it. Some saints' faces are actually blocked by the support poles. These saints are not a generic conga-line of Byzantine icons, but a milling crowd of 30 individuals with expressive faces. Some look straight out, some are in profile, and some turn at that difficult-to-draw three-quarter angle, grabbing onto the canopy poles. And the Virgin's brooch is painted so well that it almost looks... uh, real.

With unbeatable Florence to the north, Siena expanded south. Facing the *Maestà* is Simone Martini's *Guidoriccio da Fogliano*. It's the year "MCCCXXVIII" (1328), and Siena's renowned mercenary general—one of Martini's compatriots—rides across a barren landscape and surveys the imposing castle that his armies have just conquered. He has just successfully finished a six-month-long siege—see his camp on the right. This is one of Europe's first secular portraits. (Guido and his horse have the same tailor.)

The Surrender of the Castle of Giuncarico, by Duccio (1314), shows a man in green about to hand over his sword to the Sienese general (not pictured—the fresco was obliterated when it was covered by a later fresco). In the background is the man's castle and village on a rocky outcrop. Duccio's *Surrender* apparently inspired the 3-D landscape of *Guidoriccio da Fogliano*.

Also in the room (painted between the arches) are frescoes of two saints with local connections, St. Catherine (see page 306) and St. Bernardino (1380–1444). Bernardino's charismatic sermons in Siena could hold a Campo crowd for several days. At sunset, he'd say we'll continue at sunrise...and people came back. He brought together sworn enemies to share a *bacio di pace*—kiss of peace.

• *Continue into the next room.*

Room of Peace
(Sala della Pace, a.k.a. Sala dei Nove)

This is the room where the Council of Nine met. Looking down on the oligarchy during their meetings were two fascinating frescoes showing the *Effects of Good and Bad Government,* by Ambrogio Lorenzetti (1337–1340).

Good Government (on the short wall) is represented by a stately, bearded man on a throne, surrounded by virtuous females, notably the central virtue Peace (Pax), who lounges back on a pile of discarded armor. Justice holds a scale, with angels on either side, to execute her judgments. Wrongdoers (lower right) are rounded up by the authorities. At the foot of the stage, prominent Sienese file by. Concordia (below the figure of Justice) makes society just and equal with the wooden plane on her lap.

On the long wall (with the better-preserved fresco), notice the whistle-while-you-work happiness of the utopian community ruled by the utopian government. The city and the countryside are exactly the same width (20 feet), an indication that they work together and need each other. Amid Siena's skyline (Duomo at upper left), young people dance to the beat of a tambourine, workers repair roofs, a professor teaches, and the conversation flows. The blessings of a good government extend even to the countryside, which feels safe and prosperous. The fields are tilled, the Via Francigena is busy, and angels fly overhead. Study this intimate and rare look at medieval commerce.

But under *Bad Government* (other long wall, damaged fresco), a horned, fanged, wine-drinking devil sets the vices loose ("Avarice," "Vainglory"). Arsonists torch homes and fields, soldiers rape and pillage, crime is rampant, fields are barren, and frescoes get damaged. The only person still working is making weapons. Justice slumps at the devil's feet, bound and too depressed to look up. The message: Without justice, there can be no prosperity.

The rural view out the window (looking south, not to Il Campo) from this room is essentially the same view as from the top of the big stairs you'll pass as you exit—enjoy it from here.

SIENA SLEEPING, EATING, AND CONNECTIONS

Sleeping in Siena

Finding a room in Siena is tough during Easter (April 4 in 2010) or the Palio (July 2 and Aug 16). Many hotels won't take reservations until the end of May for the Palio, and even then they might require a four-night stay. If you're traveling any other time of year, you should still call ahead, as all the guidebooks list Siena's few budget places. While day-tripping tour groups turn the town into a Gothic amusement park in midsummer, Siena is basically yours in the evenings and off-season.

Most of the listed hotels lie between Il Campo and the Church of San Domenico. Part of Siena's charm is its lively, festive character—this means that all hotels can be plagued with noise, even (and sometimes especially) the hotels in the pedestrian-only zone. If tranquility is important for your sanity, ask for a room that's off the street, or consider staying at one of the recommended places outside the center.

Simple Places near Il Campo

Most of these listings are forgettable but inexpensive, and just a horse wreck away from one of Italy's most wonderful civic spaces.

$$ Palazzo Masi is a modern B&B run by husband-and-wife team Alizzardo and Daniela. Just steps away from Il Campo, it has six pleasant, quiet rooms and shared common areas on the second and third floors of a renovated medieval 14th-century townhouse (D-€80, Db-€120, these rates promised to readers through 2010 if you book direct, discounts for 4 or more nights, cash only; take the road to the far right of City Hall as you're facing it and head down Casato di Sotto for about 50 yards to #29; mobile 349-600-9155, www.palazzomasi.it, info@palazzomasi.it).

Sleep Code

(€1 = about $1.40, country code: 39)
S = Single, **D** = Double/Twin, **T** = Triple, **Q** = Quad, **b** = bathroom,
s = shower only.

   Breakfast is not included unless noted. If your hotel doesn't provide breakfast, eat at a bar on Il Campo or near your hotel. Credit cards are generally accepted, but I note in the listings if they aren't. (If not, there are ATMs all over town.) Hotel staff generally speak English unless noted otherwise.

   To help you easily sort through these listings, I've divided the rooms into three categories based on the price for a standard double room with bath:

   $$$ Higher Priced—Most rooms €130 or more.
   $$ Moderately Priced—Most rooms between €90–130.
   $ Lower Priced—Most rooms €90 or less.

$$ Palazzo Bruchi B&B offers six tranquil rooms in a 17th-century palazzo overlooking the Tuscan countryside. There's one fancy, spacious room *(luxe)* that features Old World, heavy walnut furnishings and period paintings. The other six rooms are smaller and simpler, with bright, cheery decor and views of the quiet interior courtyard. Camilla takes good care of her guests (Sb-€80–90, Db-€100, *luxe* Db/Tb-€150, Tb-€120–175, 4 percent cash discount, includes breakfast, free Wi-Fi; take Via Banchi di Sotto until it turns into Via Pantaneto, located on left, just before the Church of San Giorgio at #105; tel. & fax 0577-287-342, www .palazzobruchi.it, masignani@hotmail.com).

$ Albergo Tre Donzelle is a fine budget value with 20 plain, institutional, well-worn rooms. Don't hang out here...think of Il Campo, a block away, as your terrace (S-€38, D-€49, Db-€60, T-€70, Tb-€85, no rooms available for Palio; with your back to the tower, head away from Il Campo toward 2:00 to Via Donzelle 5; tel. 0577-280-358, www.tredonzelle.com, info@tredonzelle.com).

$ Piccolo Hotel Etruria has 20 decent air-conditioned rooms but not much soul. The hotel is a bit overpriced for what it is, though well-located and sleepable (S-€50, Sb-€55, Db-€90, Tb-€120, Qb-€150, optional breakfast-€6, curfew at 1:00 in the morning, one-night reservations not accepted more than a month in advance, next to recommended Albergo Tre Donzelle at Via Donzelle 1–3, tel. 0577-288-088, fax 0577-288-461, www.hoteletruria .com, info@hoteletruria.com, Fattorini family).

Siena Hotels

1. Palazzo Masi & Launderette
2. To Palazzo Bruchi B&B
3. Albergo Tre Donzelle
4. Piccolo Hotel Etruria
5. Locanda Garibaldi
6. Hotel Cannon d'Oro
7. To Hotel Duomo & Pensione Palazzo Ravizza
8. To Hotel Villa Elda & Hotel Villa Liberty
9. Hotel Chiusarelli
10. Alma Domus
11. Albergo Bernini
12. Internet Cafés (2)
13. Launderette

$ Locanda Garibaldi is a modest, characteristically Sienese place. Gentle Marcello rents seven pleasant rooms up a funky, artsy staircase (Db-€75, Tb-€95, only takes reservations a month in advance, half a block downhill from Il Campo at Via Giovanni Dupre 18, tel. 0577-284-204, Marcello and Sonia speak a little English).

$ Hotel Cannon d'Oro, a few blocks up Via Banchi di Sopra, has 30 airy and comfortable rooms, but is a bit noisy and group-friendly (Sb-€71, Db-€90, Tb-€115, Qb-€136, these discounted prices good with this book through 2010, family deals, includes breakfast, a couple blocks from the bus hub at Via Montanini 28, tel. 0577-44-321, fax 0577-280-868, www.cannondoro.com, info @cannondoro.com, Maurizio).

Sleeping Fancy, Southwest of Il Campo

These two classy and well-run places are a 10-minute walk from Il Campo.

$$$ Hotel Duomo has 20 spacious rooms and a bizarre floor plan (Sb-€125, Db-€150, Db suite-€200, Tb-€200, Qb-€250, includes breakfast, air-con, elevator, Internet access, picnic-friendly roof terrace, free parking; follow Via di Città, which becomes Via Stalloreggi, to #38; tel. 0577-289-088, fax 0577-43-043, www .hotelduomo.it, booking@hotelduomo.it, Svetlana and Vasilika). If arriving by train, take a taxi (€8) or bus #3 to the Porta Tufi stop, just a few minutes' walk from the hotel; if driving, go to Porta San Marco, turn right, and follow signs to the hotel—drop your bags, then park in the nearby Il Campo lot.

$$$ Pensione Palazzo Ravizza is elegant and friendly, with an aristocratic feel and a peaceful garden (Sb-€150, small loft Db-€150, standard Db-€200, superior Db-€230, Tb-€280, family suites-€320, see website for room differences, rooms in back overlook countryside, includes breakfast, air-con, elevator, Internet access, free parking, Via Piano dei Mantellini 34, tel. 0577-280-462, fax 0577-221-597, www.palazzoravizza.com, bureau@palazzoravizza.it).

Near San Domenico Church

These hotels are within a 10-minute walk northwest of Il Campo. Albergo Bernini and Alma Domus, which offer views of the old town and cathedral, are about the best values in town.

$$$ Hotel Villa Elda rents 11 bright and light rooms in a newly renovated villa. Its amenities include a bottle of wine at check-in. Classy, stately, and overpriced, it's in a fine neighborhood just a few minutes' walk past the Church of San Domenico (Db-€80–180, more with view, extra person-€40, includes breakfast, air-con, garden and view terrace, Viale Ventiquattro Maggio 10, tel. 0577-247-927, www.villaeldasiena.it, info@villaeldasiena.it).

$$$ Hotel Chiusarelli, with 49 rooms in a beautiful building, has a handy location but is on a very busy street, making it a last resort. Expect traffic noise at night—ask for a quieter room in the back (can be guaranteed with reservation). The bells of San Domenico are your 7:00 wake-up call. Readers report that the staff is indifferent (Sb-€91, Db-€132, Tb-€175, ask for Rick Steves discount when you book, air-con, rental bikes-€4/half-day, across from San Domenico at Viale Curtatone 15, tel. 0577-280-562, fax 0577-271-177, www.chiusarelli.com, info@chiusarelli.com).

$$ Hotel Villa Liberty, a bit farther out, is a former private mansion with 18 big, bright, comfortable rooms and lots of street noise (Sb-€70, Db-€120, air-con, elevator, free Internet access, bar, courtyard, free and easy street parking, facing fortress at Viale V. Veneto 11, tel. 0577-44-966, fax 0577-44-770, www.villaliberty.it, info@villaliberty.it).

$ Alma Domus is a nun-run hotel offering 43 clean, quiet little rooms for a steal. Bright lamps, quaint balconies, fine views, grand public rooms, top security, and a pleasant atmosphere make this a great value—but they offer only a limited numbers of doubles. The 10:00 checkout time is strict, but they will store your luggage in their secure courtyard (Sb-€45, Db-€75, Tb-€95, Qb-€110, breakfast included, cash only, ask for view room—*con vista,* central air-con, elevator, Internet access, suggested 1:00 in the morning curfew; from San Domenico, walk downhill toward the view with the church on your right, turn left down Via Camporegio, make a U-turn at the little chapel down the brick steps to Via Camporegio 37; tel. 0577-44-177, fax 0577-47-601, www.hotelalmadomus.it, info@hotelalmadomus.it).

$ Albergo Bernini makes you part of a Sienese family in a modest, clean home with nine traditional rooms (ask for a quiet room away from the restaurant). Giovanni, wife Daniela, and their three daughters welcome you to their spectacular view terrace for breakfast and picnic lunches and dinners (Sb-€78, D-€65, Db-€85, less in winter, optional breakfast-€7.50, cash only, non-smoking, free Internet access, suggested midnight curfew, on the main Il Campo–San Domenico drag at Via Sapienza 15, tel. & fax 0577-289-047, www.albergobernini.com, hbernin@tin.it). When booked up, they may have some charming, bigger, but more expensive apartments available (Db-€100, non-smoking, located just a few steps downhill from Albergo).

Farther from the Center

City buses will get you to any of the following places. See locations on the map on page 293.

$$$ Hotel Santa Caterina is a three-star, 18th-century place. Professionally run with real attention to quality, most of the hotel's 22 comfortable rooms were recently renovated, and there's a delightful garden outside (Sb-€105, small Db-€105, Db-€145, Tb-€195, prices promised with this book through 2010—ask for Rick Steves rate when you reserve, includes buffet breakfast, air-con, fridge in room, elevator, garden side is quieter, but street side—with multipaned windows—isn't bad, parking-€15/day—request when you reserve, 100 yards outside Porta Romana city gate at Via E.S. Piccolomini 7, tel. 0577-221-105, fax 0577-271-087, www.hscsiena.it, info@hscsiena.it, Lorenza and Andrea). To get to and from downtown Siena, catch shuttle bus #A. To connect with the bus and train stations, take bus #2 to Piazza del Sale and then transfer to #17.

$$$ Frances' Lodge is a small farmhouse B&B less than a mile out of Siena. Franca and Franco rent five modern rooms and two apartment suites in a rustic-yet-elegant old place with an inviting breakfast room, peaceful garden, eight acres of olive trees and vineyards, and great views of Siena and its countryside—even from the swimming pool (small Db-€160, Db-€190, Db suite-€200, Tb-€210–220, Tb suite-€250, Qb suite-€300, these prices promised to Rick Steves readers through 2010, includes great breakfast, air-con-€10, free parking, Strada di Valdipugna 2, tel. 0577-281-061, mobile 337-671-1608, www.franceslodge.it). It's an easy five-minute bus ride from the center (shuttle bus #B) or €10 by taxi. Consider having an al fresco picnic dinner there, complete with view.

$$ Hotel Porta Romana is at the edge of town off a busy road. Fourteen rooms face the open countryside, and breakfast is served in the garden (Sb-€90, Db-€110, Qb-€130, extra person-€20, 10 percent Rick Steves discount if you book direct, cash preferred, Internet access, free parking, 50 yards from convenient connection to town center via shuttle bus #A—desk has tickets, Via E.S. Piccolomini 35, tel. 0577-42299, fax 0577-232-905, www.hotelporta romana.com, info@hotelportaromana.com, Marco and Evelia).

$$ Hotel San Marco, just outside Porta San Marco, has 28 pleasing, modern rooms with all the comforts. While it's easiest to drive here, city bus #54 stops 100 yards from the hotel every 15 minutes (Db-€120, discounts for 3 or more nights, air-con, free parking, Via Massetana 70, tel. 0577-271-556, fax 0577-271-826, www.sanmarcosiena.it, info@sanmarcosiena.it).

$ Guidoriccio Youth Hostel, which has 100 cheap beds and an institutional ambience, welcomes anyone (€20/bed in doubles, triples, and dorms with sheets; co-ed rooms, includes breakfast, Internet access and Wi-Fi, self-service laundry-€6, lock-out 10:00–14:00; take bus #10 or #77 from train station or bus #10 or #15 from Piazza Gramsci—about 20 min to Via Fiorentina 89 in Stellino neighborhood, tel. 0577-52212, fax 0577-50277, www.ostellosiena.it, info@ostellosiena.it).

Outside of Siena

The following accommodations are set in the lush, peaceful countryside surrounding Siena, and are best for those traveling by car (see locations on map on page 293).

$$$ Borgo Argenina is a well-maintained, pricey splurge of a B&B. Run by helpful Elena Nappa, it's 20 minutes north of Siena by car in the Chianti region (Db-€170, beautiful gardens, tel. 0577-747-117, fax 0577-747-228, www.borgoargenina.it, info @borgoargenina.it).

$$ Il Canto del Sole is a lovingly restored 18th-century farmhouse turned family-friendly *agriturismo* located about six miles outside of the Porta Romana city gate. Run by Laura, Luciano, and their boy Marco, it features six bright and airy rooms and two apartments with original antique furnishings, a saltwater swimming pool, a game room, and bike rentals (Db-€90–110, Tb-€130, extra bed-€15, apartment-€220, air-con in apartments only, Val di Villa Canina 1292, 53014 Loc. Cuna, tel. 0577-375-127, fax 0577-373-378, www.ilcantodelsole.com, info@ilcantodelsole.com). Optional five-course dinner is available by request for €20 (wine is extra).

$ Agriturismo Poggio Salvi has three pleasant, spacious apartments—rentable only by the week—set in a grassy field near the tiny burg of Poggio Salvi, 15 minutes southwest of Siena. Dwellings are separate with modern conveniences (rentals from Sat–Sat, €625/2 people and €970/4 people during high season, Loc. Poggio Salvi 249, 53010 San Rocco a Pilli, tel. & fax 0577-349-443, mobile 333-290-7890, www.poggiosalvi.net, info@poggio salvi.net).

Eating in Siena

Sienese restaurants are reasonable by Florentine and Venetian standards. You can enjoy ordering high on the menu here without going broke.

Dining in the Old Town

Antica Osteria Da Divo is *the* place for a dressy and atmospheric €45 meal. The kitchen is creative, the ambience is candlelit, and the food is fresh and top-notch. While the cuisine is flamboyant and almost over-the-top, they serve up my favorite splurge dinner in town. Chef Pino is fanatic about fresh ingredients, enjoys giving traditional dishes his creative spin, and is understandably proud of his desserts (daily 12:00–14:30 & 19:00–22:30, closed Sun in summer and Tue in winter, reservations smart; facing Baptistery door, take the far right street and walk one long curving block to Via Franciosa 29; tel. 0577-284-381). Those dining here with this book

Siena Restaurants

EATING IN SIENA

1. Antica Osteria Da Divo
2. Hostaria Il Carroccio
3. Osteria Boccon del Prete
4. Trattoria La Torre, Key Largo Bar, Ciao Cafeteria & Spizzico Pizza
5. To Taverna San Giuseppe
6. To Osteria Nonna Gina
7. Trattoria Papei
8. Ristorante Guidoriccio
9. Osteria la Chiacchera
10. Osteria Trombicche
11. La Taverna Di Cecco
12. Locanda Garibaldi
13. Pizzeria La Speranza & Bar Paninoteca San Paolo
14. Bar il Palio
15. Il Bandierino
16. Osteria Liberamente
17. Costarella Gelateria
18. Antica Pizzicheria al Palazzo della Chigiana
19. Consorzio Agrario Siena Grocery
20. Enoteca Italiana

can finish with a complimentary biscotti and *vin santo* or coffee (upon request).

Hostaria Il Carroccio seats guests in an artsy, sea-foam-green dining room and serves elegantly presented, traditional "slow food" recipes with innovative flair at affordable prices (€7 pastas, €15 *secondi*, €30 tasting menu—minimum two people, reservations wise, Thu–Tue 12:30–15:00 & 19:30–22:00, closed Wed, Via Casato di Sotto 32, tel. 0577-41-165).

Osteria Boccon del Prete puts an artistic spin on Tuscan favorites using the freshest seasonal ingredients. Their sultry dining room is intimate and tiny, making reservations a must (Mon–Sat 12:30–15:00 & 19:30–22:00, closed Sun, Via S. Pietro 17, tel. 0577-280-388).

Eating Traditional and Rustic in the Old Town

Trattoria La Torre is a thriving *casalinga* (home-cooking) eatery, popular for its homemade pasta, plates of which entice eaters as they enter. The sound of its busy open kitchen adds to the conviviality. Ten tables are packed under one medieval brick arch. Ask for a written menu—otherwise the owner likes to just recite his long string of dishes (Fri–Wed 12:00–15:00 & 19:00–21:30, closed Thu, just steps below Il Campo at Via Salicotto 7, tel. 0577-287-548, Alberto Boccini).

Taverna San Giuseppe, a local favorite, offers modern Tuscan cuisine in a chic grotto atmosphere. Check the posters tacked around the entry for daily specials. Reserve or arrive early to get a table (€8 pastas, €14 *secondi*, Mon–Sat 12:00–14:30 & 19:00–22:00, closed Sun, reservations wise, can be hot and stuffy, 7-min climb up street to the right of City Hall at Via Giovanni Dupre 132, tel. 0577-42-286).

Osteria Nonna Gina wins praise from locals for its good-quality, rustic cuisine and reasonable prices (€8 pastas, €8 *secondi*, Tue–Sun 12:30–14:30 & 19:30–22:30, closed Mon, 10-min walk from Il Campo—two blocks beyond Hotel Duomo—at Piano dei Mantellini 2, tel. 0577-287-247). While the front room is charming, I'd avoid the basement.

Trattoria Papei is a Sienese favorite, featuring a bright, bustling family atmosphere and friendly servers dishing out generous portions of rib-stickin' Tuscan specialties and grilled meats (daily 12:00–15:00 & 19:00–22:30, closed Mon off-season, Piazza del Mercato 6, tel. 0577-280-894).

Ristorante Guidoriccio, just a few steps below Il Campo, feels warm and welcoming. You'll get smiling service from Ercole and Elisabetta (€8 pastas, €13 *secondi*, Mon–Sat 12:30–14:30 & 19:00–22:30, closed Sun, air-con, Via Giovanni Dupre 2, tel. 0577-44-350).

Osteria la Chiacchera is a youthful hole-in-the-brick-wall that plays hip music and serves "peasant food" at peasant prices on simple tables and paper placemats. It's an eat-it-and-beat-it, pasta-slinging place, with rickety outside tables clinging to the steep, stepped lane (€5 pastas, €7 *secondi*, daily 12:00–15:30 & 19:00–24:00, great cakes, skip the *trippa*—tripe, down the street to the left of Pension Bernini at Costa di San Antonio 4, tel. 0577-280-631).

Osteria Trombicche is cheap and small, with tight indoor seating and two tiny outdoor tables from which to watch the street scene. They serve fast, hearty food to a young crowd (€5 *ribollita*—bean-and-vegetable soup, €6–12 vegetarian sampler plates, Mon–Sat 11:00–22:00, closed Sun, Via delle Terme 66, tel. 0577-288-089).

La Taverna Di Cecco is a clean, comfortable, little eatery where earnest Luca serves tasty dishes made from fresh ingredients for a fair price. Try the yummy salads and traditional Sienese specialties (€8 pastas, €12 *secondi*, daily 12:00–15:00 & 19:00–24:00, Via Cecco Angiolieri 19, tel. 0577-288-518).

Locanda Garibaldi, just around the corner from Il Campo, gives you a chance to imagine Siena before the tourist hordes discovered it. Join Marcello, kindly wife Sonia, and their son for an unpretentious Sienese meal in a rustic setting, while the TV murmurs quietly in the corner. The pasta is handmade, the house wine is cheap, and the almond pie *(torta di mandorle)* is sweet and crunchy (€6 pastas, €9 *secondi*, €20 fixed-price meal with house wine, Sun–Fri 12:00–14:00 & 19:00–21:00, closed Sat, Via Giovanni Dupre 18, tel. 0577-284-204).

Eating on Il Campo

If you choose to eat (or drink) on perhaps the finest town square in Italy, you'll pay a premium, meet waiters who don't need to hustle, and get mediocre food. And yet I recommend it. The clamshell-shaped square is lined with venerable cafés, bars, restaurants, and pizzerias. **Caffè Fonte Gaia,** long the classic place to see and be seen, is now a bit tired. **Pizzeria La Speranza** serves good but pricey pizzas with full-frontal views. **Bar il Palio** is best for drinks (straight prices, no cover, decent waiters, great perch). For value, everyone agrees: it's **Il Bandierino,** with the square's best food but worst view. Their *pici* (pee-chee), a fat Sienese spaghetti, is good (€9 salads, €11 pizzas, €13 pastas; no cover but a 20 percent service fee, daily 11:00–23:00, tel. 0577-282-217). For a trendy vibe popular with young people, pick the dynamic little **Osteria Liberamente** (fine wine by the glass, cocktails with good tapas, breakfasts, noisy music inside but great outdoor tables, tel. 0577-274-733). If your hotel doesn't serve breakfast or if you'd like something more memorable, consider breakfast on Il Campo—there are plenty of options. A cappuccino and a *cornetto* (croissant) run about €5–6.

Drinks or Snacks from Balconies Overlooking Il Campo

Three places have skinny balconies with benches overlooking the main square for their customers. Sipping a coffee or nibbling a pastry here while marveling at the Il Campo scene is one of my favorite things to do in Europe. And it's very cheap. Survey these three places from Il Campo (from the base of the tower, imagine a 12-hour clock—they are at 10:00, high noon, and 3:00, respectively).

The little **Costarella Gelateria,** on the corner of Via di Città and Costa dei Barbieri, has good ice cream, drinks, and light snacks such as cute little €1.50 sandwiches (Fri–Wed 8:00–late, closes at 24:00 and all day Thu in off-season, Via di Città 33).

Bar Paninoteca San Paolo has a youthful pub ambience and a row of stools overlooking the square. It serves big salads and 50 kinds of sandwiches, hot and cold (€3.50 each, €0.50 extra if you sit outside, order and pay at the counter, food served daily 12:00–2:00, on Vicolo di S. Paolo at the stairs leading down to the top of Il Campo).

Key Largo Bar has two benches in the corner offering a great secret perch (daily 7:00–22:00 or until midnight in summer, on the corner of Via Rinaldini). Buy your drink or snack at the bar (no extra charge to sit), climb upstairs, and slide the ancient bar to open the door. Suddenly you're imagining Palio ponies zipping wildly around the corner.

Eating Cheaply in the Center

Antica Pizzicheria al Palazzo della Chigiana may be the official name, but I bet locals just call it Antonio's. For most of his life, frenzied Antonio has carved salami and cheese for the neighborhood. Most of the day a hungry line spills onto the street as locals wait for their sandwiches: meat and cheese sold by the weight, and a glass of good Chianti (€4). Antonio and his boys offer a big cheese-and-meat plate (about €18 for 30 minutes of eating) and pull out a tiny tabletop in the corner so you can munch or sip while standing and watch the ham-hock-y scene. Lately he's also put a small table outside (daily 8:00–20:00, Via di Città 95, tel. 0577-289-164). Even if you don't get a sandwich, pop in to inhale the commotion or peruse Antonio's gifty traditional edibles.

Ciao Cafeteria, at the bottom of Il Campo, offers good-value, self-service lunches, but no ambience or views (daily 12:00–15:00). The crowded **Spizzico,** a pizza counter in the front half of Ciao, serves huge, inexpensive quarter-pizzas; on sunny days, people take the pizza—trays and all—out on Il Campo for a picnic (daily 11:00–21:00, to left of City Tower as you face it).

Budget eaters look for *pizza al taglio* shops, scattered throughout Siena, selling pizza by the slice. Of all the grocery shops, the biggest is **Consorzio Agrario Siena** (Mon–Sat 7:30–19:30, sometimes open Sun, a block off Piazza Matteotti, toward Il Campo at Via Pianigiani 5).

Connections

Siena has sparse train connections but is a great hub for buses to the hill towns, though frequency drops on Sundays and holidays. For most, Florence is the gateway to Siena. Even if you are a railpass user, connect these two cities by bus—it's faster than the train, and Siena's bus station is more convenient and central than its train station. The Sena bus company has special promotional fares on its website: www.senabus.it.

From Siena by Train to: Florence (direct trains hourly, 1.5 hrs, €6; bus is better), **Pisa** (change at Empoli: Pisa–Empoli, roughly 2/hr, 45 min; Empoli–Siena, hourly, 1 hr, €7), **Rome** (nearly hourly, 3–4 hrs, transfer in Florence or Chiusi, €13–26 depending on type of train), **Orvieto** (12/day, 2–3 hrs, change in Chiusi). For more information, visit www.trenitalia.com.

By Bus to: Florence (2/hr, 1.25-hr *corse rapide* buses are faster than the train, avoid the 2-hr *diretta* buses unless you have time to enjoy the beautiful scenery en route, €7, tickets available at *tabacchi* shops if bus-ticket office is closed, Florence buses depart from in front of NH Excelsior Hotel on Piazza Gramsci), **San Gimignano** (8/day, 1.25 hrs, €5.30, by Tra-In bus, tickets sometimes available at *tabacchi* shops), **Assisi** (2/day, 2 hrs, €11, by Sena bus, buses depart from the train station, morning bus goes direct to Assisi, afternoon bus might terminate 3 miles below Assisi at Santa Maria degli Angeli, where a city bus finishes the ride), **Rome** (8/day, 3 hrs, €20, by Sena bus, arrives at Rome's Tiburtina station on Metro line B with easy connections to the central Termini train station), **Milan** (4/day, 4 hrs, €29, by Sena bus, departs from Siena's train station, arrives at Milan's Cadorna Station with Metro access and direct trains to Malpensa Airport), **Pisa** (2/day, €14, by Sena bus).

Some buses depart Siena from Piazza Gramsci; others leave from the train station (confirm when you purchase your ticket). You can get tickets for Tra-In buses and Sena buses at the train station's bus-ticket kiosk (cash only, Mon–Sat 6:15–20:15, Sun 7:30–12:30 & 14:30–18:30). You can also buy tickets at **Sottopassaggio la Lizza,** located under Piazza Gramsci—look for stairwells to the underground passageway in front of NH Excelsior Hotel (credit cards accepted, Tra-In bus office: Mon–Sat 6:30–19:30, Sun 7:30–19:30,

tel. 0577-204-246, toll-free tel. 800-570-530, w
.it; Sena bus office: Mon–Sat 7:15–19:45, Sun 15:00–19:30, if Sena
ticket office is closed, buy tickets next door at Tra-In office, tel. 0577-208-282, www.senabus.it). If necessary, you can buy tickets from the driver (€3 surcharge).

Sottopassaggio la Lizza also has luggage storage (€3/half-day, €5.50/day, open daily 7:00–19:00, no overnight storage), posted bus schedules, TV monitors listing all imminent departures for several bus companies, and WCs (€0.50). On schedules, the fastest buses are marked *rapida*. I'd stick with these. Note that if a schedule lists your departure point as either Via Tozzi or Piazza la Lizza, you actually catch the bus at Piazza Gramsci (Via Tozzi is the street that runs alongside Piazza Gramsci, and Piazza la Lizza is the name of the bus-hub square). Confusing? Absolutely.

PISA

In A.D. 1200, Pisa's power peaked. For nearly three centuries (1000–1300), Pisa rivaled Venice and Genoa as a sea-trading power, exchanging European goods for luxury items in Muslim lands. As a port near the mouth of the Arno River (six miles from the coast), the city enjoyed easy access to the Mediterranean, plus the protection of sitting a bit upstream. The Romans had made it a navy base, and by medieval times it was a major player.

Pisa's 150-foot galleys cruised the Mediterranean, gaining control of the islands of Corsica, Sardinia, and Sicily, and trading with Europeans, Muslims, and Byzantine Christians as far south as North Africa and as far east as Syria. European Crusaders hired Pisan boats to carry them and their supplies as they headed off to conquer the Muslim-held Holy Land. The Pisan "Republic" prided itself on its independence from both popes and emperors. The city used its sea-trading wealth to build the grand monuments of the Field of Miracles, including the now-famous Leaning Tower.

But the Pisan fleet was routed in battle by Genoa (1284, at Meloria, off Livorno), their overseas outposts were taken away, the port silted up, and Pisa was left high and dry, with only its Field of Miracles and its university keeping it on the map.

Pisa's three important sights—the Duomo, Baptistery, and the Tower—float regally on the best lawn in Italy. The style throughout is Pisa's very own "Pisan Romanesque." Even as the church was being built, Piazza del Duomo was nicknamed the "Campo dei Miracoli," or Field of Miracles, for the grandness of the undertaking.

The Tower has reopened after a decade of restoration and topple-prevention. To ascend, you'll have to make a reservation when you buy your €15 ticket (for details, see page 347).

Pisa

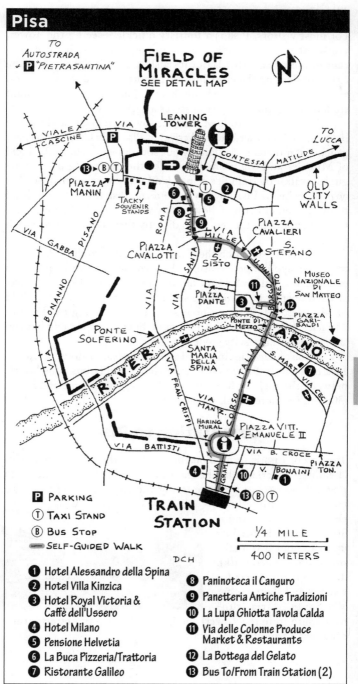

TO
AUTOSTRADA
& **P** "PIETRASANTINA"

FIELD OF
MIRACLES
SEE DETAIL MAP

N

LEANING
TOWER

VIALE
CASCINE

VIA

P

TO
LUCCA

CONTESSA MATILDE

OLD
CITY
WALLS

13 B T

PIAZZA
MANIN

TACKY
SOUVENIR
STANDS

6

ROMA

T 5

2

8

SANTA MARIA

9

VIA
MILLE

PIAZZA
CAVALIERI

S.
STEFANO

PIAZZA
CAVALOTTI

S. SISTO

U. DINI

VIA GABBA

VIA PISANO

BONANNO PISANO

VIA

VIA

PIAZZA
DANTE

11

BORGO STRETTO

MUSEO
NAZIONALE
DI
SAN MATTEO

12

PIAZZA
GARI-
BALDI

3

PONTE
SOLFERINO

PONTE DI
MEZZO

RIVER

ARNO

SANTA
MARIA
DELLA
SPINA

VIA FRAN CRISPI

VIA ITALIA

S. MART.

7

VIA CECI

VIA
MANZ.

HARING
MURAL

CORSO ITALIA

PIAZZA VITT.
EMANUELE II

i

VIA BATTISTI

4

VIA GRAM.

PIAZZA
TON.

VIA B. CROCE

10

V. BONAINI

1

13 B T

P PARKING

T TAXI STAND

B BUS STOP

SELF-GUIDED WALK

TRAIN
STATION

¼ MILE

400 METERS

DCH

1 Hotel Alessandro della Spina

2 Hotel Villa Kinzica

3 Hotel Royal Victoria &
Caffè dell'Ussero

4 Hotel Milano

5 Pensione Helvetia

6 La Buca Pizzeria/Trattoria

7 Ristorante Galileo

8 Paninoteca il Canguro

9 Panetteria Antiche Tradizioni

10 La Lupa Ghiotta Tavola Calda

11 Via delle Colonne Produce
Market & Restaurants

12 La Bottega del Gelato

13 Bus To/From Train Station (2)

PISA

Planning Your Time

For most visitors, Pisa is a touristy quickie—seeing the Tower, visiting the square, and wandering through the church are 90 percent of their Pisan thrill. But it's a shame to skip the rest of the city. Considering the city's historic importance and the wonderful ambience created by its rich architectural heritage and the vibrant student population, the city deserves a half-day visit.

By car, it's best to leave the freeway at *Pisa Nord* and use the big parking lot (described in "Arrival in Pisa—By Car," on the next page). From there, a regular city bus shuttles you to both the Field of Miracles and the train station (for the beginning of my self-guided walk). By train, it's a snap (and train travelers may need to change trains in Pisa anyway). From the Pisa train station, head to the Tower, either by following my walk through the town center, or hopping on the bus to go directly there (a 15-min ride each way).

If you want to climb the Tower, go straight to the ticket office to snag an appointment—usually for a couple of hours later. For an extra €2, you can book a time online (at least two weeks in advance) at www.opapisa.it. If you'll be seeing both the town and the Field of Miracles, plan on a six-hour stop. If just blitzing the Field of Miracles, three hours is the minimum. Spending the night lets you savor a great Italian city scene.

If you're day-tripping to Pisa from Lucca, or doing a Lucca/Pisa day trip from Florence, note that a handy bus runs hourly between the Field of Miracles and Lucca, saving time and hassle (30 min, €3; more details on page 389).

Orientation to Pisa

The city of Pisa is framed on the north by the Field of Miracles (Leaning Tower) and by the train station on the south. The Arno River flows east to west, bisecting the city. Walking from the train station directly to the Tower takes about 30 minutes (but allow up to an hour if you take my recommended walk). The two main streets for tourists and shoppers are Via Santa Maria (run-  ning south from the Tower) and Corso Italia/Borgo Stretto (running north from the train station).

Tourist Information

One TI is about 200 yards from the train station—exit and walk straight up the left side of the street to the big, circular Piazza Vittorio Emanuele II. The TI is on the left, around the corner from #16 (Mon–Fri 9:00–19:00, Sat 9:00–13:30, closed Sun, www .pisaturismo.it). Another, less-enthusiastic TI is east of the Tower, in the Duomo Museum (daily 10:00–19:00). There's also a TI at the airport (daily 11:00–23:00).

Arrival in Pisa

By Train: If checking baggage upon arrival, look for *deposito bagagli*—as you get off the train, it's to the right at the far end of platform 1, past the police office (€3/bag for 12 hours, daily 6:00–21:00, they photocopy your passport to check ID, ignore the nonfunctional lockers—installed just days before 9/11 and never used).

To get to the Field of Miracles from the station, you can **walk** (get free map from TI, 30 min direct, 60 min if you follow my walk on the next page), take a **taxi** (€6–8, tel. 050-541-600, taxi stand at station), or go by **bus.** Take bus LAM Rossa (4–6/hr, after 20:00 3/hr, 15 min), which stops across the street from the train station, in front of Jolly Hotel. Buy a €1 bus ticket from the *tabacchi*/magazine kiosk in the train station's main hall or at any *tabacchi* shop (€1.50 if you buy it on board, smart to have exact change, good for 1 hour, round-trip permitted). Before getting on the bus, confirm that it is indeed going to "Campo dei Miracoli" (ask driver, a local, or TI) or risk taking a long tour of Pisa's suburbs. The correct buses let you off at Piazza Manin, in front of the gate to the Field of Miracles; drivers make sure tourists don't miss the stop.

To return to the train station from the Tower, catch the bus in front of the BNL bank, across the street from where you got off (again, confirm the destination). You'll also find a taxi stand 30 yards from the Tower (at Bar Duomo).

Note that Pisa has a smaller Pisa S. Rossore station that's just four blocks from the Tower and Field of Miracles. Not all trains stop here, but if yours does, hop off. Follow Viale delle Cascine east, continuing as it turns into Via Contessa Matilde and follow signs to *La Torre,* or just head toward the dome of the Baptistery. Remember, there's a TI at the Duomo Museum.

By Car: Driving in the city center will likely net you a steep fine (cameras catch you and the city sends you a ticket by mail). Instead, use the big Pietrasantina parking lot, designed for tour buses (which pay €110 to park) and tourists with cars (who park for free). To reach the parking lot, exit the autostrada at *Pisa Nord* and follow signs to *Pisa* (on the left). Pass the second traffic

PISA

light and turn left toward the city center. Go straight, following the *Bus Parking* signs, until you see the gas station. The parking lot is on the left. Here you'll find a cafeteria, WC, lots of big buses, and a city bus stop for bus LAM Rossa, which shuttles visitors to the sights (4–6/hr, bus stop: Torre 2, buy €1 ticket at parking-lot cafeteria or on board for an extra charge) and on to the train station.

By Plane: From Pisa's airport, take bus LAM Rossa (€1, 4–6/hr, after 20:00 3/hr, 15 min) or a taxi (€10–12) into town.

Helpful Hints

Markets: An open-air produce market attracts picnickers to Piazza della Vettovaglie, one block north of the Arno River near Ponte di Mezzo (Mon–Sat 7:00–18:00, closed Sun). A street market bustles on Wednesday and Saturday mornings between Via del Brennero and Via Paparrelle (8:00–13:00, just outside of wall, about 6 blocks east of the Tower).

Festivals: The month of June has many events, culminating in a celebration for Pisa's patron saint (June 16–17).

Local Guide: Dottore Vincenzo Riolo is a great guide for Pisa and the surrounding area (€130/3 hours, mobile 338-211-2939, www.pisatour.it, info@pisatour.it).

Tours: To get beyond the tourist mobs and understand the cultural powerhouse that was Pisa, consider the "Walking in Pisa" tour. Local guides lead a two- to three-hour walking tour in English (and Italian) that covers the city rather than the famous Tower sights. It ends with an overview at the Field of Miracles, from where you can visit the Tower, cathedral, and Baptistery on your own (€14, Mon and Sat at 10:15, no advance booking required, meet at Piazza XX Settembre—the Town Hall square across the river from Piazza Garibaldi, tel. 050-830-253, mobile 328-144-6855 after hours, www.pisatour.it, Vincenzo).

Self-Guided Walk

Welcome to Pisa: From the Train Station to the Tower

A leisurely one-hour stroll from the station to the Tower is a great way to get acquainted with the more subtle virtues of this Renaissance city. Because almost none of the hordes who descend daily on the Tower bothers with the rest of the town, you'll find most of Pisa to be delightfully untouristy—a student-filled, classy, Old World town with an Arno-scape much like its upstream rival, Florence. Pisa is pretty small, with just 100,000 people. But its 45,000 students keep it lively, especially at night.

• *From the station, walk north up Viale Gramsci to the circular square called...*

Piazza Vittorio Emanuele II

As Pisa was considered strategic in World War II, both the train station and its main bridge were targeted. For that reason 40 percent of this district was destroyed.

The entire wall of a building just to the left of the piazza was painted by New York artist Keith Haring in 1989 to create *Tutto Mondo (Whole Wide World)*. Haring (who died of AIDS in 1990) brought New York City graffiti into the mainstream. This painting is a celebration of diversity, chaos, and the liveliness of our world, vibrating with energy. On the piazza, you'll also find a TI.

• *Walk up Corso Italia to the river.*

Corso Italia

Cutting through the center of town, this is Pisa's main drag. As it leaves Piazza Vittorio Emanuele II, look to the right to see the circa-1960 wall map of Pisa with a steam train (on the wall of a bar on the corner). You'll also see plenty of youthful fashions, as kids are out making the scene here. Be on guard for pickpockets—too young to arrest, they can only be kicked out of town. Pushed out of their former happy hunting grounds, the Field of Miracles, they now work the crowds here, often dressed as tourists.

• *Follow the pedestrianized Corso Italia straight north to the Arno River and Ponte di Mezzo. Stop in the center of the bridge.*

Ponte di Mezzo

This modern bridge, constructed on the same site where the Romans built one, marks the center of Pisa. In the Middle Ages, this bridge (like Florence's Ponte Vecchio) was lined with shops. It's been destroyed several times by floods and in 1943 by British and American bombers. Enjoy the view from the center of the bridge, with its long lines of elegant mansions recalling days of trading glory—the cityscape feels a bit like Venice's Grand Canal. Pisa sits on shifting delta sand, making construction tricky. The entire town leans. With innovative arches above ground and below, architects didn't stop the leaning—but they have made buildings that wobble without being threatened.

• *Cross the bridge to...*

Piazza Garibaldi

This square is named for the charismatic leader of the Risorgimento, the unification movement that led to Italian independence in 1870. Knowing Pisa was strongly nationalist, Garibaldi came here when wounded to be nursed back to health. Many Pisans died in the national struggle. You can side-trip about 100 yards downstream to **Caffè dell'Ussero** (famous for its fine 14th-century red terra-cotta original facade, at #28) and browse its time-warp interior, lined with portraits and documents from the struggle for Italian independence. **La Bottega del Gelato,** Pisa's favorite gelato place, is on Piazza Garibaldi (daily 11:30–24:00).

• *Continue north up the elegantly arcaded...*

Borgo Stretto

Welcome to Pisa's main shopping street. On the right, the Church of St. Michael, with its fine Pisan Romanesque facade, still sports some 16th-century graffiti. I'll bet you can see some modern graffiti across the street. Students have been pushing their causes here—or simply defacing things—for five centuries.

From here look farther up the street and notice how it undulates like a flowing river. In the sixth century B.C., Pisa was born when two parallel rivers were connected by canals. This street echoes the flow of one of those canals. An 11th-century landslide rerouted the second river, destroying ancient Pisa, and the entire city regenerated.

• *After a few steps, detour left onto Via delle Colonne, and walk one block down to...*

Piazza delle Vettovaglie

Pisa's historic market square is lively day and night. Its Renaissance loggia hosted the fish and vegetable market for generations. Now the stalls are set up just beyond, at Piazza Uomobuono (Mon–Sat 7:00–18:00, closed Sun). You could cobble together a picnic from the sandwich shops and fruit-and-veggie stalls ringing these squares.

• *Continue north on Borgo Stretto another 100 yards, passing an ugly bomb site on the right, with its horrible 1960s reconstruction. Take the second left on nondescript Via Ulisse Dini (it's not obvious—turn left immediately after the arcade's end, just before the pharmacy). This leads to Pisa's historic core, Piazza dei Cavalieri.*

Piazza dei Cavalieri

With its old clock and colorfully decorated palace, this piazza was once the seat of the independent Republic of Pisa's government. In around 1500, Florence decapitated Pisa and made this square the training place for the knights of its navy. The statue of Cosimo I de' Medici shows the Florentine who ruled Pisa in the 16th

century. With a foot on a dolphin, he reminded all who passed that the Florentine navy controlled the sea—at least a little of it. The frescoes on the exterior of the square's buildings, though damaged by salty sea air and years of neglect, reflect Pisa's fading glory under the Medicis.

With Napoleon, this complex of grand buildings became part of the University of Pisa. The university is one of Europe's oldest, with roots in a law school that dates back as far as the 11th century. In the mid-16th century, the city was a hotbed of controversy, as spacey professors like Galileo Galilei studied the solar system—with results that challenged the church's powerful doctrine. More recently, the blind tenor Andrea Bocelli attended law school in Pisa before embarking on his well-known musical career.

From here, take Via Corsica (to the left of the clock). The humble Church of San Sisto, ahead on the left (side entrance on Via Corsica) is worth a quick look. With simple bricks, assorted reused columns, heavy walls, and few windows, this was the typical Romanesque style before the more lavish Pisan Romanesque of the Field of Miracles structures.

Follow Via Corsica as it turns into Via dei Mille, and then turn right on Via Santa Maria, which leads north, through increasingly touristy claptrap, directly to the Field of Miracles and the Tower.

Sights in Pisa

▲▲▲**Leaning Tower**—A 15-foot lean from the vertical makes the Tower one of Europe's most recognizable images. You can see it for free; it's always viewable. And, after years of stabilization efforts, it's open again if you want to climb it for a fee (€15, kids under 8 not allowed, daily March 9:00–18:00, April–Sept 8:30–20:30, mid-May–mid-Sept until 23:00, Oct 9:00–19:00, Nov–Feb 10:00–17:00, ticket office opens 30 min early, last entry 30 min before closing, reservations required, www.opapisa.it).

✪ See the Pisa Tower Tour chapter.

▲▲▲**Field of Miracles (Campo dei Miracoli)**—Scattered

across a golf-course-green lawn are five grand buildings: the cathedral (or Duomo), its bell tower (the Leaning Tower), the Baptistery, the hospital (today's Museum of the Sinopias), and the Camposanto Cemetery. The buildings are constructed from

Field of Miracles Tickets

Pisa has a combo-ticket scheme designed to get you into its neglected secondary sights: the Baptistery, Camposanto Cemetery, Duomo Museum, and Museum of the Sinopias (fresco pattern museum).

For €5, you get your choice of one of the following: the Baptistery, Camposanto Cemetery, Museum of the Sinopias, or Duomo Museum; for two of these sights or one plus the Duomo, the cost is €6; for three of the above you pay €8; and for the works, you'll pay €10 (credit cards accepted). By comparison, the Duomo alone is a bargain (€2).

You can buy any of these tickets either behind the Leaning Tower or at the Museum of the Sinopias (near Baptistery, almost suffocated by souvenir stands). Both ticket offices have big, yellow, triangle-shaped signs.

No matter what ticket you get, you'll have to pay an additional €15 if you want to climb the Tower. Tickets for the Tower are sold at the ticket offices or online at least two weeks in advance at www.opapisa.it (€2 fee).

similar materials—bright white marble—and have comparable decoration. Each has a simple ground floor and rows of delicate columns and arches that form open-air arcades, giving the Campo a pleasant visual unity.

The style is dubbed Pisan Romanesque. Where traditional Romanesque has a heavy fortress-like feel—thick walls, barrel arches, few windows—Pisan Romanesque is light and elegant. At ground level, most of the structures have simple half-columns and arches. On the upper levels, you'll see a little of everything—tight rows of thin columns; pointed Gothic gables and prickly spires; Byzantine mosaics and horseshoe arches; and geometric designs (such as diamonds) and striped colored marbles inspired by mosques in Muslim lands.

Architecturally, the Campo is unique and exotic. Theologically, the Campo's buildings mark the main events of every Pisan's life: christened in the Baptistery, married in the Duomo, honored in ceremonies at the Tower, healed in the hospital, and buried in the Camposanto Cemetery.

Lining this field of artistic pearls is a gauntlet of Europe's tackiest souvenir stands, as well as dozens of amateur mimes "propping up" the Leaning Tower while tourists take photos.

⦿ See the Pisa Duomo Tour chapter and Field of Miracles Tour chapter.

▲▲**Duomo (Cathedral)**—The gargantuan Pisan Romanesque church has a Pisano pulpit, modest dress code, and no baggage check

(€2, Mon–Sat March 10:00–18:00, April–Sept 10:00–20:00, Oct 10:00–19:00, Nov–Feb 10:00–17:00; Sun 13:00–17:30 all year; last entry 30 min before closing).

⦿ See the Pisa Duomo Tour chapter.

The next four sights are covered in more detail within the ⦿ Field of Miracles Tour chapter. Individual entry tickets are €5 for each sight but most visitors buy one of the various combo-tickets described above to save money.

▲**Baptistery**—The round Baptistery, located in front of the Duomo, has superb acoustics and another fine Pisano pulpit (daily March 9:00–18:00, April–Sept 8:00–20:00, Oct 9:00–19:00, Nov–Feb 10:00–17:00, last entry 30 min before closing).

Camposanto Cemetery—Lined with faint frescoes, this ancient cemetery on the north side of the Campo is famous for its "Holy Land" dirt, said to reduce a body to a skeleton within a day. Artillery fire during World War II set the lead roof ablaze, greatly damaging the building and its frescoes (same hours as Baptistery).

Museum of the Sinopias (Museo delle Sinopie)—Across from the Baptistery, housed in a 13th-century hospital (with its entrance nearly obscured by souvenir stands), this museum displays some of the original sketches (made on walls) that were used to make the frescoes in the Camposanto Cemetery. This museum comes with two free, short, introductory videos that you can watch even without a ticket. Good students might want to start here first for this orientation (same hours as Baptistery).

Duomo Museum (Museo dell'Opera del Duomo)—This museum behind the Leaning Tower is big on Pisan art, displaying treasures of the cathedral, paintings, silverware, and sculptures (from the 12th to 14th centuries, particularly by the Pisano dynasty), as well as ancient Egyptian, Etruscan, and Roman artifacts (same hours as Baptistery, Piazza Arcivescovado 18).

Panoramic Walk on the Wall—This much-advertised walk includes just a small section of the 12th-century wall and isn't worth your time or €4 (Mon–Fri 10:00–14:00, Sat–Sun 10:00–14:00 & 15:00–19:00, shorter hours off-season, entrance near the Baptistery at Porta Leone).

Museo Nazionale di San Matteo—On the river and in a former convent, this art museum displays 12th- to 15th-century sculptures, illuminated manuscripts, and paintings on wood by Martini, Masaccio, and others. This fine collection—especially its painted wood crucifixes—gives you a chance to see Pisan innovation in 11th- to 13th-century art, before Florence took the lead (€4, Tue–Sun 8:30–19:00, off-season Sun only until 13:00, closed Mon, near Piazza San Paolo at Lungarno Mediceo, a 5-min walk upriver from the main bridge, tel. 050-541-865).

PISA

PISA TOWER TOUR

You've seen it in TV ads, in movies, and on posters, key chains, and souvenir dishes—now it's time to see it in the flesh. And, the funny thing is, it's one iconic image that really looks like its famous reproductions.

The off-kilter Tower parallels Pisa's history. It was started when Pisa was at its peak: one of the world's richest, most powerful, and most sophisticated cities. They'd built their huge cathedral to reflect Pisa's superpower status, and the cathedral's bell tower—the Leaning Tower—was the perfect complement. But as Pisa's power declined, the Tower reclined, and ever since, both have required a great deal of effort to prop up. However, after a recent renovation, the Tower's been stabilized. You can admire it in all its cockeyed glory and even climb to the top for a commanding view.

Orientation

Cost: Free to look; €15 to go inside and climb to the top (restrictions apply to youth; see "Reservations to Climb the Tower," next page).

Hours: Always viewable from the outside. It's open to climb daily March 9:00–18:00, April–Sept 8:30–20:30, mid-May–mid-Sept until 23:00, Oct 9:00–19:00, Nov–Feb 10:00–17:00, ticket office opens 30 min early, last entry 30 min before closing.

Getting There: From the main train station, you can walk (30 min), take a taxi (€6–8), or catch bus LAM Rossa (€1, 15-min ride).

Remember, if your train stops at the smaller Pisa S. Rossore station, get off there and you're only about four blocks from the Tower (head for the Baptistery's dome).

If you're traveling by car, see "Arrival in Pisa," on page 343.

Reservations to Climb the Tower: Every 30 minutes, 30 people can clamber up the 294 tilting stairs to the top. Note that children under age eight are not allowed to go up. Children ages 8–12 must be accompanied by—and hold hands at all times with—an adult. Teenagers between 12 and 18 are allowed with an adult.

You can reserve in person or, for an extra €2, book a time at www.opapisa.it.

Online bookings are accepted no more than 45 days—and no fewer than 14 days—in advance. You must pick up your ticket(s) at least 30 minutes before your time slot. Show up 10 minutes before your appointment at the meeting point outside the ticket office.

To reserve in person, go to the ticket office behind the Tower, on the left in the yellow building, or to the Museum of the Sinopias ticket office hidden behind the souvenir stalls. You choose a 30-minute time slot for your visit. If you visit in summer, it will likely be a couple of hours before you're able to go up (see the rest of the monuments and grab lunch while waiting). The wait is usually much shorter at the beginning or end of the day.

Baggage Check: You can't take any bags up the Tower, but day-bag-size lockers are available at the ticket office—show your Tower ticket to check your bag. You may check your bag 10 minutes before your reservation time and must pick it up immediately after your Tower visit.

The Climb: You wind your way up the outside of the Tower along a spiraling ramp. For your 30-minute time slot, figure about 10 minutes to climb and 10 to descend, leaving about 10 minutes for vertigo at the top. Even though it's technically a "guided" visit, that only means you're accompanied by a museum guard who makes sure you don't stay up past your scheduled appointment time.

Caution: There are skinny railings, the steps are slanted, and rain makes the marble slippery. Anyone with balance issues of any sort should think twice before ascending.

Starring: The Tower's frilly Pisan Romanesque look and its famous lean.

The Tour Begins

Yep, There It Is

Rising up alongside the cathedral, the Tower is nearly 200 feet tall and 55 feet wide, weighing 14,000 tons and currently leaning at a five-degree angle (15 feet off the vertical axis). It started to lean almost immediately after construction began. There are eight

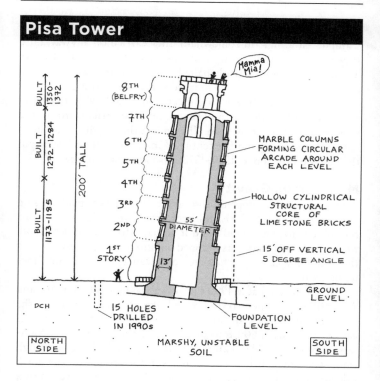

Pisa Tower

BUILT 1350–1372

BUILT 1272–1284

BUILT 1173–1185

200' TALL

Mamma Mia!

8TH (BELFRY)

7TH

6TH

5TH

4TH

3RD

2ND

1ST STORY

55' DIAMETER

13'

MARBLE COLUMNS FORMING CIRCULAR ARCADE AROUND EACH LEVEL

HOLLOW CYLINDRICAL STRUCTURAL CORE OF LIMESTONE BRICKS

15' OFF VERTICAL 5 DEGREE ANGLE

GROUND LEVEL

DCH

15' HOLES DRILLED IN 1990s

FOUNDATION LEVEL

NORTH SIDE

MARSHY, UNSTABLE SOIL

SOUTH SIDE

stories—a simple base, six stories of columns (forming arcades), and a belfry on top. The inner structural core is a hollow cylinder built of limestone bricks, faced with white marble barged here from San Giuliano, northeast of the city. The thin columns of the open-air arcades make the heavy Tower seem light and graceful.

The Building of the Tower

The Tower was built over two centuries by at least three different architects. You can see how each successive architect tried to

correct the leaning problem—once halfway up (after the fourth story), once at the belfry on the top.

The first stones were laid in 1173, probably under the direction of the architect Bonanno Pisano (who also designed the Duomo's bronze back door). Five years later, just as they'd finished the base and the first arcade, someone said, "Is it just me, or does that look crooked?" The heavy Tower—resting on a very shallow 13-foot foundation—was obviously sinking on the south side into the marshy, multilayered, unstable soil. (Actually, all the Campo's buildings tilt somewhat.) They carried on anyway, until they'd finished four stories (the base, plus three arcade floors). Then, construction suddenly halted—no one knows why—and for a century the Tower sat half-finished and visibly leaning.

Around 1272, the next architect continued, trying to correct the problem by angling the next three stories backward, in the opposite direction of the lean. The project then again sat mysteriously idle for nearly another century. Finally, Tommaso Pisano put the belfry on the top (c. 1350–1372), also kinking it backward.

Man Versus Gravity

After the Tower's completion, several attempts were made to stop its slow-motion fall. The architect/artist/writer Giorgio Vasari reinforced the base (1550), and it actually worked. But in 1838, well-intentioned engineers pumped out groundwater, destabilizing the Tower and causing it to increase its lean at a rate of a millimeter per year.

It got so bad that in 1990 the Tower was closed for repairs, and $30 million was spent trying to stabilize it. Engineers dried the soil with steam pipes, anchored the Tower to the ground with steel cables, and buried 600 tons of lead on the north side as a counterweight (not visible)—all with little success. The breakthrough came when they drilled 15-foot holes in the ground on the north side and sucked out sixty tons of soil, allowing the Tower to sink on the north side and straighten out its lean by about six inches.

As well as gravity, erosion threatens the Tower. Since its construction, 135 of the Tower's 180 marble columns have had to be replaced. Stone decay, deposits of lime and calcium phosphate, accumulations of dirt and moss, cracking from the stress of the lean—all of these are factors in its decline.

Thanks to the Tower's lean, there are special trouble spots. The lower south side (which is protected from cleansing rain and wind) is black from dirty airborne particles, while the stone on the upper areas, though clean, has more decay (from eroding rain and wind).

The Tower, now stabilized, is getting cleaned. Cracks are filled, and accumulations removed, using atomized water sprays and poultices of various solvents.

All the work to shore up, straighten, and clean the Tower has probably turned the clock back a few centuries. In fact, art historians figure it leans today as much as it did for Galileo.

PISA DUOMO TOUR

The huge Pisan Romanesque cathedral, with its carved pulpit by Giovanni Pisano, is artistically more important than its more famous bell tower.

Orientation

Cost: €2 (see "Field of Miracles Tickets" sidebar on page 348 for combo-ticket info).

Hours: The Duomo is open daily—Mon–Sat March 10:00–18:00, April–Sept 10:00–20:00, Oct 10:00–19:00, Nov–Feb 10:00–17:00; Sun 13:00–17:30 all year; last entry 30 min before closing.

Dress Code: Shorts are OK as long as they're not too short, and shoulders should be covered (although it's not really enforced).

Baggage: Big backpacks are not allowed, nor is storage provided. If you have a day bag, carry it.

Length of This Tour: Allow one hour.

The Tour Begins

❶ Exterior

The Duomo is the centerpiece of the Field of Miracles' complex of religious buildings. Begun in 1063, it was financed by a galley-load of booty ransacked that year from the Muslim-held capital of Palermo, Sicily. The architect Buschetto created the style of Pisan Romanesque that set the tone for the Baptistery and Tower. Five decades later (1118), the architect Rainaldo added the impressive main-entrance facade (which also leans out about a foot).

The lower half of the church is simple Romanesque, with

blind arches. The upper half has four rows of columns that form arcades. Stripes of black-and-white marble, mosaics, stone inlay, and even recycled Roman tombstones complete the decoration.

• *Tourists enter the church at the facade, opposite the Baptistery.*

❷ Nave

The 320-foot nave was the longest in Christendom when it was built. The model comes from traditional Roman basilicas—68 Corinthian columns of granite (most shipped from Sardinia in 1063) that divide the nave into five aisles. But the striped marble and arches-on-columns give it an exotic, almost mosque-like feel. Dim light filters in from the small upper windows of the galleries, where the women worshipped. The gilded coffered ceiling has shields of Florence's Medicis, including the round symbols (pills). This powerful family—who began as medics, later became cloth merchants, and finally bankers—took over Pisa after its glory days.

• *In the apse (behind the altar) is the...*

❸ Apse Mosaic

The mosaic (c. 1300, partly done by Cimabue) shows Christ as the Ruler of All (Pantocrator) between Mary and John the Evangelist. The Pantocrator image of Christ is a bit foreign to Protestants, Catholics, and secularists, but is standard fare among Eastern Orthodox Christians—that is, the "Byzantine" people who were Pisa's partners in trade.

As King of the Universe, Christ sits on a throne, facing directly out with penetrating eyes. He wears a halo divided with a cross, worn only by Christ. In his left hand is a Bible open to the verse *"Ego Lux Sum Mundi"*—"I am the light of the world." While his feet crush the devil in serpent form, Christ blesses us with his right hand. His fingers form the Greek letters *chi* and *rho*, the first two letters of "Christos." The thumb (almost) touches the fingers, symbolizing how Christ unites both his divinity and his humanity.

❹ Dome

Looking up into the dome, the heavens open, and rings of saints and angels spiral up to a hazy God. Beneath the dome is an inlaid-marble, Cosmati-style mosaic floor. The modern (and therefore controversial) marble altar and pulpit were carved by a Florentine artist in 2002.

• *Near the center of the church you'll find...*

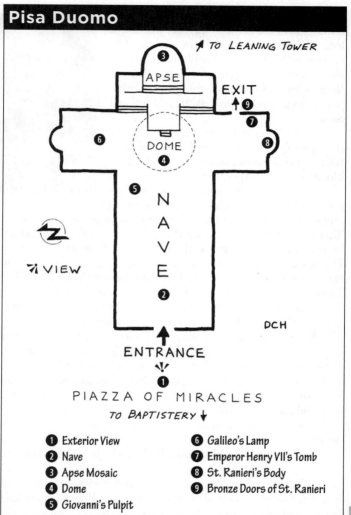

Pisa Duomo

TO LEANING TOWER

APSE

EXIT

DOME

VIEW

N
A
V
E

DCH

ENTRANCE

PIAZZA OF MIRACLES
TO BAPTISTERY

❶ Exterior View
❷ Nave
❸ Apse Mosaic
❹ Dome
❺ Giovanni's Pulpit
❻ Galileo's Lamp
❼ Emperor Henry VII's Tomb
❽ St. Ranieri's Body
❾ Bronze Doors of St. Ranieri

PISA DUOMO

❺ Giovanni's Pulpit (1301–1311)

The 15-foot-tall, octagonal pulpit by Giovanni Pisano (c. 1250–1319) is the last, biggest, and most complex of the four pulpits by the Pisano father-and-son team. Giovanni's father, Nicola, started the family tradition four decades earlier, carving the pulpit in the Baptistery. Giovanni grew up working side-by-side with his dad on numerous projects. Now on his own, he crams everything he's learned into his crowning achievement.

Giovanni left no stone uncarved in his pursuit of beauty. Four hundred intricately sculpted figures smother the pulpit, blurring the architectural outlines. In addition, the relief panels are actually curved, making it look less like an octagon than a circle. The creamy-white Carrara marble has the look and feel of carved French ivories, which the Pisanos loved. Originally, this and the other pulpits were frosted with paint, gilding, and colored pastes.

At the base, lions roar and crouch over their prey, symbolizing how Christ (the lion) triumphs over Satan (the horse, as in the Four Horsemen of the Apocalypse).

Four of the pulpit's support "columns" are statues. The central "column" features three graceful ladies representing Faith, Hope, and Charity, the three pillars of Christianity. They in turn stand on the sturdy base of knowledge, represented by the liberal arts taught at the U. of Pisa. Another "column" is Hercules, standing *contrapposto*, nude, holding his club and lion skin. Nearby, Lady Church suckles the babies of the Old and New Testaments, while at her feet are the Four Virtues, including Justice (with her scales), Moderation (modestly covering her nakedness), Courage (holding a lion), and Wisdom (with a horn of plenty).

Around the top of the pulpit, Christ's life unfolds in a series of panels saturated with carvings. The panels tilt out from the top, so the viewer below has a better look, and they're bordered on top with a heavy cornice as a backdrop. Since the panels are curved and unframed, you "read" Christ's life less like a nine-frame comic strip and more like a continuous scroll.

The story unfolds from left to right, beginning at the back near the stairs:

1. Story of Elizabeth and Zechariah: John the Baptist's parents.

2. Nativity: Mary lounges across a bed, unfazed by labor and delivery. Her pose is clearly inspired by carved Roman sarcophagi (which you can see in the Camposanto Cemetery), showing the dearly departed relaxing for eternity atop their coffins. Mary and the babe are surrounded by angels (above) and shepherds (right).

3. Adoration of the Magi: The wise men ride in with horses and camels.

4. Presentation in the Temple (left side): Joseph and Mary hold baby Jesus between them. On the right side of the panel, Giovanni adds the next scene in the story, when the nuclear family gets on a donkey and escapes into Egypt.

5. Massacre of the Innocents: Herod (at the top) turns and gestures dramatically, ordering the slaughter of all babies. A mother (bottom left corner) grabs her head in despair. Giovanni uses thick lips and big noses to let the faces speak the full range of human emotions. The soldiers in the tangled chaos are almost freestanding.

6. Kiss of Judas: Jesus is betrayed by a kiss (left side).

7. Crucifixion: An emaciated Christ is mourned by his followers, who turn every which way. A Roman horseman (bottom right corner) rides directly away from us—an example of Renaissance "foreshortening" a century before its time.

8. and 9. Last Judgment: Christ sits in the center, the dead rise from their graves, and he sends the good to heaven (left) and the bad to hell (right).

Giovanni was a better pure sculptor than his father. Armed with more sophisticated chisels, he could cut even deeper into the marble, freeing heads from the marble backdrop, creating almost-freestanding, 3-D figures. Where Nicola shows figures either facing forward or in profile, Giovanni mastered the difficult three-quarters angle.

If the pulpit seems a bit cluttered and asymmetrical, blame Mussolini. Originally, Giovanni built the pulpit standing on the right side of the altar (the traditional location). But after a massive fire in 1595 (when the roof burned), the pulpit was disassembled and stored away for three centuries. In 1926, they pulled it out of storage, reassembled it on this spot...and ended up with pieces left over (now in other museums), leading scholars to debate the current look.

• *Hanging from the ceiling of the north transept (to the left of the altar) is...*

❻ Galileo's Lamp

The bronze incense burner is said to be the one (actually, this is a replacement for the original) that caught teenage Galileo's attention one day in church. Someone left a church door open, and a gust of wind set the lamp swinging. Galileo timed the swings, and realized that the burner swung back and forth in the same amount of time regardless of how wide the arc. (This pendulum motion was a constant that allowed Galileo to measure this ever-changing universe.)

Galileo Galilei (1564–1642) was born in Pisa, grew up here on Via Giuseppe Giusti (where the family home still stands, adorned with a humble plaque), and taught math at the university (1584–1591). Legend says he threw things off the Tower to time their falls, fascinated by gravity.

• *Find the following two sights in the right (south) transept, near the back of the church.*

❼ Emperor Henry VII's Tomb

In the left corner of the south transept, pause at the tomb of Holy Roman Emperor Henry VII, whose untimely death plunged Pisa into its centuries-long decline. Henry lies sleeping, arms folded, his head turned to the side, resting on a soft pillow.

This German king (c. 1275–1313) invaded Italy and was welcomed by Pisans as a nonpartisan leader who could bring peace to Italy's warring Guelphs and Ghibellines. In 1312, he was crowned Emperor by the pope in Rome. He returned to his base in Pisa and was preparing to polish off the last opposition when he caught a fever (or was poisoned by a priest) and died. Ghibelline Pisa was suddenly at the mercy of Guelph rivals such as rising Florence, and Pisa never recovered.

❽ St. Ranieri's Body

In a glass-lined casket on the altar, Pisa's patron saint lies mummified, encased in silver at his head and feet, with his hair shirt covering his body. The silver, mask-like face dates from 2000 and is as realistic as possible—derived from an FBI-style computer scan of Ranieri's skull.

Ranieri Scuggeri (1117–1161) was born into the city of Pisa at its peak, when the Field of Miracles was a construction zone. (Ranieri was one year old when this Duomo was consecrated in thanks for Pisa's lucrative victory over the Muslims.) The son of a rich sea-trader, Ranieri chose the life of a hard-partying, popular, touring musician. Backstage one night, he met a mysterious stranger who changed his life. Ranieri was inspired to take his musical instrument and set it on fire, while opening his arms to the heavens (à la Jimi Hendrix). He returned to his father's shipping business and amassed a fortune. Then, one day, he smelled something funky—his own money. He gave it all away, joined a monastery, and put on a hair shirt.

The former wandering troubadour, traveling salesman, and pilgrimaging monk finally settled down in his hometown of Pisa. He devoured the Bible, then used his showmanship to wow audiences here—in the Duomo—when he took stage atop the pulpit to deliver spirited sermons.

Ranieri, honored in grand style on June 16 and 17, is cause for Pisa's biggest local event—the Luminara—celebrated along the Arno with tens of thousands of candles lining the buildings and floating on the river. The next day, rowing teams play a game of capture-the-flag, racing to a boat in the Arno and shinnying up a long rope to claim the prize.

• Exit the church at the back end, where you'll find the...

❾ Bronze Doors of St. Ranieri
(*Porta San Ranieri,* outside facing the Tower)

Designed by Bonanno Pisano (c. 1186)—thought by some historians to have been the Tower's first architect—the doors have 24

different panels that show Christ's story using the same simple, skinny figures found in Byzantine icons. (The doors are actually copies; the originals are housed—but not always on display—in the Duomo Museum.)

The story begins in the lower right panel ("Magis"), as the three Wise Men ride up a hill, heading toward...the panel to the left, where tiny baby Jesus lays in a manger while angels and shepherds look down from above. Above the manger scene, King Herod ("Erodi") sits under a canopy (in Pisan Romanesque style) and orders a soldier to raise his sword to kill all potential Messiahs. The terrified mother pulls her hair out. In the panel to the right, John the Baptist stands under a swaying palm and baptizes the adult Jesus, who wears the rippling River Jordan like a blanket.

Cast using the lost-wax technique, these doors were an inspiration for Lorenzo Ghiberti's bronze doors in Florence.

FIELD OF MIRACLES TOUR

Campo dei Miracoli

Imagine arriving in Pisa as a sailor in the 11th century, when the Arno came to just outside the walls surrounding this square, the church here was the biggest in the world, and this ensemble in gleaming white marble was the most impressive space in Christendom. Calling it the Field of Miracles (Campo dei Miracoli) would not have been hyperbole.

The Leaning Tower nearly steals the show from the massive cathedral, which muscles out the other sights. But don't neglect the rest of the Field of Miracles: the Baptistery, Camposanto Cemetery, Museum of the Sinopias, and the Duomo Museum.

Orientation

Cost: €10 combo-ticket includes all of the sights, plus the Duomo (credit cards accepted, see "Field of Miracles Tickets" sidebar on page 348).

Hours: All monuments on this tour share the same schedule: Daily March 9:00–18:00, April–Sept 8:00–20:00, Oct 9:00–19:00, Nov–Feb 10:00–17:00, last entry 30 min before closing.

Location: The Baptistery is located in front of the Duomo's facade. The Camposanto Cemetery is behind the church on the north side of the Field of Miracles. The Museum of the Sinopias is hidden behind souvenir stands, across the street from the Baptistery entrance. The Duomo Museum is housed behind the Tower.

Length of This Tour: Allow two hours.

Pisa's Field of Miracles

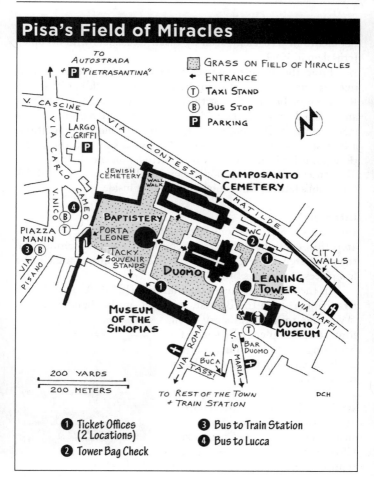

TO AUTOSTRADA
🅿 "PIETRASANTINA"

░░ GRASS ON FIELD OF MIRACLES
← ENTRANCE
Ⓣ TAXI STAND
Ⓑ BUS STOP
🅿 PARKING

N

V. CASCINE

VIA CARLO CAMEO

LARGO C.GRIFFI
🅿

V. NICO

VIA CONTESSA

JEWISH CEMETERY

WALL WALK

❹
Ⓑ

PIAZZA MANIN
❸ Ⓑ
Ⓣ

VIA PISANO

BAPTISTERY

PORTA LEONE

TACKY SOUVENIR STANDS

Duomo

❶

CAMPOSANTO CEMETERY

VIA MATILDE

WC
❷

❶

LEANING TOWER

CITY WALLS

VIA MAFFI

🅹

MUSEUM OF THE SINOPIAS

VIA ROMA

V. S. MARIA

LA BUCA TASSI

BAR DUOMO

Ⓣ

DUOMO MUSEUM

🅹

200 YARDS
200 METERS

TO REST OF THE TOWN + TRAIN STATION

DCH

❶ Ticket Offices (2 Locations)
❷ Tower Bag Check
❸ Bus to Train Station
❹ Bus to Lucca

The Tour Begins

Baptistery

Pisa's Baptistery is Italy's biggest. It's interesting for its pulpit and interior ambience, and especially great for its acoustics.

Exterior

The building is 180 feet tall—John the Baptist on top looks eye-to-eye with the tourists atop the nearly 200-foot Leaning Tower. Notice that the Baptistery leans nearly six feet to the north (the Tower leans 15 feet to the south). The building

FIELD OF MIRACLES

(begun 1153) is modeled on the circular domed Church of the Holy Sepulchre in Jerusalem, seen by Pisan Crusaders who occupied Jerusalem in 1099.

From the outside, you see three distinct sections, reflecting changing tastes that span the years spent building it: simple Romanesque blind arches at the base (1153), ornate Gothic spires and pointed arches in the middle (1250), and a Renaissance dome (15th century). The roofing looks unfinished but was intentionally designed with red tiles on the seaward side and the more-prestigious lead tiles (which would corrode) on the sheltered side. The statues of the midsection are by Nicola Pisano (c. 1220–1278, Giovanni's father), who sculpted the pulpit inside.

Interior

Inside, it's simple, spacious, and baptized with light. Tall arches atop thin columns once again echo the Campo's architectural theme of arches above blank spaces. The columns encircle just a few pieces of religious furniture.

In the center sits the **octagonal font** (1246). A statue of the first baptist, John the Baptist, stretches out his hand and says, "Welcome to my Baptistery." The font contains plenty of space for baptizing adults by immersion (the medieval custom), plus four wells for dunking babies.

Baptismal fonts—where sinners symbolically die and are reborn— are traditionally octagons. The shape suggests a cross (symbolizing Christ's death), and the eight sides represent the eighth day of Christ's ordeal, when he was resurrected. The font's sides, carved with inlaid multicolored marble, feature circle-in-a-square patterns, indicating the interlocking of heaven and earth. The circles are studded with interesting faces, both human and animal. Behind the font, the altar features similar inlaid-marble work.

Nicola Pisano's Pulpit

Is this the world's first Renaissance sculpture? It's the first authenticated (signed) work by the "Giotto of sculpture," working in what came to be called the Renaissance style. The freestanding sculpture has classical columns, realistic people and animals, and 3-D effects in the carved panels.

The 15-foot-tall, hexagonal pulpit is by Nicola Pisano, and the earliest (1260) and simplest of the four pulpits by the Pisano father-and-son team. Nicola, born in southern Italy, settled in

Pisa, where he found steady work. Ten-year-old Giovanni learned the art of pulpit-making here at the feet of his father.

The speaker's platform stands on columns that rest on the backs of animals, representing Christianity's triumph over paganism. The white Carrara-marble panels are framed by dark rose-colored marble, making a pleasant contrast. Originally, this and the other pulpits were touched up with paint, gilding, and colored pastes.

The relief panels, with scenes from the life of Christ, are more readable than the Duomo pulpit. They show bigger, simpler figures in dark-marble "frames." Read left to right, starting from the back:

1. Nativity: Mary reclines across a bed like a Roman matron, a pose inspired by Roman sarcophagi, which had been found around Pisa in Nicola's day (on display in the Camposanto Cemetery).

2. Adoration of the Magi: The Three Kings kneel before baby Jesus in simple profile; but notice the strong 3-D of the horses' heads coming straight out of the panel. Just below this relief, note the small statue of Hercules. Many art historians consider this the first Renaissance carving. Sculpted in 1260—200 years before Michelangelo—it's a nude depiction of a pagan character, with a realistic body standing in a believable *contrapposto* pose. This was clearly inspired by carvings found on ancient sarcophagi.

3. Presentation in the Temple: It lacks the star of the scene, baby Jesus, who got broken off, but on the panel's right side, a powerful, bearded man in a voluminous robe epitomizes Nicola's solemn classical style.

4. Crucifixion: Everyone faces either straight out or in profile; the Roman in front actually has to look back over his shoulder to razz Jesus.

5. Last Judgment: Christ reigns over crowded, barely controlled chaos. The pulpit's lectern is an eagle clutching its prey, echoing the "triumph of Christianity" theme of the base.

Acoustics

Make a sound in here and it echoes for a good 10 seconds. A priest standing at the baptismal font (or a security guard today) can sing three tones within the 10 seconds—"Ave Maria"—and make a chord, singing haunting harmonies with himself. This medieval form of digital delay is due to the 250-foot-wide dome. Recent computer analysis suggests that the 15th-century architects who built the dome intended this building to function not just as a Baptistery, but also as a musical instrument. A security guard sings every half-hour, starting at 8:30. Climb 75 steps to the interior gallery (midway up) for an impressive view back down on the baptismal font.

Camposanto Cemetery

The long white building (1278–1465) with a nondescript entrance borders the Field of Miracles on the north. This site has been a cemetery since ancient times. Highlights are the building's cloistered interior courtyard, some ancient sarcophagi, and the large 14th-century fresco *The Triumph of Death* (same hours as Baptistery).

Inside is a delightful open-air **courtyard,** surrounded by an arcade with intricately carved tracery in the arches. The courtyard's grass grows on special dirt (said to turn a body into bones in a single day) shipped here by returning Crusaders from Jerusalem's Mount Calvary, where Christ was crucified.

The arcade floor is paved with the **coats of arms** of some 600 dearly departed Pisans. In death all are equal—the most humble peasant (or tourist) can walk upon these VIP tombstones. Today much of the marble flooring is scarred, the result of lead melting from the roof during WWII bombing.

Displayed in the arcade are dozens of ancient Roman sarcophagi. These coffins, which originally held dead Romans, were reused by medieval big shots. In anticipation of death, a wealthy Pisan would shop around, choose a good sarcophagus, and chip his message into it. When he died, his marble box was placed with the others around the exterior of the cathedral. Great sculptors such as Nicola and Giovanni Pisano passed them daily, gaining inspiration.

Circle the courtyard clockwise, noticing **traces of fresco** on the bare-brick walls. (We'll see some reconstructed frescoes later.) The huge **chains** on the west wall once stretched across the mouth of Pisa's harbor as a defense. Then Genoa attacked, broke the chains, carried them off as a war trophy, and gave them to Pisa's arch-rival Florence. After unification, they were returned to Pisa as a token of friendship.

Straight ahead is the cemetery's oldest object, an ochre-colored Greek tombstone. This **stele,** dating from the time of Alexander the Great (fourth century B.C.), shows a woman (seated) who's just given birth. A maid (standing) shows the baby while the mother gazes adoringly.

In the floor 10 yards away, by the corner of the courtyard, is a **pavement slab** dedicated to an American artist, Deane Keller. After serving in Italy during World War II, he helped rebuild the Camposanto Cemetery and restore its frescoes.

On the wall in the corner, what looks like a big faded **bull's-eye** is the politically correct 14th-century view of the universe—everything held by Christ, with the earth clearly in the center.

At the back of the courtyard (opposite where you entered), step through the door to see **photos** of the bombed-out Camposanto. By the summer of 1944, Allied troops had pushed Nazi forces to the north bank of the Arno, and German Field Marshal Kesselring dug in at Pisa, surrounded by the United States' 91st Infantry. Germans and Americans lobbed artillery shells at each other. (The Americans even considered blowing up the Leaning Tower—the "Tiltin' Hilton" was suspected to be the German lookout point.) Most of the Field of Miracles was miraculously unscathed, but the Camposanto took a direct hit with a Yankee incendiary grenade. It melted the lead-covered arcade roof and peeled historic frescoes from the walls—one of the many tragic art losses of World War II. The Americans liberated the city on September 2 and rebuilt the Camposanto. Some of the much-damaged frescoes are displayed in the adjoining room. (After careful restoration, these are now slowly and steadily being returned to their original spots on the walls of the Camposanto.)

The 1,000-square-foot *Triumph of Death* (on the left wall, c. 1350, artist unknown) captures Pisa's mood in the wake of the bubonic plague (1348), which killed one in three Pisans. Well-dressed ladies and gents (left half of the painting) are riding gaily through the countryside when they come across three coffins with corpses (bottom left). Confronted with death, they each react differently—a woman puts her hand thoughtfully to her chin, a man holds his nose against the stench, while a horse leans in for a better whiff. Above them, a monk scours the Bible for the meaning of death. Mr. Death, a winged demon with a scythe, stands to the right of center and eyes his future victims.

In the right half of the painting, young people gather in a garden (bottom right) to play music (symbolizing earthly pleasure), oblivious to the death around them. Winged demons swoop down from above to pluck souls from a pile of corpses, while winged angels fight them for the souls. The action continues in the next fresco (the room's far wall), where Jesus and Mary judge the dead at the Last Judgment. The wicked are led away to hell (the right wall of the room) to be tortured by a horned Satan. Grim stuff, but appropriate for the Camposanto's permanent residents.

As you leave the fresco room, look left to see a third-century A.D. **Roman sarcophagus** carved with mythological scenes. Near the corner, another sarcophagus features a couple—the deceased—relaxing atop their coffin.

Stepping back into the piazza, consider how this richly artistic but utilitarian square fit into the big picture of life. The ensemble around you includes the Baptistery, the cathedral, the bell tower, the hospital (present-day Museum of the Sinopias), and the Christian cemetery you just visited. The Jewish cemetery is adjacent but just outside the walls. Pisa, a pragmatic port town, needed the money and business connections of the Jews and treated them relatively well for the age. Unlike Rome or Venice, there was no Jewish ghetto here in the Middle Ages.

Museum of the Sinopias

Housed in a 13th-century hospital, this museum (Museo delle Sinopie) features the preparatory sketches (sinopias) for the Camposanto's WWII-damaged frescoes. If you loved *The Triumph of Death* and others in the Camposanto, or if you're interested in fresco technique, this museum is worthwhile. If not, you'll wonder why you're here.

Whether you pay to go in or not, you can watch two free videos in the entry lobby that serve to orient you to the square: a 10-minute 3-D computer tour of the complex, and a 15-minute story of the Tower, its tilt, and its fix.

Just past the ticket-taker, you'll see the multi-ringed, Earth-centric, Ptolemaic universe of the *Theological Cosmography*. Continue to your right to find a faint *Crucifixion* and scenes from the Old Testament. At the end of the long hall, climb the stairs to the next floor to find (midway along the right wall) the red-tinted sinopias for *The Triumph of Death* and the *Last Judgment and Hell*.

Sinopias are sketches in red paint painted directly on the wall, designed to guide the making of the final colored fresco. The master always did the sinopia himself. It was a way for him (and for those who paid for the work) to see exactly how the scene would look in its designated spot. If it wasn't quite right, the master changed a detail here and there. Next, assistants made a "cartoon" by tracing the sinopia onto large sheets of paper *(cartone)*. Then the sinopia was plastered over. To put the drawing back on the wall, assistants perforated the drawing on the cartoon, hung the cartoon over the wall, and dabbed it with a powdered bag of charcoal. This process printed dotted lines onto the newly plastered wall, re-creating the cartoon. While the plaster was still wet, the master and his team quickly filled in the color and details, producing the final frescoes (now on display at the Camposanto). These sinopias—never meant to be seen—were uncovered by the bombing and restoration of the Camposanto and brought here.

Duomo Museum

Near the Tower is the entrance to the Duomo Museum (Museo dell'Opera del Duomo), which houses many of the original statues and much of the artwork that once adorned the Campo's buildings (where copies stand today), notably the statues by Nicola and Giovanni Pisano. You can stand face-to-face with the Pisanos' very human busts that once ringed the outside of the Baptistery. Giovanni Pisano's stone *Madonna del Colloquio* solemnly exchanges gazes with baby Jesus in her arms. The most charming piece is Giovanni's carved ivory *Madonna and Child*. Mary leans back gracefully to admire baby Jesus, her pose matching what she's carved from—an elephant's tusk. Here, too, are the Duomo's original 12th-century bronze doors of St. Ranieri, with scenes from the life of Jesus, done by Bonanno Pisano.

You'll see a mythical sculpted hippogriff (a medieval jackalope) and other oddities brought back from the Holy Land by Pisan Crusaders. The museum also has several large-scale wooden models of the Duomo, Baptistery, and Tower. The church treasury is here, with vestments, chalices, and bishops' staves.

On the next floor up are the illuminated manuscripts, along with fine inlaid woodwork that once graced the choir stalls of the sacristy. The collection of antiquities includes Etruscan funerary urns with reclining people—the inspiration for the Roman sarcophagi that inspired the Pisanos. Beyond the Etruscan collection are beautiful small-scale copies of the Camposanto frescoes, painted in the 1830s. There's also a scene that shows what the building looked like inside before it was bombed.

The museum's interior courtyard has a two-story, tourist-free view of the Tower, Duomo, and Baptistery.

PISA SLEEPING, EATING, AND CONNECTIONS

Sleeping in Pisa

To locate these hotels, see the map on page 341.

$$$ Hotel Alessandro della Spina, in a nondescript neighborhood near the train station, has 16 elegant and colorful rooms, each named after a flower (Sb-€120, Db-€140, discounts off-season and for drop-ins, air-con, free parking; head straight out of train station, turn right on Viale F. Bonaini, and take the third right on Via Alessandro della Spina to find the hotel on your left at #5; tel. 050-502-777, fax 050-20583, www.hoteldellaspina.it, info @hoteldellaspina.it).

$$ Hotel Villa Kinzica, with 30 tired but decent rooms and indifferent management, is just steps away from the Field of Miracles—ask for a room with a view of the Tower (Sb-€78, Db-€108, Tb-€124, Qb-€135, air-con, elevator, attached restaurant, Piazza Arcivescovado 2, tel. 050-560-419, fax 050-551-204, www.hotelvillakinzica.it, info@hotelvillakinzica.it).

$$ Hotel Royal Victoria, a classy place on the Arno River, is conveniently located dead-center between the Tower and main train station (D-€80, standard Db-€100, better Db-€130, suite-€190, family room-€200, prices higher mid-June and mid-April, Lungarno Pacinotti 12, tel. 050-940-111, fax 050-940-180, www .royalvictoria.it, mail@royalvictoria.it, Piegaja family).

$ Hotel Milano, near the train station, offers 10 spacious, tidy rooms; ask for a room off the street when you book (D-€55, Db-€78, breakfast extra, air-con, Via Mascagni 14, tel. 050-23-162, fax 050-44-237, www.hotelmilano.pisa.it, info@hotelmilano .pisa.it).

$ Pensione Helvetia is a no-frills, homey, clean, and quiet inn just 100 yards from the Tower. Its 29 economical rooms are

Sleep Code

(€1 = about $1.40, country code: 39)
S = Single, **D** = Double/Twin, **T** = Triple, **Q** = Quad, **b** = bathroom,
s = shower only.
Unless otherwise noted, credit cards are accepted, breakfast is included, and English is generally spoken.
  To help you sort easily through these listings, I've divided the rooms into three categories based on the price for a standard double room with bath:

$$$ Higher Priced—Most rooms €120 or more.
  $$ Moderately Priced—Most rooms between €80-120.
    $ Lower Priced—Most rooms €80 or less.

spread over four floors (no elevator); the lower your room number, the lower your altitude. Reservations are accepted by phone only; let them know your arrival time since they don't ask for deposits to secure reservations (S-€35, Sb-€50, D-€45, Db-€62, optional breakfast-€5, ceiling fans, Via Don G. Boschi 31, tel. 050-553-084).

Eating in Pisa

For a quick lunch or dinner, the pizzeria/trattoria **La Buca,** just a block from the Tower, is adequate and convenient (Sat–Thu 12:00–15:00 & 19:00–22:30, closed Fri, at Via Santa Maria 171 and Via A. G. Tassi 6b, tel. 050-560-660).

  Ristorante Galileo, south of the Arno, has excellent pizza (dinner only) and pasta (€6–8, Wed–Mon 12:30–15:30 & 19:30–23:30, closed Sun at lunch and all day Tue, Via Silvestri 12, tel. 050-28287).

  At **Paninoteca il Canguro,** friendly Fabio makes warm, hearty sandwiches to order. Try the popular primavera sandwich (Mon–Fri 10:00–24:00, Sat 10:30–21:00, closed Sun, Via Santa Maria 151, tel. 050-561-942).

  Panetteria Antiche Tradizioni is a sandwich/bread shop with complete fixings for a picnic on the lawn at the Field of Miracles or a sit-down lunch ordered from their menu (limited pastas, soups, and salads). Build your own sandwich with home-made bread or focaccia, then choose fruit from the counter, fresh pastries from the window, and cold drinks or wine to round out your meal (daily 8:00–20:00, Via Santa Maria 66, mobile 347-675-2940).

  Drop by cheery **La Lupa Ghiotta Tavola Calda** for a cheap, fast, and tasty meal a few steps from the train station. It's got everything you'd want from a *ristorante* at half the price with faster service (build your own salad—5 ingredients for €4.50; Mon and Wed–Sat 12:15–15:00 & 19:15–23:30, Tue 12:15–15:00 only, closed Sun, Viale F. Bonaini 113, tel. 050-21018).

The street that houses the daily market, **Via delle Colonne** (a block north of the Arno, west of Borgo Stretto), has a few atmospheric, mid-priced restaurants and several fun, greasy take-out options.

Connections

From Pisa by Train to: Florence (2–3/hr, 1.25 hrs, €6), **Rome** (at least hourly, many change in Florence, 3–4 hrs), **La Spezia,** gateway to Cinque Terre (about hourly, 1–1.5 hr), **Siena** (change at Empoli: Pisa–Empoli, roughly 2/hr, 45 min; Empoli–Siena, hourly, 1 hr, €7), **Lucca** (roughly 2/hr Mon–Sat, hourly on Sun, more with changes in Viareggio, 30 min). Even the fastest trains stop in Pisa, so you might change trains here whether you plan to stop or not.

By Bus to Lucca: A handy bus connects the Field of Miracles with Lucca's Piazzale Verdi in 30 minutes with hourly departures (in Pisa, wait at the Vai Bus signpost, immediately outside the wall behind the Baptistery; buy €3 ticket on bus). This makes a half-day side-trip to Pisa from Lucca particularly easy.

By Car: The drive between Pisa and Florence is that rare case where the non-autostrada highway (free, more direct, and at least as fast) is a better deal than the autostrada.

Pisa's Airport: For information on Pisa's Galileo Galilei Airport, see page 283.

LUCCA

Surrounded by well-preserved ramparts, layered with history, alternately quaint and urbane, Lucca charms its visitors. The city is a paradox. Though it hasn't been involved in a war since 1430, it is Italy's most impressive fortress city, encircled by a perfectly intact wall. Most cities tear down their wall to make way for modern traffic. But Lucca's wall effectively keeps out both traffic and, it seems, the stress of the modern world. Locals are very protective of their wall, which they enjoy like a community roof garden.

Lucca, known for being Europe's leading producer of toilet paper and Kleenex (with a monopoly on the special machinery that makes it), has no single monumental sight to attract tourists. It's simply a uniquely human and undamaged, never-bombed city. Romanesque churches seem to be around every corner, as do fun-loving and shady piazzas filled with soccer-playing children. Still, it's hard to focus on anything in particular within the walls.

Locals say Lucca is like a cake with a cherry filling in the middle...every slice is equally good. Despite Lucca's charm, few tourists seem to put it on their maps, and it remains a city for the Lucchesi (loo-KAY-zee).

Orientation to Lucca

Tourist Information

The main TI is just inside the Porta Santa Maria gate, on Piazza Santa Maria (daily April–Oct 9:00–20:00, Nov–March 9:00–12:30 & 15:00–18:30, pricey Internet access, WCs, train tickets, no-fee room booking, Piazza Santa Maria 35, tel. 0583-919-931, www .luccatourist.it, info@luccaturismo.it).

Another TI, on Piazzale Verdi, offers information, a no-fee room-booking service, walking tours, and baggage check (daily 9:00–18:00, off-season 9:00–17:30, bike rental, 80-min city-walk audioguide-€9, additional audioguide-€3 more; bag storage-€1.50/ hr per bag, they need to photocopy your passport; futuristic WC, tel. 0583-583-150).

A third TI, at Piazza Curtatone, has the handiest baggage check near the train station (daily 10:00–13:30 & 14:30–17:30, bag storage-€1.50/day per bag, some rental bikes; exit the station, cross the square, and it's just ahead on the right; tel. 0583-583-150).

Arrival in Lucca

To reach the city center from the **train** station, walk toward the walls and head left, to the entry at Porta San Pietro. Taxis are sparse, but try calling 0583-333-434 or 0583-491-349. There is no baggage check at the train station, but there is one at the TI in nearby Piazza Curtatone (see "Tourist Information," above).

Drivers: The key for drivers—don't try to drive within the walls. The old town is ringed by lots. Try parking lots at Porta Santa Maria and Porta Sant'Anna (€1/hr), or consider parking outside the gates near the train station or on the boulevard surrounding the city. Lucca's TIs have maps showing the location of free parking lots just outside the walls. Overnight parking (20:00–8:00) is free in the lots at Porta Santa Maria and Porta Sant'Anna and €1.50/night at Ex-Caserma Mazzini, just inside Porta Elisa.

Helpful Hints

Combo-Tickets: A €6 combo-ticket includes visits to the Ilaria del Carretto tomb in San Martino Cathedral (€2), Cathedral Museum (€4), and San Giovanni Church (€2.50). A €5 ticket combines the Guinigi Tower (€3.50) and the Clock Tower (€3.50). Yet another combo-ticket covers Palazzo Mansi and Villa Guinigi for €6.50 and is valid for three days (€4 each if purchased separately).

Shops and Museums Alert: Shops close most of Sunday and Monday mornings. Many museums are closed on Monday as well.

Markets: Lucca's atmospheric markets are worth visiting. Every third Sunday and the preceding Saturday of the month, one of the largest **antiques markets** in Italy unfurls in the blocks from Piazza Antelminelli to Piazza San Giovanni (8:00–19:00). The last weekend of the month, local artisans sell **arts and crafts** throughout the town (also 8:00–19:00). At the **general market,** held Wednesdays and Saturdays, you'll find produce and household goods (8:30–13:00, from Porta Elisa to Porta San Jacopo on Via dei Bacchettoni).

Concerts: San Giovanni Church hosts one-hour concerts featuring a pianist and singers performing highlights from hometown composer Giacomo Puccini (tickets €16.50 in advance, plenty available at the door for €15, nightly in peak season at 19:00; get schedule at church, TI, or your hotel, or check www.puccinielasualucca.com).

Festival: On September 13 and 14, the city celebrates Volto Santo ("Holy Face"), with a procession of the treasured local crucifix and a fair in Piazza Antelminelli.

Internet Access: You can get online at the main TI (see "Tourist Information," above) or at **Betty Blue,** a wine bar handy to the recommended launderette (€4.50/hr, two terminals and cables to plug in your laptop, Thu–Tue 11:00–24:00, closed Wed, Via del Gonfalone 16, tel. 0583-492-166).

Laundry: Lavanderia Self-Service Niagara is just off Piazza Santa Maria at Via Rosi 26 (daily 7:00–23:00).

Bike Rental: Several places with identical prices cluster around Piazza Santa Maria (€2.50/hr, €12.50/day, tandem bikes available, free helmets, open daily about 9:00–19:30 or sunset). These easygoing shops rent good bikes: **Antonio Poli** (Piazza Santa Maria 42, tel. 0583-493-787, enthusiastic Cristiana) and **Cicli Bizzarri** (Piazza Santa Maria 32, tel. 0583-496-682, Australian Dely). Closer to the train station, you can rent a bike at the **Piazza Curtatone TI** (they have just a few) or at **Promo Turist** at Porta San Pietro (same rates and hours as the competition, Via Francesco Carrara, mobile 348-380-0126, Marco). A one-hour rental gives you two leisurely loops around the ramparts.

Local Guide: Gabriele Calabrese knows and shares his hometown well (mobile 347-788-0667, www.turislucca.com, turis lucca@turislucca.com).

Sights in Lucca

▲▲**Bike the Ramparts**—Lucca's most remarkable feature, its Renaissance wall, is also its most enjoyable attraction—especially when circled on a rental bike. Stretching for 2.5 miles, this is an ideal place to come for an overview of the city by foot or bike.

Lucca has had a protective wall for 2,000 years. You can read three walls into today's map: the first rectangular Roman wall, the later medieval wall (nearly the size of today's), and the 16th-century Renaissance wall which survives today.

With the advent of cannons, thin medieval walls were

Lucca

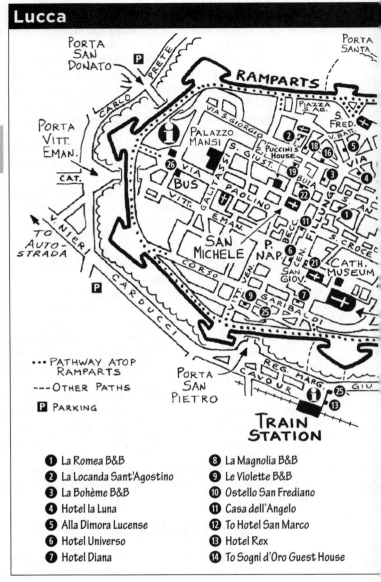

LUCCA

···· PATHWAY ATOP RAMPARTS
---- OTHER PATHS
P PARKING

1. La Romea B&B
2. La Locanda Sant'Agostino
3. La Bohème B&B
4. Hotel la Luna
5. Alla Dimora Lucense
6. Hotel Universo
7. Hotel Diana
8. La Magnolia B&B
9. Le Violette B&B
10. Ostello San Frediano
11. Casa dell'Angelo
12. To Hotel San Marco
13. Hotel Rex
14. To Sogni d'Oro Guest House

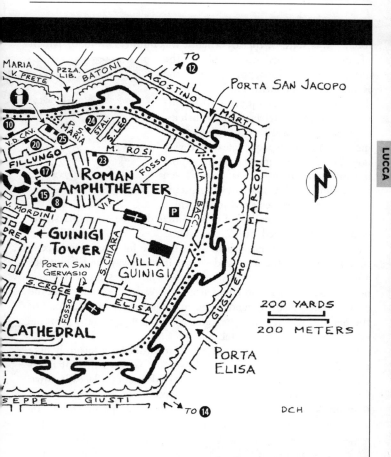

LUCCA

⑮ Ristorante Canuleia
⑯ Locanda di Bacco &
   Osteria Via San Giorgio
⑰ Vineria I Santi &
   Osteria Baralla
⑱ Vecchia Trattoria Buralli
⑲ Trattoria da Leo

⑳ Bella 'Mbriana
㉑ Il Cuore Enogastronomia
㉒ Pizzeria da Felice
㉓ Launderette
㉔ Betty Blue (Internet Access)
㉕ Bike Rentals (3)
㉖ Bus to Pisa's Leaning Tower

suddenly vulnerable. A new design—the same one that stands today—was state-of-the-art when it was built (1550–1650). Much of the old medieval wall (look for the old stones) was incorporated into the Renaissance wall (with uniform bricks). The new wall was squat: a 100-foot-wide mound of dirt faced with bricks, engineered to absorb a cannonball pummeling. The townspeople cleared a wide no-man's-land around the town, exposing any attackers from a distance. Eleven heart-shaped bastions (inviting picnic areas today) were designed to minimize

exposure to cannonballs and to maximize defense capabilities. The ramparts were armed with 130 cannons.

The town invested a third of its income for more than a century to construct the wall, and—since it kept away the Florentines and nasty Pisans—it was considered a fine investment. In fact, nobody ever bothered to try to attack the wall. Locals say that the only time it actually defended the city was during an 1812 flood of the Serchio River, when the gates were sandbagged and its ramparts kept out the high water.

Today, the ramparts seem made-to-order for a leisurely bike ride (20-min pedal, wonderfully smooth). You can rent bikes cheaply and easily from one of several bike-rental places in town (see "Helpful Hints," earlier in this chapter).

Roman Amphitheater—Just off the main shopping street, the architectural ghost of a Roman amphitheater can be felt in the

delightful Piazza Anfiteatro. With the fall of Rome, the theater (which seated 10,000) was gradually cannibalized for its stones and inhabited by a mishmash of huts. The huts were cleared away at the end of the 19th century to better appreciate the town's illustrious past. Today, the square is

a circle of touristy shops and mediocre restaurants that becomes a lively bar-and-café scene after dark. Today's street level is nine feet above the original arena floor. The only bits of surviving Roman stonework are a few arches on the northern exterior (at Via Fillungo 42 and on Via Anfiteatro).

Via Fillungo—This main pedestrian drag stretches southwest from the Roman amphitheater. The street to stroll, Via Fillungo takes you from the amphitheater almost all the way to the cathedral. Along the way, you'll get a taste of Lucca's rich past, including several elegant, century-old storefronts. Many of the original storefront paintings, reliefs, and mosaics survive—even if today's shopkeeper sells something entirely different.

At #97 is a classic old **jewelry store** with a rare storefront that has kept its T-shaped arrangement (when closed, you see a wooden T, and during open hours it unfolds with a fine old-time display). This design dates from a time when the merchant sold his goods in front, did his work in the back, and lived upstairs.

Di Simo Caffè at #58 has long been the hangout of Lucca's artistic and intellectual elite. Composer and hometown boy Giacomo Puccini tapped his foot while sipping coffee here. Pop in to check out the 1880s ambience (handy €10 buffet lunch served daily 12:30–14:30).

A surviving five-story **tower house** is at #67. Remember, there was a time when nearly every corner sported its own tower. The stubby stones that still stick out once supported wooden staircases (there were no interior connections between floors). So many towers cast shadows over this part of town that the street just before it is called Via Buia (Dark Street). Look left down Via San Andrea for a peek at the town's tallest tower, Guinigi, in the distance—with its characteristic oak trees sprouting from the top.

At #45 and #43, you'll see two more good examples of tower houses. Across the street, the **Clock Tower** (Torre delle Ore) has a hand-wound Swiss clock that has clanged four times an hour since 1754 (€3.50 to climb up and see the mechanism flip into action on the quarter hour, €5 combo-ticket includes Guinigi Tower, April–Sept daily 9:30–18:30, closed Oct–March, corner of Via Fillungo and Via del'Arancio).

The intersection of Via Fillungo and Via Roma/Via Santa Croce marks the center of town (where the two original Roman roads crossed). As you go right down Via Roma, you'll pass the fine Edison Bookstore before reaching Piazza San Michele.

Piazza San Michele—This square has been the center of town since Roman times, when it was the forum. It's dominated by the Church of San Michele. Towering above the church's fancy Pisan

Romanesque facade, the archangel Michael stands ready to flap his wings—which he actually did on special occasions.

The square is surrounded by an architectural hodgepodge. The loggia, which dates from 1495, is the first Renaissance building in town. The Bertoldi Agency (#5; in front of the church), famous for its exports to the US—both oil and immigrants—sports an Art Nouveau facade that celebrates both Amerigo Vespucci and Cristoforo Colombo.

You'll notice that no statues of big shots decorate Lucca squares. That's because unlike Venice, Florence, and Milan—which were dominated by a few powerful dynasties—Lucca was traditionally run by an oligarchy of a hundred leading families. But after Italian unification, when leaders were fond of saying, "We have created Italy...now we need to create Italians," stirring statues of national heroes popped up everywhere—even in Lucca. The statue on Piazza San Michele is a two-bit local guy, dredged up centuries after his death because he favored strong central government.

Look back at the church facade, which also has an element of patriotism—designed to give roots and legitimacy to Italian statehood. It's decorated with the faces of heroes in the Italian independence and unification movement: Victor Emmanuel II (above the short red column on the right), the Count of Cavour (next to Victor, above the column with black zigzags), Giuseppe Mazzini, and Dante.

▲San Martino Cathedral—This cathedral, begun in the 11th century, is an entertaining mix of architectural and artistic styles. Its elaborate Pisan Romanesque **facade**—featuring Christian teaching scenes, animals, and candy-cane-striped columns—dominates the piazza. The facade's central figure is St. Martin, a Roman military officer from Hungary who, by offering his cloak to a beggar, more fully understood the beauty of Christian compassion. (The impressive original, a fine example of Romanesque sculpture, hides from pollution just inside, to the right of the main entrance.) Each of the columns on the facade is unique. Notice how the facade is asymmetrical: The 11th-century bell tower was already in place when the rest of the cathedral was built, so the builders cheated on the right side to make it fit the space. Over the right portal (as if leaning against the older tower), the architect Guideo from Como holds a document declaring that he finished the facade in 1204. On the right (at eye level on the pilaster), a labyrinth is set into the wall. The maze relates to the struggle and challenge our souls face in finding salvation. (French pilgrims on their way to Rome could

relate to this, as it's the same pattern they knew from the floor of the church at Chartres.) The Latin plaque just left of the main door is where moneychangers and spice traders met to seal deals

The History of Lucca

Lucca began as a Roman settlement. In fact, the grid layout of the streets (and the shadow of an amphitheater) survives from Roman times. Trace the rectangular Roman wall—indicated by today's streets—on the map. As in typical Roman towns, two main roads quartered the fortified town, crossing at what was the forum (main market and religious/political center)—today's Piazza San Michele.

Christianity came here early; it's said that the first bishop of Lucca was a disciple of St. Peter. While churches were built here as early as the fourth century, the majority of Lucca's elegant Romanesque churches date from about the 12th century.

Feisty Lucca, though never a real power, enjoyed a long period of independence (maintained by clever diplomacy). Aside from 30 years of being ruled from Pisa in the 14th century, Lucca was basically an independent city-state until Napoleon came to town.

In the Middle Ages, wealthy Lucca's economy was built on the silk industry, dominated by the Guinigi (gwee-NEE-gee) family. Without silk, Lucca would have been just another sleepy Italian town. In 1500, the town had 3,000 silk looms employing 25,000 workers. Banking was also big. Many pilgrims stopped here on their way to the Holy Land, deposited their money for safety...and never returned to pick it up.

In its heyday, Lucca packed 160 towers—one on nearly every corner—and 70 churches within its walls. Each tower was the home of a wealthy merchant family. Towers were many stories tall, with single rooms stacked atop each other: ground-floor shop, upstairs living room, and top-floor fire-safe kitchen, all connected by exterior wooden staircases. The rooftop was generally a vegetable garden with trees providing shade. Later, the wealthy city folk moved into the countryside, trading away life in their city palazzos to establish farm estates complete with fancy villas. (You can visit some of these villas today—the TI has a brochure—but they're convenient only for drivers and are generally not worth the cost of admission.)

In 1799, Napoleon stormed into Italy and took a liking to Lucca. He liked it so much that he gave it to his sister as a gift. It was later passed on to Napoleon's widow, Marie Louise. With a feminine sensitivity, Marie Louise was partially responsible for turning the city's imposing (but no longer particularly useful) fortified wall into a fine city park that is much enjoyed today.

(on the doorstep of the church—to underscore the reliability of their promises). Notice the date: *An Dni MCXI* (A.D. 1111).

The **interior** features Gothic arches, Renaissance paintings, and stained glass from the 19th century. On the left side of the nave, a small, elaborate, birdcage-like temple contains the wooden crucifix—beloved by locals—called Volto Santo. It's said to have been sculpted by Nicodemus in Jerusalem and set afloat in an unmanned boat that landed on the coast of Tuscany, from where wild oxen miraculously carried it to Lucca in 782. The sculpture (which is actually 12th-century Byzantine-style) has quite a jewelry collection, which you can see in the Cathedral Museum (next listing).

On the right side of the nave, the sacristy houses the enchantingly beautiful **memorial tomb of Ilaria del Carretto** by Jacopo della Quercia (1407). Pick up a handy English description to the right of the door as you enter the sacristy. This young bride of silk baron Paolo Guinigi is decked out in the latest, most expensive fashions, with the requisite little dog curled up at her feet in eternal sleep. She's so realistic that the statue was nicknamed "Sleeping Beauty." Her nose is partially worn off because of a long-standing tradition of lonely young ladies rubbing it for luck in finding a boyfriend (cathedral—free, Ilaria tomb—€2, €6 combo-ticket includes Cathedral Museum and San Giovanni Church, Mon–Fri 9:30–17:45, Sat 9:30–18:45; Sun open sporadically between Masses: 9:30–10:45 & 12:00–17:45; Piazza San Martino).

Cathedral Museum (Museo della Cattedrale)—This beautifully presented museum houses original paintings, sculptures, and vestments from the cathedral and other Lucca churches. The first room displays jewelry made to dress up the Volto Santo crucifix, including gigantic gilded silver shoes. Upstairs, notice the fine red brocaded silk—a reminder that this precious fabric is what brought riches and power to the city. The exhibits in this museum have very brief descriptions and are meaningful only with the €1 audioguide—if you're not in the mood to listen, skip the place altogether (€4, €6 combo-ticket includes Ilaria tomb and San Giovanni Church, April–Oct daily 10:00–18:00; Nov–March Mon–Fri 10:00–14:00, Sat–Sun 10:00–17:00; to the left of the cathedral as you're facing it, Piazza Antelminelli).

San Giovanni Church—This first cathedral of Lucca is interesting only for its archaeological finds. The entire floor of the 12th-century church has been excavated in recent decades, revealing layers of Roman houses, ancient hot tubs that date back to the time of Christ, early churches, and theological graffiti. Eager students can request an English translation of the floor plans from the ticket office to learn what's what. As you climb under the church's present-day floor and wander the lanes of Roman Lucca, remember that the entire city sits on similar ruins (€2.50, €6 combo-ticket includes Ilaria tomb and Cathedral Museum, audioguide-€1; mid-March–Oct daily 10:00–18:00; Nov–mid-March Sat–Sun 10:00–17:00, closed Mon–Fri; see concert info in "Helpful Hints," page 374; kitty-corner from cathedral at Piazza San Giovanni).

Church of San Frediano—This impressive church was built in 1112 by the pope to counter Lucca's bishop and his spiffy cathedral. Lucca was the first Mediterranean stop on the pilgrim route from northern Europe, and the pope wanted to remind pilgrims that the action, the glory, and the papacy awaited them in Rome. Therefore, he had the church made "Roman-esque." The pure marble facade frames an early Christian Roman-style mosaic of Christ with his 12 apostles. Step inside and you're struck by the sight of 40 powerful (if recycled) ancient Roman columns. The message: Lucca may be impressive, but the finale of your pilgrimage—in Rome—is worth the hike.

Lucca 383

Inside, there's a notable piece of art in each corner: At rear left is the 12th-century baptistery, with some interesting Church propaganda showing the story of Moses (the evil Egyptians are played by Holy Roman Empire troops). At rear right is St. Zita's actual body, put there in 1278. At front left is a particularly elegant Virgin Mary, depicted at the moment she gets the news that she'll bring the Messiah into the world (carved and painted by Lucchesi artist Matteo Civitali, c. 1460). And at front right is a painting on wood of the *Assumption of the Virgin* (c. 1510), with Doubting Thomas receiving Mary's red belt as she ascends so he'll doubt no more. The pinball-machine composition serves as a virtual catalog of the fine silk material produced in Lucca—a major industry in the 16th century (free, daily 9:00–12:00 & 15:00–17:00, Piazza San Frediano, tel. 0583-493-627).

Palazzo Mansi—Minor paintings by Tintoretto, Pontormo, Veronese, and others vie for attention, but the palace itself—a sumptuously furnished and decorated 17th-century confection— steals the show. This is your chance to appreciate the wealth of Lucca's silk merchants (€4, €6.50 combo-ticket includes Villa

Guinigi, Tue–Sat 8:30–19:30, Sun 8:30–13:30, closed Mon, no photos, request English booklet at ticket desk, Via Galli Tassi 43, tel. 0583-55-570). All visitors must be accompanied by a museum custodian, so there may be a bit of a wait during high season.

Guinigi Tower (Torre Guinigi)—Many Tuscan towns have towers, but none is quite like the Guinigi family's. Up 227 steps is a small garden with fragrant trees surrounded by fantastic views (€3.50, €5 combo-ticket includes Clock Tower, likely open daily

April–Sept 9:00–19:30, Oct 10:00–18:00, Nov–March 9:30–16:30, Via Sant'Andrea 41).

Puccini's House—Opera enthusiasts (but nobody else) will want to visit the home where Giacomo Puccini (1858–1924) grew up, but—tragedy—it's closed. A pitched battle is going on between Puccini's grandniece—who actually owns the house and wants to renovate the museum—and the city of Lucca, which wants to preserve the house unchanged. Until one or the other relents, the museum's curtains will remain closed.

Villa Guinigi—Built by Paolo Guinigi in 1418, the family villa is now a stark, abandoned-feeling museum displaying a hodge-podge of Etruscan artifacts, religious sculptures, paintings, inlaid woodwork, and ceramics. Monumental paintings by the multi-talented Giorgio Vasari are the best reason to visit (€4, €6.50 combo-ticket includes Palazzo Mansi, Tue–Sat 8:30–19:30, Sun 8:30–13:30, closed Mon, may have to wait in high season for a museum custodian to accompany you, Via della Quarquonia, tel. 0583-496-033).

Sleeping in Lucca

Fancy Little Boutique B&Bs Within the Walls

$$$ La Romea B&B, in an air-conditioned, restored, 14th-century palazzo near Guinigi Tower, feels like a royal splurge. Its four posh rooms and one suite are lavishly decorated in handsome colors, and surround a big plush lounge with stately Venetian-style floors (Db-€100–130 depending on season, big suite-€160, extra bed-€20–25, 3 percent cheaper with cash, Wi-Fi; from Via Fillungo, take Via Sant'Andrea to the Church of Sant'Andrea and turn right on Vicolo delle Ventaglie to #2; tel. 0583-464-175, www.laromea.com, info@laromea.com, Giulio and wife Gaia).

$$$ La Locanda Sant'Agostino, run by gracious Sarah, has three romantic and spacious rooms. The vine-draped terrace and quaint views invite you to relax (Db-€160, extra bed-€25, 5 percent discount with cash and this book, air-con, Internet access and Wi-Fi, from Via Fillungo take Via San Giorgio to Piazza Sant'Agostino 3, best to reserve by email, tel. & fax 0583-467-884, www.locandasantagostino.it, info@locandasantagostino.it). Sarah's husband, Irio, runs an antiques shop—as reflected in the tasteful furnishings.

$$$ La Bohème B&B has a cozy yet elegant ambience, offering six large, charming, chandeliered rooms, each painted with a different rich color scheme (Db-€120, less off-season, 10 percent discount with cash and this book, air-con, free Wi-Fi, Via del Moro 2, tel. & fax 0583-462-404, www.boheme.it, info@boheme.it, Sara).

Sleep Code

(€1 = about $1.40, country code: 39)
S = Single, **D** = Double/Twin, **T** = Triple, **Q** = Quad, **b** = bathroom,
s = shower only.

Unless otherwise noted, credit cards are accepted, English is spoken, and breakfast is included (but usually optional).

   To help you sort easily through these listings, I've divided the rooms into three categories based on the price for a standard double room with bath:

$$$ Higher Priced—Most rooms €120 or more.
$$ Moderately Priced—Most rooms between €80–120.
$ Lower Priced—Most rooms €80 or less.

Sleeping More Forgettably Within the Walls

$$ Hotel la Luna, run by the Barbieri family, has 29 classy, spotless rooms in the heart of the city. Updated rooms are split between two adjacent buildings right off of the main shopping street (Sb-€83, Db-€113, suite-€175, these prices for Rick Steves' readers, overpriced breakfast-€10, air-con, elevator, parking-€15/day, Via Fillungo at Corte Compagni 12, tel. 0583-493-634, fax 0583-490-021, www.hotellaluna.com, info@hotellaluna.com, lovely Lulu gives you a warm reception).

$$ Alla Dimora Lucense's seven new rooms are bright, modern, clean, and peaceful, with all the comforts. Enjoy their relaxing, sunny interior courtyard (Db-€115, suite for 2–4 people-€150–200, overpriced optional breakfast-€9, air-con, half a block from Via Fillungo at Via Fontana 17, tel. 0583-495-722, fax 0583-441-210, www.dimoralucense.it, info@dimoralucense.it).

$$ Hotel Universo, renting 56 rooms right on Piazza Napoleone and facing the theatre and Palazzo Ducale, is a 19th-century town fixture. While it clearly was once elegant, now it's old and tired, with a big Old World lounge and soft prices ("comfort" Db-€100, "superior" Db-€130, Wi-Fi, Piazza del Giglio 1, tel. 0583-493-678, www.universolucca.com, info @universolucca.com).

$ Hotel Diana is a dreary little family-run hotel, with nine rooms in the main building and another six slightly nicer, soundproofed, and air-conditioned rooms in the annex just around the corner (D-€50, Db-€67, annex Db-€85, south of the cathedral at Via del Molinetto 11, tel. 0583-492-202, fax 0583-467-795, www .albergodiana.com, info@albergodiana.com).

$ La Magnolia B&B offers five basic rooms with an intimate atmosphere and relaxing garden. It's buried in a ramshackle old palace in a central location (Sb-€55–65, Db-€75–85, includes breakfast at nearby bar, 5 percent discount with cash and this book, a block behind amphitheater at Via Mordini 63, tel. 0583-467-111, www.lamagnolia.com, info@lamagnolia.com, Andrea and Laura).

$ At Le Violette B&B, friendly Anna (who's still learning English; her granddaughter Sara speaks English) will settle you into one of her six homey rooms near the train station inside Porta San Pietro (D-€60, Db-€75, extra bed-€15, communal kitchen, €5 to use washer and dryer, Via della Polveriera 6, tel. 0583-493-594, mobile 349-823-4645, fax 0583-429-305, www.leviolette.it, leviolette@virgilio.it).

$ Ostello San Frediano, in a central, sprawling ex-convent with a peaceful garden, is a cut above the average hostel. Older travelers feel comfortable here. Its 28 rooms are bright and modern, and some have fun lofts (140 beds, Db-€55, Qb-€100, €20 beds in 6- to 8-person dorms, includes sheets, €3 extra/night for non-members, cash only, lockers, no curfew, Internet access, cheap restaurant, free parking, Via della Cavallerizza 12, tel. 0583-469-957, fax 0583-461-007, www.ostellolucca.it, info@ostellolucca.it).

$ Casa dell'Angelo has four simple, economical rooms up two steep flights of stairs in the heart of Lucca (D-€50, Db-€65, no breakfast, can be noisy—ask for a quiet room when you book, Corte dell'Angelo 13, mobile 333-498-3045, fax 0583-957-612, www.luccarooms.com, info@luccarooms.com). From Via Roma, pass under the arch across from #11, turn right, and find #13 at the end of the courtyard.

Outside the Walls

$$$ Hotel San Marco, a seven-minute walk outside the Porta Santa Maria, is a postmodern place decorated à la Stanley Kubrick. Its 42 rooms are sleek, with all the comforts (Sb-€87, Db-€126, includes nice breakfast spread, air-con, elevator, pool, bikes-€5/half-day, free parking, taxi from station-€6, Via San Marco 368, tel. 0583-495-010, fax 0583-490-513, www.hotelsanmarcolucca.com, info@hotelsanmarcolucca.com).

$$ Hotel Rex rents 25 rooms in a practical modern building on the train station square. While in the modern world, you're just 200 yards away from the old town and get more space for a better price (Db-€90–100, air-con, Wi-Fi, a few steps from the train station at Piazza Ricasoli 19, tel. 0583-955-443, www.hotelrexlucca.com, info@hotelrexlucca.com).

$ Sogni d'Oro Guest House ("Sleep like Gold"), run by Davide, is a handy budget option for drivers, with five basic rooms and a cheery communal kitchen (grocery store next door). It's a 10-minute walk from the train station and a five-minute walk from the city walls (D-€50, Db-€65, €5/person discount with cash;

free shuttle to and from station with advance notice—then call when your train arrives in Lucca; from the station, head straight out to Viale Regina Margherita and turn right, follow the main boulevard as it turns into Viale Giuseppe Giusti, at the curve turn right onto Via Antonio Cantore to #169; tel. 0583-467-768, mobile 333-498-3045, fax 0583-957-612, www.bbsognidoro.com, info @bbsognidoro.com).

Eating in Lucca

Ristorante Canuleia makes everything fresh in their small kitchen. While the portions aren't huge, the food is tasty. You can eat in their dressy little dining room or outside on the garden courtyard (€9 pastas, €15 *secondi,* Mon–Sat 12:30–14:00 & 19:30–21:30, closed Sun, Via Canuleia 14, tel. 0583-467-470, reserve for dinner).

Locanda di Bacco is a smart, woodsy bistro, where hardworking hostess Daniela puts an innovative twist on traditional dishes. The menu changes with market availability, but typical Lucchese specialties are always offered, as are Daniela's homemade desserts (€10 pastas, €13 *secondi,* Wed–Mon 12:00–15:00 & 19:30–22:30, closed Tue, Via San Giorgio 36, tel. 0583-493-136, reserve for dinner).

Vineria I Santi is pricey but good if you appreciate quality food and fine wine, and just want to lay back and be pampered. Leonardo serves food with a sexy jazz ambience that would work well in a bordello. Relax in the peaceful indoors among wine bottles, or on a quiet square outside (€10 pastas, €18 *secondi,* closed Tue, Via Anfiteatro 29, tel. 0583-496-124).

Osteria Via San Giorgio, owned by Locanda di Bacco's Daniela and her brother Piero, is a cheery family eatery specializing in fish. Sample the splittable *antipasto fantasia*—five small courses such as *ceviche* (seafood salad), scallops au gratin, squid sautéed with potatoes, or whatever else was caught that day in Viareggio. Dinner-size salads are bright and fresh, pasta is homemade, and Daniela's desserts tempt (Tue–Sun 12:00–16:00 & 19:00–22:30, closed Mon, Via San Giorgio 26, tel. 0583-953-233).

Vecchia Trattoria Buralli, on quiet Piazza Sant'Agostino, is a good bet for traditional cooking and juicy steaks, with fine indoor and piazza seating (€6 pastas, €10 *secondi,* €14–30 fixed-price meals, Thu–Tue 12:00–14:45 & 19:15–22:30, closed Wed, Piazza Sant'Agostino 10, tel. 0583-950-611).

Osteria Baralla, a few steps from the Roman amphitheater, is popular with locals for its quality mid-priced meals. They have a breezy, spacious dining room under medieval vaults, and a few quiet tables on the pedestrian street (Mon–Sat 12:30–14:15

Specialties in Lucca

Lucca has some tasty specialties worth seeking out. *Ceci* (CHEH-chee), also called *cecina* (cheh-CHEE-nah), makes an ideal cheap snack any time of day. This garbanzo-bean crepe is sold in pizza shops and is best accompanied by a nip of red wine.

Farro, a grain (spelt) dating back to ancient Roman cuisine, shows up in restaurants in soups or as a creamy rice-like dish *(risotto di farro).*

Tordelli, the Lucchesi version of *tortelli,* is homemade ravioli. It's traditionally stuffed with meat and served with more meat sauce, but chefs creatively pair cheeses and vegetables, too.

Meat, not fish, is the star at most restaurants, especially steak, which is listed on menus as *filetto di manzo* (filet), *tagliata di manzo* (thin slices of grilled tenderloin), or the king of steaks, *bistecca alla fiorentina.* Order *al sangue* (rare), *medio* (medium rare), *cotto* (medium), or *ben cotto* (well). Anything more than *al sangue* is considered a travesty for steak connoisseurs.

Note that steaks (as well as fish) are often sold by weight, noted on menus as *s.q.* (according to quantity ordered) or *l'etto* (cost per 100 grams—250 grams is about an 8-ounce steak). *Buon appetito!*

& 19:30–22:15, closed Sun, reservations smart for dinner, Via Anfiteatro 7/9, tel. 0583-440-240).

Trattoria da Leo, a cousin of Vecchia Trattoria Buralli, packs in chatty locals for typical, cheap home-cooking in a hash-slingin' Mel's-diner atmosphere. This place is a high-energy winner...you know it's going to be good as soon as you step in. Arrive early or reserve in advance (€6 pastas, €10 *secondi,* daily 12:00–14:30 & 19:30–22:30, cash only, exit Piazza San Salvatore on Via Asili and take the first left to Via Tegrimi 1, tel. 0583-492-236).

Bella 'Mbriana focuses on doing one thing very well: turning out piping-hot, wood-fired pizzas to happy locals in a welcoming wood-paneled dining room. Order and pay at the counter, take a number, and they'll call you when your pizza's ready. Consider take-out to munch on the nearby walls. Prices range from €5 for your basic *Napolitano* to €8 for their specialty, with buffalo mozzarella and other gourmet ingredients (Wed–Mon 12:30–14:30 & 18:30–23:30, closed Tue, to the right as you face San Frediano Church, Via della Cavalerizza 29, tel. 0583-495-565).

Il Cuore Enogastronomia is a bustling delicatessen in the heart of Lucca, with ready-to-eat lasagna, saucy meatballs, grilled and roasted vegetables, vegetable soufflés, Tuscan bean soup, fruit salads, and more, sold by weight and dished up in disposable trays to go. Ask them to heat your order *(riscaldare)*. Picnic on nearby Piazza Napoleone. To accommodate curious traveling foodies on a budget who want to eat right there, they can assemble a €10 "Degustation plate"—point to direct the construction from among the array of tasty treats under the glass (Tue–Sun 9:30–19:30, closed Mon, Via del Battistero 2, tel. 0583-495-425).

Pizzeria da Felice is a little mom-and-pop hole-in-the-wall serving *cecina* (chickpea crepes) and slices of freshly baked pizza to throngs of snackers. Grab a *cecina* and a short glass of wine for €2.50 (Mon–Sat 10:00–20:30, closed Sun and 3 weeks in Aug, Via Buia 12, tel. 0583-494-986).

Connections

From Lucca by Train to: Florence (2/hr, 1.5 hrs, €5), **Pisa** (roughly 2/hr Mon–Sat, hourly on Sun, more with changes in Viareggio, 30 min, bus is better), **Milan** (2/hr except Sun, 4–5 hrs, transfer in Florence or Prato), **Rome** (2/hr except Sun, 4 hrs, change in Florence or Pisa).

From Lucca by Bus to Pisa: Direct buses from Lucca's Piazzale Verdi drop you right at the Leaning Tower, making Pisa an easy day trip (hourly, 30 min, €3). Even with a car, I'd opt for this much faster and cheaper option. For more on Pisa, see the Pisa chapters.

TUSCAN HILL TOWNS

Tuscany is rich in history, and proud locals will remind you that their ancestors, the Etruscans, were thriving long before anyone had heard of Julius Caesar. The region offers a delightful mix of scenic beauty and rich history...and a taste of the rustic Italian good life.

Many of the hill towns—so emblematic of Tuscany—trace their roots to Etruscan times (well before ancient Rome). Others date from the fall of Rome, when barbarian invasions chased lowland towns-folk to the hills, where they built fortified communities. The Middle Ages were formative times for many cities, when warring factions divided towns between those loyal to the pope (Guelphs) and the Holy Roman Emperor (Ghibellines). Cities developed monumental defensive walls and built great towers. Then, the Black Death swept through Tuscany in 1348 and devastated the region. The plague, plus the increasing dominance of Florence, turned many bustling cities into docile backwaters. Ironically, what was bad news in the 14th century is good news today: The hill towns enjoy a tourist-fueled affluence and retain a unique, medieval charm.

Tuscan towns are best enjoyed by adapting to the pace of the countryside. So, slow...down...and savor the delights that Tuscany offers. Spend the night if you can, as many hill towns are mobbed by day-trippers from Florence and Siena.

But how in Dante's name does a traveler choose from the liter-ally hundreds of Tuscan hill towns? I've listed some of my favorites in this chapter. The one(s) you visit will depend on your interests, time, and mode of transportation.

Multi-towered San Gimignano is a classic, but because it's such an easy hill town to visit (75-min bus ride from Florence), peak-season crowds can overwhelm the town's charms. For rustic vitality not trampled by tourist crowds, out-of-the-way Volterra is the clear winner. Wine aficionados head for Montalcino and

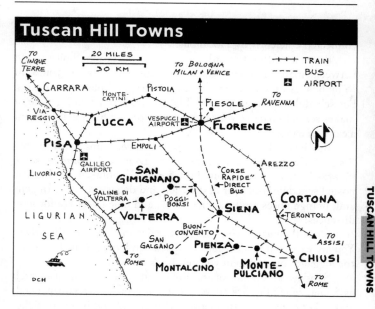

Tuscan Hill Towns

Montepulciano—each a happy gauntlet of wine shops and art galleries (Montepulciano being my favorite). Fans of architecture and urban design appreciate Pienza's well-planned streets and squares. Art-lovers and those enamored by Frances Mayes' memoir *(Under the Tuscan Sun)* make the pilgrimage to Cortona.

One of the greatest Tuscan treats—the food—varies wildly depending on where you are. The areas around Florence and Siena are famed for serving hearty "farmer food," but as you move west, dishes become lighter, based more on seafood and grains. Each town proudly boasts local specialties—ask for the *"specialità della città."* While Siena is the town that excels at sweets, you can find good local desserts anywhere (watch for the phrase *"fatta in casa,"* or homemade). Wine is good throughout Tuscany, with pleasing selections for both amateurs and connoisseurs. (See the "Wines in Tuscany" sidebar later in this chapter for a description of Tuscan wines.)

Getting Around Tuscany

Bigger destinations (such as Cortona) are doable by public transportation. Most hill towns are easier and more efficient to visit by car.

By Bus or Train

Traveling by public transportation is cheap and connects you with the locals. While trains link some of the towns, hill towns—being on hills—don't quite fit the railroad plan. Stations are likely to be in the valley a couple of miles from the town center, usually connected efficiently by a local bus.

Buses are often the only public-transportation choice to get between small hill towns. You can usually get anywhere you want to by bus, as long as you're not in a hurry, and plan ahead using bus schedules (pick up at local TIs). If you're pinched for time, it makes sense to narrow your focus to one or two hill towns, or rent a car to see more.

Buy bus tickets at newsstands or *tabacchi* shops (with the big *T* signs). Confirm the departure point *("Dov'è la fermata?")*—some piazzas have more than one bus stop, so double-check that the posted schedule lists your destination and departure time. In general, orange buses are local city buses, and blue buses are for long distances.

Once the bus arrives, confirm the destination with the driver. You are expected to stow big backpacks underneath the bus (open the luggage compartment yourself if it's closed).

Sundays and holidays are problematic; even from cities such as Siena, schedules are sparse, departing buses are jam-packed, and ticket offices are often closed. Plan ahead and buy your ticket in advance. Most travel agencies book bus and train tickets with little or no commission.

By Car

Exploring small-town Tuscany by car can be a great experience. But since a car is an expensive, worthless headache in Florence and Siena, wait to pick up your car until the last big city you visit (or pick it up at the nearest airport to avoid big-city traffic). Then use the car for lacing together the hill towns and exploring the countryside. For information on renting a car, see page 284.

Be warned that Italian drivers can be aggressive. They tailgate as if it were required. They pass where Americans are taught not to—on blind corners and just before tunnels. Roads have narrow shoulders or none at all. On roads too narrow for two vehicles, the larger one has the right-of-way. Fortunately, driving in the Tuscan countryside is less stressful than driving through Italy's urban areas, but you'll need to be on the alert nonetheless.

A good map and a semiskilled navigator are essential. Freeways (such as the toll autostrada and the non-toll *superstrada*) provide the fastest way to connect two points, but the smaller roads, including the super-scenic S-222 through the heart of the Chianti region (connecting Florence and Siena), are more rewarding. For more joyrides—from Siena to Montalcino, and from Montalcino to Montepulciano—see "Crete Senese Drives" on page 448.

Buy a big, detailed Tuscany road map (at a newsstand or gas station). Although roads are numbered on maps, actual road signs don't list route numbers. Instead, roads are indicated by blue signs with a city name on them (for example, if you want to take the road heading west out of Montepulciano—marked route S-146 on your map—you'd follow signs to Pienza, the next town along this route). The signs are inconsistent: They may direct you to the nearest big city or simply the next town along the route. If you end up on a truckers' route, you might see provocatively dressed women standing by the side of the road; they're not having car trouble.

Parking throughout Tuscany can be challenging. Some towns don't allow nonresidents to park in the city center, so you'll need to leave your car outside the walls and walk into town. Don't drive or park in any area with signs reading *Zona Traffico Limitato (ZTL)*—often above a red circle. Your license plate will be photographed and a hefty (€100-plus) ticket mailed to your home address in the US. If your hotel is within a *ZTL*, your hotelier can register your car as an authorized vehicle or direct you to parking outside the restricted zone.

Parking lots, indicated by big blue *P* signs, are usually free and plentiful outside city walls. In some towns, you can park on the street; nearby kiosks sell "pay and display" tickets. I'd advise, when possible, parking in guarded lots, which are worth the expense to reduce the threat of theft (no guarantees, though). Wherever you park, be sure that all of your valuables are out of sight and locked in the trunk, or even better, with you or in your room. Thieves easily recognize rental cars and assume they are filled with a tourist's gear.

Sleeping in Tuscany
Hotels, Rooms, and Apartments
Smaller towns offer few hotels to choose from. Prices are lower than in Florence, but a nice double will still run about €80, including breakfast. Many towns have an abundance of *affitacamere*, or rental rooms. This can be anything from a set of keys and a basic bed to a cozy B&B with your own Tuscan grandmother. TIs book rooms and apartments and have lists of each. Private rooms are generally a good budget option, but since they vary in quality, shop around to find the best value. It's always OK to ask to see the room before you commit. Apartments usually offer a couple of bedrooms, a sitting area, and a teensy *cucinetta*, typically stocked with dishes and flatware—a great value for families traveling together who'd rather cook than eat out all the time.

Wines in Tuscany

The region of Tuscany produces some of the most famous and tastiest wines in Italy. The characteristics of the soil, tempera-ture, and exposure make each wine unique to its area. Even if you don't often drink wine, try some in Tuscany.

Choosing a wine can be intimidating, but the Italian government tries to help you choose something decent, even if you're clueless. In general, wines are designated by one of four categories:

Vino da Tavola (table wine) is the lowest grade—drink this one with pizza. While inexpensive *vino della casa,* or "house wines," fall into this category, they can be decent. Many restau-rants, even modest ones, take pride in their house wine, bottling their own or working with local wineries.

Denominazione di Origine Controllata (DOC), a cut above table wine, is usually cheap, but can be surprisingly good. More than 700 wines have earned the DOC designation. You'll see plenty of DOC wines in Tuscany, since many come from the Chianti region, located between Florence and Siena.

Denominazione di Origine Controllata e Guarantita (DOCG) is the highest grade, and can be identified by the pink or green

Agriturismo

Agriturismo (agricultural tourism), or rural B&Bs, began in the 1980s as a way for small farmers to survive in a modern economy where, like in the US, so many are run out of business by giant agricultural corpo-rations. By renting rooms to travelers, farmers can remain on their land and continue to produce food. A peaceful home base for exploring the region, these rural Italian B&Bs are ideal

for those traveling by car—especially families.

It's wise to book several months in advance for high season (May–Sept). Weeklong stays are preferred in July and August, but shorter stays are possible off-season. In the winter, you might be charged extra for heat, so confirm the price ahead of time. Payment policies vary, but generally a 25 percent deposit is required (lost if label on the neck and the scary price tag on the shelf. Only 21 wines in Italy can be called DOCG. They're generally a good bet if you want a quality wine, but you don't know anything else about the winemaker.

A recently created category called **Indicazione Geografica Tipica** (IGT) is a broad group of wines that range from basic to some of Italy's best. It includes the "Super Tuscans"—wines that don't follow the strict "recipe" required for DOC or DOCG status, but that give local vintners more opportunity to be creative. Super Tuscans are made from a mix of international grapes (such as cabernet sauvignon) grown in Tuscany and aged in small oak barrels for only two years. The result is a lively full-bodied wine that dances all over your head...and is worth the steep price.

Visit a Tuscan *enoteca* (wine bar) and sample some of these wines side-by-side to figure out what you like—and what suits your pocketbook.

Words to Live by, or...How to Describe Wine in Italian

dry	*secco*	SAY-koh
sweet	*dolce*	DOHL-chay
earthy	*terroso*	tay-ROH-zoh
fruity	*fruttoso*	froo-TOH-zoh
full-bodied	*corposo*	kor-POH-zoh
elegant	*elegante*	ay-lay-GAHN-tay

you cancel), and the balance is due one month before arrival.

As the name implies, *agriturismi* are in the countryside, although some are located within a mile of town. Most are family-run and vary wildly in quality. Some properties are rustic, while others are downright luxurious, offering amenities such as swimming pools and riding stables. The rooms are usually clean and comfortable. Breakfast is often included, and *mezza pensione* (half-pension, which in this case, means a home-cooked dinner) might be built into the price whether you want it or not. Most places serve tasty homegrown food; some are vegetarian or organic, others are gourmet. Kitchenettes are often available to cook up your own feast.

To qualify officially as an *agriturismo,* the farm must still generate more money from its farm activities, thereby insuring that the land is worked and preserved.

Some farmhouse B&Bs are simply that, and are not really working farms, though are still fine places to stay. But if you want the real thing, make sure the owners call their place an *agriturismo.*

Tips for Enjoying an *Agriturismo* Farmhouse Stay

- To sleep cheap, avoid peak season. Rental prices follow the old rule of supply and demand. For instance, a Tuscan farmhouse that rents for as much as $2,000 a week at peak times can go for as little as $700 in late September or October.

- Make sure your trip fits their requirements. Many properties rent on a traditional Saturday-to-Saturday time period. You might be unable to rent for a different or shorter time, especially during peak season.

- If you want amenities, be willing to pay more. A private pool can add substantially to the cost but, at the height of summer, could be worth every extra euro.

- Consider renting a rural apartment rather than an entire villa or farmhouse. Often the owners have renovated an original rambling farmhouse or medieval estate into a series of well-constructed apartments with private kitchens, bathrooms, living areas, and outdoor terraces. They usually share a common pool.

- You will need private transportation, such as a rental car, to fully enjoy—or even reach—your accommodations.

- To make the most of your time, ask an expert—the owner—for suggestions on local restaurants, sights, and activities. Make sure you know how to operate the appliances.

- Slow down. One of the joys of staying for at least a week in one location is you can develop a true *dolce far niente* (sweetness of doing nothing) attitude. If it rains, grab a book from the in-house library and curl up on the sofa.

- While your time in the countryside may not be action-packed, staying put in one spot leaves you open to the unexpected pleasures that come when you just let the days unwind without a plan.

In this chapter, I've listed some *agriturismi* and farmhouses under the towns that they're nearest, but there are many, many more. Local TIs can give you a list of farms in their area, and many *agriturismi* now have their own websites. For a sampling, visit www.agriturismoitaly.it or do a Web search for *agriturismo*. One booking agency among many is Farm Holidays in Tuscany (closed Sat–Sun, tel. 0564-417-418, www.byfarmholidays.com, info@byfarmholidays.com).

North Tuscany

San Gimignano

The epitome of a Tuscan hill town, with 14 medieval towers still standing (out of an original 60 or so), San Gimignano (sahn jee-meen-YAH-noh) is a per-fectly preserved tourist trap. There are no impor-tant interiors to sightsee, and the town is packed with crass commercial-ism. The locals seem cor-rupted by the easy money of tourism, and most

of the rustic is faux. The fact that this small town supports two torture museums is a comment on the caliber of the masses who choose to visit. But San Gimignano is so easy to reach and visually so beautiful that it remains a good stop. I find the place enchanting at night.

In the 13th century, back in the days of Romeo and Juliet, feuding noble families ran the towns. They'd periodically battle things out from the protection of their respective family towers. Pointy skylines, like San Gimignano's, were the norm in medieval Tuscany.

San Gimignano's cuisine is mostly what you might find in Siena—typical Tuscan home cooking. *Cinghiale* (cheeng-GAH-lay, wild boar) is served in almost every way: stews, soups, cutlets, and, my favorite, as salami. Most shops will give you a sample before you commit to buying. The city is well known for having some of the best saffron in Italy; look for it on menus at finer restaurants (it's fairly expensive). Although Tuscany is normally a red-wine region, the most famous Tuscan white wine comes from here: the inexpensive, light and fruity Vernaccia di San Gimignano. Look for the green "DOCG" label around the neck for the best quality (see "Wines in Tuscany" sidebar earlier in this chapter).

Orientation to San Gimignano

While the basic three-star sight here is the town of San Gimignano itself, there are a few worthwhile stops. From the town gate, head straight up the traffic-free town's cobbled main drag to Piazza della Cisterna (with its 13th-century well). The town sights cluster around the adjoining Piazza del Duomo.

TUSCAN HILL TOWNS

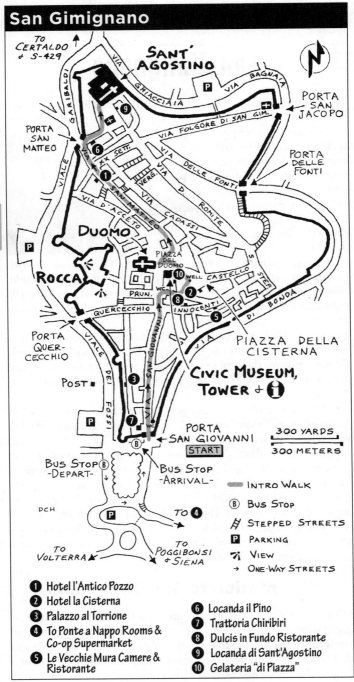

San Gimignano

300 YARDS
300 METERS

- 🟥🟥 INTRO WALK
- ⓑ BUS STOP
- ⧣ STEPPED STREETS
- 🄿 PARKING
- 🟄 VIEW
- → ONE-WAY STREETS

1. Hotel l'Antico Pozzo
2. Hotel la Cisterna
3. Palazzo al Torrione
4. To Ponte a Nappo Rooms & Co-op Supermarket
5. Le Vecchie Mura Camere & Ristorante
6. Locanda il Pino
7. Trattoria Chiribiri
8. Dulcis in Fundo Ristorante
9. Locanda di Sant'Agostino
10. Gelateria "di Piazza"

Tourist Information: The helpful TI is in the old center on Piazza del Duomo (daily March–Oct 9:00–13:00 & 15:00–19:00, Nov–Feb 9:00–13:00 & 14:00–18:00, free maps, sells bus tickets, books rooms, tel. 0577-940-008, www.sangimignano.com). The TI rents **audioguides** (€5 for meaty, easy-to-share 2-hour tour, takes you into Civic Museum but focuses mostly on exteriors and architecture).

The town offers a two-hour **guided walk** in English and Italian several days a week (April–Oct Sat–Sun at 11:00, €20; includes admission to Civic Museum and Tower; pay and meet at TI).

Arrival in San Gimignano: The bus stops at the main town gate, Porta San Giovanni. There's no baggage storage anywhere in town, so you're better off leaving your bags in Siena or Florence. You can't drive within the walled town. There are three pay lots a short walk outside the walls; the handiest is Parcheggio Montemaggio, just outside Porta San Giovanni. The one below the roundabout and Co-op supermarket is least expensive (€1/hr, €6/day, Giubileo 1).

Helpful Hints: Thursday is market day on Piazza del Duomo (8:00–13:00), but for local merchants, every day is a sales frenzy. A public WC is just off Piazza della Cisterna (€0.50), and another is around the corner from Porta San Giovanni. A little electric shuttle bus does its laps all day from Porta San Giovanni to Piazza della Cisterna to Porta San Matteo (€0.50, 2/hr, buy ticket from TI, *tabacchi* shop, or from coin-operated machine on bus).

Self-Guided Walk

Welcome to San Gimignano

This quick walking tour will take you across town from the bus stop at Porta San Giovanni through the town's main squares to the Duomo, and on to the Sant'Agostino Church.

• Start, as most tourists do, at the Porta San Giovanni gate at the bottom end of town.

Porta San Giovanni: San Gimignano lies about 25 miles from both Siena and Florence, a good stop for pilgrims en route to those cities, and on a naturally fortified hilltop that encouraged settlement. The town's walls were built in the 13th century, with gates like this that helped regulate who came and went. Today, modern posts keep out all but service and emergency vehicles. The small square just outside the gate features a memorial to the town's WWII dead. Follow the pilgrims' route (and flood of modern tourists) through the gate and up the main drag.

About 100 yards up, on the right, is a pilgrims' shelter (12th-century, Pisan Romanesque). The Maltese cross indicates that this was built by the Knights of Malta. It was one of 11 such shelters in town. Today, only the wall of this shelter remains.

• *Carry on, up to the town's central Piazza della Cisterna. Sit on the steps of the well.*

Piazza della Cisterna: The piazza is named for the cistern that is served by the old well standing in the center of this square.
A clever system of pipes drained rainwater from the nearby rooftops into the underground cistern. This square has been the center of the town since the ninth century. Turn in a slow circle and observe the commotion of rustic-yet-proud facades crowding in a tight huddle around the well. Imagine  this square in pilgrimage times, lined by inns and taverns for the town's guests. Now finger the grooves in the lip of the well and imagine generations of maids and children fetching water. Each Thursday, the square fills with a market—as it has for more than a thousand years.

• *Notice San Gimignano's famous towers.*

The Towers: Of the original 60 or so towers, only 14 survive. Before effective city walls were developed, rich people fortified  their own homes with these towers: They provided a handy refuge when ruffians and rival city-states were sacking the town. These towers became a standard part of medieval skylines. Even after town walls were built, the towers continued to rise—now to fortify noble families feuding within a town (Montague and Capulet–style).

In the 14th century, San Gimignano's good times turned very bad. In the year 1300, about 13,000 people lived within the walls. Then in 1348, a six-month plague decimated the population, leaving the once-mighty town with barely 4,000 survivors. Once fiercely independent, now crushed and demoralized, San Gimignano came under Florence's control and was forced to tear down its towers. (The Banca Toscana building occupies the remains of one such toppled tower.) And, to add injury to injury, Florence redirected the vital trade route away from San Gimignano. The town never recovered, and poverty left it in a 14th-century architectural time warp. That well-preserved cityscape, ironically, is responsible for the town's prosperity today.

• *From the well, walk 30 yards uphill to the adjoining square with the cathedral.*

Piazza del Duomo: The square faces the former cathedral. The twin towers to the right are 10th-century, among the first in

town. The stubby tower opposite the church is typical of a merchant's tower: main door on ground floor, warehouse upstairs, holes to hold beams that once supported wooden balconies and exterior staircases, heavy stone on the first floor, cheaper and lighter brick for upper stories.

• *On the piazza are the Civic Museum and Tower, worth checking out (see "Sights in San Gimignano," next page). You'll also see the...*

Duomo (or Collegiata): Walk inside San Gimignano's Romanesque cathedral. Sienese Gothic art (14th century) lines the nave with parallel themes, Old Testament on the left and New Testament on the right. (For example: the suffering of Job opposite the suffering of Jesus, Creation facing the Annunciation, and the birth of Adam facing the Nativity.) This is a classic use of art to teach. Study the fine Creation series (top left). Many scenes are portrayed with a local 14th-century "slice of life" setting, to help lay townspeople relate to Jesus—in the same way that many white Christians are more comfortable thinking of Jesus as Caucasian (€3.50, €5.50 combo-ticket includes mediocre Religious Art Museum, daily April–Oct 9:30–19:30, Nov–March 9:30–17:00).

From the church, hike uphill (passing the church on your left) following signs to *Rocca e Parco di Montestaffoli.* Keep walking until you enter a peaceful hilltop park and olive grove within the shell of a 14th-century fortress. On the far side, a few steps take you to the top of a little tower (free) for the best views of San Gimignano's skyline; the far end of town and the Sant'Agostino Church (where this walk ends); and a commanding 360-degree view of the Tuscan countryside. San Gimignano is surrounded by olives, grapes, cypress trees, and—in the Middle Ages—lots of wild dangers. Back then, farmers lived inside the walls and were thankful for the protection.

• *Return to the bottom of Piazza del Duomo, turn left, and continue your walk across town, cutting under the double arch (from the town's first wall). In around 1200 this defined the end of town. The Church of San Bartolo stood just outside the wall. The Maltese cross indicates that it likely served as a hostel for pilgrims. Continuing on down Via San Matteo, you pass a fascinating array of stone facades from the 13th and 14th centuries—now a happy cancan of wine shops and galleries. Eventually you reach...*

Sant'Agostino Church: This tranquil church, at the opposite end of town (built by the Augustinians who arrived in 1260), has fewer crowds and more soul. Behind the altar, a lovely fresco cycle by Benozzo Gozzoli (who painted the exquisite Chapel of the Magi in the Medici-Riccardi Palace in Florence) tells of the life of St. Augustine, a North African monk who preached simplicity. The kind, English-speaking friars (from Britain and the US) are happy to tell you about their church and way of life, and also have Mass in English on Sundays at 11:00. Pace the tranquil cloister before heading back into the tourist mobs (free, €0.50 lights the frescoes, daily April–Oct 7:00–12:00 & 15:00–19:00, until 18:00 Nov–March). Their fine little shop, with books on the church and its art, is worth a look.

Sights in San Gimignano

Civic Museum and Tower (Museo Civico and Torre Grossa)—This small, fun museum, consisting of just three unfurnished rooms and a tower, is inside City Hall (Palazzo Comunale). The main room, called Sala di Consiglio (a.k.a. Danti Hall), is covered in festive frescoes, including the *Maestà* by Lippo Memmi. This virtual copy of Simone Martini's *Maestà* in Siena proves that Memmi doesn't have quite the same talent as his famous brother-in-law. Upstairs, the Pinacoteca displays a classy little painting collection, with a 1422 altarpiece by Taddeo di Bartolo honoring St. Gimignano. You can see the saint, with the town—bristling with towers—in his hands, surrounded by events from his life.

As you exit, be sure to stop by the Mayor's Room (Camera del Podesta). Frescoed in 1310 by Memmo di Filippuccio, it offers an intimate and candid peek into the 14th century. The theme: profane love. As you enter, look to the left corner where a young man is ready to experience the world. He hits his parents up for a bag of money and is free. Almost immediately he's entrapped by two prostitutes, who lead him into a tent where he loses his money (above the window), is turned out, and is beaten. Above the door from left to right you see a parade of better choices: marriage, the cradle of love, the bride led to the groom's house, and newlyweds bathing together and retiring happily to their bed.

The highlight for most visitors is a chance to climb the **Tower** (Torre Grossa). The city's tallest tower, 200 feet and 218 steps up, rewards those who climb it with a commanding view. You leave via a delightful stony loggia and court-

yard out back (€5, includes museum and tower, audioguide-€2, daily March–Oct 9:30–19:00, Nov–Feb 10:00–17:30, Piazza del Duomo).

Sleeping in San Gimignano

Although the town is a zoo during the daytime, locals outnumber tourists when evening comes, and San Gimignano becomes peaceful and enjoyable. Drivers can load/unload near their hotels, then park outside the walls in recommended lots. Hotel websites provide instructions.

$$$ Hotel l'Antico Pozzo is an elegantly restored, 15th-century townhouse with 18 tranquil, comfortable rooms, a peaceful interior courtyard terrace, and an elite air (Db-€140 and higher depending on the room, air-con, elevator, near Porta San Matteo at Via San Matteo 87, tel. 0577-942-014, fax 0577-942-117, www.anticopozzo .com).

$$$ Hotel la Cisterna, right on Piazza della Cisterna, offers 49 predictable rooms, some with panoramic view terraces (Sb-€72, Db-€100, Db with view-€118, Db with view terrace-€135, 10 percent discount with this book, buffet breakfast, air-con, elevator, Wi-Fi, good restaurant with great view, closed Jan–Feb, Piazza della Cisterna 23, tel. 0577-940-328, fax 0577-942-080, www .hotelcisterna.it, info@hotelcisterna.it, Alessio).

$$$ Palazzo al Torrione, just inside Porta San Giovanni, is quiet and handy, and generally better than most hotels, though they don't have a full-time reception. Their 10 modern rooms are spacious and tastefully appointed (Db-€80, terrace Db–€100, Tb-€98, terrace Tb–€113, family suite, 10 percent discount with this book, breakfast-€5, communal kitchen, parking-€5, inside and left of gate at Via Berignano 76; operated from *tabacchi* shop 2 blocks away, on the main drag at Via San Giovanni 59; tel. 0577-940-480, mobile 338-938-1656, fax 0577-955-605, www.palazzoaltorrione.com, palazzoaltorrione@palazzoaltorrione.com, Vanna and Francesco).

$$ Ponte a Nappo, run by enterprising Carla Rossi (who doesn't speak English) and her son Francesco (who does), has seven comfortable rooms and two apartments in a kid-friendly farmhouse. Located a long half-mile below town, this place has killer views (Db-€100, 2–6 person apartment-€120–220, air-con extra, free Wi-Fi, parking, pool, free loaner bikes, 15-min walk or 5-min drive from Porta San Giovanni, tel. 0577-955-041, mobile 349-882-1565, fax 0577-941-268, www.accommodation-sangimignano .it, info@rossicarla.it). A picnic dinner—lounging on their comfy garden furniture as the sun sets—is good Tuscan living. About 100 yards below the monument square at Porta San Giovanni, find Via Vecchia (not left or right, but down a tiny road) and follow it down

Sleep Code

(€1 = about $1.40, country code: 39)

S = Single, **D** = Double/Twin, **T** = Triple, **Q** = Quad, **b** = bathroom, **s** = shower only. Unless otherwise noted, credit cards are accepted and breakfast is included (but usually optional). English is generally spoken, but I've noted exceptions.

To help you sort easily through these listings, I've divided the rooms into three categories based on the price for a standard double room with bath:

$$$ Higher Priced—Most rooms €100 or more.

$$ Moderately Priced—Most rooms between €70–100.

$ Lower Priced—Most rooms €70 or less.

a dirt road for five minutes by car. They also rent a dozen or so rooms and apartments in town (each described on their website).

$ Le Vecchie Mura Camere offers three good rooms above their restaurant in the old town (Db-€60, air-con, no breakfast, Via Piandornella 15, tel. 0577-940-270, www.vecchiemura.it, info @vecchiemura.it, Bagnai family).

$ Locanda il Pino is tiny (five rooms), but has a big living room. It's dank but super-clean, quiet, and run by English-speaking Elena and her family above their elegant restaurant just inside Porta San Matteo (Db-€55, no breakfast, easy parking just outside the gate, Via Cellolese 4, tel. 0577-940-415, locanda @ristoranteilpino.it). While far from the bus stop, this is a good value for those with a car.

Eating in San Gimignano

Trattoria Chiribiri, just inside Porta San Giovanni, serves homemade pastas and desserts at remarkably fair prices. It's petite with tight seating and, while hot in the summer, is a fine value (daily 11:00–23:00, Piazza della Madonna 1, tel. 0577-941-948).

Dulcis in Fundo Ristorante, small and family-run, proudly serves local cuisine with a modern twist, gourmet presentation, and slow food values in a jazz ambience (€12 pastas, €15 *secondi,* meals served from 12:30 and 19:30, closed Wed, Vicolo degli Innocenti 21, tel. 0577-941-919).

Le Vecchie Mura Ristorante is my choice for good service, great prices, tasty home-cooking, and the ultimate view. It's romantic indoors or out. They have a dressy, modern interior where you can dine with a view of the busy stainless-steel kitchen under rustic vaults, but I'd come for the incredible cliffside garden terrace. Cliffside tables are worth reserving in advance by calling or dropping by: Ask for "front view" (€8 pastas, €12 *secondi,* open only for dinner from 18:00, last order at 22:00, closed Tue, Via Piandornella 15, tel. 0577-940-270, Bagnai family).

Locanda di Sant'Agostino spills out onto the peaceful square, facing Sant'Agostino Church. It's cheap and cheery, serving lunch and dinner daily—a great place for salads, pizza, or a rustic dish of pasta. Dripping with wheat stalks and atmosphere on the inside, there's shady on-the-square seating outside (daily 11:00–22:00, closed Jan, Piazza Sant'Agostino 15, tel. 0577-943-141, Genziana and sons).

Picnics: The big, modern **Co-op supermarket** sells all you need for a nice spread (Mon–Sat 8:30–20:00, closed Sun, at parking lot below Porta San Giovanni). Or browse the little shops guarded by wild boar heads within the town walls; they sell boar meat *(cinghiale).* Pick up 100 grams (about a quarter pound) of boar, cheese, bread, and wine and enjoy a picnic in the garden at the Rocca or the park outside Porta San Giovanni. To cap the evening and sweeten your late-night city stroll, stop by **Gelateria "di Piazza"** on Piazza della Cisterna (at #4).

Connections

Bus tickets are sold at the bar just inside the town gate or at the TI.

From San Gimignano by Bus to: Florence (hourly, 1.25–2 hrs, change in Poggibonsi, less on Sat–Sun, €6), **Siena** (8 direct/ day, 1.25 hrs), **Volterra** (4/day Mon–Sat; on Sun only 1/day— usually crowded—with no return to San Gimignano; 2 hrs, change in Colle Val d'Elsa).

By Car: San Gimignano is an easy 45-minute drive from Florence (take the A1 exit marked *Firenze Certosa,* then a right past tollbooth following *Siena per 4 corsie* sign; exit the freeway at Poggibonsi). From San Gimignano, it's a scenic and windy half-hour drive to Volterra.

Volterra

Encircled by impressive walls and topped with a grand fortress, Volterra sits high above the rich farmland. More than 2,000 years ago, Volterra was one of the most important Etruscan cities, a city much larger than the one we see today. Greek-trained Etruscan artists worked here, leaving a significant stash of art, particularly funerary urns. Eventually Volterra was absorbed into the Roman

Empire, and for centuries it was an independent city-state. Volterra fought bitterly against the Florentines, but like many Tuscan towns, it lost in the end and was given a fortress atop the city to "protect" its citizens.

Unlike other famous towns in Tuscany, Volterra feels not cutesy or touristy...but real, vibrant, and almost oblivious to the allure of the tourist dollar. A refreshing break from its more commercial neighbors, it's my favorite small town in Tuscany.

Orientation to Volterra

Compact and walkable, the city stretches out from the pleasant Piazza dei Priori to the old city gates.

Tourist Information: The helpful TI is on the main square, at Piazza dei Priori 19 (daily 10:00–13:00 & 14:00–18:00, tel. 0588-87257). The TI's excellent €5 audioguide narrates 20 stops (2-for-1 discount on audioguides with this book).

Arrival in Volterra: Buses stop at Piazza Martiri della Libertà in the town center. Drivers will find the town ringed with easy numbered parking lots (#2 is free, #3 is most likely to have a place but comes with a steeper hike into town). The most central lots are the pay lots at Porta Fiorentina and underground at Piazza Martiri della Libertà (€1.50/hr or €11/24 hrs).

Helpful Hints

Market Day: Market day is Saturday morning near the Roman Theater (8:00–13:00, in Piazza dei Priori in winter).

Festivals: Volterra's Medieval Festival takes place the third Sunday of August (Aug 15 in 2010). Fall is a popular time for food festivals—check with the TI for dates and events planned.

Internet Access: Web & Wine has a few terminals and fine wine by the glass (€3/hr, no minimum, summer daily 9:30–1:00 in the morning, off-season closed Thu, Via Porta all'Arco 11–15, tel. 0588-81531, www.webandwine.com, Lallo speaks English). **Enjoy Café** has a couple of terminals in their basement (daily 6:30–23:00, Piazza dei Martiri 3, tel. 0588-80530).

Local Guide: American **Annie Adair** married into the local community, organizes American marriages in Tuscany, is an excellent private guide, and can organize wine and food tours (€105/half-day, €210/day, tel. 0588-87774, mobile 347-143-5004, www.tuscantour.com, info@tuscantour.com).

Sights in Volterra

▲▲Guided Volterra Walk—Annie Adair and her colleagues offer a great one-hour introductory English-only walking tour of Volterra for €5. The walk touches on Volterra's Etruscan, Roman, and medieval history, as well as the contemporary cultural scene (April–Sept daily, rain or shine, at 18:00; depart from Piazza Martiri della Libertà, at the bus terminal above the underground parking lot; no need to reserve—just show up, they need a minimum of 4 people—or €20—to make the tour go, www .volterrawalkingtour.com or www.tuscantour.com, info@volterra walkingtour.com). There's no better way to spend €5 and one hour in this city.

▲▲Self-Guided Historic Town Walk—You can easily lace the town's top sights and my descriptions together to make your own handy little town walk. Here's the spine of the walk (all described in this order below): Start with the Etruscan Arch, browse up what I call "Artisan Lane," follow my tour of Via Matteotti, side-trip to the main square and Duomo, head over to the Etruscan Museum and Alabaster Workshop, and finish with a drink under all the bras with Bruno and Lucio at La Vena di Vino. The town's other sights are easily grafted onto this route.

▲"Porta all'Arco" Etruscan Arch—Volterra's most famous sight is its Etruscan arch, built of massive, volcanic *tuff* stones

in the fourth century B.C. (For more information on tuff, see the sidebar on page 410). Volterra's original wall was four miles around—twice the size of the wall that encircles it today. With 25,000 people, Volterra was a key Etruscan trade center—one of 12 leading towns that made up the Etruscan *Dodecapolis* (a league of Etruscan cities). The three seriously eroded heads, dating from the first century B.C., show what happens when you leave something outside for 2,000 years. The newer stones are part of the 13th-century city wall, which incorporated parts of the much older Etruscan wall.

A plaque just outside remembers June 30, 1944. That night, Nazi forces were planning to blow up the arch to slow the Allied advance. To save their treasured landmark, Volterrans ripped up the stones that pave Via Porta all'Arco and plugged the gate, managing to convince the Nazi commander that there was no need to blow up the arch. Today, all the stones are back in their places, and, like silent heroes, they welcome you through the oldest standing

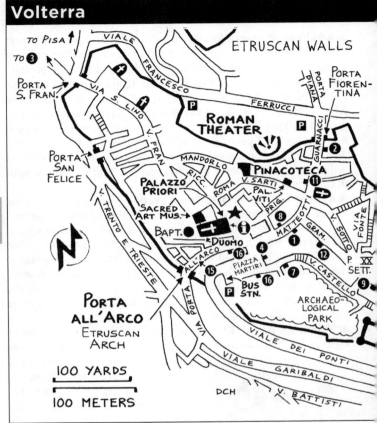

Volterra

TO PISA
TO ③
VIALE FRANCESCO
ETRUSCAN WALLS
PORTA S. FRAN.
VIA S. LINO
PORTA DIANA
PORTA FIORENTINA
FERRUCCI
ROMAN THEATER
GUARNACCI
PORTA SAN FELICE
VIA S. FRAN.
MANDORLO
RICC.
ROMA
V. SARTI
PINACOTECA ⑪
⓫
PALAZZO PRIORI
PAL. VITI PRIG.
⑧
MATTEOTTI
GRAM.
V. SOTTO
VIA FONTE
SACRED ART MUS.
BAPT. ⊕
DUOMO
④
①
⑯
②
V. TRENTO E TRIESTE
PORTA ALL'ARCO
⑯
PIAZZA MARTIRI
⑮
⑦
V. CASTELLO
⑫
P. XX SETT.
⑨
BUS STN.
⑯
ARCHAEOLOGICAL PARK
PORTA ALL'ARCO ETRUSCAN ARCH
VIALE DEI PONTI
VIALE GARIBALDI
DCH
V. BATTISTI

100 YARDS
100 METERS

Etruscan gate into Volterra. Locals claim this as the only surviving round arch of the Etruscan age, and believe this is where Romans got the idea for using a keystone in their arches.

Artisan Lane—Via Porta all'Arco (which leads to and from the Etruscan arch) is lined with interesting shops featuring the work of artisans and producers. Because of its alabaster heritage, Volterra attracted artisans and artists, who brought with them a rich variety of crafts (shops generally open Mon–Sat 10:00–13:00 & 16:00–19:00, closed Sun; the TI produces a free booklet called *Handicraft in Volterra*).

From the Etruscan Arch, browse your way up the hill, checking out these shops (listed from bottom to top): a co-op of producers of cheese, salami, and oil, letting you buy direct at farm prices (#52); alabaster shops (#57 and #45); book bindery and papery (#26); jewelry (#25); etchings and silk screening (#23); leather (#16); Web & Wine (Internet access; #11–15); and bronze work (#6).

🔭 VIEW
P PARKING
★ PIAZZA DEI PRIORI
||||| STAIRS

1 Albergo Etruria
2 Hotel La Locanda
3 To Albergo Villa Nencini
4 Albergo Nazionale
5 Seminario Vescovile Sant'Andrea
6 To Volterra Youth Hostel & Trattoria da Bado
7 Ristorante Enoteca del Duca
8 La Vecchia Lira
9 Ristorante Il Sacco Fiorentino
10 La Vena di Vino Wine Bar (Wine Tasting with Bruno & Lucio)
11 Ombra della Sera & Pizzeria Tavernetta
12 DeSpar Market
13 Alab'Arte Alabaster Showroom
14 Alab'Arte Alabaster Workshop
15 "Artisan Lane"
16 Internet Cafés (2)

▲**Via Matteotti**—The town's main drag, named after the popular Socialist leader killed by the Fascists in 1924, provides a good cultural scavenger hunt. The street starts 30 yards from Palazzo dei Priori (City Hall and cathedral, described later in this chapter).

At #1, there's a typical Italian bank security door. (Step in and say, "Beam me up, Scotty.") Look up and all around. Find the medieval griffin torch holder—symbol of Volterra—and imagine it holding a lit torch. The pharmacy sports the symbol of its medieval guild. As you head down Via Matteotti, notice how the doors show centuries of refitting work.

At #2, look up and imagine heavy beams cantilevered out, supporting extra wooden rooms, and balconies crowding out over the street. Throughout Tuscany, today's stark and stony old building fronts once supported a tangle of wooden extensions. Doors that once led to these extra rooms are now partially bricked up to make windows. Contemplate urban density in the 14th century,

Italy Is Made of Tuff Stuff

Tuff is a light-colored volcanic rock that is common in Italy. A part of Tuscany is even called the "Tuff Area." The seven hills of Rome are made of tuff, and quarried blocks of this stone can be seen in the Colosseum, Pantheon, and Castel Sant'Angelo. Just outside of Rome, the catacombs were carved from tuff. Sorrento rises above the sea on a tuff outcrop. Orvieto, Civita di Bagnoregio (pictured), and many other hill towns perch on bluffs of tuff.

The Italian word for tuff is *tufo*. Italy's early inhabitants, including the Etruscans and Romans, carved caves, tunnels, burial niches, and even roads out of tuff. Blocks of this rock (called *tufi*) were quarried to make houses and walls. Tuff is soft and easy to carve when it's first exposed to air, but hardens later, which makes it a good building stone.

Italy's tuff-producing volcanoes resulted from a lot of tectonic-plate bumping and grinding. This violent geologic history is reflected in Italy's volcanoes, like Vesuvius and Etna, and earthquakes such as the 2009 quake in the L'Aquila area northeast of Rome.

Tuff is actually just a big hardened pile of old volcanic ash. When volcanoes hold magma that contains a lot of water, they erupt explosively (think heat + water = steam = POW!). The exploded rock material gets blasted out as hot volcanic ash, which settles on the surrounding landscape, piles up, and over time welds together into the rock called tuff.

So when you're visiting an area in Italy of ancient caves or catacombs built out of this material, you'll know that at least once (and maybe more) upon a time, it was a site of a lot of volcanic activity.

before the plague thinned out the population. Be careful: There's a wild boar (a local delicacy) at #10.

At #12, notice how the typical palace, once the home of a single rich family, is now occupied by many middle-class families (judging from the line of doorbells). After the social revolution in the 18th century and the rise of the middle class, former palaces were condominium-ized. Even so, like in *Dr. Zhivago*, the original family still lives here. Apartment #1 is the home of Count Guidi.

At #16, pop in to an alabaster showroom. Alabaster, mined nearby, has long been a big industry here. Volterra alabaster—

softer and more porous than marble—was sliced thin to serve as windows for Italy's medieval churches.

At #19, La Vecchia Lira is a lively cafeteria (listed in "Eating in Volterra," later in this section). The Bar L'Incontro across the street is a favorite for homemade gelato and pastries.

Across the way, up Vicolo delle Prigioni, is a fun bakery *(panificio)*. They're happy to sell small quantities if you want to try the local *cantuccini* (almond biscotti) or munch a cannoli.

At #51, a bit of Etruscan wall is artfully used to display more alabaster art. And #56B is the alabaster art gallery of Paolo Sabatini.

Locals gather early each evening at #57 for the best cocktails in town—served with free munchies. The cinema is across the street. Movies in Italy are rarely in *versione originale*. Italians are used to getting their movies dubbed into Italian.

At #66, the end of the street is marked by another Tuscan tower. This noble house has a ground floor with no interior access to the safe upper floors. Rope ladders were used to get upstairs. The tiny door was wide enough to let in your skinny friends...but definitely not anyone wearing armor and carrying big weapons.

Across the street stands the ancient Church of St. Michael. After long years of barbarian chaos, the Lombards moved in from the north and asserted law and order in places like Volterra. That generally included building a Christian church on the old Roman forum to symbolically claim and tame the center of town. The church standing here today is Romanesque, dating from the 12th century. Find the crude little guys under its eaves—they've been making faces at the passing crowds for 800 years.

Duomo—A common arrangement in the Middle Ages was for the church to face the baptistery (you couldn't enter the church until you were baptized)...and for the hospital to face the cemetery. All of these overlooked the same square. That's how it is in Pisa. And that's how it is here.

This 12th-century church is not as elaborate as its cousin in Pisa, but the simple facade and central nave flanked by monolithic stone columns are beautiful examples of the Pisan Romanesque style. The chapel to the left of the entry has painted terra-cotta statue groups. The interior was decorated mostly in the late 16th century, during Florentine rule under the Medici family. You'll see a lot of the Medici coat of arms (with the six pills, representing the family's first trade—as doctors, or *medici*). The 12th-century marble pulpit is beautifully carved. All of the apostles are together except Judas, who's under the table with the evil dragon (his name is the only one not carved onto the relief).

Just before the pulpit (in the Rosary Chapel, on the left), check out the *Annunciation* by Fra Bartolomeo (who was a student of Fra Angelico and painted this in 1497). Bartolomeo delicately gives worshippers a way to see Mary "conceived by the Holy Spirit." Note the vibrant colors, exaggerated perspective, and Mary's *contrapposto* pose—all attributes of the Renaissance.

To the right of the main altar is a dreamy painted-and-gilded-wood *Deposition* (Jesus being taken down from the cross), restored to its original form. Painted in 1228, a generation before Giotto, it shows emotion and motion way ahead of its time.

The glowing windows in the transept and behind the altar are sheets of alabaster. These, along with the recorded Gregorian chants, add to the church's wonderful ambience (free, daily 8:00–12:30 & 15:00–17:00).

Sacred Art Museum—This humble four-room museum collects sacred art from deconsecrated churches and small, unguarded churches from nearby villages (€8 combo-ticket includes Etruscan Museum and Pinacoteca, daily 9:00–13:00 & 15:00–18:00, morning only in winter, well-explained in English, next to the Duomo at Via Roma 1).

▲▲Etruscan Museum (Museo Etrusco Guarnacci)—Filled top to bottom with rare Etruscan artifacts, this museum—even with few English explanations and its dusty, almost neglectful, old-school style—makes it easy to appreciate how advanced this pre-Roman culture was.

The collection starts with pre-Etruscan Villanovian artifacts (c. 1500 B.C.), but its highlight is a seemingly endless collection of Etruscan funerary urns (designed to contain the ashes of cremated loved ones).

Each urn is tenderly carved with a unique scene, offering a peek into the still-mysterious Etruscan society. While contemporaries of the Greeks, the Etruscans were more libertine. Their religion was less demanding, and their women were a respected part of both the social and public spheres. Women and men alike are depicted lounging on Etruscan urns. While they seem to be just hanging out, the  lounging dead were actually offering the gods a banquet—in order to gain their favor in the transition to the next life. The outcome of the banquet had eternal consequences.

On urns dating from the seventh to the first century B.C., the dearly departed are often depicted holding scrolls, blank wax tablets (symbolizing blank new lives in the next world), and libation cups—offering wine to the gods. Realistic scenes show the fabled horseback-and-carriage ride to the underworld, where the dead are greeted by Caron, with his hammer and pointy ears. While the finer urns are carved of alabaster, most are made of volcanic tuff. Most lids are mismatched—casualties of reckless 18th- and 19th-century archaeology. Look at the faces, and imagine the lives they lived and the loved ones they left behind.

On the top floor is a re-created grave site, with several urns and artifacts that would have been buried with the deceased. Some of these were funeral dowry (called *corredo*) that the dead would pack along. You'll see artifacts such as mirrors, coins, hardware for vases, votive statues, pots, pans, and jewelry.

Fans of Alberto Giacometti will be amazed at how the tall, skinny figure called *The Shadow of Night (L'Ombra della Sera)* looks just like the modern Swiss sculptor's work—but is 2,500 years older (€8 combo-ticket includes—like it or not—the Pinacoteca and Sacred Art Museum, daily 9:00–19:00, Nov–March closes at 13:45, ask at the ticket window for mildly interesting English pamphlet, €3 audioguide fleshes out your visit well, Via Don Minzoni 15, tel. 0588-86347). An alabaster showroom and a recommended wine bar are across the street; see listings on page 416–417.

Pinacoteca—This museum fills a 14th-century palace with fine paintings that feel more Florentine than Sienese—a reminder of whose domain this town was in. Its highlights are Luca Signorelli's beautifully lit *Annunciation*, an example of classic High Renaissance (from the town cathedral), and (to the right) *Deposition from the Cross*, the groundbreaking Mannerist work by Rosso Fiorentino (note the elongated bodies and harsh emotional lighting and colors). Notice also Ghirlandaio's *Christ in Glory*. The two devout-looking kneeling women are actually pagan, pre-Christian Etruscan demigoddesses, Attinea and Greciniana, but the church identified them as obscure saints to make the painting acceptable (€8 combo-ticket includes Etruscan and Sacred Art museums, daily April–Oct 9:00–19:00, Nov–March closes at 13:45, Via dei Sarti 1, tel. 0588-87580).

Palazzo Viti—Go behind the rustic, heavy, stone walls of the city and see how the nobility lived (in this case, rich from 19th-century alabaster wealth). One of the finest private residential buildings in Italy, with 12 rooms open to the public, Palazzo Viti feels remarkably lived in because it is. You'll also find Senora Viti herself selling admission tickets. It's no wonder this time warp is so popular with Italian movie directors. While exquisite, it's pricey. But remember, you're helping keep a noble family in leotards (€5, pick up the loaner English description, daily April–Oct 10:00–13:00 & 14:30–18:30, closed in winter, Via dei Sarti 41, tel. 0588-84047).

Roman Theater—Built in about 10 B.C., this well-preserved theater is considered to have some of the best acoustics of its kind.

Under the Etruscan Sun
(c. 900 B.C.–A.D. 1)

Around 550 B.C.—just before the Golden Age of Greece—the Etruscan people of central Italy had their own Golden Age. Though their origins are mysterious, their mix of Greek-style art with Roman-style customs helped lay a civilized foundation for the rise of Rome. As you travel through Tuscany (from "Etruscan") you'll find traces of this long-lost people.

Etruscan tombs and artifacts are still being discovered, often by farmers in the countryside. Museums in Volterra and Cortona house fine collections of urns, pottery, and devotional figures. You can visit several domed tombs outside of Cortona.

The Etruscans first appeared in the ninth century B.C., when a number of cities sprouted up in sparsely populated Tuscany and Umbria, including today's hill towns of Cortona, Chiusi, and Volterra. Perhaps they were immigrants from Turkey, but more likely they were local farmers who moved to the city, became traders and craftsmen, and welcomed new ideas from Greece.

More technologically advanced than their neighbors, the Etruscans mined metal, exporting it around the Mediterranean, both as crude ingots and as some of the finest-crafted jewelry in the known world. They drained and irrigated large tracts of land, creating the fertile farmland of central Italy's breadbasket. With their disciplined army, warships, merchant vessels, and (from the Greek perspective) pirate galleys, they ruled central Italy and the major ports along the Tyrrhenian Sea. For nearly two centuries (c. 700–500 B.C.), much of Italy lived a golden age of peace and prosperity under the Etruscan sun.

Judging from the many luxury items that have survived, the Etruscans enjoyed the good life. Frescoes show men and women looking remarkably like how the Greeks and Romans described them: healthy, vibrant, and well-dressed, playing flutes, dancing with birds, or playing party games. Etruscan artists celebrated individual people, showing their wrinkles, crooked noses, silly smiles, and funny haircuts.

Thousands upon thousands of surviving ceramic plates, cups, and vases attest to the importance of food. Men and women ate together, propped on their elbows on dining couches, surrounded by colorful frescoes and terra-cotta tiles. According to contemporary accounts, the Etruscans were Europe's best-dressed people, even their slaves. The banqueters were entertained with music and dancing, and they were served by elegant and well-treated slaves.

Scholars today have deciphered the Etruscans' Greek-style alphabet and some individual words, but they have yet to fully master the grammar or crack the code.

Much of what we know of the Etruscans comes from their tombs, often clustered in a necropolis. The tomb was a home in the hereafter, fully furnished for the afterlife, complete with all the deceased's belongings. The sarcophagus might have a statue

The Etruscan Empire

N

BOLOGNA ■

Ravenna •

A D R I A T I C

S E A

A P P E N I N E

M T N S.

La Spezia

Florence

Pisa

A R N O R.

FIESOLE

VOLTERRA ■

CORTONA ■
(M)

Siena •

■ PERUGIA

T Y R R H E N I A N

S E A

POPULONIA ■

CHIUSI ■
(M)

■ VETULONIA

ORVIETO ■
(M)

ELBA

■ ROSELLE

BOLSENA

30 MILES

• VULCI

50 KM

T I B E R R.

TARQUINIA ■

VEIO ■

■ ETRUSCAN CITIES

• Modern Cities

(M) ETRUSCAN MUSEUM

- - - BORDER OF TUSCANY

CERVETERI ■

Rome
(M)

DCH

on the lid of the deceased at a banquet—lying across a dining couch, spooning with his wife, smiles on their faces, living the good life for all eternity.

Seven decades of wars with the Greeks (545–474 B.C.) disrupted the trade routes and drained the Etruscan League, just as a new Mediterranean power was emerging...Rome. In 509 B.C., the Romans overthrew their Etruscan king, and Rome expanded, capturing Etruscan cities one by one (the last in 264 B.C.). Etruscan resisters were killed, the survivors intermarried with Romans, their kids grew up speaking Latin, and the culture became Romanized. By Julius Caesar's time, the only remnants of Etruscan culture were Etruscan priests, who became Rome's professional soothsayers, or fortune-tellers. Interestingly, the Etruscan prophets had foreseen their own demise, having predicted that Etruscan civilization would last 10 centuries.

But Etruscan culture lived on in Roman religion (pantheon of gods, household gods, and divination rituals), art (realism), lifestyle (the banquet), and in a taste for Greek styles—the mix that became our "Western civilization."

Because of the fine aerial view you get from the city wall promenade, you may find it unnecessary to pay admission to enter. Belly up to the 13th-century wall and look down. The wall that you're standing on divided the theater from the town center...so, naturally, the theater became the town dump. Over time, the theater was forgotten—covered in the garbage of Volterra. Luckily, it was rediscovered in the 1950s.

The stage wall was standard Roman design—with three levels from which actors would appear: one for humans, one for heroes, and the top one for gods. Parts of two levels still stand. Gods leaped out onto the third level for the last time in the fourth century A.D., when the town decided to abandon the theater and to use its stones to build fancy baths instead. You can see the remains of the baths behind the theater, including the round sauna with brick supports to raise the heated floor (€2.50, but you can view the theater free from Via Lungo le Mure, April–Oct daily 10:30–17:30, Nov–March Sat–Sun only 10:00–16:00).

From the vantage point on the city wall promenade, you can trace Volterra's vast Etruscan wall. Find the church in the distance, on the left, and notice the stones just below. They are from the Etruscan wall that followed the ridge into the valley and defined Volterra five centuries before Christ.

Palazzo dei Priori—Volterra's City Hall (c. 1209) claims to be the oldest of any Tuscan city-state. It clearly inspired the more famous Palazzo Vecchio in Florence. Town halls like this were emblematic of an era when city-states were powerful. They were architectural exclamation points declaring that, around here, no pope or emperor called the shots. Towns such as Volterra were truly city-states—proudly independent and relatively democratic. They had their own armies, taxes, and even weights and measures. Notice the horizontal "cane" cut into the City Hall wall. For a thousand years, this square hosted a market and the "cane" was the local yardstick. When not in use for meetings or weddings, the city council chambers—lavishly painted and lit with fun dragon lamps as they have been for centuries of town meetings—are open to visitors (€1, daily April–Oct 10:30–17:30, Nov–March Sat–Sun only 10:00–17:00).

▲Alabaster Workshop—Alab'Arte offers a fun peek into the art of alabaster. Their showroom is across from the Etruscan Museum. A block downhill is their powdery workshop, where you can watch Roberto Chiti and Giorgio Finazzo at work. They are delighted to share their art with visitors. Lighting shows off the translucent quality of the

Vampire Volterra

Sitting on its stony main square at midnight, watching bats dart about as if they own the place, I realize there really is something supernatural about Volterra. The cliffs of Volterra inspired Dante's "cliffs of hell." In the winter, the town's vibrancy is smothered under a deadening cloak of clouds. The name Volterra means "land that floats"—referring to the clouds that often seem to cut it off from the rest of the world below.

The people of Volterra live in a cloud of mystery, too. Their favorite cookie, crunchy with almonds, is called Ossi di Morta ("bones of the dead"). The only disco the town ever had was named Catacombs. And in the 1970s, when Volterra was the set of a wildly popular TV horror series called *Ritratto di Donna Velata (Portrait of a Veiled Woman)*, all of Italy tuned in to Volterra every week for a good scare.

Lately the town is attracting international attention for its connection to the bestselling *Twilight* series of vampire romance novels and movies. Part of the second movie, *New Moon* (2009), is set in Volterra. Even though it was actually filmed in Montepulciano, the Volterra TI plays a video clip of the cast of *Twilight* dutifully saying how much they love Volterra.

Already the town is seeing lots of Twilighters, who come not for the Etruscan Museum, but to run across the sun-drenched square at noon. Some hope the movie will stir up lots more vampire tourism.

stone and the expertise of these artists (showroom—daily 10:30–13:00 & 15:30–19:00, Via Don Minzoni 18; workshop—Mon–Sat 9:30–13:00 & 15:00–19:00, closed Sun, Via Orti Sant'Agostino 28; tel. 0588-85506). For more artisans in action, visit the "Artisan Lane" described earlier, or ask the TI for their list of the town's many workshops open to the public.

▲La Vena di Vino (Wine Tasting with Bruno and Lucio)—
La Vena di Vino, also just across from the Etruscan Museum, is a fun *enoteca* where two guys have devoted themselves to the wonders of wine and share it with a fun-loving passion. Each day Bruno and Lucio open six or eight bottles, serve your choice by the glass, pair it with characteristic munchies, and offer fine music (guitars available for patrons) and an unusual decor (the place is strewn with bras). Hang out here with the local characters. This is your chance to try the

Super Tuscan—a creative mix of international grapes grown in Tuscany. According to Bruno, "While the Brunello (€6 a glass) is just right for wild boar, the Super Tuscan (also €6) is just right for meditation." They can make you a fine sandwich or plate of meats and cheeses (Wed–Mon 10:00–1:00 in the morning, closed Tue, 3- and 5-glass wine tastings, Via Don Minzoni 30, tel. 0588-81491). While Volterra is famously quiet late at night, this place is full of action. There's a vintage dentists' chair attached to the karaoke machine downstairs.

Medici Fortress and Archaeological Park—The Parco Archeologico marks what was the acropolis of Volterra from 1500 B.C. until A.D. 1472, when Florence conquered the pesky city and burned its political and historic center, turning it into a grassy commons (today's park) and building the adjacent Medici Fortezza. The old fortress—a symbol of Florentine dominance—now keeps people in rather than out. It's a maximum-security prison housing only about 60 special prisoners. (Note that when you're driving from San Gimignano to Volterra, you pass another big, modern prison—almost surreal in the midst of all the Tuscan wonder.) Authorities prefer to keep organized crime figures locked up far away from their family ties in Sicily.

Sleeping in Volterra

(€1 = about $1.40, country code: 39)

$$ Albergo Etruria, on Volterra's main drag, rents 21 fresh, modern, and spacious rooms within an ancient stone structure. They have a welcoming TV lounge and a peaceful garden out back. Request a quiet room off the street (Sb-€70, Db-€90, Tb-€110, 10 percent discount with cash and this book, fans, Wi-Fi, Via Matteotti 32, tel. 0588-87377, fax 0588-92784, www.albergoetruria .it, info@albergoetruria.it, Lisa and Giuseppina are fine hosts).

$$ Hotel La Locanda is well-located and rents 18 decent rooms (Db-€89–99, air-con, Wi-Fi, Via Guarnacci 24/28, tel. 0588-81547, www.hotel-lalocanda.com, staff@hotel-lalocanda .com).

$$ Albergo Villa Nencini, just outside of town, is big, modern, and professional, with 36 fine rooms. A few rooms have terraces and many have views. There's also a large pool and free parking (Sb-€67, Db-€88, Tb-€115, 10 percent discount with cash and this book, Borgo Santo Stefano 55, a 15-min uphill walk to main square, tel. 0588-86386, fax 0588-80601, www.villanencini .it, info@villanencini.it, Nencini family).

$$ Albergo Nazionale, with 38 big rooms, is simple, a little musty, short on smiles, popular with school groups, and steps from the bus stop (Sb-€60–65, Db-€75-85, Tb-€100, less off-season,

Via dei Marchesi 11, tel. 0588-86284, fax 0588-84097, www.hotel nazionale-volterra.it, info@hotelnazionale-volterra.it).

$ Seminario Vescovile Sant'Andrea has been training priests for 500 years. Today, the remaining eight priests still train students, and their 16 rooms—separated by vast and holy halls—are rented very cheap to travelers (S-€15, Sb-€20, D-€28, Db-€36, T-€42, Tb-€54, breakfast-€3, elevator, closes at 24:00, groups welcome, free parking, easy 7-min walk from Etruscan Museum, Viale Vittorio Veneto 2, tel. 0588-86028, semvescovile@diocesi volterra.it).

$ Volterra Youth Hostel fills a wing of the restored Convent of San Girolamo with 85 beds. It's spacious and has lots of services, but it's a 15-minute hike out of town, in a boring area, and no cheaper than the more-memorable seminary option closer to town (bed in 6-bed dorm-€17, Db-€60, breakfast-€3, lockers, tel. 0588-86613, www.ostellovolterra.it, info@ostellovolterra.it).

Eating in Volterra

Menus feature a Volterran take on regional dishes. *Zuppa alla Volterrana* is a fresh vegetable-and-bread soup, similar to *ribollita* (except that it isn't made from leftovers). *Torta di ceci*, also known as *cecina*, is a savory-pancake-like dish made with garbanzo beans. Those with more adventurous palates dive into *trippa* (tripe; comes in a bowl like stew), the traditional breakfast of the alabaster carvers.

Ristorante Enoteca del Duca, with a locally respected chef named Genuino, serves well-presented and creative Tuscan cuisine. You can dine under a medieval arch with walls lined with wine bottles, in a stark dining room (with a Etruscan statuette at each table), or on a nice little patio out back. It's a good place for truffles, and has a fine wine list and friendly staff. The spacious seating, dressy clientele, and calm atmosphere make this a good choice for a romantic meal (€42 food-sampler fixed-price meal, €10 pastas, €17 *secondi*, Wed–Mon 12:30–15:00 & 19:30–22:00, closed Tue, near City Hall at Via di Castello 2, tel. 0588-81510).

Trattoria da Bado, a 10-minute hike out of town, is every local's favorite for its *tipica cucina Volterrana*. Giacomo and family offer a rustic atmosphere and serve food with no pretense—"the way you wish your mamma cooks" (meals from 12:30 and 19:30, closed Wed, Borgo San Lazzero 9, tel. 0588-86477, reserve before you go as it's often full).

La Vecchia Lira, bright and cheery, is a classy self-serve eatery that's a hit with locals as a quick and cheap lunch spot by day, and a fancier restaurant at night (Fri–Wed 12:00–14:30 & 19:00–22:30, closed Thu, Via Matteotti 19, tel. 0588-86180, Lamberto and Massimo).

Ristorante il Sacco Fiorentino is a local favorite for traditional cuisine and seafood specials (€8 pastas, €15 *secondi*, Thu–Tue 12:00–14:45 & 19:00–21:45, closed Wed, Piazza XX Settembre 18, tel. 0588-88537).

La Vena di Vino is an *enoteca* serving up simple and traditional dishes and the best of Tuscan wine in a fun atmosphere (closed Tue; see listing in "Sights in Volterra," earlier; Via Don Minzoni 30, tel. 0588-81491).

Pizzerias: **Ombra della Sera** dishes out what local kids consider the best pizza in town. At €6 and big enough to split, they make a cheap date (Tue–Sun 12:00–15:00 & 19:00–22:00, closed Mon, Via Guarnacci 16, tel. 0588-85274).

Pizzeria Tavernetta, next door, is more romantic, with delightful indoor and on-the-street seating. Marco, who looks like Billy Joel, serves splittable €7 pizzas (closed Tue, Via Guarnacci 14, tel. 0588-87630).

Picnics: You can assemble a picnic at the few *alimentari* around town (try Despar Market at Via Gramsci 12, Thu–Tue 7:30–13:30 & 17:00–20:00, Wed only 7:30–13:30) and eat in the breezy Archaeological Park.

Connections

The nearest train station is in **Saline di Volterra,** a 15-minute bus ride away (7/day, 4/day Sun). In Volterra, buses come and go from Piazza Martiri della Libertà (buy tickets at any *tabacchi* shop).

From Volterra by Bus to: Florence (4/day, 2/day Sun, 2 hrs, change in Colle Val d'Elsa), **Siena** (4/day, 1/day Sun, 2 hrs, change in Colle Val d'Elsa), **San Gimignano** (4/day, 2/day Sun, 2 hrs, change in Colle Val d'Elsa), **Pisa** (9/day, 2 hrs, change in Pontedera). For Siena, Florence, and San Gimignano, C.P.T. bus tickets get you only as far as Colle Val d'Elsa (4/day, 50 min, €2.50); you must then buy another ticket (from another bus company) at the newsstand near the bus stop.

South Tuscany

Montalcino

On a hill overlooking vineyards and valleys, Montalcino—famous for its delicious and pricey Brunello di Montalcino red wines—is a must for wine lovers. Everyone touring this area seems to be relaxed and in an easy groove…as if enjoying a little wine buzz.

In the Middle Ages, Montalcino (mohn-tahl-CHEE-noh) was considered Siena's biggest ally. Originally allied with Florence, the town switched sides after the Sienese beat up Florence in the Battle of Montaperti in 1260. The Sienese persuaded the Montalcini to join their side by forcing them to sleep one night in the bloody Florentine-strewn battlefield.

Montalcino prospered under Siena, but like its ally, it waned after the Medici family took control of the region. The village became a humble place. Then, in the late 19th century, the Biondi Santi family created a fine, dark red wine, calling it "the brunette" (Brunello). Today's affluence is due to the town's much-sought-after wine.

Non–wine-lovers may find Montalcino a bit too focused on *vino,* but one sip of Brunello makes even wine skeptics believe that Bacchus was onto something. Note that Rosso di Montalcino (a younger version of Brunello) is also very good, at half the price. Those with a sweet tooth will enjoy crunching the Ossi di Morta ("bones of the dead") cookies popular in Tuscany.

Orientation to Montalcino

Sitting atop a hill amidst a sea of vineyards, Montalcino is surrounded by walls and dominated by the Fortezza (a.k.a. "La Rocca"). From here, roads lead down into the two main squares: Piazza Garibaldi and Piazza del Popolo.

Tourist Information: The TI, just off Piazza Garibaldi in the City Hall, can find you a room (Db-€50–80) for no fee. They have information on taxi service to nearby towns, abbeys, and monasteries (daily 10:00–13:00 & 14:00–17:40, tel. & fax 0577-849-331, www.prolocomontalcino.it).

Arrival in Montalcino: The bus station is on Piazza Cavour, about 300 yards from the town center. Drivers coming in for a short visit should drive right through the old gate under the fortress (follow signs to *Fortezza;* it looks almost forbidden) and grab a spot in the pay lot at the fortress (€1.50/hr, free 20:00–8:00). Otherwise, park for free a short walk away.

Helpful Hints: Market day is Friday (7:00–13:00) on Viale della Libertà. Day-trippers be warned: Montalcino has no baggage storage. In a jam, try the TI.

Sights in Montalcino

Fortezza—This 14th-century fort, built under the rule of Siena, is now little more than an empty shell. People visit for its *enoteca* (wine bar—see "Wine Tasting and Wineries," page 425). You can climb the ramparts to enjoy a panoramic view of the Asso and Orcia valleys, or enjoy a picnic in the park surrounding the fort (€4 for rampart walk, €6 combo-ticket includes Civic Museum—sold only at museum, daily 9:00–20:00).

Piazza del Popolo—All roads in tiny Montalcino seem to lead to the main square, Piazza del Popolo (literally "People's Square"). Since 1888, Caffè Fiaschetteria Italiana has been the elegant place to enjoy a drink (see listing in "Eating in Montalcino," later in this section). Its founder, inspired by Café Florian in Venice, brought fine coffee to this humble town of woodcutters.

The City Hall was the fortified seat of government. It's decorated by the coats of arms of judges who, in the interest of fairness, were from outside of town. Like Siena, Montalcino was a republic in the Middle Ages. When Florentines took Siena in 1555, Siena's ruling class retreated here and held out for four more years. The Medici coat of arms (with the six pills) superseding all the others is a reminder that in 1559 Florence finally took Montalcino.

The one-handed clock was the norm until 200 years ago. For five centuries the arcaded loggia hosted the town market. And, of course, it's fun to simply observe the *passeggiata*—these days mostly a parade of tourists here for the wine.

Civic Museum (Museo Civico)—Gothic sacred art is the star of this museum, with works from Montalcino's heyday, the 13th to 16th centuries. Most of the art was created by local artists. Among the museum's highlights are a glazed terra-cotta altarpiece and statue of San Sebastian by Andrea della Robbia. The ground floor is best, with an impressive collection of crucifixes (€4.50, €6 combo-ticket includes rampart walk at Fortezza, Tue–Sun 10:00–13:00 & 14:00–17:50, closed Mon, Via Ricasoli 31, to the right of Sant'Agostino Church, tel. 0577-846-014).

Montalcino

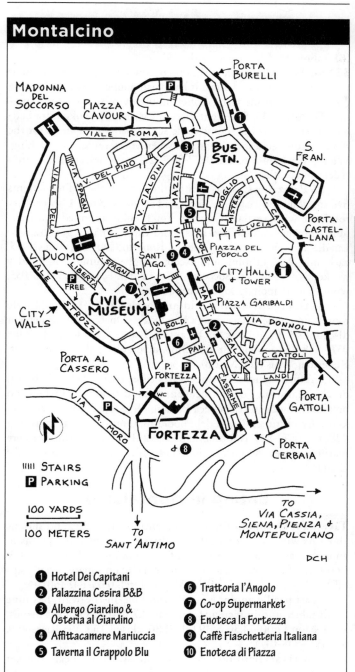

① Hotel Dei Capitani

② Palazzina Cesira B&B

③ Albergo Giardino & Osteria al Giardino

④ Affittacamere Mariuccia

⑤ Taverna il Grappolo Blu

⑥ Trattoria l'Angolo

⑦ Co-op Supermarket

⑧ Enoteca la Fortezza

⑨ Caffè Fiaschetteria Italiana

⑩ Enoteca di Piazza

TUSCAN HILL TOWNS

Sleeping in Montalcino

(€1 = about $1.40, country code: 39)

$$ Hotel Dei Capitani, at the end of town near the bus station, is well-run and rents 29 rooms. It has plush public spaces, an inviting pool, and a cliffside terrace offering plenty of reasons for lounging (Db-€105–115, 8 percent discount with this book, extra bed-€30, air-con, half the rooms come with vast Tuscan views for the same price—request a view room when you reserve, free parking, Wi-Fi, Via Lapini 6, tel. 0577-847-227, www.deicapitani.it, info @deicapitani.it).

$$ Palazzina Cesira, right in the heart of the old town, rents five spacious and tastefully decorated rooms in a fine 13th-century residence with a palatial lounge. You'll enjoy a refined and tranquil ambience, a nice breakfast, and the chance to get to know Lucilla and her American husband Roberto (Db-€95, suites-€115, cash only, 2-night minimum except 3-night minimum on holiday weekends, Wi-Fi, Via Soccorso Saloni 2, tel. & fax 0577-846-055, www.montalcinoitaly.com, p.cesira@tin.it).

$ Albergo Giardino, old and basic, has nine big simple rooms, no public spaces, and a fine locale (Db-€55–60, 10 percent discount with this book, no breakfast, Piazza Cavour 4, tel. & fax 0577-848-257, mobile 338-684-3163, albergoilgiardino@virgilio.it, Roberto and his dad, Mario).

$ Affittacamere Mariuccia has three basic, Ikea-chic rooms on the main drag over a heaven-scented bakery (Db-€44, no breakfast, check-in at Enoteca Pierangioli before 20:00 or let them know arrival time, Piazza del Popolo 16, rooms across the street at #28, tel. 0577-849-113, mobile 348-392-4780, www.affittacamere mariuccia.it, enotecapierangioli@hotmail.com, Alessandro speaks English).

Eating in Montalcino

Taverna il Grappolo Blu is unpretentious, friendly, and serious about its wine, serving local specialties and vegetarian options to an enthusiastic crowd (€8 pastas, €12 *secondi*, daily 12:00–15:00 & 19:00–22:00, reservations smart, near the main square, a few steps off Via Mazzini at Scale di Via Moglio 1, tel. 0577-847-150).

Trattoria l'Angolo, a family-run hole-in-the-wall, has nine small tables and homemade desserts (€7 pastas, €8 meat dishes, Wed–Mon 12:00–14:30 & 19:00–21:30, closed Tue, Via Ricasoli 9, tel. 0577-848-017).

Osteria al Giardino is small and dressy, serving near-gourmet creative Tuscan cuisine at the bus-station end of town. Owner and chef Giovanni Luca makes everything fresh, from the bread to the desserts, always has a veggie option, and offers a tasting *menu* (€10 pastas, €14 *secondi*, Mon–Sat 12:30–14:30 & 19:30–21:45, closed Sun, Piazza Cavour 1, tel. 0577-849-076). Giovanni's wife, Paola, runs the dining room.

Gather ingredients for a picnic at the **Co-op supermarket** on Via Sant'Agostino (just off Via Ricasoli in front of Sant'Agostino Church, closed Sun), then enjoy your feast up at the Madonna del Soccorso Church, with vast territorial views.

Wine Tasting and Wineries

Enoteca la Fortezza offers a chance to taste top-end wines by the glass, each with an English explanation. While wine snobs turn up their noses, the medieval setting inside Montalcino's fort is a hit for most visitors. Spoil yourself with Brunello in the cozy *enoteca* or at an outdoor table (€12 for 3 tastings; €5–9 sampler plates of cheeses, *salumi*, honeys, and olive oil; daily 9:00–20:00, closes at 18:00 in off-season, inside the Fortezza, tel. 0577-849-211, www.enotecalafortezza.it).

Caffè Fiaschetteria Italiana was founded by Ferruccio Biondi Santi, who created the famous Brunello wine. The wine library in the back of the café boasts many local wine choices. A meeting place since 1888, this grand café also serves light lunches and espresso to tourists and locals alike (€6–15 for a glass of Brunello and plate of snacks; same prices inside, outside, or in back room; daily 7:30–23:00, Piazza del Popolo 6, tel. 0577-849-043). And if it's coffee you need, this place—with its classic 1961 espresso machine—is considered the best in town.

Enoteca di Piazza is one of a chain of wine shops with a fun system of mechanical wine dispensers. You get a card that keeps track of the samples you take, and you'll pay from €1 to €9 for each 50-gram taste of 100 different wines kept fresh in the fancy machines. The only nibbles are saltine-type crackers. They hope you'll buy a bottle of the samples you like (rule of thumb: a bottle costs about 10 times the cost of the sample), and are happy to educate you in English. While the place feels a little formulaic and sterile, it's a fun experience and the wine is great (daily 9:00–20:00, just off Piazza del Popolo at Via Matteotti 43, tel. 0577-848-104, www.enotecadipiazza.com).

Wineries: While there are plenty of *enoteche,* there are no real wineries inside the city. The nearby countryside, however, is littered with them, and some offer tastings. While some require an appointment, many also are happy to serve a glass to potential buyers and show them around. **Banfi,** huge and the most touristy, produces well-respected wines (daily 10:00–18:00, tours Mon–Fri at 16:00, reserve in advance, 10-min drive south of Montalcino in Sant'Angelo Scalo, tel. 0577-840-111, www.castellobanfi.com, reservations@banfi.it).

The Montalcino TI can give you a list of more than 150 regional wineries. Or check with the vintners' consortium (tel. 0577-848-246, www.consorziobrunellodimontalcino.it, info @consorziobrunellodimontalcino.it).

Connections

The nearest train station is a 30-minute bus ride (running nearly hourly) away in Buonconvento. Montalcino's bus station is on Piazza Cavour, within the town walls. Bus tickets are sold at the bar on Piazza Cavour or at *tabacchi* shops, but not on board. Check schedules at the TI or the bus station.

From Montalcino by Bus to: Siena (6/day, 1.5 hrs, €3.20), **Pienza** (5/day, none on Sun, change to line #114 in Torrenieri, 60 min plus changing time), **Sant'Antimo** (3/day, none on Sat–Sun, 15 min, €1.50, buy tickets on board). Anyone going to Florence changes in Siena.

Pienza

Set on a crest, surrounded by green, rolling hills, the small town of Pienza packs a lot of Renaissance punch. In the 1400s, locally born

Pope Pius II of the Piccolomini family decided to remodel his birthplace in the style that was all the rage: Renaissance. Propelled by papal clout, the town of Corsignano was transformed—in only five years' time—into a jewel of Renaissance architecture. It was renamed Pienza, after Pope Pius. The plan was to remodel the entire town, but work ended in 1464 when both the pope and his architect, Bernardo Rossellino, died. Their vision—what you see today—was completed a century later. The architectural focal point is the square, Piazza Pio II, surrounded by the Duomo and the pope's family residence, Palazzo Piccolomini. While Piazza Pio II is Pienza's pride and joy, the entire town—a mix of old stonework, potted plants, and grand views—is fun to explore, especially with a camera or sketchpad in hand. You can walk each lane in the tiny town in a few minutes.

Cute as the town is, it also feels a bit greedy and is entirely given over to snaring the tourist dollar. Because of that, I'd recommend popping in to enjoy the setting, and perhaps touring the palace, but not lingering for an overnight.

Nearly every shop sells the town's specialty: Pecorino cheese. This pungent sheep's cheese is available fresh *(fresco)* or aged *(secco)*, and sometimes contains other ingredients, such as truffles or peppers. Look on menus for warm *(al forno* or *alla griglia)* Pecorino, often topped with honey or pears and served with bread. Along with a glass of local wine, this just might lead you to a new understanding of *la dolce vita.*

Tourist Information: The TI is 10 yards up the street from Piazza Pio II, inside the Diocesan Museum (daily 10:00–13:00 & 15:00–18:00, shorter hours Nov–March, tel. 0578-749-905).

Arrival in Pienza: Free street parking is available—if you can find it. Otherwise you can park at the large lot near Largo Roma outside of the old town (€1.50/hr, often completely full in the morning).

Helpful Hints: Market day is Friday morning. A public WC is just outside the town gate on Piazza Dante Alighieri.

Sights in Pienza

▲**Piazza Pio II**—One of Italy's classic piazzas, this square is famous for its elegance and artistic unity. The square and the surrounding buildings were all designed by Rossellino to form an "outdoor room." Spinning around clockwise, you'll see the City Hall (13th-century bell tower with a Renaissance facade and a fine loggia), the Bishop's Palace (now an art museum), the Duomo, and the Piccolomini family palace. Just to the left of the church, a lane leads to the best viewpoint in town.

Duomo—Its classic, symmetrical Renaissance facade—dated 1462 with the Piccolomini family coat of arms immodestly front and center—dominates Piazza Pio II. The interior is charming, with several Gothic altarpieces and painted arches. Windows feature the crest of Pius II, with five half-moons advertising the number of crusades that his family funded. The interior art is Sienese Gothic on the cusp of the Renaissance. As the local clay and *tufo* stone were not ideal building material for the foundation, the church is slouching. See the cracks in the apse walls, and get seasick behind the main altar.

▲▲**Palazzo Piccolomini**—The home of Pius II (see page 316 in the Siena Duomo Tour chapter) and the Piccolomini family (until 1962) can be visited with a guided tour. While the 30-minute tour (in English and Italian, call ahead for tour schedule) visits only six rooms and the loggia, it offers a fascinating slice of 15th-century aristocratic life and is the sightseeing highlight of the town. In fact, it's the most impressive small-town palace experience I've found in Tuscany. You can check out the well-preserved, painted courtyard for free. In Renaissance times, most buildings were covered with elaborate paintings like these (€7, Tue–Sun 10:00–13:00 & 14:00–18:30, closed Mon and in winter, tel. 0578-748-392).

Diocesan Museum (Museo Diocesano)—This collection of religious paintings from local churches fills the cardinal's Renaissance palace. The art is provincial Sienese, displayed in chronological order from the 12th through 17th centuries, conveniently all on one floor (€4; mid-March–Dec Wed–Mon 10:00–13:00 & 15:00–19:00, closed Tue; Jan–mid-March open Sat–Sun only, Corso il Rossellino 30).

View Terrace—Facing the church, a lane leads left to the panoramic promenade. Views from the terrace include the Tuscan countryside and Monte Amiata, the largest mountain in southern Tuscany, in the distance.

Connections

Bus tickets are sold at the bar just inside Pienza's town gate (or pay a little extra and buy tickets from the driver). Montepulciano is the nearest transportation hub to other points.

From Pienza by Bus to: Siena (5/day, none on Sun, 1.5 hrs), **Montepulciano** (9/day, 30 min).

Montepulciano

Curving its way along a ridge, Montepulciano (mohn-tay-pull-chee-AH-noh) delights visitors with *vino* and views. Alternately under Sienese and Florentine rule, the city still retains its medieval *contrade* districts, each with a mascot and flag. The neighborhoods compete the last Sunday of August in the Bravio delle Botti, where teams of men push large wine casks uphill from Piazza Marzocco to Piazza Grande, all hoping to win a banner and bragging rights.

The city is a collage of architectural styles, but the elegant San Biagio Church, at the base of the hill, is its most impressive Renaissance building. Most visitors ignore the architecture and focus more on the city's other creative accomplishment, the tasty Vino Nobile di Montepulciano red wine.

Orientation to Montepulciano

The commercial action in Montepulciano centers in the lower town, mostly along Via di Gracciano nel Corso (nicknamed Corso). Strolling here you'll find cheap eateries, gift shops, and tourist traps. The back streets are worth exploring. The main square at the top of town is Piazza Grande. Standing proudly above all the touristy sales energy, it has a more noble, Florentine feel.

Tourist Information: The TI is near the bus station, in Piazza Don Minzoni. It books wine tours, hotels, and rooms for no fee; sells train tickets; and can book one of the town's two taxis (Mon–Sat 9:30–12:30 & 15:00–18:00, Sun 9:30–12:30, daily until 20:00 in summer, tel. 0578-757-341, www.proloco montepulciano.it).

Note that there's a more central office that looks like a TI, but is actually a privately run "Strada del Vino" (Wine Road) agency. They don't have city info, but provide wine-road maps and organize **wine tours** in the city, and minibus winery tours farther afield. They offer other tours (olive oil, cheese, and slow food), cooking classes, and more, depending on season and demand (Mon–Fri 10:00–13:00 & 15:00–18:00, closed Sat–Sun, Piazza Grande 7, tel. 0578-717-484, www.stradavinonobile.it).

Arrival in Montepulciano: Most visits begin at the fortified Porta al Prato gate, near the bus station. From the gate, it's a 15-minute walk uphill along the Corso, the bustling main drag (note the Etruscan reliefs on the foundation of Palazzo Bucelli— see photo on previous page) to the main square, Piazza Grande. If you arrive at the bus station, an orange shuttle bus can take you to Piazza Grande (3/hr); it's a good strategy to take the bus up and walk back down.

Drivers arriving by car should park outside the walls (don't try to tackle the tiny roads inside the city), either at the bus station or the numerous lots on the edge of town. For a free spot near the top of the hill, follow signs for lots #7 and #8. If you're sleeping in town, your hotelier will give you a permit to park within the walls.

Helpful Hints: Market day is Thursday. There's no official baggage storage in town, but the TI might let you leave bags with them if they have space. Public WCs are located at the TI, next to Palazzo Comunale, and at the Church of St. Augustine. Check your email at Internet Train (Mon–Sat 10:30–13:30 & 16:00–19:30, closed Sun, Via Gracciano 26, tel. 0578-717-253). A self-service laundry is at Via del Paolino 2 (daily 8:00–22:00, tel. 0578-717-544).

Sights in Montepulciano

Piazza Grande—This pleasant, lively piazza is surrounded by a grab bag of architectural sights. The medieval Palazzo Comunale

may remind you of Palazzo Vecchio in Florence—that's because Florence dominated this town in the 15th and 16th centuries. The crenellations along the roof were never intended to hide soldiers—they're meant just to symbolize power. A cistern system fed by rainwater draining from surrounding palaces supplied the courtyard's fine well. Check out its 19th-century pulleys, the grills to keep animals from contaminating the water supply, and the Medici coat of arms (with lions symbolizing political power of Florence).

Climbing the **tower** rewards you with a windy but commanding view from the terrace below the clock. Go into the Palazzo Comunale, head up the stairs to your left, and pay on the second floor (€2, daily 10:00–18:00, closed in winter). The Palazzo de' Nobili-Tarugi is a Renaissance arcaded confection; meanwhile, the unfinished Duomo looks glumly on, wishing the city hadn't run out of money for its facade. The Contucci Palace (left of the church) is lucky enough to have a 16th-century Renaissance facade. The Contucci family still lives in their palace, producing and selling their own wine. The town is fortunate to be graced with so many bold and noble palazzos—Florentine nobility favored Montepulciano as a breezy and relaxed place for a secondary residence.

Duomo—This church's unfinished facade—rough stonework left waiting for the final marble veneer—is not that unusual. Many churches were built just to the point where they had a functional interior, and then, for various practical reasons, the facades were left unfinished. But step inside and you'll be rewarded with some fine art. A beautiful Andrea della Robbia glazed-terra-cotta *Altar of the Lilies* is behind the baptismal font (on the left as you enter). The high altar features a luminous, early-Renaissance Assumption triptych by the Sienese artist Taddeo di Bartolo. Showing Mary in her dreamy eternal sleep as she ascends to be crowned by Jesus, it illustrates how Siena clung to the Gothic aesthetic—elaborate gold leaf and lacy pointed arches—to show heavenly grandeur at the expense of realism (daily 9:00–13:00 & 15:00–18:00).

▲▲Contucci Cantina—Montepulciano's most popular attraction isn't made of stone...it's the famous wine, Vino Nobile. This robust red can be tasted in any of the cantinas lining Via Ricci and Via di

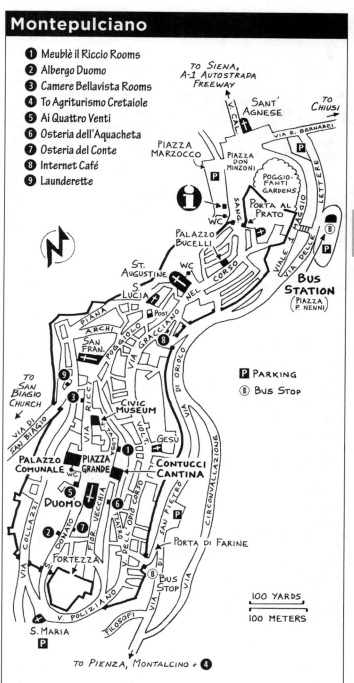

Montepulciano

1. Meublè il Riccio Rooms
2. Albergo Duomo
3. Camere Bellavista Rooms
4. To Agriturismo Cretaiole
5. Ai Quattro Venti
6. Osteria dell'Aquacheta
7. Osteria del Conte
8. Internet Café
9. Launderette

TO SIENA,
A-1 AUTOSTRADA
FREEWAY

TO CHIUSI

SANT' AGNESE

VIA E. BERNABEI

PIAZZA MARZOCCO

PIAZZA DON MINZONI

POGGIO-FANTI GARDENS

PORTA AL PRATO

PALAZZO BUCELLI

ST. AUGUSTINE

S. LUCIA

CORSO

NEL

VIALE I MAGGIO

VIA DELLE LETTERE

BUS STATION
(PIAZZA P. NENNI)

PIANA

ARCHI

POGGIOLO

SAN FRAN.

VIA GRACCIANO

Post

VIA DI ORIOLO

TO SAN BIAGIO CHURCH

VIA DI SAN BIAGIO

VIA RICCI

CIVIC MUSEUM

VIA DI ITALOSA

GESÙ

PALAZZO COMUNALE

PIAZZA GRANDE

CONTUCCI CANTINA

VIA DEL OPIO CORSO

DUOMO

FIOR. VECCHIA

SAN PIETRO

VIA DELL' OPIO CORSO

CIRCONVALLAZIONE

PARKING

BUS STOP

VIA COLLAZZI

DONATO

FORTEZZA

TEATRO

PORTA DI FARINE

BUS STOP

VIA POLIZIANO

FILOSOFI

S. MARIA

100 YARDS

100 METERS

TO PIENZA, MONTALCINO + 4

TUSCAN HILL TOWNS

Gracciano nel Corso, but the cantina in the basement of the Contucci Palace is both historic and fun. While the palace has a formal wine-tasting showroom facing the square, head down the lane on the right to the actual cellars, where you'll meet lively Adamo, who has been making wine since 1953 and welcomes tourists into his cellar. While at the palace, you may meet Andrea Contucci, whose family has lived here since the 11th century. He loves to share his family's products with the public. Adamo and Signor Contucci usually have a dozen bottles open (free drop-in tasting, daily 8:30–12:30 & 14:30–18:30, Piazza Grande 7, tel. 0578-757-006).

After sipping a little wine with Adamo, explore the palace basement, with its 13th-century vaults. Originally part of the town's wall, these chambers have been filled since the 1500s with huge barrels of wine. Dozens of barrels of Croatian, Italian, and French oak (1,000–2,500 liters each) cradle the wine through a two-year in-the-barrel aging process, while the wine picks up the personality of the wood. After about 35 years, an exhausted barrel has nothing left to offer its wine, so it's retired. Adamo explains that the French oak gives the wine "pure elegance," the Croatian is more masculine, and the Italian oak is a marriage of the two. Each barrel is labeled with the size in liters, the year the wine was barreled, and the percentage of alcohol (determined by how much sun shone in that year). "Nobile"-grade wine needs a minimum of 13 percent alcohol.

Civic Museum (Museo Civico)—Small and eclectic, the highlight of this forgettable museum is its colorful Andrea della Robbia ceramic altarpieces and Etruscan artifacts (€4.20, Tue–Sun 10:00–13:00 & 15:00–18:00, closed Mon, no English, Via Ricci 10, tel. 0578-717-300).

San Biagio Church—Just outside of town, down a picturesque driveway lined with cypresses, this church—designed by Antonio da Sangallo and built of locally quarried travertine—is Renaissance perfection. The proportions of the Greek cross floor plan give the building a pleasing rhythmic quality. Bramante, who designed St. Peter's at the Vatican in 1516, was inspired by this dome. The lone tower was supposed to have a twin, but it was never built. The soaring interior, with a high dome and lantern, creates a fine Renaissance space (normally daily 9:00–13:00 & 15:00–18:00). Walk around the building to study the freestanding towers. Consider a picnic or snooze on the grass in back. The street called Via di San Biagio, leading from the church up into town, makes for an enjoyable, if challenging, walk.

Sleeping in Montepulciano

(€1 = about $1.40, country code: 39)

$$ Mueblè il Riccio ("hedgehog" in Italian) is medieval-elegant, with six modern and spotless rooms, an awesome roof terrace, and friendly owners (Sb-€80, Db-€100, Tb-€116, breakfast-€8, air-con, Internet access and Wi-Fi, limited free parking—request when you reserve, a block below the main square at Via Talosa 21, tel. & fax 0578-757-713, www.ilriccio.net, info@ilriccio.net, Gió and Ivana speak English). Gió and his son Iacopo give country tours (€30/hr) in one of their classic Italian cars; for tour details, see their website. Ivana makes wonderful breakfast tarts.

$$ Albergo Duomo, renting 13 rooms, is big, modern, and forgettable (Db-€90, Tb-€115, family deals, Internet, free parking, Via di San Donato 14, tel. 0578-757-473, www.albergoduomo.it, albergoduomo@libero.it).

$ Camere Bellavista has 10 basic rooms, some with better views than others. Room 6 has a view terrace worth reserving (Db-€65, terrace Db-€80, optional breakfast at a bar in the piazza-€3, cash only, housekeeping only for stays of 3 or more days, no elevator, Via Ricci 25, no reception—call before arriving, mobile 347-823-2314, fax 0578-716-341, bellavista@bccmp.com, little English spoken).

Between Montepulciano and Montalcino: A Green Acres *Agriturismo* Holiday

$$ Agriturismo Cretaiole, in pristine farmland on the Montalcino–Pienza road, is warmly run by Isabella and her husband,

Carlo. This family-friendly farm, deeply rooted in the culture, welcomes visitors for weeklong stays (generally Sat–Sat) in six comfortable apartments. Eager to share their local traditions, they create a community of about 14–20 travelers who are looking for a rich cultural education. Isabella offers cooking demonstrations and leads guests in hands-on truffle hunting, grape and olive harvesting, and gardening. Carlo's father, Luciano, is in charge of the grappa. While there's no swimming pool—for philosophical reasons— many thoughtful touches and extras, such as Wi-Fi, mountain bikes, and loaner mobile phones, are provided (Db-€630/week, small Db apartment-€840/week, large Db apartment-€1100, same apartment for four-€1,250, prices soft mid-Nov–mid-March, non-included activities are fairly priced, tel. & fax 0578-748-083, Isabella's mobile 338-740-9245, www.cretaiole.it, info@cretaiole .it). It's on the Montalcino–Pienza road (S-146), about 11 miles out of Montalcino, and about three miles out of Pienza. While they prefer weeklong stays, when things are slow they may accept guests for as few as three nights (for this you must book less than a month in advance, Db-€100, 3-night minimum).

Eating in Montepulciano

Ai Quattro Venti is fresh, flavorful, fun, and right on Piazza Grande, offering good indoor and outdoor seating (€8.50 pastas, Fri–Wed 12:30–14:30 & 19:30–22:30, closed Thu, next to City Hall on Piazza Grande, tel. 0578-717-231).

Osteria dell'Aquacheta is a carnivore's dream come true, famous among locals for its excellent beef steaks. Its long narrow room is jammed with shared tables and tight seating, with an open fire in back and a big hunk of red beef laying on the counter like a corpse on a gurney. Giulio, with a pencil tucked into his ponytail, whacks off slabs with a cleaver, confirms the weight and price with the diner, and tosses them on the grill—seven minutes per side. Steaks are sold by the weight (€3/100 grams, or *etto,* one kilo is about the smallest they serve, two can split it for €30). They also serve hearty €6 pastas and salads and a fine house wine (Wed–Mon 12:30–15:00 & 19:30–22:30, closed Tue, Via del Teatro 22, tel. 0578-758-443). In the tradition of old trattorias, they serve one glass, which you use alternately for wine and water.

Osteria del Conte, an attractive but humble family-run bistro, offers a €30 four-course dinner of local specialties including wine, as well as à la carte options and cooking like mom's (€7 pastas, €12 *secondi,* indoor and outdoor seating, Thu–Tue 12:30–14:30 & 19:30–21:30, closed Wed, Via S. Donato 19, tel. 0578-756-062).

Connections

All buses leave from Piazza Pietro Nenni. Check www.sienamo bilita.it for schedules.

From Montepulciano by Bus to: Florence (3/day with a change in Bettole), **Siena** (8/day, 1.25 hrs, none on Sun), **Pienza**

(9/day, 30 min). There are hourly bus connections to **Chiusi,** a town on the main Florence–Rome rail line; Chiusi is a much better bet than the distant Montepulciano station (5 miles away), which is served only by milk-run trains. Buses connect Montepulciano's bus station and its train station (8/day, none on Sun).

To Montalcino: This connection is problematic by public transportation—consider asking at the TI for a taxi. Although expensive (about €50), a taxi could make sense for two or more people. Otherwise you can take a bus to Buonconvento, then change to get to Montalcino (2 hrs). **Drivers** find route S-146 to Montalcino particularly scenic (see "Crete Senese Drives" at the end of this chapter).

Cortona

Cortona blankets a 1,700-foot hill surrounded by dramatic Tuscan and Umbrian views. Frances Mayes' books, such as *Under the Tuscan Sun,* placed this town in the touristic limelight, just as Peter Mayle's books popularized the Luberon region in France. But long before Mayes ever published a book, Cortona was popular with Romantics and considered one of the classic Tuscan hill towns. Unlike San Gimignano, Cortona maintains a rustic and gritty personality—even with its long history of foreigners who, enamored

with its Tuscan charm, made this their adopted home.

The city began as one of the largest Etruscan settlements, the remains of which can be seen at the base of the city walls, as well as in the nearby tombs. It grew to its present size in the 13th to 16th centuries, when it was a colorful and crowded city, eventually allied with Florence. The farmland that fills almost every view from the city was marshy and uninhabitable until about 200 years ago, when it was drained and turned into some of Tuscany's most fertile land.

Art-lovers know Cortona as the home of Renaissance painter Luca Signorelli, Baroque master Pietro da Cortona (Berretini), and the 20th-century Futurist artist Gino Severini. The city's museums and churches reveal many of the works of these native sons.

Orientation to Cortona

Most of the main sights, shops, and restaurants cluster around the level streets on the Piazza Garibaldi–Piazza del Duomo axis, but Cortona will have you huffing and puffing up some steep hills.

Tourist Information: The helpful TI is on the main drag at Via Nazionale 42 (April–Oct daily 9:00–13:00 & 15:00–19:00, shorter hours and closed Sun off-season, sells train and bus tickets, tel. 0575-630-352, www.apt.arezzo.it).

Arrival in Cortona: Train travelers arrive at Camucia-Cortona train station, a long, strenuous walk from the town on roads with no sidewalks. Fortunately, buses are generally timed with the arrival of the train and zip you right up to town in 10 minutes (2/hr, €1, buy tickets at newsstand 200 yards from station). Buses stop at Piazza Garibaldi. From here, it's a level five-minute walk down bustling, shop-lined Via Nazionale (stop by the TI) to Piazza della Repubblica, the heart of the town, dominated by City Hall (Palazzo del Comune). From this square, a two-minute stroll leads you past the interesting Etruscan Museum and theater to Piazza del Duomo, where you'll find the recommended Diocesan Museum. Steep streets, many of them stepped, go from Piazza della Repubblica up to the San Niccolò and Santa Margherita churches and the Medici Fortress (a 30-minute climb from Piazza della Repubblica).

Drivers will find several free lots right outside the walls. Viale Battisti may be your best bet. A new free lot just after the big Santo Spirito Church has an escalator leading to Piazza Garibaldi. Piazza Garibaldi itself has a handful of pay spots (marked by blue lines, pay & display, cheap, free 20:00–8:00). The small town is actually very long, and it can be smart to drive to the top for sightseeing up there (parking at Santa Margherita Basilica).

Helpful Hints: Market day is Saturday on Piazza Signorelli (early–14:00). The town has no baggage storage, so try asking nicely at a hotel or museum to store your bag there. The best public WC is located in Piazza del Duomo, under St. Margherita's statue.

Local Guide: Giovanni Adreani exudes energy and a love of his city and Tuscan high culture. He is great at bringing the fine points of the city to life and can take visitors around in his car for no extra price. As this region is speckled with underappreciated charms, having Giovanni for a day as your driver/guide promises to be a fascinating experience (€110/half-day, €200/day, tel. 0575-630-665, mobile 347-176-2830, www.adreanigiovanni.com, adreanigiovanni@alice.it).

Cooking Classes: Husband-and-wife team Romano and Agostina hold morning hands-on cooking and cheese-making classes in the kitchen of their Ristorante La Bucaccia (see "Eating in Cortona," later in this section). In the three-hour class you'll prepare two *antipasti*, two types of pasta, an entrée, and a dessert, which you then get to eat (€60–70/person, classes start at 9:30, book in advance, Via Ghibellina 17, tel. 0575-606-039, www .labucaccia.it).

Self-Guided Walk

Welcome to Cortona

This introductory walking tour will take you from Piazza Garibaldi, up the main strip, to the town center, its piazzas, and the Duomo.

• *Start at the bus stop in...*

Piazza Garibaldi: Many visits start and finish in this square, thanks to its bus stop. While the piazza, bulging like a big turret out from the town fortifications, looks like part of an old rampart, it's really a souvenir of those early French and English Romantics—the ones who first created the notion of a dreamy, idyllic Tuscany. During the Napoleonic age, the French built this balcony (and the scenic little park behind the adjacent San Domenico Church) simply to enjoy a commanding view of the Tuscan countryside.

With Umbria about a mile away, Cortona marks the end of Tuscany. This is a major cultural divide, as Cortona was the last town in Charlemagne's empire and the last under Medici rule. Umbria, just to the south, was papal territory for centuries. These deep-seated cultural disparities were a great challenge for the visionaries who unified the fractured region to create the modern nation of Italy during the 1860s. A statue in the center of this square honors one of the heroes of the struggle for Italian unification—the brilliant revolutionary general, Giuseppe Garibaldi.

Enjoy the commanding view from here. Assisi is just over the ridge on the left. Lake Trasimeno peeks from behind the hill, looking quite normal today. But, according to legend, it was blood-red after Hannibal defeated the Romans here in 217 B.C., and 15,000 died in the battle. The only sizable town you can see, on the right, is Montepulciano. Cortona is still defined by its Etruscan walls—remnants of these walls, with stones laid 2,500 years ago, stretch from here in both directions.

Frances Mayes put Cortona on the map for many Americans with her book and the movie *Under the Tuscan Sun*. The book describes her real-life experience buying, fixing up, and living in a rundown villa

Cortona

in Cortona with her husband, Ed. The movie romanticized the story, turning Frances into a single, recently divorced writer who restores the villa and her peace of mind. Frances' villa (pictured on previous page) isn't "under the Tuscan sun" very often; it's named "Bramasole"—literally, "craving sun." On the wrong side of the hill, it's in the shade after 15:00. She and her husband still live there part of each year and are respected members of their adopted community (outside the walls, behind the hill on the left).

• *From this square, head into town along...*

Via Nazionale: The only level road in town, locals have nick-named Via Nazionale the *ruga piana* (flat wrinkle). This is the main commercial street in this town of 2,500, and it's been that way for a long time. Every shop seems to have a medieval cellar or an Etruscan well. Notice the crumbling sandstone door frames. The entire town is constructed out of this grainy, eroding rock.

• *Via Nazionale leads to...*

PORTA
MONTANINA

TO
MEDICI
FORTRESS

P BAR

VIA
S. CROCE

SAN
NICCOLÒ

V. CANTUCCE

SANTA
MARGHERITA

PORTA
BERADA

100 YARDS

100 METERS

CITY
WALLS

PUBLIC
GARDENS

TO CAMUCIA
& TERONTOLA
(NEAREST TRAIN
STATIONS)

❶ Albergo San Luca & Parking
❷ Rugapiana Vacanze B&B
❸ Casa Betania
❹ Istituto Santa Margherita
❺ San Marco Hostel
❻ Casa Kita
❼ To Casa San Martino,
   La Villetta di San Martino B&B
   & Castello di Montegualandro
❽ Trattoria la Grotta
❾ Ristorante La Loggetta
❿ Ristorante La Bucaccia
⓫ Ristorante Dolce Maria
⓬ Fufluns Tavern Pizzeria
⓭ Osteria del Teatro
⓮ Enoteca la Saletta
⓯ DeSpar Market Molesini

▬▬ INTRO WALK
P PARKING
→ ENTRY POINT
   TO SIGHTS

⟍ VIEW
⫼⫼ STAIRS
Ⓑ BUS STOP

TUSCAN HILL TOWNS

Piazza della Repubblica: The City Hall faces Cortona's main square. Note how the City Hall is a clever hodgepodge of twin medieval towers, with a bell tower added to connect them, and a grand staircase to lend some gravitas. Notice also the fine wood balconies on the left. In the Middle Ages, wooden extensions such as balconies were common features on the region's stone buildings. These balconies (not original, but rebuilt in the 19th century) would have fit right into the medieval cityscape. These days, you usually see only the holes that once supported the long-gone wooden beams.

This spot has been the town center since Etruscan times. Four centuries before Christ, an important street led from here up to the hill-capping temple. Later, the square became the Roman forum. Opposite the City Hall is the handy DeSpar Market Molesini, good for cheap sandwiches (described in "Eating in Cortona," later in this section). Above that is the loggia—once a fish market, now a recommended restaurant.

• *The second half of the square, to the right of the City Hall, is...*

Piazza Signorelli: Dominated by Casali Palace, this square was the headquarters of the Florentine captains who used to control the city. Peek into the palace entrance for a look at the coats of arms. Every six months, Florence would send a new captain to Cortona, who would help establish his rule by inserting his family coat of arms into the palace's wall. These date from the 15th to the 17th century, and were once painted with bright colors. Cortona's fine Etruscan Museum (listed in "Sights in Cortona") is in the Casali Palace courtyard, which is lined with many more of these family coats of arms. The inviting Caffè del Teatro fills the loggia of the theater that is named for the town's most famous artist, Luca Signorelli.

• *Head down the street just to the right of the museum to...*

Piazza del Duomo: Here you'll find the Diocesan Museum (listed under "Sights in Cortona"), cathedral, and a statue of St. Margherita. If the cathedral seems a little underwhelming and tucked away, that's because it is. Cortona loves its hometown saint, Margherita, and put the energy it would normally invest in its cathedral into the Santa Margherita Basilica, at the top of the hill. Margherita was a 13th-century rich girl who took good care of the poor and was an early follower of St. Francis and St. Clare. Many locals believe that Margherita protected Cortona from WWII bombs.

The Piazza del Duomo terrace comes with a commanding view of the Tuscan countryside. Find the town cemetery in the distance. If you were standing here before the time of Napoleon, you'd be surrounded by tombstones. But Cortona's graveyards—like other urban graveyards throughout Napoleon's realm—were cleaned out in the early 1800s to reclaim land and improve hygiene.

• *Next, enter the...*

Duomo: The Cortona cathedral is not—strictly speaking—a cathedral, because it no longer has a bishop. The white-and-gray Florentine Renaissance–style interior is mucked up with lots of Baroque chapels filling once-spacious side niches. In the rear (on the right) is an altar cluttered with relics. Technically, any Catholic altar, in order to be consecrated, needs a relic embedded in it. Go ahead—gently lift up the tablecloth. The priest here doesn't mind. You'll see a little marble patch that holds a bit of a saint (daily 7:30–13:00 & 15:00–18:30, shorter hours in winter, closed during Mass).

• *From here, you can visit the nearby Diocesan Museum or head back toward Piazza della Repubblica to visit the Etruscan Museum in Piazza Signorelli (both listed in "Sights in Cortona," next page), or to get a bite to eat (see "Eating in Cortona," later in this section).*

Sights in Cortona

▲Etruscan Museum (Museo dell'Accademia Etrusca)—
Located in the 13th-century Casali Palace, this fine gallery
(established in 1727) is one of the first dedicated to artifacts from
the Etruscan civilization. You'll see an exhibit on the Roman
settlement and take a virtual tour of the Etruscan "Il Sodo"
tombs. The Cortona Tablet (*Tabula Cortonensis*, second century
B.C.), a 200-word contract inscribed in bronze, contains dozens of
Etruscan words archaeologists had never seen before its discovery
in 1992. Along with lots of gold and jewelry, you'll find a seventh-
century B.C. grater (for some really old Parmesan cheese) and a
magnificent fourth-century B.C. bronze oil lamp with 16 spouts,
set in a small, four-pillared temple. The library of the Etruscan
Academy, founded in 1727 to promote an understanding of the
city through the study of archaeology, is upstairs. This eclectic
museum also has an Egyptian section, fine Roman mosaics, and a
room dedicated to modern abstract works by Severini, all lovingly
described in English (€8, €10 combo-ticket includes Diocesan
Museum, April–Oct daily 10:00–19:00; Nov–March Tue–Sun
10:00–17:00, closed Mon; Casali Palace on Piazza Signorelli, tel.
0575-637-235).

▲Diocesan Museum (Museo Diocesano)—This collection
of art from the town's many churches has works by Fra Angelico
and Pietro Lorenzetti, and masterpieces by hometown hero and
Renaissance master Luca Signorelli.

Don't miss Fra Angelico's sumptuous *Annunciation*. In this
scene, Mary says, "Yes," consenting to bear God's son. Notice how
the house sits on a pillow of flowers...the new Eden. The old Eden,
featuring the expulsion of Adam and Eve from Paradise, is in the
upper left. The painting comes with comic strip–like narration of
scenes from Mary's life: The angel's words are top and bottom,
while Mary's answer is upside down (logically, since it's directed to
God, who would be reading while looking down from heaven).

The crucifix (by Pietro Lorenzetti, c. 1325, just to the right
of the Fra Angelico) is impressive in its severity. Notice the grip-
ping realism—even the tendons in Jesus' arms are pulled tight.
Another highlight is Luca Signorelli's *Mourning of the Dead Christ
(Compianto sul Cristo Morto)*. Signorelli was a generation ahead
of Michelangelo and, with his passion for painting ideas, was an
inspiration for the young artist. Everything in his painting has a
meaning: The skull of Adam sits under the sacrifice of Jesus; the
hammer represents the Passion (the Crucifixion leading to the
Resurrection); the lake is blood; and so on. I don't understand all
of the medieval symbolism, but it is intense (€5, €10 combo-ticket

includes Etruscan Museum, helpful audioguide-€3, April–Oct daily 10:00–19:00; Nov–March Tue–Sun 10:00–17:00, closed Mon; Piazza del Duomo 1, tel. 0575-62-830). For more on Signorelli, see page 440.

Church of St. Francis—Established by St. Francis' best friend, Brother Elias, this church dates from the 13th century. The wooden beams of the ceiling are original. While the place was redecorated in the Baroque age, some of the original frescoes that once wallpapered the church peek through the whitewash in a chapel on the left. Francis fans visit for its precious Franciscan relics. To the left of the altar, you'll find one of Francis' tunics, his pillow (inside a fancy cover), and his gospel book. Behind the altar is Elias' very simple tomb. It reads "Frate Elia da Cortona." Notice how the entire high altar seems designed to frame its precious relic—a piece of the cross Elias brought back from his visit to the patriarch in Constantinople. You're welcome to climb the altar for a close-up look (Mon–Fri 9:00–17:30, Sat 10:00–17:30, Sun 9:00–10:00 & 11:00–19:00).

San Niccolò Church—Signorelli enthusiasts will want to make the pilgrimage up to this tiny church. Ring the bell, and the caretaker might give you a short tour in Italian (€1 donation, daily in summer 9:00–12:00 & 15:00–19:00, off-season until 17:00). The highlight of this humble church is an altarpiece painted on both sides by Signorelli. The caretaker activates a tricky arm mechanism that moves the picture away from the wall to reveal the painting behind it.

Santa Margherita Basilica—From San Niccolò Church, a steep path leads uphill 10 minutes to this basilica, which houses the remains of Margherita, the town's favorite saint. St. Margherita, an unwed mother from Montepulciano, found her calling with the Franciscans in Cortona, tending to the sick and poor. The well-preserved and remarkably emotional 13th-century crucifix on the right is the cross that, according to legend, talked to Margherita (daily 9:00–12:00 & 15:00–19:00, tel. 0575-603-116).

Still need more altitude? Head uphill five more minutes to the Medici Fortezza (€3, usually open daily mid-March–June and Sept 9:00–12:00 & 15:00–18:00, July–Aug until 19:00, closed Oct–early March). The views are stunning, stretching all the way to distant Lago Trasimeno.

Etruscan Tombs near Cortona—Guided tours to nearby "Il Sodo" tombs (called *melone* for their melon-like shape) are complicated to arrange. But the excavation site and bits of the ruins are easy to visit and can be seen from outside the fence in the morning. It's just a couple miles out of Cortona on the Arezzo road (R-71), at the edge of Camucia at the foot of the Cortona hill; ask anyone for "Il Sodo."

Sleeping in Cortona

(€1 = about $1.40, country code: 39)

$$$ Albergo San Luca, perched on the side of a cliff, has 57 modern, business-class, impersonal rooms, half with stunning views of Lago Trasimeno. While tired and a bit run-down, it's friendly and conveniently located right at the bus stop (Sb-€85, Db-€120, Tb-€150, request a view room when you reserve, popular with Americans and groups, Piazza Garibaldi 1, tel. 0575-630-460, fax 0575-630-105, www.sanlucacortona.com, info @sanlucacortona.com). If driving, there's a small public parking lot at the hotel where you might find a spot (cheap and easy meters).

$$ Rugapiana Vacanze B&B rents four doubles and four apartments, each described separately on their website. Located on Cortona's main drag, it's beautifully furnished with all the thoughtful touches (apartment or Db-€95 with breakfast at a nearby bar, 10 percent discount with this book, family suites, Wi-Fi, Via Nazionale 63, tel. & fax 0575-630-712, mobile 340-808-6879, www.rugapianavacanze.com, info@rugapianavacanze .com, Massimo).

$ Casa Betania, a big, wistful convent with an inviting view terrace, rents 27 fine rooms (mostly twin beds) for the best price in town. While it's primarily for "thoughtful travelers," anyone looking for a peaceful place to call home will feel welcome in this pilgrims' resort (S-€32, D-€44, Db-€48, Tb-€66, extra bed-€20, breakfast-€4, parking, about a third of a mile out of town, a few minutes' walk below Piazza Garibaldi at Via Gino Severini 50, tel. & fax 0575-630-423, www.casaperferiebetania.com, info@casa perferiebetania.com, Lao).

$ Istituto Santa Margherita, run by the Serve di Maria Riparatrici sisters, rents 22 cheap and simple rooms in a smaller and more institutional-feeling convent across the street (Sb-€40, Db-€54, Tb-€70, Qb-€80, breakfast-€4, free parking, Viale Cesare Battisti 15, tel. & fax 0575-630-336, comunitacortona@smr.it).

$ San Marco Hostel, at the top of town, is housed in a remodeled 13th-century palace (bed in dorm-€14, in 2-bed and 4-bed rooms-€18, includes breakfast, lockout 10:00–14:00, Via Maffei 57, tel. & fax 0575-601-392, www.cortonahostel.com, ostellocortona @libero.it).

$ Casa Kita, renting four fine rooms, is a homely place at the edge of town with breathtaking views from its terrace (Db-€60, 100 yards below Piazza Garibaldi at Vicolo degli Orti 7, tel. 389-557-9893, www.casakita.com, info@casakita.com, Lorenzini family).

Near Cortona

$$$ Casa San Martino, a 30-minute drive east of Cortona near the isolated village of Lisciano Niccone, is a 250-year-old countryside farmhouse run as a B&B by American Italophile Lois Martin. While Lois reserves the summer (June–Aug) for people staying at least one week, she'll take guests staying a minimum of three nights the rest of the year (Db-€140, 10 percent discount for my readers—mention this book when you reserve, pool, Casa San Martino 19, Lisciano Niccone, tel. 075-844-288, fax 075-844-422, www.tuscanyvacation.com, csm@tuscanyvacation.com).

$$$ Castello di Montegualandro, a well-preserved castle on a hill opposite Cortona, overlooks the lake and countryside. The Marti family rents four charming medieval apartments, formerly peasants' quarters, inside the peaceful castle walls. Each one is unique and named for its former use—the Fornaci's sunken living room used to be a kiln (apartments range from €400–450 for 3-night minimum stay, €700–800/wk, cash only; for a 5-night stay, mention this book for a 7 percent discount; 10 percent discount for longer stays; 10 min southeast of Cortona in Tuoro sul Trasimeno, tel. & fax 075-823-0267, www.montegualandro.com, info@monte gualandro.com).

$$ La Villetta di San Martino B&B is a tidy place run by Lois' neighbors, Ernestine and Gisbert Schwanke (Db-€80, 2-night minimum, cash only, common kitchen and sitting room, San Martino 36, tel. & fax 075-844-309, www.tuscanyvacation .com, erni@netemedia.net).

Eating in Cortona

Trattoria la Grotta, just off Piazza della Repubblica, is a traditional place serving daily specials to an enthusiastic clientele under grotto-like vaults (€7 pastas, €8 meat dishes, good wine by the glass, Wed–Mon 12:00–14:30 & 19:00–22:30, closed Tue, Piazza Baldelli 3, tel. 0575-630-271).

Ristorante La Loggetta serves up big portions of well-presented Tuscan cuisine on the loggia overlooking Piazza della Repubblica. While they have fine indoor seating, I'd eat here for the chance to gaze at the square over a meal (€8 pastas, €7–15 meat dishes, Thu–Tue 12:30–15:00 & 19:30–23:00, closed Wed, Piazza Pescheria 3, tel. 0575-630-575).

Ristorante La Bucaccia is a family-run eatery set in a rustic, medieval wine cellar. It's dressy and romantic. They take great pride in their Chianina beef entrées and homemade pastas (€9 pastas, €15 entrées, daily 12:00–15:30 & 19:00–24:00, show this book for a 5 percent discount, Via Ghibellina 17, tel. 0575-606-039). With an evangelical pride in their food, Romano hosts and his wife Agostina cooks.

Ristorante Dolce Maria (Sweet Mary) offers an affordable, limited menu of Tuscan fare focused on quality seasonal produce. Eat in a minimalist, sunlit dining room or tucked away in a tranquil, secret courtyard (€8 pastas, €15 *secondi*, daily 12:00–14:30 & 19:00–22:30, Via Ghini 14, tel. 0575-62091, Luigi).

Fufluns Tavern Pizzeria (that's the Etruscan name for Dionysus) is easy-going, friendly, and remarkably unpretentious for its location in the town center. It's popular with locals for its good, inexpensive Tuscan cooking and friendly staff (cheap, lots of €6 pizza and pasta plus big salads, good house wine, Wed–Mon 12:15–14:30 & 19:15–22:30, closed Tue, a block below Piazza della Repubblica at Via Ghibellina 3, tel. 057-560-4140).

Osteria del Teatro tries very hard to create a romantic Old World atmosphere and does it well. Chef Emiliano serves nicely presented and tasty international and local cuisine (taking creative liberties with traditions). There's good outdoor seating, too (Thu–Tue 12:30–14:30 & 19:30–21:30, closed Wed, 2 blocks uphill from the main square at Via Maffei 2, tel. 0575-630-556).

Enoteca la Saletta, dark and classy, is good for fine wine and a light meal. You can sit inside surrounded by wine bottles or outside to people-watch on the town's main drag (daily 7:30–24:00, meals served 12:00–24:00, Via Nazionale 26, tel. 0575-603-366).

For a Picnic: On the main square, the chic little **DeSpar Market Molesini** makes tasty sandwiches (see list on counter and order by number) and sells whatever you might want for a picnic (daily including Sun morning, Piazza della Repubblica 23). Munch your picnic across the square on the steps of the City Hall, or just past Piazza Garibaldi in the public gardens behind San Domenico Church.

Connections

Cortona has good train connections with the rest of Italy through its Camucia-Cortona station. To get to the train station at the foot of the hill, take a taxi or hop the bus (€1, 2/hr between Piazza Garibaldi and station, buy tickets at newsstand or *tabacchi* shop, or buy from driver at double the price). Note that some only take you as far as the newsstand *(edicola)* 200 yards in front of the station.

From Cortona by Train to: Rome (14/day, 2 hrs), **Florence** (hourly, 1.5 hrs), **Assisi** (7/day, 1.25 hrs), **Montepulciano** (10/day, 1–1.25 hrs, change in Chiusi—because few buses serve Montepulciano's town center from its distant train station, it's better to go by train to Chiusi, then by hourly bus to Montepulciano), **Chiusi** (hourly, 30 min). Most trains stop at the Camucia-Cortona train station, but some trains to/from Rome and Florence stop at

Terontola, 10 miles away (bus to/from Cortona runs hourly during the week, 4/day on Sun, €2, tel. 800-115-605 or call the TI to confirm times).

More Tuscan Sights

▲Galgano Monastery

Of southern Tuscany's several evocative monasteries, San Galgano is the best. Set in a forested area called the Montagnolo (medium-size mountains), the isolated abbey and chapel are postcard-perfect.

St. Galgano was a 12th-century saint who renounced his past as a knight to become a hermit. Lacking a cross to display, he created his own by miraculously burying his sword up to its hilt into a stone, à la King Arthur, but in reverse. After his death, a large Cistercian monastery complex grew. Today, all you'll see is the roofless, ruined abbey and, on a nearby hill, the Chapel of San Galgano with its fascinating dome and sword in the stone.

Getting There: Although a bus reportedly comes here from Siena, this sight is realistically accessible only for drivers. It's just outside of Monticiano (not Montalcino), about an hour south of Siena. A warning to the queasy: These roads are curvy.

The Abbey: This picturesque, Cistercian abbey was once a powerful institution in Tuscany. Known for their skill as builders, the Cistercians oversaw the construction of Siena's cathedral. But after losing most of its population in the plague of 1348, the abbey never really recovered and was eventually deconsecrated.

The Cistercian order was centered in France, and the architecture of the abbey shows a heavy French influence. Notice the large, high windows and the pointy, delicate arches. This is pure French Gothic, a style that never fully caught on in Italy (compare it with the chunky, elaborately decorated cathedral in Siena, built about the same time).

As you enter the church, notice the small section of the cloister wall to the left. This used to surround the garden, and was the only place where the monks were allowed to talk, for one hour each day. From inside the church, the empty windows frame the view of the chapel up on the hill.

The Chapel: A path from the abbey leads up the hill to the Chapel of San Galgano. The unique, beehive-like interior houses

St. Galgano's sword and stone, recently confirmed to date back to the 12th century. Don't try and pull the sword from the stone—the small chapel to the left displays the severed arms of the last guy who tried. The chapel also contains some deteriorated frescoes and more interesting *sinopie* (fresco sketches). The adjacent gift shop sells a little bit of everything, from wine to postcards to herbs, some of it monk-made (free, summer daily 9:00–20:00, shoulder season until 18:30, erratic hours Nov–Dec, closed Jan–Feb, tel. 0577-756-738). For a quick snack, a small, touristy bar at the end of the driveway is your only option.

Other, more accessible Tuscan monasteries worth visiting include Sant'Antimo (6 miles south of Montalcino) and Monte Oliveto Maggiore (15 miles south of Siena, mentioned in "Crete Senese Drives," on the next page).

▲Chiusi

This small hill town (rated ▲▲ for Etruscan fans) was once one of the most important Etruscan cities. Today, it's a key train junction and a pleasant, workaday Italian village with an enjoyable historic center and few tourists.

The region's trains (to Florence, Siena, Orvieto, and Assisi) go through or change at this hub, making Chiusi an easy day trip. Buses link the train station with the town center two miles away (depart every 40 min, tickets at *tabacchi* shop). Easy and free parking lots are a five-minute walk from the center.

The **TI** is on the main square (May–Sept Tue–Sun 10:00–13:00 & 15:00–17:00, closed Mon, shorter hours off-season, tel. 0578-227-667).

The **Archaeological Museum,** just off the main square, thoughtfully presents a high-quality collection with plenty of explanations in English. The collection of funerary urns, some in painted terra-cotta and some in *pietra fetida* ("stinky stone"), are remarkably intact (€4, July–Sept daily 9:00–20:00, Oct–June until 14:00, Via Porsenna 93, tel. 0578-20177). The museum also arranges tours to visit tombs outside of town. One of the tombs is multi-chambered, with several sarcophagi. Another, the **Tomba della Scimmia** (Tomb of the Monkey), has some well-preserved frescoes. Visiting the tombs requires a guide, a car, and an advance reservation (€2, Tue, Thu, and Sat at 11:00 and 15:30; 25 visitors per tour).

Troglodyte alert! The **Cathedral Museum** on the main square has a dark, underground labyrinth of Etruscan tunnels. The mandatory guided tour of the tunnels ends in a large Roman cistern from which you can climb the church bell tower for an expansive view of the countryside (museum-€2, labyrinth-€3, combo-ticket-€4, daily June–Oct 9:30–12:30 & 16:00–19:00, Nov–May 9:30–12:30 only, 30-min tunnel tours run every 40 min during museum hours, Piazza Duomo 1, tel. 0578-226-490).

Craving more underground fun? The **Museo Civico** provides hourly tours of the Etruscan water system, which includes an underground lake (€3; May–Oct Tue–Sun at 10:15, 11:30, 12:45, 15:15, 16:30, and 17:45; closed Mon, fewer tours off-season, call to confirm times, Via II Ciminia 1, tel. 0578-227-667, mobile 348-522-6337).

▲Florence American Cemetery and Memorial

The compelling sight of endless rows of white marble crosses and Stars of David recalls the heroism of the young Americans who fought so valiantly to free Italy (and ultimately Europe) from the grip of fascism. This particular cemetery is the final resting place of more than 4,000 Americans who died in the liberation of Italy during World War II. Climb the hill past the perfectly manicured lawn lined with grave markers, to the memorial, where maps and a history of the Italian campaign detail the Allied advance (daily 9:00–17:00; 7.5 miles south of  Florence, off Via Cassia, which parallels the *superstrada* between Florence and Siena, 2 miles south of Florence Certosa exit on A-1 autostrada; tel. 055-202-0020, www.abmc.gov). Buses from Florence stop just outside the cemetery.

▲▲Crete Senese Drives

South of Siena, the hilly area known as the "Sienese Crests" is full of colorful fields and curvy, scenic roads. You'll see an endless parade of classic Tuscan scenes, rolling hills topped with medieval towns, olive groves, rustic stone farmhouses, and a skyline punctuated with cypress trees. You won't find many wineries here, since the clay soil is better for wheat and sunflowers, but you will find the pristine, panoramic Tuscan countryside that you find on calendars and postcards.

During the spring, the fields are painted in yellow and green with fava beans and broom, dotted by red poppies on the fringes. Sunflowers decorate the area during June and July, and expanses of windblown grass fill the landscape almost all year.

Most roads to the southeast of Siena will give you a taste of this area, but one of the most scenic stretches is the Lauretan road (Siena–Asciano–San Giovanni d'Asso, #438 on road maps; you can also take S-2—Via Cassia—toward Rome and turn off at *Asciano* sign, either way allows you to easily continue to Montalcino). You'll come across plenty of turnouts for panoramic photo opportunities on this road, as well as a few roadside picnic areas.

For a break from the winding road, about 15 miles from Siena, you'll find the quaint and non-touristy village of **Asciano**. With a medieval town center and several interesting churches and museums, this town offers a rare look at everyday Tuscan living—and a great place for lunch (TI open Mon–Fri 10:30–13:00 & 15:00–18:00, Sat–Sun 10:30–13:00, at Corso Matteotti 18, tel. 0577-719-510). If you're in town on Saturday, gather a picnic at the outdoor market (Via Amendola, 8:00–13:00).

Five miles south of Asciano, the **Abbey of Monte Oliveto Maggiore** houses a famous fresco cycle of the life of St. Benedict, painted by Renaissance masters Il Sodoma and Luca Signorelli (free, daily April–Oct 9:45–12:00 & 15:15–18:00, Nov–March closes at 17:00, Gregorian chanting Sun at 11:00 and Mon–Sat at 18:15, call to confirm, tel. 0577-707-611). Once you reach the town of **San Giovanni d'Asso,** it's only another 12 miles southwest to Montalcino.

Another scenic drive is the lovely stretch between Montalcino and Montepulciano (S-146 on road maps). This route alternates between the grassy hills of the Crete Senese and sunbathed vineyards of the Orcia River valley. Stop by Pienza en route.

Sleeping in the Crete Senese: **Agriturismo il Molinello** rents five apartments, two built over a medieval mill. Hardworking Alessandro and Elisa share their organic produce and offer weekly wine tastings for a minimum of four people. From May through October, they offer free guided tours of Siena on Tuesday afternoons. With children, friendly dogs, toys, and a swimming pool, this is ideal for families (Qb-€70–100, apartment for up to 8-€150–180, optional breakfast-€8, one-week stay required in summer, discounts and no minimum stay off-season, free Internet access, mountain-bike rentals, biking maps and guided bike tours, near Asciano, 30 min southeast of Siena, tel. 0577-704-791, mobile 335-692-5720, fax 0577-705-605, www.molinello.com, info @molinello.com).

FIORENZA

FLORENTINE HISTORY

Two Millennia in Five Pages

59 B.C.–A.D. 1200: Roman, Early Christian, Medieval

It's the usual Rome story—military outpost, thriving provincial capital, conversion to Christianity, overrun by barbarians—except Florence really didn't fall. Proud medieval Florentines traced their roots back to civilized Rome, and the city remained a Tuscan commercial center during the Dark Ages.

Sights

- Piazza della Repubblica (the old Forum)
- Find the ancient Roman military camp on today's street map. You can still see the rectangular grid plan—lined up with compass points, rather than the river.
- Baptistery (built c. 1050), likely on site of Roman temple
- Roman and Etruscan fragments (Duomo Museum)

1200s: Urban Growth

Woolen cloth manufacture, trade, and banking made urban merchants—organized into guilds—more powerful than rural, feudal nobles. Florence, now a largely independent city-state, allied with nearby cities.

Sights
- Bargello (it was built as the City Hall)
- Santa Croce and Santa Maria Novella churches
- Baptistery interior mosaics

1300s: Prosperity, Plague, Recovery

As part of a budding democracy with civic pride, Florence's guilds and merchants financed major construction projects (some begun in the late 1200s). But the population of 90,000 was suddenly cut nearly in half by the Black Death (bubonic plague) of 1348. Recovery was slowed by more plagues, bank failures, and political rivalries.

FLORENTINE HISTORY

Sights
- Duomo and Campanile (original decorations in Duomo Museum)
- Palazzo Vecchio
- Orsanmichele Church
- Santa Croce, Santa Maria Novella, and Giotto's bell-tower design (Campanile) and his paintings in Uffizi

1400s: Renaissance and Medicis

While 1500 marks Europe's Renaissance, in Florence—where the whole revival of classical culture got its start—the Renaissance

began and ended in the 1400s (the Quattrocento). The Medicis (MED-ee-chees), a rich textile-and-banking family whose wealth gave them political leverage around Europe, ruled the most prosperous city in Italy, appeasing the masses with philanthropy and public art.

Sights
- Brunelleschi's Duomo dome and Pazzi Chapel
- Donatello's statues in Bargello, Duomo Museum, and on Orsanmichele exterior
- Ghiberti's two bronze doors on Baptistery (originals in Duomo Museum)

Church Architecture

History comes to life when you visit a centuries-old church. Knowing a few simple terms will enrich your experience. Note that not every church will have every feature, and that a "cathedral" isn't a type of church architecture, but rather a governing center for a local bishop.

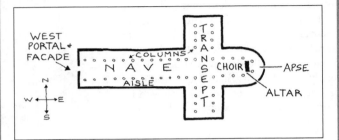

Aisles: The long, generally low-ceilinged arcades that flank the nave.

Altar: The raised area with a ceremonial table (often adorned with candles or a crucifix), where the priest prepares and serves the bread and wine for Communion.

Apse: The space beyond the altar, generally bordered with small chapels.

Choir: A cozy area, often screened off, located within the church nave and near the high altar where services are sung in a more intimate setting.

Cloister: A square-shaped series of hallways surrounding an open-air courtyard, traditionally where monks and nuns got fresh air.

Facade: The outer wall of the church's main (west) entrance, viewable from outside and generally highly decorated.

Groin Vault: An arched ceiling formed where two equal barrel vaults meet at right angles. Less common usage: term for a medieval jock strap.

Narthex: The area (portico or foyer) between the main entry and the nave.

Nave: The long, central section of the church (running west to east, from the entrance to the altar) where, in medieval times, the congregation stood through the service.

Transept: The north–south part of the church, which crosses (perpendicularly) the east–west nave. In a traditional Latin cross-shaped floor plan, the transept forms the "arms" of the cross.

West Portal: The main entry to the church (on the west end, opposite the main altar).

- Botticelli's paintings in Uffizi
- The Uffizi, tracing painting history from medieval to Michelangelo
- The Bargello, tracing sculpture history
- Masaccio's frescoes in Santa Maria Novella and Brancacci Chapel
- Fra Angelico paintings (and Savonarola history) in San Marco Museum

1500–1800: Decline, Medici Dukes, Renaissance Goes South

Bankrupt, the anti-democratic Medicis were exiled to Rome, where they married into royalty and returned—backed by foreign powers—as even less democratic nobles. The "Renaissance spirit" moved elsewhere, taking Michelangelo, Leonardo, and Raphael with it. In succeeding centuries, the Medici dukes ruled an economically and politically declining city, but still financed art.

Sights

- Michelangelo's Florentine works—*David*, Medici Chapels, and Laurentian Library
- Pitti Palace and Boboli Gardens (the later Medici palace)
- Later paintings (Uffizi) and statues (Bargello)
- Destruction of the original Duomo facade (Duomo Museum)
- Medici Chapels—pompous tombs of (mostly) later Medicis
- Ponte Vecchio cleaned up for jewelry shops
- Baroque interiors of many older churches
- Galileo's finger, telescopes, and experiments in the Galileo Science Museum

1800s: Italian Unification

After years of rule by Austrian nobles, Florence peacefully booted the *ausländer*s and joined the Italian unification movement. It even served briefly as modern Italy's capital (1865–1870). Artistic revival of both medieval (Neo-Gothic) and Renaissance (Neoclassical) styles.

Sights

- Duomo's current Neo-Gothic facade
- Piazza della Repubblica (commemorating unification) with its fine 19th-century cafés

1900s to Today: Uncontrolled Urbanization, Urban Renewal

Population growth, rapid industrialization, WWII destruction, and the 20-foot-high flood of 1966 made Florence a chaotic, noisy, dirty, traffic-choked city. In the last 30 years, however, the tourist zone has been cleaned and cleared, museums revamped, hours extended, and the people have adapted to welcoming foreign visitors. Now if they could just do something about those Vespas....

Florence Timeline

500 B.C.–A.D. 1000: Etruscans, Romans, and "Barbarians"

c. 550 B.C.	Etruscans settle in Fiesole, near Florence.
59 B.C.	Julius Caesar establishes the Roman town of Florentia (meaning "flowering" or "flourishing") at a convenient crossing point on the Arno River.
c. A.D. 200	Thriving Roman city, pop. 10,000.
c. 350	In the wake of Constantine's legalization of Christianity, Bishop (and Saint) Zenobius builds a church where the Duomo stands today.
450	Rome falls. Ostrogoths from the east, Byzantines from modern-day Turkey, and Germanic barbarians sweep through in waves. But Florence survives as a small trading town.
800	Charlemagne's Franks sweep through; he becomes the first Holy Roman Emperor. Florence is part of the Empire for the next 300 years, and is the regional capital (rather than Fiesole).

1000–1400: Medieval Rise and Political Squabbles

c. 1050	Baptistery built, likely on site of ancient Roman temple.
1100	Matilda, Countess of Tuscany, allies with the pope and rises against the German-based Holy Roman Empire, gaining independence for Florence.

Guelphs vs. Ghibellines

In medieval times, Italy was divided between two competing political factions, characterized by thes differences:

	Guelphs	Ghibellines
Leader	Pope	Emperor
Constituency	Middle-class merchants and craftsmen	Aristocrats of feudal order
Economics	Urban (new economy)	Rural (traditional economy)
Politics	Independence of city-states under local Italian leaders	Unification of small states under traditional dukes and kings

Their conflict had more to do with power than ideology. (It wasn't what you believed, but with whom you were allied.) The names could mean something different depending on the particular place and time.

1200 Florence is the leading city in Tuscany, thriving on wool manufacture, trade, banking, and money lending.

1215 Political assassination of Buondelmonte epitomizes power struggles among nobles (Ghibellines), rich merchants and craftsmen (Guelphs), and laborers. The different factions seek support from outsiders—Guelphs ally with pope, Ghibellines with emperor. In general, Ghibellines dominate in first half of 1200s.

1222–1235 Florentine armies defeat Pisa, Siena, and Pistoia. Florence is the dominant city-state in Tuscany, heading a rich, commercial marketplace.

1252 Gold florin minted, one of Europe's strongest currencies.

1266 Merchants and craftsmen (Guelphs), organized into guilds, oust nobles and establish the primo popolo, the first "rule by the people."

1293 Guelphs solidify rule by the rich middle class, establishing a constitution that forbids nobles and laborers from holding office. The Ghibellines are gone, but bitter political infighting continues, with Florence divided between Black and White Guelphs.

1296 Construction begins on the Duomo. Santa Croce and Santa Maria Novella are also being built.

1302	The poet Dante, a prominent White Guelph, is exiled. Traveling around Europe and Italy, he writes his epic poem, *The Divine Comedy*.
1347	Florence's population is 90,000, making it one of Europe's biggest cities.
1348	Population nearly halved after the horrific bubonic plague. In addition, recent bank failures and ongoing political squabbles make recovery more difficult.
1378	The Ciompi revolt, led by wool-factory workers, is suppressed by rich merchant families. The guilds (workers' unions) lose power as a few wealthy families rise—the Strozzi, Ricci, Alberti, and...Medici.

1400s, The "Quattrocento": A Prosperous Renaissance City Under Medici Princes

1401	Baptistery door competition energizes an already civic-minded city.
1406	Florence, by conquering Pisa, gains a port and becomes a sea-trading power.
1421	Giovanni de' Medici, a shrewd businessman, expands the Medici family business from wool manufacture into banking.
1434	Cosimo the Elder (Giovanni's son) returns triumphant from exile to rule Florence. Outwardly, he honors the Florentine constitution, but, in fact, he uses his great wealth to rule as a tyrant, buying popularity with lavish patronage of public art.
1436	Dedication of the Duomo, topped by Brunelleschi's dome.
1440	Battle of Anghiari—Florence defeats Milan.
c. 1440	Donatello's *David*.
1458	Cosimo the Elder creates a rubber-stamp Council of the Hundred.
1464	Cosimo's son, Piero the Gouty, rules stiffly but ably.
1469	Lorenzo the Magnificent, Cosimo's grandson, rules over the most powerful city in Italy. He is a popular politician but a so-so businessman.
1492	Lorenzo dies. Many Medici banks go bankrupt. Lorenzo's son, Piero the Unfortunate, faces an invasion force from France and appears to side with the foreigners.
1494	Reviled for being morally, financially, and politically bankrupt, the Medici family is exiled. In the political vacuum, the monk Girolamo

Savonarola appears as a voice of moral authority. He reestablishes the Florentine constitution.

1498 Savonarola is hanged and burned on Piazza della Signoria by political enemies and a citizenry tired of his morally strict rule. The constitution-driven republic continues.

1500–1800: The "Later" Medicis Oversee Florence's Decline

1501 Michelangelo begins sculpting *David*.

1512 The Medici family, having established a power base in Rome, returns to take political power as tyrants, backed by the pope and the Spanish army of Holy Roman Emperor Charles V.

1513 Lorenzo the Magnificent's son, Giovanni, becomes Pope Leo X.

1523 Lorenzo's nephew becomes Pope Clement VII.

1527 Renegade, unpaid, mercenary troops loot Rome. In the political chaos that follows, Florentines drive the Medicis from Florence, reestablishing a republic.

1530 After a yearlong siege, Pope Clement VII and Charles V retake Florence, abolishing the republic and reinstalling Medici rulers.

1533 The Medicis marry off Catherine de' Medici to the future King Henry II of France.

1537 Cosimo the Younger, a Medici descended from Cosimo the Elder's brother, is made Duke of Florence. He and his wife, Eleanor of Toledo, rule as tyrannical nobles but beautify the city with the Uffizi, a renovated Palazzo Vecchio, and a rebuilt Pitti Palace.

1574 Francesco I becomes duke, soon to be followed by various Ferdinandos and Cosimos. Florence is now a minor player in world affairs, a small dukedom with a stagnant economy.

1587 The medieval facade of the Duomo is torn down. It remains bare brick for the next 200 years while different proposals are debated.

1600 Maria de' Medici marries Henry IV to become Queen of France.

1610–1633 Galileo, backed by the Medici family, works in Florence.

1737 Gian Gastone, the last of the Medici line, dies. Florence is ruled by Austrian Habsburg nobles.

1800–Present: Florence Enters the Modern World

1799   Napoleon "liberates" the city, briefly establishing a pseudo-democracy with his sister as duchess.

1814   Napoleon falls, and the city returns to Austrian rule, under a distant descendant of the Medici family.

1848   Florentine citizens join an uprising all over Italy against foreign rule. The Risorgimento is on.

1860   Florence joins the kingdom of Victor Emmanuel II, forming the nucleus of united, democratic, modern Italy.

1865   Florence is made Italy's capital.

1870   Rome is liberated and becomes the de facto capital of a unified Italy (officially in 1871).

1944   Under Nazi occupation as the Allies close in, all of the Arno bridges except Ponte Vecchio are blown up.

1966   A disastrous flood, up to nearly 20 feet high, covers the city's buildings and art treasures in mud. The city is a cultural, economic, and touristic mess. An international effort of volunteer "mud angels" slowly brings these treasures back into view.

1993   The Mafia tries to strike terror with a bomb that destroys a section of the Uffizi, but the museum and the city recover. With a thriving university, Internet cafés, and sparkling clean museums, Florence is a model cultural destination.

2010   You visit Florence, the art capital of Europe.

Renaissance Florence: Cradle of the Modern World

There was something dynamic about the Florentines. Pope Boniface VIII said there were five elements: earth, air, fire, water... and Florentines. For 200 years, starting in the early 1300s, their city was a cultural hub.

Florence's contributions to Western culture are immense: the whole revival of the arts, humanism, and science after centuries of medieval superstition and oppression; the seeds of democracy; the modern Italian language (which grew out of the popular Florentine dialect); the art of Botticelli, Leonardo, and Michelangelo; the writings of Machiavelli, Boccaccio, and Dante; and the explorations of Amerigo Vespucci, who gave his name to a newly discovered continent. Florentines considered themselves descendants of the highly cultured people of the Roman Empire. But Florence, even in its Golden Age, was always a mixture of lustiness and refinement. The streets were filled with tough-talking, hardened, illiterate merchants who strode about singing verses from Dante's *Divine Comedy*.

Florentine culture came from money, and that money came from the wool trade, silk factories, and banking. The city had a large middle class and strong guilds (labor unions for skilled craftsmen). Success was a matter of civic pride, and Florentines showed that pride in the mountains of money they spent to rebuild and beautify the city.

Technically, Florence was a republic, ruled by elected citizens rather than nobility. While there was some opportunity for upward mobility among the middle class, most power was in the hands of a few wealthy banking families. The most powerful was the Medici family. The Medici bank had branches in 10 European cities, including London, Geneva, Bruges (Belgium), and Lyon (France). The pope kept his checking account in the Rome branch. The Florentine florin was the monetary standard of the continent.

Florence dominated Italy economically and culturally, but not militarily. The independent Italian city-states squabbled and remained scattered until the nationalist movement four centuries later. (When someone suggested to the Renaissance Florentine Niccolò Machiavelli that the Italian city-states might unite against their common enemy, France, he wrote back, "Don't make me laugh.")

Lorenzo de' Medici (1449–1492), inheritor of the family's wealth and power and his grandfather Cosimo's love of art, was a central figure of the Golden Age. He was young (20 when he took power), athletic, and intelligent, in addition to being a poet, horseman, musician, and leader. He wrote love songs and humorous dirty songs to be performed loudly and badly at carnival time. His marathon drinking bouts and illicit love affairs were legendary. He learned Greek and Latin and read the classics, yet his great passion was hunting. He was the Renaissance Man—a man of knowledge and action, a patron of the arts, and a scholar and man of the world. He was Lorenzo the Magnificent.

Lorenzo epitomized the Florentine spirit of optimism. Born on New Year's Day and raised in the lap of luxury (Donatello's *David* stood in the family courtyard) by loving parents, he grew up feeling that there was nothing he couldn't do. Florentines saw themselves as part of a "new age," a great undertaking of discovery and progress in man's history. They boasted that within the city walls, there were more "nobly gifted souls than the world has seen in the entire thousand years before." These people invented the term "Dark Ages" for the era that preceded theirs.

Lorenzo surrounded himself with Florence's best and brightest. They created an informal "Platonic Academy," based on that of ancient Greece, to meet over a glass of wine under the stars at the

Medici villa and discuss literature, art, music, and politics—witty conversation was considered an art in itself.

Their "neo-Platonic" philosophy stressed the goodness of man and the created world; they believed in a common truth behind all religion. The Academy was more than just an excuse to go out with the guys: The members were convinced that their discussions were changing the world and improving their souls.

Sandro Botticelli was a member of the Platonic Academy. He painted scenes from the classical myths that the group read, weaving contemporary figures and events into the ancient subjects. He gloried in the nude body, which he considered God's greatest creation.

Artists such as Botticelli thrived on the patronage of wealthy individuals, government, the Church, and guilds. Botticelli commanded as much as 100 florins for one work, enough to live on for a year in high style, which he did for many years. In Botticelli's art we see the lightness, gaiety, and optimism of Lorenzo's court.

Another of Lorenzo's protégés was the young **Michelangelo Buonarroti.** Impressed with his work, Lorenzo took the poor, unlearned 13-year-old boy into the Medici household and treated him like a son.

Michelangelo's playmates were the Medici children, later to become Popes Leo X and Clement VII, who would give him important commissions. For all the encouragement, education, and contacts Michelangelo received, his most important gift from Lorenzo was simply a place at the dinner table, where Michelangelo could absorb the words of the great men of the time and their love of art for art's sake.

Even with all the art and philosophy of the Renaissance, violence, disease, and warfare were present in medieval proportions. For the lower classes, life was as harsh as it had always been. Many artists and scholars wore swords and daggers as part of everyday dress. This was the time of the ruthless tactics of the Borgias (known for murdering their political enemies) and of other families battling for power. Lorenzo himself barely escaped assassination in the cathedral during Easter Mass; his brother died in the attack.

The center of the Renaissance gradually shifted to Rome, but its artists were mostly Florentine. In the 15th century, the Holy City of Rome was a dirty, decaying, crime-infested place. Then a series of popes, including Lorenzo's son and nephew, launched a building and beautification campaign. They used fat commissions (and outright orders) to lure Michelangelo, Raphael, and others to Rome. The Florentine Renaissance headed south.

APPENDIX

Contents

Tourist Information

The Italian national tourist offices **in the US** are a wealth of information. Before your trip, scan their website (www.italiantourism .com) or contact the nearest Italian tourist office to briefly describe your trip and request information. They'll mail you a general interest brochure and you can download many other brochures free of charge at their website. If you have a specific problem, they're a good source of sympathy.

In New York: Tel. 212/245-5618, brochure hotline tel. 212/245-4822, fax 212/586-9249, enitny@italiantourism.com; 630 Fifth Ave. #1565, New York, NY 10111.

In Illinois: Tel. 312/644-0996, brochure hotline tel. 312/644-0990, fax 312/644-3019, enitch@italiantourism.com; 500 N. Michigan Ave. #506, Chicago, IL 60611.

In California: Tel. 310/820-1898, brochure hotline tel. 310/820-0098, fax 310/820-6357, enitla@italiantourism.com; 12400 Wilshire Blvd. #550, Los Angeles, CA 90025.

In Florence, your best first stop is generally the tourist information office (abbreviated **TI** in this book); branches are located across from the train station, near Santa Croce Church, and on Via Cavour (listed on page 35). Useful websites are www.firenze turismo.it (Florence tourist information), www.polomuseale .firenze.it (Florence museum information), and www.museumsin florence.com (more Florence museum information).

Communicating

Many Italians—especially those in the tourist trade and in big cities such as Florence—speak English. Still, you'll get better treatment if you learn and use Italian pleasantries. For a list of survival phrases, see page 481.

Telephones

Smart travelers use the telephone to reserve or reconfirm rooms, get tourist information, reserve restaurants, confirm tour times, or phone home. Generally the easiest, cheapest way to call home is to use an international phone card purchased in Italy. This section covers dialing instructions, phone cards, and types of phones.

How to Dial

Calling from the US to Italy, or vice versa, is simple—once you break the code. The European calling chart later in this chapter will walk you through it.

Dialing Within Italy

Italy has a direct-dial phone system (no area codes). To call anywhere within Italy, just dial the number. For example, the number of one of my recommended Florence hotels is 055-289-592. That's the number you dial whether you're calling it from Florence's train station or from Rome. Keep in mind that Italian phone numbers vary in length; a hotel can have, say, an eight-digit phone number and a nine-digit fax number.

Dialing Internationally to or from Italy

If you want to make an international call, follow these steps:

1. Dial the international access code (00 if you're calling from Europe, 011 from the US or Canada).

2. Dial the country code of the country you're calling (39 for Italy, or 1 for the US or Canada).

3. Dial the local number. Note that in most European countries, you have to drop the zero at the beginning of the local number—but in Italy, you dial it.

Calling from the US to Italy: To call the Florence hotel from the US, dial 011 (the US international access code), 39 (Italy's country code), then 055-289-592.

Calling from Italy to the US: To call my office in Edmonds, Washington, from Italy, I dial 00 (Europe's international access code), 1 (the US country code), 425 (Edmonds' area code), and 771-8303.

Note: You might see a + in front of a European number. When dialing the number, replace the + with the international access code of the country you're calling from (00 from Europe, 011 from the US or Canada).

Public Phones and Hotel-Room Phones

To make calls from public phones, you'll need a prepaid phone card. There are two different kinds of phone cards: international and insertable. (Coin-op phones are virtually extinct.) Both types of phone card work only in Italy. If you have a live card at the end of your trip, give it to another traveler to use up.

International Phone Cards: These are the cheapest way to make international calls from Europe—with the best cards, it costs literally pennies a minute. They also work for local calls. To use the card, you'll dial a toll-free access number, then type in your scratch-to-reveal PIN code. You can use international phone cards from any type of phone, even your hotel-room phone. To avoid being charged by the hotel for the call, be sure to dial the *freephone* number (starts with "80") provided on the card rather than the "local access" number.

You can buy the cards at small newsstand kiosks, *tabacchi* (tobacco) shops, Internet cafés, hostels, and hole-in-the-wall long-distance phone shops. Because there are so many brand names, simply ask for an international phone card (*carta telefonica prepagata internazionale,* KAR-tah teh-leh-FOHN-ee-kah pray-pah-GAH-tah in-ter-naht-zee-oh-NAH-lay). Tell the vendor where you'll be making most calls (*"per Stati Uniti"*—to America), and he'll select the brand with the best deal.

Buy a lower denomination in case the card is a dud. I've had good luck with the Europa card, which offers up to 350 minutes from Italy to the US for €5.

Insertable Phone Cards: This type of card can only be used at a pay phone. These Telecom cards, considered "official" since they're sold by Italy's phone company, give you the best deal for calls within Italy and are reasonable for international calls. You can buy Telecom cards (in denominations of €5 or €10) at *tabacchi* shops, post offices, and machines near phone booths (many phone booths have signs indicating where the nearest phone-card sales outlet is located).

European Calling Chart

Just smile and dial, using this key:
AC = Area Code, LN = Local Number.

European Country	Calling long distance within ...	Calling from the US or Canada to ...	Calling from a European country to ...
Austria	AC + LN	011 + 43 + AC (without the initial zero) + LN	00 + 43 + AC (without the initial zero) + LN
Belgium	LN	011 + 32 + LN (without initial zero)	00 + 32 + LN (without initial zero)
Bosnia-Herzegovina	AC + LN	011 + 387 + AC (without initial zero) + LN	00 + 387 + AC (without initial zero) + LN
Britain	AC + LN	011 + 44 + AC (without initial zero) + LN	00 + 44 + AC (without initial zero) + LN
Croatia	AC + LN	011 + 385 + AC (without initial zero) + LN	00 + 385 + AC (without initial zero) + LN
Czech Republic	LN	011 + 420 + LN	00 + 420 + LN
Denmark	LN	011 + 45 + LN	00 + 45 + LN
Estonia	LN	011 + 372 + LN	00 + 372 + LN
Finland	AC + LN	011 + 358 + AC (without initial zero) + LN	999 + 358 + AC (without initial zero) + LN
France	LN	011 + 33 + LN (without initial zero)	00 + 33 + LN (without initial zero)
Germany	AC + LN	011 + 49 + AC (without initial zero) + LN	00 + 49 + AC (without initial zero) + LN
Gibraltar	LN	011 + 350 + LN	00 + 350 + LN
Greece	LN	011 + 30 + LN	00 + 30 + LN
Hungary	06 + AC + LN	011 + 36 + AC + LN	00 + 36 + AC + LN
Ireland	AC + LN	011 + 353 + AC (without initial zero) + LN	00 + 353 + AC (without initial zero) + LN
Italy	LN	011 + 39 + LN	00 + 39 + LN

European Country	Calling long distance within ...	Calling from the US or Canada to ...	Calling from a European country to ...
Montenegro	AC + LN	011 + 382 + AC (without initial zero) + LN	00 + 382 + AC (without initial zero) + LN
Morocco	LN	011 + 212 + LN (without initial zero)	00 + 212 + LN (without initial zero)
Netherlands	AC + LN	011 + 31 + AC (without initial zero) + LN	00 + 31 + AC (without initial zero) + LN
Norway	LN	011 + 47 + LN	00 + 47 + LN
Poland	LN	011 + 48 + LN (without initial zero)	00 + 48 + LN (without initial zero)
Portugal	LN	011 + 351 + LN	00 + 351 + LN
Slovakia	AC + LN	011 + 421 + AC (without initial zero) + LN	00 + 421 + AC (without initial zero) + LN
Slovenia	AC + LN	011 + 386 + AC (without initial zero) + LN	00 + 386 + AC (without initial zero) + LN
Spain	LN	011 + 34 + LN	00 + 34 + LN
Sweden	AC + LN	011 + 46 + AC (without initial zero) + LN	00 + 46 + AC (without initial zero) + LN
Switzerland	LN	011 + 41 + LN (without initial zero)	00 + 41 + LN (without initial zero)
Turkey	AC (if no initial zero is included, add one) + LN	011 + 90 + AC (without initial zero) + LN	00 + 90 + AC (without initial zero) + LN

- The instructions above apply whether you're calling a land line or mobile phone.
- The international access codes (the first numbers you dial when making an international call) are 011 if you're calling from the US or Canada, or 00 if you're calling from virtually anywhere in Europe (except Finland, where it's 999).
- To call the US or Canada from Europe, dial 00, then 1 (the country code for the US and Canada), then the area code and number. In short, 00 + 1 + AC + LN = Hi, Mom!

Rip off the perforated corner to "activate" the card, and then physically insert it into a slot in the pay phone. It displays how much money you have remaining on the card. Then just dial away. The price of the call is automatically deducted while you talk.

Hotel-Room Phones: Calling from your room can be cheap for local calls (ask for the rates at the front desk first), but is often a rip-off for long-distance calls (unless you use an international phone card, explained earlier). Incoming calls are free, making this a cheap way for friends and family to stay in touch (provided they have a good long-distance plan for calls to Europe—and a list of your hotels' phone numbers).

US Calling Cards: These cards, such as the ones offered by AT&T, Verizon, or Sprint, are the worst option. You'll nearly always save a lot of money by using a local phone card instead.

Metered Phones: In Italy, some call shops have phones with meters. You can talk all you want, then pay the bill when you leave—but be sure you know the rates before you have a lengthy conversation.

Mobile Phones

Many travelers enjoy the convenience of traveling with a mobile phone. For more in-depth information than I include below, see www.ricksteves.com/phones.

Using Your Mobile Phone: Your US mobile phone works in Europe if it's GSM-enabled, tri-band or quad-band, and on a calling plan that includes international calls. For example, with a T-Mobile phone, you'll pay $1 per minute to make or receive a call, and about $0.35 apiece for text messages.

You can save money if your phone is electronically "unlocked"—then you can simply buy a **SIM card** (a fingernail-sized chip that stores the phone's information) in Europe. SIM cards, which give you a European phone number and some prepaid calling time, are sold at mobile-phone stores and some newsstand kiosks for about €4–8. You may need to show ID, such as your passport, when you buy a SIM card. Simply insert the SIM card in your phone (usually in a slot behind the battery), and it'll work like a European mobile phone. When buying a SIM card, always ask about fees for domestic and international calls, roaming charges, and how to check your credit balance and buy more time.

Many **smartphones,** such as the iPhone or BlackBerry, work in Europe—but beware of sky-high fees, especially for data downloading (checking email, browsing the Internet, watching videos, and so on). Ask your provider in advance how to avoid unwittingly "roaming" your way to a huge bill. Some applications allow for cheap or free smartphone calls over a Wi-Fi connection (see "Calling over the Internet," on the next page).

Using a European Mobile Phone: Local mobile-phone shops all over Europe sell basic phones for around €35–75. (My Italian guides tell me that TIM is a reliable Italian mobile-phone company.) You'll also need to buy a SIM card and prepaid credit for making calls. If you remain in the phone's home country, domestic calls are reasonable, and incoming calls are free. You'll pay more if you're "roaming" in another country. If your phone is "unlocked," you can swap out its SIM card for a new one in other countries.

Calling over the Internet

Some things that seem too good to be true...actually are true. If you're traveling with a laptop, make calls using VoIP (Voice over Internet Protocol). With VoIP, two computers act as the phones, and the Internet-based calls are free (or you can pay a few cents to call from your computer to a telephone). The major providers are Skype (www.skype.com) and Google Talk (www.google.com /talk).

Useful Phone Numbers

Italy's toll-free numbers start with "80". These "80" numbers—called *freephone* or *numero verde* (green number)—can be dialed free from any phone without using a phone card. Note that you can't call Italy's toll-free numbers from America, nor can you count on reaching America's toll-free numbers from Italy.

Any Italian phone number that starts with "8" but isn't followed by a "0" is a toll call, generally costing €0.10–0.50 per minute.

Embassies and Consulates
US Consulate: tel. 055-266-951 (Mon–Fri 8:30–12:30, closed Sat–Sun and US and Italian holidays, Lungarno Vespucci 38, Florence, http://florence.usconsulate.gov)
US Embassy: 24-hour emergency line—tel. 06-46741, non-emergency—tel. 06-4674-2406 (Via Vittorio Veneto 119/A, Rome, www.usembassy.it)
Canadian Embassy: tel. 06-854-441 (Via Zara 30, Rome, www .international.gc.ca)

Emergency Needs
English-speaking police help: 113
Ambulance: 118
Road Service: 116

Travel Advisories
US Department of State: tel. 202/647-5225, www.travel.state.gov
Canadian Department of Foreign Affairs: Canadian tel. 800-267-6788, www.dfait-maeci.gc.ca
US Centers for Disease Control and Prevention: tel. 800-CDC-INFO (800-232-4636), www.cdc.gov/travel

Directory Assistance
Telephone Help (in English; free directory assistance): 170
Directory Assistance (for €0.50, an Italian-speaking robot gives the number twice, very clearly): 12

Internet Access

Many hotels offer a computer in the lobby with Internet access for guests. Smaller places may sometimes let you sit at their desk for a few minutes just to check your email, if you ask politely. For those traveling with a laptop, your hotel may have Wi-Fi (wireless Internet access) or a port in your room for plugging in a cable. Most hotels offer Wi-Fi for free; others charge by the minute. If your hotel doesn't have access, ask your hotelier to direct you to the nearest place to get online. Internet cafés and little hole-in-the-wall Internet-access shops (offering a few computers, no food, and cheap prices) are common in most cities.

Because of an anti-terrorism law in Italy, you may be asked to show your passport (carry it in your money belt) when using a public Internet terminal at an Internet café or in a hotel lobby. The proprietor likely will make a copy of your passport.

Mail

While you can arrange for mail delivery to your hotel (allow 10 days for a letter to arrive), phoning and emailing are so easy that I've dispensed with mail stops altogether. Mail service in Italy has improved over the last few years, but even so, mail nothing precious from an Italian post office. Federal Express makes pricey two-day deliveries.

Resources

Resources from Rick Steves

Florence & Tuscany 2010 is one of more than 30 titles in a series of **books** on European travel, which includes country guidebooks, city guidebooks (Venice, Rome, Paris, London, etc.), and my budget-travel skills handbook, *Rick Steves' Europe Through the Back Door*. My phrase books—for Italian, French, German, Spanish, and Portuguese—are practical and budget-oriented. My other books are *Europe 101* (a crash course on art and history, newly expanded

and in full color), *Travel as a Political Act* (a travelogue sprinkled with tips for bringing home a global perspective), *European Christmas* (on traditional and modern-day celebrations), and *Postcards from Europe* (a fun memoir of my travels over 25 years). For a complete list of my books, see the inside of the last page of this book.

My **TV series**, *Rick Steves' Europe*, covers European destinations in 100 shows, with 14 episodes on Italy, including four on Florence and Tuscany. My weekly **public radio** show, *Travel with Rick Steves*, features interviews with travel experts from around the world, including several hours on Italy and Italian culture. All the TV scripts and radio shows (which are easy and free to download to an iPod or other MP3 player) are at www.ricksteves.com.

Take advantage of my free self-guided **audio tours** for Florence—of the Renaissance Walk, the Accademia *(David)*, and the Uffizi Gallery. Simply download them from www.ricksteves.com or iTunes (search for "Rick Steves' tours" in the iTunes Store), then transfer them to your iPod or other MP3 player. If your travels take you beyond Florence, we also offer audio tours of the major sights in Rome, Venice, Paris, and London.

Maps

The black-and-white maps in this book, designed by my well-traveled staff, are concise and simple. The maps are intended to help you locate recommended places and get to local TIs, where you can pick up a more in-depth map (usually free) of the city or region. More detailed maps are also sold at newsstands and bookstores—look before you buy to be sure the map has the level of detail you want. For drivers, I'd recommend a 1:200,000- or 1:300,000-scale map.

Other Guidebooks

For most travelers, this book has more than enough information. But if you'll be exploring beyond my recommended neighborhoods and destinations, $30 for extra maps and books can be money well-spent.

The following books are worthwhile, though are not updated annually; check the publication date before you buy. The Access

At our travel website, you'll find a wealth of free information on European destinations, including fresh monthly news and helpful tips from thousands of fellow travelers. You'll also find my latest guidebook updates (www.ricksteves.com/update) and my travel blog.

Our **online Travel Store** offers travel bags and accessories specially designed by me and my staff to help you travel smarter and lighter. These include my popular carry-on bags (roll-aboard and rucksack versions), money belts, totes, toiletries kits, adapters, other accessories, and a wide selection of guidebooks, planning maps, and DVDs.

Choosing the right **railpass** for your trip—amidst hundreds of options—can drive you nutty. We'll help you choose the best pass for your needs, plus give you a bunch of free extras.

Rick Steves' Europe Through the Back Door travel company offers **tours** with more than three dozen itineraries and about 300 departures reaching the best destinations in this book...and beyond. Our Italy tours include "the best of" in 17 days, Village Italy in 14 days, South Italy in 13 days, Venice–Florence–Rome in 10 days, the Heart of Italy in 9 days, Sicily in 9 days, and a week-long Rome tour. You'll enjoy great guides, a fun bunch of travel partners (with small groups of generally around 28), and plenty of room to spread out in a big, comfy bus. You'll find European adventures to fit every vacation length. For all the details, and to get our Tour Catalog and a free Rick Steves Tour Experience DVD (filmed on location during an actual tour), visit www.ricksteves.com or call us at 425/608-4217.

guide (which combines Florence and Venice) is well-researched, organized by neighborhood, and color-coded for sights, hotels, and restaurants. Focusing mainly on sights, the colorful Eyewitness guide on Florence and Tuscany is fun for its great graphics and photos, but it's relatively skimpy on content and weighs a ton. You can buy it in Florence (no more expensive than in the US) or simply borrow it for a minute from other travelers at certain sights to make sure that you're aware of that place's highlights.

If you'll be traveling elsewhere in Italy, consider these books in the Rick Steves series: *Italy, Rome,* and *Venice.*

Recommended Books and Movies

To get the feel of Florence and Tuscany past and present, check out a few of these books or films:

Non-Fiction

Among the classics of Italian literature with particular relevance to Florence are Niccolò Machiavelli's *The Prince* and *Florentine Histories.*

For a historical overview of the whole city, try *The City of Florence* (R. W. B. Lewis), which has a biographer's perspective. In *Florence: A Portrait,* Michael Levey writes with a curator's expertise. *The Stones of Florence* bubbles with Mary McCarthy's wit.

Architecture fans should consider reading the novel-like *Brunelleschi's Dome* (Ross King) or *The Architecture of the Italian Renaissance* (Peter Murray), which presents a (not too dry) textbook overview. For an academic take on Italian art history, try *The Lives of the Artists* (Giorgio Vasari) or *Italian Renaissance Art* (Laurie Schneider Adams).

Christopher Hibbert tells of the intrigues of Florence's first family in *The House of Medici* (his *Florence* is also recommended). *Fortune Is a River* (Roger D. Masters) describes a scheme between Machiavelli and da Vinci to re-route the Arno (which, thankfully, never happened).

If you'll be traveling to the area outside of Florence, consider the sensuous travel memoir, *The Hills of Tuscany* (Ferenc Máté). Also worthwhile is *A Tuscan Childhood* (Kinta Beevor), about growing up in a sun-drenched villa. *Under the Tuscan Sun* was a bestseller for Frances Mayes (and is better than the movie of the same name). Another memoir on the adventure of renovating a Tuscan farmhouse is *A Small Place in Italy* (Eric Newby).

Fiction

Florence was a favorite destination for European aristocrats and artists in the 19th and early 20th centuries. The Italian influence lives on in classics written during that time, including George

Eliot's *Romola* and E. M. Forster's *A Room with a View*.

For a modern read, consider *The Passion of Artemisia*, by Susan Vreeland (who also wrote the bestselling *Girl in Hyacinth Blue*) and *The Sixteen Pleasures* (Robert Hellenga), set during the great floods that wracked the city in 1966. *Birth of Venus*, by Sarah Dunant, chronicles the story of a teen girl striving to survive Savonarola's reign. *Galileo's Daughter* (Dava Sobel) is based on the real-life letters between the scientist and his daughter.

Page-turning mysteries set in Florence include *A Rich Full Death* (Michael Dibdin), *Death of an Englishman* (Magdalen Nabb), *The Dante Game* (Jane Langton), and *Bella Donna* (Barbara Cherne). For a fun Michelangelo potboiler, try *The Agony and the Ecstasy* (Irving Stone).

The Light in the Piazza (Elizabeth Spencer), the story of a mother and daughter visiting in the 1950s, was a movie (from 1962) and recently became an award-winning Broadway musical.

And for the lover of classical tales, Giovanni Boccaccio's *Decameron*, written in the mid-1300s, is set in plague-ridden medieval Florence.

Films

For a well-done Shakespeare flick that was filmed in Tuscany, try *Much Ado About Nothing* (1993), which is actually set in Sicily. *A Room with a View* (1986) captures the charm of the book of the same name (see above). *Under the Tuscan Sun*—filled with eye-candy views—falls flat in comparison. Oscar-winning *Life Is Beautiful* (1997) has sections set in a Tuscan town. The warm-hearted Italian epic *Best of Youth* (2003) takes place in several Italian locations, including Florence and rural Tuscany.

If you'll be traveling to San Gimignano, consider watching these films set in that locale: *Prince of Foxes* (1949) and *Where Angels Fear to Tread* (1991). Two films by Franco Zeffirelli were also set in "San G": *Brother Sun, Sister Moon* (1972) and *Tea with Mussolini* (1999).

If Siena is on your itinerary, try *Palio* (1932), *Stealing Beauty* (1996), and *Up at the Villa* (2000), which also has scenes set in Florence. *The English Patient* (1996) was partially shot in Montepulciano, as was the vampire romance, *New Moon* (2009). Filmed in Lucca, *The Triumph of Love* (2001) has a baroque feel, while *The Portrait of a Lady* (1996) stays true to Henry James' bleak novel.

In 2005, PBS produced an excellent docudrama about Florence's first family, *Medici: Godfathers of the Renaissance* (with a fine website: www.pbs.org/empires/medici).

2010

JANUARY
S	M	T	W	T	F	S
					1	2
3	4	5	6	7	8	9
10	11	12	13	14	15	16
17	18	19	20	21	22	23
24/31	25	26	27	28	29	30

FEBRUARY
S	M	T	W	T	F	S
	1	2	3	4	5	6
7	8	9	10	11	12	13
14	15	16	17	18	19	20
21	22	23	24	25	26	27
28						

MARCH
S	M	T	W	T	F	S
	1	2	3	4	5	6
7	8	9	10	11	12	13
14	15	16	17	18	19	20
21	22	23	24	25	26	27
28	29	30	31			

APRIL
S	M	T	W	T	F	S
				1	2	3
4	5	6	7	8	9	10
11	12	13	14	15	16	17
18	19	20	21	22	23	24
25	26	27	28	29	30	

MAY
S	M	T	W	T	F	S
						1
2	3	4	5	6	7	8
9	10	11	12	13	14	15
16	17	18	19	20	21	22
23/30	24/31	25	26	27	28	29

JUNE
S	M	T	W	T	F	S
		1	2	3	4	5
6	7	8	9	10	11	12
13	14	15	16	17	18	19
20	21	22	23	24	25	26
27	28	29	30			

JULY
S	M	T	W	T	F	S
				1	2	3
4	5	6	7	8	9	10
11	12	13	14	15	16	17
18	19	20	21	22	23	24
25	26	27	28	29	30	31

AUGUST
S	M	T	W	T	F	S
1	2	3	4	5	6	7
8	9	10	11	12	13	14
15	16	17	18	19	20	21
22	23	24	25	26	27	28
29	30	31				

SEPTEMBER
S	M	T	W	T	F	S
			1	2	3	4
5	6	7	8	9	10	11
12	13	14	15	16	17	18
19	20	21	22	23	24	25
26	27	28	29	30		

OCTOBER
S	M	T	W	T	F	S
					1	2
3	4	5	6	7	8	9
10	11	12	13	14	15	16
17	18	19	20	21	22	23
24/31	25	26	27	28	29	30

NOVEMBER
S	M	T	W	T	F	S
	1	2	3	4	5	6
7	8	9	10	11	12	13
14	15	16	17	18	19	20
21	22	23	24	25	26	27
28	29	30				

DECEMBER
S	M	T	W	T	F	S
			1	2	3	4
5	6	7	8	9	10	11
12	13	14	15	16	17	18
19	20	21	22	23	24	25
26	27	28	29	30	31	

APPENDIX

Holidays and Festivals

Italy celebrates many holidays, which close sights and bring crowds. Each town has a local festival honoring its patron saint.

Your best source for general information is the Florence tourist information office (www.firenzeturismo.it). You could also check with Italy's national tourist offices (www.italiantourism .com), listed at the beginning of this chapter.

Italian Holidays in 2010

Note that this isn't a complete list. In Italy, holidays strike without warning. Speaking of strikes, they can disrupt even the most carefully planned trip. Be on the lookout for posters that indicate when a strike *(sciopero)* is coming.

Jan 1	New Year's Day
Jan 6	Epiphany
Jan	Florence fashion convention

Mid-Feb	Carnival Celebrations/Mardi Gras in Florence (costumed parades, street water fights, jousting competitions)
March	Italy's Cultural Heritage Week (check www.beniculturali.it for dates)
April 4	Easter Sunday. Explosion of the Cart (Scoppio del Carro) in Florence (fireworks, bonfire in wooden cart)
April 5	Easter Monday
April 25	Italian Liberation Day
May 1	Labor Day
May 13	Ascension Day
Mid-May	Cricket Festival in Florence (music, entertainment, food, crickets sold in cages)
June	Florence fashion convention
June 1–30	Annual Flower Display in Florence (carpet of flowers on the main square, Piazza della Signoria)
June 2	Anniversary of the Republic
June 16–17	Festival of St. Ranieri in Pisa
June 24	Festival of St. John in Florence (parades, dances, boat races). Also Calcio Fiorentino (costumed soccer game on Florence's Piazza Santa Croce)
Late June–early Sept	Florence's annual outdoor cinema season (contemporary films)
July–Aug	Annual Florence Dance Festival
July 2	Palio horse race in Siena
Aug 15	Assumption of Mary (Ferragosto)
Aug 16	Palio horse race in Siena
Sept, first week	Festa della Rificolona in Florence (children's procession with lanterns, street performances, parade)
Sept 13–14	Volto Santo in Lucca (procession and fair)
Oct	Musica dei Popoli Festival in Florence (ethnic and folk music and dances, www.flog.it/mus_pope.htm)
Nov 1	All Saints' Day
Dec 8	Feast of the Immaculate Conception
Dec 25	Christmas
Dec 26	St. Stephen's Day

Conversions and Climate

Numbers and Stumblers

- Europeans write a few of their numbers differently than we do. 1 = 1, 4 = 4, 7 = 7.
- In Europe, dates appear as day/month/year, so Christmas is 25/12/10.
- Commas are decimal points, and decimal points are commas. A dollar and a half is 1,50, and there are 5.280 feet in a mile.
- When pointing, use your whole hand, palm down.
- When counting with fingers, start with your thumb. If you hold up your first finger to request one item, you'll probably get two.
- What Americans call the second floor of a building is the first floor in Europe.
- On escalators and moving sidewalks, Europeans keep the left "lane" open for passing. Keep to the right.

Roman Numerals

In the US, you'll see Roman numerals—which originated in ancient Rome—used for copyright dates, clocks, and the Super Bowl. In Italy, you're likely to observe these numbers chiseled on statues and buildings. If you want to do some numeric detective work, here's how: In Roman numerals, as in ours, the highest numbers (thousands, hundreds) come first, followed by smaller numbers. Many numbers are made by combining numerals into sets: V = 5, so VIII = 8 (5 plus 3). Roman numerals follow a sub-traction principle for multiples of four (4, 40, 400, etc.) and nine (9, 90, 900, etc.); the number four, for example, is written as IV (1 subtracted from 5), rather than IIII. The number nine is IX (1 subtracted from 10).

Rick Steves' Florence & Tuscany 2010—written in Roman numerals—would translate as *Rick Steves' Florence & Tuscany MMX*. Big numbers such as dates can look daunting at first. The easiest way to handle them is to read the numbers in discrete chunks. For example, Michelangelo was born in MCDLXXV. Break it down: M (1,000) + CD (100 subtracted from 500, or 400) + LXX (50 + 10 + 10, or 70) + V (5) = 1475. It was a very good year.

M = 1000	XL = 40
CM = 900	X = 10
D = 500	IX = 9
CD = 400	V = 5
C = 100	IV = 4
XC = 90	I = duh
L = 50	

APPENDIX

Metric Conversions (approximate)

A kilogram is 2.2 pounds, and 1 liter is about a quart, or almost four to a gallon. A kilometer is six-tenths of a mile. I figure kilometers to miles by cutting them in half and adding back 10 percent of the original (120 km: 60 + 12 = 72 miles, 300 km: 150 + 30 = 180 miles).

1 foot = 0.3 meter	1 square yard = 0.8 square meter
1 yard = 0.9 meter	1 square mile = 2.6 square kilometers
1 mile = 1.6 kilometers	1 ounce = 28 grams
1 centimeter = 0.4 inch	1 quart = 0.95 liter
1 meter = 39.4 inches	1 kilogram = 2.2 pounds
1 kilometer = 0.62 mile	32°F = 0°C

Clothing Sizes

When shopping for clothing, use these US-to-European comparisons as general guidelines (but note that no conversion is perfect).

- Women's dresses and blouses: Add 30 (US size 10 = European size 40)
- Men's suits and jackets: Add 10 (US size 40 regular = European size 50)
- Men's shirts: Multiply by 2 and add about 8 (US size 15 collar = European size 38)
- Women's shoes: Add about 30 (US size 8 = European size 38½)
- Men's shoes: Add 32–34 (US size 9 = European size 41; US size 11 = European size 45)

Florence's Climate

First line—average daily high; second line—average daily low; third line—days of no rain. For more detailed statistics, check www.worldclimate.com.

J	F	M	A	M	J	J	A	S	O	N	D
40°	46°	56°	65°	74°	80°	84°	82°	75°	63°	51°	43°
32°	35°	43°	49°	57°	63°	67°	66°	61°	52°	43°	35°
25	21	24	22	23	21	25	24	25	23	20	24

APPENDIX

Temperature Conversion:
Fahrenheit and Celsius

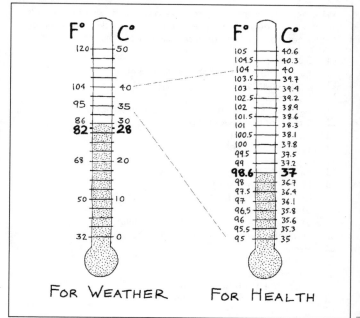

FOR WEATHER   FOR HEALTH

Europe takes its temperature using the Celsius scale, while we opt for Fahrenheit. For a rough conversion from Celsius to Fahrenheit, double the number and add 30. For weather, remember that 28°C is 82°F—perfect. For health, 37°C is just right.

Essential Packing Checklist

Whether you're traveling for five days or five weeks, here's what you'll need to bring. Remember to pack light to enjoy the sweet freedom of true mobility. Happy travels!

❑   5 shirts
❑   1 sweater or lightweight fleece jacket
❑   2 pairs pants
❑   1 pair shorts
❑   1 swimsuit (women only—men can use shorts)
❑   5 pairs underwear and socks
❑   1 pair shoes
❑   1 rainproof jacket
❑   Tie or scarf
❑   Money belt
❑   Money—your mix of:
    ❑   Debit card for ATM withdrawals
    ❑   Credit card
    ❑   Hard cash in US dollars ($20 bills)
❑   Documents (and back-up photocopies)
❑   Passport
❑   Printout of airline e-ticket
❑   Driver's license
❑   Student ID and hostel card
❑   Railpass/car rental voucher
❑   Insurance details
❑   Daypack
❑   Sealable plastic baggies
❑   Camera and related gear
❑   Empty water bottle
❑   Wristwatch and alarm clock
❑   Earplugs
❑   First-aid kit
❑   Medicine (labeled)
❑   Extra glasses/contacts and prescriptions
❑   Sunscreen and sunglasses
❑   Toiletries kit
❑   Soap
❑   Laundry soap
❑   Clothesline
❑   Small towel
❑   Sewing kit
❑   Travel information
❑   Necessary map(s)
❑   Address list (email and mailing addresses)
❑   Postcards and photos from home
❑   Notepad and pen
❑   Journal

If you plan to carry on your luggage, note that all liquids must be in three-ounce or smaller containers and fit within a single quart-size baggie. For details, see www.tsa.gov/travelers.

Hotel Reservation

To: _____   _____
                    hotel   *email or fax*

From:_____   _____
                    name   *email or fax*

Today's date: _____ /_____ /_____
                         day   *month*   *year*

Dear Hotel _____ ,
Please make this reservation for me:

Name: _____

Total # of people: _____   # of rooms: _____   # of nights: _____

Arriving: _____ /_____ /_____   My time of arrival (24-hr clock): _____
                 day   *month*   *year*   (I will telephone if I will be late)

Departing: ____ /____ /____
                   day   *month*   *year*

Room(s): Single____   Double ____   Twin ____   Triple ____   Quad____

With: Toilet ____   Shower ____ Bath ____   Sink only____

Special needs: View____ Quiet____ Cheapest ____ Ground Floor____

Please email or fax confirmation of my reservation, along with the type of
room reserved and the price. Please also inform me of your cancellation
policy. After I hear from you, I will quickly send my credit-card information
as a deposit to hold the room. Thank you.

_____
Name

_____
Address

_____
City   *State*   *Zip Code*   *Country*

*Before hoteliers can make your reservation, they want to know the informa-
tion listed above. You can use this form as the basis for your email, or you can
photocopy this page, fill in the information, and send it as a fax (also available
online at www.ricksteves.com/reservation).*

Italian Survival Phrases

Good day.	**Buon giorno.**	bwohn JOR-noh
Do you speak English?	**Parla inglese?**	PAR-lah een-GLAY-zay
Yes. / No.	**Sì. / No.**	see / noh
I (don't) understand.	**(Non) capisco.**	(nohn) kah-PEES-koh
Please.	**Per favore.**	pehr fah-VOH-ray
Thank you.	**Grazie.**	GRAHT-seeay
You're welcome.	**Prego.**	PRAY-go
I'm sorry.	**Mi dispiace.**	mee dee-speeAH-chay
Excuse me.	**Mi scusi.**	mee SKOO-zee
(No) problem.	**(Non) c'è un problema.**	(nohn) cheh oon proh-BLAY-mah
Good.	**Va bene.**	vah BEHN-ay
Goodbye.	**Arrivederci.**	ah-ree-vay-DEHR-chee
one / two	**uno / due**	OO-noh / DOO-ay
three / four	**tre / quattro**	tray / KWAH-troh
five / six	**cinque / sei**	CHEENG-kway / SEHee
seven / eight	**sette / otto**	SEHT-tay / OT-toh
nine / ten	**nove / dieci**	NOV-ay / deeAY-chee
How much is it?	**Quanto costa?**	KWAHN-toh KOS-tah
Write it?	**Me lo scrive?**	may loh SKREE-vay
Is it free?	**È gratis?**	eh GRAH-tees
Is it included?	**È incluso?**	eh een-KLOO-zoh
Where can I buy / find...?	**Dove posso comprare / trovare...?**	DOH-vay POS-soh kohm-PRAH-ray / troh-VAH-ray
I'd like / We'd like...	**Vorrei / Vorremmo...**	vor-REHee / vor-RAY-moh
...a room.	**...una camera.**	OO-nah KAH-meh-rah
...a ticket to ___.	**...un biglietto per ___.**	oon beel-YEHT-toh pehr
Is it possible?	**È possibile?**	eh poh-SEE-bee-lay
Where is...?	**Dov'è...?**	DOH-veh
...the train station	**...la stazione**	lah staht-seeOH-nay
...the bus station	**...la stazione degli autobus**	lah staht-seeOH-nay DAYL-yee OW-toh-boos
...tourist information	**...informazioni per turisti**	een-for-maht-seeOH-nee pehr too-REE-stee
...the toilet	**...la toilette**	lah twah-LEHT-tay
men	**uomini, signori**	WOH-mee-nee, seen-YOH-ree
women	**donne, signore**	DON-nay, seen-YOH-ray
left / right	**sinistra / destra**	see-NEE-strah / DEHS-trah
straight	**sempre diritto**	SEHM-pray dee-REE-toh
When do you open / close?	**A che ora aprite / chiudete?**	ah kay OH-rah ah-PREE-tay / keeoo-DAY-tay
At what time?	**A che ora?**	ah kay OH-rah
Just a moment.	**Un momento.**	oon moh-MAYN-toh
now / soon / later	**adesso / presto / tardi**	ah-DEHS-soh / PREHS-toh / TAR-dee

In the Restaurant

I'd like...	Vorrei...	vor-REHee
We'd like...	Vorremmo...	vor-RAY-moh
...to reserve...	...prenotare...	pray-noh-TAH-ray
...a table for one / two.	...un tavolo per uno / due.	oon TAH-voh-loh pehr OO-noh / DOO-ay
Non-smoking.	Non fumare.	nohn foo-MAH-ray
Is this seat free?	È libero questo posto?	eh LEE-bay-roh KWEHS-toh POH-stoh
The menu (in English), please.	Il menù (in inglese), per favore.	eel may-NOO (een een-GLAY-zay) pehr fah-VOH-ray
service (not) included	servizio (non) incluso	sehr-VEET-seeoh (nohn) een-KLOO-zoh
cover charge	pane e coperto	PAH-nay ay koh-PEHR-toh
to go	da portar via	dah POR-tar VEE-ah
with / without	con / senza	kohn / SEHN-sah
and / or	e / o	ay / oh
menu (of the day)	menù (del giorno)	may-NOO (dayl JOR-noh)
specialty of the house	specialità della casa	spay-chah-lee-TAH DEHL-lah KAH-zah
first course (pasta, soup)	primo piatto	PREE-moh peeAH-toh
main course (meat, fish)	secondo piatto	say-KOHN-doh peeAH-toh
side dishes	contorni	kohn-TOR-nee
bread	pane	PAH-nay
cheese	formaggio	for-MAH-joh
sandwich	panino	pah-NEE-noh
soup	minestra, zuppa	mee-NEHS-trah, TSOO-pah
salad	insalata	een-sah-LAH-tah
meat	carne	KAR-nay
chicken	pollo	POH-loh
fish	pesce	PEH-shay
seafood	frutti di mare	FROO-tee dee MAH-ray
fruit / vegetables	frutta / legumi	FROO-tah / lay-GOO-mee
dessert	dolci	DOHL-chee
tap water	acqua del rubinetto	AH-kwah dayl roo-bee-NAY-toh
mineral water	acqua minerale	AH-kwah mee-nay-RAH-lay
milk	latte	LAH-tay
(orange) juice	succo (d'arancia)	SOO-koh (dah-RAHN-chah)
coffee / tea	caffè / tè	kah-FEH / teh
wine	vino	VEE-noh
red / white	rosso / bianco	ROH-soh / beeAHN-koh
glass / bottle	bicchiere / bottiglia	bee-keeAY-ray / boh-TEEL-yah
beer	birra	BEE-rah
Cheers!	Cin cin!	cheen cheen
More. / Another.	Ancora un po.' / Un altro.	ahn-KOH-rah oon poh / oon AHL-troh
The same.	Lo stesso.	loh STEHS-soh
The bill, please.	Il conto, per favore.	eel KOHN-toh pehr fah-VOH-ray
tip	mancia	MAHN-chah
Delicious!	Delizioso!	day-leet-seeOH-zoh

For hundreds more pages of survival phrases for your trip to Italy, check out *Rick Steves' Italian Phrase Book & Dictionary* or *Rick Steves' French, Italian, and German Phrase Book*.

INDEX

INDEX

MAP INDEX

MAP INDEX

▸ Plan Your Trip

Browse thousands of articles and a wealth of money-saving tips for planning your dream trip. You'll find up-to-date information on Europe's best destinations, packing smart, getting around, finding rooms, staying healthy, avoiding scams and more.

▸ Eurail Passes

Find out, step-by-step, if a rail pass makes sense for your trip—and how to avoid buying more than you need. Get a bunch of free extras!

▸ Graffiti Wall & Travelers' Helpline

Learn, ask, share—our online community of savvy travelers is a great resource for first-time travelers to Europe, as well as seasoned pros.

urn your travel dreams into affordable reality

Free Audio Tours & Travel Newsletter

Get your nose out of this guide-book and focus on what you'll be seeing with Rick's free audio tours of the greatest sights in Paris, Rome, Florence and Venice.

Subscribe to our free *Travel News* e-newsletter, and get monthly articles from Rick on what's happening in Europe.

▶ Great Gear from Rick's Travel Store

Pack light and right—on a budget—with Rick's custom-designed carry-on bags, roll-aboards, day packs, travel accessories, guidebooks, journals, maps and DVDs of his TV shows.

130 Fourth Avenue North, PO Box 2009 • Edmonds, WA 98020 USA
Phone: (425) 771-8303 • Fax: (425) 771-0833 • www.ricksteves.com

Rick Steves

www.ricksteves.com

TRAVEL SKILLS
Europe Through the Back Door

EUROPE GUIDES
Best of Europe
Eastern Europe
Europe 101
European Christmas
Postcards from Europe

COUNTRY GUIDES
Croatia & Slovenia
England
France
Germany
Great Britain
Ireland
Italy
Portugal
Scandinavia
Spain
Switzerland

CITY & REGIONAL GUIDES
Amsterdam, Bruges & Brussels
Athens & The Peloponnese
Budapest
Florence & Tuscany
Istanbul
London
Paris
Prague & The Czech Republic
Provence & The French Riviera
Rome
Venice
Vienna, Salzburg & Tirol

PHRASE BOOKS & DICTIONARIES
French
French, Italian & German
German
Italian
Portuguese
Spanish

RICK STEVES' EUROPE DVDs
Austria & The Alps
Eastern Europe
England
Europe
France & Benelux
Germany & Scandinavia
Greece, Turkey, Israel & Egypt
Ireland & Scotland
Italy's Cities
Italy's Countryside
Rick Steves' European Christmas
Spain & Portugal
Travel Skills & "The Making Of"

PLANNING MAPS
Britain, Ireland & London
Europe
France & Paris
Germany, Austria & Switzerland
Ireland
Italy
Spain & Portugal

JOURNALS
Rick Steves' Pocket Travel Journal
Rick Steves' Travel Journal

RICK STEVES APPS FOR THE iPHONE OR iPOD TOUCH

With these apps you can:

➤ Spin the compass icon to switch views between sights, hotels, and restaurant selections—and get details on cost, hours, address, and phone number.

➤ Tap any point on the screen to read Rick's detailed information, including history and suggested viewpoints.

➤ Get a deeper view into Rick's tours with audio and video segments.

Go to iTunes to download the following apps:

Rick Steves' Louvre Tour

Rick Steves' Historic Paris Walk

Rick Steves' Orsay Museum Tour

Rick Steves' Versailles

Rick Steves' Ancient Rome Tour

Rick Steves' St. Peter's Basilica Tour

Once downloaded, these apps are completely self-contained on your iPhone or iPod Touch, so you will not incur pricey roaming charges during use overseas.

Rick Steves books and DVDs are available at bookstores and through online booksellers.
Rick Steves guidebooks are published by Avalon Travel, a member of the Perseus Books Group.
Rick Steves apps are produced by Übermind, a boutique Seattle-based software consultancy firm.

Credits

Researchers
To update this book, Rick and Gene relied on the help of...

Ben Cameron

Ben experienced his first taste of European travel when he was three, exploring medieval castles with his parents. Returning after graduation, he was hooked and has spent much of his time since exploring Europe independently and leading tours for Rick Steves. When not living out of his backpack, he splits his time between Rome and Seattle.

Helen Inman

After graduating with a law degree, Helen left England for the Mediterranean, finding sunshine, vibrant energy, and Latin culture and languages. Before working as a guide for Rick Steves tours and as a guidebook researcher, she enjoyed five years in Italy. She now lives in Spain, where she thrives on a diet of dancing, laughter, *cava*, and seafood.

Rick Steves' Guidebook Series

Country Guides

Rick Steves' Best of Europe
Rick Steves' Croatia & Slovenia
Rick Steves' Eastern Europe
Rick Steves' England
Rick Steves' France
Rick Steves' Germany
Rick Steves' Great Britain
Rick Steves' Ireland
Rick Steves' Italy
Rick Steves' Portugal
Rick Steves' Scandinavia
Rick Steves' Spain
Rick Steves' Switzerland

City and Regional Guides

Rick Steves' Amsterdam, Bruges & Brussels
Rick Steves' Athens & the Peloponnese
Rick Steves' Budapest
Rick Steves' Florence & Tuscany
Rick Steves' Istanbul
Rick Steves' London
Rick Steves' Paris
Rick Steves' Prague & the Czech Republic
Rick Steves' Provence & the French Riviera
Rick Steves' Rome
Rick Steves' Venice
Rick Steves' Vienna, Salzburg & Tirol

Rick Steves' Phrase Books

French
French/Italian/German
German
Italian
Portuguese
Spanish

Other Books

Rick Steves' Europe 101: History and Art for the Traveler
Rick Steves' Europe Through the Back Door
Rick Steves' European Christmas
Rick Steves' Postcards from Europe
Rick Steves' Travel as a Political Act

Avalon Travel
a member of the Perseus Books Group
1700 Fourth Street
Berkeley, CA 94710

Text © 2009 by Rick Steves.
Maps © 2009 Europe Through the Back Door.
First printing September 2009.
Photos are used by permission and are the property of the original copyright owners.

Printed in the United States of America by Worzalla

Portions of this book were originally published in *Rick Steves' Mona Winks* © 2001, 1998, 1996, 1993, 1988 by Rick Steves and Gene Openshaw, and in *Rick Steves' Italy* © 2009, 2008, 2007, 2006, 2005, 2004, 2003, 2002, 2001 by Rick Steves.

ISBN (13): 978-1-59880-284-9
ISSN: 1538-1609

For the latest on Rick's lectures, guidebooks, tours, public radio show, and public television series, contact Europe Through the Back Door, Box 2009, Edmonds, WA 98020, tel. 425/771-8303, fax 425/771-0833, www.ricksteves.com, rick@ricksteves.com.

Europe Through the Back Door Managing Editor: Risa Laib
ETBD Editors: Jennifer Madison Davis, Tom Griffin, Cathy McDonald, Gretchen Strauch, Sarah McCormic
Avalon Travel Senior Editor and Series Manager: Madhu Prasher
Avalon Travel Project Editor: Kelly Lydick
Research Assistance: Ben Cameron, Helen Inman
Copy Editor: Kay Elliott
Proofreader: Jennifer Malnick
Indexer: Claire Splan
Production & Typesetting: McGuire Barber Design
Cover Design: Kimberly Glyder Design
Graphic Content Director: Laura VanDeventer
Maps & Graphics: David C. Hoerlein, Laura VanDeventer, Lauren Mills, Barb Geisler, Mike Morgenfeld
Front Cover Photo: Duomo at Night © Laura VanDeventer
Front Matter Color Photo: p. i, View of Florence © Rick Steves; p. iii, Siena Duomo © Mike Potter
Interior Photography: Rick Steves, Gene Openshaw, David C. Hoerlein, Jennifer Hauseman, Mary Carlson